CONFLICT AND COOPERATION
Evolving Theories of International Relations

CONFLICT AND COOPERATION

Evolving Theories of International Relations

Marc A. Genest
University of Rhode Island

Harcourt Brace College Publishers

Fort Worth   Philadelphia   San Diego   New York   Orlando   Austin   San Antonio
Toronto   Montreal   London   Sydney   Tokyo

Publisher	Ted Buchholz
Editor in Chief	Christopher P. Klein
Acquisitions Editor	David Tatom
Developmental Editor	Fritz Schanz
Project Editor	Barbara Moreland
Production Manager	Jane Tyndall Ponceti
Art Director	Garry Harman
Permissions Editor	Sheila Shutter

ISBN: 0-15-501500-1

Library of Congress Catalog Card Number: 95-60348

Address for Editorial Correspondence: Harcourt Brace College Publishers, 301 Commerce Street, Suite 3700, Fort Worth, TX 76102.

Address for Orders: Harcourt Brace & Company, 6277 Sea Harbor Drive, Orlando, FL 32887. 1-800-782-4479, or 1-800-433-0001 (in Florida).

(Copyright Acknowledgments begin on page 581, which constitutes a continuation of this copyright page.)

Printed in the United States of America
5 6 7 8 9 0 1 2 3 4 039 9 8 7 6 5 4 3 2 1

PREFACE

The end of the Cold War is undoubtedly one of the great transforming events of world history. Scholars are still grappling with how to explain the dramatic changes that have altered boundaries on world maps, marked the end of the ideological and geopolitical struggle between the Soviet Union and the United States, and fundamentally reshaped international politics—all without a major war. Taken together, these astonishing events have provided us with an important opportunity from which to step back and reexamine our study of world politics. Perhaps no other period in time so clearly epitomizes the title of (and need for) this book, *Conflict and Cooperation: Evolving Theories of International Relations*. Our past and present are full of vivid accounts of war and conflict. Yet we sometimes forget that our history has been equally characterized by cooperation between people and states. Just as these relationships evolve, so too must our theories about the world, how it operates, and our place within it.

The purpose of this book is to present and discuss classic offerings in international relations theory as well as contemporary selections that propose new ways of interpreting human behavior. This type of theorizing is part of a long-standing tradition in history—attempting to answer the question, "Why do people (and, hence, states) act the way they do?" In answering that question, theories of international relations provide frameworks that enable scholars and statesmen to describe, analyze, and predict the behavior of states. The ultimate purpose of such theories is to help formulate effective policies.

The difference between this book of readings and others that focus on international relations theory lies in both its organization and user friendliness. These two characteristics are actually linked. First, the organization is based on three traditional levels of analysis: system, state, and individual, and because many other main textbooks and curricula are structured according to levels of analysis, this reader serves as a *practical* complement. Also, this reader serves as an important *theoretical* complement because the levels serve as important conceptual tools that provide explanations and points of focus; thus, the structure of this book helps to simplify and organize our thinking about complex international phenomena.

The second difference between this book of readings and others is its user friendliness. Because the intent is to provide a survey of some important classical and contemporary contributions to international relations theories, the level of reading is somewhat sophisticated. But, rather than omitting challenging articles, a number of pedagogical tools have been provided to assist the student in the learning process.

First, the introduction to the book discusses the nature of international relations theory, theory formulation, and the levels of analysis; this discussion sets the stage for the entire volume. Second, each of the three parts of the book opens with an overview of the given level of analysis and of the general characteristics of the theories falling within that level. Third, a box, which summarizes the core components of each theory, is placed at the beginning of each chapter. This box promotes quick understanding of, as well as comparisons among, theories. Fourth, each chapter contains a substantial introduction, which is central to the pedagogical emphasis of this book. These introductions discuss the development, characteristics, and strengths and weaknesses of each theory; in addition, they discuss the readings, their individual themes, and their contributions to the theories. Fifth, each reading is accompanied by a headnote that provides a brief description of the reading and a biography of the author. Sixth, two questions at the end of each reading may be used for class discussion or writing assignments. Last, key terms are noted in bold type throughout the chapter introductions and are listed, with their definitions, at the end of each chapter's introduction.

This reader is divided into three parts: system, state, and individual levels of analysis, and including the introductory chapter, it has 10 chapters and 45 readings. Part I covers the System Level of Analysis. Chapter 2 on Realist Theory presents classic as well as neoclassic realism, and includes, among others, such thinkers as Thucydides, Machiavelli, Morgenthau, and Waltz. Chapter 3 on Transnationalist Theory presents the institutional and economic branches of transnationalism. Such writers as Wilson, Russett, and Sutterlin show how international institutions and law have a vital role in affecting the behavior of states, and Nye, Keohane, and Reich discuss the growing influence of economic interdependence and nonstate actors in fostering cooperation and in guiding world economic policy. Chapter 4 on Class System Theory includes articles on Marxism, imperialism, dependency, and the roots and implications of the collapse of the former Soviet Union. Selections are from such writers as Marx, Wallerstein, and Halliday.

The State Level of Analysis is the subject of Part II. Chapter 5 on Political Cultural Theory first focuses on regimes and their influence in determining a country's domestic and foreign policy behavior; of note is Fukuyama's end of history thesis. The chapter then focuses on the civilizationists' arguments, as expressed by Huntington, which emphasize the impact of culture (e.g., ethnicity, race, religion, language, and traditions) in shaping the nature of a country and its policies. Chapter 6 on Decision-making Process Theory shifts to a discussion of how the nuts and bolts of state governance affect a country's behavior. The influence of bureaucracies and policymaking structures are discussed by such authors as Snyder, Sapin, Bruck, and Levy.

Part III on the Individual Level of Analysis is the final section of the book. Chapter 7 on Human Nature Theory includes classic works on the basic nature of mankind and on how this nature affects our relations with one another; selections are from Aristotle, Hobbes, and Freud. Chapter 8 on Cognitive Theory presents readings on the interaction between nature and nurture. Lasswell and Hermann discuss the effects of personality traits on foreign policy; Jervis analyzes the role of shared perceptions; and Lagon describes the post-Cold War change in shared beliefs among elite leadership groups. Chapter 9 on Feminist Theory in International Relations provides excerpts from pioneering efforts to reinterpret the nature of world politics; these show how and to what effect feminist perspectives and women have been excluded from international affairs. In one article, Peterson and Runyan show the influence of masculinist interpretations on the study and conduct of global politics; in another article, Tickner argues that gender bias in international relations is reinforced, in part, by how the discipline is taught. Chapter 10 on Peace Studies Theory also offers a new approach to the study of international relations; it embraces sociological analysis, Gandhian nonviolence, and epistemology. Stephenson traces the evolution of peace studies and describes it as a distinct discipline, and Crews and Stein separately discuss the goals of peace studies and the varied approaches it employs.

It is vital in our changing environment to acquaint new students of international relations with contemporary approaches in world affairs. This collection of readings is one of the few comprehensive sources that offers selections on such important post-Cold War theories as political culture (regimist and civilizationist), feminism, and peace studies. With current shifts in international politics resulting from the breakdown of the Soviet Union and of the bipolar global environment of the Cold War, new theories of international affairs now have more opportunity to be considered in the academic and policymaking communities.

Acknowledgments

I would like to thank the following reviewers for their valuable suggestions: Ralph G. Carter, Texas Christian University; Larry Elowitz, Georgia College; Howard P. Lehman, University of Utah; Joseph Lepgold, Georgetown University; Susan Stoudinger Northcutt, University of South Florida-Tampa; Henry A. Shockley, Boston University; Randolph M. Siverson, University of California-Davis; Donald A. Sylvan, Ohio State University-Columbus; Mary Ann Tetreault, Old Dominion University; Paul A. Tharp, University of Oklahoma; Herbert K. Tillema, University of Missouri-Columbia.

I owe special thanks to Mark Lagon, Adjunct Professor at Georgetown University and Research Assistant Associate at the American Enterprise Institute for his useful suggestions and contributions concerning the structure and content of the text. I also thank my colleague Art Stein from the University of Rhode Island for his insightful comments and contributions to Chapter 10. Over the course of this project, I have received wonderful support from my research assistant Todd Anderson, as well as from David Munoz-Storer, and Armando Heredia, all of whom performed above and beyond my expectations. I am also sincerely grateful to the University of Rhode Island, its Political Science Department, and its students for providing an academic environment that supports both scholarship and teaching.

From the beginning to the end of this project, the staff of Harcourt Brace have been a pleasure to work with. I would like to thank David Tatom, Acquisitions Editor, for his faith in the viability of this project. A special thanks goes to Fritz Schanz who played the dual role of Developmental Editor and diplomat as he managed to convince me that deadlines are flexible, but not imaginary. I also thank Barbara Moreland, Project Editor, for efficiently managing editorial and production responsibilities.

Finally, I would like to thank Marcy Marceau Genest, a truly wonderful wife and colleague. Her love, support, and editorial expertise have been invaluable. I consider this her book, as well as mine.

TABLE OF CONTENTS

State Level International Relations Theories

Individual Level International Relations Theories

CONFLICT AND COOPERATION
Evolving Theories of International Relations

Chapter 1

INTRODUCTION

WHAT IS INTERNATIONAL RELATIONS THEORY?

More than ever, our lives today are shaped by the world in which we live and the people, or groups of people, that surround us. We have formed boundaries, cultures, and communities that define what we call nations. The relationship of nations and their behavior toward one another, international relations, is what makes up our human history.

Scholars throughout that history have studied the human condition—assessing, evaluating, and even predicting patterns of behavior—using and developing various theories. A **theory** is a proposition, or set of propositions, that tries to analyze, explain or predict something. An **international relations theory,** then, is defined as a set of principles and guidelines used to analyze both world events and relations between states. International relations scholars often interchange various terms with theory, such as *paradigm, model, image,* or *perspective.* Whatever the words, the important thing to remember is that theories help to assess past and present conditions and, in turn, provide a reasonable basis for predicting future trends.

The development of international relations theory could be compared to a laboratory experiment. A scientist uses his knowledge of specific elements and their properties to predict how they might behave in various combinations and under specific conditions, as well as to produce a certain reaction or outcome. Theories about international relations are formed in a similar way. In this case, though, the laboratory is the international system as a whole, and we must speculate about the behavior of the states and individuals within it.

Theories of international relations can be grouped into two broad categories: explanatory theories and prescriptive theories. As the name implies, **explanatory theories** try to explain events and circumstances. They are based on description and evaluation of past events, conditions, and patterns of behavior. Scholars form a theory based on how nations have acted and interacted in the past in order to predict what their future behavior might be. For example, many theorists have studied past wars, trying to find certain patterns of behavior that might tell them why war is such a perennial problem in international relations. One popular international relations theory, realism, can be considered an explanatory theory.

Prescriptive theories, also referred to as normative theories, do not discount the value of historical experience but also incorporate moral principles and the setting of goals. A **prescriptive theory** is a set of principles or guidelines that contain overt value judgements about how the world ought to be, rather than how the world actually is. Prescriptive theory often involves the development of standards or principles for the conduct of international relations. Based on both past and contemporary conditions and patterns, theories prescribe or suggest a particular course of action, policy, or doctrine. This prescription is designed to improve and enhance relations between states within the international system. Peace studies is an example of this category of prescriptive theories. Many theories, such as transnationalism and class system theory, actually cross over, incorporating both the explanatory method and prescription.

Finally, it is important to note that a theory may be correct, incorrect, or even partially correct. In the end, it is up to the individual student to decide for him- or herself which theory or theories provide the most accurate and useful guidelines for understanding the course of global politics.

How Is International Relations Theory Formed?

We have discussed what international relations theory is, now let us address the question of how it is formed. In putting together different theories of international relations, social scientists and scholars of world affairs consider a number of factors. They are not simply looking at distinct, isolated events that have occurred over the course of history. They must also take into account the various elements that acted as the driving force of the crises.

These elements provide important clues in discovering how a crisis originated. The nature of the states and system when not in crisis can serve as a starting point for the investigation. That is, the specific details of a crisis lose their meaning if we do not know what led up to the event and what happened afterwards.

Scholars begin with what is called a hypothesis. For all intents and purposes, a **hypothesis** is essentially an educated guess or proposition about how or why something—an event or specific set of conditions—occurred. A hypothesis must, however, have a certain degree of probability; if one does not believe something to be possible, there is no point in determining its likelihood.

The hypothesis is then put to the test using certain methods. The methodology commonly employed in the development of international relations theory consists of several components, used either singly or in combination: analysis of historical events, conditions, or progressions; reasoned deduction based on the facts or evidence; and assessment of quantitative data.

By using these techniques, scholars and students of international relations come up with theories about the behavior and interaction of states. These theories might be explained through case studies. A **case study** uses a specific event, set of circumstances, or period of time to introduce and/or exemplify the key concepts of a given theory. A **concept** is an idea, thought or notion derived from the theory.

There can be no absolutes in theorizing about international relations, particularly given the vaguaries and random actions that can, and do, occur in human interaction. Unlike many stable, constant elements of a laboratory experiment—whether solids, gases or liquids—the world is an ever-changing environment. A theory of international relations may well be relevant and applicable during a specific period of history with a specific set of circumstances. New theories, however, must be periodically adapted and applied to our changing environment. Quite apart from simply invalidating the "old" theory, this continuous theoretical growth instead speaks to the exciting, even limitless, possibilities for examining, evaluating, and developing international relations theory.

LEVELS OF ANALYSIS: A METHOD FOR STUDYING INTERNATIONAL RELATIONS THEORY

One apparently lasting methodology for studying international relations theory is what is known as the levels of analysis. Developed originally in the 1950s by Kenneth Waltz, **levels of analysis** is exactly what it says—a method for examining international relations theory based on three different "units of measure," in purely scientific terms, or "levels." These levels are—from broad to narrow in scope—system level, state level, and individual level. That is, each theory or set of theories associated with a given level emphasizes the characteristics, conditions, and confines of that particular level in understanding and explaining world events and relations between states.[1]

Different levels focus on different questions. The system level of analysis looks at the international environment and how that shapes the pattern of interaction between countries. At the system level of analysis, questions center on how the distribution of military and economic power among states affect the course of international relations. Also, how does the global political environment affect the behavior of states? The second level examines how states make foreign policy. This level asks two fundamental questions: First, are some types of governments more prone to war than others? Second, does the competition for influence over policy-making between interest groups and within bureaucracies have a significant impact on a state's foreign policy? Finally, individual level analyses center on whether and how the characteristics, values, and perspectives of individual leaders affect their foreign policy decisions.

The levels of analysis concept is a tool to assist us in our examination of international relations. It helps us understand that international politics is the result of numerous sources. Each level features a different view of the event or events we are examining. It is like taking a picture from different distances. The system level approach will give you a sense of the broad features of the environment and provide the widest perspective, but will give very little detail of the individual parts. The state level can be compared to a photograph taken from several steps closer. We can now distinguish between the objects in the photograph though specific details remain

---

[1] Some works on international relations theory have identified as many as six different levels of analysis: individual, roles, government, society, international relations, and the world system. See Bruce Russet and Harvey Starr's *World Politics: The Menu For Choice,* 4th edition (New York: W. H. Freeman and Company, 1992), pp. 11–17. For this reader, Kenneth Waltz's original three levels provide students with a clearer, more basic framework for studying international relations theory.

unclear. The individual level provides the closest look at our subject, offering terrific detail, but eliminating the perspective provided by the broader views. Like the different photographs, all three levels of analysis have unique value. When taken together they provide the most accurate and complete understanding of international relations.

For an international relations example, we see that the origins of the Cold War cannot be analyzed properly without the proper context—the role of certain key individual leaders, the types of countries involved, and how the structure of the international system shaped or constrained the behavior of the United States and the Soviet Union. This provides perspective on the causes and ramifications of the event itself.

At the beginning of the Cold War, many countries were still suffering from the effects of World War II. Great Britain was weak from the effort of defeating Nazi Germany, and all three of the traditional European powers—Great Britain, France, and Germany—were trying to rebuild from the rubble of countless battles and bombings. Indeed, after the United States dropped the first two atomic bombs on Japan in 1945, all of the former Axis Powers (Germany, Italy, and Japan) who had initiated World War II had been defeated.

Only two nations at this time were strong enough to take leading roles on the international stage: the United States and the Soviet Union. But the styles of government in these two states were at opposite ends of the political spectrum and were not at all compatible. In the democratic United States, individual rights were and are valued and protected. Checks and balances within the government and on the government ensure these individual freedoms, yet provide a structure for national self-determination. Reliance on capitalist economic principles with free trade and open markets both helps to support American-style democracy and is supported by the democratic process.

The communist government of the Soviet Union emphasized collective rights over individual rights and freedoms. Power flowed from the center of the political structure and was dictatorial in nature, particularly under the rule of Joseph Stalin in the early Cold War years. Along with this centralized political authority came centralized economic planning. That is, the government owns the "means of production"—from factories and farms to tools and other equipment. Essentially, everyone in the Soviet Union was an employee of the state, and private ownership was kept to a bare minimum.

So, in the broadest sense, we see that the world was in a very delicate position at the beginning of the Cold War. The traditional European powers of Great Britain, France, and Germany were recovering from the damage of World War II. Only the United States and the Soviet Union were powerful enough to influence world politics.

The problem lay in the extreme differences of the two nations. Each state wanted to channel the course of international politics in its own direction and rebuild the world in its own image. For the Soviet Union, that image was communist. For the United States, the image was democratic capitalism. These differences and the power vacuum created by the weakness of the other states in the international system contributed to the competition and confrontation of the United States and Soviet Union.

In addition to the weakness of the system and the confrontational relationship between the two countries, we might also take a step closer and speculate about the psychological motivations of individual leaders. With Joseph Stalin as head of the Soviet Union during this period, his need for absolute authority, as well as his insecurities and ruthlessness, shaped both his decisions and Soviet foreign policy. These tendencies, combined with Stalin's documented fear of the West, compounded—and was compounded by—the shaky condition of the international system and the inevitable friction between the two competing political-economic systems.

On the American side, the fact that Harry Truman quite suddenly became president of the United States upon the death of Franklin Roosevelt could have made him feel somewhat anxious about the need to appear decisive and in control. His state of mind with respect to the Soviet Union might be best described in his own words: "If the Soviets do not wish to join us, they could go to Hell." This attitude may have exacerbated hostility between the two nations and made cooperation much less likely in the post–World War II environment.

Let us now reexamine our example on the origins of the Cold War within the levels of analysis framework. On a system level, the United States and the Soviet Union were the two most powerful states left standing in the post-war world. The global situation was in turmoil. Formerly strong nations were helpless in the wake of a massive war effort.

So, we have two strong powers dominating the international system. Looking at the situation from a state level perspective, conflict between the democratic United States and the communist Soviet Union is not surprising. The countries had radically different political and economic structures with neither, at that point, willing to compromise.

Finally, on an individual level, there was a serious mistrust on the part of both President Truman and Soviet leader Stalin. There was an almost cyclical reinforcement between these different levels of analysis and interaction. Competition between the United States and the Soviet Union was natural because of their differences. This competition reinforced those differences and fed the fears and wariness of the individual leaders.

Overall, we see that there are points to be made at each level of analysis with respect to this example. Let us now examine the specifics of each level—system, state, and individual—and the theories of international relations that go along with them.

System Level

Beginning with the broadest method, the theories associated with **system level analysis**—realist, transnationalist, and class system—tend to suggest that relations between states can be explained by factors that influence the system as a whole and by the characteristics and proclivities of the system itself. Allocation of power among states or groups of states, economic interdependence, and distribution of wealth are some of the general factors used in system level analysis. The dynamic created both within and by the system then shapes the relations of states and individuals.

For example, one type of system level theory is known as the realist school of thought. Realist theory emphasizes that the distribution of power in the international system shapes the behavior of the states within it. Some realists focus on the structure of the international system and the fact that there is no international authority to achieve and maintain global peace and stability among nations. Realists call this condition—the absence of an over-arching government in the system—anarchy. States, then, are forced to be self-reliant and use their own power—or establish a mutually beneficial alliance structure with other states—to preserve their independence. Power—its uneven distribution in the system and the quest of states for it—shapes the behavior of nations and alliances.

The first scholar to remark on the importance of power and shifts in power was the Greek historian Thucydides, in 461 B.C. Using the rivalry between the city-states of Athens and Sparta as his case study, Thucydides found that, not only do uneven rates of development and levels of power create tension between nations, but that generally ''strong states do what they have the power to do and weak states accept what they must.'' And with no international government in place to preserve law and order, as well as the rights of the weak, it is understandable that power—its acquisition and preservation—becomes an important commodity.

If the realists are generally pessimistic in their view of power and the anarchic nature of the international system, a second group of theorists, whom we shall call the transnationalists, take a somewhat brighter view. Though transnationalists, like the realists, accept that the world is anarchic, they also suggest that this condition is not static and the system can be changed. Transnationalists base this assumption on the notion that, though there is no over-arching government in the international system, there does exist a harmony of interests among nations. This harmony of interests implies that the incentive to cooperate with one another is stronger than the incentive for conflict. Creating international organizations and international law can build on these bonds and further promote good relations between states.

Transnationalists that advocate this kind of institutional approach—that is, the creation of international political organizations and international law—are known as institutional transnationalists (sometimes referred to as idealists). Proponents of this theory are looking to establish an international society, in which hostility and mistrust no longer characterize relations among states. Selfishness is replaced by mutual respect and understanding.

Despite their faith in the ability of these organizations and the rule of law to help avoid conflict, institutional transnationalists acknowledge that some friction within the system is inevitable. At these times, states can come together under what they call collective security. The term *collective security* suggests that if all states agree to join together to defend the independence of every state in the international community, then their collective ability to rebuff the aggression of a single state is greatly enhanced. Similar to the old adage about safety in numbers, collective security provides for the safety and security of its members.

According to institutional transnationalists, cooperation and collective security can be established through the use of international organizations. International organizations, such as the United Nations, are geared more toward political-military goals and stability. These organizations are designed to preserve and enforce specific rules and norms in global politics. Economic transnationalists, on the other hand, emphasize the importance of other transnational actors, such as multi-national corporations (MNCs). MNCs build bonds between nations based on economics and trade. Economic transnationalists contend that by expanding international economic ties, all nations will have a stake in preserving peace and promoting stability. In short, while the institutional and economic branches of transnationalism emphasize different mechanisms and actors, they both focus on the common goal of building international cooperation.

One final theory in our presentation of system-level analyses is based primarily on an economic foundation. Class system theory suggests that the distribution of wealth within the international system shapes the system itself. Among class system theorists, it is generally accepted that this shape is capitalist. In the world capitalist system, wealthy people and wealthy countries mold global affairs to their own benefit. This perpetuates a cycle of dependency among poor and weak states.

Karl Marx and V. I. Lenin were perhaps the best known advocates of this theory. They contended that this exploitation crossed state boundaries and would eventually unite the working class, or proletariat, in an international revolution against imperialist domination. Conflict, then, occurs primarily on an economic basis—the global exploitation of the poor by the wealthy and by the imperialist force of capitalism.

State Level

State level analysis brings the examination of relations between states and the formulation of international relations theory a step closer. **State level** emphasizes the nature and characteristics of individual states in evaluating the dynamics of global politics and the international system. As we see in our example on the origins of the Cold War, the fundamental differences between communist states and capitalist democracies can be a source of tension.

Both the two major state level theories that we will discuss in this book—political regime theory and decision-making process theory—emphasize the domestic factors of nations in their international behavior. These factors include the type of government and how it operates, level of citizen participation, sense of popular well-being, and the adaptability of the state to both internal and external pressures and changes.

In political regime theory, the central question is whether the type of government of a nation has an impact on that nation's foreign policy. More specifically, we might ask, do authoritarian regimes behave more belligerently or are they more prone to conflict or war than democracies?

Bruce Russett and Francis Fukuyama argue that different types of governments do behave differently, and democracies are, indeed, less likely to go to war than authoritarian or totalitarian regimes. They generally attribute this to the fact that the political ideals forming the basis of democracies incorporate a great respect for human rights, the value of international law, and the resolution of conflict through negotiation. Since democratic leaders must answer to a popular mandate, foreign policy conforms to these principles as closely as possible.

The other state level theory presented, decision-making process theory, emphasizes not the type of government but the characteristics of the bureaucratic machine

KEY CONCEPTS

Case study   uses a specific event, set of circumstances or period of time to introduce and/or exemplify the key concepts of a given theory.

Concept   is an idea, thought or notion derived from a theory.

Explanatory theories   try to explain events and circumstances. They are based on description and evaluation of past events, conditions, and patterns of behavior. Scholars form a theory based on how nations have acted and interacted in the past in order to predict what their future behavior might be.

Hypothesis   is essentially an educated guess or proposition about how or why something—an event or specific set of conditions—occurred. A hypothesis must, however, have a certain degree of probability.

Individual level analysis   is an approach to understanding international relations that focuses on the role and impact of particular individuals, or looks for explanations based on "human nature," or common characteristics of all individuals.

International relations theory   is a set of principles and guidelines used to analyze both world events and relations between states. The theories help to assess past and present conditions and, in turn, provide a reasonable basis for predicting future trends.

Levels of analysis   is a method for examining international relations theory based on three different perspectives or levels. These levels are, from

(continued)

itself. That is, how do governments make foreign policy and how does that, in turn, affect foreign policy?

Process theorists contend that decisions are quite often the result of compromise between competing factions or groups within the government bureaucracy. An example might be the influence of the military industrial complex in the United States' defense and foreign policy-making. That is, companies that specialize in manufacturing military hardware and the different branches of the military all have a stake in maintaining some influence over the country's defense and foreign policy. The role of these factions in the government and the competition between them are important contributing factors to the politics of the state.

Individual Level

The third and final level of analysis takes a look at the role of the individual in society. **Individual level** approaches to understanding international politics emphasize the

(continued from previous page)

broad to narrow in scope, system level, state level, and individual level. Each theory or set of theories associated with a given level emphasizes the characteristics, conditions, and confines of that particular level in understanding and explaining world events and relations between states.

Prescriptive theory   is a set of principles and guidelines that contain overt value judgements about how the world ought to be, rather than how the world actually is. Prescriptive theory often involves the development of standards or principles for the conduct of international relations. Based on both past and contemporary conditions and patterns, these theories prescribe or suggest a particular course of action, policy, or doctrine. This prescription is designed to improve and enhance relations between states within the international system.

State level analysis   is an analytical approach to international relations that focuses on the domestic or internal causes of state actions. State level theories attempt to explain international relations by emphasizing the internal workings of the state itself.

System level analysis   attempts to explain international relations by focusing on the manner in which the structure of the international system (global distribution of resources among states) shapes or constrains the actions of states. System level theories contend that relations between states can be explained by factors that influence the system as a whole and by the characteristics and proclivities of the system itself.

Theory   is a proposition or set of propositions that tries to analyze, explain, or predict something.

common characteristics of all individuals, often referred to as "human nature," or they look for explanations based on the impact that particular individuals have on the foreign policy of a given state.

Individual level explanations examine the human actor in several different ways. The first approach looks at the base characteristics of human nature in general. According to Thomas Hobbes, it is the nature of the individual, which is naturally insecure and aggressive, that shapes, defines, and characterizes society and government. The second analyzes the motives, principles, and preconceptions of individuals. Thomas Carlyle once said, "The history of the world is but the biography of great men." This notion suggests that the perceptions, misperceptions, and behavior of individual leaders can have a dramatic impact on the actions of a state. These actions then create ripples through the international system as a whole.

Using these guidelines, this study will look at four theoretical treatments of international relations based on the individual level of analysis: human nature, the nature of the individual, gender roles, and the mitigation of human aggression. The articles in this section offer a range of viewpoints. From pessimists, such as Thomas Hobbes, one is left with the impression that man is by nature aggressive and driven in a quest for power. Only strong governments, he suggests, can mitigate these tendencies and preserve domestic and international stability.

An alternate approach addresses the ability of a single leader or personality to shape the actions of a nation. In so doing, that individual is able to alter the course of political interaction on a global scale. The rise and fall of Adolf Hitler is one of the most vivid contemporary examples of such a leader, but he is certainly not alone. From George Washington to Winston Churchill, from Lenin to Mao Tse Tung to Kim II Sung, individuals have made, and no doubt will continue to make, their marks on the international system.

Something that all these examples have in common is their gender. We will present several articles that address the issue of gender in international politics. Are men more prone to aggression and a quest for power than women? Similarly, do women generally emphasize cooperation and resolution through negotiation? Certainly, these questions offer an interesting new perspective on some old theoretical questions.

Finally, an optimistic perspective of the individual is set forth in the last section. As part of the relatively new field of Peace Studies, Arthur Stein characterizes humans as potentially "good" and capable of positively transforming individuals, societies, and the world in general. The theory of Peace Studies more broadly focuses on building harmonious relations among both individuals and states. The premise asserts that if certain prescriptions are followed, a more peaceful and stable world may be created. Individual enlightenment, accordingly, is the key.

The difference between Waltz's three levels of analysis for international relations theory is one not of exclusivity but, rather, emphasis. No single level by itself can provide a complete explanation of events and changes in world politics. Each level organizes the facts in its own particular fashion, and each level focuses on different facts. Only by examining what scholars and proponents of all three levels have said about individuals, their societies, as well as the global environment, can we hope to create a more complete picture of our world and our future.

One final note, the articles in this book have been placed into either the system, state, or individual level of analysis. The levels of analysis methodology is an analytical tool used to clarify and order our exploration of the different dimensions of international relations theory. However, students should be aware that many of the theorists presented in this volume incorporate some of the basic assumptions of more than one level of analysis. For example, Hans Morganthau, a realist, is categorized as a system level theorist even though he had strong views about human nature and the role of governments in shaping foreign policy. His overall emphasis, though, was primarily directed at the behavior of states as shaped by the international system. So, again it is a matter of emphasis, rather than exclusivity, that allows us to categorize theories according to the three levels of analysis.

1.   Man, the State and War

Kenneth N. Waltz

In this selection Kenneth N. Waltz identifies three alternative "images," or "levels of analysis," that can be used to explain the causes of war: individual, state, and international systems. Waltz concludes that, although the immediate causes of war are found in the individual and state levels, the permissive cause of war is the anarchic nature of the international system. This excerpt is from *Man, the State and War* (1959).

Kenneth N. Waltz is Ford Professor of Political Science at the University of California, Berkeley. His other books include *Foreign Policy and Democratic Politics: The American and British Experience* (1967, reissued 1992), *Theory of International Politics* (1979), and numerous essays.

INTRODUCTION

Asking who won a given war, someone has said, is like asking who won the San Francisco earthquake. That in wars there is no victory but only varying degrees of defeat is a proposition that has gained increasing acceptance in the twentieth century. But are wars also akin to earthquakes in being natural occurrences whose control or elimination is beyond the wit of man? Few would admit that they are, yet attempts to eliminate war, however nobly inspired and assiduously pursued, have brought little more than fleeting moments of peace among states. There is an apparent disproportion between effort and product, between desire and result. The peace wish, we are told, runs strong and deep among the Russian people; and we are convinced that the same can be said of Americans. From these statements there is some comfort to be derived, but in the light of history and of current events as well it is difficult to believe that the wish will father the condition desired.

Social scientists, realizing from their studies how firmly the present is tied to the past and how intimately the parts of a system depend upon each other, are inclined to be conservative in estimating the possibilities of achieving a radically better world. If one asks whether we can now have peace where in the past there has been war, the answers are most often pessimistic. Perhaps this is the wrong question. And indeed the answers will be somewhat less discouraging if instead the following questions are put: Are there ways of decreasing the incidence of war, of increasing the chances of peace? Can we have peace more often in the future than in the past?

Peace is one among a number of ends simultaneously entertained. The means by which peace can be sought are many. The end is pursued and the means are applied under varying conditions. Even though one may find it hard to believe that there are ways to peace not yet tried by statesmen or advocated by publicists, the very complexity of the problem suggests the possibility of combining activities in different ways in the hope that some combination will lead us closer to the goal. Is one then led to conclude that the wisdom of the statesman lies in trying first one policy and then another, in doing what the moment seems to require? An affirmative reply would suggest that the hope for improvement lies in policy divorced from analysis, in action removed from thought. Yet each attempt to alleviate a condition implies some idea of its causes: to explain how peace can be more readily achieved requires an understanding of the causes of war. It is such an understanding that we shall seek in the following pages.

THE FIRST IMAGE: INTERNATIONAL CONFLICT AND HUMAN BEHAVIOR

There is deceit and cunning and from these wars arise.

—CONFUCIUS

According to the first image of international relations, the focus of the important causes of war is found in the nature and behavior of man. Wars result from selfishness, from misdirected aggressive impulses, from stupidity. Other causes are secondary and have to be interpreted in the light of these factors. If these are the primary causes of war, then the elimination of war must come through uplifting and enlightening men or securing their psychic-social readjustment. This estimate of causes and cures has been dominant in the writings of many serious students of human affairs from Confucius to present-day pacifists. It is the leitmotif

of many modern behavioral scientists as well.

Prescriptions associated with first-image analyses need not be identical in content, as a few examples will indicate. Henry Wadsworth Longfellow, moved to poetic expression by a visit to the arsenal at Springfield, set down the following thoughts:

> Were half the power that fills the world
> with terror,
> Were half the wealth bestowed on camps
> and courts,
> Given to redeem the human mind from
> error,
> There were no need of arsenals or forts.

Implicit in these lines is the idea that the people will insist that the right policies be adopted if only they know what the right policies are. Their instincts are good, though their present gullibility may prompt them to follow false leaders. By attributing present difficulties to a defect in knowledge, education becomes the remedy for war. The idea is wide-spread. Beverly Nichols, a pacifist writing in the 1930s, thought that if Norman Angell "could be made educational dictator of the world, war would vanish like the morning mist, in a single generation."[1] In 1920, a conference of Friends, unwilling to rely upon intellectual development alone, called upon the people of the world to replace self-seeking with the spirit of sacrifice, cooperation, and trust.[2] Bertrand Russell, at about the same time and in much the same vein, saw a decline in the possessive instincts as a prerequisite to peace.[3] By others, increasing the chances of peace has been said to require not so much a change in "instincts" as a channeling of energies that are presently expended in the destructive folly of war.

If there were something that men would rather do than fight, they would cease to fight altogether. Aristophanes saw the point. If the women of Athens would deny themselves to husbands and lovers, their men would have to choose between the pleasures of the couch and the exhilarating experiences of the battlefield. Aristophanes thought he knew the men, and women, of Athens well enough to make the outcome a foregone conclusion. William James was in the same tradition. War, in his view, is rooted in man's bellicose nature, which is the product of centuries-old tradition. His nature cannot be changed or his drives suppressed, but they can be diverted. As alternatives to military service James suggests drafting the youth of the world to mine coal and man ships, to build skyscrapers and roads, to wash dishes and clothes. While his estimate of what diversions would be sufficient is at once less realistic and more seriously intended than that of Aristophanes, his remedy is clearly the same in type.[4]

The prescriptions vary, but common to them all is the thought that in order to achieve a more peaceful world men must be changed, whether in their moral-intellectual outlook or in their psychic-social behavior. One may, however, agree with the first-image analysis of causes without admitting the possibility of practicable prescriptions for their removal. Among those who accept a first-image explanation of war there are both optimists and pessimists, those who think the possibilities of progress so great that wars will end before the next generation is dead and those who think that wars will continue to occur though by them we may all die.

THE SECOND IMAGE: INTERNATIONAL CONFLICT AND THE INTERNAL STRUCTURE OF STATES

However conceived in an image of the world, foreign policy is a phase of domestic policy, an inescapable phase.

—CHARLES BEARD, *A Foreign Policy for America*

The first image did not exclude the influence of the state, but the role of the state was introduced as a consideration less important than, and to be explained in terms of, human behavior. According to the first image, to say that the state acts is to speak metonymically. We say that the state acts when we mean that the people in it act, just as we say that the pot boils when we mean that the water in it boils. The preceding [section] concentrated on the contents rather than the container; the present [section] alters the balance of emphasis in favor of the latter. To continue the figure: Water running out of a faucet is chemically the same as water in a container, but once the water is in a container, it can be made to "behave" in different ways. It can be turned into steam and used to power an engine, or, if the water is sealed in and heated to extreme temperatures, it can become the instrument of a destructive explosion. Wars would not exist were human nature not what it is, but neither would Sunday schools and brothels, philanthropic organizations and criminal gangs. Since everything is related to human nature, to explain anything one must consider more than human nature. The events to be explained are so many and so varied that human nature cannot possibly be the single determinant.

The attempt to explain everything by psychology meant, in the end, that psychology succeeded in explaining nothing. And adding sociology to the analysis simply substitutes the error of sociologism for the error of psychologism. Where Spinoza, for example, erred by leaving out of his personal estimate of cause all reference to the causal role of social structures, sociologists have, in approaching the problem of war and peace, often erred in omitting all reference to the political framework within which individual and social actions occur. The conclusion is obvious: to understand war and peace political analysis must be used to supplement and order the findings of psychology and sociology. What kind of political analysis is needed? For possible explanations of the occurrence or non-occurrence of war, one can look to international politics (since war occurs among states), or one can look to the states themselves (since it is in the name of the state that the fighting is actually done). The former approach is postponed [until the next section]; according to the second image, the internal organization of states is the key to understanding war and peace.

One explanation of the second-image type is illustrated as follows. War most often promotes the internal unity of each state involved. The state plagued by internal strife may then, instead of waiting for the accidental attack, seek the war that will bring internal peace. Bodin saw this clearly, for he concludes that "the best way of preserving a state, and guaranteeing it against sedition, rebellion, and civil war is to keep the subjects in amity one with another, and to this end, to find an enemy against whom they can make common cause." And he saw historical evidence that the principle had been applied, especially by the Romans, who "could find no better antidote to civil war, nor one more certain in its effects, than to oppose an enemy to the citizens."[5] Secretary of State William Henry Seward followed this reasoning when, in order to promote unity within the country, he urged upon Lincoln a vigorous foreign policy, which included the possibility of declaring war on Spain and France.[6] Mikhail Skobelev, an influential Russian military officer of the third quarter of the nineteenth century, varied the theme but slightly when he argued that the Russian monarchy was doomed unless it could produce major military successes abroad.[7]

The use of internal defects to explain those external acts of the state that bring war can take many forms. Such explanation may be related to a type of government that is thought to be generically bad. For example, it is often thought that the deprivations imposed by despots upon their subjects produce tensions that may find expression in foreign adventure. Or the explanation may be given in terms of defects in a government not itself considered bad. Thus it has been argued that the restrictions placed upon a government in order to protect the prescribed rights of its citizens act as impediments to the making and executing of foreign policy. These restrictions, laudable in original purpose, may have the unfortunate effect of making difficult or impossible the effective action of that government for the maintenance of peace in the world.[8] And, as a final example, explanation may be made in terms of geographic or economic deprivation or in terms of deprivations too vaguely defined to be labeled at all. Thus a nation may argue that it has not attained its "natural" frontiers, that such frontiers are necessary to its security, that war to extend the state to its deserved compass is justified or even necessary.[9] The possible variations on this theme have been made familiar by the "have-not" arguments so popular in this century. Such arguments have been used both to explain why "deprived" countries undertake war and to urge the satiated to make the compensatory adjustments thought necessary if peace is to be perpetuated.[10]

The examples just given illustrate in abundant variety one part of the second image, the idea that defects in states cause wars among them. But in just what ways should the structure of states be changed? What definition of the "good" state is to serve as a standard? Among those who have taken this approach to international relations there is a great variety of definitions. Karl Marx defines "good" in terms of ownership of the means of production; Immanuel Kant in terms of abstract principles of right; Woodrow Wilson in terms of national self-determination and modern democratic organization. Though each definition singles out different items as crucial, all are united in asserting that if, and only if, substantially all states reform will world peace result. That is, the reform prescribed is considered the sufficient basis for world peace. This, of course, does not exhaust the subject. Marx, for example, believed that states would disappear shortly after they became socialist. The problem of war, if war is defined as violent conflict among states, would then no longer exist. Kant believed that republican states would voluntarily agree to be governed in their dealings by a code of law drawn up by the states themselves. Wilson urged a variety of requisites to peace, such as improved international understanding,

collective security and disarmament, a world confederation of states. But history proved to Wilson that one cannot expect the steadfast cooperation of undemocratic states in any such program for peace.

For each of these men, the reform of states in the ways prescribed is taken to be the *sine qua non* of world peace. The examples given could be multiplied. Classical economists as well as socialists, aristocrats and monarchists as well as democrats, empiricists and realists as well as transcendental idealists—all can furnish examples of men who have believed that peace can be had only if a given pattern of internal organization becomes widespread. Is it that democracies spell peace, but we have had wars because there have never been enough democracies of the right kind? Or that the socialist form of government contains within it the guarantee of peace, but so far there have never been any true socialist governments?[11] If either question were answered in the affirmative, then one would have to assess the merits of different prescriptions and try to decide just which one, or which combination, contains the elusive secret formula for peace. The import of our criticism, however, is that no prescription for international relations written entirely in terms of the second image can be valid, that the approach itself is faulty. Our criticisms of the liberals apply to all theories that would rely on the generalization of one pattern of state and society to bring peace to the world.

Bad states lead to war. As previously said, there is a large and important sense in which this is true. The obverse of this statement, that good states mean peace in the world, is an extremely doubtful proposition. The difficulty, endemic with the second image of international relations, is the same in kind as the difficulty encountered in the first image. There the statement that men make the societies, including the international society, in which they live was criticized not simply as being wrong but as being incomplete. One must add that the societies they live in make men. And it is the same in international relations. The actions of states, or, more accurately, of men acting for states, make up the substance of international relations. But the international political environment has much to do with the ways in which states behave. The influence to be assigned to the internal structure of states in attempting to solve the war–peace equation cannot be determined until the significance of the international environment has been reconsidered.

THE THIRD IMAGE: INTERNATIONAL CONFLICT AND INTERNATIONAL ANARCHY

For what can be done against force without force?

—CICERO, *The Letters to His Friends*

With many sovereign states, with no system of law enforceable among them, with each state judging its grievances and ambitions according to the dictates of its own reason or desire—conflict, sometimes leading to war, is bound to occur. To achieve a favorable outcome from such conflict a state has to rely on its own devices, the relative efficiency of which must be its constant concern. This, the idea of the third image, is to be examined [here]. It is not an esoteric idea; it is not a new idea. Thucydides implied it when

he wrote that it was "the growth of the Athenian power, which terrified the Lacedaemonians and forced them into war."[12] John Adams implied it when he wrote to the citizens of Petersburg, Virginia, that "a war with France, if just and necessary, might wean us from fond and blind affections, which no Nation ought ever to feel towards another, as our experience in more than one instance abundantly testifies."[13] There is an obvious relation between the concern over relative power position expressed by Thucydides and the admonition of John Adams that love affairs between states are inappropriate and dangerous. This relation is made explicit in Frederick Dunn's statement that "so long as the notion of self-help persists, the aim of maintaining the power position of the nation is paramount to all other considerations."[14]

In anarchy there is no automatic harmony. The three preceding statements reflect this fact. A state will use force to attain its goals if, after assessing the prospects for success, it values those goals more than it values the pleasures of peace. Because each state is the final judge of its own cause, any state may at any time use force to implement its policies. Because any state may at any time use force, all states must constantly be ready either to counter force with force or to pay the cost of weakness. The requirements of state action are, in this view, imposed by the circumstances in which all states exist.

In a manner of speaking, all three images are a part of nature. So fundamental are man, the state, and the state system in any attempt to understand international relations that seldom does an analyst, however wedded to one image, entirely overlook the other two. Still, emphasis on one image may distort one's interpretation of the others. It is, for example, not uncommon to find those inclined to see the world in terms of either the first or the second image countering the oft-made argument that arms breed not war but security, and possibly even peace, by pointing out that the argument is a compound of dishonest myth, to cover the interests of politicians, armament makers, and others, and honest illusion entertained by patriots sincerely interested in the safety of their states. To dispel the illusion, Cobden, to recall one of the many who have argued this way, once pointed out that doubling armaments, if everyone does it, makes no state more secure and, similarly, that none would be endangered if all military establishments were simultaneously reduced by, say, 50 percent.[15] Putting aside the thought that the arithmetic is not necessarily an accurate reflection of what the situation would be, this argument illustrates a supposedly practical application of the first and second images. Whether by educating citizens and leaders of the separate states or by improving the organization of each of them, a condition is sought in which the lesson here adumbrated becomes the basis for the policies of states. The result?—disarmament, and thus economy, together with peace, and thus security, for all states. If some states display a willingness to pare down their military establishments, other states will be able to pursue similar policies. In emphasizing the interdependence of the policies of all states, the argument pays heed to the third image. The optimism is, however, the result of ignoring some inherent difficulties. [Here Waltz takes up Rousseau's view of man in the early state of nature.—*Ed.*]

In the early state of nature, men were sufficiently dispersed to make any pattern of cooperation unnecessary. But finally the combination of increased numbers and the usual natural hazards posed, in a variety of situations, the proposition: cooperate or die. Rousseau illustrates the line of reasoning with the simplest example. The example is worth reproducing, for it is the point of departure for the establishment of government and contains the basis for his explanation of conflict in international relations as well. Assume that five men who have acquired a rudimentary ability to speak and to understand each other happen to come together at a time when all of them suffer from hunger. The hunger of each will be satisfied by the fifth part of a stag, so they "agree" to cooperate in a project to trap one. But also the hunger of any one of them will be satisfied by a hare, so, as a hare comes within reach, one of them grabs it. The defector obtains the means of satisfying his hunger but in doing so permits the stag to escape. His immediate interest prevails over consideration for his fellows.[16]

The story is simple; the implications are tremendous. In cooperative action, even where all agree on the goal and have an equal interest in the project, one cannot rely on others. Spinoza linked conflict causally to man's imperfect reason. Montesquieu and Rousseau counter Spinoza's analysis with the proposition that the sources of conflict are not so much in the minds of men as they are in the nature of social activity. The difficulty is to some extent verbal. Rousseau grants that if we knew how to receive the true justice that comes from God, "we should need neither government nor laws."[17] This corresponds to Spinoza's proposition that "men in so far as they live in obedience to reason, necessarily live always in harmony one with another."[18]

The idea is a truism. If men were perfect, their perfection would be reflected in all of their calculations and actions. Each could rely on the behavior of others, and all decisions would be made on principles that would preserve a true harmony of interests. Spinoza emphasizes not the difficulties inherent in mediating conflicting interests but the defectiveness of man's reason that prevents their consistently making decisions that would be in the interest of each and for the good of all. Rousseau faces the same problem. He imagines how men must have behaved as they began to depend on one another to meet their daily needs. As long as each provided for his own wants, there could be no conflict; whenever the combination of natural obstacles and growth in population made cooperation necessary, conflict arose. Thus in the stag-hunt example, the tension between one man's immediate interest and the general interest of the group is resolved by the unilateral action of the one man. To the extent that he was motivated by a feeling of hunger, his act is one of passion. Reason would have told him that his long-run interest depends on establishing, through experience, the conviction that cooperative action will benefit all of the participants. But reason also tells him that if he forgoes the hare, the man next to him might leave his post to chase it, leaving the first man with nothing but food for thought on the folly of being loyal.

The problem is now posed in more significant terms. If harmony is to exist in anarchy, not only must I be perfectly rational but I must be able to assume that everyone else is too. Otherwise there is no basis for rational calculation. To allow in my calculation for the irrational acts of others can lead to no determinate solutions, but to attempt to act on a rational calculation without making such an allowance may lead to my own undoing. The latter argument is reflected in Rousseau's comments on the proposition that "a people of true Christians would form the most perfect society imaginable." In the first place he points out that such a society "would not be a society of men." Moreover, he says, "For the state to be peaceable and for harmony to be maintained, *all* the citizens *without exception* would have to be [equally] good Christians; if by ill hap there should be a single self-seeker or hypocrite . . . he would certainly get the better of his pious compatriots."[19]

If we define cooperative action as rational and any deviation from it irrational, we must agree with Spinoza that conflict results from the irrationality of men. But if we examine the requirements of rational action, we find that even in an example as simple as the stag hunt we have to assume that the reason of each leads to an identical definition of interest, that each will draw the same conclusion as to the methods appropriate to meet the original situation, that all will agree instantly on the action required by any chance incidents that raise the question of altering the original plan, and that each can rely completely on the steadfastness of purpose of all the others. Perfectly rational action requires not only the perception that our welfare is tied up with the welfare of others but also a perfect appraisal of details so that we can answer the question: Just *how* in each situation is it tied up with everyone else's? Rousseau agrees with Spinoza in refusing to label the act of the rabbit-snatcher either good or bad; unlike Spinoza, he also refuses to label it either rational or irrational. He has noticed that the difficulty is not only in the actors but also in the situations they face. While by no means ignoring the part that avarice and ambition play in the birth and growth of conflict,[20] Rousseau's analysis makes clear the extent to which conflict appears inevitably in the social affairs of men.

In short, the proposition that irrationality is the cause of all the world's troubles, in the sense that a world of perfectly rational men would know no disagreements and no conflicts, is, as Rousseau implies, as true as it is irrelevant. Since the world cannot be defined in terms of perfection, the very real problem of how to achieve an approximation to harmony in cooperative and competitive activity is always with us and, lacking the possibility of perfection, it is a problem that cannot be solved simply by changing men. Rousseau's conclusion, which is also the heart of his theory of international relations, is accurately though somewhat abstractly summarized in the following statement: That among particularities accidents will occur is not accidental but necessary.[21] And this, in turn, is simply another way of saying that in anarchy there is no automatic harmony.

If anarchy is the problem, then there are only two possible solutions: (1) to impose an effective control on the separate and imperfect states; (2) to remove states from the sphere of the accidental, that is, to define the good state as so perfect that it will no longer be particular. Kant tried to compromise by making states good enough to obey a set of laws to which they have volunteered their assent. Rousseau, whom on this point Kant failed to follow, emphasizes the particular nature of even the good state and, in so doing, makes apparent the futility of the solution Kant suggests.[22] He also makes possible a theory of international relations that in general terms explains the

behavior of all states, whether good or bad.[23]

In the stag-hunt example, the will of the rabbit-snatcher was rational and predictable from his own point of view. From the point of view of the rest of the group, it was arbitrary and capricious. So of any individual state, a will perfectly good for itself may provoke the violent resistance of other states.[24] The application of Rousseau's theory to international politics is stated with eloquence and clarity in his commentaries on Saint-Pierre and in a short work entitled *The State of War*. His application bears out the preceding analysis. The states of Europe, he writes, "touch each other at so many points that no one of them can move without giving a jar to all the rest; their variances are all the more deadly, as their ties are more closely woven." They "must inevitably fall into quarrels and dissensions at the first changes that come about." And if we ask why they must "inevitably" clash, Rousseau answers: Because their union is "formed and maintained by nothing better than chance." The nations of Europe are willful units in close juxtaposition with rules neither clear nor enforceable to guide them. The public law of Europe is but "a mass of contradictory rules which nothing but the right of the stronger can reduce to order: so that in the absence of any sure clue to guide her, reason is bound, in every case of doubt, to obey the promptings of self-interest—which in itself would make war inevitable, even if all parties desired to be just." In this condition, it is foolhardy to expect automatic harmony of interest and automatic agreement and acquiescence in rights and duties. In a real sense there is a "union of the nations of Europe," but "the imperfections of this association make the state of those who belong to it worse than it would be if they formed no community at all."[25]

The argument is clear. For individuals the bloodiest stage of history was the period just prior to the establishment of society. At that point they had lost the virtues of the savage without having acquired those of the citizen. The late stage of the state of nature is necessarily a state of war. The nations of Europe are precisely in that stage.[26]

What then is cause: the capricious acts of the separate states or the system within which they exist? Rousseau emphasizes the latter:

> Every one can see that what unites any form of society is community of interests, and what disintegrates [it] is their conflict; that either tendency may be changed or modified by a thousand accidents; and therefore that, as soon as a society is founded, some coercive power must be provided to co-ordinate the actions of its members and give to their common interests and mutual obligations that firmness and consistency which they could never acquire of themselves.[27]

But to emphasize the importance of political structure is not to say that the acts that bring about conflict and lead to the use of force are of no importance. It is the specific acts that are the immediate causes of war,[28] the general structure that permits them to exist and wreak their disasters. To eliminate every vestige of selfishness, perversity, and stupidity in nations would serve to establish perpetual peace, but to try directly to eliminate all the immediate causes of war without altering the structure of the "union of Europe" is utopian.

What alteration of structure is required? The idea that a voluntary federation, such as Kant later proposed, could keep peace among states, Rousseau rejects emphatically. Instead, he says, the remedy for war among states "is to be found only in such a form of federal Government as shall unite nations by bonds similar to those which already unite their individual members, and place the one no less than the other under the authority of the Law."[29] Kant made similar statements only to amend them out of existence once he came to consider the reality of such a federation. Rousseau does not modify his principle, as is made clear in the following quotation, every point of which is a contradiction of Kant's program for the pacific federation:

> The Federation [that is to replace the "free and voluntary association which now unites the States of Europe"] must embrace all the important Powers in its membership; it must have a Legislative Body, with powers to pass laws and ordinances binding upon all its members; it must have a coercive force capable of compelling every State to obey its common resolves whether in the way of command or of prohibition; finally, it must be strong and firm enough to make it impossible for any member to withdraw at his own pleasure the moment he conceives his private interest to clash with that of the whole body.[30]

It is easy to poke holes in the solution offered by Rousseau. The most vulnerable point is revealed by the questions: How could the federation enforce its law on the states that comprise it without waging war against them? and How likely is it that the effective force will always be on the side of the federation? To answer these questions Rousseau argues that the states of Europe are in a condition of balance sufficiently fine to prevent any one state or combination of states from pre-

1. Man, the State and War 21

vailing over the others. For this reason, the necessary margin of force will always rest with the federation itself. The best critical consideration of the inherent weakness of a federation of states in which the law of the federation has to be enforced on the states who are its members is contained in the *Federalist Papers.* The arguments are convincing, but they need not be reviewed here. The practical weakness of Rousseau's recommended solution does not obscure the merit of his theoretical analysis of war as a consequence of international anarchy.

CONCLUSION

The third image, like the first two, leads directly to a utopian prescription. In each image a cause is identified in terms of which all others are to be understood. The force of the logical relation between the third image and the world-government prescription is great enough to cause some to argue not only the merits of world government but also the ease with which it can be realized.[51] It is of course true that with world government there would no longer be international wars, though with an ineffective world government there would no doubt be civil wars. It is likewise true, reverting to the first two images, that without the imperfections of the separate states there would not be wars, just as it is true that a society of perfectly rational beings, or of perfect Christians, would never know violent conflict. These statements are, unfortunately, as trivial as they are true. They have the unchallengeable quality of airtight tautologies: perfectly good states or men will not do bad things; within an effective organization highly damaging deviant behavior is not permitted. The near perfection required by concentra-

tion upon a single cause accounts for a number of otherwise puzzling facts: the pessimism of St. Augustine, the failure of the behavioral scientists as prescribers for peace, the reliance of many liberals on the forces of history to produce a result not conceivably to be produced by the consciously directed efforts of men, the tendency of socialists to identify a corrupting element every time harmony in socialist action fails to appear. It also helps to explain the often rapid alternation of hope and despair among those who most fully adopt a single-cause approach to this or to almost any other problem. The belief that to make the world better requires changing the factors that operate within a precisely defined realm leads to despair whenever it becomes apparent that changes there, if possible at all, will come slowly and with insufficient force. One is constantly defeated by the double problem of demonstrating how the "necessary changes" can be produced and of substantiating the assertion that the changes described as necessary would be sufficient to accomplish the object in view.

The contrary assertion, that all causes may be interrelated, is an argument against assuming that there is a single cause that can be isolated by analysis and eliminated or controlled by wisely constructed policy. It is also an argument against working with one or several hypotheses without bearing in mind the interrelation of all causes. The prescriptions directly derived from a single image are incomplete because they are based upon partial analyses. The partial quality of each image sets up a tension that drives one toward inclusion of the others. With the first image the direction of change, representing Locke's perspective as against Plato's, is from men to societies and states. The second image catches up both elements. Men make states, *and* states make men; but this is still a limited view. One is led to a search for the more inclusive nexus of causes, for states are shaped by the international environment as are men by both the national and international environments. Most of those whom we have considered in preceding [sections] have not written entirely in terms of one image. That we have thus far been dealing with the consequences arising from differing degrees of emphasis accounts for the complexity of preceding [sections] but now makes somewhat easier the task of suggesting how the images can be interrelated without distorting any one of them.

The First and Second Images in Relation to the Third

It may be true that the Soviet Union poses the greatest threat of war at the present time. It is not true that were the Soviet Union to disappear the remaining states could easily live at peace. We have known wars for centuries; the Soviet Union has existed only for decades. But some states, and perhaps some forms of the state, are more peacefully inclined than others. Would not the multiplication of peacefully inclined states at least warrant the hope that the period between major wars might be extended? By emphasizing the relevance of the framework of action, the third image makes clear the misleading quality of such partial analyses and of the hopes that are often based upon them. The act that by individual moral standards would be applauded may, when performed by a state, be an invitation to the war we seek to avoid. The third image, taken not as a theory of world government but as a theory of the

conditioning effects of the state system itself, alerts us to the fact that so far as increasing the chances of peace is concerned there is no such thing as an act good in itself. The pacification of the Hukbalahaps was a clear and direct contribution to the peace and order of the Philippine state. In international politics a partial "solution," such as one major country becoming pacifistic, might be a real contribution to world peace; but it might as easily hasten the coming of another major war.

The third image, as reflected in the writings of Rousseau, is based on an analysis of the consequences arising from the framework of state action. Rousseau's explanation of the origin of war among states is, in broad outline, the final one so long as we operate within a nation–state system. It is a final explanation because it does not hinge on accidental causes— irrationalities in men, defects in states— but upon his theory of the framework within which *any* accident can bring about a war. That state A wants certain things that it can get only by war does not explain war. Such a desire may or may not lead to war. My wanting a million dollars does not cause me to rob a bank, but if it were easier to rob banks, such desires would lead to much more bank robbing. This does not alter the fact that some people will and some will not attempt to rob banks no matter what the law enforcement situation is. We still have to look to motivation and circumstance in order to explain individual acts. Nevertheless one can predict that, other things being equal, a weakening of law enforcement agencies will lead to an increase in crime. From this point of view it is social structure—institutionalized restraints and institutionalized methods of altering and adjusting interests—that counts. And it counts in a way different from the ways usually associated with the word "cause." What causes a man to rob a bank are such things as the desire for money, a disrespect for social properties, a certain boldness. But if obstacles to the operation of these causes are built sufficiently high, nine out of ten would-be bank robbers will live their lives peacefully plying their legitimate trades. If the framework is to be called cause at all, it had best be specified that it is a permissive or underlying cause of war.

Applied to international politics this becomes, in words previously used to summarize Rousseau, the proposition that wars occur because there is nothing to prevent them. Rousseau's analysis explains the recurrence of war without explaining any given war. He tells us that war may at any moment occur, and he tells us why this is so. But the structure of the state system does not directly cause state A to attack state B. Whether or not that attack occurs will depend on a number of special circumstances— location, size, power, interest, type of government, past history and tradition— each of which will influence the actions of both states. If they fight against each other it will be for reasons especially defined for the occasion by each of them. These special reasons become the immediate, or efficient, causes of war. These immediate causes of war are contained in the first and second images. States are motivated to attack each other and to defend themselves by the reason and/or passion of the comparatively few who make policies for states and of the many more who influence the few. Some states, by virtue of their internal conditions, are both more proficient in war and more inclined to put their proficiency to the test. Variations in the factors included

in the first and second images are important, indeed crucial, in the making and breaking of periods of peace—the immediate causes of every war must be either the acts of individuals or the acts of states.

If every war is preceded by acts that we can identify (or at least try to identify) as cause, then why can we not eliminate wars by modifying individual or state behavior? This is the line of thinking followed by those who say: To end war, improve men; or: To end war, improve states. But in such prescriptions the role of the international environment is easily distorted. How can some of the acting units improve while others continue to follow their old and often predatory ways? The simplistic assumption of many liberals, that history moves relentlessly toward the millennium, is refuted if the international environment makes it difficult almost to the point of impossibility for states to behave in ways that are progressively more moral. Two points are omitted from the prescriptions we considered under the first and second images: (1) If an effect is produced by two or more causes, the effect is not permanently eliminated by removing one of them. If wars occur because men are less than perfectly rational and because states are less than perfectly formed, to improve only states may do little to decrease the number and intensity of wars. The error here is in identifying one cause where two or more may operate. (2) An endeavor launched against one cause to the neglect of others may make the situation worse instead of better. Thus, as the Western democracies became more inclined to peace, Hitler became more belligerent. The increased propensity to peace of some participants in international politics may increase, rather than decrease, the likelihood of war. This illustrates the role of the permissive cause, the international environment. If there were but two loci of cause involved, men and states, we could be sure that the appearance of more peacefully inclined states would, at worst, not damage the cause of world peace. Whether or not a remedy proposed is truly a remedy or actually worse than none at all depends, however, on the content and timing of the acts of all states. This is made clear in the third image.

War may result because state A has something that state B wants. The efficient cause of the war is the desire of state B; the permissive cause is the fact that there is nothing to prevent state B from undertaking the risks of war. In a different circumstance, the interrelation of efficient and permissive causes becomes still closer. State A may fear that if it does not cut state B down a peg now, it may be unable to do so ten years from now. State A becomes the aggressor in the present because it fears what state B may be able to do in the future. The efficient cause of such a war is derived from the cause that we have labeled permissive. In the first case, conflicts arise from disputes born of specific issues. In an age of hydrogen bombs, no single issue may be worth the risk of full-scale war. Settlement, even on bad grounds, is preferable to self-destruction. The use of reason would seem to require the adoption of a doctrine of "non-recourse to force." One whose reason leads him down this path is following the trail blazed by Cobden when in 1849 he pointed out "that it is almost impossible, on looking back for the last hundred years, to tell precisely what any war was about," and thus implied that Englishmen should never have become involved in them.[32] He is falling into the trap that ensnared A. A. Milne when he explained the First World War as a war in which ten million men died because Austria-Hungary sought, unsuccessfully, to avenge the death of one archduke.[33] He is succumbing to the illusion of Sir Edward Grey, who, in the memoirs he wrote some thirty years ago, hoped that the horrors of the First World War would make it possible for nations "to find at least one common ground on which they should come together in confident understanding: an agreement that, in the disputes between them, war must be ruled out as a means of settlement that entails ruin."[34]

It is true that the immediate causes of many wars are trivial. If we focus upon them, the failure to agree to settlement without force appears to be the ultimate folly. But it is not often true that the immediate causes provide sufficient explanation for the wars that have occurred. And if it is not simply particular disputes that produce wars, rational settlement of them cannot eliminate war. For, as Winston Churchill has written, "small matters are only the symptoms of the dangerous disease, and are only important for that reason. Behind them lie the interests, the passions and the destiny of mighty races of men; and long antagonisms express themselves in trifles."[35] Nevertheless Churchill may be justified in hoping that the fear induced by a "balance of terror" will produce a temporary truce. Advancing technology makes war more horrible and presumably increases the desire for peace; the very rapidity of the advance makes for uncertainty in everyone's military planning and destroys the possibility of an accurate estimate of the likely opposing forces. Fear and permanent peace are more difficult to equate. Each major advance in the technology of war has found its prophet ready to proclaim that war is no longer possible: Alfred Nobel and dynamite, for example, or Benjamin Franklin and the lighter-than-air balloon. There may well have been a prophet to proclaim the end of tribal warfare when the spear was invented and another to make a similar prediction when poison was first added to its tip. Unfortunately, these prophets have all been false. The development of atomic and hydrogen weapons may nurture the peace wish of some, the war sentiment of others. In the United States and elsewhere after the Second World War, a muted theme of foreign-policy debate was the necessity of preventive war—drop the bomb quickly before the likely opponent in a future war has time to make one of his own. Even with two or more states equipped with similar weapon systems, a momentary shift in the balance of terror, giving a decisive military advantage temporarily to one state, may tempt it to seize the moment in order to escape from fear. And the temptation would be proportionate to the fear itself. Finally, mutual fear of big weapons may produce, instead of peace, a spate of smaller wars.

The fear of modern weapons, of the danger of destroying the civilizations of the world, is not sufficient to establish the conditions of peace identified in our discussions of the three images of international relations. One can equate fear with world peace only if the peace wish exists in all states and is uniformly expressed in their policies. But peace is the primary goal of few men or states. If it were the primary goal of even a single state, that state could have peace at any time—simply by surrendering. But, as John Foster Dulles so often warned, "Peace can be a cover whereby evil men perpetrate diabolical wrongs."[36] The

issue in a given dispute may not be: Who shall gain from it? It may instead be: Who shall dominate the world? In such circumstances, the best course of even reasonable men is difficult to define; their ability always to contrive solutions without force, impossible to assume. If solutions in terms of none of the three images is presently—if ever—possible, then reason can work only within the framework that is suggested by viewing the first and second images in the perspective of the third, a perspective well and simply set forth in the *Federalist Papers,* especially in those written by Hamilton and Jay.

What would happen, Jay asks, if the thirteen states, instead of combining as one state, should form themselves into several confederations? He answers:

> Instead of their being "joined in affection" and free from all apprehension of different "interests," envy and jealousy would soon extinguish confidence and affection, and the partial interests of each confederation, instead of the general interests of all America, would be the only objects of their policy and pursuits. Hence, like most *bordering* nations, they would always be either involved in disputes and war, or live in the constant apprehension of them.[37]

International anarchy, Jay is here saying, is the explanation for international war. But not international anarchy alone. Hamilton adds that to presume a lack of hostile motives among states is to forget that men are "ambitious, vindictive, and rapacious." A monarchical state may go to war because the vanity of its king leads him to seek glory in military victory; a republic may go to war because of the folly of its assembly or because of its commercial interests. That the king may be vain, the assembly foolish, or the commercial interests irreconcilable: none of these is inevitable. However, so many and so varied are the causes of war among states that "to look for a continuation of harmony between a number of independent, unconnected sovereigns in the same neighborhood, would be to disregard the uniform course of human events, and to set at defiance the accumulated experience of the ages."[38]

Jay and Hamilton found in the history of the Western state system confirmation for the conclusion that among separate sovereign states there is constant possibility of war. The third image gives a theoretical basis for the same conclusion. It reveals why, in the absence of tremendous changes in the factors included in the first and second images, war will be perpetually associated with the existence of separate sovereign states. The obvious conclusion of a third-image analysis is that world government is the remedy for world war. The remedy, though it may be unassailable in logic, is unattainable in practice. The third image may provide a utopian approach to world politics. It may also provide a realistic approach, and one that avoids the tendency of some realists to attribute the necessary amorality, or even immorality, of world politics to the inherently bad character of man. If everyone's strategy depends upon everyone else's, then the Hitlers determine in part the action, or better, reaction, of those whose ends are worthy and whose means are fastidious. No matter how good their intentions, policy makers must bear in mind the implications of the third image, which can be stated in summary form as follows: Each state pursues its own interests, however defined, in ways it judges best. Force is a means of achieving the external ends of states because there exists no consistent, reliable pro-

cess of reconciling the conflicts of interest that inevitably arise among similar units in a condition of anarchy. A foreign policy based on this image of international relations is neither moral nor immoral, but embodies merely a reasoned response to the world about us. The third image describes the framework of world politics, but without the first and second images there can be no knowledge of the forces that determine policy; the first and second images describe the forces in world politics, but without the third image it is impossible to assess their importance or predict their results.

NOTES

1. Beverly Nichols, *Cry Havoc!* (New York: Doubleday, Doran & Co., 1933), p. 164.
2. Margaret E. Hirst, *The Quakers in Peace and War* (London: Swarthmore Press, 1923), pp. 521-25.
3. Bertrand Russell, *Political Ideals* (New York: Century Co., 1971), p. 42. In one way or another the thought recurs in Lord Russell's many writings on international relations.
4. William James, "The Moral Equivalent of War," in *Memories and Studies* (New York: Longmans, Green and Co., 1912), pp. 262-72, 290.
5. Jean Bodin, *Six Books of the Commonwealth,* abridged and trans. M. J. Tooley (Oxford: Basil Blackwell, n.d.), p. 168.
6. "Some Thoughts for the President's Consideration," Apr. 1, 1861, in *Documents of American History,* ed. Henry Steele Commager, 3d ed. (New York: F. S. Crofts & Co., 1946), p. 392.
7. Hans Herzfeld, "Bismarck und die Skobelewespisode," *Historische Zeitschrift* 142 (1930): 279-302.
8. Cf. Robert E. Sherwood, *Roosevelt and Hopkins* (New York: Harper and Brothers, 1948), pp. 67-68, 102, 126, 133-36, 272, and esp. 931; and Secretary of State

Hay's statement in Henry Adams, *The Education of Henry Adams* (New York: Book League of America, 1928), p. 374. Note that in this case the fault is one that is thought to decrease the ability of a country to implement a peaceful policy. In the other examples, the defect is thought to increase the propensity of a country to go to war.

9. Cf. Bertrand Russell, who in 1917 wrote: "There can be no good international system until the boundaries of states coincide as nearly as possible with the boundaries of nations" (*Political Ideals,* p. 146).

10. Frank H. Simonds and Brooks Emery, *The Great Powers in World Politics* (New York: American Book Co., 1939), passim; W. S. Thompson, *Danger Spots in World Population* (New York: Alfred A. Knopf, 1930), esp. the Preface and chaps. 1 and 13.

11. Cf. Vladimir Dedijer, "Albania, Soviet Pawn," *Foreign Affairs* 30 (1951): 104: socialism, but not Soviet Union state capitalism, means peace.

12. Thucydides, *History of the Peloponnesian War,* trans. B. Jowett, 2d ed. (London: Oxford University Press, 1900), bk. 1, par. 23.

13. John Adams to the citizens of the town of Petersburg, Virginia, June 6, 1798, reprinted in the program for the visit of William Howard Taft, Petersburg, May 19, 1909.

14. Frederick S. Dunn, *Peaceful Change* (New York: Council on Foreign Relations, 1937), p. 13.

15. Richard Cobden, esp. *Speeches on Peace, Financial Reform, Colonial Reform and Other Subjects Delivered during 1849* (London: James Gilbert, n.d.), p. 135.

16. Jean Jaques Rousseau, *The Social Contract and Discourses,* trans, G. D. H. Cole, Everyman's Library Edition (New York: E. P. Dutton and Co., 1950); see esp. *Inequality,* pp. 234 ff.

17. Ibid., p. 34.

18. Benedict de Spinoza, *The Chief Works of Benedict de Spinoza,* trans. R. H. M. Elwes, 2 vols. (New York: Dover Publications, 1951), *Ethics,* pt. 4, prop. 35, proof.

19. Rousseau, *Social Contract and Discourses,* pp. 135–36 (bk. 4, chap. 8), italics added. The word "equally" is necessary for an accurate rendering of the French text but docs not appear in the translation cited.

20. Jean Jacques Rousseau, *A Lasting Peace through the Federation of Europe and the State of War,* trans. C. E. Vaughan (London: Constable and Co., 1917), p. 72.

21. This parallels Hegel's formulation: "It is to what is by nature accidental that accidents happen, and the fate whereby they happen is thus a necessity" [G. W. F.] Hegel, *Philosophy of Right,* trans. T. M. Knox (Oxford: Clarendon Press, 1942), sec. 324].

22. Kant is more willing to admit the force of this criticism than is generally realized.

23. This is not, of course, to say that no differences in state behavior follow from the different constitutions and situations of states. This point raises the question of the relation of the third image to the second, which will be discussed below.

24. Rousseau, *Social Contract and Discourses,* pp. 290–91.

25. Rousseau, *A Lasting Peace,* pp. 46–48, 58–59.

26. Ibid., pp. 38, 46–47. On p. 121, Rousseau distinguishes between the "state of war," which always exists among states, and war proper, which manifests itself in the settled intention to destroy the enemy state.

27. Ibid., p. 49.

28. In ibid., p. 69, Rousseau presents his exhaustive list of such causes.

29. Ibid., pp. 38–39.

30. Ibid., pp. 59–60.

31. Cf. Karl Popper, *The Open Society and Its Enemies* (Princeton: Princeton University Press, 1950), pp. 158–59; and William Esslinger, *Politics and Science* (New York: Philosophical Library, 1955), passim.

32. Richard Cobden, *Speeches on Questions of Public Policy,* 2 vols., ed. John Bright and James E. Thorold Rogers (London: Macmillan & Co., 1870), 2: 165.

33. A. A. Milne, *Peace and War* (New York: E. P. Dutton & Co., 1934), p. 11.

34. Edward Grey, *Twenty-Five Years,* 2 vols. (New York: Frederick A. Stokes Co., 1925), 2: 285.

35. Winston Churchill, *The World Crisis,* 1911–1914, 4 vols. (New York: Charles Scribner's Sons, 1923–29), 1: 52.

36. "Excerpts from Dulles Address on Peace," Washington, D.C., Apr. 11, 1955, in *New York Times,* Apr. 12, 1955, p. 6.

37. Alexander Hamilton, John Jay, and James Madison, *The Federalist* (New York: Modern Library, 1941), pp. 23–24 (no. 5).

38. Ibid., pp. 27–28 (no. 6); cf. p. 18 (no. 4, Jay) and pp. 34–40 (no. 7, Hamilton).

QUESTIONS

1. Which image do you think offers the best explanation for war and why?

2. Why does Waltz distinguish between the "immediate" causes of war and the "permissive" causes of war?

2.   The Level-of-Analysis Problem in International Relations

J. David Singer

In this article, J. David Singer focuses on state- and system-level explanations for the study of international relations. Singer argues that a theoretical model of international politics should be able to describe, to explain, and to predict. He then examines the two alternative levels of analysis and concludes that both models are useful for different purposes, and both make significant contributions to our understanding of international politics. This selection is from *The International System: Theoretical Essays* (1961).

   J. David Singer is a professor of international relations at the University of Michigan. His other works include *Deterrence, Arms Control and Disarmament: Toward a Synthesis in National Security Policy* (1962), and *Explaining War* (1979).

In any area of scholarly inquiry, there are always several ways in which the phenomena under study may be sorted and arranged for purposes of systemic analysis. Whether in the physical or social sciences, the observer may choose to focus upon the parts or upon the whole, upon the components or upon the system. He may, for example, choose between the flowers or the garden, the rocks or the quarry, the trees or the forest, the houses or the neighborhood, the cars or the traffic jam, the delinquents or the gang, the legislators or the legislative, and so on.[1] Whether he selects the micro- or macrolevel of analysis is ostensibly a mere matter of methodological or conceptual convenience. Yet the choice often turns out to be quite difficult, and may well become a central issue within the discipline concerned. The complexity and significance of these level-of-analysis decisions are readily suggested by the long-standing controversies between social psychology and sociology, personality-oriented and culture-oriented anthropology, or micro- and macro-economics, to mention but a few. In the vernacular of general systems theory, the observer is always confronted with a system, its sub-systems, and their respective environments, and while he may choose as his system any cluster of phenomena from the most minute organism to the universe itself, such choice cannot be merely a function of whim or caprice, habit or familiarity.[2] The responsible scholar must be prepared to evaluate the relative utility—conceptual and methodological—of the various alternatives open to him, and to appraise the manifold implications of the level of analysis finally selected. So it is with international relations.

But whereas the pros and cons of the various possible levels of analysis have been debated exhaustively in many of the social sciences, the issue has scarcely been raised among students of our emerging discipline.[3] Such tranquillity may be seen by some as a reassuring indication that the issue is not germane to our field, and by others as evidence that it has already been resolved, but this writer perceives the quietude with a measure of concern. He is quite per-suaded of its relevance and certain that it has yet to be resolved. Rather, it is contended that the issue has been ignored by scholars still steeped in the intuitive and artistic tradition of the humanities or enmeshed in the web of "practical" policy. We have, in our texts and elsewhere, roamed up and down the ladder of organizational complexity with remarkable abandon, focusing upon the total system, international organizations, regions, coalitions, extra-national associations, nations, domestic pressure groups, social classes, elites, and individuals as the needs of the moment required. And though most of us have tended to settle upon the nation as our most comfortable resting place, we have retained our propensity for vertical drift, failing to appreciate the value of a stable point of focus.[4] Whether this lack of concern is a function of the relative infancy of the discipline or the nature of the intellectual traditions from whence it springs, it nevertheless remains a significant variable in the general sluggishness which characterizes the development of theory in the study of relations among nations. It is the purpose of this paper to raise the issue, articulate the alternatives, and examine the theoretical implications and consequences of two of the more widely employed levels of analysis: the international system and the national sub-systems.

I. THE REQUIREMENTS OF AN ANALYTICAL MODEL

Prior to an examination of the theoretical implications of the level of analysis or orientation employed in our model, it might be worthwhile to discuss the uses to which any such model might be put, and the requirements which such uses might expect of it.

Obviously, we would demand that it offer a highly accurate *description* of the phenomena under consideration. Therefore the scheme must present as complete and undistorted a picture of these phenomena as is possible; it must correlate with objective reality and coincide with our empirical referents to the highest possible degree. Yet we know that such accurate representation of a complex and wide-ranging body of phenomena is extremely difficult. Perhaps a useful illustration may be borrowed from cartography; the oblate spheroid which the planet earth most closely represents is not transferable to the two-dimensional surface of a map without *some* distortion. Thus, the Mercator projection exaggerates distance and distorts direction at an increasing rate as we move north or south *from* the equator, while the polar gnomonic projection suffers from these same debilities as we move *toward* the equator. Neither offers therefore a wholly accurate presentation, yet each is true enough to reality to be quite useful for certain specific purposes. The same sort of tolerance is necessary in evaluating any analytical model for the study of international relations; if we must sacrifice total representational accuracy, the problem is to decide where distortion is least dysfunctional and where such accuracy is absolutely essential.

These decisions are, in turn, a function of the second requirement of any such model—a capacity to *explain* the relationships among the phenomena under investigation. Here our concern is not so much with accuracy of description as with validity of explanation. Our model must have such analytical capabilities as to treat the causal relationships in a fashion which is not only valid and thorough, but parsimonious; this latter requirement is often overlooked, yet its implications for research strategy are not inconsequential.[5] It should be asserted here that the primary purpose of theory is to explain, and when descriptive and explanatory requirements are in conflict, the latter ought to be given priority, even at the cost of some representational inaccuracy.

Finally, we may legitimately demand that any analytical model offer the promise of reliable *prediction.* In mentioning this requirement last, there is no implication that it is the most demanding or difficult of the three. Despite the popular belief to the contrary, prediction demands less of one's model than does explanation or even description. For example, any informed layman can predict that pressure on the accelerator of a slowly moving car will increase its speed; that more or less of the moon will be visible tonight than last night; or that the normal human will flinch when confronted with an impending blow. These *predictions* do not require a particularly elegant or sophisticated model of the universe, but their *explanation* demands far more than most of us carry around in our minds. Likewise, we can predict with impressive reliability that any nation will respond to military attack in kind, but a description and understanding of the processes and factors leading to such a response are considerably more elusive, despite the gross simplicity of the acts themselves.

Having articulated rather briefly the requirements of an adequate analytical model, we might turn now to a consideration of the ways in which one's choice of analytical focus impinges upon such a model and affects its descriptive, explanatory, and predictive adequacy.

II. THE INTERNATIONAL SYSTEM AS LEVEL OF ANALYSIS

Beginning with the systemic level of analysis, we find in the total international system a partially familiar and highly promising point of focus. First of all, it is the most comprehensive of levels available, encompassing the totality of interactions which take place within the system and its environment. By focusing on the system, we are enabled to study the patterns of interaction which the system reveals, and to generalize about such phenomena as the creation and dissolution of coalitions, the frequency and duration of specific power configurations, modifications in its stability, its responsiveness to changes in formal political institutions, and the norms and folklore which it manifests as a societal system. In other words, the systemic level of analysis, and only this level, permits us to examine international relations in the whole, with a comprehensiveness that is of necessity lost when our focus is shifted to a lower, and more partial, level. For descriptive purposes, then, it offers both advantages and disadvantages; the former flow from its comprehensiveness, and the latter from the necessary dearth of detail.

As to explanatory capability, the system-oriented model poses some genuine difficulties. In the first place, it tends to lead the observer into a position which exaggerates the impact of the system upon the national actors and, conversely, discounts the impact of the actors on the system. This is, of course, by no means inevitable; one could conceivably look upon the system as a rather passive environment in which dynamic states act out their relationships rather than as a socio-political entity with a dynamic of its own. But there is a natural tendency to endow that upon which we focus our attention with somewhat greater potential than it might normally be expected to have. Thus, we tend to move, in a system-oriented model, away from notions implying much national autonomy and independence of choice and toward a more deterministic orientation.

Secondly, this particular level of analysis almost inevitably requires that we postulate a high degree of uniformity in the foreign policy operational codes of our national actors. By definition, we allow little room for divergence in the behavior of our parts when we focus upon the whole. It is no coincidence that our most prominent theoretician—and one of the very few text writers focusing upon the international system—should "assume that [all] statesmen think and act in terms of interest defined as power."[6] If this single-minded behavior be interpreted literally and narrowly, we have a simplistic image comparable to economic man or sexual man, and if it be defined broadly, we are no better off than the psychologist whose human model pursues "self-realization" or "maximization of gain"; all such gross models suffer from the same fatal weakness as the utilitarian's "pleasure-pain" principle. Just as individuals differ widely in what they deem to be pleasure and pain, or gain and loss, nations may differ widely in what they consider to be the national interest, and we end up having to break down and refine the larger category. Moreover, Professor Morgenthau finds himself compelled to go still further and disavow the relevance of both motives and ideological preferences in national behavior, and these represent two of the more useful dimensions in differentiating among the several nations in our international system. By eschewing any empirical concern with the domestic and internal variations within the separate nations, the system-oriented approach tends to produce a sort of "black box" or "billiard ball" concept of the national actors.[7] By discounting—or denying—the differences among nations, or by positing the near-impossibility of observing many of these differences at work within them,[8] one concludes with a highly homogenized image of our nations in the international system. And though this may be an inadequate foundation upon which to base any *causal* statements, it offers a reasonably adequate basis for *correlative* statements. More specifically, it permits us to observe and measure correlations between certain forces or stimuli which seem to impinge upon the nation and the behavior patterns which are the apparent consequence of these stimuli. But one must stress the limitations implied in the word "apparent"; what is thought to be the consequence of a given stimulus may only be a coincidence or artifact, and until one investigates the major elements in the causal link—no matter how persuasive the deductive logic—one may speak only of correlation, not of consequence.

Moreover, by avoiding the multitudinous pitfalls of intra-nation observation, one emerges with a singularly manageable model, requiring as it does little of the methodological sophistication or onerous empiricism called for when one probes beneath the behavioral externalities of the actor. Finally, as has already been suggested in the introduction, the systemic orientation should prove to be reasonably satisfactory as a basis for prediction, even if such prediction is to extend beyond the characteristics of the system and attempt anticipatory statements regarding the actors themselves; this assumes, of course, that the actors are characterized and their behavior predicted in relatively gross and general terms.

These, then, are some of the more significant implications of a model which focuses upon the international system as a whole. Let us turn now to the more familiar of our two orientations, the national state itself.

III. THE NATIONAL STATE AS LEVEL OF ANALYSIS

The other level of analysis to be considered in this paper is the national state—our primary actor in international relations. This is clearly the traditional focus among Western students, and is the one which dominates almost all of the texts employed in English-speaking colleges and universities.

Its most obvious advantage is that it permits significant differentiation among our actors in the international system. Because it does not require the attribution of great similarity to the national actors, it encourages the observer to examine them in greater detail. The favorable results of such intensive analysis cannot be overlooked, as it is only when the actors are studied in some depth that we are able to make really valid generalizations of a comparative nature. And though the systemic model does not necessarily preclude comparison and contrast among the national sub-systems, it usually eventuates in rather gross comparisons based on relatively crude dimensions and characteristics. On the other hand, there is no assurance that the nation-oriented approach will produce a sophisticated model for the comparative study of foreign policy; with perhaps the exception of the Haas and Whiting study,[9] none of our major texts makes a serious and successful effort to describe and explain national behavior in terms of most of the significant variables by which such behavior might be comparatively analyzed. But this would seem to be a function, not of the level of analysis employed, but of our general unfamiliarity with the other social sciences (in which comparison is a major preoccupation) and of the retarded state of comparative government and politics, a field in which most international relations specialists are likely to have had some experience.

But just as the nation-as-actor focus permits us to avoid the inaccurate homogenization which often flows from the systemic focus, it also may lead us into the opposite type of distortion—a marked exaggeration of the differences among our sub-systemic actors. While it is evident that neither of these extremes is conducive to the development of a sophisticated comparison of foreign policies, and such comparison requires a balanced preoccupation with both similarity and difference, the danger seems to be greatest when we succumb to the tendency to overdifferentiate; comparison and contrast can proceed only from observed uniformities.[10]

One of the additional liabilities which flow in turn from the pressure to overdifferentiate is that of Ptolemaic parochialism. Thus, in over-emphasizing the differences among the many national states, the observer is prone to attribute many of what he conceives to be virtues to his own nation and the vices to others, especially the adversaries of the moment. That this ethnocentrism is by no means

an idle fear is borne out by perusal of the major international relations texts published in the United States since 1945. Not only is the world often perceived through the prism of the American national interest, but an inordinate degree of attention (if not spleen) is directed toward the Soviet Union; it would hardly be amiss to observe that most of these might qualify equally well as studies in American foreign policy. The scientific inadequacies of this sort of "we–they" orientation hardly require elaboration, yet they remain a potent danger in any utilization of the national actor model.

Another significant implication of the subsystemic orientation is that it is only within its particular framework that we can expect any useful application of the decision-making approach.[11] Not all of us, of course, will find its inapplicability a major loss; considering the criticism which has been leveled at the decision-making approach, and the failure of most of us to attempt its application, one might conclude that it is no loss at all. But the important thing to note here is that a system-oriented model would not offer a hospitable framework for such a detailed and comparative approach to the study of international relations, no matter what our appraisal of the decision-making approach might be.

Another and perhaps more subtle implication of selecting the nation as our focus or level of analysis is that it raises the entire question of goals, motivation, and purpose in national policy.[12] Though it may well be a peculiarity of the Western philosophical tradition, we seem to exhibit, when confronted with the need to explain individual or collective behavior, a strong proclivity for a goal-seeking approach. The question of whether national behavior is purposive or not seems to require discussion in two distinct (but not always exclusive) dimensions.

Firstly, there is the more obvious issue of whether those who act on behalf of the nation in formulating and executing foreign policy consciously pursue rather concrete goals. And it would be difficult to deny, for example, that these role-fulfilling individuals envisage certain specific outcomes which they hope to realize by pursuing a particular strategy. In this sense, then, nations may be said to be goal-seeking organisms which exhibit purposive behavior.

However, purposiveness may be viewed in a somewhat different light, by asking whether it is not merely an intellectual construct that man imputes to himself by reason of his vain addiction to the free-will doctrine as he searches for characteristics which distinguish him from physical matter and the lower animals. And having attributed this conscious goal-pursuing behavior to himself as an individual, it may be argued that man then proceeds to project this attribute to the social organizations of which he is a member. The question would seem to distill down to whether man and his societies pursue goals of their own choosing or are moved toward those imposed upon them by forces which are primarily beyond their control.[13] Another way of stating the dilemma would be to ask whether we are concerned with the ends which men and nations strive for or the ends toward which they are impelled by the past and present characteristics of their social and physical milieu. Obviously, we are using the terms "ends," "goals," and "purpose" in two rather distinct ways; one refers to those which are

consciously envisaged and more or less rationally pursued, and the other to those of which the actor has little knowledge but toward which he is nevertheless propelled.

Taking a middle ground in what is essentially a specific case of the free will vs. determinism debate, one can agree that nations move toward outcomes of which they have little knowledge and over which they have less control, but that they nevertheless do prefer, and therefore select, particular outcomes and *attempt* to realize them by conscious formulation of strategies.

Also involved in the goal-seeking problem when we employ the nation-oriented model is the question of how and why certain nations pursue specific sorts of goals. While the question may be ignored in the system-oriented model or resolved by attributing identical goals to all national actors, the nation-as-actor approach demands that we investigate the processes by which national goals are selected, the internal and external factors that impinge on those processes, and the institutional framework from which they emerge. It is worthy of note that despite the strong predilection for the nation-oriented model in most of our texts, empirical or even deductive analyses of these processes are conspicuously few.[14] Again, one might attribute these lacunae to the methodological and conceptual inadequacies of the graduate training which international relations specialists traditionally receive.[15] But in any event, goals and motivations are both dependent and independent variables, and if we intend to explain a nation's foreign policy, we cannot settle for the mere postulation of these goals; we are compelled to go back a step and inquire into their genesis and the process by which they become the crucial variables that they seem to be in the behavior of nations.

There is still another dilemma involved in our selection of the nation-as-actor model, and that concerns the phenomenological issue: do we examine our actor's behavior in terms of the objective factors which allegedly influence that behavior, or do we do so in terms of the actor's *perception* of these "objective factors"? Though these two approaches are not completely exclusive of one another, they proceed from greatly different and often incompatible assumptions, and produce markedly divergent models of national behavior.[16]

The first of these assumptions concerns the broad question of social causation. One view holds that individuals and groups respond in a quasi-deterministic fashion to the realities of physical environment, the acts or power of other individuals or groups, and similar "objective" and "real" forces or stimuli. An opposite view holds that individuals and groups are not influenced in their behavior by such objective forces, but by the fashion in which these forces are perceived and evaluated, however distorted or incomplete such perceptions may be. For adherents of this position, the only reality is the phenomenal—that which is discerned by the human senses; forces that are not discerned do not exist for that actor, and those that do exist do so only in the fashion in which they are perceived. Though it is difficult to accept the position that an individual, a group, or a nation is affected by such forces as climate, distance, or a neighbor's physical power only insofar as they are recognized and appraised, one must concede that perceptions will certainly affect the manner in which such forces are responded to. As has often been pointed out, an individual will fall to the ground when he steps out of a tenth-story window regardless of his perception of gravitational forces, but on the other hand such perception is a major factor in whether or not he steps out of the window in the first place.[17] The point here is that if we embrace a phenomenological view of causation, we will tend to utilize a phenomenological model for explanatory purposes.

The second assumption which bears on one's predilection for the phenomenological approach is more restricted, and is primarily a methodological one. Thus, it may be argued that any description of national behavior in a given international situation would be highly incomplete were it to ignore the link between the external forces at work upon the nation and its general foreign policy behavior. Furthermore, if our concern extends beyond the mere description of "what happens" to the realm of explanation, it could be contended that such omission of the cognitive and the perceptual linkage would be ontologically disastrous. How, it might be asked, can one speak of "causes" of a nation's policies when one has ignored the media by which external conditions and factors are translated into a policy decision? We may observe correlations between all sorts of forces in the international system and the behavior of nations, but their causal relationship must remain strictly deductive and hypothetical in the absence of empirical investigation into the causal chain which allegedly links the two. Therefore, even if we are satisfied with the less-than-complete descriptive capabilities of a non-phenomenological model, we are still drawn to it if we are to make any progress in explanation.

The contrary view would hold that the above argument proceeds from an erroneous comprehension of the nature of explanation in social science. One is by no means required to trace every perception, transmission, and receipt between stimulus and response or input and output in order to explain the behavior of the nation or any other human group. Furthermore, who is to say that empirical observation—subject as it is to a host of errors—is any better a basis of explanation than informed deduction, inference, or analogy? Isn't an explanation which flows logically from a coherent theoretical model just as reliable as one based upon a misleading and elusive body of data, most of which is susceptible to analysis only by techniques and concepts foreign to political science and history?

This leads, in turn, to the third of the premises relevant to one's stand on the phenomenological issue: are the dimensions and characteristics of the policy-makers' phenomenal field empirically discernible? Or, more accurately, even if we are convinced that their perceptions and beliefs constitute a crucial variable in the explanation of a nation's foreign policy, can they be observed in an accurate and systematic fashion?[18] Furthermore, are we not required by the phenomenological model to go beyond a classification and description of such variables, and be drawn into the tangled web of relationships out of which they emerge? If we believe that these phenomenal variables are systematically observable, are explainable, and can be fitted into our explanation of a nation's behavior in the international system, then there is a further tendency to embrace the phenomenological approach. If not, or if we are convinced that the gathering of such data is inefficient or uneconomical, we will tend to shy clear of it.

The fourth issue in the phenomenological dispute concerns the very nature of the nation as an actor in international relations. Who or what is it that we study? Is it a distinct social entity with well-defined boundaries—a unity unto itself? Or is it an agglomeration of individuals, institutions, customs, and procedures? It should be quite evident that those who view the nation or the state as an integral social unit could not attach much utility to the phenomenological approach, particularly if they are prone to concretize or reify the abstraction. Such abstractions are incapable of perception, cognition, or anticipation (unless, of course, the reification goes so far as to anthropomorphize and assign to the abstraction such attributes as will, mind, or personality). On the other hand, if the nation or state is seen as a group of individuals operating within an institutional framework, then it makes perfect sense to focus on the phenomenal field of those individuals who participate in the policy-making process. In other words, *people* are capable of experiences, images, and expectations, while institutional abstractions are not, except in the metaphorical sense. Thus, if our actor cannot even have a phenomenal field, there is little point in employing a phenomenological approach.[19]

These, then, are some of the questions around which the phenomenological issue would seem to revolve. Those of us who think of social forces as operative regardless of the actor's awareness, who believe that explanation need not include all of the steps in a causal chain, who are dubious of the practicality of gathering phenomenal data, or who visualize the nation as a distinct entity apart from its individual members, will tend to reject the phenomenological approach.[20] Logically, only those who disagree with each of the above four assumptions would be *compelled* to adopt the approach. Disagreement with any one would be *sufficient* grounds for so doing.

The above represent some of the more significant implications and fascinating problems raised by the adoption of our second model. They seem to indicate that this subsystemic orientation is likely to produce richer description and more satisfactory (from the empiricist's point of view) explanation of international relations, though its predictive power would appear no greater than the systemic orientation. But the descriptive and explanatory advantages are achieved only at the price of considerable methodological complexity.

IV. CONCLUSION

Having discussed some of the descriptive, explanatory, and predictive capabilities of these two possible levels of analysis, it might now be useful to assess the relative utility of the two and attempt some general statement as to their prospective contributions to greater theoretical growth in the study of international relations.

In terms of description, we find that the systemic level produces a more comprehensive and total picture of international relations than does the national or sub-systemic level. On the other hand, the atomized and less coherent image produced by the lower level of analysis is somewhat balanced by its richer detail, greater depth, and more intensive portrayal.[21] As to explanation, there seems little doubt that the sub-systemic or actor orientation is considerably more fruitful,

permitting as it does a more thorough investigation of the processes by which foreign policies are made. Here we are enabled to go beyond the limitations imposed by the systemic level and to replace mere correlation with the more significant causation. And in terms of prediction, both orientations seem to offer a similar degree of promise. Here the issue is a function of what we seek to predict. Thus the policy-maker will tend to prefer predictions about the way in which nation x or y will react to a contemplated move on his own nation's part, while the scholar will probably prefer either generalized predictions regarding the behavior of a given class of nations or those regarding the system itself.

Does this summary add up to an overriding case for one or another of the two models? It would seem not. For a staggering variety of reasons the scholar may be more interested in one level than another at any given time and will undoubtedly shift his orientation according to his research needs. So the problem is really not one of deciding which level is most valuable to the discipline as a whole and then demanding that it be adhered to from now unto eternity.[22] Rather, it is one of realizing that there *is* this preliminary conceptual issue and that it must be temporarily resolved prior to any given research undertaking. And it must also be stressed that we have dealt here only with two of the more common orientations, and that many others are available and perhaps even more fruitful potentially than either of those selected here. Moreover, the international system gives many indications of prospective change, and it may well be that existing institutional forms will take on new characteristics or that new ones will appear to take their place. As a matter of fact, if incapacity to perform its functions leads to the transformation or decay of an institution, we may expect a steady deterioration and even ultimate disappearance of the national state as a significant actor in the world political system.

However, even if the case for one or another of the possible levels of analysis cannot be made with any certainty, one must nevertheless maintain a continuing awareness as to their use. We may utilize one level here and another there, but we cannot afford to shift our orientation in the midst of a study. And when we do in fact make an original selection or replace one with another at appropriate times, we must do so with a full awareness of the descriptive, explanatory, and predictive implications of such choice.

A final point remains to be discussed. Despite this lengthy exegesis, one might still be prone to inquire whether this is not merely a sterile exercise in verbal gymnastics. What, it might be asked, is the difference between the two levels of analysis if the empirical referents remain essentially the same? Or, to put it another way, is there any difference between international relations and comparative foreign policy? Perhaps a few illustrations will illuminate the subtle but important differences which emerge when one's level of analysis shifts. One might, for example, postulate that when the international system is characterized by political conflict between two of its most powerful actors, there is a strong tendency for the system to bipolarize. This is a systemic-oriented proposition. A sub-systemic proposition, dealing with the same general empirical referents, would state that when a powerful actor finds itself in political conflict with another of approximate parity, it will tend to exert

pressure on its weaker neighbors to join its coalition. Each proposition, assuming it is true, is theoretically useful by itself, but each is verified by a different intellectual operation. Moreover—and this is the crucial thing for theoretical development—one could not add these two kinds of statements together to achieve a cumulative growth of empirical generalizations.

To illustrate further, one could, at the systemic level, postulate that when the distribution of power in the international system is highly diffused, it is more stable than when the discernible clustering of well-defined coalitions occurs. And at the sub-systemic or national level, the same empirical phenomena would produce this sort of proposition: when a nation's decision-makers find it difficult to categorize other nations readily as friend or foe, they tend to behave toward all in a more uniform and moderate fashion. Now, taking these two sets of propositions, how much cumulative usefulness would arise from attempting to merge and codify the systemic proposition from the first illustration with the sub-systemic proposition from the second, or vice versa? Representing different levels of analysis and couched in different frames of reference, they would defy theoretical integration; one may well be a corollary of the other, but they are not immediately combinable. A prior translation from one level to another must take place.

This, it is submitted, is quite crucial for the theoretical development of our discipline. With all of the current emphasis on the need for more empirical and data-gathering research as a prerequisite to theory-building, one finds little concern with the relationship among these separate and discrete data-gathering activities. Even if we were to declare a moratorium on deductive and speculative research for the next decade, and all of us were to labor diligently in the vineyards of historical and contemporary data, the state of international relations theory would probably be no more advanced at that time than it is now, unless such empirical activity becomes far more systematic. And "systematic" is used here to indicate the cumulative growth of inductive and deductive generalizations into an impressive array of statements conceptually related to one another and flowing from some common frame of reference. What that frame of reference should be, or will be, cannot be said with much certainty, but it does seem clear that it must exist. As long as we evade some of these crucial *a priori* decisions, our empiricism will amount to little more than an ever-growing potpourri of discrete, disparate, non-comparable, and isolated bits of information or extremely low-level generalizations. And, as such, they will make little contribution to the growth of a theory of international relations.

NOTES

1. As Kurt Lewin observed in his classic contribution to the social sciences: "The first prerequisite of a successful observation in any science is a definite understanding about what size of unit one is going to observe at a given time." *Field Theory in Social Science,* New York, 1951, I, p. 157.

2. For a useful introductory statement on the definitional and taxonomic problems in a general systems approach, see the papers by Ludwig von Bertalanffy, "General System Theory," and Kenneth Boulding, "General System Theory: The Skeleton of Science," in Society for the Advancement of General Systems Theory, *General Systems,* Ann Arbor, Mich., 1956, I, part I.

3. An important pioneering attempt to deal with some of the implications of one's level of analysis, however, is Kenneth N. Waltz, *Man, the State, and War,* New York, 1959. But Waltz restricts himself to a consideration of these implications as they impinge on the question of the causes of war. See also this writer's review of Waltz, "International Conflict: Three Levels of Analysis," *World Politics,* XII (April 1960), pp. 453–61.

4. Even during the debate between "realism" and "idealism" the analytical implications of the various levels of analysis received only the scantiest attention; rather the emphasis seems to have been at the two extremes of pragmatic policy and speculative metaphysics.

5. For example, one critic of the decision-making model formulated by Richard C. Snyder, H. W. Bruck, and Burton Sapin, in *Decision-Making as an Approach to the Study of International Politics* (Princeton, N.J., 1954), points out that no single researcher could deal with all the variables in that model and expect to complete more than a very few comparative studies in his lifetime. See Herbert McClosky, "Concerning Strategies for a Science of International Politics," *World Politics,* VIII (January 1956), pp. 281–95. In defense, however, one might call attention to the relative ease with which many of Snyder's categories could be collapsed into more inclusive ones, as was apparently done in the subsequent case study (see note 11 below). Perhaps a more telling criticism of the monograph is McClosky's comment that "Until a greater measure of theory is introduced into the proposal and the relations among variables are specified more concretely, it is likely to remain little more than a setting-out of categories and, like any taxonomy, fairly limited in its utility" (p. 291).

6. Hans J. Morgenthau, *Politics Among Nations,* 3rd ed., New York, 1960, pp. 5–7. Obviously, his model does not preclude the use of power as a dimension for the differentiation of nations.

7. The "black box" figure comes from some of the simpler versions of S-R psychology, in which the observer more or less ignores what goes on within the individual and concentrates upon the correlation between stimulus and response; these are viewed as empirically verifiable, whereas cognition, perception, and other mental processes have to be imputed to the individual with a heavy reliance on these assumed "intervening variables." The "billiard ball" figure seems to carry the same sort of connotation, and is best employed by Arnold Wolfers in "The Actors in International Politics" in William T. R. Fox, ed., *Theoretical Aspects of International Relations,* Notre Dame, Ind., 1959, pp. 83–106. See also, in this context, Richard C. Synder, "International Relations Theory—Continued," *World Politics,* XIII (January 1961), pp. 300–12; and J. David Singer, "Theorizing About Theory in International Politics," *Journal of Conflict Resolution,* IV (December 1960), pp. 431–42. Both are review articles dealing with the Fox anthology.

8. Morgenthau observes, for example, that it is "futile" to search for motives because they are "the most illusive of psychological data, distorted as they are, frequently beyond recognition, by the interests and emotions of actor and observer alike" (*op.cit.,* p. 6).

9. Ernst B. Haas and Allen S. Whiting, *Dynamics of International Relations,* New York, 1956.

10. A frequent by-product of this tendency to overdifferentiate is what Waltz calls the "second-image fallacy," in which one explains the peaceful or bellicose nature of a nation's foreign policy exclusively in terms of its domestic economic, political, or social characteristics (*op.cit.,* chs. 4 and 5).

11. Its most well-known and successful statement is found in Synder *et al., op.cit.* Much of this model is utilized in the text which Snyder wrote with Edgar S. Furniss, Jr., *American Foreign Policy: Formulation, Principles, and Programs,* New York, 1954. A more specific application is found in Snyder and Glenn D. Paige, "The United States Decision to Resist Aggression in Korea: The Application of an Analytical Scheme," *Administrative Science Quarterly,* III (December 1958), pp. 341–78. For those interested in this approach, very useful is Paul Wasserman and Fred S. Silander, *Decision-Making: An Annotated Bibliography,* Ithaca, N.Y., 1958.

12. And if the decision-making version of this model is employed, the issue is unavoidable. See the discussion of motivation in Snyder, Bruck, and Sapin, *op.cit.,* pp. 92–117; note that 25 of the 49 pages on "The Major Determinants of Action" are devoted to motives.

13. A highly suggestive, but more abstract treatment of this teleological question is in Talcott Parsons, *The Structure of Social Action,* 2nd ed., Glencoe, Ill., 1949, especially in his analysis of Durkheim and Weber. It is interesting to note that for Parsons an act implies, *inter alia,* "a future state of affairs toward which the process of action is oriented," and he therefore comments that "in this sense and this sense only, the schema of action is inherently teleological" (p. 44).

14. Among the exceptions are Haas and Whiting, *op.cit.,* chs. 2 and 3; and some of the chapters in Roy C. Macridis, ed., *Foreign Policy in World Politics,* Englewood Cliffs, N.J., 1958, especially that on West Germany by Karl Deutsch and Lewis Edinger.

15. As early as 1934, Edith E. Ware noted that ". . . the study of international relations is no longer entirely a subject for political science or law, but that economics, history, sociology, geography—all the social sciences—are called upon to contribute

towards the understanding . . . of the international system." See *The Study of International Relations in the United States,* New York, 1934, p. 172. For some contemporary suggestions, see Karl Deutsch, "The Place of Behavioral Sciences in Graduate Training in International Relations," *Behavioral Science,* III (July 1958), pp. 278–84; and J. David Singer, "The Relevance of the Behavioral Sciences to the Study of International Relations," *ibid.,* VI (October 1961), pp. 324–35.

16. The father of phenomenological philosophy is generally acknowledged to be Edmund Husserl (1859–1938), author of *Ideas: General Introduction to Pure Phenomenology,* New York, 1931, trans. by W. R. Boyce Gibson; the original was published in 1913 under the title *Ideen zu einer reinen Phänomenologie und Phänomenologischen Philosophie.* Application of this approach to social psychology has come primarily through the work of Koffka and Lewin.

17. This issue has been raised from time to time in all of the social sciences, but for an excellent discussion of it in terms of the present problem, see Harold and Margaret Sprout, *Man-Milieu Relationship Hypotheses in the Context of International Politics,* Princeton University, Center of International Studies, 1956, pp. 63–71.

18. This is another of the criticisms leveled at the decision-making approach which, almost by definition, seems compelled to adopt some form of the phenomenological model. For a comprehensive treatment of the elements involved in human perception, see Karl Zener *et al.,* eds., "Interrelationships Between Perception and Personality: A Symposium," *Journal of Personality,* XVIII (1949), pp. 1–266.

19. Many of these issues are raised in the ongoing debate over "methodological individualism," and are discussed cogently in Ernest Nagel, *The Structure of Science,* New York, 1961, pp. 535–46.

20. Parenthetically, holders of these specific views should also be less inclined to adopt the national or sub-systemic model in the first place.

21. In a review article dealing with two of the more recent and provocative efforts toward theory (Morton A. Kaplan, *System and Process in International Politics,* New York, 1957, and George Liska, *International Equilibrium,* Cambridge, Mass., 1957), Charles P. Kindleberger adds a further—if not altogether persuasive—argument in favor of the lower, sub-systemic level of analysis: "The total system is infinitely complex with everything interacting. One can discuss it intelligently, therefore, only bit by bit." "Scientific International Politics," *World Politics,* XI (October 1958), p. 86.

22. It should also be kept in mind that one could conceivably develop a theoretical model which successfully embraces both of these levels of analysis without sacrificing conceptual clarity and internal consistency. In this writer's view, such has not been done to date, though Kaplan's *System and Process in International Politics* seems to come fairly close.

QUESTIONS

1. What does Singer mean when he says that both models are useful for different purposes?

2. Compare and contrast the two levels of analysis provided in Singer's essay. What are the strengths and weaknesses of the two models?

System Level International Relations Theories

In the preceding section, we introduced the levels of analysis methodology used in the study of international relations theory. In this section, as well as the sections that follow, we will take a closer look at each of these levels and provide some of the classic readings from the available literature.

We focus here on theories from the system level of analysis. System level theorists assume that international relations is best understood by taking a broad, global perspective. They look at the nature of the system as a whole, and how states behave within that system. The system, then, sets the standard; it conditions and constrains the behavior of those who operate within it.

There are three major system level theories that we present in this section: realism, transnationalism, and class system. Since each of these theories is discussed in detail in the following chapters, we will simply provide a brief overview here of how they characterize the international system and the role of states and other major actors in that system.

Realist theory focuses on power. It looks at how the distribution of power, quest for power, and ability to preserve power within the system supercede other goals and dictate the behavior of states and organizations. Some realists argue that this situation creates and perpetuates a system in which there are no overarching authorities to maintain order on a global scale. States arms themselves and form strategic military alliances for security and self-preservation. This sense of "everyone for him- or herself" tends to strengthen a system dominated by the drive for upward mobility in a hierarchy of power.

Our second theory, transnationalism, does not dispute that the international system lacks a global authority to instill order and regulate the behavior of states. Transnationalists, though, point out that this does not necessarily have to be the case. There are a number of instances where states have positive incentives to cooperate with one another—trade and other economic partnerships or environmental and conservation efforts, for example. Another aspect of transnationalist theory points out that international organizations, such as the United Nations, do exist to help bring order to the global community and could be strengthened and expanded.

The final system level theory is what we have termed class system theory. As the name implies, this theory focuses on the distribution of wealth throughout the world and how that distribution—usually uneven—creates economic classes of people that transcend state boundaries. Essentially, the world is segregated by economics into "haves" and "have-nots." Under such conditions the wealthy classes in different countries have more in common with one another than with the poorer classes of their own nation. They also have a substantial stake in preserving the existing system. Conflict occurs along economic class lines on a global basis, cutting across state boundaries, as the poorer classes revolt against economic imperialism.

These theories all provide unique perspectives on the system and the behavior of states within it. In the coming chapters, we will discuss the readings, highlight important terms and concepts, and look at some of the strengths and weaknesses of each paradigm. An effective theory of international relations—whether system, state, or individual level—provides not only a frame of reference for looking at past events but a method for analyzing current conditions and making projections about our future.

Chapter 2

REALIST THEORY

COMPONENTS OF REALIST THEORY

Focus of Analysis ········▶	• Struggle for power among states in an anarchic international system
Major Actors ········▶	• States
Behavior of States ········▶	• Rational, unitary actors
Goals of States ········▶	• Enhance power and security
View of Human Nature ········▶	• Pessimistic
Condition of International System ········▶	• Anarchic • Self-help system
Key Concepts ········▶	• Security dilemma; Balance of power; Power politics; Anarchy; Self-help system; Rational actor

INTRODUCTION

Realism is the oldest theory for understanding and explaining international politics. The roots of this school of thought extend back nearly 2,500 years. The fundamental principles and inferences of realism can be found in the writings of the ancient Greek historian Thucydides and the Italian Renaissance political philosopher Niccolo Machiavelli. Many contemporary scholars, including Hans Morgenthau, E. H. Carr, and Kenneth Waltz, have further explored and developed realist principles.

Indeed, the realist school of thought so predominated the study of international politics in the post–World War II era that it became the theoretical basis for United States foreign policy during the Cold War. The list of practitioners includes some of the most influential people in the American foreign policy establishment. George Kennan, U.S. envoy to the Soviet Union during World War II and chief architect of the Containment Doctrine, used the realist balance of power concept in constructing the American policy to contain Soviet influence in the Cold War years. American presidents, such as Harry Truman, Dwight Eisenhower, and Richard Nixon, as well as Secretaries of State John Foster Dulles and Henry Kissinger, all relied to a significant extent on realist principles in shaping their foreign policy decisions.

Many scholars argue that the influence of realism over statesmen is evidence of the strength and utility of its principles. They contend that leaders rely on realist theory because it presents a "realistic" view of international relations and focuses on how the world *is,* rather than how it *ought* to be. They believe that a careful and objective assessment of world history is important because the fundamental characteristics and behavior of countries have remained essentially unchanged. Thus, realist scholars attempt to discern patterns of behavior among states in the past and then use these observations to analyze and predict the behavior and actions of nations in contemporary international politics.

For realists, power is the key factor in understanding international relations. Global politics is considered a contest for power among states. A state's power is measured primarily in terms of its military capabilities. International diplomacy is based on **power politics**, in which force or the threat of force is the primary method states use to further their interests. According to realists, international relations is a struggle for power and security among competing states. It is the responsibility of each nation-state to provide for its own defense and security. Thus, states are compelled to base foreign policy decisions on considerations of power and security, rather than morality or ideals.

CLASSICAL REALISM

In his work *The History of the Peloponnesian War,* the Greek scholar and historian, Thucydides, was one of the first to distinguish these realist principles. He used the war between the city-states of Athens and Sparta as a case study for his analysis. Thucydides described the underlying cause of war between Athens and Sparta in clear terms: "What made war inevitable was the growth of Athenian power and the fear which this caused in Sparta." Sparta was wary of the innovative and dynamic nature of Athenian society, which was growing and modernizing both economically and militarily. The Spartans perceived a shift in the balance of power between the two states. The **balance of power** principle contends that if two or more states, or coalitions of states, maintain an even distribution of power, neither side can be confident of victory should conflict arise. Under such conditions, we would presume that states might be reluctant to initiate or pursue a military resolution to their differences with other states. In this way, balance and peace in the system would be preserved.

Returning to Thucydides' example, Sparta began to strengthen its position militarily in response to the vitality of Athens. The Athenians then grew fearful of their rival's arms build-up and responded in a similar fashion. War between Athens and Sparta erupted shortly thereafter. Thucydides recorded and analyzed these events to provide a background on the nature of war for future historians and scholars.

One of those who followed was the Italian philosopher Niccolo Machiavelli. Machiavelli is considered the first modern political theorist because, in traditional realist fashion, he sought to describe politics as it is, not as it ought to be. In his book *The Prince,* Machiavelli sought to separate politics from ethics because he wished to provide a practical and objective account of the political process.

In addition, Machiavelli made two other notable contributions to realism. First, his view that humans are "wicked" became one of the central tenants of classical realism. In *The Prince,* Machiavelli wrote that the "gulf between how one should live and how one does live is so wide that a man who neglects what is done for what should be done learns the way to self-destruction rather than self-preservation." Second, this pessimistic assessment of human nature led Machiavelli to emphasize the importance of military power and national security. The survival of the state, as represented figuratively by the prince, is the most important goal in politics. Machiavelli argued that "it is unreasonable to expect that an armed man should obey one who is not or that an unarmed man should remain safe and secure when his servants are armed." Certainly, this statement demonstrates his conviction that those who hold the reins of power must be prepared to contend with threats to their rule. That is, leaders who neglect national security do so not only at their own peril but also jeopardize the security of the state as a whole.

More contemporary scholars, Edward Hallet Carr and Hans Morgenthau based their view of international politics, to a significant extent, on many of the observations found in the writings of Thucydides, Machiavelli, and other classical theorists. E. H. Carr's work, *The Twenty Years' Crisis,* was completed in 1939 only a few months before World War II erupted in Europe. Like Thucydides' discussion of the Peloponnesian War, Carr's work focused on the "underlying" causes of the conflict. In this selection taken from *The Twenty Years' Crisis,* Carr critiques the strengths and weaknesses of both idealism and realism, concluding that any "sound political thought must be based on elements of both utopia [idealism] and reality [realism]."[2]

In his book, *Politics Among Nations,* Hans Morganthau used the principles of classical realism to both analyze and shape geopolitics of 1948. In doing so, Morgenthau created a more scientific approach to the study and practice of foreign affairs in our contemporary age.

Morgenthau, like Machiavelli, maintained that insecurity, aggression, and war are recurring themes of international politics and that these themes are ultimately rooted in human nature. Morgenthau, again like his realist predecessors, recognized that, on a fundamental level, conflict was driven not by political or ideological differences as much as man's desire to dominate his fellow man. He suggested that "statesmen think

---

[2] Edward Hallet Carr, *The Twenty Years' Crisis* (New York: Harper & Row, 1964), p. 93.

and act in terms of power."[3] One common characteristic of all states, Morgenthau assumed, was their tendency to behave as rational actors. According to the **rational actor** assumption, states pursue attainable, prudent goals that are commensurate with their power (capability) to achieve. Likewise, a state's foreign policy is based on prudent calculations of national interest.

Morgenthau's prescription for a "rational theory of international politics" was based on the notion of "interest defined as power." That is, in a system consisting of individual states or blocs of states struggling for power, Morgenthau suggested that the "ever present threat of large-scale violence" had in the past, and could in the future, be contained by pursuing a balance-of-power strategy. As discussed earlier, this strategy contends that, if two or more coalitions of states maintain a roughly equal distribution of power, no single state can be confident in its ability to win a war. Consequently, all states would be reluctant to initiate conflict—balance, order, and peace would, in theory, be preserved.

The selection by George Kennan provides an excellent example of the application of realist principles to the formulation of American foreign policy. In 1946, George Kennan, an American diplomat serving in Moscow, sent his now famous "long telegram" to Washington. The telegram was a detailed assessment of the sources of Soviet conduct. One year later, using the pseudonym of X, Kennan's argument was published in the highly respected journal *Foreign Affairs*. His ideas provided the intellectual and geopolitical foundation for the United States postwar policy of "containment," aimed at curbing Soviet expansionism. Kennan's analysis and policy recommendations relied upon the realist concepts of both power politics and balance of power.

NEO-REALISM

Some contemporary proponents of realist theory, known as neo-realists, suggest that it is not just the uneven development or distribution of power among states—like that between Athens and Sparta—that leads to conflict. Neo-realists differ from classical realists on one basic point. They believe that the struggle for power is the result of the structure of the international system as a whole, rather than the nature of man. Specifically, the problem is found in the anarchic nature of the international system. The term **anarchy** refers to the lack of a central authority or government to enforce law and order between states and throughout the globe.

Kenneth Waltz, founder of neo-realist theory, suggests that this lack of central authority is key to understanding the international system and international relations theory. According to Waltz, states are compelled to base their foreign policy on national security considerations because they are ultimately responsible for their own survival. Since there is no overarching world government to enforce peace, states

---

[3] Hans J. Morgenthau, *Politics Among Nations* (McGraw-Hill, 1993), p. 5.

exist in a **self-help system.** Like the call on a sinking ship, the anarchic nature of the international system leaves "every state for itself."

This type of self-help situation leads to a security dilemma. A **security dilemma** is the result of fear, insecurity, and lack of trust among states living in an anarchic international system. States arm themselves in order to pursue the rational goal of self-preservation. But by arming themselves, more fear and insecurity is created among other states. These states, in turn, also increase their armaments. Even though a state may be arming itself for purely defensive purposes, this process makes all states within the system less secure and fuels an arms race. We see that each state may be acting rationally on an individual basis, but, collectively, their actions lead to unintended consequences. At the very least, these consequences can include an expensive and wasteful arms race, and, in the end, such actions can even lead to war.

Many of the assumptions of neo-realism outlined above can be found in the piece by Kenneth Waltz, in which he discusses the relevance of nuclear weapons. In this selection, Waltz assesses the role conventional and nuclear weapons play in deterring war. He asserts that nuclear weapons are "a tremendous force for peace" since states that possess them are less likely to go to war than those relying solely on conventional arms. Fear over the devastation of nuclear weapons is so overwhelming that deterrence is actually enhanced.

The final two readings by Fareed Zakaria and Robert Tucker discuss the continuing relevance of realism in the post–Cold War era. Both authors question the utility of realism as an explanation for contemporary world politics. The realist focus on the military capabilities of states and power politics are evaluated and deemed insufficient explanations for current trends in international relations. It is interesting to note, however, that both Zakaria and Tucker also advise caution against discarding out of hand all of the lessons provided by realist theory.

A CRITIQUE OF REALIST THEORY

As we have discussed, classical realism and the more contemporary neo-realism offer important and unique insights into the essential characteristics of international relations. Like any theory of international relations, however, the realist paradigm has both strengths and weaknesses. From a practical standpoint, realist theory offers a set of simple, straightforward principles that have guided statesmen in their decision making for many years. These pragmatic guidelines strip away moral and idealistic notions of how states *should* act or how international dialogue *ought* to be conducted. Rather, the focus is on how nations actually *do* behave within the international system, both individually and collectively.

Realism also has some valid strengths from a historical, scholarly standpoint. From the ancient Greek philosopher Thucydides to contemporary scholars like Hans Morgenthau and Kenneth Waltz, there is certainly a wide body of historical evidence to support the realists' supposition that states are locked in a struggle for power that can, and often does, lead to war.

Realists contend, as well, that history tends to favor their approach to international relations theory. The conflict between Athens and Sparta, the series of events and decisions preceding World War I, and the conditions that led to the Cold War could all serve as case studies and provide data to support an argument for realism.

That so much of history can be used to support the realist perspective and that so many leaders and policymakers have relied on realist principles are valid, if somewhat self-serving, raises testament to the strength of the theory. We must also acknowledge, however, some problems in applying realism to conditions in our world today. As we shall see in the next chapter, transnationalist theorists argue that realism places too great an emphasis on conflict, while underestimating the role of international institutions in promoting cooperation. The nature of international competition has changed, and war is no longer considered a natural extension of politics among major powers. Perhaps most dramatically, nuclear weapons have made the pursuit of power using war or armed conflict dangerous and costly. It is fairly safe to assume that war between two nuclear powers would be unwinnable.

Aside from the devastating consequences, the use of force—under most conditions—is less acceptable in today's increasingly interdependent world. In its emphasis on conflict, realist theory tends to ignore the current expansion of cooperation between states. Further, the international conditions that allow for, indeed, even promote cooperation between nations challenge the neo-realist notion of anarchy. Certain generally accepted rules and norms—as well as the institutions that establish and uphold them—play an important role in facilitating and promoting an appropriate climate for cooperation. Anarchy, even anarchy ordered by a specific power structure as neo-realists describe, does not offer an adequate explanation for the kind of cooperation and transnational linkages so common in our contemporary world.

With this idea of extended cooperation, we can see some other weaknesses of realist theory. States are no longer the only important actors on the international stage. International organizations, like the United Nations, and non-governmental organizations, such as multi-national corporations and environmental organizations, perform important functions in maintaining stability and expanding cooperation worldwide.

And we must question, too, whether states, particularly under these more complex global conditions, can be considered truly unitary actors in the realist sense. Can a nation be viewed monolithically, able to make coherent decisions based strictly on considerations of the national interest? The politics of a state, both internal and external, are more likely a messy business, full of compromise and competing interests. That the actions of a state reflect rational, consistent cost-benefit calculations based purely on self-interest, as realist theory suggests, is, at the very least, difficult to prove.

One final weakness in the case for realism is the theory's inability to account for peaceful change. According to realists, change in the international system can only come about from, and is often the catalyst for, war. In the wake of the Cold War and peaceful dissolution of the Soviet Union, we might say that realism is left holding the theoretical bag on the phenomenon of peaceful change.

Late twentieth-century society is more and more characterized by the spread of consumerism and free exchange of ideas and technology, by expanded economic and political ties, and by growth through cooperation and conflict resolution through peaceful means. Without some sort of modification, proponents of realist theory might be put in a difficult position if these trends continue into and beyond the year 2000. In response, realists would question whether the international politics of today are, indeed, so different from the past. The recent tragedies in Bosnia, Somalia, and Rowanda, to name just a few, provide ample evidence that violence and conflict are still very much a part of our world.

KEY CONCEPTS

Anarchy   refers to the lack of a central authority or government to enforce law and order between states throughout the globe.

Balance of power   is a policy aimed at maintaining the international status quo. According to this theory, peace and stability are best preserved when power is distributed among five or more states and no single state has a preponderance of military power

Neo-realism   is a variant of realism and contends that the struggle for power among states is the result of the anarchic structure of the international system as a whole, rather than the nature of man.

Power politics   are policies in which force, or the threat of force, is the primary method used to further a state's interests. According to realists, international relations is a struggle for power and security among competing states,

Rational actor   refers to the realist assumption that states generally pursue attainable, prudent goals that are commensurate with their power (capability) to achieve.

Security dilemma   is the result of fear, insecurity, and lack of trust among states living in an anarchic international system. States arm themselves in order to pursue the rational goal of self-preservation. But by arming themselves, more fear and insecurity is created among other states. These states, in turn, also increase their armaments. Even though a state may be arming itself for purely defensive purposes, this process makes all states within the system less secure and fuels an arms race.

Self-help system   is a neo-realist concept that, in an anarchic international system where there is no overarching global authority (like a world government) to enforce peace and stability, each state is responsible for its own survival and cannot rely on the help of other states.

3.   The History of the Peloponnesian War

Thucydides

In this famous excerpt, known as the Melian Dialogue, Thucydides describes the conference between Athenian diplomats and Melian officials in which the Athenians are attempting to persuade the Melians to join the war against Sparta. This discussion contains some of the most important elements of the realist view of the relationship between strong and weak states. While the Melians rely on moral arguments, the Athenians, representing the more powerful state, warn the Melians that the "strong do what they have the power to do and the weak accept what they have to accept." In the end, the Melian plea for fair play and justice fails, and all the men of Melos are killed and the women and children are enslaved. This selection is from *History of the Peloponnesian War.*

Thucydides (460–400 B.C.) was an Athenian historian and is credited with being the founder of international relations theory. He is also one of the first scholars to be identified with the Realist tradition.

Thucydides the Athenian wrote the history of the war fought between Athens and Sparta, beginning the account at the very outbreak of the war, in the belief that it was going to be a great war and more worth writing about than any of those which had taken place in the past. My belief was based on the fact that the two sides were at the very height of their power and preparedness, and I saw, too, that the rest of the Hellenic world was committed to one side or the other; even those who were not immediately engaged were deliberating on the courses which they were to take later. This was the greatest disturbance in the history of the Hellenes, affecting also a large part of the non-Hellenic world, and indeed, I might almost say, the whole of mankind. For though I have found it impossible, because of its remoteness in time, to acquire a really precise knowledge of the distant past or even of the history preceding our own period, yet, after looking back into it as far as I can, all the evidence leads me to conclude that these periods were not great periods either in warfare or in anything else.

. . . So for a long time the state of affairs everywhere in Hellas was such that nothing very remarkable could be done by any combination of powers and that even the individual cities were lacking in enterprise.

Finally, however, the Spartans put down tyranny in the rest of Greece, most of which had been governed by tyrants for much longer than Athens. From the time when the Dorians first settled in Sparta there had been a particularly long period of political disunity; yet the Spartan constitution goes back to a very early date, and the country has never been ruled by tyrants. For rather more than 400 years, dating from the end of the late war, they have had the same system of government, and this has been not only a source of internal strength, but has enabled them to intervene in the affairs of other states.

Not many years after the end of tyrannies in Hellas the battle of Marathon was fought between the Persians and the Athenians. Ten years later the foreign enemy returned with his vast armada for the conquest of Hellas, and at this moment of peril the Spartans, since they were the leading power, were in command of the allied Hellenic forces. In face of the invasion the Athenians decided to abandon their city; they broke up their homes, took to their ships, and became a people of sailors. It was by a common effort that the foreign invasion was repelled; but not long afterwards the Hellenes—both those who had fought in the war together and those who later revolted from the King of Persia—split into two divisions, one group following Athens and the other Sparta. These were clearly the two most powerful states, one being supreme on land, the other on the sea. For a short time the war-time alliance held together, but it was not long before quarrels took place and Athens and Sparta, each with her own allies, were at war with each other, while among the rest of the Hellenes states that had their own differences now joined one or other of the two sides. So from the end of the Persian War till the beginning of the Peloponnesian War, though there were some intervals of peace, on the whole these two Powers were either fighting with each other or putting down revolts among their allies. They were consequently in a high state of military preparedness and had gained their military experience in the hard school of danger.

The Spartans did not make their allies pay tribute, but saw to it that they were governed by oligarchies who would work in the Spartan interest. Athens, on the other hand, had in the course of time taken over the fleets of her allies (except for those of Chios and Lesbos) and had made them pay contributions of money instead. Thus the forces available to Athens alone for this war were greater than the combined forces had ever been when the alliance was still intact.

In investigating past history, and in forming the conclusions which I have formed, it must be admitted that one cannot rely on every detail which has come down to us by way of tradition. People are inclined to accept all stories of ancient times in an uncritical way—even when these stories concern their own native countries. Most people in Athens, for instance, are under the impression that Hipparchus, who was killed by Harmodius and Aristogiton, was tyrant at the time, not realizing that it was Hippias who was the eldest and the chief of the sons of Pisistratus, and that Hipparchus and Thessalus were his younger brothers. What happened was this: on the very day that had been fixed for their attempt, indeed at the very last moment, Harmodius and Aristogiton had reason to believe that Hippias had been informed of the plot by some of the conspirators. Believing him to have been forewarned, they kept away from him, but, as they wanted to perform some daring exploit before they were arrested themselves, they killed Hipparchus when they found him by the Leocorium organizing the Panathenaic procession.

The rest of the Hellenes, too, make many incorrect assumptions not only about the dimly remembered past, but also about contemporary history. For instance, there is a general belief that the kings of Sparta are each entitled to two votes, whereas in fact they have only one;

and it is believed, too, that the Spartans have a company of troops called 'Pitanate'. Such a company has never existed. Most people, in fact, will not take trouble in finding out the truth, but are much more inclined to accept the first story they hear.

However, I do not think that one will be far wrong in accepting the conclusions I have reached from the evidence which I have put forward. It is better evidence than that of the poets, who exaggerate the importance of their themes, or of the prose chroniclers, who are less interested in telling the truth than in catching the attention of their public, whose authorities cannot be checked, and whose subject-matter, owing to the passage of time, is mostly lost in the unreliable streams of mythology. We may claim instead to have used only the plainest evidence and to have reached conclusions which are reasonably accurate, considering that we have been dealing with ancient history. As for this present war, even though people are apt to think that the war in which they are fighting is the greatest of all wars and, when it is over, to relapse again into their admiration of the past, nevertheless, if one looks at the facts themselves, one will see that this was the greatest war of all.

In this history I have made use of set speeches some of which were delivered just before and others during the war. I have found it difficult to remember the precise words used in the speeches which I listened to myself and my various informants have experienced the same difficulty; so my method has been, while keeping as closely as possible to the general sense of the words that were actually used, to make the speakers say what, in my opinion, was called for by each situation.

And with regard to my factual reporting of the events of the war I have made it a principle not to write down the first story that came my way, and not even to be guided by my own general impressions; either I was present myself at the events which I have described or else I heard of them from eye-witnesses whose reports I have checked with as much thoroughness as possible. Not that even so the truth was easy to discover: different eye-witnesses give different accounts of the same events, speaking out of partiality for one side or the other or else from imperfect memories. And it may well be that my history will seem less easy to read because of the absence in it of a romantic element. It will be enough for me, however, if these words of mine are judged useful by those who want to understand clearly the events which happened in the past and which (human nature being what it is) will, at some time or other and in much the same ways, be repeated in the future. My work is not a piece of writing designed to meet the taste of an immediate public, but was done to last for ever.

The greatest war in the past was the Persian War; yet in this war the decision was reached quickly as a result of two naval battles and two battles on land. The Pcloponnesian War, on the other hand, not only lasted for a long time, but throughout its course brought with it unprecedented suffering for Hellas. Never before had so many cities been captured and then devastated, whether by foreign armies or by the Hellenic powers themselves (some of these cities, after capture, were resettled with new inhabitants); never had there been so many exiles; never such loss of life—both in the actual warfare and in internal revolutions. Old stories of past prodigies, which had not found much confirmation in recent experience, now became credible. Wide areas, for instance, were affected by violent earthquakes; there were more frequent eclipses of the sun than had ever been recorded before; in various parts of the country there were extensive droughts followed by famine; and there was the plague which did more harm and destroyed more life than almost any other single factor. All these calamities fell together upon the Hellenes after the outbreak of war.

War began when the Athenians and the Peloponnesians broke the Thirty Years Truce which had been made after the capture of Euboea. As to the reasons why they broke the truce, I propose first to give an account of the causes of complaint which they had against each other and of the specific instances where their interests clashed: this is in order that there should be no doubt in anyone's mind about what led to this great war falling upon the Hellenes. But the real reason for the war is, in my opinion, most likely to be disguised by such an argument. What made war inevitable was the growth of Athenian power and the fear which this caused in Sparta. As for the reasons for breaking the truce and declaring war which were openly expressed by each side, they are as follows. . . .

THE MELIAN DIALOGUE

Next summer Alcibiades sailed to Argos with twenty ships and seized 300 Argive citizens who were still suspected of being pro-Spartan. These were put by the Athenians into the nearby islands under Athenian control.

The Athenians also made an expedition against the island of Melos. They had thirty of their own ships, six from Chios, and two from Lesbos; 1,200 hoplites, 300 archers, and twenty mounted archers, all from Athens; and about 1,500 hoplites from the allies and the islanders.

The Melians are a colony from Sparta. They had refused to join the Athenian empire like the other islanders, and at first had remained neutral without helping either side; but afterwards, when the Athenians had brought force to bear on them by laying waste their land, they had become open enemies of Athens.

Now the generals Cleomedes, the son of Lycomedes, and Tisias, the son of Tisimachus, encamped with the above force in Melian territory and, before doing any harm to the land, first of all sent representatives to negotiate. The Melians did not invite these representatives to speak before the people, but asked them to make the statement for which they had come in front of the governing body and the few. The Athenian representatives then spoke as follows:

"So we are not to speak before the people, no doubt in case the mass of the people should hear once and for all and without interruption an argument from us which is both persuasive and incontrovertible, and should so be led astray. This, we realize, is your motive in bringing us here to speak before the few. Now suppose that you who sit here should make assurance doubly sure. Suppose that you, too, should refrain from dealing with every point in detail in a set speech, and should instead interrupt us whenever we say something controversial and deal with that before going on to the next point? Tell us first whether you approve of this suggestion of ours."

The Council of the Melians replied as follows:

"No one can object to each of us putting forward our own views in a calm atmosphere. That is perfectly reasonable. What is scarcely consistent with such a proposal is the present threat, indeed the certainty, of your making war on us. We see that you have come prepared to judge the argument yourselves, and that the likely end of it all will be either war, if we prove that we are in the right, and so refuse to surrender, or else slavery."

Athenians: If you are going to spend the time in enumerating your suspicions about the future, or if you have met here for any other reason except to look the facts in the face and on the basis of these facts to consider how you can save your city from destruction, there is no point in our going on with this discussion. If, however, you will do as we suggest, then we will speak on.

Melians: It is natural and understandable that people who are placed as we are should have recourse to all kinds of arguments and different points of view. However, you are right in saying that we are met together here to discuss the safety of our country and, if you will have it so, the discussion shall proceed on the lines that you have laid down.

Athenians: Then we on our side will use no fine phrases saying, for example, that we have a right to our empire because we defeated the Persians, or that we have come against you now because of the injuries you have done us—a great mass of words that nobody would believe. And we ask you on your side not to imagine that you will influence us by saying that you, though a colony of Sparta, have not joined Sparta in the war, or that you have never done us any harm. Instead we recommend that you should try to get what it is possible for you to get, taking into consideration what we both really do think; since you know as well as we do that, when these matters are discussed by practical people, the standard of justice depends on the equality of power to compel and that in fact the strong do what they have the power to do and the weak accept what they have to accept.

Melians: Then in our view (since you force us to leave justice out of account and to confine ourselves to self-interest)—in our view it is at any rate useful that you should not destroy a principle that is to the general good of all men—namely, that in the case of all who fall into danger there should be such a thing as fair play and just dealing, and that such people should be allowed to use and to profit by arguments that fall short of a mathematical accuracy. And this is a principle which affects you as much as anybody, since your own fall would be visited by the most terrible vengeance and would be an example to the world.

Athenians: As for us, even assuming that our empire does come to an end, we are not despondent about what would happen next. One is not so much frightened of being conquered by a power which rules over others, as Sparta does (not that we are concerned with Sparta now), as of what would happen if a ruling power is attacked and defeated by its own subjects. So far as this point is concerned, you can leave it to us to face the risks involved. What we shall do now is to show you that it is for the good of our own empire that we are here and that it is for the preservation of your city that we shall say what we are going to say. We do not want any trouble in bringing you into our empire, and we want you to be spared for the good both of yourselves and of ourselves.

Melians: And how could it be just as good for us to be the slaves as for you to be the masters?

Athenians: You, by giving in, would save yourselves from disaster; we, by not destroying you, would be able to profit from you.

Melians: So you would not agree to our being neutral, friends instead of enemies, but allies of neither side?

Athenians: No, because it is not so much your hostility that injures us; it is rather the case that, if we were on friendly terms with you, our subjects would regard that as a sign of weakness in us, whereas your hatred is evidence of our power.

Melians: Is that your subjects' idea of fair play—that no distinction should be made between people who are quite unconnected with you and people who are mostly your own colonists or else rebels whom you have conquered?

Athenians: So far as right and wrong are concerned they think that there is no difference between the two, that those who still preserve their independence do so because they are strong, and that if we fail to attack them it is because we are afraid. So that by conquering you we shall increase not only the size but the security of our empire. We rule the sea and you are islanders, and weaker islanders too than the others; it is therefore particularly important that you should not escape.

Melians: But do you think there is no security for you in what we suggest? For here again, since you will not let us mention justice, but tell us to give in to your interests, we, too, must tell you what our interests are and, if yours and ours happen to coincide, we must try to persuade you of the fact. Is it not certain that you will make enemies of all states who are at present neutral, when they see what is happening here and naturally conclude that in course of time you will attack them too? Does not this mean that you are strengthening the enemies you have already and are forcing others to become your enemies even against their intentions and their inclinations?

Athenians: As a matter of fact we are not so much frightened of states on the continent. They have their liberty, and this means that it will be a long time before they begin to take precautions against us. We are more concerned about islanders like yourselves, who are still unsubdued, or subjects who have already become embittered by the constraint which our empire imposes on them. These are the people who are most likely to act in a reckless manner and to bring themselves and us, too, into the most obvious danger.

Melians: Then surely, if such hazards are taken by you to keep your empire and by your subjects to escape from it, we who are still free would show ourselves great cowards and weaklings if we failed to face everything that comes rather than submit to slavery.

Athenians: No, not if you are sensible. This is no fair fight, with honour on one side and shame on the other. It is rather a question of saving your lives and not resisting those who are far too strong for you.

Melians: Yet we know that in war fortune sometimes makes the odds more level than could be expected from the difference in numbers of the two sides. And if we surrender, then all our hope is lost at once, whereas, so long as we remain in action, there is still a hope that we may yet stand upright.

Athenians: Hope, that comforter in danger! If one already has solid advantages to fall back upon, one can indulge in hope. It may do harm, but will not destroy one. But hope is by nature an expensive commodity, and those who are risking their all on one cast find out what it means only when they are already ruined; it never fails them in the period when such a knowledge would enable them to take precautions. Do not let this happen to you, you who are weak and whose fate depends on a single movement of the scale. And do not be like those people who, as so commonly happens, miss the chance of saving themselves in a human and practical way, and, when every clear and distinct hope has left them in their adversity, turn to what is blind and vague, to prophecies and oracles and such things which by encouraging hope lead men to ruin.

Melians: It is difficult, and you may be sure that we know it, for us to oppose your power and fortune, unless the terms be equal. Nevertheless we trust that the gods will give us fortune as good as yours, because we are standing for what is right against what is wrong; and as for what we lack in power, we trust that it will be made up for by our alliance with the Spartans, who are bound, if for no other reason, then for honour's sake, and because we are their kinsmen, to come to our help. Our confidence, therefore, is not so entirely irrational as you think.

Athenians: So far as the favour of the gods is concerned, we think we have as much right to that as you have. Our aims and our actions are perfectly consistent with the beliefs men hold about the gods and with the principles which govern their own conduct. Our opinion of the gods and our knowledge of men lead us to conclude that it is a general and necessary law of nature to rule whatever one can. This is not a law that we made ourselves, nor were we the first to act upon

it when it was made. We found it already in existence, and we shall leave it to exist for ever among those who come after us. We are merely acting in accordance with it, and we know that you or anybody else with the same power as ours would be acting in precisely the same way. And therefore, so far as the gods are concerned, we see no good reason why we should fear to be at a disadvantage. But with regard to your views about Sparta and your confidence that she, out of a sense of honour, will come to your aid, we must say that we congratulate you on your simplicity but do not envy you your folly. In matters that concern themselves or their own constitution the Spartans are quite remarkably good; as for their relations with others, that is a long story, but it can be expressed shortly and clearly by saying that of all people we know the Spartans are most conspicuous for believing that what they like doing is honourable and what suits their interests is just. And this kind of attitude is not going to be of much help to you in your absurd quest for safety at the moment.

Melians: But this is the very point where we can feel most sure. Their own self-interest will make them refuse to betray their own colonists, the Melians, for that would mean losing the confidence of their friends among the Hellenes and doing good to their enemies.

Athenians: You seem to forget that if one follows one's self-interest one wants to be safe, whereas the path of justice and honour involves one in danger. And, where danger is concerned, the Spartans are not, as a rule, very venturesome.

Melians: But we think that they would even endanger themselves for our sake and count the risk more worth taking than in the case of others, because we are so close to the Peloponnese that they could operate more easily, and because they can depend on us more than on others, since we are of the same race and share the same feelings.

Athenians: Goodwill shown by the party that is asking for help does not mean security for the prospective ally. What is looked for is a positive preponderance of power in action. And the Spartans pay attention to this point even more than others do. Certainly they distrust their own native resources so much that when they attack a neighbour they bring a great army of allies with them. It is hardly likely therefore that, while we are in control of the sea, they will cross over to an island.

Melians: But they still might send others. The Cretan sea is a wide one, and it is harder for those who control it to intercept others than for those who want to slip through to do so safely. And even if they were to fail in this, they would turn against your own land and against those of your allies left unvisited by Bras idas. So, instead of troubling about a country which has nothing to do with you, you will find trouble nearer home, among your allies, and in your own country.

Athenians: It is a possibility, something that has in fact happened before. It may happen in your case, but you are well aware that the Athenians have never yet relinquished a single siege operation through fear of others. But we are somewhat shocked to find that, though you announced your intention of discussing how you could preserve yourselves, in all this talk you have said absolutely nothing which could justify a man in thinking that he could be preserved. Your chief points are concerned with what you hope may happen in the future, while your actual resources are too scanty to give you a chance of survival against the forces that are opposed to you at this moment. You will therefore be showing an extraordinary lack of common sense if, after you have asked us to retire from this meeting, you still fail to reach a conclusion wiser than anything you have mentioned so far. Do not be led astray by a false sense of honour—a thing which often brings men to ruin when they are faced with an obvious danger that somehow affects their pride. For in many cases men have still been able to see the dangers ahead of them, but this thing called dishonour, this word, by its own force of seduction, has drawn them into a state where they have surrendered to an idea, while in fact they have fallen voluntarily into irrevocable disaster, in dishonour that is all the more dishonourable because it has come to them from their own folly rather than their misfortune. You, if you take the right view, will be careful to avoid this. You will see that there is nothing disgraceful in giving way to the greatest city in Hellas when she is offering you such reasonable terms—alliance on a tribute-paying basis and liberty to enjoy your own property. And, when you are allowed to choose between war and safety, you will not be so insensitively arrogant as to make the wrong choice. This is the safe rule—to stand up to one's equals, to behave with deference towards one's superiors, and to treat one's inferiors with moderation. Think it over again, then, when we have withdrawn from the meeting, and let this be a point that constantly recurs to your minds—that you are discussing the fate of your country, that you have only one country, and that its future for good or ill depends on this one single decision which you are going to make.

The Athenians then withdrew from the discussion. The Melians, left to themselves, reached a conclusion which was much the same as they had indicated in their previous replies. Their answer was as follows:

"Our decision, Athenians, is just the same as it was at first. We are not prepared to give up in a short moment the liberty which our city has enjoyed from its foundation for 700 years. We put our trust in the fortune that the gods will send and which has saved us up to now, and in the help of men—that is, of the Spartans; and so we shall try to save ourselves. But we invite you to allow us to be friends of yours and enemies to neither side, to make a treaty which shall be agreeable to both you and us, and so to leave our country."

The Melians made this reply, and the Athenians, just as they were breaking off the discussion, said:

"Well, at any rate, judging from this decision of yours, you seem to us quite unique in your ability to consider the future as something more certain than what is before your eyes, and to see uncertainties as realities, simply because you would like them to be so. As you have staked most on and trusted most in Spartans, luck, and hopes, so in all these you will find yourselves most completely deluded."

The Athenian representatives then went back to the army, and the Athenian generals, finding that the Melians would not submit, immediately commenced hostilities and built a wall completely round the city of Melos, dividing the work out among the various states. Later they left behind a garrison of some of their own and some allied troops to blockade the place by land and sea, and with the greater part of their army re-turned home. The force left behind stayed on and continued with the siege.

About the same time the Argives invaded Phliasia and were ambushed by the Phliasians and the exiles from Argos, losing about eighty men.

Then, too, the Athenians at Pylos captured a great quantity of plunder from Spartan territory. Not even after this did the Spartans renounce the treaty and make war, but they issued a proclamation saying that any of their people who wished to do so were free to make raids on the Athenians. The Corinthians also made some attacks on the Athenians because of private quarrels of their own, but the rest of the Peloponnesians stayed quiet.

Meanwhile the Melians made a night attack and captured the part of the Athenian lines opposite the market-place. They killed some of the troops, and then, after bringing in corn and everything else useful that they could lay their hands on, retired again and made no further move, while the Athenians took measures to make their blockade more efficient in future. So the summer came to an end.

In the following winter the Spartans planned to invade the territory of Argos, but when the sacrifices for crossing the frontier turned out unfavourably, they gave up the expedition. The fact that they had intended to invade made the Argives suspect certain people in their city, some of whom they arrested, though others succeeded in escaping.

About this same time the Melians again captured another part of the Athenian lines where there were only a few of the garrison on guard. As a result of this, another force came out afterwards from Athens under the command of Philocrates, the son of Demeas. Siege operations were now carried on vigorously and, as there was also some treachery from inside, the Melians surrendered unconditionally to the Athenians, who put to death all the men of military age whom they took, and sold the women and children as slaves. Melos itself they took over for themselves, sending out later a colony of 500 men.

QUESTIONS

1. What are the main points the Melians make to the Athenians in the dialogue?

2. Do you agree with the maxim that, in international politics, the "strong do what they have the power to do and the weak accept what they have to accept"?

4. The Prince

Niccolo Machiavelli

In this excerpt, Niccolo Machiavelli offers his recommendations on how a ruler should lead a nation. Based on historical observation, Machiavelli suggests that a leader must, at times, take measures that might otherwise be considered unacceptable to preserve the security of the state. For Machiavelli, the successful ruler makes the security and power of the state superior to all considerations of morality and ethics. This selection is from *The Prince* (1513).

Niccolo Machiavelli (1469–1527) was influenced by many of the ancient Greek and Roman works in writing his classic work *The Prince*. Machiavelli's sixteenth-century Italy was divided among several city-states—similar to Thucydides' Greece. Machiavelli served as a civil servant and diplomat until the Republic of Florence was defeated in 1512. Forced from public life, Machiavelli devoted himself to writing and completed *The Prince* (1513), *Discourses on the First Decade of Livy* (1514) and *The History of Florence* (1525).

THE THINGS FOR WHICH MEN, AND ESPECIALLY PRINCES, ARE PRAISED OR BLAMED

It now remains for us to see how a prince must govern his conduct towards his subjects or his friends. I know that this has often been written about before, and so I hope it will not be thought presumptuous for me to do so, as, especially in discussing this subject, I draw up an original set of rules. But since my intention is to say something that will prove of practical use to the inquirer, I have thought it proper to represent things as they are in real truth, rather than as they are imagined. Many have dreamed up republics and principalities which have never in truth been known to exist; the gulf between how one should live and how one does live is so wide that a man who neglects what is actually done for what should be done learns the way to self-destruction rather than self-preservation. The fact is that a man who wants to act virtuously in every way necessarily comes to grief among so many who are not virtuous. Therefore if a prince wants to maintain his rule he must learn how not to be virtuous, and to make use of this or not according to need.

So leaving aside imaginary things, and referring only to those which truly exist, I say that whenever men are discussed (and especially princes, who are more exposed to view), they are noted for various qualities which earn them either praise or condemnation. Some, for example, are held to be generous, and others miserly (I use the Tuscan word rather than the word avaricious: we call a man who is mean with what he possesses, miserly, and a man who wants to plunder others, avaricious).[1] Some are held to be benefactors, others are called grasping; some cruel, some compassionate; one man faithless, another faithful; one man effeminate and cowardly, another fierce and courageous; one man courteous, another proud; one man lascivious, another pure; one guileless, another crafty; one stubborn, another flexible; one grave, another frivolous; one religious, another sceptical; and so forth. I know everyone will agree that it would be most laudable if a prince possessed all the qualities deemed to be good among those I have enumerated. But, because of conditions in the world, princes cannot have those qualities, or observe them completely. So a prince has of ne-

cessity to be so prudent that he knows how to escape the evil reputation attached to those vices which could lose him his state, and how to avoid those vices which are not so dangerous, if he possibly can; but, if he cannot, he need not worry so much about the latter. And then, he must not flinch from being blamed for vices which are necessary for safeguarding the state. This is because, taking everything into account, he will find that some of the things that appear to be virtues will, if he practises them, ruin him, and some of the things that appear to be vices will bring him security and prosperity.

GENEROSITY AND PARSIMONY

So, starting with the first of the qualities I enumerated above, I say it would be splendid if one had a reputation for generosity; nonetheless if you do in fact earn a reputation for generosity you will come to grief. This is because if your generosity is good and sincere it may pass unnoticed and it will not save you from being reproached for its opposite. If you want to acquire a reputation for generosity, therefore, you have to be ostentatiously lavish; and a prince acting in that fashion will soon squander all his resources, only to be forced in the end, if he wants to maintain his reputation, to lay excessive burdens on the people, to impose extortionate taxes, and to do everything else he can to raise money. This will start to make his subjects hate him, and, since he will have impoverished himself, he will be generally despised. As a result, because of this generosity of his, having injured many and rewarded few, he will be vulnerable to the first minor setback, and the first real danger he encounters will bring him to grief. When he realizes this and tries to retrace his path he will immediately be reputed a miser.

So as a prince cannot practise the virtue of generosity in such a way that he is noted for it, except to his cost, he should if he is prudent not mind being called a miser. In time he will be recognized as being essentially a generous man, seeing that because of his parsimony his existing revenues are enough for him, he can defend himself against an aggressor, and he can embark on enterprises without burdening the people. So he proves himself generous to all those from whom he takes nothing, and they are innumerable, and miserly towards all those to whom he gives nothing, and they are few. In our own times great things have been accomplished only by those who have been held miserly, and the others have met disaster. Pope Julius II made use of a reputation for generosity to win the papacy but subsequently he made no effort to maintain this reputation, because he wanted to be able to finance his wars. The present king of France has been able to wage so many wars without taxing his subjects excessively only because his long-standing parsimony enabled him to meet the additional expenses involved. Were the present king of Spain renowned for his generosity he would not have started and successfully concluded so many enterprises.

So a prince must think little of it, if he incurs the name of miser, so as not to rob his subjects, to be able to defend himself, not to become poor and despicable, not to be forced to grow rapacious. Miserliness is one of those vices which sustain his rule. Someone may object: Caesar came to power by virtue of his generosity, and many others, because they practised and were known for their generosity, have risen to the very highest

positions. My answer to this is as follows. Either you are already a prince, or you are on the way to becoming one. In the first case, your generosity will be to your cost; in the second, it is certainly necessary to have a reputation for generosity. Caesar was one of those who wanted to establish his own rule over Rome; but if, after he had established it, he had remained alive and not moderated his expenditure he would have fallen from power.

Again, someone may retort: there have been many princes who have won great successes with their armies, and who have had the reputation of being extremely generous. My reply to this is: the prince gives away what is his own or his subjects', or else what belongs to others. In the first case he should be frugal; in the second, he should indulge his generosity to the full. The prince who campaigns with his armies, who lives by pillaging, sacking, and extortion, disposes of what belongs to aliens; and he must be open-handed, otherwise the soldiers would refuse to follow him. And you can be more liberal with what does not belong to you or your subjects, as Caesar, Cyrus, and Alexander were. Giving away what belongs to strangers in no way affects your standing at home; rather it increases it. You hurt yourself only when you give away what is your own. There is nothing so self-defeating as generosity: in the act of practising it, you lose the ability to do so, and you become either poor and despised or, seeking to escape poverty, rapacious and hated. A prince must try to avoid, above all else, being despised and hated; and generosity results in your being both. Therefore it is wiser to incur the reputation of being a miser, which invites ignominy but not hatred, than to be forced by seeking a name for generosity to incur a reputation for rapacity, which brings you hatred as well as ignominy.

CRUELTY AND COMPASSION; AND WHETHER IT IS BETTER TO BE LOVED THAN FEARED, OR THE REVERSE

Taking others of the qualities I enumerated above, I say that a prince must want to have a reputation for compassion rather than for cruelty: nonetheless, he must be careful that he does not make bad use of compassion. Cesare Borgia was accounted cruel; nevertheless, this cruelty of his reformed the Romagna, brought it unity, and restored order and obedience. On reflection, it will be seen that there was more compassion in Cesare than in the Florentine people, who, to escape being called cruel, allowed Pistoia to be devastated.[2] So a prince must not worry if he incurs reproach for his cruelty so long as he keeps his subjects united and loyal. By making an example or two he will prove more compassionate than those who, being too compassionate, allow disorders which lead to murder and rapine. These nearly always harm the whole community, whereas executions ordered by a prince only affect individuals. A new prince, of all rulers, finds it impossible to avoid a reputation for cruelty, because of the abundant dangers inherent in a newly won state. Vergil, through the mouth of Dido, says:

> *Res dura, et regni novitas me talia cogunt Moliri, et late fines custode tueri.*[3]

Nonetheless, a prince must be slow to take action, and must watch that he does not come to be afraid of his own shadow; his behaviour must be tempered by humanity and prudence so that over-confidence does not make him rash or excessive distrust make him unbearable.

From this arises the following question: whether it is better to be loved than feared, or the reverse. The answer is that one would like to be both the one and the other; but because it is difficult to combine them, it is far better to be feared than loved if you cannot be both. One can make this generalization about men: they are ungrateful, fickle, liars, and deceivers, they shun danger and are greedy for profit; while you treat them well, they are yours. They would shed their blood for you, risk their property, their lives, their children, so long, as I said above, as danger is remote; but when you are in danger they turn against you. Any prince who has come to depend entirely on promises and has taken no other precautions ensures his own ruin; friendship which is bought with money and not with greatness and nobility of mind is paid for, but it does not last and it yields nothing. Men worry less about doing an injury to one who makes himself loved than to one who makes himself feared. The bond of love is one which men, wretched creatures that they are, break when it is to their advantage to do so; but fear is strengthened by a dread of punishment which is always effective.

The prince must nonetheless make himself feared in such a way that, if he is not loved, at least he escapes being hated. For fear is quite compatible with an absence of hatred; and the prince can always avoid hatred if he abstains from the property of his subjects and citizens and from their women. If, even so, it proves necessary to execute someone, this is to be done only when there is proper justification and manifest reason for it. But above all a prince must abstain from the property of others; because men sooner forget the death of their father than the loss of their patrimony. It is always possible to find pretexts for confiscating someone's property; and a prince who starts to live by rapine always finds pretexts for seizing what belongs to others. On the other hand, pretexts for executing someone are harder to find and they are less easily sustained.

However, when a prince is campaigning with his soldiers and is in command of a large army then he need not worry about having a reputation for cruelty; because, without such a reputation, no army was ever kept united and disciplined. Among the admirable achievements of Hannibal is included this: that although he led a huge army, made up of countless different races, on foreign campaigns, there was never any dissension, either among the troops themselves or against their leader, whether things were going well or badly. For this, his inhuman cruelty was wholly responsible. It was this, along with his countless other qualities, which made him feared and respected by his soldiers. If it had not been for his cruelty, his other qualities would not have been enough. The historians, having given little thought to this, on the one hand admire what Hannibal achieved, and on the other condemn what made his achievements possible.

That his other qualities would not have been enough by themselves can be proved by looking at Scipio, a man unique in his own time and through all recorded history. His armies mutinied against him in Spain, and the only reason for this was his excessive leniency, which allowed his soldiers more licence than was good for military discipline. Fabius Maximus reproached him for this in the Senate and called him a corrupter of the Roman legions. Again, when the Locri were plundered by one of Scipio's officers, he neither gave them satisfaction nor punished his officer's insubordination; and this was all because of his having too lenient a nature. By way of excuse for him some senators argued that many men were better at not making mistakes themselves than at correcting them in others. But in time Scipio's lenient nature would have spoilt his fame and glory had he continued to indulge it during his command; when he lived under orders from the Senate, however, this fatal characteristic of his was not only concealed but even brought him glory.

So, on this question of being loved or feared, I conclude that since some men love as they please but fear when the prince pleases, a wise prince should rely on what he controls, not on what he cannot control. He must only endeavour, as I said, to escape being hated.

NOTES

1. The two words Machiavelli uses are *misero* and *avaro*.
2. Pistoia was a subject-city of Florence, which forcibly restored order there when conflict broke out between two rival factions in 1501–02. Machiavelli was concerned with this business at first hand.
3. "Harsh necessity, and the newness of my kingdom, force me to do such things and to guard my frontiers everywhere." *Aeneid* i, 563.

QUESTIONS

1. Why does Machiavelli recommend that it is better for a leader to be feared, rather than liked?

2. Can Machiavelli's Prince be considered a tyrant? Why or why not?

5. The Twenty Years' Crisis

Edward Hallet Carr

In this selection, Edward Hallet Carr discusses what we might call a combined approach to international relations theory. He suggests the moral and ethical standards that guide states' behavior should moderate and work in concert with the realist goals of power and security. By applying an ethical perspective in the pursuit of national security, a state's quest for power, based on reasons of imperialism or pure self-aggrandizement, are recognized as illegitimate and unacceptable in a moral context. This selection is from *The Twenty Years' Crisis: 1919–1939* (1946).

Edward Hallet Carr (1892–1982) served as a diplomat in the British Foreign Office and assistant editor of the *London Times* in the 1940s, before becoming a university professor. His other books include the fourteen-volume *History of Soviet Russia, The Russian Revolution: Lenin to Stalin* (1979), and *Studies on Revolution* (1963).

THE LIMITATIONS OF REALISM

The exposure by realist criticism of the hollowness of the utopian edifice is the first task of the political thinker. It is only when the sham has been demolished that there can be any hope of raising a more solid structure in its place. But we cannot ultimately find a resting place in pure realism; for realism, though logically overwhelming, does not provide us with the springs of action which are necessary even to the pursuit of thought. Indeed, realism itself, if we attack it with its own weapons, often turns out in practice to be just as much conditioned as any other mode of thought. In politics, the belief that certain facts are unalterable or certain trends irresistible commonly reflects a lack of desire or lack of interest to change or resist them. The impossibility of being a consistent and thorough-going realist is one of the most certain and most curious lessons of political science. Consistent realism excludes four things which appear to be essential ingredients of all effective political thinking: a finite goal, an emotional appeal, a right of moral judgment and a ground for action.

The conception of politics as an infinite process seems in the long run uncongenial or incomprehensible to the human mind. Every political thinker who wishes to make an appeal to his contemporaries is consciously or unconsciously led to posit a finite goal. Treitschke declared that the "terrible thing" about Machiavelli's teaching was "not the immorality of the methods he recommends, but the lack of content of the state, which exists only in order to exist."[1] In fact, Machiavelli is not so consistent. His realism breaks down in the last chapter of *The Prince,* which is entitled "An Exhortation to free Italy from the Barbarians"— a goal whose necessity could be deduced from no realist premise. Marx, having dissolved human thought and action into the relativism of the dialectic, postulates the absolute goal of a classless society where the dialectic no longer operates— that one far-off event towards which, in true Victorian fashion, he believed the whole creation to be moving. The realist thus ends by negating his own postulate and assuming an ultimate reality outside the historical process. Engels was one of the first to level this charge against Hegel. "The whole dogmatic content of the Hegelian system is declared to be absolute truth in contradiction to his dialectical method, which dissolves all dogmatism."[2] But Marx lays himself open to precisely the same criticism when he brings the process of dialectical materialism to an end with the victory of the proletariat. Thus utopianism penetrates the citadel of realism; and to envisage a continuing, but not infinite, process towards a finite goal is shewn to be a condition of political thought. The greater the emotional stress, the nearer and more concrete is the goal. The first world war was rendered tolerable by the belief that it was the last of wars. Woodrow Wilson's moral authority was built up on the conviction, shared by himself, that he pos-

sessed the key to a just, comprehensive and final settlement of the political ills of mankind. It is noteworthy that almost all religions agree in postulating an ultimate state of complete blessedness.

The finite goal, assuming the character of an apocalyptic vision, thereby acquires an emotional, irrational appeal which realism itself cannot justify or explain. Everyone knows Marx's famous prediction of the future classless paradise:

> When work ceases to be merely a means of life and becomes the first living need; when, with the all-round development of the individual, productive forces also develop, and all the sources of collective wealth flow in free abundance—then only will it be possible to transcend completely the narrow horizon of *bourgeois* right, and society can inscribe on its banner: From each according to his capacities, to each according to his needs.[3]

Sorel proclaimed the necessity of a "myth" to make revolutionary teaching effective; and Soviet Russia has exploited for this purpose the myth, first of world revolution, and more recently of the "socialist fatherland." There is much to be said for Professor Laski's view that "communism has made its way by its idealism, and not by its realism, by its spiritual promise, not by its materialistic prospects."[4] A modern theologian has analysed the situation with almost cynical clear-sightedness:

> Without the ultrarational hopes and passions of religion, no society will have the courage to conquer despair and attempt the impossible; for the vision of a just society is an impossible one, which can be approximated only by those who do not regard it as impossible. The truest visions of religion are illusions, which

may be partly realised by being resolutely believed.[5]

And this again closely echoes a passage in *Mein Kampf* in which Hitler contrasts the "programme-maker" with the politician:

> His [i.e. the programme-maker's] significance lies almost wholly in the future, and he is often what one means by the word '*weltfremd*' [unpractical, utopian]. For if the art of the politician is really the art of the possible, then the programme-maker belongs to those of whom it is said that they please the gods only if they ask and demand from them the impossible.[6]

Credo quia impossibile becomes a category of political thinking.

Consistent realism, as has already been noted, involves acceptance of the whole historical process and precludes moral judgments on it. As we have seen, men are generally prepared to accept the judgment of history on the past, praising success and condemning failure. This test is also widely applied to contemporary politics. Such institutions as the League of Nations, or the Soviet or Fascist régimes, are to a considerable extent judged by their capacity to achieve what they profess to achieve; and the legitimacy of this test is implicitly admitted by their own propaganda, which constantly seeks to exaggerate their successes and minimise their failures. Yet it is clear that mankind as a whole is not prepared to accept this rational test as a universally valid basis of political judgment. The belief that whatever succeeds is right, and has only to be understood to be approved, must, if consistently held, empty thought of purpose, and thereby sterilise and ultimately destroy it. Nor do those whose philosophy appears to exclude the possibility of moral judgments in fact

refrain from pronouncing them. Frederick the Great, having explained that treaties should be observed for the reason that "one can trick only once," goes on to call the breaking of treaties "a bad and knavish policy," though there is nothing in his thesis to justify the moral epithet.[7] Marx, whose philosophy appeared to demonstrate that capitalists could only act in a certain way, spends many pages—some of the most effective in *Capital*—in denouncing the wickedness of capitalists for behaving in precisely that way. The necessity, recognised by all politicians, both in domestic and in international affairs, for cloaking interests in a guise of moral principles is in itself a symptom of the inadequacy of realism. Every age claims the right to create its own values, and to pass judgments in the light of them; and even if it uses realist weapons to dissolve other values, it still believes in the absolute character of its own. It refuses to accept the implication of realism that the word "ought" is meaningless.

Most of all, consistent realism breaks down because it fails to provide any ground for purposive or meaningful action. If the sequence of cause and effect is sufficiently rigid to permit of the "scientific prediction" of events, if our thought is irrevocably conditioned by our status and our interests, then both action and thought become devoid of purpose. If, as Schopenhauer maintains, "the true philosophy of history consists of the insight that, throughout the jumble of all these ceaseless changes, we have ever before our eyes the same unchanging being, pursuing the same course to-day, yesterday and for ever,"[8] then passive contemplation is all that remains to the individual. Such a conclusion is plainly repugnant to the most deep-seated belief of man about himself. That human affairs can be directed and modified by human action and human thought is a postulate so fundamental that its rejection seems scarcely compatible with existence as a human being. Nor is it in fact rejected by those realists who have left their mark on history. Machiavelli, when he exhorted his compatriots to be good Italians, clearly assumed that they were free to follow or ignore his advice. Marx, by birth and training a *bourgeois,* believed himself free to think and act like a proletarian, and regarded it as his mission to persuade others, whom he assumed to be equally free, to think and act likewise. Lenin, who wrote of the imminence of world revolution as a "scientific prediction," admitted elsewhere that "no situations exist from which there is absolutely no way out."[9] In moments of crisis, Lenin appealed to his followers in terms which might equally well have been used by so thorough-going a believer in the power of the human will as Mussolini or by any other leader of any period: "At the decisive moment and in the decisive place, you *must prove* the stronger, you must *be victorious.*"[10] Every realist, whatever his professions, is ultimately compelled to believe not only that there is something which man ought to think and do, but that there is something which he can think and do, and that his thought and action are neither mechanical nor meaningless.

We return therefore to the conclusion that any sound political thought must be based on elements of both utopia and reality. Where utopianism has become a hollow and intolerable sham, which serves merely as a disguise for the interests of the privileged, the realist performs an indispensable service in unmasking it. But pure realism can offer nothing but a naked struggle for power which makes any kind of international society impossible. Having demolished the current utopia with the weapons of realism, we still need to build a new utopia of our own, which will one day fall to the same weapons. The human will will continue to seek an escape from the logical consequences of realism in the vision of an international order which, as soon as it crystallises itself into concrete political form, becomes tainted with self-interest and hypocrisy, and must once more be attacked with the instruments of realism.

Here, then, is the complexity, the fascination and the tragedy of all political life. Politics are made up of two elements—utopia and reality—belonging to two different planes which can never meet. There is no greater barrier to clear political thinking than failure to distinguish between ideals, which are utopia, and institutions, which are reality. The communist who set communism against democracy was usually thinking of communism as a pure ideal of equality and brotherhood, and of democracy as an institution which existed in Great Britain, France or the United States and which exhibited the vested interests, the inequalities and the oppression inherent in all political institutions. The democrat who made the same comparison was in fact comparing an ideal pattern of democracy laid up in heaven with communism as an institution existing in Soviet Russia with its class-divisions, its heresy-hunts and its concentration camps. The comparison, made in each case between an ideal and an institution, is irrelevant and makes no sense. The ideal, once it is embodied in an institution, ceases to be an ideal and becomes the expression of a selfish interest, which must be destroyed in the name of a new ideal. This constant interaction of irreconcileable forces is the stuff of politics. Every political situation contains mutually incompatible elements of utopia and reality, of morality and power.

This point will emerge more clearly from the analysis of the nature of politics which we have now to undertake.

NOTES

1. Treitschke, *Aufsätze,* iv. p. 428.
2. Engels, *Ludwig Feuerbach* (Engl. transl.), p. 23.
3. Marx and Engels, *Works* (Russian ed.), xv. p. 275.
4. Laski, *Communism,* p. 250.
5. R. Niebuhr, *Moral Man and Immoral Society,* p. 81.
6. Hitler, *Mein Kampf,* p. 231.
7. *Anti-Machiavel,* p. 248.
8. Schopenhauer, *Welt als Wille und Vorstellung,* ii. ch. 38.
9. Lenin, *Works* (2nd Russian ed.), xxv. p. 340.
10. Lenin, *Collected Works* (Engl. transl.), xxi. pt. i. p. 68.

QUESTIONS

1. Explain three factors that identify how power and morality can be separated from each other.

2. Does Carr's thesis differ from Machiavelli's recommendations in *The Prince* for the use of power? Explain.

6.   Politics Among Nations

Hans J. Morgenthau

In this reading Hans J. Morgenthau, one of the great contemporary scholars of realist theory, suggests that politics are "governed by objective laws" and that it is possible to develop a "rational theory that reflects . . . these objective laws." Morgenthau's key points are that international politics is a struggle for power among states with competing interests and that states define their interest in terms of power. This selection is from *Politics Among Nations: The Struggle for Power and Peace* (1978).

Hans J. Morgenthau (1904–1980) practiced and taught law in Frankfurt, Germany. He left to teach at the University of Geneva a year before Adolph Hitler came to power. From there, he went to Madrid and then to the United States, in 1937. Morgenthau taught first at Brooklyn College and the University of Kansas City before being appointed to the University of Chicago in 1943. Morgenthau's other works include *In Defense of the National Interest* (1951), *The Purpose of American Politics* (1960), *Politics in the Twentieth Century* (1962), *A New Foreign Policy for the United States* (1969), and *Science: Servant Or Master?* (1972).

ON THE SIX PRINCIPLES OF POLITICAL REALISM

1. Political realism believes that politics, like society in general, is governed by objective laws that have their roots in human nature. In order to improve society it is first necessary to understand the laws by which society lives. The operation of these laws being impervious to our preferences, men will challenge them only at the risk of failure.

Realism, believing as it does in the objectivity of the laws of politics, must also believe in the possibility of developing a rational theory that reflects, however imperfectly and one-sidedly, these objective laws. It believes also, then, in the possibility of distinguishing in politics between truth and opinion—between what is true objectively and rationally, supported by evidence and illuminated by reason, and what is only a subjective judgment, divorced from the facts as they are and informed by prejudice and wishful thinking.

Human nature, in which the laws of politics have their roots, has not changed since the classical philosophies of China, India, and Greece endeavored to discover these laws. Hence, novelty is not necessarily a virtue in political theory, nor is old age a defect. The fact that a theory of politics, if there be such a theory, has never been heard of before tends to create a presumption against, rather than in favor of, its soundness. Conversely, the fact that a theory of politics was developed hundreds or even thousands of years ago—as was the theory of the balance of power—does not create a presumption that it must be outmoded and obsolete. A theory of politics must be subjected to the dual test of reason and experience. To dismiss such a theory because it had its flowering in centuries past is to present not a rational argument but a modernistic prejudice that takes for granted the superiority of the present over the past. To dispose of the revival of such a theory as a "fashion" or "fad" is tantamount to assuming that in matters political we can have opinions but no truths.

For realism, theory consists in ascertaining facts and giving them meaning through reason. It assumes that the character of a foreign policy can be ascertained only through the examination of the political acts performed and of the foreseeable consequences of these acts. Thus we can find out what statesmen have actually done, and from the foreseeable consequences of their acts we can surmise what their objectives might have been.

Yet examination of the facts is not enough. To give meaning to the factual raw material of foreign policy, we must approach political reality with a kind of rational outline, a map that suggests to us the possible meanings of foreign policy. In other words, we put ourselves in the position of a statesman who must meet a certain problem of foreign policy under certain circumstances, and we ask ourselves what the rational alternatives are from which a statesman may choose who must meet this problem under these circumstances (presuming always that he acts in a rational manner), and which of these rational alternatives this particular statesman, acting under these circumstances, is likely to choose. It is the testing of this rational hypothesis against the actual facts and their consequences that gives theoretical meaning to the facts of international politics.

2. The main signpost that helps political realism to find its way through the landscape of international politics is the concept of interest defined in terms of power. This concept provides the link between reason trying to understand international politics and the facts to be understood. It sets politics as an autonomous sphere of action and understanding apart from other spheres, such as economics (understood in terms of interest defined as wealth), ethics, aesthetics, or religion. Without such a concept a theory of politics, international or domestic, would be altogether impossible, for without it we could not distinguish between political and nonpolitical facts, nor could we bring at least a measure of systemic order to the political sphere.

We assume that statesmen think and act in terms of interest defined as power, and the evidence of history bears that assumption out. That assumption allows us to retrace and anticipate, as it were, the steps a statesman—past, present, or future—has taken or will take on the political scene. We look over his shoulder when he writes his dispatches; we listen in on his conversation with other statesmen; we read and anticipate his very thoughts. Thinking in terms of interest defined as power, we think as he does, and as disinterested observers we understand his thoughts and actions perhaps better than he, the actor on the political scene, does himself.

The concept of interest defined as power imposes intellectual discipline upon the observer, infuses rational order into the subject matter of politics, and thus makes the theoretical understanding of politics possible. On the side of the actor, it provides for rational discipline in action and creates that astounding continuity in foreign policy which makes American, British, or Russian foreign policy appear as an intelligible, rational continuum, by and large consistent within itself, regardless of the different motives, preferences, and intellectual and moral qualities of successive statesmen. A realist theory of international politics, then, will guard against two popular fallacies: the concern with motives and the concern with ideological preferences.

To search for the clue to foreign policy exclusively in the motives of statesmen is both futile and deceptive. It is futile because motives are the most illusive of psychological data, distorted as they are, frequently beyond recognition, by the interests and emotions of actor and observer alike. Do we really know what our own motives are? And what do we know of the motives of others?

Yet even if we had access to the real motives of statesmen, that knowledge would help us little in understanding foreign policies, and might well lead us astray. It is true that the knowledge of the statesman's motives may give us one among many clues as to what the direction of his foreign policy might be. It cannot give us, however, the one clue by which to predict his foreign policies. History shows no exact and necessary correlation between the quality of motives and the quality of foreign policy. This is true in both moral and political terms.

We cannot conclude from the good intentions of a statesman that his foreign policies will be either morally praiseworthy or politically successful. Judging his motives, we can say that he will not intentionally pursue policies that are morally wrong, but we can say nothing about the probability of their success. If we want to know the moral and political qualities of his actions, we must know them, not his motives. How often have statesmen been motivated by the desire to improve the world, and ended by making it worse? And how often have they sought one goal, and ended by achieving something they neither expected nor desired?

Neville Chamberlain's politics of appeasement were, as far as we can judge, inspired by good motives; he was probably less motivated by considerations of personal power than were many other British prime ministers, and he sought to preserve peace and to assure the happiness of all concerned. Yet his policies helped to make the Second World War inevitable, and to bring untold miseries to millions of people. Sir Winston Churchill's motives, on the other hand, were much less universal in scope and much more narrowly directed toward personal and national power, yet the foreign policies that sprang from these inferior motives were certainly superior in moral and political quality to those pursued by his predecessor. Judged by his motives, Robespierre was one of the most virtuous men who ever lived. Yet it was the utopian radicalism of that very virtue that made him kill those less virtuous than himself, brought him to the scaffold, and destroyed the revolution of which he was a leader.

Good motives give assurance against deliberately bad policies; they do not guarantee the moral goodness and political success of the policies they inspire. What is important to know, if one wants to understand foreign policy, is not pri-marily the motives of a statesman, but his intellectual ability to comprehend the essentials of foreign policy, as well as his political ability to translate what he has comprehended into successful political action. It follows that while ethics in the abstract judges the moral qualities of motives, political theory must judge the political qualities of intellect, will, and action.

A realist theory of international politics will also avoid the other popular fallacy of equating the foreign policies of a statesman with his philosophic or political sympathies, and of deducing the former from the latter. Statesmen, especially under contemporary conditions, may well make a habit of presenting their foreign policies in terms of their philosophic and political sympathies in order to gain popular support for them. Yet they will distinguish with Lincoln between their *"official* duty," which is to think and act in terms of the national interest, and their *"personal* wish," which is to see their own moral values and political principles realized throughout the world. Political realism does not require, nor does it condone, indifference to political ideals and moral principles, but it requires indeed a sharp distinction between the desirable and the possible—between what is desirable everywhere and at all times and what is possible under the concrete circumstances of time and place.

It stands to reason that not all foreign policies have always followed so rational, objective, and unemotional a course. The contingent elements of personality, prejudice, and subjective preference, and of all the weaknesses of intellect and will which flesh is heir to, are bound to deflect foreign policies from their rational course. Especially where foreign policy is conducted under the conditions of democratic control, the need to marshal popular emotions to the support of foreign policy cannot fail to impair the rationality of foreign policy itself. Yet a theory of foreign policy which aims at rationality must for the time being, as it were, abstract from these irrational elements and seek to paint a picture of foreign policy which presents the rational essence to be found in experience, without the contingent deviations from rationality which are also found in experience.

Deviations from rationality which are not the result of the personal whim or the personal psychopathology of the policy maker may appear contingent only from the vantage point of rationality, but may themselves be elements in a coherent system of irrationality. The possibility of constructing, as it were, a counter-theory of irrational politics is worth exploring.

When one reflects upon the development of American thinking on foreign policy, one is struck by the persistence of mistaken attitudes that have survived— under whatever guises—both intellectual argument and political experience. Once that wonder, in true Aristotelian fashion, has been transformed into the quest for rational understanding, the quest yields a conclusion both comforting and disturbing: we are here in the presence of intellectual defects shared by all of us in different ways and degrees. Together they provide the outline of a kind of pathology of international politics. When the human mind approaches reality with the purpose of taking action, of which the political encounter is one of the outstanding instances, it is often led astray by any of four common mental phenomena: residues of formerly adequate modes of thought and action now rendered obsolete by a new social reality; demonological interpretations of reality

which substitute a fictitious reality—peopled by evil persons rather than seemingly intractable issues—for the actual one; refusal to come to terms with a threatening state of affairs by denying it through illusory verbalization; reliance upon the infinite malleability of a seemingly obstreperous reality.

Man responds to social situations with repetitive patterns. The same situation, recognized in its identity with previous situations, evokes the same response. The mind, as it were, holds in readiness a number of patterns appropriate for different situations; it then requires only the identification of a particular case to apply to it the preformed pattern appropriate to it. Thus the human mind follows the principle of economy of effort, obviating an examination *de novo* of each individual situation and the pattern of thought and action appropriate to it. Yet when matters are subject to dynamic change, traditional patterns are no longer appropriate: they must be replaced by new ones reflecting such change. Otherwise a gap will open between traditional patterns and new realities, and thought and action will be misguided.

On the international plane it is no exaggeration to say that the very structure of international relations—as reflected in political institutions, diplomatic procedures, and legal arrangements—has tended to become at variance with, and in large measure irrelevant to, the reality of international politics. While the former assumes the "sovereign equality" of all nations, the latter is dominated by an extreme inequality of nations, two of which are called super-powers because they hold in their hands the unprecedented power of total destruction, and many of which are called "ministates" because their power is minuscule even compared with that of the traditional nation states. It is this contrast and incompatibility between the reality of international politics and the concepts, institutions, and procedures designed to make intelligible and control the former, which has caused, at least below the great-power level, the unmanageability of international relations which borders on anarchy. International terrorism and the different government reactions to it, the involvement of foreign governments in the Lebanese civil war, the military operations of the United States in Southeast Asia, and the military intervention of the Soviet Union in Eastern Europe cannot be explained or justified by reference to traditional concepts, institutions, and procedures.

All these situations have one characteristic in common. The modern fact of interdependence requires a political order which takes that fact into account, while in reality the legal and institutional superstructure, harking back to the nineteenth century, assumes the existence of a multiplicity of self-sufficient, impenetrable, sovereign nation states. These residues of an obsolescent legal and institutional order not only stand in the way of a rational transformation of international relations in light of the inequality of power and the interdependence of interests, but they also render precarious, if not impossible, more rational policies within the defective framework of such a system.

It is a characteristic of primitive thinking to personalize social problems. That tendency is particularly strong when the problem appears not to be susceptible to rational understanding and successful manipulation. When a particular person or group of persons is identified with the recalcitrant difficulty, that may

seem to render the problem both intellectually accessible and susceptible of solution. Thus belief in Satan as the source of evil makes us "understand" the nature of evil by focusing the search for its origin and control upon a particular person whose physical existence we assume. The complexity of political conflict precludes such simple solutions. Natural catastrophes will not be prevented by burning witches; the threat of a powerful Germany to establish hegemony over Europe will not be averted by getting rid of a succession of German leaders. But by identifying the issue with certain persons over whom we have—or hope to have—control, we reduce the problem, both intellectually and pragmatically, to manageable proportions. Once we have identified certain individuals and groups of individuals as the source of evil, we appear to have understood the causal nexus that leads from the individuals to the social problem; that apparent understanding suggests the apparent solution: Eliminate the individuals "responsible" for it, and you have solved the problem.

Superstition still holds sway over our relations within society. The demonological pattern of thought and action has now been transferred to other fields of human action closed to the kind of rational enquiry and action that have driven superstition from our relations with nature. As William Graham Sumner put it, "The amount of superstition is not much changed, but it now attaches to politics, not to religion."[1] The numerous failures of the United States to recognize and respond to the polycentric nature of Communism is a prime example of this defect. The corollary of this indiscriminate opposition to Communism is the indiscriminate support of governments and movements that profess and practice anti-Communism. American policies in Asia and Latin America have derived from this simplistic position. The Vietnam War and our inability to come to terms with mainland China find here their rationale. So do the theory and practice of counterinsurgency, including large-scale assassinations under the Phoenix program in Vietnam and the actual or attempted assassinations of individual statesmen. Signs of a similar approach have been evident more recently in Central America.

The demonological approach to foreign policy strengthens another pathological tendency, which is the refusal to acknowledge and cope effectively with a threatening reality. The demonological approach has shifted our attention and concern towards the adherents of Communism—individuals at home and abroad, political movements, foreign governments—and away from the real threat: the power of states, Communist or not. McCarthyism not only provided the most pervasive American example of the demonological approach but was also one of the most extreme examples of this kind of misjudgment: it substituted the largely illusory threat of domestic subversion for the real threat of Russian power.

Finally, it is part of this approach to politics to believe that no problems—however hopeless they may appear—are really insoluble, given well-meaning, well-financed, and competent efforts. I have tried elsewhere to lay bare the intellectual and historical roots of this belief,[2] here I limit myself to pointing out its persistent strength despite much experience to the contrary, such as the Vietnam War and the general decline of American power. This preference for economic solutions to political and military problems is powerfully reinforced by

the interests of potential recipients of economic support, who prefer the obviously profitable transfer of economic advantages to painful and risky diplomatic bargaining.

The difference between international politics as it actually is and a rational theory derived from it is like the difference between a photograph and a painted portrait. The photograph shows everything that can be seen by the naked eye; the painted portrait does not show everything that can be seen by the naked eye, but it shows, or at least seeks to show, one thing that the naked eye cannot see: the human essence of the person portrayed.

Political realism contains not only a theoretical but also a normative element. It knows that political reality is replete with contingencies and systemic irrationalities and points to the typical influences they exert upon foreign policy. Yet it shares with all social theory the need, for the sake of theoretical understanding, to stress the rational elements of political reality; for it is these rational elements that make reality intelligible for theory. Political realism presents the theoretical construct of a rational foreign policy which experience can never completely achieve.

At the same time political realism considers a rational foreign policy to be good foreign policy; for only a rational foreign policy minimizes risks and maximizes benefits and, hence, complies both with the moral precept of prudence and the political requirement of success. Political realism wants the photographic picture of the political world to resemble as much as possible its painted portrait. Aware of the inevitable gap between good—that is, rational—foreign policy and foreign policy as it actually is, political realism maintains not only that theory must focus upon the rational elements of political reality, but also that foreign policy ought to be rational in view of its own moral and practical purposes.

Hence, it is no argument against the theory here presented that actual foreign policy does not or cannot live up to it. That argument misunderstands the intention of this book, which is to present not an indiscriminate description of political reality, but a rational theory of international politics. Far from being invalidated by the fact that, for instance, a perfect balance of power policy will scarcely be found in reality, it assumes that reality, being deficient in this respect, must be understood and evaluated as an approximation to an ideal system of balance of power.

3. Realism assumes that its key concept of interest defined as power is an objective category which is universally valid, but it does not endow that concept with a meaning that is fixed once and for all. The idea of interest is indeed of the essence of politics and is unaffected by the circumstances of time and place. Thucydides' statement, born of the experiences of ancient Greece, that "identity of interests is the surest of bonds whether between states or individuals" was taken up in the nineteenth century by Lord Salisbury's remark that "the only bond of union that endures" among nations is "the absence of all clashing interests." It was erected into a general principle of government by George Washington:

> A small knowledge of human nature will convince us, that, with far the greatest part of mankind, interest is the governing principle; and that almost every man is more or less, under its influence. Motives of public virtue may for a time, or in particular instances, actuate men to the observance of a conduct purely disinterested; but they are not of themselves sufficient to produce persevering conformity to the refined dictates and obligations of social duty. Few men are capable of making a continual sacrifice of all views of private interest, or advantage, to the common good. It is vain to exclaim against the depravity of human nature on this account; the fact is so, the experience of every age and nation has proved it and we must in a great measure, change the constitution of man, before we can make it otherwise. No institution, not built on the presumptive truth of these maxims can succeed.[3]

It was echoed and enlarged upon in our century by Max Weber's observation:

> Interests (material and ideal), not ideas, dominate directly the actions of men. Yet the "images of the world" created by these ideas have very often served as switches determining the tracks on which the dynamism of interests kept actions moving.[4]

Yet the kind of interest determining political action in a particular period of history depends upon the political and cultural context within which foreign policy is formulated. The goals that might be pursued by nations in their foreign policy can run the whole gamut of objectives any nation has ever pursued or might possibly pursue.

The same observations apply to the concept of power. Its content and the manner of its use are determined by the political and cultural environment. Power may comprise anything that establishes and maintains the control of man over man. Thus power covers all social relationships which serve that end, from physical violence to the most subtle psychological ties by which one mind controls another. Power covers the domination of man by man, both when it is disciplined by moral ends and controlled by constitutional safeguards, as in Western democracies, and when it is that untamed and barbaric force which finds its laws in nothing but its own strength and its sole justification in its aggrandizement.

Political realism does not assume that the contemporary conditions under which foreign policy operates, with their extreme instability and the ever present threat of large-scale violence, cannot be changed. The balance of power, for instance, is indeed a perennial element of all pluralistic societies, as the authors of *The Federalist* papers well knew; yet it is capable of operating, as it does in the United States, under the conditions of relative stability and peaceful conflict. If the factors that have given rise to these conditions can be duplicated on the international scene, similar conditions of stability and peace will then prevail there, as they have over long stretches of history among certain nations.

What is true of the general character of international relations is also true of the nation state as the ultimate point of reference of contemporary foreign policy. While the realist indeed believes that interest is the perennial standard by which political action must be judged and directed, the contemporary connection between interest and the nation state is a product of history, and is therefore bound to disappear in the course of history. Nothing in the realist position militates against the assumption that the present division of the political world into nation states will be replaced by larger units of a quite different character, more in keeping with the technical po-

tentialities and the moral requirements of the contemporary world.

The realist parts company with other schools of thought before the all-important question of how the contemporary world is to be transformed. The realist is persuaded that this transformation can be achieved only through the workmanlike manipulation of the perennial forces that have shaped the past as they will the future. The realist cannot be persuaded that we can bring about that transformation by confronting a political reality that has its own laws with an abstract ideal that refuses to take those laws into account.

4. Political realism is aware of the moral significance of political action. It is also aware of the ineluctable tension between the moral command and the requirements of successful political action. And it is unwilling to gloss over and obliterate that tension and thus to obfuscate both the moral and the political issue by making it appear as though the stark facts of politics were morally more satisfying than they actually are, and the moral law less exacting that it actually is.

Realism maintains that universal moral principles cannot be applied to the actions of states in their abstract universal formulation, but that they must be filtered through the concrete circumstances of time and place. The individual may say for himself: "*Fiat justitia, pereat mundus* (Let justice be done, even if the world perish)," but the state has no right to say so in the name of those who are in its care. Both individual and state must judge political action by universal moral principles, such as that of liberty. Yet while the individual has a moral right to sacrifice himself in defense of such a moral principle, the state has no right to let its moral disapprobation of the infringement of liberty get in the way of successful political action, itself inspired by the moral principle of national survival. There can be no political morality without prudence; that is, without consideration of the political consequences of seemingly moral action. Realism, then, considers prudence—the weighing of the consequences of alternative political actions—to be the supreme virtue in politics. Ethics in the abstract judges action by its conformity with the moral law; political ethics judges action by its political consequences. Classical and medieval philosophy knew this, and so did Lincoln when he said:

> I do the very best I know how, the very best I can, and I mean to keep doing so until the end. If the end brings me out all right, what is said against me won't amount to anything. If the end brings me out wrong, ten angels swearing I was right would make no difference.

5. Political realism refuses to identify the moral aspirations of a particular nation with the moral laws that govern the universe. As it distinguishes between truth and opinion, so it distinguishes between truth and idolatry. All nations are tempted—and few have been able to resist the temptation for long—to clothe their own particular aspirations and actions in the moral purposes of the universe. To know that nations are subject to the moral law is one thing, while to pretend to know with certainty what is good and evil in the relations among nations is quite another. There is a world of difference between the belief that all nations stand under the judgment of God, inscrutable to the human mind, and the blasphemous conviction that God is always on one's side and that what one wills oneself cannot fail to be willed by God also.

The lighthearted equation between a particular nationalism and the counsels of Providence is morally indefensible, for it is that very sin of pride against which the Greek tragedians and the Biblical prophets have warned rulers and ruled. That equation is also politically pernicious, for it is liable to engender the distortion in judgment which, in the blindness of crusading frenzy, destroys nations and civilizations—in the name of moral principle, ideal, or God himself.

On the other hand, it is exactly the concept of interest defined in terms of power that saves us from both that moral excess and that political folly. For if we look at all nations, our own included, as political entities pursuing their respective interests defined in terms of power, we are able to do justice to all of them. And we are able to do justice to all of them in a dual sense: We are able to judge other nations as we judge our own and, having judged them in this fashion, we are then capable of pursuing policies that respect the interests of other nations, while protecting and promoting those of our own. Moderation in policy cannot fail to reflect the moderation of moral judgment.

6. The difference, then, between political realism and other schools of thought is real, and it is profound. However much of the theory of political realism may have been misunderstood and misinterpreted, there is no gainsaying its distinctive intellectual and moral attitude to matters political.

Intellectually, the political realist maintains the autonomy of the political sphere, as the economist, the lawyer, the moralist maintain theirs. He thinks in terms of interest defined as power, as the economist thinks in terms of interest defined as wealth; the lawyer, of the conformity of action with legal rules; the moralist, of the conformity of action with moral principles. The economist asks: "How does this policy affect the wealth of society, or a segment of it?" The lawyer asks: "Is this policy in accord with the rules of law?" The moralist asks: "Is this policy in accord with moral principles?" And the political realist asks: "How does this policy affect the power of the nation?" (Or of the federal government, of Congress, of the party, of agriculture, as the case may be.)

The political realist is not unaware of the existence and relevance of standards of thought other than political ones. As political realist, he cannot but subordinate these other standards to those of politics. And he parts company with other schools when they impose standards of thought appropriate to other spheres upon the political sphere. It is here that political realism takes issue with the "legalistic-moralistic approach" to international politics. That this issue is not, as has been contended, a mere figment of the imagination, but goes to the very core of the controversy, can be shown from many historical examples. Three will suffice to make the point.[5]

In 1939 the Soviet Union attacked Finland. This action confronted France and Great Britain with two issues, one legal, the other political. Did that action violate the Covenant of the League of Nations and, if it did, what countermeasures should France and Great Britain take? The legal question could easily be answered in the affirmative, for obviously the Soviet Union had done what was prohibited by the Covenant. The answer to the political question depends, first, upon the manner in which the Russian action affected the interests of France and Great Britain; second upon the existing

distribution of power between France and Great Britain, on the one hand, and the Soviet Union and other potentially hostile nations, especially Germany, on the other; and, third, upon the influence that the countermeasures were likely to have upon the interests of France and Great Britain and the future distribution of power. France and Great Britain, as the leading members of the League of Nations, saw to it that the Soviet Union was expelled from the League, and they were prevented from joining Finland in the war against the Soviet Union only by Sweden's refusal to allow their troops to pass through Swedish territory on their way to Finland. If this refusal by Sweden had not saved them, France and Great Britain would shortly have found themselves at war with the Soviet Union and Germany at the same time.

The policy of France and Great Britain was a classic example of legalism in that they allowed the answer to the legal question, legitimate within its sphere, to determine their political actions. Instead of asking both questions, that of law and that of power, they asked only the question of law; and the answer they received could have no bearing on the issue that their very existence might have depended upon.

The second example illustrates the "moralistic approach" to international politics. It concerns the international status of the Communist government of China. The rise of that government confronted the Western world with two issues, one moral, the other political. Were the nature and policies of that government in accord with the moral principles of the Western world? Should the Western world deal with such a government? The answer to the first question could not fail to be in the negative. Yet it did not follow with necessity that the answer to the second question should also be in the negative. The standard of thought applied to the first—the moral—question was simply to test the nature and the policies of the Communist government of China by the principles of Western morality. On the other hand, the second—the political—question had to be subjected to the complicated test of the interests involved and the power available on either side, and of the bearing of one or the other course of action upon these interests and power. The application of this test could well have led to the conclusion that it would be wiser not to deal with the Communist government of China. To arrive at this conclusion by neglecting this test altogether and answering the political question in terms of the moral issue was indeed a classic example of the "moralistic approach" to international politics.

The third case illustrates strikingly the contrast between realism and the legalistic-moralistic approach to foreign policy. Great Britain, as one of the guarantors of the neutrality of Belgium, went to war with Germany in August 1914 because Germany had violated the neutrality of Belgium. The British action could be justified either in realistic or legalistic-moralistic terms. That is to say, one could argue realistically that for centuries it had been axiomatic for British foreign policy to prevent the control of the Low Countries by a hostile power. It was then not so much the violation of Belgium's neutrality per se as the hostile intentions of the violator which provided the rationale for British intervention. If the violator had been another nation but Germany, Great Britain might well have refrained from intervening. This is the position taken by Sir Edward Grey, British Foreign Secretary during that period. Under Secretary for Foreign Affairs Hardinge remarked to him in 1908: "If France violated Belgian neutrality in a war against Germany, it is doubtful whether England or Russia would move a finger to maintain Belgian neutrality, while if the neutrality of Belgium was violated by Germany, it is probable that the converse would be the case." Whereupon Sir Edward Grey replied: "This is to the point." Yet one could also take the legalistic and moralistic position that the violation of Belgium's neutrality per se, because of its legal and moral defects and regardless of the interests at stake and of the identity of the violator, justified British and, for that matter, American intervention. This was the position which Theodore Roosevelt took in his letter to Sir Edward Grey of January 22, 1915:

> To me the crux of the situation has been Belgium. If England or France had acted toward Belgium as Germany has acted I should have opposed them, exactly as I now oppose Germany. I have emphatically approved your action as a model for what should be done by those who believe that treaties should be observed in good faith and that there is such a thing as international morality. I take this position as an American who is no more an Englishman than he is a German, who endeavors loyally to serve the interests of his own country, but who also endeavors to do what he can for justice and decency as regards mankind at large, and who therefore feels obliged to judge all other nations by their conduct on any given occasion.

This realist defense of the autonomy of the political sphere against its subversion by other modes of thought does not imply disregard for the existence and importance of these other modes of thought. It rather implies that each should be assigned its proper sphere and function. Political realism is based upon a pluralistic conception of human nature. Real man is a composite of "economic man," "political man," "moral man," "religious man," etc. A man who was nothing but "political man" would be a beast, for he would be completely lacking in moral restraints. A man who was nothing but "moral man" would be a fool, for he would be completely lacking in prudence. A man who was nothing but "religious man" would be a saint, for he would be completely lacking in worldly desires.

Recognizing that these different facets of human nature exist, political realism also recognizes that in order to understand one of them one has to deal with it on its own terms. That is to say, if I want to understand "religious man," I must for the time being abstract from the other aspects of human nature and deal with its religious aspect as if it were the only one. Furthermore, I must apply to the religious sphere the standards of thought appropriate to it, always remaining aware of the existence of other standards and their actual influence upon the religious qualities of man. What is true of this facet of human nature is true of all the others. No modern economist, for instance would conceive of his science and its relations to other sciences of man in any other way. It is exactly through such a process of emancipation from other standards of thought, and the development of one appropriate to its subject matter, that economics has developed as an autonomous theory of the economic activities of man. To contribute to a similar development in the field of politics is indeed the purpose of political realism.

It is in the nature of things that a theory of politics which is based upon such principles will not meet with unanimous approval—nor does, for that matter, such a foreign policy. For theory and policy alike run counter to two trends in our culture which are not able to reconcile themselves to the assumptions and results of a rational, objective theory of politics. One of these trends disparages the role of power in society on grounds that stem from the experience and philosophy of the nineteenth century. . . . The other trend, opposed to the realist theory and practice of politics, stems from the very relationship that exists, and must exist, between the human mind and the political sphere. . . . The human mind in its day-by-day operations cannot bear to look the truth of politics straight in the face. It must disguise, distort, belittle, and embellish the truth—the more so, the more the individual is actively involved in the processes of politics, and particularly in those of international politics. For only by deceiving himself about the nature of politics and the role he plays on the political scene is man able to live contentedly as a political animal with himself and his fellow men.

Thus it is inevitable that a theory which tries to understand international politics as it actually is and as it ought to be in view of its intrinsic nature, rather than as people would like to see it, must overcome a psychological resistance that most other branches of learning need not face. A book devoted to the theoretical understanding of international politics therefore requires a special explanation and justification.

NOTES

1. "Mores of the Present and Future," in *War and Other Essays* (New Haven: Yale University Press, 1911), p. 159.

2. *Scientific Man versus Power Politics* (Chicago: University of Chicago Press, 1946).

3. *The Writings of George Washington,* edited by John C. Fitzpatrick (Washington: United States Printing Office, 1931–44), Vol. X, p. 363.

4. Marianne Weber, *Max Weber* (Tuebingen: J. C. B. Mohr, 1926), pp. 347–8. See also Max Weber, *Gesammelte Aufsätze zur Religionssoziologie* (Tuebingen: J. C. B. Mohr, 1920), p. 252.

5. See the other examples discussed in Hans J. Morgenthau, "Another 'Great Debate': The National Interest of the United States," *The American Political Science Review,* Vol. XLVI (December 1952), pp. 979 ff. See also Hans J. Morgenthau, *Politics in the 20th Century,* Vol. 1, *The Decline of Democratic Politics* (Chicago: University of Chicago Press, 1962), pp. 79 ff; and abridged edition (Chicago: University of Chicago Press, 1971), pp. 204 ff.

QUESTIONS

1. What does Morgenthau mean by the phrase "international relations is the concept of interest defined in terms of power"?

2. Compare and contrast Morgenthau's view of the role of ethics in international politics with that of Machiavelli. What are the similarities and differences between the two theorists?

7.   The Sources of Soviet Conduct

George Kennan

In his famous "X" article, George Kennan lays out the framework for the policy of containment—a strategy adopted by the United States in the aftermath of World War II to prevent the spread of Soviet communism. Kennan points out the weaknesses of the Soviet Union's political and economic infrastructure, recommending that the United States contain Soviet military, political, and moral influence worldwide. This selection is from the journal *Foreign Affairs* (1946).

George Kennan, professor emeritus of the School of Historical Studies at the Institute for Advanced Study in Princeton, New Jersey, has also written *Realities of American Foreign Policy 1900–1950* (1951), *Russia, The Atom and The West* (1958), and *On Dealing With the Communist World* (1964), in addition to many contributions to journals of international affairs. Kennan also served as United States Ambassador to Yugoslavia from 1961 to 1963.

The political personality of Soviet power as we know it today is the product of ideology and circumstances: ideology inherited by the present Soviet leaders from the movement in which they had their political origin, and circumstances of the power which they now have exercised for nearly three decades in Russia. There can be few tasks of psychological analysis more difficult than to try to trace the interaction of these two forces and the relative role of each in the determination of official Soviet conduct. Yet the attempt must be made if that conduct is to be understood and effectively countered.

It is difficult to summarize the set of ideological concepts with which the Soviet leaders came into power. Marxian ideology, in its Russian-Communist projection, has always been in process of subtle evolution. The materials on which it bases itself are extensive and complex. But the outstanding features of Communist thought as it existed in 1916 may perhaps be summarized as follows: (a) that the central factor in the life of man, the factor which determines the character of public life and the "physiognomy of society," is the system by which material goods are produced and exchanged; (b) that the capitalist system of production is a nefarious one which inevitably leads to the exploitation of the working class by the capital-owning class and is incapable of developing adequately the economic resources of society or of distributing fairly the material goods produced by human labor; (c) that capitalism contains the seeds of its own destruction and must, in view of the inability of the capital-owning class to adjust itself to economic change, result eventually and inescapably in a revolutionary transfer of power to the working class; and (d) that

imperialism, the final phase of capitalism, leads directly to war and revolution.

The rest may be outlined in Lenin's own words: "Unevenness of economic and political development is the inflexible law of capitalism. It follows from this that the victory of Socialism may come originally in a few capitalist countries or even in a single capitalist country. The victorious proletariat of that country, having expropriated the capitalists and having organized Socialist production at home, would rise against the remaining capitalist world, drawing to itself in the process the oppressed classes of other countries."[1] It must be noted that there was no assumption that capitalism would perish without proletarian revolution. A final push was needed from a revolutionary proletariat movement in order to tip over the tottering structure. But it was regarded as inevitable that sooner or later that push be given.

For 50 years prior to the outbreak of the Revolution, this pattern of thought had exercised great fascination for the members of the Russian revolutionary movement. Frustrated, discontented, hopeless of finding self-expression—or too impatient to seek it—in the confining limits of the Tsarist political system, yet lacking wide popular support for their choice of bloody revolution as a means of social betterment, these revolutionists found in Marxist theory a highly convenient rationalization for their own instinctive desires. It afforded pseudo-scientific justification for their impatience, for their categoric denial of all value in the Tsarist system, for their yearning for power and revenge and for their inclination to cut corners in the pursuit of it. It is therefore no wonder that they had come to believe implicitly in the truth and soundness of the Marxian-Leninist teachings, so congenial to their own impulses and emotions. Their sincerity need not be impugned. This is a phenomenon as old as human nature itself. It has never been more aptly described than by Edward Gibbon, who wrote in "The Decline and Fall of the Roman Empire": "From enthusiasm to imposture the step is perilous and slippery; the demon of Socrates affords a memorable instance how a wise man may deceive himself, how a good man may deceive others, how the conscience may slumber in a mixed and middle state between self-illusion and voluntary fraud." And it was with this set of conceptions that the members of the Bolshevik Party entered into power.

Now it must be noted that through all the years of preparation for revolution, the attention of these men, as indeed of Marx himself, had been centered less on the future form which Socialism[2] would take than on the necessary overthrow of rival power which, in their view, had to precede the introduction of Socialism. Their views, therefore, on the positive program to be put into effect, once power was attained, were for the most part nebulous, visionary and impractical. Beyond the nationalization of industry and the expropriation of large private capital holdings there was no agreed program. The treatment of the peasantry, which according to the Marxist formulation was not of the proletariat, had always been a vague spot in the pattern of Communist thought; and it remained an object of controversy and vacillation for the first ten years of Communist power.

The circumstances of the immediate post-revolution period—the existence in Russia of civil war and foreign intervention, together with the obvious fact that the Communists represented only a tiny minority of the Russian people—made the establishment of dictatorial power a necessity. The experiment with "war Communism" and the abrupt attempt to eliminate private production and trade had unfortunate economic consequences and caused further bitterness against the new revolutionary régime. While the temporary relaxation of the effort to communize Russia, represented by the New Economic Policy, alleviated some of this economic distress and thereby served its purpose, it also made it evident that the "capitalistic sector of society" was still prepared to profit at once from any relaxation of governmental pressure, and would, if permitted to continue to exist, always constitute a powerful opposing element to the Soviet régime and a serious rival for influence in the country. Somewhat the same situation prevailed with respect to the individual peasant who, in his own small way, was also a private producer.

Lenin, had he lived, might have proved a great enough man to reconcile these conflicting forces to the ultimate benefit of Russian society, though this is questionable. But be that as it may, Stalin, and those whom he led in the struggle for succession to Lenin's position of leadership, were not the men to tolerate rival political forces in the sphere of power which they coveted. Their sense of insecurity was too great. Their particular brand of fanaticism, unmodified by any of the Anglo-Saxon traditions of compromise, was too fierce and too jealous to envisage any permanent sharing of power. From the Russian-Asiatic world out of which they had emerged they carried with them a skepticism as to the possibilities of permanent and peaceful coexistence of rival forces. Easily persuaded of their own doctrinaire "rightness," they insisted on the submission or destruction of all competing power. Outside of the Communist Party, Russian society was to have no rigidity. There were to be no forms of collective human activity or association which would not be dominated by the Party. No other force in Russian society was to be permitted to achieve vitality or integrity. Only the Party was to have structure. All else was to be an amorphous mass.

And within the Party the same principle was to apply. The mass of Party members might go through the motions of election, deliberation, decision and action; but in these motions they were to be animated not by their own individual wills but by the awesome breath of the Party leadership and the overbrooding presence of "the word."

Let it be stressed again that subjectively these men probably did not seek absolutism for its own sake. They doubtless believed—and found it easy to believe—that they alone knew what was good for society and that they would accomplish that good once their power was secure and unchallengeable. But in seeking that security of their own rule they were prepared to recognize no restrictions, either of God or man, on the character of their methods. And until such time as that security might be achieved, they placed far down on their scale of operational priorities the comforts and happiness of the peoples entrusted to their care.

Now the outstanding circumstance concerning the Soviet régime is that down to the present day this process of political consolidation has never been completed and the men in the Kremlin have continued to be predominantly absorbed with the struggle to secure and make absolute the power which they seized in November 1917. They have endeavored to secure it primarily against forces at home, within Soviet society itself. But they have also endeavored to secure it against the outside world. For ideology, as we have seen, taught them that the outside world was hostile and that it was their duty eventually to overthrow the political forces beyond their borders. The powerful hands of Russian history and tradition reached up to sustain them in this feeling. Finally, their own aggressive intransigence with respect to the outside world began to find its own reaction; and they were soon forced, to use another Gibbonesque phrase, "to chastise the contumacy" which they themselves had provoked. It is an undeniable privilege of every man to prove himself right in the thesis that the world is his enemy; for if he reiterates it frequently enough and makes it the background of his conduct he is bound eventually to be right.

Now it lies in the nature of the mental world of the Soviet leaders, as well as in the character of their ideology, that no opposition to them can be officially recognized as having any merit or justification whatsoever. Such opposition can flow, in theory, only from the hostile and incorrigible forces of dying capitalism. As long as remnants of capitalism were officially recognized as existing in Russia, it was possible to place on them, as an internal element, part of the blame for the maintenance of a dictatorial form of society. But as these remnants were liquidated, little by little, this justification fell away; and when it was indicated officially that they had been finally destroyed, it disappeared altogether. And this fact created one of the most basic of the compulsions which came to act upon the Soviet régime: since capitalism no longer existed in Russia and since it could not be admitted that there could be serious or widespread opposition to the Kremlin springing spontaneously from the liberated masses under its authority, it became necessary to justify the retention of the dictatorship by stressing the menace of capitalism abroad.

This began at an early date. In 1924 Stalin specifically defended the retention of the "organs of suppression," meaning, among others, the army and the secret police, on the ground that "as long as there is a capitalist encirclement there will be danger of intervention with all the consequences that flow from that danger." In accordance with that theory, and from that time on, all internal opposition forces in Russia have consistently been portrayed as the agents of foreign forces of reaction antagonistic to Soviet power.

By the same token, tremendous emphasis has been placed on the original Communist thesis of a basic antagonism between the capitalist and Socialist worlds. It is clear, from many indications, that this emphasis is not founded in reality. The real facts concerning it have been confused by the existence abroad of genuine resentment provoked by Soviet philosophy and tactics and occasionally by the existence of great centers of military power, notably the Nazi régime in Germany and the Japanese Government of the late 1930's, which did indeed have aggressive designs against the Soviet Union. But there is ample evidence that the stress laid in Moscow on the menace confronting Soviet society from the world outside its borders is founded not in the realities of foreign antagonism but in the necessity of explaining away the maintenance of dictatorial authority at home.

Now the maintenance of this pattern of Soviet power, namely, the pursuit of unlimited authority domestically, accompanied by the cultivation of the semi-myth of implacable foreign hostility, has gone far to shape the actual machinery of Soviet power as we know it today. Internal organs of administration which did not serve this purpose withered on the vine. Organs which did serve this purpose became vastly swollen. The security of Soviet power came to rest on the iron discipline of the Party, on the severity and ubiquity of the secret police, and on the uncompromising economic monopolism of the state. The "organs of suppression," in which the Soviet leaders had sought security from rival forces, became in large measure the masters of those whom they were designed to serve. Today the major part of the structure of Soviet power is committed to the perfection of the dictatorship and to the maintenance of the concept of Russia as in a state of siege, with the enemy lowering beyond the walls. And the millions of human beings who form that part of the structure of power must defend at all costs this concept of Russia's position, for without it they are themselves superfluous.

As things stand today, the rulers can no longer dream of parting with these organs of suppression. The quest for absolute power, pursued now for nearly three decades with a ruthlessness unparalleled (in scope at least) in modern times, has again produced internally, as it did externally, its own reaction. The excesses of the police apparatus have fanned the potential opposition to the régime into something far greater and more dangerous than it could have been before those excesses began.

But least of all can the rulers dispense with the fiction by which the maintenance of dictatorial power has been defended. For this fiction has been canonized in Soviet philosophy by the excesses already committed in its name; and it is now anchored in the Soviet structure of thought by bonds far greater than those of mere ideology.

II

So much for the historical background. What does it spell in terms of the political personality of Soviet power as we know it today?

Of the original ideology, nothing has been officially junked. Belief is maintained in the basic badness of capitalism, in the inevitability of its destruction, in the obligation of the proletariat to assist in that destruction and to take power into its own hands. But stress has come to be laid primarily on those concepts which relate most specifically to the Soviet régime itself: to its position as the sole truly Socialist régime in a dark and misguided world, and to the relationships of power within it.

The first of these concepts is that of the innate antagonism between capitalism and Socialism. We have seen how deeply that concept has become imbedded in foundations of Soviet power. It has profound implications for Russia's conduct as a member of international society. It means that there can never be on Moscow's side any sincere assumption of a community of aims between the Soviet Union and powers which are regarded as capitalist. It must invariably be assumed in Moscow that the aims of the capitalist world are antagonistic to the Soviet ré-

gime, and therefore to the interests of the peoples it controls. If the Soviet Government occasionally sets its signature to documents which would indicate the contrary, this is to be regarded as a tactical manœuvre permissible in dealing with the enemy (who is without honor) and should be taken in the spirit of *caveat emptor*. Basically, the antagonism remains. It is postulated. And from it flow many of the phenomena which we find disturbing in the Kremlin's conduct of foreign policy: the secretiveness, the lack of frankness, the duplicity, the wary suspiciousness, and the basic unfriendliness of purpose. These phenomena are there to stay, for the foreseeable future. There can be variations of degree and of emphasis. When there is something the Russians want from us, one or the other of these features of their policy may be thrust temporarily into the background; and when that happens there will always be Americans who will leap forward with gleeful announcements that "the Russians have changed," and some who will even try to take credit for having brought about such "changes." But we should not be misled by tactical manœuvres. These characteristics of Soviet policy, like the postulate from which they flow, are basic to the internal nature of Soviet power, and will be with us, whether in the foreground or the background, until the internal nature of Soviet power is changed.

This means that we are going to continue for a long time to find the Russians difficult to deal with. It does not mean that they should be considered as embarked upon a do-or-die program to overthrow our society by a given date. The theory of the inevitability of the eventual fall of capitalism has the fortunate connotation that there is no hurry about it. The forces of progress can take their time in preparing the final *coup de grâce*. Meanwhile, what is vital is that the "Socialist fatherland"—that oasis of power which has been already won for Socialism in the person of the Soviet Union—should be cherished and defended by all good Communists at home and abroad, its fortunes promoted, its enemies badgered and confounded. The promotion of premature, "adventuristic" revolutionary projects abroad which might embarrass Soviet power in any way would be an inexcusable, even a counter-revolutionary act. The cause of Socialism is the support and promotion of Soviet power, as defined in Moscow.

This brings us to the second of the concepts important to contemporary Soviet outlook. That is the infallibility of the Kremlin. The Soviet concept of power, which permits no focal points of organization outside the Party itself, requires that the Party leadership remain in theory the sole repository of truth. For if truth were to be found elsewhere, there would be justification for its expression in organized activity. But it is precisely that which the Kremlin cannot and will not permit.

The leadership of the Communist Party is therefore always right, and has been always right ever since in 1929 Stalin formalized his personal power by announcing that decisions of the Politburo were being taken unanimously.

On the principle of infallibility there rests the iron discipline of the Communist Party. In fact, the two concepts are mutually self-supporting. Perfect discipline requires recognition of infallibility. Infallibility requires the observance of discipline. And the two together go far to determine the behaviorism of the entire Soviet apparatus of power. But their effect cannot be understood unless a third

factor be taken into account: namely, the fact that the leadership is at liberty to put forward for tactical purposes any particular thesis which it finds useful to the cause at any particular moment and to require the faithful and unquestioning acceptance of that thesis by the members of the movement as a whole. This means that truth is not a constant but is actually created, for all intents and purposes, by the Soviet leaders themselves. It may vary from week to week, from month to month. It is nothing absolute and immutable—nothing which flows from objective reality. It is only the most recent manifestation of the wisdom of those in whom the ultimate wisdom is supposed to reside, because they represent the logic of history. The accumulative effect of these factors is to give to the whole subordinate apparatus of Soviet power an unshakeable stubbornness and steadfastness in its orientation. This orientation can be changed at will by the Kremlin but by no other power. Once a given party line has been laid down on a given issue of current policy, the whole Soviet governmental machine, including the mechanism of diplomacy, moves inexorably along the prescribed path, like a persistent toy automobile wound up and headed in a given direction, stopping only when it meets with some unanswerable force. The individuals who are the components of this machine are unamenable to argument or reason which comes to them from outside sources. Their whole training has taught them to mistrust and discount the glib persuasiveness of the outside world. Like the white dog before the phonograph, they hear only the "master's voice." And if they are to be called off from the purposes last dictated to them, it is the master who must call them off. Thus the foreign representative cannot hope that his words will make any impression on them. The most that he can hope is that they will be transmitted to those at the top, who are capable of changing the party line. But even those are not likely to be swayed by any normal logic in the words of the bourgeois representative. Since there can be no appeal to common purposes, there can be no appeal to common mental approaches. For this reason, facts speak louder than words to the ears of the Kremlin; and words carry the greatest weight when they have the ring of reflecting, or being backed up by, facts of unchallengeable validity.

But we have seen that the Kremlin is under no ideological compulsion to accomplish its purposes in a hurry. Like the Church, it is dealing in ideological concepts which are of long-term validity, and it can afford to be patient. It has no right to risk the existing achievements of the revolution for the sake of vain baubles of the future. The very teachings of Lenin himself require great caution and flexibility in the pursuit of Communist purposes. Again, these precepts are fortified by the lessons of Russian history: of centuries of obscure battles between nomadic forces over the stretches of a vast unfortified plain. Here caution, circumspection, flexibility and deception are the valuable qualities; and their value finds natural appreciation in the Russian or the oriental mind. Thus the Kremlin has no compunction about retreating in the face of superior force. And being under the compulsion of no timetable, it does not get panicky under the necessity for such retreat. Its political action is a fluid stream which moves constantly, wherever it is permitted to move, toward a given goal. Its main concern is to make sure that it has filled every nook and cranny available

to it in the basin of world power. But if it finds unassailable barriers in its path, it accepts these philosophically and accommodates itself to them. The main thing is that there should always be pressure, unceasing constant pressure, toward the desired goal. There is no trace of any feeling in Soviet psychology that that goal must be reached at any given time.

These considerations make Soviet diplomacy at once easier and more difficult to deal with than the diplomacy of individual aggressive leaders like Napoleon and Hitler. On the one hand it is more sensitive to contrary force, more ready to yield on individual sectors of the diplomatic front when that force is felt to be too strong, and thus more rational in the logic and rhetoric of power. On the other hand it cannot be easily defeated or discouraged by a single victory on the part of its opponents. And the patient persistence by which it is animated means that it can be effectively countered not by sporadic acts which represent the momentary whims of democratic opinion but only by intelligent long-range policies on the part of Russia's adversaries—policies no less steady in their purpose, and no less variegated and resourceful in their application, than those of the Soviet Union itself.

In these circumstances it is clear that the main element of any United States policy toward the Soviet Union must be that of a long-term, patient but firm and vigilant containment of Russian expansive tendencies. It is important to note, however, that such a policy has nothing to do with outward histrionics: with threats or blustering or superfluous gestures of outward "toughness." While the Kremlin is basically flexible in its reaction to political realities, it is by no means unamenable to considerations of prestige. Like almost any other government, it can be placed by tactless and threatening gestures in a position where it cannot afford to yield even though this might be dictated by its sense of realism. The Russian leaders are keen judges of human psychology, and as such they are highly conscious that loss of temper and of self-control is never a source of strength in political affairs. They are quick to exploit such evidences of weakness. For these reasons, it is a *sine qua non* of successful dealing with Russia that the foreign government in question should remain at all times cool and collected and that its demands on Russian policy should be put forward in such a manner as to leave the way open for a compliance not too detrimental to Russian prestige.

III

In the light of the above, it will be clearly seen that the Soviet pressure against the free institutions of the western world is something that can be contained by the adroit and vigilant application of counterforce at a series of constantly shifting geographical and political points, corresponding to the shifts and manœuvres of Soviet policy, but which cannot be charmed or talked out of existence. The Russians look forward to a duel of infinite duration, and they see that already they have scored great successes. It must be borne in mind that there was a time when the Communist Party represented far more of a minority in the sphere of Russian national life than Soviet power today represents in the world community.

But if ideology convinces the rulers of Russia that truth is on their side and that they can therefore afford to wait, those of us on whom that ideology has no claim are free to examine objectively the validity of that premise. The Soviet thesis not only implies complete lack of control by the west over its own economic destiny, it likewise assumes Russian unity, discipline and patience over an infinite period. Let us bring this apocalyptic vision down to earth, and suppose that the western world finds the strength and resourcefulness to contain Soviet power over a period of ten to fifteen years. What does that spell for Russia itself?

The Soviet leaders, taking advantage of the contributions of modern technique to the arts of despotism, have solved the question of obedience within the confines of their power. Few challenge their authority; and even those who do are unable to make that challenge valid as against the organs of suppression of the state.

The Kremlin has also proved able to accomplish its purpose of building up in Russia, regardless of the interests of the inhabitants, an industrial foundation of heavy metallurgy, which is, to be sure, not yet complete but which is nevertheless continuing to grow and is approaching those of the other major industrial countries. All of this, however, both the maintenance of internal political security and the building of heavy industry, has been carried out at a terrible cost in human life and in human hopes and energies. It has necessitated the use of forced labor on a scale unprecedented in modern times under conditions of peace. It has involved the neglect or abuse of other phases of Soviet economic life, particularly agriculture, consumers' goods production, housing and transportation.

To all that, the war has added its tremendous toll of destruction, death and human exhaustion. In consequence of this, we have in Russia today a population which is physically and spiritually tired. The mass of the people are disillusioned, skeptical and no longer as accessible as they once were to the magical attraction which Soviet power still radiates to its followers abroad. The avidity with which people seized upon the slight respite accorded to the Church for tactical reasons during the war was eloquent testimony to the fact that their capacity for faith and devotion found little expression in the purposes of the régime.

In these circumstances, there are limits to the physical and nervous strength of people themselves. These limits are absolute ones, and are binding even for the cruelest dictatorship, because beyond them people cannot be driven. The forced labor camps and the other agencies of constraint provide temporary means of compelling people to work longer hours than their own volition or mere economic pressure would dictate; but if people survive them at all they become old before their time and must be considered as human casualties to the demands of dictatorship. In either case their best powers are no longer available to society and can no longer be enlisted in the service of the state.

Here only the younger generation can help. The younger generation, despite all vicissitudes and sufferings, is numerous and vigorous; and the Russians are a talented people. But it still remains to be seen what will be the effects on mature performance of the abnormal emotional strains of childhood which Soviet dictatorship created and which were enormously increased by the war. Such things as normal security and placidity of home environment have practically ceased to exist in the Soviet Union outside of the most remote farms and villages. And observers are not yet sure whether that is not going to leave its mark on the over-all capacity of the generation now coming into maturity.

In addition to this, we have the fact that Soviet economic development, while it can list certain formidable achievements, has been precariously spotty and uneven. Russian Communists who speak of the "uneven development of capitalism" should blush at the contemplation of their own national economy. Here certain branches of economic life, such as the metallurgical and machine industries, have been pushed out of all proportion to other sectors of economy. Here is a nation striving to become in a short period one of the great industrial nations of the world while it still has no highway network worthy of the name and only a relatively primitive network of railways. Much has been done to increase efficiency of labor and to teach primitive peasants something about the operation of machines. But maintenance is still a crying deficiency of all Soviet economy. Construction is hasty and poor in quality. Depreciation must be enormous. And in vast sectors of economic life it has not yet been possible to instill into labor anything like that general culture of production and technical self-respect which characterizes the skilled worker of the west.

It is difficult to see how these deficiencies can be corrected at an early date by a tired and dispirited population working largely under the shadow of fear and compulsion. And as long as they are not overcome, Russia will remain economically a vulnerable, and in a certain sense an impotent, nation, capable of exporting its enthusiasms and of radiating the strange charm of its primitive political vitality but unable to back up those articles of export by the real evidences of material power and prosperity.

Meanwhile, a great uncertainty hangs over the political life of the Soviet Union. That is the uncertainty involved in the transfer of power from one individual or group of individuals to others.

This is, of course, outstandingly the problem of the personal position of Stalin. We must remember that his succession to Lenin's pinnacle of preëminence in the Communist movement was the only such transfer of individual authority which the Soviet Union has experienced. That transfer took 12 years to consolidate. It cost the lives of millions of people and shook the state to its foundations. The attendant tremors were felt all through the international revolutionary movement, to the disadvantage of the Kremlin itself.

It is always possible that another transfer of preëminent power may take place quietly and inconspicuously, with no repercussions anywhere. But again, it is possible that the questions involved may unleash, to use some of Lenin's words, one of those "incredibly swift transitions" from "delicate deceit" to "wild violence" which characterize Russian history, and may shake Soviet power to its foundations.

But this is not only a question of Stalin himself. There has been, since 1938, a dangerous congealment of political life in the higher circles of Soviet power. The All-Union Congress of Soviets, in theory the supreme body of the Party, is supposed to meet not less often than once in three years. It will soon be eight full years since its last meeting. During this period membership in the Party has numerically doubled. Party mortality during the war was enormous; and today well over half of the Party members are persons who have entered since the last Party congress was held. Meanwhile, the same small group of men has carried on at the top through an amazing series of national vicissitudes. Surely there is some reason why the experiences of the war brought basic political changes to every one of the great governments of the west. Surely the causes of that phenomenon are basic enough to be present somewhere in the obscurity of Soviet political life, as well. And yet no recognition has been given to these causes in Russia.

It must be surmised from this that even within so highly disciplined an organization as the Communist Party there must be a growing divergence in age, outlook and interest between the great mass of Party members, only so recently recruited into the movement, and the little self-perpetuating clique of men at the top, whom most of these Party members have never met, with whom they have never conversed, and with whom they can have no political intimacy.

Who can say whether, in these circumstances, the eventual rejuvenation of the higher spheres of authority (which can only be a matter of time) can take place smoothly and peacefully, or whether rivals in the quest for higher power will not eventually reach down into these politically immature and inexperienced masses in order to find support for their respective claims? If this were ever to happen, strange consequences could flow for the Communist Party: for the membership at large has been exercised only in the practices of iron discipline and obedience and not in the arts of compromise and accommodation. And if disunity were ever to seize and paralyze the Party, the chaos and weakness of Russian society would be revealed in forms beyond description. For we have seen that Soviet power is only a crust concealing an amorphous mass of human beings among whom no independent organizational structure is tolerated. In Russia there is not even such a thing as local government. The present generation of Russians have never known spontaneity of collective action. If, consequently, anything were ever to occur to disrupt the unity and efficacy of the Party as a political instrument, Soviet Russia might be changed overnight from one of the strongest to one of the weakest and most pitiable of national societies.

Thus the future of Soviet power may not be by any means as secure as Russian capacity for self-delusion would make it appear to the men in the Kremlin. That they can keep power themselves, they have demonstrated. That they can quietly and easily turn it over to others remains to be proved. Meanwhile, the hardships of their rule and the vicissitudes of international life have taken a heavy toll of the strength and hopes of the great people on whom their power rests. It is curious to note that the ideological power of Soviet authority is strongest today in areas beyond the frontiers of Russia, beyond the reach of its police power. This phenomenon brings to mind a comparison used by Thomas Mann in his great novel "Buddenbrooks." Observing that human institutions often show the greatest outward brilliance at a moment when inner decay is in reality farthest advanced, he compared the Buddenbrook family, in the days of its greatest glamour, to one of those stars whose light shines most brightly on this world when in reality it has long since ceased to exist. And who can say with assurance that the strong light still cast by the Kremlin on the dissatisfied peoples of the western world is

not the powerful afterglow of a constellation which is in actuality on the wane? This cannot be proved. And it cannot be disproved. But the possibility remains (and in the opinion of this writer it is a strong one) that Soviet power, like the capitalist world of its conception, bears within it the seeds of its own decay, and that the sprouting of these seeds is well advanced.

IV

It is clear that the United States cannot expect in the foreseeable future to enjoy political intimacy with the Soviet régime. It must continue to regard the Soviet Union as a rival, not a partner, in the political arena. It must continue to expect that Soviet policies will reflect no abstract love of peace and stability, no real faith in the possibility of a permanent happy coexistence of the Socialist and capitalist worlds, but rather a cautious, persistent pressure toward the disruption and weakening of all rival influence and rival power.

Balanced against this are the facts that Russia, as opposed to the western world in general, is still by far the weaker party, that Soviet policy is highly flexible, and that Soviet society may well contain deficiencies which will eventually weaken its own total potential. This would of itself warrant the United States entering with reasonable confidence upon a policy of firm containment, designed to confront the Russians with unalterable counter-force at every point where they show signs of encroaching upon the interests of a peaceful and stable world.

But in actuality the possibilities for American policy are by no means limited to holding the line and hoping for the best. It is entirely possible for the United States to influence by its actions the internal developments, both within Russia and throughout the international Communist movement, by which Russian policy is largely determined. This is not only a question of the modest measure of informational activity which this government can conduct in the Soviet Union and elsewhere, although that, too, is important. It is rather a question of the degree to which the United States can create among the peoples of the world generally the impression of a country which knows what it wants, which is coping successfully with the problems of its internal life and with the responsibilities of a World Power, and which has a spiritual vitality capable of holding its own among the major ideological currents of the time. To the extent that such an impression can be created and maintained, the aims of Russian Communism must appear sterile and quixotic, the hopes and enthusiasm of Moscow's supporters must wane, and added strain must be imposed on the Kremlin's foreign policies. For the palsied decrepitude of the capitalist world is the keystone of Communist philosophy. Even the failure of the United States to experience the early economic depression which the ravens of the Red Square have been predicting with such complacent confidence since hostilities ceased would have deep and important repercussions throughout the Communist world.

By the same token, exhibitions of indecision, disunity and internal disintegration within this country have an exhilarating effect on the whole Communist movement. At each evidence of these tendencies, a thrill of hope and excitement goes through the Communist world; a new jauntiness can be noted in the Moscow tread; new groups of foreign supporters climb on to what they can only view as the band wagon of international politics; and Russian pressure increases all along the line in international affairs.

It would be an exaggeration to say that American behavior unassisted and alone could exercise a power of life and death over the Communist movement and bring about the early fall of Soviet power in Russia. But the United States has it in its power to increase enormously the strains under which Soviet policy must operate, to force upon the Kremlin a far greater degree of moderation and circumspection than it has had to observe in recent years, and in this way to promote tendencies which must eventually find their outlet in either the break-up or the gradual mellowing of Soviet power. For no mystical, Messianic movement— and particularly not that of the Kremlin— can face frustration indefinitely without eventually adjusting itself in one way or another to the logic of that state of affairs.

Thus the decision will really fall in large measure in this country itself. The issue of Soviet-American relations is in essence a test of the over-all worth of the United States as a nation among nations. To avoid destruction the United States need only measure up to its own best traditions and prove itself worthy of preservation as a great nation.

Surely, there was never a fairer test of national quality than this. In the light of these circumstances, the thoughtful observer of Russian-American relations will find no cause for complaint in the Kremlin's challenge to American society. He will rather experience a certain gratitude to a Providence which, by providing the American people with this implacable challenge, has made their entire security as a nation dependent on their pulling themselves together and accepting the responsibilities of moral and political leadership that history plainly intended them to bear.

NOTES

1. "Concerning the Slogans of the United States of Europe," August 1915. Official Soviet edition of Lenin's works.
2. Here and elsewhere in this paper "Socialism" refers to Marxist or Leninist Communism, not to liberal Socialism of the Second International variety.

QUESTIONS

1. What weaknesses does Kennan associate with the Soviet Union?

2. Can the view presented in the "X" article be considered realist? Why or why not?

---

8.   Nuclear Myths and Political Realities

Kenneth N. Waltz

In this article, Kenneth N. Waltz compares and contrasts the impact that conventional and nuclear weapons have on deterring states from going to war. Waltz contends that nuclear weapons are "a tremendous force for peace" because states that possess nuclear weapons are less likely to go to war than those that rely solely on conventional arms. In sum, nuclear weapons enhance deterrence because the consequences of nuclear war are so devastating and frightening. This selection is from the *Quarterly Journal of the American Political Science Association* (1990).

Kenneth N. Waltz is Ford Professor of Political Science at the University of California, Berkeley. He has authored several books, which include *Foreign Policy and Democratic Politics: The American and British Experience* (1967, reprinted in 1992), *Theory of International Politics* (1979), as well as numerous essays.

Nuclear weapons have been given a bad name not just by the Left, as one might have expected, but by the Center and Right as well. Throughout the long life of NATO, calls for strengthening conventional forces have been recurrently heard, reflecting and furthering debate about the wisdom of relying on nuclear deterrence. Doubts were spread more widely when McGeorge Bundy, George Kennan, Robert McNamara, and Gerald Smith published their argument for adopting a NATO policy of "no first use" (Bundy et al. 1982). From the Right came glib talk about the need to be prepared to fight a protracted nuclear war in order to "deter" the Soviet Union and proclaiming the possibility of doing so. Brigadier General Louis Guifridda, when he was director of the Federal Emergency Management Agency, well described the Reagan administration's intended nuclear stance: "The administration," he said, "categorically rejected the short war. We're trying to inject a long-war mentality" (Dowd 1984). Such statements, which scared people at home and abroad out of their wits, quickly disappeared from public discourse. Nevertheless, preparation to carry the policy through proceeded apace. In 1982 Secretary of Defense Caspar Weinberger signed the five-year Defense Guidance Plan, which was to provide the means of sustaining a nuclear war; and in March of that year an elaborate war game dubbed Ivy League "showed" that it could be done (Pringle and Arkin 1983, 22–40). Finally, in March of 1983 President Reagan offered his vision of a world in which defensive systems would render nuclear weapons obsolete.

With their immense destructive power, nuclear weapons are bound to make people uneasy. Decades of fuzzy thinking in high places about what deterrence is, how it works, and what it can and cannot do have deepened the nuclear malaise. Forty-some years after the first atomic bombs fell on Japan, we have yet to come to grips with the strategic implications of nuclear weapons. I apply nuclear reasoning to military policy and in doing so contrast the logic of conventional and nuclear weapons.

Uneasiness over nuclear weapons and the search for alternative means of security stem in large measure from widespread failure to understand the nature and requirements of deterrence. Not unexpectedly, the language of strategic discourse has deteriorated over the decades. This happens whenever discussion enters the political arena, where words take on meanings and colorations reflecting the preferences of their users. Early in the nuclear era *deterrence* carried its dictionary definition, dissuading someone from an action by frightening that person with the consequences of the action. To deter an adversary from attacking one need have only a force that can survive a first strike and strike back hard enough to outweigh any gain the aggressor had hoped to realize. Deterrence in its pure form entails no ability to defend; a deterrent strategy promises not to fend off an aggressor but to damage or destroy things the aggressor holds dear. Both defense and deterrence are strategies that a status quo country may follow, hoping to dissuade a state from attacking. They are different strategies designed to accomplish a common end in different ways, using different weapons differently deployed. Wars can be prevented, as they can be caused, in various ways.

Deterrence antedates nuclear weapons, but in a conventional world deterrent threats are problematic. Stanley Baldwin warned in the middle 1930s when he was prime minister of England that the bomber would always get through, a thought that helped to demoralize England. It proved seriously misleading in the war that soon followed. Bombers have to make their way past fighter planes and through ground fire before finding their targets and hitting them quite squarely. Nuclear weapons purify deterrent strategies by removing elements of defense and war-fighting. Nuclear warheads eliminate the necessity of fighting and remove the possibility of defending, because only a small number of warheads need to reach their targets.

Ironically, as multiplication of missiles increased the ease with which destructive blows can be delivered, the distinction between deterrence and defense began to blur. Early in President Kennedy's administration, Secretary McNamara began to promote a strategy of Flexible Response, which was halfheartedly adopted by NATO in 1967. Flexible Response calls for the ability to meet threats at all levels from irregular warfare to conventional warfare to nuclear warfare. In the 1970s and 1980s more and more emphasis was placed on the need to fight and defend at all levels in order to "deter." The melding of defense, warfighting, and deterrence overlooks a simple truth about nuclear weapons proclaimed in the book title *The Absolute Weapon* (Brodie 1946). Nuclear weapons can carry out their deterrent task no matter what other countries do. If one nuclear power were able to destroy almost all of another's strategic warheads with practical certainty or defend against all but a few strategic warheads coming in, nuclear weapons would not be absolute. But because so much explosive power comes in such small packages, the invulnerability of a sufficient number of warheads is easy to achieve and the delivery of fairly large numbers of warheads impossible to thwart, both now and as far into the future as anyone can see. The absolute quality of nuclear weapons sharply sets a nuclear world off from a conventional one.

WHAT DETERS?

Most discussions of deterrence are based on the belief that deterrence is difficult to achieve. In the Eisenhower years "massive retaliation" was the phrase popularly used to describe the response we would supposedly make to a Soviet Union attack. Deterrence must be difficult if the threat of massive retaliation is required to achieve it. As the Soviet Union's arsenal grew, MAD (mutual assured destruction) became the acronym of choice, thus preserving the notion that deterrence depends on being willing and able to destroy much, if not most, of a country.

That one must be able to destroy a country in order to deter it is an odd notion, though of distinguished lineage. During the 1950s emphasis was put on the *massive* in *massive retaliation*. Beginning in the 1960s the emphasis was put on the *assured destruction* in the doctrine of MAD. Thus viewed, deterrence becomes a monstrous policy, as innumerable critics have charged. One quotation can stand for many others. In a warning to NATO defense ministers that became famous, Henry Kissinger counseled the European allies not to keep "asking us to multiply strategic assurances that we cannot possibly mean or if we do mean, we should not want to execute because if we execute, we risk the destruction of civilization" (1981, 240). The notion that the failure of deterrence would lead to national suicide or to mutual annihilation betrays a misunderstanding of both political behavior and nuclear realities.

Introducing the Eisenhower administration's New Look policy in January of 1954, John Foster Dulles gave the impression that aggression anywhere would elicit heavy nuclear retaliation. Just three months later, he sensibly amended the policy. Nuclear deterrence, Dulles and many others quickly came to realize, works not against minor aggression at the periphery, but only against major aggression at the center, of international politics. Moreover, to deter major aggression, Dulles now said, "the probable hurt" need only "outbalance the probable gain" (1954, 359). Like Brodie before him, Dulles based deterrence on the principle of proportionality: "Let the punishment fit the crime."

What would we expect the United States to do if the Soviet Union launched a major conventional attack against vital U.S. interests—say, in Western Europe? Military actions have to be related to an objective. Because of the awesome power of nuclear weapons, the pressure to use them in ways that achieve the objective at hand while doing and suffering a minimum of destruction would be immense. It is preposterous to think that if a Soviet attack broke through NATO's defenses, the United States would strike thousands of Soviet military targets or hundreds of Soviet cities. Doing so would serve no purpose. Who would want to make a bad situation worse by launching wantonly destructive attacks on a country that can strike back with comparable force, or, for that matter, on a country that could not do so? In the event, we might strike a target or two—military or industrial—chosen to keep casualties low. If the Soviet Union had run the preposterous risk of attacking the center of Europe believing it could escape retaliation, we would thus show them that they were wrong while conveying the idea that more would follow if they persisted. Among countries with abundant nuclear weapons, none can gain an advantage by striking first. The purpose of demonstration shots is simply to remind everyone— should anyone forget—that catastrophe threatens. Some people purport to believe that if a few warheads go off, many will follow. This would seem to be the least likely of all the unlikely possibilities.

That no country gains by destroying another's cities and then seeing a comparable number of its own destroyed in return is obvious to everyone.

Despite widespread beliefs to the contrary, deterrence does not depend on destroying cities. Deterrence depends on what one *can* do, not on what one *will* do. What deters is the fact that we can do as much damage to them as we choose, and they to us. The country suffering the retaliatory attack cannot limit the damage done to it; only the retaliator can do that.

With nuclear weapons, countries need threaten to use only a small amount of force. This is so because once the willingness to use a little force is shown, the adversary knows how easily more can be added. This is not true with conventional weapons. Therefore, it is often useful for a country to threaten to use great force if conflict should lead to war. The stance may be intended as a deterrent one, but the ability to carry the threat through is problematic. With conventional weapons, countries tend to emphasize the first phase of war. Striking hard to achieve a quick victory may decrease the cost of war. With nuclear weapons, political leaders worry not about what may happen in the first phase of fighting but about what may happen in the end. As Clausewitz wrote, if war should ever approach the absolute, it would become "imperative . . . not to take the first step without considering what may be the last" (1976, 584).

Since war now approaches the absolute, it is hardly surprising that President Kennedy echoed Clausewitz' words during the Cuban Missile Crisis of 1962. "It isn't the first step that concerns me," he said, "but both sides escalating to the fourth and fifth step—and we don't go to the sixth because there is no one around to do so" (R. Kennedy 1969, 98). In conventional crises, leaders may sensibly seek one advantage or another. They may bluff by threatening escalatory steps they are in fact unwilling to take. They may try one stratagem or another and run considerable risks. Since none of the parties to the struggle can predict what the outcome will be, they may have good reason to prolong crises, even crises entailing the risk of war. A conventional country enjoying military superiority is tempted to use it before other countries right the military balance. A nuclear country enjoying superiority is reluctant to use it because no one can promise the full success of a disarming first strike. As Henry Kissinger retrospectively said of the Cuban Missile Crisis, the Soviet Union had only "60–70 truly strategic weapons while we had something like 2,000 in missiles and bombs." But, he added, "with some proportion of Soviet delivery vehicles surviving, the Soviet Union could do horrendous damage to the United States" (Kissinger 1979, 18). In other words, we could not be sure that our two thousand weapons would destroy almost all of their sixty or seventy. Even with numbers immensely disproportionate, a small force strongly inhibits the use of a large one.

The catastrophe promised by nuclear war contrasts sharply with the extreme difficulty of predicting outcomes among conventional competitors. This makes one wonder about the claimed dependence of deterrence on perceptions and the alleged problem of credibility. In conventional competitions, the comparative qualities of troops, weaponry, strategies, and leaders are difficult to gauge. So complex is the fighting of wars with conventional weapons that their outcomes have

been extremely difficult to predict. Wars start more easily because the uncertainties of their outcomes make it easier for the leaders of states to entertain illusions of victory at supportable cost. In contrast, contemplating war when the use of nuclear weapons is possible focuses one's attention not on the probability of victory but on the possibility of annihilation. Because catastrophic outcomes of nuclear exchanges are easy to imagine, leaders of states will shrink in horror from initiating them. With nuclear weapons, stability and peace rest on easy calculations of what one country can do to another. Anyone—political leader or man in the street—can see that catastrophe lurks if events spiral out of control and nuclear warheads begin to fly. The problem of the credibility of deterrence, a big worry in a conventional world, disappears in a nuclear one.

Yet the credibility of deterrence has been a constant U.S. worry. The worry is a hangover from the 1930s. Concern over credibility, and the related efforts to show resolve in crises or wars where only peripheral interests are at stake were reinforced because the formative experiences of most of the policy makers of the 1950s and 1960s took place in the 1930s. In rearming Germany, in reoccupying the Rhineland, in annexing Austria, and in dismantling Czechoslovakia, Hitler went to the brink and won. "We must not let that happen again" was the lesson learned, but in a nuclear world the lesson no longer applies. Despite rhetoric to the contrary, practice accords with nuclear logic because its persuasive force is so strong, and the possible consequences of ignoring it so grave. Thus, John Foster Dulles, who proclaimed that maintaining peace requires the courage to go the brink of war, shrank from the precipice during the Hungarian uprising of 1956. And so it has been every time that events even remotely threatened to get out of hand at the center of international politics.

Still, strategists' and commentators' minds prove to be impressively fertile. The imagined difficulties of deterrence multiply apace. One example will do: Paul Nitze argued in the late 1970s that, given a certain balance of strategic forces, the Soviet Union's supposed goal of world domination, and its presumed willingness to run great risks, the Soviet Union might launch a first strike against our land-based missiles, our bombers on the ground, and our strategic submarines in port. The Soviet Union's strike would tilt the balance of strategic forces sharply against us. Rather than retaliate, our president might decide to acquiesce; that is, we might be self-deterred (1988, 357-60). Nitze's scenario is based on faulty assumptions, unfounded distinctions, and preposterous notions about how governments behave. Soviet leaders, according to him, may have concluded from the trend in the balance of nuclear forces in the middle 1970s that our relatively small warheads and their civil defense would enable the Soviet Union to limit the casualties resulting from our retaliation to 3% or 4% of their population. Their hope for such a "happy" outcome would presumably rest on the confidence that their first strike would be well timed and accurate and that their intelligence agencies would have revealed the exact location of almost all of their intended targets. In short, their leaders would have to believe that all would go well in a huge, unrehearsed missile barrage, that the United States would fail to launch on warning, and that if by chance they had failed to "deter our deterrent," they would still be able to limit casualties to only ten million people or so.[1] But how could they entertain such a hope when by Nitze's own estimate their first strike would have left us with two thousand warheads in our submarine force in addition to warheads carried by surviving bombers?

Nitze's fear rested on the distinction between counterforce strikes and countervalue strikes—strikes aimed at weapons and strikes aimed at cities. Because the Soviet Union's first strike would be counterforce, any U.S. president would seemingly have good reason to refrain from retaliation, thus avoiding the loss of cities still held hostage by the Soviet Union's remaining strategic forces. But this thought overlooks the fact that once strategic missiles numbered in the low hundreds are fired, the counterforce-countervalue distinction blurs. One would no longer know what the attacker's intended targets might be. The Soviet Union's counterforce strike would require that thousands, not hundreds, of warheads be fired. Moreover, the extent of their casualties, should we decide to retaliate, would depend on how many of our warheads we chose to fire, what targets we aimed at, and whether we used ground bursts to increase fallout. Several hundred warheads could destroy either the United States or the Soviet Union as ongoing societies. The assumptions made in the effort to make a Soviet first strike appear possible are ridiculous. How could the Soviet Union—or any country, for that matter—somehow bring itself to run stupendous risks in the presence of nuclear weapons? What objectives might its leaders seek that could justify the risks entailed? Answering these questions sensibly leads one to conclude that deterrence is deeply stable. Those who favor increasing the strength of our strategic forces, however, shift to a different question. "The crucial question," according to Nitze, "is whether a future U.S. president should be left with only the option of deciding within minutes, or at most within two or three hours, to retaliate after a counterforce attack in a manner certain to result not only in military defeat for the United States but in wholly disproportionate and truly irremediable destruction to the American people" (1988, 357). One of the marvels of the nuclear age is how easily those who write about the unreliability of deterrence focus on the retaliator's possible inhibitions and play down the attacker's obvious risks. Doing so makes deterrence seem hard and leads to arguments for increasing our military spending in order "to deny the Soviet Union the possibility of a successful war-fighting capability" (1988, 360), a strategic capability that the Soviet Union has never remotely approached.

We do not need ever-larger forces to deter. Smaller forces, so long as they are invulnerable, would be quite sufficient. Yet the vulnerability of fixed, land-based missiles has proved worrisome. Those who do the worrying dwell on the vulnerability of one class of weapon. The militarily important question, however, is not about the vulnerability of one class of weapon but about the vulnerability of a whole strategic-weapons system. Submarine-launched missiles make land-based missiles invulnerable since destroying only the latter would leave thousands of strategic warheads intact. To overlook this again reflects conventional thinking. In the absence of a dominant weapon, the vulnerability of one weapon or another may be a big problem. If the means of protecting sea-lanes of communications were destroyed, for example, we would be unable to deploy and support troops abroad. The problem disappears in a nuclear world. Destroying a portion of one's strategic force means little if sufficient weapons for deterrence survive.

Thinking about deterrence is often faulted for being abstract and deductive, for not being grounded in experience. The criticism is an odd one, since all statements about the military implications of nuclear weapons are inferred from their characteristics. Deterrers from Brodie onward have drawn conclusions from the all-but-unimaginable increase in easily delivered firepower that nuclear warheads embody. Those who in the nuclear era apply lessons learned in conventional warfare make the more problematic claim that despite profound changes in military technology the classic principles of warfare endure (Rose 1980, 102–106). We all, happily, lack the benefit of experience. Moreover, just as deterrent logic is abstract and deductive, so too are the weaknesses attributed to it. Scenarios showing how deterrence might fail are not only abstract but also far-fetched. Deterrence rests on simple propositions and relies on forces obviously sufficient for their purpose.

DETERRING THE SOVIET UNION

Underlying much of the concern about the reliability of nuclear deterrence is the conviction that the Soviet Union is especially hard to deter. Three main reasons are given for believing this. First, the Soviet Union's ambitions are said to be unlimited. In 1984 Secretary of Defense Caspar Weinberger, when asked why the Soviet Union armed itself so heavily, answered the question bluntly, "World domination, it's that simple" (Rosenthal 1989). Second, her military doctrine seemed to contemplate the possibility of fighting and winning combined conventional and nuclear war, while rejecting the doctrine of deterrence. Third, the Soviet Union has appeared to many people in the West to be striving for military superiority.

These three points make a surprisingly weak case, even though it has been widely accepted. Ambitions aside, looking at the Soviet Union's behavior one is impressed with its caution when acting where conflict might lead to the use of major force. Leaders of the Soviet Union may hope that they can one day turn the world to communism. Although the Soviet Union's intentions may be extraordinary, her behavior has not been. Everyone agrees that except in the military sector, the Soviet Union is the lagging competitor in a two-party race. The Soviet Union has been opportunistic and disruptive, but one expects the lagging party to score a point or two whenever it can. The Soviet Union has not scored many. Her limited international successes should not obscure the fact that what the Soviet Union has done mostly since 1948 is lose.

The second point rests on basic misunderstandings about deterrence. It has often been argued that we could not rely on deterrence when the Soviet Union was rejecting the doctrine. One of the drawbacks of the "theory" of assured destruction, according to Henry Kissinger, was that "the Soviets did not believe it" (1981, 238). The efficacy of nuclear deterrence, however, does not depend on anyone's accepting it. Secretaries of defense nevertheless continue to worry that Soviet values, perceptions, and calculations may be different from ours. Thus, Secretary of Defense Harold Brown, worried by the Soviets' emphasis "on the ac-

quisition of war-winning capabilities," concluded that we must "continue to adapt and update our countervailing capabilities so that the Soviets will clearly understand that we will never allow them to use their nuclear forces to achieve any aggressive aim at an acceptable cost" (1980, 83).

The belief that the Soviet Union's having an aggressive military doctrine makes her especially hard to deter is another hangover from conventional days. Germany and Japan in the 1930s were hard to deter, but then the instruments for deterrence were not available. We can fairly say that their leaders were less averse to running risks than most political leaders are. But that is no warrant for believing that had they been confronted with second-strike nuclear forces, they would have been so foolhardy as to risk the sudden destruction of their countries. The decision to challenge the vital interests of a nuclear state, whether by major conventional assault or by nuclear first strike, would be a collective decision involving a number of political and military leaders. One would have to believe that a whole set of leaders might suddenly go mad. Rulers like to continue to rule. Except in the relatively few countries of settled democratic institutions, one is struck by how tenaciously rulers cling to power. We have no reason to expect Russian leaders to be any different. The notion that Russian leaders might risk losing even a small number of cities by questing militarily for uncertain gains is fanciful. Malenkov and Khrushchev lost their positions for lesser failures.

With conventional weapons a status quo country must ask itself how much power it must harness to its policy in order to dissuade an especially aggressive state from striking. Countries willing to

introduce nuclear weapons might then prove irresistible, and they would be fired in the chaos of defeat with little chance of limited and discriminant use. Early use would promise surer control and closer limitation of damage. In a nuclear world a conventional war-fighting strategy would appear to be the worst possible one, more dangerous than a strategy of relying on deterrence.

Attempts to gain escalation dominance, like efforts to raise the nuclear threshold, betray a failure to appreciate the strategic implications of nuclear weapons. Escalation dominance, so it is said, requires a "seamless web of capabilities" up and down "the escalation ladder." Earlier, it had been thought that the credibility of deterrence would be greater if some rungs of the escalation ladder were missing. The inability to fight at some levels would make the threat to use higher levels of force easy to credit. But again, since credibility is not a problem, this scarcely matters militarily. Filling in the missing rungs neither helps nor hurts. Escalation dominance is useful for countries contending with conventional weapons only. Dominance, however, is difficult to achieve in the absence of a decisive weapon. Among nuclear adversaries the question of dominance is pointless because one second-strike force cannot dominate another. Since strategic nuclear weapons will always prevail, the game of escalation dominance cannot be played. Everyone knows that anyone can quickly move to the top rung of the ladder. Because anyone can do so, all of the parties in a serious crisis have an overriding incentive to ask themselves one question: How can we get out of this mess without nuclear warheads' exploding? The presence of nuclear weapons forces

them to figure out how to deescalate, not how to escalate.

To gain escalation dominance, if that were imaginable, would require the ability to fight nuclear wars. War-fighting strategies imply that nuclear weapons are not absolute but relative, so that the country with more and better nuclear weapons could in some unspecified way prevail. No one, however, has shown how such a war could be fought. Indeed, Desmond Ball has argued that a nuclear war could not be sustained beyond the exchange of strategic warheads numbered not in the hundreds but in the tens (1981, 9). After a small number of exchanges no one would know what was going on or be able to maintain control. Yet nuclear weapons save us from our folly: fanciful strategies are irrelevant because no one will run the appalling risk of testing them.

Deterrence has been faulted for its lack of credibility, its dependence on perceptions, its destructive implications, and its inability to cover interests abroad. The trouble with deterrence, however, lies elsewhere: the trouble with deterrence is that it can be implemented cheaply. The claim that we need a seamless web of capabilities in order to deter does serve one purpose: it keeps military budgets wondrously high. Efforts to fashion a defensive and war-fighting strategy for NATO are pointless because deterrence prevails and futile because strategy cannot transcend the military conditions that nuclear weapons create.

NUCLEAR ARMS AND DISARMAMENT

The probability of major war among states having nuclear weapons approaches zero. But the "real war" may, as William James claimed, lie in the preparation for waging it. The logic of deterrence, if followed, circumscribes the causes of "real wars" (1968, 23). Nuclear weapons make it possible for a state to limit the size of its strategic forces as long as other states are unable to achieve disarming first-strike capabilities by improving their forces.

Within very wide ranges, a nuclear balance is insensitive to variation in numbers and size of warheads. This has occasionally been seen by responsible officials. Harold Brown, when he was secretary of defense, said that purely deterrent forces "can be relatively modest, and their size can perhaps be made substantially, though not completely, insensitive to changes in the posture of an opponent." Somehow, he nevertheless managed to argue that we need "to design our forces on the basis of essential equivalents" (1979, 75–76). Typically, over the past three decades secretaries of defense have sought, albeit vainly, the superiority that would supposedly give us a war-fighting capability. But they have failed to explain what we can do with twelve thousand strategic nuclear warheads that we could not do with two thousand or an even smaller number. What difference does it make if we have two thousand strategic weapons and the Soviet Union has four thousand? We thought our deterrent did not deter very much and did not work with sufficient reliability just as we were reaching a peak of numerical superiority in the mid-1960s. Flexible response, with emphasis on conventional arms, was a policy produced in our era of nuclear plenty. "Superiority" and "parity" have had the same effect on our policy.

Many who urge us to build ever more strategic weapons in effect admit the military irrelevance of additional forces when, as so often, they give political rather than military reasons for doing so: spending less, it is said, would signal weakness of will. Yet militarily, only one perception counts, namely, the perception that a country has second-strike forces. Nuclear weapons make it possible for states to escape the dynamics of arms racing; yet the United States and the Soviet Union have multiplied their weaponry far beyond the requirements of deterrence. Each has obsessively measured its strategic forces against the other's. The arms competition between them has arisen from failure to appreciate the implications of nuclear weapons for military strategy and, no doubt, from internal military and political pressures in both countries.

Many of the obstacles to arms reduction among conventional powers disappear or dwindle among nuclear nations. For the former, the careful comparison of the quantities and qualities of forces is important. Because this is not so with nuclear weapons, the problem of verifying agreements largely disappears. Provisions for verification may be necessary in order to persuade the Senate to ratify an agreement, but the possibility of noncompliance is not very worrisome. Agreements that reduce one category of conventional weapons may shift competition to other types of weapons and lead to increases in their numbers and capabilities. Because with nuclear weapons sufficiency is easily defined, there is no military reason for reductions in some weapons to result in increases in others. Conventionally, multiparty agreements are hard to arrive at because each party has to consider how shifting alignments may alter the balance of forces if agreements are reached to reduce them. In a world of second-strike nuclear forces, alliances have little effect on the strategic balance. The Soviet Union's failure to insist that British, French, and Chinese forces be counted in strategic arms negotiations may reflect its appreciation of this point. Finally, conventional powers have to compare weapons of uncertain effectiveness. Arms agreements are difficult to reach because their provisions may bear directly on the prospects for victory or defeat. Because in a nuclear world peace is maintained by the presence of deterrent forces, strategic arms agreements do not have military but economic and political, significance. They can benefit countries economically and help to improve their relations.

A minority of U.S. military analysts have understood the folly of maintaining more nuclear weapons than deterrence requires. In the Soviet Union, Mikhail Gorbachev and some others have put forth the notion of "reasonable sufficiency," defined as having a strategic force roughly equal to ours and able to inflict unacceptable damage in retaliation. Edward Warner points out that some civilian analysts have gone further, "suggesting that as long as the USSR had a secure second-strike capability that could inflict unacceptable damage, it would not have to be concerned about maintaining approximate numerical parity with U.S. strategic nuclear forces" (1989, 21). If leaders in both countries come to accept the minority view—and also realize that a deterrent force greatly reduces conventional requirements on central fronts—both countries can enjoy security at much lower cost.

STRATEGIC DEFENSE

Strategic defenses would radically change the propositions advanced here. The Strategic Defense Initiative, in Reagan's vision, was to provide an area defense that would protect the entire population of the United States. Strategic defenses were to pose an absolute defense against what have been absolute weapons, thus rendering them obsolete. The consequences that would follow from mounting such a defense boggle the mind. That a perfect defense against nuclear weapons could be deployed and sustained is inconceivable. This is so for two reasons: (1) it is impossible, and (2) if it were possible, it wouldn't last.

Nuclear weapons are small and light; they are easy to move, easy to hide, and easy to deliver in a variety of ways. Even an unimaginably perfect defense against ballistic missiles would fail to negate nuclear weapons. Such a defense would instead put a premium on the other side's ability to deliver nuclear weapons in different ways: firing missiles on depressed trajectories, carrying bombs in suitcases, placing nuclear warheads on freighters to be anchored in American harbors. Indeed, someone has suggested that the Soviet Union can always hide warheads in bales of marijuana, knowing we cannot keep them from crossing our borders. To have even modestly effective defenses we would, among other things, have to become a police state. We would have to go to extraordinary lengths to police our borders and exercise control within them. Presumably, the Soviet Union does these things better than we do. It is impossible to imagine that an area defense can be a success because there are so many ways to thwart it. In no way can we prevent the Soviet Union from exploding nuclear warheads on or in the United States if it is determined to do so.

Second, let us imagine for a moment that an airtight defense, however defined, is about to be deployed by one country or the other. The closer one country came to deploying such a defense, the harder the other would work to overcome it. When he was secretary of defense, Robert McNamara argued that the appropriate response to a Soviet defensive deployment would be to expand our deterrent force. More recently, Caspar Weinberger and Mikhail Gorbachev have made similar statements. Any country deploying a defense effective for a moment cannot expect it to remain so. The ease of delivering nuclear warheads and the destructiveness of small numbers of them make the durability of defenses highly suspect.

The logic of strategic defense is the logic of conventional weaponry. Conventional strategies pit weapons against weapons. That is exactly what a strategic defense would do, thereby recreating the temptations and instabilities that have plagued countries armed only with conventional weapons. If the United States and the Soviet Union deploy defensive systems, each will worry—no doubt excessively—about the balance of offensive and defensive capabilities. Each will fear that the other may score an offensive or defensive breakthrough. If one side should do so, it might be tempted to strike in order to exploit its temporary advantage. The dreaded specter of the hair trigger would reappear. Under such circumstances a defensive system would serve as the shield that makes the sword useful. An offensive-defensive race would introduce many uncertainties. A country enjoying a momentary defensive advantage would be tempted to strike in the forlorn hope that its defenses would be able to handle a ragged and reduced response to its first strike. Both countries would prepare to launch on warning

while obsessively weighing the balance between offensive and defensive forces.

Finally, let us imagine what is most unimaginable of all—that both sides deploy defenses that are impregnable and durable. Such defenses would make the world safe for World War III—fought presumably in the manner of World War II but with conventional weapons of much greater destructive power.

Still, some have argued that even if some American cities remain vulnerable, defenses are very good for the cities they do cover. The claim is spurious. In response to the Soviet Union's deploying antiballistic missiles to protect Moscow, we multiplied the number of missiles aimed at that city. We expect to overcome their defenses and still deliver the "required" number of warheads. The result of defending cities may be that more warheads strike them. This is especially so because both they and we, working on worst-case assumptions, are likely to overestimate the number of missiles that the other country's system will be able to shoot down. Strategic defenses are likely to increase the damage done.

Most knowledgeable people believe that an almost leak-proof defense cannot be built. Many, however, believe that if improved hard-point defenses result from the SDI program, they will have justified its price. Defense of missiles and of command, control, and communications installations will strengthen deterrence, so the argument goes. That would be a solution, all right; but we lack a problem to go with it: deterrence is vibrantly healthy. If the Soviet Union believes that even one Trident submarine would survive its first strike, it will be deterred.[3] Since we do not need hard-point defenses, we should not buy them. The deployment of such defenses by one side would be seen by the other as the first step in deploying an area defense. Strategic considerations should dominate technical ones. In a nuclear world defensive systems are predictably destabilizing. It would be folly to move from a condition of stable deterrence to one of unstable defense.

CONCLUSION

Nuclear weapons dissuade states from going to war more surely than conventional weapons do. In a conventional world, states going to war can at once believe that they may win and that, should they lose, the price of defeat will be bearable. World Wars I and II called the latter belief into question before atomic bombs were ever dropped. If the United States and the Soviet Union were now armed only with conventional weapons, the lesson of those wars would be strongly remembered—especially by Russia, since she has suffered more in war than we have. If the atom had never been split, the United States and the Soviet Union would still have much to fear from each other. The stark opposition of countries of continental size armed with ever-more-destructive conventional weapons would strongly constrain them. Yet in a conventional world even forceful and tragic lessons have proved to be exceedingly difficult for states to learn. Recurrently in modern history one great power or another has looked as though it might become dangerously strong (Louis XIV's and Napolean's France, Wilhelm II's and Hitler's Germany). Each time, an opposing coalition formed, if belatedly, and turned the expansive state back. The lesson would seem to be clear: in international politics, success leads to failure. The excessive accumulation of power by one state or coalition of states elicits the opposition of others. The leaders of expansionist states have nevertheless been able to persuade themselves that skillful diplomacy and clever strategy might enable them to transcend the normal processes of balance-of-power politics. The Schlieffen Plan, for example, seemed to offer a strategy that would enable Germany to engage enemies on two fronts, serially: Germany would defeat France before Russia could mobilize fully and move westward in force. Later, Hitler, while denouncing the "boobs" of Wilhelmine Germany for getting themselves into a war on two fronts, reenacted their errors.

How can we perpetuate peace without solving the problem of war? This is the question that states with nuclear weapons must constantly answer. Nuclear states continue to complete militarily. With each state tending to its security interests as best it can, war is constantly possible. Although the possibility of war remains, nuclear weapons have drastically reduced the probability of its being fought by the states that have them. Wars that might bring nuclear weapons into play have become extraordinarily hard to start. Over the centuries great powers have fought more wars, and lesser states have fought fewer: the frequency of war has correlated less closely with the attributes of states than with their international standing. Yet because of a profound change in military technology, waging war has more and more become the privilege of poor and weak states. Nuclear weapons have reversed the fates of strong and weak states. Never since the Treaty of Westphalia in 1648, which conventionally marks the beginning of modern history, have great powers enjoyed a longer period of peace than we have known since the Second World War. One can scarcely believe that the presence of nuclear weapons does not greatly help to explain this happy condition.

NOTES

This essay was presented as the presidential address at the annual meeting of the American Political Science Association in Washington, 1988. David Schleicher's penetrating criticisms and constructive suggestions helped me greatly in writing it.

1. Nitze blandly adds that if we do launch on warning, "the estimates in the Soviet civil defense manuals are overoptimistic from the Soviet viewpoint" (1988, 357).
2. Quaint ideas die hard. In the fall of 1989 NATO resisted discussing naval disarmament with the Soviet Union because of the need for forces to guard the sea-lanes to Europe (Lewis 1988).
3. An Ohio-class Trident submarine carries twenty-four missiles, each with eight warheads.

REFERENCES

Ball, Desmond. 1981. "Counterforce Targeting: How New? How Viable?" *Arms Control Today* 11:1–9.

Brodie, Bernard, ed. 1946. *The Absolute Weapon.* New York: Harcourt, Brace.

Brodie, Bernard. 1957. "More about Limited War." *World Politics* 10:112–22.

Brodie, Bernard. 1973. *War and Politics.* New York: Macmillan.

Brooks, Linton F. 1988. "Naval Power and National Security." In *The Use of Force,* 3d ed., ed. Robert J. Art and Kenneth N. Waltz. Lanham, MD: University Press of America.

Brown, Harold. 1979. *Annual Report, Fiscal Year 1980.* Washington. U.S. Department of Defense.

Brown, Harold. 1980. *Annual Report, Fiscal Year 1981.* Washington: U.S. Department of Defense.

Bundy, McGeorge, George F. Kennan, Robert S. McNamara, and Gerard Smith. 1982. "Nuclear Weapons and the Atlantic Alliance." *Foreign Affairs* 60:753–68.

Clausewitz, Carl von. 1976. *On War.* Trans. Michael Howard and Peter Paret. Princeton: Princeton University Press.

Dowd, Maureen. 1984. "Ferraro Suggests Reagan Go Home." *New York Times* 22 September.

Dulles, John Foster. 1954. "Policy for Security and Peace." *Foreign Affairs* 32:353–64.

Howard, Michael. 1981. "On Fighting a Nuclear War." *International Security* 5:3–17.

James, William. 1968. "The Moral Equivalent of War." In *War: Studies from Psychology, Sociology, Anthropology,* 2d ed., ed. Leon Bramson and George W. Goethals. New York: Basic Books.

Kahn, Herman. 1960. *On Thermonuclear War.* Princeton: Princeton University Press.

Kennedy, Robert F. 1969. *Thirteen Days.* New York: Norton.

Kissinger, Henry. 1979. "Kissinger's Critique." *Economist* 3 February.

Kissinger, Henry. 1981. *For the Record: Selected Statements, 1977–1980.* Boston: Little, Brown.

Lewis, Paul. 1938. "Soviet Official Says Talks on Arms Should Emphasize Cuts in Navies." *New York Times* 19 October.

Nitze, Paul H. 1988. "Deterring Our Deterrent." In *The Use of Force,* 3d ed., ed. Robert J. Art and Kenneth N. Waltz. Lanham, MD: University Press of America.

Pringle, Peter, and William Arkin. 1983. S.I.O.P.: *The Secret of U.S. Plan for Nuclear War.* New York: Norton.

Rose, John P. 1980. *The Evolution of U.S. Army Nuclear Doctrine, 1945–1980.* Boulder: Westview.

Rosenthal, Andrew. 1989. "Pentagon Report Softens Soviet Menace." *New York Times* 28 September.

Warner, Edward L. III. 1989. "New Thinking and Old Realities in Soviet Defense Policy." *Survival* 31:13–33.

QUESTIONS

1. Based on Waltz's writings, how have nuclear weapons been a stabilizing force for those nations that possess them? Why?

2. Does Waltz remain consistent with the realist perspective from his previous work, *Man, The State and War?*

9. Is Realism Finished?

Fareed Zakaria

In this article, Fareed Zakaria outlines the current debate on the future application of realism in explaining the nature of the international system. By defining both realism and liberal pluralism (institutional transnationalism), Zakaria provides a foundation for understanding this important theoretical debate. With the end of the Cold War, he sees economic growth and power replacing the influence of military capability in the international system. He acknowledges, however, that it would be imprudent at this time to discard completely the tenets of realist theory. This selection is from the journal *National Interest* (1992).

Fareed Zakaria is the managing editor of *Foreign Affairs.*

For the third time this century the United States has waged and won a world war. And for the third time the postwar environment brings with it calls that this nation transcend international politics rather than engage in it. As in 1918 and 1945, the end of a great struggle against an evil empire has brought with it the hope that a new world order can arise, if only we assist in its creation. Leading statesmen and publicists now urge, as they did twice before, that American foreign policy be based not merely on preserving the peace and protecting America's interests but on collective security, international law, democratization, and other noble causes. In some versions, the goal of American diplomacy is nothing less than a wholly democratic world that lives in perpetual peace.

The school of thought that has traditionally cast doubt on the ability of the United States—or any country—to make the world anew is "realism," a term usually prefixed in the mouths of its detractors with the words "cold-blooded" or "heartless." Its adherents are charged with all manner of crimes from coddling dictators to spurning America's "true" values. The hall of shame to which realists are assigned includes controversial luminaries like Richard Nixon and Henry Kissinger, academics like Hans Morgenthau and Raymond Aron, and of course George Bush. Today its critics have branded realism obsolete, a relic of the days of courts and princes, an approach out-of-sync with a world of borderless economies, peace-loving democracies, and global crises like the greenhouse effect.

In fact realism has been attacked in similar terms for hundreds of years, and despite recurrent onslaughts from liberals, Marxists, pacifists, environmentalists, deconstructionists, and others, it persists as the fundamental method of analyzing world politics. Indeed as one liberal theorist notes, "these critiques seem only to confirm the centrality of Realist thinking in the international political thought of the West." The public debate on this subject, however, has been shallow, dominated by name-calling on both sides (realists are not averse to branding their opponents woolly-minded dreamers). This is unfortunate because a serious discussion of first principles in international relations raises crucial issues about war, peace, and foreign policy.

Although the distinction between the two has often been blurred, realism is not so much a normative guide for for-eign policy as an explanation of how the world works, a theory of international relations. From this understanding of world politics one could propose different foreign policies depending on the kind of risks, tradeoffs, and goals one seeks—in fact realists have often disagreed on specific policy issues. One could, alternately, regard realism as a pivotal but incomplete understanding of inter-state relations and set out to supplement its sparc analysis with additional factors (which is this writer's position). Or one might reject the entire framework and replace it with something else. Whatever one's final conclusions, it is worth asking at the start: What is realism?

THE CAUSES OF WAR

A theory of how the world works must be able to explain the most persistent and disturbing feature of international history: the periodic recurrence of war. One strand of realist thought locates the roots of international conflict in human nature. Drawing on the Christian philosophical tradition running from St. Augustine to Reinhold Niebuhr, this view is associated with modern realist thought mainly because of the writings of Hans Morgenthau, the German emigré political scientist who dominated the postwar study of international relations in America. Morgenthau wrote against a backdrop of Anglo-American idealist thinking which had declared war to be unnatural, caused by nefarious interest-groups, a defective intellectual environment, and misinformation. Conflict was like a disease; it could be eliminated if men and nations were properly socialized. One prominent English thinker, Alfred Zimmern, even suggested establishing an international lending library to educate properly the next generation of cosmopolitan statesmen.

In a withering critique of these "utopians," Morgenthau argued that war was the result of "forces inherent in human nature." "The ubiquity of evil in human actions," he said, inevitably led human organizations to struggle for power, transforming "churches into political organizations . . . revolutions into dictatorships . . . and love for country into imperialism." Morgenthau moved the discussion of war away from Enlightenment rationalism with its view of human perfectibility, towards an older, darker Western tradition in which "the sinfulness of man is conceived not as an accidental disturbance of the order of the world sure to be overcome by a gradual development toward the good, but as an inescapable necessity." Although he pointed to other causes of conflict, this one loomed largest in his work and became the most widely caricatured, cited whenever critics wish to charge that realism rests on a fundamentally cynical view of humankind.

Other realists, however, have long believed that Morgenthau's focus on an *animus dominandi* is at best incomplete. As today's leading realist scholar, Kenneth Waltz, points out, if human nature explains the recurrent episodes of conflict in the world, does it not also explain the many periods of peace? "Human nature may in some sense have been the cause of war in 1914, but by the same token it was the cause of peace in 1910. In the intervening years many things changed, but human nature did not." While the evil in humans may be the fundamental cause of war, the good in them is the fundamental cause of peace. Human nature cannot explain why some eras are more war-ravaged than others;

nor why domestic politics, while conflictual, is usually non-violent.

THE INTERNATIONAL SYSTEM

The other, more important, tradition in realist thought, running from Thucydides through Hobbes and Rousseau, explains the persistence of war by the situation in which states exist. The international system is anarchic, with no overarching authority providing security and order. In such a "self-help" system each state must rely on its own resources to survive and flourish, and in this uncertain climate competition and conflicts of interest abound. Because there is no authoritative, impartial method of settling these disputes—i.e. no world government—states are their own judges, juries, and hangmen, and often resort to force to achieve their security interests. War persists in this view because "nothing exists to prevent it."

The defining characteristic of realism has always been its belief that the international system is different and separate from the domestic one, and that this competitive atmosphere exerts a powerful influence on states. Everything else is a footnote to this observation. In the sixteenth century, diplomats and scholars of the Italian city-states noticed that their external relations followed a pattern determined by their relative power positions. A century later the Huguenot Prince Henri de Rohan spoke of the need for princes to follow the "national interest," because it represented the dictates of the international system: "The Princes command people," he explained, "and the Interest commands the Prince." Two centuries after that the great Austrian statesman Metternich argued that "the society of states [is] the essential condition of the modern world."

This strand of realism is often termed "structural realism" or "neorealism." It treats the international system as a distinct analytic concept. Because this realm has no ruler, its cardinal feature is the distribution of power within it, determining who can do what to whom. Thus the distribution of power has a potent influence on world politics. The seminal example of systemic pressures affecting international outcomes, indeed creating a pattern of history, is the recurrent formation of *balances of power.* The logic of competition under anarchy suggests that states, jealous of their independence, will balance against a rising, threatening great power, rather than jump on its bandwagon.

The broad outline of modern European history bears out this generalization. There have been five unsuccessful attempts by individual powers at continental hegemony. The Hapsburg bid for mastery of the continent in the seventeenth century was thwarted by a combination of powers; France's attempts at dominance in the eighteenth and early nineteenth century were finally defeated by the Quadruple Alliance; Germany's two massive campaigns to conquer Europe ended in failure in the two World Wars; and the Soviet Union's quest for domination of large parts of Eurasia collapsed under the pressure of a worldwide anti-Soviet alliance. The pattern of aspiring hegemons and neighbors who gang up on them is not limited to modern Europe. The fundamental cause of the Peloponnesian War was, in Thucydides' oft-quoted phrase, "the rise of Athens and the fear which this caused in Sparta."

While realists debate how strong systemic influences are on a state's foreign policies, most agree that *in crises* and *in the long run* they tend to dominate other factors. Of course states pursue goals unrelated to their physical security, such as economic welfare. They often form alliances for reasons of ideological affinity. They make many foreign policy decisions because of domestic pressures. But because the stakes in the realm of international security are so high—ultimately national survival itself—in a crisis they usually respond to the strategic environment rather than to their ideological preferences. Thus when Nazi Germany invaded the Soviet Union, the Western world's most ardent anticommunist, Winston Churchill, quickly embraced Stalin's regime as an ally. Thirty years later Richard Nixon, a charter member of the "Who Lost China?" Republicans, went to Beijing to forge an anti-Soviet alliance with a communist elite fresh from perpetrating the barbarisms of the Cultural Revolution. Most recently, when President Bush needed a united Arab front to back his anti-Iraq campaign he travelled to Damascus to befriend Hafez Assad of Syria, a man his administration had boycotted for years and branded a terrorist.

This discussion raises one of the great misconceptions about realism. Critics, even well-meaning ones, have been puzzled by the fact that realists often assert that the international system pushes states to act in a certain manner; yet these same realists can be found urging the United States to follow one course rather than another. Robert W. Tucker asks, "If the national interest is so objective, if it is analogous in nature to gravity, then what is the reason for the repeated failure of statesmen to see what is self-evident?" Why do realists keep imploring statesmen to do what they will be forced to do anyway? The answer is simple. Realists do not believe that states always follow systemic pressures; they do believe that states that ignore these pressures pay a price. As Henri de Rohan said in 1640, "According [as the national interest] is well understood, it maketh states to live or die."

States exist in the international system in much the same way that firms do in a free market. Markets impose certain imperatives on firms—most basically, look out for your interests, keep an eye on the competition, and maximize your profits. Most firms follow these incentives and disincentives. Those that do not, in the long run, go bust. The international realm works differently, but not much. States rise and fall more frequently than we may think. In the sixteenth century there were over 500 states in Europe. After 300 conflict-ridden years there were fewer than thirty. Over the last century all of the great multinational empires have collapsed and there are now close to 200 member-states of the United Nations. Of course, just as some firms perish for technological or structural reasons, some states have been victims of forces beyond their control, e.g. the rise of sea power favored island and coastal nations. But, just as many firms go bankrupt through bad management, so do nations. Eighteenth-century Poland miscalculated the capabilities and intentions of its neighbors; the result was that it disappeared from the map of Europe for over a hundred years.

For the great powers, the international system resembles an oligopolist market, with its handful of large actors, more than it does a free one. Because their size insulates them from the effects of any one error or change, death rates for firms in such markets are low; Ford did not close down after the Edsel fiasco. Instead, mistakes result in large losses, which erode a firm's market position. Similarly, when great powers err they bleed rather than die. If they truly overextend themselves, as Germany and the Soviet Union did in this century, they can be reduced to second-rank status for a generation. If they are very strong and make smaller errors—e.g. Britain in the Boer War or the U.S. in Vietnam—they will still pay a price in the blood and treasure of their citizens.

For great powers survival is usually assured. Freed of this basic constraint, they often concern themselves with goals beyond security, such as spreading their beliefs or religion abroad. There is nothing intrinsically wrong with spending "surplus power" on non-security related goals. For example, America's vigorous promotion of democracy abroad is a noble cause. But from Versailles to Vietnam, idealistic statesmen, distracted by the grandeur of their goals, have neglected prudence and calculation. Realists worry that it is too easy, when pursuing such policies, to ignore basic systemic discipline and to forget that in the uncertain environment of world politics, misperceptions, unintended consequences, and Murphy's laws abound. Hence, while most realists were early and strong supporters of containment, many were also early critics of the Vietnam War. What realists often suggest as a grand strategy for states is the foreign policy equivalent of a long-term strategy for a big business. It eschews dramatic short-term profits and risky investments in return for smaller but more lasting gains, long-term profits, and security. It is the grand strategy of Warren Buffet rather than Donald Trump.

Good great power strategy is rare, but two models can be emulated—Britain during the nineteenth century and America since World War II. The roll call of Europe's aspiring hegemons listed earlier omitted these two names because they did not invite upon themselves the large countervailing coalitions that the others did. Alone among modern great powers, these two countries were able to remain utterly dominant in the world without causing rivals to collude against them. The reason is simple: America and, to a lesser extent, Great Britain followed policies that concentrated on essentials, building economic power at home and commercial links abroad. Each was the most important power of its time but did not try to destroy other great powers. (In fact, at the turn of the century Britain chose to appease both America in the Western hemisphere and Russia in Central Asia.) They intervened when vital interests were at stake, most dramatically when the European balance of power was threatened, denying Germany and the Soviet Union conquest of the continent. By husbanding their own power and using it with wisdom and restraint, Britain and America outlasted all their rivals.

THE CHALLENGE FROM POLITICAL LIBERALISM

From the days of the Greeks some philosophers have argued that international relations are determined not by states' power positions but by their internal characteristics. In the last two centuries this viewpoint evolved into a coherent critique of realism, and by the early twentieth century, liberal and Marxist variations of this view became quite popular.

Two specific issues crystallized this disagreement, in arguments that continue to this day: Britain's great surge of imperialism in the 1880s and 1890s; and Germany's attempt to dominate Europe in World War I. The British liberal J.A. Hobson set forth a powerful argument, later adapted by Lenin, that the economic and social structure of British capitalism caused Britain's "scramble for Africa." At the same time various German scholars argued that the roots of German *Weltpolitik* lay in that country's part-feudal, part-industrial socio-economic structure. Despite their cynical view of domestic politics, these critiques were in a larger sense of a product of Enlightenment optimism. If war and expansion were caused by diseased societies, then they could be cured. Turning states towards Marxism or democracy, depending on one's politics, would hasten the millennium.

Over the centuries, critics of realism have associated various internal causes with imperialism and war. When most of the world's great powers were religious monarchies, they claimed that religion caused war; but states became increasingly secular and war persisted. Then they said that it was kings who caused war; yet monarchies vanished and war did not. Marxist-Leninists proclaimed that capitalism caused war, pointing to the many imperial powers at the time that were capitalist. But many equally imperial regimes were not capitalist at all, Japan and Russia for example. (A more difficult problem for dialecticians was the fact that communist states proved as expansionist as any in history.) Today, it is the turn of nationalism to bear the blame. These various theories of imperialism and war are partially true in the sense that many of the factors identified—religion, capitalism, or fascism—had close connections with specific wars. But they do not explain the larger phenomenon of war itself. Let us be clear: realists believe that while "bad" states cause wars, they do not cause *War*.[1] If a particular domestic regime were the cause of war in general, how could it be that in the thousands of years of recorded history every kind of regime known to man has engaged in war and expansion? Monarchies, oligarchies, aristocracies, republics, city-states, nation-states, holy empires, dictatorships, and even democracies have gone to war regularly and with roughly uniform zeal.

Marxism having been discredited in both theory and practice, the most important challenge to realist thought now comes from political liberalism, which argues that democracies are inherently more pacific than other regimes and that a world of democracies would hence be one of "perpetual peace." These ideas were first put forth by Emmanuel Kant and have been revived and adapted by political scientist Michael Doyle. Kant wrote that republics would not war on one another, and Doyle claims that the last two centuries bear out the generalization that no democracy has ever gone to war with another democracy. One can quibble with the specifics—the War of 1812 is skipped by defining Britain as undemocratic at the time; the American Civil War doesn't count either—but the correlation is impressive, and if it holds up over the next decades it will pose a serious problem for realism.

For an international theorist the existence of peace among democracies leads less to self-congratulation than to further questioning. Why don't they fight each other? Is it that they abhor violence? Or is it that ordinary people won't pay for costly expansionism? Or is it, as Francis Fukuyama claims, in Joseph Schumpeter's tradition, that "imperialism and war are related to a certain social class, the class of masters, otherwise known as the aristocracy, who derived their social status from their willingness to risk their lives in bygone days." All three arguments, however, should make democracies more peaceful across the board, towards all other countries. In fact democracies have been more war-prone than other regimes—they fight wars more often and with greater fury than the average state. Only in relations with each other do democracies keep the peace.

Even though the logic behind the "liberal peace" is still unclear, it would be foolish dogmatism not to recognize that important trends have changed the world over the last two centuries, making the Western capitalist democracies less war-prone than they have ever been. They are fat, contented, unwilling to spend thousands of lives in military adventures, and, when dealing with each other, less susceptible to the egotism, insecurity, and paranoia which often lead to war. Bitter rivalries and struggles for influence among liberal democracies will develop in the world ahead; but these conflicts of interests will not turn into conflicts of armies as long as the political and economic conditions in which the Western states live remain unchanged. Similar progress towards great power peace was made in the nineteenth century, another era of spectacular economic and political progress. Then came economic rivalries, depressions, xenophobia, nationalism, and war. If the prosperous economic order of the post-1945 world were to crumble, the liberal peace might not survive the strain.

The Challenge from Economic Liberalism

Economic liberalism is the dominant Anglo-American perspective on economic affairs. Over the last two centuries it has replaced all other modes of economic thought in Europe. More recently it has gained adherents across the globe as other nations have tried to copy the Western world's staggering growth. Economic liberalism is defined by its reliance on the concept of the market. It assumes that free markets occur naturally and spontaneously, and that the unfettered exchange of goods, money, and services is the most efficient way of organizing economic life, domestically and internationally. Liberals may differ on how much efficiency should be sacrificed for other social goals—spending on the poor, for example—but all of them, Keynesians and supply siders alike, accept that the market and its pricing mechanism are the most efficient available system of allocating resources. The individual pursuit of self-interest, in this view, leads to general economic welfare; as Bernard Mandeville put it in 1706, "Private vice is public virtue." If nations allow free exchange the world economic pie will keep growing bigger. Of course some nations will gain more than others, just as within a nation comparative advantages and relative efficiencies make some millionaires and leave others paupers.

Post-war realists like Morgenthau and Kissinger thought little about economics. The Soviet threat was a political, military, and ideological one and they dealt with it on those terms. But earlier realists, from Thucydides to Alexander Hamilton to E.H. Carr, were always vitally concerned with economics. This school of thought has recently been revived in a sophisti-cated manner by Robert Gilpin of Princeton University. Modern realists have an ambiguous relationship towards economic liberalism. Virtually all contemporary American realists happen to be liberals in the sense that they believe that the market and its pricing mechanism allow for maximum economic efficiency. Almost all of them are economic liberals in a deeper, normative sense in that they value individual freedom and limited government. They believe that free markets create the greatest wealth possible, and that an international economy characterized by the free exchange of people, capital, and goods holds the greatest prospect for world economic growth and welfare (in this they depart from realists like Hamilton, List, and Bismarck).

But realists believe that the distribution of power is the most important fact of international life. Thus the widespread practice of particular economic and political arrangements are the result of the preferences of the world's dominant states. Realists do not believe that free markets arise spontaneously, nor that the liberal economic world is a "normal" or natural state of affairs. Instead they see this beneficent arrangement as the product of the power and liberal preferences of the world's two economic hegemons, Britain in the nineteenth century and America in the twentieth century. The *Pax Britannica* lasted approximately from the repeal of the Corn Laws through World War I. The global economic system was unhinged in the 1930s because British power had collapsed and America failed to step into the void. The spectacular growth of the OECD economies from the late 1940s to the present has rested on five American-made pillars: the political and military protection provided by the United States; the West's unity, itself based on fear of the Soviet threat; the dollar's pivotal role in the international monetary system; the free trade system, also sponsored by the United States; and American foreign aid and direct investment.

American hegemony, though still unrivalled, has already begun eroding, largely from forces beyond its control—the uneven nature of international growth, the pace of technological change, and free-rider advantages for other countries. Some American policies and practices have also hurt. By the 1960s the United States was consuming more and investing less, and the massive Keynesian state intervention of that era coupled with the Vietnam War accelerated this trend. By the 1970s American productivity growth rates, once the envy of the world at 3 percent, had declined to 0.8 percent, behind Germany, Japan, and the Newly Industrializing Countries (NICs). This shift in relative economic power had clear political consequences. The world monetary system came apart with the collapse of Bretton Woods, and is now kept patched together by ad hoc arrangements and summit meetings. The free-trade system is under similar pressure, as bilateralism, sectoral protectionism, and regional blocs are on the rise. Moreover, Japan appears both less able and willing to help create and maintain the post-war, liberal, economic order.

Some people see the international economic ills of the last fifteen years as being caused by specific problems and policies—such as Vietnam, the oil shocks, and the budget deficits. Realists tend to see the growing disharmony of the OECD countries as the result of structural problems, which threaten to get worse. With the end of the Cold War, concerns about relative military gains have given way to concerns about relative economic gains. The United States was once willing to encourage Japan and Western Europe to grow robustly (in fact, faster than its own economy) so as to stand as a bulwark against the Soviet Union. Today the victorious OECD powers are increasingly worried about each other's competitive position and their global market-share in key industries.

Where liberals might assume that great powers will be satisfied with absolute economic gains—rising standards of living for their citizens—regardless of whether they are doing better than other states, realists know that international influence stems from *relative* national power. Take one example: Britain grew impressively over the last century at an average rate of 1.75 percent. The average citizen in Britain today enjoys a much higher standard of living than did his Victorian predecessor. But other industrial nations grew just a little faster than Britain, the United States by an average of 2.25 percent during the same period. The result: while Victorian Britain strode the world like a colossus, Britain today limps hesitantly, bringing up the rear of the great power club.

SOURCES OF OPTIMISM

Two liberal schools argue against the pessimism implied in this realist perspective on political economy; both have some merit. The first believes that interdependence, the increasingly intertwined nature of national economies and societies, has created countless incentives for peace and cooperation. Wars between nations that trade, manufacture, invest, and research together would be too disruptive for statesmen to contemplate; they would be forced to find peaceful solutions to their troubles. Clearly there is some truth to the notion that commerce creates the sentiments and interests that make war less likely.

Interdependence, however, is double-edged. While it creates incentives for peace, it also gives rise to the irritations, frictions, and conflicts that can lead to war. The great powers of nineteenth century Europe were far more integrated, in every sense, than their counterparts since 1945. Asa Briggs has called that age of *truly* borderless commerce and travel "the belle epoque of interdependence." Using a simple economic measure of interdependence—exports plus imports as a percentage of GNP—we see that nineteenth-century Britain, France, Germany, and Italy ranged between 33 and 52 percent. Observing this happy state of affairs, the British liberal Norman Angell explained that war among the advanced European nations had become unthinkably costly and was therefore obsolete. His book, *The Great Illusion,* was published in 1913.

Using the same measure of trade as a percentage of GNP, during the Cold War the United States and the Soviet Union ranged between a modest 8 and 14 percent, a dramatically lower level of interdependence than in nineteenth-century Europe. In fact one might argue that the Cold War was relatively peaceful precisely *because* the two superpowers had such little contact with each other and were largely independent of the rest of the world (both having large internal economies). Had there been constant contact between these two arch-enemies there would have been constant friction and many more Berlin and Cuban crises. One need only look at Yugoslavia, a nation that was consciously made as economically, politically, and ethnically intertwined as possible, to recognize that the quiet caress of interdependence can sometimes turn into a deadly embrace.

The second source of optimism derives from a faith in international institutions. Harvard political scientist Robert Keohane argues that cooperation can continue even after the decline of a hegemon, as long as the major powers commit themselves to international institutions and regimes that will recognize and implement their common long-term interests. This would ensure continued prosperity for the major powers and provide a hospitable environment for the fledgling capitalist democracies around the globe. The occasions for conflict inherent in multipolar anarchy would still exist, but they would be moderated by growth, democracy, and multi-lateral problem-solving.

The institutionalist viewpoint is often caricatured by realists as a naive belief that peace derives from membership in world bodies like the League of Nations and the UN. In fact recent writings in this tradition have made more modest claims that are firmly grounded in realist logic. They proceed from the assumption that anarchy and uncertainty are the cause of inter-state conflict, and propose solutions that ameliorate these two conditions. International regimes serve to regularize cooperation, reduce transactions costs, and provide institutional support for multilateral policies. These regimes often play a positive role in international life, but they cannot make member-states choose international over national interests. During the recent monetary crisis in Europe, for example, Germany put its own economic interests over those of Europe as a whole.

The happiest prospect for the future of the world economy is that the United

States, Japan, and Germany join together and rejuvenate the liberal international economy, placing it on a firmer footing. This is America's preeminent strategic challenge in the next decade, and it is not a futile one. Each of the major powers has a strong interest in an open world economy and there exist many trends that will keep those interests alive. Grand strategy, however, must be based not simply on a best-case scenario but on other likely ones as well. America, having long struggled with the question of how a politically liberal state operates in a realist world, must now consider what an economically liberal state might have to do in an increasingly mercantilist world.

THE PROBLEM OF PEACEFUL CHANGE

As we have demonstrated, in an anarchic world the distribution of power has powerful effects on international events. Changes in this distribution, therefore, have serious, system-wide repercussions; witness how the collapse of the USSR has influenced politics from the Middle East to South Africa to Nicaragua. But the distribution of power is in constant flux, and this dynamic condition ensures that world politics can never stay the same. For all kinds of reasons—technological change, demography, and leadership skills among them—*uneven economic growth* is a permanent feature of international life. Nations rise and fall, and they do so at different paces. The new rich want influence commensurate with their wealth, the newly impoverished hold more territory or prestige than they can afford. The lack of a supranational authority ensures that states will take it upon themselves to sort these matters out, often resorting to force.

Great powers have a vested interest in systemic peace. First, a general war would be ruinous for most of them. Second, stability and predictability are the foundations on which the material and moral welfare of their citizens rests (America has a special interest in a peaceful world because it provides the best breeding ground for democracy and capitalism). Thus the great power statesman's responsibilities are threefold: to maximize his country's security and influence in the world; to allow for the inevitable shifts in international power and prestige; and finally, to preclude or preempt a general war. These three tasks are rarely harmonious, which is why E.H. Carr termed the central dilemma of international relations "the problem of peaceful change."

In this century the most commonly proposed solution to this problem has been collective security: a binding system of laws by which all nations commit themselves to the defense of *any* nation attacked. The criticisms of collective security are well-known: no system can work if it requires that states go to war, expending blood and treasure, for reasons that they regard as peripheral to their own security. More generally, collective security is a static concept; it attempts to outlaw the inevitable frictions of a dynamic world. The international hierarchy cannot be frozen circa 1945, with first rank powers like Germany and Japan placed on the same footing as Bolivia and Costa Rica.

A more modest proposal would be to return to a concert of great powers, a loose, informal, arrangement for cooperation. It would operate in much the same way as the nineteenth-century concert of Europe did; making the assumption that while each great power has its own distinct interests, they all agree that a large-scale war should be prevented. In each region, the relevant great power would undertake to provide "public goods" for its neighbors, chiefly security. The benefits are obvious—peace and the conditions for political and economic progress—and, additionally for the great power, international prestige. The system is likely to work better than it did in the nineteenth century because, unlike then, the great powers today are governed by fairly responsible regimes. Of the seven—America, Japan, Germany, Russia, China, France, and England— none appears to harbor major territorial grievances; most are liberal, capitalist democracies, and none presents a radically different ideology, which would make it a "revolutionary" state. Such revisionism as exists is limited to demands for clout in global economic affairs, international organizations, etc.—concerns that can be satisfied more easily and peaceably than, say, the claim on Alsace-Lorraine.[2]

In practical terms, for this concert to work, Japan and Germany must be integrated into the ranks of the great powers, even if that means eventually encouraging them to take on military responsibilities. If the concert is to work through the United Nations, as it should, those two states must become permanent members of the Security Council with veto powers. It also requires a frank recognition that, unlike under a system of collective security, there will not be a universal commitment to respond to *every* act of aggression, regardless of cost or location. Those conflicts that threaten to spill over into general conflagrations will require concerted responses. Other flare-ups may be regional in nature giving only one or two of them the interests and incentives to get involved. Regional balancing and

discrimination will take the place of the global deterrence of the Cold War.

Concerts of power have often been criticized for their ad hoc nature. They are, of course, only as good as their members, but in the absence of a world government, that will be true of any system of peace-making. It is argued that concerts are too flexible, tolerating minor conflicts to minimize the possibility of a major one. They are seen to represent an old idea that seeks not to eradicate war, but merely to keep it in temporary abeyance, a "second best" solution compared to more ambitious schemes that hold out the prospect of a permanent end to international violence. This is true. The realist statesman assumes that there is no final solution to the problem of war. He tries instead to avoid wars between great powers; to pursue his nation's interests; and to mediate change in world politics using diplomacy and, if need be, force. Conflict, in his view, will persist in international life whatever scheme one concocts. Better an admittedly sloppy, "second-best" arrangement that works most of the time, than an intricate mechanism, beautiful in abstraction, that collapses under the stress of international life.

MORALITY AND FOREIGN POLICY

The great Italian statesman Count Cavour is reported to have said to a friend, "If we were to do for ourselves what we are doing for Italy, we should be great rogues." Many of the critics of realism have judged Cavour and his ilk to be rogues anyway, the most popular criticism of realism being that it is immoral or at best amoral. Its advocates supposedly reject the conjoining of politics and morality, and preach instead a gospel of naked self-interest, brute force, and national advantage. Like the Athenians in Thucydides' Melian dialogue, realists are said to embrace unabashedly the belief that might makes right: "the strong do what they can and the weak do what they must." This critique rings loudest in America, a country defined by its liberal roots, and uneasy with what is often portrayed as a cynical European art. (Critics of realism prefer the German term *realpolitik* to make that point). It remains for most Americans *the* problem with—the cause for rejecting—realism. This is a caricature of serious realism. Far from being philosophic skeptics, realists like Max Weber, Reinhold Niebuhr, and Hans Morgenthau have devoted years of their lives and hundreds of pages of text in order to establish moral imperatives in the international arena. It is no accident that today's most prominent realist statesman, Henry Kissinger, and its most prominent realist scholar, Kenneth Waltz, have both written serious works on Emmanuel Kant. No realist thinker believes that morality is bunk or that politics and morality are incompatible.

From Thucydides on, however, realists have recognized that the domestic sphere is so different from the international one that standards of morality devised for the former cannot be applied easily to the latter. Domestic morality rests on an ordered polity and an accepted social framework. By contrast, "international relations," in Stanley Hoffmann's words, "is a competition of groups with no consensus among them, and no power above them." It is a realm with no uniform social, political, or moral system; comprised of groups with widely different values and philosophical traditions, and with great inequalities of status and power. In *Duties Beyond Borders,* Hoffmann's eloquent exhortation for greater moral sensibility in foreign policy, he concedes that because of these differences, "moral opportunities for the statesman in world affairs are quite limited." A moral statesman operating in a realist world must hence keep in mind three caveats—chaos, competition, and caution.

Chaos. The moral responsibilities of international life are different from those of domestic life. In an anarchic world, order is the essential precondition for other ideals to flourish. This concern with the consequences of chaos underlies Henry Kissinger's approving use of Goethe: "If I had to choose between justice and disorder on the one hand, and injustice and order on the other, I would always choose the latter." Though the quotation is a cruel overstatement, those who scorn entirely its hierarchy of values would be well advised to ask themselves whether they would prefer to live in Yugoslavia under Tito or in Yugoslavia today; in Somalia under a tin-pot dictator or in Somalia today. It is easy to celebrate, from the safety of suburban America, every breakdown of unsavory authority in the belief that it will usher in a new birth of freedom. Often, however, it brings chaos, death, and destruction—not the best breeding grounds for liberty.

Competition. States must rely upon their own devices for their security. This creates constraints on moral action that do not exist in a civil society with a governmental authority. Were human beings forced to live in a world without laws or governments, we would expect different standards of behavior of them than we do now. Self-defense, even within an ordered polity, justifies otherwise illegal actions. In fact, states routinely behave in ways that, in other contexts, would be considered rank immorality. They spy, they betray trusts, they cheat, and they consciously plan to do great violence to one another. Cavour was not being cynical; he was making a careful distinction between what he might legitimately do for himself on the one hand, and for Italy on the other. The competitive nature of international life ensures that if one country *alone* acts out of moral rather than strategic concerns, it will encourage others to seek advantage.

Caution. Misperceptions and unintended consequences are a constant feature of the uncertain global milieu, and statesmen are forced to act with greater caution and modesty then they would in domestic affairs. Max Weber explained the difference between the "ethic of intentions" and the "ethic of responsibility." The ethic of intentions does not ask about the consequences of its actions; it draws its sanction and its morality from the purity of the statesman's intentions. The ethic of responsibility, however, acknowledges that the statesman must "give an account of the foreseeable results of his action." It recognizes that in the international realm the road to hell is frequently paved with good intentions. But the statesman will, and should, be held responsible for the consequences of his actions.

This political prudence also suggests a certain kind of moral humility. It is all too easy to brand your opponent immoral when discussing complex issues of international responsibility. Take, again, the debate over American policy in what was Yugoslavia. Morality could not have been the deciding factor for the proponents of American intervention. Yugoslavia is no worse in moral terms than most of the ethnic wars that are taking place, and have taken place, in Africa, Central Asia, and Southeast Asia over the last fifteen years. In terms of numbers of deaths, brutality, and the conscious nature of the violence, the Yugoslavian tragedy is on the low end of a sad scale. Thus the interventionists must have decided that *this* tragedy alone merited a response for other reasons; fears of a wider war or political instability in Europe, a desire for strict collective security, or even empathy for the suffering of white Europeans. These criteria may or may not be valid; in any event, they are not moral ones. Having selected Yugoslavia for largely non-moral reasons, however, these debaters have had no compunction about using *exclusively* moral pronouncements to shame their opponents. Kant denounced this kind of "political moralism"—the manipulative use of morality for political ends.

Morality has an important place in foreign policy. International constraints are rarely so tight that national survival is a state's only concern. In fact, most great powers have ample room for maneuver. As important, any politics that is devoid of purposive action degenerates into sterile selfishness. America's foreign policy in particular is properly concerned with ideals and principles, and the world is a better place because of the spread of Anglo-American values. But the conditions for a steady global movement towards capitalism and democracy are better served by quiet purpose than sensational emotionalism. The changes wrought by foreign economic, social, and political ties in a closed society are often more lasting than any superficial concessions gained by hectoring its government. Incremental progress, while not dramatic, is often the most enduring.

During the Cold War diplomacy was war by other means. But this victory of coercive diplomacy took forty-five years, nine American administrations, a worldwide alliance, and at least five trillion dollars. Today, without a strategic or ideological threat that warrants a new cold war, American diplomacy should return to its traditional tasks: securing American power and interests, and strengthening the conditions for economic and political development across the world. In that order.

NOTES

1. The confusion over a similar kind of distinction between history and History has led to the almost universal misunderstanding of Francis Fukuyama's thesis in his "The End of History."

2. China is clearly the odd man out, though in the international arena its behavior has been cautious. Because of a combination of uncertainty over its future, and the confluence of fast-growing nations, disparate regime types, border problems, and historical animosities, East Asia is likely to be the most unstable region in the world over the next fifteen years.

QUESTIONS

1. Identify the major points outlined by Zakaria in his essay that support replacing realism as the primary theory on the international system.

2. How might Hans Morgenthau respond to this argument?

10.   Realism and the New Consensus

Robert W. Tucker

In this article, Robert W. Tucker provides a historical basis for the policy of realism in the United States. With the end of the Cold War, Robert Tucker identifies a "new foreign policy consensus" that questions the utility of realism in transforming and promoting a new world order. He cautions, however, that certain tenets of realism should be preserved to prevent the formulation and adoption of unwise foreign policy. This selection is from the journal *National Interest* (1992).

Robert W. Tucker is professor of American Diplomacy with the Nitze School of Advanced International Studies at Johns Hopkins University. He is co-author of *The Imperial Temptation* (1992), with David C. Hendrickson.

Political realism has seldom found much favor in American thinking on foreign policy. Historians may remind us that the Founding Fathers thought and acted in terms of interest and power, that is was this country's first president who cautioned that, "No nation is to be trusted farther than it is bound by its interests"— a statement that presumably applied to the new American nation as much as to others—and that Washington's Farewell Address, so long the nation's sacred text on foreign policy, was cast in classic realist terms.

Yet the realism that undoubtedly characterized so much of early American thinking about foreign policy was not unalloyed. There was from the outset another outlook that vied with realism, that contended the American nation stood for something new under the sun, and that saw our destiny as a nation to lead the world from an old and discredited international system to a new order of things. The principles and policies of republican government were considered to be the very antithesis of the principles and policies that marked the monarchies of Europe.

The logic of reason of state was the logic of monarchies, not of republics. It was the logic of those who found in war the principal outlet for their passions and energies, and who made the fundamental rule of governments the principle of extending their territories. "Why are not republics plunged into war," Thomas Paine had asked, "but because the nature of their government does not admit of an interest distinct from that of the nation?" Paine's answer might just as well have been given by Thomas Jefferson and by the party of Jefferson, the Republicans.

The view that republics were naturally peaceful, monarchies naturally ag-

gressive, was rejected by Jefferson's great adversary, Alexander Hamilton. That the "genius of republics is pacific" seemed no more plausible to Hamilton than the equation of peace with commerce. "The causes of hostility among nations are innumerable," he argued in *The Federalist,* and they operated independently of forms of government. War was to Hamilton an inescapable fact of political life. It was to be avoided not through the absence of preparedness but through the moderation of diplomatic ambition. In this respect as well, Hamilton was at odds with Jefferson, whose diplomacy entertained grand objectives while shrinking from the means required for realizing those objectives.

It is often said that the nation's views on foreign policy are above all an amalgam of the views of Jefferson and Hamilton. But this gives to Hamilton a greater influence than the historical record warrants. Particularly in this century, it is Jefferson—or rather Jefferson's principal successor, Woodrow Wilson—who has dominated our thinking about foreign policy. Wilson articulated, as no other president has done in this century, the nation's ideals and aspirations. Wilson is the great expositor of America's distinctive reason of state, the expansion of freedom, just as he is the fount of the reformist impulse that has marked American diplomacy. It is true that America's post-World War II foreign policy embraced Hamiltonian means, the means of the old diplomacy. The essential feature of the policy of containment was the organization of power to counter power. In the pursuit of a favorable and stable balance of power, an alliance system was created and sustained over a period of four decades. The principal means employed in waging the Cold War can scarcely be seen as a vindication of either Jefferson or Wilson.

If, however, we consider the ends for which the great contest with the Soviet Union was ostensibly waged, the paramount influence of Wilson is clear. The ends held out by the Truman Doctrine—the prospect of a world in which free peoples might work out their own destinies in their own way, of a world that would make possible the lasting freedom and independence of all nations—were vintage Wilson. The Truman Doctrine reflected Wilson's belief that only a democratic world would be a truly peaceful world, just as it reflected Wilson's belief that a peaceful world could only be achieved and maintained through America's leadership.

The world that has emerged after the Cold War appears to many a striking vindication of Wilson's vision. The promise of a new international order—an order in which the principles of the consent of the governed, equality of right, and freedom from aggression are joined with the idea of America's leadership—has never seemed brighter. America's leadership, it is maintained, will no longer be expressed through a balance of power but through a community of power (the United Nations) whose working will result from this nation's hegemonic position in a progressively capitalist and democratic world that is no longer dominated by the prospect of war between the great powers.

It is around this vision of a new order that a foreign policy consensus is now forming. That this consensus is unreceptive to the outlook and counsel of political realism is not surprising. Experience indicates that realism is likely to be given a serious hearing in times of adversity, not of good fortune; that its persuasive-

ness is the result of harsh necessity, not of benign freedom. The great spokesmen of realism—from Thucydides to Max Weber—have written against the background of conflicts and disaster. In our own history, the realism of the Founding Fathers was forged in a hostile and unforgiving world. More recently, the experience of the Second World War and of the early years of the Cold War gave to realism a currency and standing that it had not enjoyed for some time.

The circumstances of the passing of the Cold War, however, are not such as to evoke a realist outlook. The task of maintaining a balance of power no longer forms the overriding imperative of American policy. Without a great power adversary, the United States is released from the necessity that was for so long the principal, if not the sole determinant of its foreign policy. For the foreseeable future, at any rate, this nation has no major military competitor; for all intents and purposes, it is freed from the requirements of the balance. At the same time, it is more than ever before the dominant military power in the world. In the reach and effectiveness of its military forces, America compares favorably with some of the greatest empires known to history. If its military power nevertheless has limits, those limits reflect domestic political constraints more than those imposed by a resistant world.

It is in—and because of—these circumstances that a new foreign policy consensus is forming today, a consensus that in time may match the vaunted Cold War consensus of a generation ago. The consensus that fell apart over Vietnam was one of ends and means. Critics eventually attacked both. America had become, the argument ran, not simply the world's policeman but a reactionary policeman. From a progressive and liberating force it had become a repressive and counter-revolutionary power. The identification of American power with reaction persisted well into the 1980s. But the collapse of the Soviet Union and its socialist satellites, and the avidity with which the developing world has embraced liberal-capitalist principles and institutions, have dealt a fatal blow to this criticism of yesterday. The skepticism with which the purposes of American policy were once viewed by the liberal left has all but disappeared. In its place, we have a Democratic president-elect who has urged that America, "lead a global alliance for democracy as united and steadfast as the global alliance that defeated communism."

More significant still is the emergence of a consensus over means. The great division in foreign policy since Vietnam reflected more a disagreement over the means of policy than over ends. It was the issue of force, of the interests for which and the conditions in which military power should be employed, that formed the nerve root of controversy. The major fault line of the foreign policy debates of a generation, that issue separated an interventionist Republican Party from a non-interventionist Democratic Party. The Gulf War, in all likelihood, marked its last appearance. That conflict promises to be to the divisions of the past generation what the war in Vietnam was to the early Cold War consensus. Long-standing democratic opponents of intervention learned a lesson that has since led to a striking shift in attitude toward force and its uses. The causes of this shift, domestic political expediency apart, are apparent. It was in large measure due to an appreciation that with the Soviet Union's

disappearance from the international scene, intervention no longer carried the risks and costs it once did. The Gulf War appeared to provide a persuasive demonstration of this lesson. But it was also seen to demonstrate that given sufficient technological superiority in arms, intervention might be undertaken quickly and almost painlessly. And it indicated that in a world no longer driven by superpower conflict, intervention under the leadership of the remaining superpower could be endowed with the kind of international legitimacy seldom enjoyed in the past.

Clearly, these are not the circumstances in which realism might be expected to flourish and there are a few signs that a new foreign policy consensus arising from them will be so informed. In the prevailing contemporary temper, realism cannot but seem curiously irrelevant. Realism is above all a profoundly conservative outlook, a classically conservative outlook. Its temper is skeptical both of human nature and of the possibilities of political action. Its emphasis is on the limitations attending the conduct of statecraft. Its principal prescription is prudence.

In almost any period, these elements of a realist outlook have formed at best an uneasy fit with American views on foreign policy. If there seems little fit at all today it is because the extraordinary success and good fortune that in recent years have attended our encounter with the world have not surprisingly encouraged traits long resistant to the insights of realism. A reformist tradition in foreign policy, more exuberant today than it has been in many years, can have little use for a view that is as skeptical as realism over the prospects for anything resembling fundamental change in the international system. A nation so deeply committed to the belief that it is a great power unlike other great powers in history, that its power is only exercised on behalf of justice and freedom, must find it difficult to accept the realist admonition that hegemonic states have always called forth the counterbalancing efforts of others and that, sooner or later, these efforts may be expected in the present instance as well. A diplomacy addicted to entertaining grand ends unmatched by adequate means may be expected to give little heed to the realist counsel of prudence in circumstances where it does clearly enjoy a vast superiority in military power over all other states. Where power is seen for all practical purposes as being virtually unlimited, what need is there for the discipline of realism?

Yet it is precisely in these circumstances that realism may be most needed, for it is in these circumstances that the limitations attending all statecraft—even the statecraft of a nation as powerful as this one—will be ignored or simply rejected. The utility of the insights afforded by realism have often been exaggerated. As a general disposition toward politics—above all, international politics—realism deals with the perennial conditions that define the activity of statecraft, not with the specific conditions that confront the statesman. It does not so much tell the political actor what he can do in a concrete situation as what he can not expect to do in almost any situation. Realism warns that successful policy can no more afford to ignore the contingent than it can the invariable. Still, it cannot deduce the specific requirements of a successful policy from necessities that are independent of time and place. This is one reason why realists, although sharing common assumptions about the nature of political

reality, have often had marked disagreements over policy.

That realism cannot provide a ready "policy guide" to success for the statesman is a defect only from the perspective of those who impose this unreasonable requirement. A far more serious charge, however, is the failure of realists to live up to the essential commitment of realism, in Machiavelli's words, "to go to the real truth of the matter" when the real truth is far reaching, even transforming, change in the international system. At a time when the international system appears to be undergoing such change, this failure may be critical. An unwillingness today to acknowledge that among liberal democratic states war may well become all but precluded as a means for resolving conflicts of interest or that nuclear weapons may rule out the possibility of major war among states that possess them can only serve to discredit realism. Both propositions may be true; there is increasing evidence to support the conclusion that they are true. Their truth would not invalidate realism, only a version of realism that insists on making the structure of the international system—that is, its decentralized or "anarchic" character—the overriding determinant of war and its persistence. The case for doing so, however, has never gone unchallenged. Today, it appears more questionable than ever.

Nor can realism resolve the great moral dilemmas of statecraft. To be sure, realism prescribes prudence and insists that the political actor concern himself with the likely consequences of his actions. But prudence may otherwise set little limit to self-interest. After all, if Churchill was prudent, so was Stalin. Prudence is compatible with almost any purposes that hold out the solid prospect of success. Realists nevertheless have often contended that realism enjoins reciprocity, and that it does so not only by virtue of its emphasis on prudence but because of its preoccupation with the limits on statecraft. There is surely some merit to these claims. Even so, realism, while mitigating, still does not resolve the moral dilemmas the conduct of foreign policy so often raises.

These considerations no more than make the point, which should be obvious enough, that there are limits to the utility of political realism. But if realism does not explain the whole of international politics and foreign policy, it still explains a great deal. Even more, it encourages an outlook toward foreign policy, that is sorely needed in a time of triumphalism and unbounded optimism. Whether it will gain the hearing it deserves, though, remains very much in doubt.

QUESTIONS

1. Why does Tucker believe that a new foreign policy consensus provides for a new theory of international relations apart from realism?

2. What alternatives does Tucker offer to replace realism?

Chapter 3

TRANSNATIONALIST THEORY

COMPONENTS OF TRANSNATIONALIST THEORY

Focus of Analysis ········▶	• Enhancing global political and economic cooperation
Major Actors ········▶	• States • International organizations • Multinational corporations (MNCs) • Non-governmental organizations (NGOs)
Behavior of States ········▶	• States not always rational actors • Compromise between various interests within the state
Goals of States ········▶	• Economic prosperity • International stability
View of Human Nature ········▶	• Optimistic
Condition of International System ········▶	• Anarchic • Possible to mitigate anarchy
Key Concepts ········▶	• International organizations; International law; Collective security; Regime; economic interdependence; Harmony of interests

INTRODUCTION

The idea of promoting global order through expanded political and economic ties leads us to our next theory, the transnationalist theory. Transnationalists point out that realism fails to offer an adequate explanation for the order that we see within our presumably anarchic system. Advocates of transnationalism argue that states cooperate as much, if not more, than they compete. And this cooperation, they assert, is more consistent than the realists' fleeting convergence of national interest among limited numbers of states. Rather, states cooperate because it is in their common interest to do so, and prosperity and stability in the international system are the direct result of that cooperation.

In addition, transnationalists believe that states are not motivated solely by national interest defined in terms of power. Unlike realism, transnationalism contends that international politics can no longer be divided into "high" and "low" politics. While the high politics of national security and military power remain important, transnationalists maintain that economic, social, and environmental issues—or low politics—have become priorities on the international agenda.

The establishment and success of international order, according to transnationalism, depends largely on four major factors: the role of international institutions; international rules and norms for behavior of states; the increasing economic interdependence between nations; and technological advancement and the growth of global communication. Transnationalists acknowledge that international institutions, rules and norms, economic interdependence, and advances in global telecommunications can neither create nor enforce the type of stable international order that might be provided by a strong world government. These elements do, however, play an indispensable role in constraining, or regulating, the behavior of nation-states within the system, as well as shaping the international environment as a whole. The transnational linkages that these four factors represent build incentives for cooperation, enhance trust between nations, and promote negotiation rather than military confrontation as a means to resolve disputes between states.

INSTITUTIONAL TRANSNATIONALISM

At this point, we must distinguish between two branches of transnationalist theory. The first branch, which we shall call **institutional transnationalism** (also referred to as *idealism*), focuses on institutionalizing global cooperation. Institutional transnationalists call for the creation of a new global power structure, supported by creating and empowering a variety of international organizations. That is, advocates of this theory believe that global cooperation is founded upon three primary factors: enhancing the role and influence of international organizations, instituting collective security, and enforcing international law. All three of these factors might be viewed as prescriptions for how states should behave, with an ultimate goal of reforming the anarchy of the international system and forging a harmonious community of nations.

A predecessor of what we now call institutional transnationalism was the classical legal scholar, Hugo Grotius. In his book *On the Law of War and Peace* (1625), Grotius contended that a fundamental "natural law" exists, and this natural law transcends the domestic law of states. **Natural law** is based on the belief that humans have basic, inalienable rights. These inalienable rights (essentially rights to life and liberty) bind states together, forming an international "society of states" linked through certain rules and norms of conduct.

For Grotius, relations between states within the system were to be based on these universal rules of international behavior—even to the point of regulating the conduct of war. This concept would later form the basis for international law in the European state system. **International law** is the codification of rules that regulate the behavior of states and set limits upon what is permissible and what is not permissible. These rules are binding on states, as well as other international actors.

Contemporary institutional transnationalism was also influenced by the idealist scholars and statesmen, who dominated the formulation and practice of international relations after World War I. The idealists believed that the relations between states in the international system needed to be fundamentally reformed to ensure that future wars might be avoided.

One notable idealist at that time was President Woodrow Wilson. He believed that the balance-of-power premise, so critical in realist theory, was unlikely to produce a stable international order. Instead, Wilson, like Grotius, wanted to build an international community of nations. This new community, based on international law and specific rules and norms of behavior, would be regulated by international institutions. The transnational linkages established by these international institutions, such as the League of Nations and, later, the United Nations, would presumably moderate—or, ideally, even eliminate—the need for power politics.

Acknowledging the need to temper such idealistic goals with the harsh realities of international politics, Wilson suggested that order within the community could be preserved through collective security. **Collective security** is a system in which states band together to safeguard the territorial independence and security of one another against aggression. That is, the use of force by a state or group of states would be curtailed by the strength of all states working through an international institution designed for that purpose. Collective security differs from balance of power politics in that it is not directed against a specific nation but against any state that threatens the *status quo.* Enforcing international law would then be a collective responsibility for the good of all states within the community.

Wilson, then, believed that order within the international system could be established through reform. The creation of effective international organizations capable of enforcing order and facilitating cooperation between states formed the basis for that reform.

Another institutional transnationalist, Hedley Bull, interpreted the nature and course of international relations in a somewhat more practical manner. Bull focused on the tools and methods by which order already exists within the system. He suggested that while anarchy could not be abolished, the behavior of states in the international system could be constrained. According to Bull, diplomacy, balance of power politics and alliances, as well as international law and institutions, all contribute to preserving order, enhancing cooperation, and promoting international ethical standards.

The reading by Louis Henkin provides some valuable insights into the contemporary institutional transnationalist concept of international law. He provides a broad overview of the role of international law in the global state system. Henkin notes that international law is a "political instrument" that helps to regulate the interactions of states. Henkin concludes that the creation and enforcement of international law are political acts that are generally the result of negotiation and compromise between different groups of states and different regions of the world.

The selection by Bruce Russert and James Sutterlin demonstrates the continuing interest among scholars in the central role of the United Nations in international politics. Russert and Sutterlin use the experiences of the Korean Conflict and the Gulf War to draw lessons about the ability of the United Nations to restore and maintain collective security. The authors discuss various options that the United Nations might adopt to enhance its effectiveness and credibility. One such recommendation is to create a permanent military force that has the capacity to carry out peacekeeping and enforcement measures that will serve under a unified Security Council command.

ECONOMIC TRANSNATIONALISM

The second branch of transnationalists emphasizes economic ties between nations as a basis to establish and preserve order within the international system. Similar to institutional transnationalism, **economic transnationalism** (also referred to as the *interdependence model*) highlights the transnational ties or linkages between states. Economic transnationalists, however, identify the increasingly integrated nature of the global economy as a major force in promoting those linkages.

With this merging of international and domestic economic interests, states, according to economic transnationalists, have become increasingly interconnected or interdependent. Interdependence is a pivotal part of economic transnationalist theory. **Interdependence** can be defined as the "mutual dependence" of nations within the international system and transnationalists argue that it is a defining characteristic of our contemporary world. The selection by Joseph Nye provides a good summary of the principle components of interdependence. Nye believes that the expansion of global trade and investment has blurred the distinction between domestic economies of individual states and of international economy as a whole. The more states interact within the global marketplace, the more their prosperity depends on the political and economic cooperation of other states.

As in any interdependent relationship, however, we must acknowledge that some states are more vulnerable than others to the ups and downs of the global economy. That is, smaller, less developed nations can be more vulnerable in such a relationship than larger, more economically diverse countries. Although interdependence generally carries substantial economic benefits, the various levels of sensitivity between nations to downturns in the international economy can create both political and economic tension.

As a practical matter, we might suggest that interdependence is based on three general assumptions: First, states are not the only key actors in international relations. International institutions; non-governmental organizations (NGOs), such as large multinational corporations (MNCs); economic cartels, such as OPEC; Greenpeace; or even large religious groups, such as the Catholic Church—all these actors take positions on the global stage. Second, the agenda of international relations is more complex and diverse than in the past. Issues such as trade, technology, and the environment can be as important as traditional national security concerns. Finally, military force plays less of a role in contemporary international politics. Economic interdependence, along with expanded political ties, have increased the value of cooperation and decreased the utility of force.

According to economic transnationalists, interdependence has transformed the nature of power in the international system. No international actor can meet its needs—whether those needs involve national security or economic prosperity—without the cooperation or participation of other states and non-state actors. Power is no longer measured solely in terms of military strength. Influence is often the result of economic flexibility or technological innovation, and leadership involves negotiating expertise and economic coordination. Interdependence has dramatically increased the incentives for cooperation, not only among states but among all international actors.

Robert Keohane, in his book *After Hegemony,* argues that international cooperation is not restricted to formal international organizations like the United Nations. Instead, cooperation often results from the creation of international regimes. A **regime** is a set of accepted rules, norms, and procedures that regulates the behavior of states and other actors in a given issue area. A regime also encompasses the international institutions, NGOs, and treaties that enhance cooperation in that area. Issues such as trade, the environment, monetary relations, etc. represent a host of different international concerns that might be targeted. Cooperation, then, according to Keohane, is based on a variety of regimes designed to meet the needs of specific issue areas.

Economic transnationalists tend to focus on international economic integration and the role of non-governmental organizations as a means to enhance this cooperation. They argue that, with greater cooperation and integration, a state's economy is merely one piece of an increasingly integrated, world-economic whole. In this **complex interdependence,** we see "more actors, more issues, greater interactions, and less hierarchy in international politics."[1] Hence, though it is important to encourage economic growth of individual nations so that they, too, might have a stake in preserving and increasing interdependence, the capacity of a single state to have decisive control over the global economy is limited.

---

[1] Joseph S. Nye, Jr., "Understanding U.S. Strength," *Foreign Policy,* 72 (Fall 1988), p. 108.

Within this interdependent economic system, the realist assumption that states are the primary actor in international relations is no longer the case in a strict sense. As we noted, economic transnationalists suggest that non-state actors—non-governmental organizations and multinational corporations—play a vital role in building and maintaining global interdependence. These organizations help to break down national boundaries and blend domestic and international political interests.

Multinational corporations are companies that have production facilities or branches in several countries. The influence of multinational corporations is twofold. First, MNCs expand and reinforce global economic and political linkages among people and groups across national borders. These organizations can have greater economic resources and international influence, than many smaller or less developed nations. Companies conducting business across state boundaries also make states more interdependent and create a new context in which countries make decisions about one another.

One thing to keep in mind, however, is that these MNCs have their own agendas, and their interests do not necessarily coincide with the interests of those states in which they conduct business. MNCs operate in the interests of their stockholders, and their goal is to maximize profits for those stockholders. For example, when General Motors decides to close a plant in Michigan and open a new plant in Mexico, the impact of this decision is felt by both nations. The United States must contend with increased unemployment, while Mexico gains job opportunities and tax revenue.

The selection by Robert Reich, an economist and Secretary of Labor in the Clinton administration, discusses the impact of multinational corporations and of transnational investment in his article, "Who Is Us?" He questions whether it matters where the headquarters of a multinational is located. Instead, Reich suggests that a more important question is where the MNC is investing in research and production. He asserts that a foreign company operating inside the United States may indeed be more beneficial to the economic well-being of Americans than an American company operating in another country. Reich's point is that ownership of the company matters less than the creation of jobs for Americans.

While MNCs might operate to further their own agenda, their well-being is linked to that of the international community in a fundamental way, which leads to our second point. MNCs need a stable international environment—an environment that facilitates trade, commerce, and international investment. In a self-reinforcing pattern, economic transnationalists suggest that force plays a smaller role in international politics because states have formed closer economic, as well as political, linkages. These linkages—and the NGOs and MNCs that help to promote them—flourish only in a stable international environment. Consequently, all members of the community have a stake in preserving order to further their own interests.

Perhaps the best way to describe this process is as a harmony of interests among states. **Harmony of interests** is the belief that the interest of all states coincides with the interest of each state. This concept is generally accepted by both institutional and economic transnationalists and focuses on the mutual advantages of cooperation between nations. For institutional transnationalists, harmony of interests emphasizes that the security of all nations is enhanced by international cooperation. For economic transnationalists, that harmony of interests revolves around the growing economic interdependence of nations. For both branches of transnationalist theory, the utility of power and military force as instruments of foreign policy has been marginalized by greater linkages and expanded cooperation—political or economic—among all nations of the international system.

A Critique of Transnationalist Theory

Critics of transnationalist theory—both institutional and economic—contend that the theory places too much emphasis on this harmony of interests. Cooperation between states, whether political, economic, or even military, is subject to a number of internal and external pressures, making success much more problematic than transnationalists might imply.

The critique of transnationalist theory tends to focus on three broad issues: basic tendencies of human nature, national security interests, and economic cooperation. With respect to human nature, realist critics suggest that transnationalism underestimates the conflictual aspects of state interests and that the benefits of cooperation can often be outweighed by fear and mistrust.

Though these feelings might be engendered by past experiences, transnationalism also fails to take into account the powerful role of nationalism in world politics. Human history—both ancient and contemporary—is, quite literally, littered with examples in which religion or ethnicity formed the basis for conflict between nations. From the Crusades to more recent events in Bosnia and Rwanda, human nature offers more complex questions than transnationalist theory is prepared to answer in this regard.

Samuel Huntington argues that conflicts arising from nationalism or ethnic strife sometimes represent a greater challenge than ideological competition.[2] Compromise and settlements are often clouded by the unavoidable intrusion of human passions—complicating already volatile situations. In an unusual sense, the end of the Cold War actually signals the beginning of new, more complex conflicts, no longer frozen or confined by the two great ideological camps. Nuclear weapons may have deterred superpower confrontation but conventional conflict between smaller states still occurs. Since the East-West coalitions have loosened, states now pursue their own narrow interests—often guided by ethnic or nationalist ideals. Transnationalism fails to take these more unpredictable factors into account in its approach to international relations theory.

Critics of transnationalist theory also argue that states cannot be expected to pursue collective gains on a consistent basis. Maintaining long-term or comprehensive

---

[2] For more details, see Samuel Huntington's article in the next section of the text.

cooperation between nations is more problematic than transnationalism implies. States—like individuals—can be attracted by relative gains, settling for less gain but more control and self-reliance than the broader cooperation of transnationalism necessitates. Also, the goals and priorities of states can change, making such an arrangement too confining or inappropriate under new or altered circumstances.

Realists tend to criticize transnationalist theory particularly with respect to our second issue—national security. The theme of national interest defined as self-interest (as opposed to transnationalism's collective interest) is evident in many past and contemporary conflicts throughout the world.

Certainly the most glaring lapses in a collective security arrangement—and, indeed, in transnationalist theory generally—occurred prior to World War II when the League of Nations failed either to prevent or offset the rise of Hitler and Mussolini. Despite idealistic goals and cooperative intent of the League of Nations, fascism gained not only a toehold but a firm grip on Western Europe that only a prolonged and costly world war could break.

In addition, the direct intervention by the United States to relieve widespread starvation in Somalia is the exception, rather than the rule, in international politics. The prolonged bloodshed in Bosnia and failure of the Western powers to mobilize either sufficient political or military force to alleviate the situation illustrates the reluctance of states to extend themselves when vital interests are not at risk. This point is clear when we recall how quickly and effectively the international community responded when Iraq threatened the vast oil reserves of Kuwait during the Persian Gulf War. It seems, then, that collective security is problematic at best. Small countries with limited economic or geopolitical value to the major powers rely on collective security only at their own considerable peril.

Similarly, realists are also skeptical of the transnationalists' notion that "low politics" have become as important as these national security issues. Certainly, the world community has become more attuned to social, environmental, and economic issues. According to realists, however, national security and the well-being of the state remain top priorities for leaders in formulating and implementing foreign and domestic policy.

Realists point to a tendency among transnational theorists to cross the line between describing the interaction of states in the international system and attributing certain patterns of behavior to certain global conditions into a more prescriptive posture. That is, transnationalists actually become advocates of their own program for global interdependence, rather than maintaining theory positions as neutral observers and analysts of international relations.

In addition, transnationalism's proposed economic interdependence is subject to criticism on several points. Realists argue that the economic integration of states ascribed by transnationalism does not necessarily lead to greater cooperation. As we discussed earlier, realists are more skeptical about the long-term success of converging state interests. Changing priorities or global conditions make the outlook for prolonged economic interdependence somewhat problematic.

Finally, proponents of class system theory, which will be discussed in greater detail in the next section, also question the assumption that interdependence

KEY CONCEPTS

Collective security   is an institutional transnationalist concept of a system of world order in which aggression against an individual state is considered aggression against all states and will be met by a collective response from all states within the system. Collective security differs from balance-of-power politics in that it is not directed against a specific nation but against any state that threatens the status quo.

Complex interdependence   is an economic transnationalist concept that assumes states are not the only important actors, social welfare issues share center stage with security issues on the global agenda, and cooperation is as dominant a characteristic of international politics as conflict.

Economic transnationalism   is a theory of international relations that highlights the economic transnational ties or linkages between states. Economic transnationalists identify the increasingly integrated nature of the global economy as a major force in international relations. According to economic transnationalists, with the merging of international and domestic economic interests, states have become increasingly interconnected or interdependent and less dependent on, or less willing to use, force or the threat of force to further their national interests.

Harmony of interests   is a transnationalist concept stating that the interest of all states coincides with the interest of each state. This concept is generally accepted by both institutional and economic transnationalists and focuses on the mutual advantages of cooperation between nations. Harmony of interests implies that the incentive to cooperate with one another is stronger than the incentive for conflict.

Interdependence   is an economic transnationalist concept that focuses on the "mutual dependence" of nations in which two or more states are mutually sensitive and vulnerable to each other's actions. Economic transna-

(continued)

facilitates greater cooperation among nations. In addition to being "Western-centric," they view interdependence as exploitative of, rather than beneficial to, less developed countries. Indeed, interdependence affects countries differently. Developing nations, such as Haiti and Botswana, are more vulnerable to the economic shifts and cultural intrusion or imperialism associated with interdependence than richer, industrialized states like the United States.

Transnationalists might respond to their critics by stating that their theory is the only systemic explanation that takes into account the changing nature of twentieth-century international relations. The realist emphasis on military power and conflict

(continued from previous page)

tionalists argue that this is a defining characteristic of our contemporary world.

Institutional transnationalism is a theory of international relations that contends global cooperation is founded upon three primary factors: enhancing the role and influence of international organizations, instituting collective security, and enforcing international law. All three of these factors might be viewed as prescriptions for how states should behave, with an ultimate goal of reforming the anarchy of the international system and forging a harmonious community of nations.

International law is the codification of rules that regulate the behavior of states and set limits upon what is permissible and what is not permissible. In theory, these rules are binding on states, as well as other international actors.

Multinational corporations (MNCs) are companies that have production facilities or branches in several countries.

Natural law is a view that there is a system of rules and principles for the conduct of human affairs founded on the belief that all people have basic, inalienable rights. In theory, these inalienable rights (essentially to life and liberty) supersede any mortal authority and cannot be legitimately denied by any government or society. Natural law is widely accepted as one of the philosophical foundations of international law.

Regime is a set of accepted rules, norms, and procedures that regulate the behavior of states and other actors in a given issue area. A regime also encompasses the international institutions, NGOs, and treaties that enhance cooperation in that area. Issues such as trade, the environment, monetary relations, etc., represent a host of different international concerns that might be targeted. International cooperation is based on a variety of regimes designed to meet the needs of specific issue areas.

and the class system focus on the exploitation of the poor by the rich are too simplistic and do not provide accurate explanations of international relations.

To the realist's critique, transnationalists would respond by saying that they do not reject many of the major tenets of realism, they simply use them as a foundation upon which to build new explanations for contemporary global politics. For example, transnationalists accept the realist notion of anarchy, but argue that the growth of international economic interdependence and expanding-role, non-state actors and international institutions have transformed world politics, making it less anarchic and more cooperative.

To the class system theorists, transnationalists would point out that they do take into account that less developed countries (LDCs) are more vulnerable than advanced industrialized states. However, they reject the argument that the global economy is structured to oppress the LDCs. Transnationalists view international relations as much more complex and subtle. They contend that the ability of individual corporations or states to control the course of international relations is more limited than the class system theorists would have you believe.

Overall, transnationalism offers a fairly flexible and nuanced explanation for contemporary international relations. Like all theories of global politics, transnationalism has gaps and weaknesses, but it does offer unique insights into the changing nature of our late twentieth-century world.

11. On the Law of War and Peace

Hugo Grotius

In this selection, Hugo Grotius posits that relations between states should be based on universal rules of international behavior—even to the point of regulating the conduct of war. This concept would later form the basis for international law in the European state system. This selection is from *The Rights of War and Peace* (1625).

Hugo Grotius (1583–1645) was a Dutch philosopher, theologian, and jurist who is generally regarded as the founder of international law.

I.   The first and most necessary divisions of war are into one kind called private, another public, and another mixed. Now public war is carried on by the person holding the sovereign power. Private war is that which is carried on by private persons without authority from the state. A mixed war is that which is carried on, on one side by public authority, and on the other by private persons. But private war, from its greater antiquity, is the first subject for inquiry.

The proofs that have been already produced, to shew that to repel violence is not repugnant to natural law, afford a satisfactory reason to justify private war, as far as the law of nature is concerned. But perhaps it may be thought that since public tribunals have been erected, private redress of wrongs is not allowable. An objection which is very just. Yet although public trials and courts of justice are not institutions of nature, but erected by the invention of men, yet as it is much more conducive to the peace of society for a matter in dispute to be decided by a disinterested person, than by the partiality and prejudice of the party aggrieved, natural justice and reason will dictate the necessity and advantage of every one's submitting to the equitable decisions of public judges. Paulus, the Lawyer, observes that "what can be done by a magistrate with the authority of the state, should never be intrusted to individuals; as private redress would give rise to greater disturbance. And "the reason," says King Theodoric, "why laws were invented, was to prevent any one from using personal violence, for wherein would peace differ from all the confusion of war, if private disputes were terminated by force?" And the law calls it force for any man to seize what he thinks his due, without seeking a legal remedy.

II.   It is a matter beyond all doubt that the liberty of private redress, which once existed, was greatly abridged after courts of justice were established. Yet there may be cases, in which private redress must be allowed, as for instance, if the way to legal justice were not open. For when the law prohibits any one from redressing his own wrongs, it can only be understood to apply to circumstances where a legal remedy exists. Now the obstruction in the way to legal redress may be either temporary or absolute. Temporary, where it is impossible for the injured party to wait for a legal remedy, without imminent danger and even destruction. As for instance, if a man were attacked in the night, or in a secret place where no assistance could be procured. Absolute, either as the right, or the fact may require. Now there are many situations, where the right must cease from the impossibility of supporting it in a legal way, as in unoccupied places, on the seas, in a wilderness, or desert island, or any other place, where there is no civil government. All legal remedy too ceases by fact, when subjects will not submit to the judge, or if he refuses openly to take cognizance of matters in dispute. The assertion that all private war is not made repugnant to the law of nature by the erection of legal tribunals, may be understood from the law given to the Jews, wherein God thus speaks by the mouth of Moses, Exod. xxii. 2. "If a thief be found breaking up, that is, by night, and be smitten that he dies, there shall no blood be shed for him, but if the sun be risen upon him, there shall be blood shed for him." Now this law, making so accurate a distinction in the merits of the case, seems not only to imply impunity for killing any one, in self-defence, but to explain a natural right, founded not on any special divine command, but on the common principles of justice. From whence other nations have plainly followed the same rule. The passage of the twelve tables is well known, undoubtedly taken from the old Athenian Law, "If a thief commit a robbery in the night, and a man kill him, he is killed lawfully." Thus by the laws of all known and civilized nations, the person is judged innocent, who kills another, forcibly attempting or endangering his life; a conspiring and universal testimony, which proves that in justifiable homicide, there is nothing repugnant to the law of nature.

IV.[1]   Public war, according to the law of nations, is either SOLEMN, that is FORMAL, or LESS SOLEMN, that is INFORMAL. The name of lawful war is commonly given to what is here called formal, in the same sense in which a regular will is opposed to a codicil, or a lawful marriage to the cohabitation of slaves. This opposition by no means implies that it is not allowed to any man, if he pleases, to make a codicil, or to slaves to cohabit in matrimony, but only, that, by the civil law, FORMAL WILLS and SOLEMN MARRIAGES, were attended with peculiar privileges and effects. These observations were the more necessary; because many, from a misconception of the word just or lawful, think that all wars, to which those epithets do not apply, are condemned as unjust and unlawful. Now to give a war the formality required by the law of nations, two things are necessary. In the first place it must be made on both sides, by the sovereign power of the state, and in the next place it must be accompanied with certain formalities. Both of which are so essential that one is insufficient without the other.

Now a public war, LESS SOLEMN, may be made without those formalities, even against private persons, and by any magistrate whatever. And indeed, considering the thing without respect to the civil law, every magistrate, in case of resistance, seems to have a right to take up arms, to maintain his authority in the execution of his office; as well as to defend the people committed to his protection. But as a whole state is by war involved in danger, it is an established law in almost all nations that no war can be made but by the authority of the sovereign in each state. There is such a law as this in the last book of Plato ON LAWS. And by the Roman law, to make war, or levy troops without a commission from the Prince was high treason. According to the Cornelian law also, enacted by Lucius

Cornelius Sylla, to do so without authority from the people amounted to the same crime. In the code of Justinian there is a constitution, made by Valentinian and Valens, that no one should bear arms without their knowledge and authority. Conformably to this rule, St. Augustin says, that as peace is most agreeable to the natural state of man, it is proper that Princes should have the sole authority to devise and execute the operations of war. Yet this general rule, like all others, in its application must always be limited by equity and discretion.

In certain cases this authority may be communicated to others. For it is a point settled beyond all doubt that subordinate magistrates may, by their officers, reduce a few disobedient and tumultuous persons to subjection, provided, that to do it, it requires not a force of such enormous magnitude as might endanger the state. Again, if the danger be so imminent as to allow of no time for an application to the sovereign executive power, here too the necessity is admitted as an exception to the general rule. Lucius Pinarius the Governor of Enna, a Sicilian garrison, presuming upon this right, upon receiving certain information that the inhabitants had formed a conspiracy to revolt to the Carthaginians, put them all to the sword, and by that means saved the place. Franciscus Victoria allows the inhabitants of a town to take up arms, even without such a case of necessity, to redress their own wrongs, which the Prince neglects to avenge, but such an opinion is justly rejected by others.

V.   Whether the circumstances, under which subordinate magistrates are authorised to use military force, can properly be called public war or not, is a matter of dispute among legal writers, some affirming and others denying it. If indeed we call no other public war, but that which is made by magisterial authority, there is no doubt but that such suppressions of tumult are public wars, and those who in such cases resist the magistrate in the execution of his office, incur the guilt of rebellion against superiors. But if public war is taken in the higher sense of FORMAL war, as it undoubtedly often is; those are not public wars; because to entitle them to the full rights of such, the declaration of the sovereign power and other requisites are wanting. Nor do the loss of property and the military executions, to which the offenders are subject, at all affect the question.[2] For those casualties are not so peculiarly attached to formal war, as to be excluded from all other kinds. For it may happen, as in an extensive empire for instance, that persons in subordinate authority, may, when attacked, or threatened with attack, have powers granted to commence military operations. In which case the war must be supposed to commence by the authority of the sovereign power; as a person is considered to be the author of a measure which by virtue of his authority he empowers another to perform. The more doubtful point is, whether, where there is no such commission, a conjecture of what is the will of the sovereign power be sufficient. This seems not admissible. For it is not sufficient to consider, what we suppose would be the Sovereign's pleasure, if he were consulted; but what would be his actual will, in matters admitting of time for deliberation, even though he were not formally consulted; if a law was to be passed upon those matters. "For though UNDER SOME PARTICULAR CIRCUMSTANCES, it may be necessary to waive consulting the will of the sovereign, yet this would by no means authorise it as a GENERAL

PRACTICE. For the safety of the state would be endangered, if subordinate powers should usurp the right of making war at their discretion.'' It was not without reason, that Cneus Manlius was accused by his Lieutenants of having made war upon the Galatians without authority from the Roman people. For though the Galatians had supplied Antiochus with troops, yet as peace had been made with him, it rested with the Roman people, and not with Manlius to determine in what manner the Galatians should be punished for assisting an enemy. Cato proposed that Julius Caesar should be delivered up to the Germans for having attacked them in violation of his promise, a proposal proceeding rather from the desire to be rid of a formidable rival, than from any principle of justice.

The case was thus; the Germans had assisted the Gauls, enemies of the Roman people, therefore they had no reason to complain of the injury done to them, if the war against the Gauls, in which they had made themselves a party concerned, was just. But Caesar ought to have contented himself with driving the Germans out of Gaul, the province assigned him, without pursuing them into their own country, especially as there was no farther danger to be apprehended from them; unless he had first consulted the Roman people. It was plain, then, the Germans had no right to demand the surrender of Caesar's person, though the Romans had a right to punish him for having exceeded his commission. On a similar occasion the Carthaginians answered the Romans; ''It is not the subject of inquiry whether Hannibal has besieged Saguntum, by his own private or by public authority, but whether justly or unjustly. For with respect to one of our own subjects it is our business to inquire by what authority he has acted; but the matter of discussion with you is, whether he has broken any treaty.'' Cicero defends the conduct of Octavius and Decimus Brutus, who had taken up arms against Antony. But though it was evident that Antony deserved to be treated as an enemy, yet they ought to have waited for the determination of the Senate and people of Rome, whether it were for the public interest not to take notice of his conduct or to punish it, to agree to terms of peace with him, or to have recourse to arms. This would have been proper; for no one is obliged to exercise the right of punishing an enemy, if it is attended with probable danger.

But even if it had been judged expedient to declare Antony an enemy, the choice of the persons to conduct the war should have been left to the Senate and people of Rome. Thus when Cassius demanded assistance of the Rhodians, according to treaty, they answered they would send it, if the senate thought proper. This refutation of Cicero's opinion will serve, along with many other instances to be met with; as an admonition not to be carried away by the opinions of the most celebrated writers, particularly the most brilliant orators, who often speak to suit the circumstances of the moment. But all political investigation requires a cool and steady judgment, not to be biased by examples, which may rather be excused than vindicated.

Since then it has already been established that no war can lawfully be made but by the sovereign power of each state, in respect to all the questions connected with war, it will be necessary to examine what that sovereign power is, and who are the persons that hold it.

VI. The moral power then of governing a state, which is called by Thucydides the civil power, is described as consisting of three parts which form the necessary substance of every state; and those are the right of making its own laws, executing them in its own manner, and appointing its own magistrates. Aristotle, in the fourth book of his Politics, comprises the sovereignty of a state in the exercise of the deliberative, executive, and judicial powers. To the deliberative branch he assigns the right of deciding upon peace or war, making or annulling treaties, and framing and passing new laws. To these he adds the power of inflicting death, banishment, and forfeiture, and of punishing also for public peculation. In the exercise of judicial power, he includes not only the punishment of crimes and misdemeanors, but the redress of civil injuries.[3] Dionysius of Halicarnassus, points out three distinguishing marks of sovereign power; and those are, the right of appointing magistrates, the right of enacting and repealing laws, and the right of making war and peace. To which, in another part, he adds the administration of justice, the supreme authority in matters of religion, and the right of calling general councils.

A true definition comprehends every possible branch of authority that can grow out of the possession and exercise of sovereign power. For the ruler of every state must exercise his authority either in person, or through the medium of others. His own personal acts must be either general or special. He may be said to do GENERAL acts in passing or repealing laws, respecting either temporal matters, or spiritual concerns, as far as the latter relate to the welfare of the state. The knowledge of these principles is called by Aristotle the masterpiece in the science of government.

The particular acts of the Sovereign are either directly of a public nature, or a private, but even the latter bear reference to his public capacity. Now the acts of the sovereign executive power of a directly public kind are the making of peace and war and treaties, and the imposition of taxes, and other similar exercises of authority over the persons and property of its subjects, which constitute the sovereignty of the state. Aristotle calls the knowledge of this practice political and deliberative science.

The private acts of the sovereign are those, in which by his authority, disputes between individuals are decided, as it is conducive to the peace of society that these should be settled. This is called by Aristotle the judicial power. Thus the acts of the sovereign are done in his name by his magistrates or other officers, among whom ambassadors are reckoned. And in the exercise of all those rights sovereign power consists.

VII. That power is called sovereign, whose actions are not subject to the controul of any other power, so as to be annulled at the pleasure of any other human will. The term ANY OTHER HUMAN WILL exempts the sovereign himself from this restriction, who may annul his own acts, as may also his successor, who enjoys the same right, having the same power and no other. We are to consider then what is the subject in which this sovereign power exists. Now the subject is in one respect common, and in another proper, as the body is the common subject of sight, the eye the proper, so the common subject of sovereign power is the state, which has already been said to be a perfect society of men.

NOTES

1. As the topics of the third section have been so fully stated in the second chapter, that section has been omitted, and the translation goes on from the second of the original to the fourth. (Translator.)

2. In case of rebellion, the subjects taken in arms, have no right to be treated as prisoners of war, but are liable to punishment as criminals.

3. "Wrongs are divisible into two sorts or species, PRIVATE WRONGS, and PUBLIC WRONGS. The former are an infringement or privation of the private or civil rights belonging to individuals, considered as individuals, and are therefore frequently termed civil injuries; the latter are a breach and violation of public rights and duties which affect the whole community considered as a community, and are distinguished by the harsher appellation of crimes and misdemeanors."—Blackst. Com. b. iii. c. i.

QUESTIONS

1. According to Grotius what is the difference between "private war" and "public war"?

2. How does Grotius define the concept of Sovereignty?

12. Fourteen Points

Woodrow Wilson

In this excerpt, President Woodrow Wilson proposes Fourteen Points as part of a broader program to establish a new international order in the wake of World War I. These Fourteen Points were presented in response to news that several of the Allies had made secret treaties designed to divide the conquered nations for geopolitical and economic gain. Wilson's plan identified the need for "open covenants of peace, openly arrived at. . . ." In this text, Wilson introduces the concept of collective security. This speech was delivered before Congress on January 8, 1918.

In addition to serving as President of the United States, Woodrow Wilson (1856–1924) was a professor of political science and president of Princeton University. He first entered politics when he was elected Governor of New Jersey in 1910. His works include *Congressional Government* and the five volume set *History of the American People*.

. . . We entered this war because violations of right had occurred which touched us to the quick and made the life of our own people impossible unless they were corrected and the world secured once for all against their recurrence.

What we demand in this war, therefore, is nothing peculiar to ourselves. It is that the world be made fit and safe to live in; and particularly that it be made safe for every peaceloving nation which, like our own, wishes to live its own life, determine its own institutions, be assured of justice and fair dealing by the other peoples of the world as against force and selfish aggression. All the peoples of the world are in effect partners in this interest, and for our own part we see very clearly that unless justice be done to others it will not be done to us. The program of the world's peace, therefore, is our program; and that program, the only possible program, as we see it, is this:

I. Open covenants of peace, openly arrived at, after which there shall be no private international understandings of any kind but diplomacy shall proceed always frankly and in the public view.

II. Absolute freedom of navigation upon the seas, outside territorial waters, alike in peace and in war, except as the seas may be closed in whole or in part by international action for the enforcement of international covenants.

III. The removal, so far as possible, of all economic barriers and the establishment of an equality of trade conditions among all the nations consenting to the peace and associating themselves for its maintenance.

IV. Adequate guarantees given and taken that national armaments will be reduced to the lowest point consistent with domestic safety.

V. A free, open-minded, and absolutely impartial adjustment of all colonial claims, based upon a strict observance of the principle that in determining all such questions of sovereignty the interests of the populations concerned must have equal weight with the equitable claims of the government whose title is to be determined.

VI. The evacuation of all Russian territory and such a settlement of all questions affecting Russia as will secure the best and freest coöperation of the other nations of the world in obtaining for her an unhampered and unembarrassed opportunity for the independent determination of her own political development and national policy and assure her of a sincere welcome into the society of free nations under institutions of her own choosing; and, more than a welcome, assistance also of every kind that she may need and may herself desire. The treatment accorded Russia by her sister nations in the months to come will be the acid test of their good will, of their comprehension of her need as distinguished from their own interests, and of intelligent and unselfish sympathy.

VII. Belgium, the whole world will agree, must be evacuated and restored, without any attempt to limit the sovereignty which she enjoys in common with all other free nations. No other single act will serve as this will serve to restore confidence among the nations in the laws which they have themselves set and determined for the government of their relations with one another. Without this healing act the whole structure and validity of international law is forever impaired.

VIII. All French territory should be freed and invaded portions restored, and the wrong done to France by Prussia in 1871 in the matter of Alsace-Lorraine, which has unsettled the peace of the world for nearly fifty years, should be righted, in order that peace may once more be made secure in the interest of all.

IX. A readjustment of the frontiers of Italy should be effected along clearly recognizable lines of nationality.

X. The peoples of Austria-Hungary, whose place among the nations we wish to see safe-guarded and assured, should be accorded the freest opportunity of autonomous development.

XI. Rumania, Serbia, and Montenegro should be evacuated; occupied territories restored; Serbia accorded free and secure access to the sea; and the relations of the several Balkan states to one another determined by friendly counsel along historically established lines of allegiance and nationality; and international guarantees of the political and economic independence and territorial integrity of the several Balkan states should be entered into.

XII. The Turkish portions of the present Ottoman Empire should be assured a secure sovereignty, but the other nationalities which are now under Turkish rule should be assured an undoubted security of life and an absolutely unmolested opportunity of autonomous development, and the Dardanelles should be permanently opened as a free passage to the ships and commerce of all nations under international guarantees.

XIII. An independent Polish state should be erected which should include the territories inhabited by indisputably Polish populations, which should be assured a free and secure access to the sea, and whose political and economic independence and territorial integrity should be guaranteed by international covenant.

XIV. A general association of nations must be formed under specific covenants for the purpose of affording mutual guarantees of political independence and territorial integrity to great and small states alike.

In regard to these essential rectifications of wrong and assertions of right we feel ourselves to be intimate partners of all the governments and peoples associated together against the imperialists. We cannot be separated in interest or divided in purpose. We stand together until the end.

For such arrangements and covenants we are willing to fight and to continue to fight until they are achieved; but only because we wish the right to prevail and desire a just and stable peace such as can be secured only by removing the chief provocations to war, which this program does remove. We have no jealousy of German greatness, and there is nothing in this program that impairs it. We grudge her no achievement or distinction of learning or of pacific enterprise such as have made her record very bright and very enviable. We do not wish to injure her or to block in any way her legitimate influence or power. We do not wish to fight her either with arms or with hostile arrangements of trade if she is willing to associate herself with us and the other peace-loving nations of the world in covenants of justice and law and fair dealing. We wish her only to accept a place of equality among the peoples of the world—the new world in which we now live—instead of a place of mastery.

Neither do we presume to suggest to her any alteration or modification of her institutions. But it is necessary, we must frankly say, and necessary as a preliminary to any intelligent dealings with her on our part that we should know whom her spokesmen speak for when they speak to us, whether for the Reichstag majority or for the military party and the men whose creed is imperial domination.

We have spoken now, surely, in terms too concrete to admit of any further doubt or question. An evident principle runs through the whole program I have outlined. It is the principle of justice to all peoples and nationalities, and their right to live on equal terms of liberty and safety with one another, whether they be strong or weak. Unless this principle be made its foundation no part of the structure of international justice can stand. The people of the United States could act upon no other principle; and to the vindication of this principle they are ready to devote their lives, their honor, and everything that they possess. The moral climax of this the culminating and final war for human liberty has come, and they are ready to put their own strength, their own highest purpose, their own integrity and devotion to the test.

QUESTIONS

1. How does Wilson's view differ from the realist perspective?

2. If the *Fourteen Points* had been approved, could World War II have been prevented?

---

13.   The Anarchical Society

Hedley Bull

In this excerpt, Hedley Bull examines three traditions of thought in international relations: Hobbesian (realist), Kantian, and Grotian (this textbook places the latter two authors into the transnationalist school of thought). For his own part, Bull combines some of the concepts we have in realist theory, such as balance of power, with other internationalist notions about the effective use of generally accepted rules and norms. This selection is from *The Anarchical Society* (1977).

Hedley Bull (1932–1985) taught at the London School of Economics and the Australian National University. He was a leading authority on both arms control issues and problems of the Third World. Bull's other works include *The Control of the Arms Race* (1961) and contributions to various international studies journals.

Does Order Exist in World Politics?

We have now made it clear what is meant in this study by order in world politics. The question we must now ask is: does it exist?

Order in world politics may one day take the form of the maintenance of elementary goals of social life in a single world society or great society of all mankind. How far the system of states is giving place to such a society, and whether or not it is desirable that it should, are questions that will be considered later in this study. It could not be seriously argued, however, that the society of all mankind is already a going concern. In the present phase we are still accustomed to thinking of order in world politics as consisting of domestic order, or order within states, and international order, or order among them.

No one would deny that there exists within some states a high degree of domestic or municipal order. It is, however, often argued that international order does not exist, except as an aspiration, and that the history of international relations consists simply of disorder or strife. To many people the idea of international order suggests not anything that has occurred in the past, but simply a possible or desirable future state of international relations, about which we might speculate or which we might work to bring about. To those who take this view a study of international order suggests simply a design for a future world, in the tradition of Sully, Cruce, St. Pierre and other irenists or peace theorists.

This present study takes as its starting-point the proposition that, on the contrary, order is part of the historical record of international relations; and in particular, that modern states have formed, and continue to form, not only a system of states but also an international society. To establish this proposition I shall begin by showing first that there has always been present, throughout the history of the modern states system, an idea of international society, proclaimed by philosophers and publicists, and present in the rhetoric of the leaders of states. Second, I shall seek to show that this idea is reflected, at least in part, in interna-

tional reality; that the idea of international society has important roots in actual international practice. Third, I shall set out the limitations of the idea of international society as a guide to the actual practice of states, the precarious and imperfect nature of the order to which it gives rise.

THE IDEA OF INTERNATIONAL SOCIETY

Throughout the history of the modern states system there have been three competing traditions of thought: the Hobbesian or realist tradition, which views international politics as a state of war; the Kantian or universalist tradition, which sees at work in international politics a potential community of mankind; and the Grotian or internationalist tradition, which views international politics as taking place within an international society. Here I shall state what is essential to the Grotian or internationalist idea of international society, and what divides it from the Hobbesian or realist tradition on the one hand, and from the Kantian or universalist tradition on the other. Each of these traditional patterns of thought embodies a description of the nature of international politics and a set of prescriptions about international conduct.

The Hobbesian tradition describes international relations as a state of war of all against all, an arena of struggle in which each state is pitted against every other. International relations, on the Hobbesian view, represent pure conflict between states and resemble a game that is wholly distributive or zero-sum: the interests of each state exclude the interests of any other. The particular international activity that, on the Hobbesian view, is most typical of international activity as a whole, or best provides the clue to it, is war itself. Thus peace, on the Hobbesian view, is a period of recuperation from the last war and preparation for the next.

The Hobbesian prescription for international conduct is that the state is free to pursue its goals in relation to other states without moral or legal restrictions of any kind. Ideas of morality and law, on this view, are valid only in the context of a society, but international life is beyond the bounds of any society. If any moral or legal goals are to be pursued in international politics, these can only be the moral or legal goals of the state itself. Either it is held (as by Machiavelli) that the state conducts foreign policy in a kind of moral and legal vacuum, or it is held (as by Hegel and his successors) that moral behaviour for the state in foreign policy lies in its own self-assertion. The only rules or principles which, for those in the Hobbesian tradition, may be said to limit or circumscribe the behaviour of states in their relations with one another are rules of prudence or expediency. Thus agreements may be kept if it is expedient to keep them, but may be broken if it is not.

The Kantian or universalist tradition, at the other extreme, takes the essential nature of international politics to lie not in conflict among states, as on the Hobbesian view, but in the transnational social bonds that link the individual human beings who are the subjects or citizens of states. The dominant theme of international relations, on the Kantian view, is only apparently the relationship among states, and is really the relationship among all men in the community of mankind—which exists potentially, even if it does not exist actually, and which when it comes into being will sweep the system of states into limbo.

Within the community of all mankind, on the universalist view, the interests of all men are one and the same; international politics, considered from this perspective, is not a purely distributive or zero-sum game, as the Hobbesians maintain, but a purely co-operative or non-zero-sum game. Conflicts of interest exist among the ruling cliques of states, but this is only at the superficial or transient level of the existing system of states; properly understood, the interests of all peoples are the same. The particular international activity which, on the Kantian view, most typifies international activity as a whole is the horizontal conflict of ideology that cuts across the boundaries of states and divides human society into two camps—the trustees of the immanent community of mankind and those who stand in its way, those who are of the true faith and the heretics, the liberators and the oppressed.

The Kantian or universalist view of international morality is that, in contrast to the Hobbesian conception, there are moral imperatives in the field of international relations limiting the action of states, but that these imperatives enjoin not coexistence and co-operation among states but rather the overthrow of the system of states and its replacement by a cosmopolitan society. The community of mankind, on the Kantian view, is not only the central reality in international politics, in the sense that the forces able to bring it into being are present; it is also the end or object of the highest moral endeavour. The rules that sustain coexistence and social intercourse among states should be ignored if the imperatives of this higher morality require it. Good faith with heretics has no meaning, except in terms of tactical convenience; between the elect and the damned, the liberators and the oppressed, the question of mutual acceptance of rights to sovereignty or independence does not arise.

What has been called the Grotian or internationalist tradition stands between the realist tradition and the universalist tradition. The Grotian tradition describes international politics in terms of a society of states or international society. As against the Hobbesian tradition, the Grotians contend that states are not engaged in simple struggle, like gladiators in an arena, but are limited in their conflicts with one another by common rules and institutions. But as against the Kantian or universalist perspective the Grotians accept the Hobbesian premise that sovereigns or states are the principal reality in international politics; the immediate members of international society are states rather than individual human beings. International politics, in the Grotian understanding, expresses neither complete conflict of interest between states nor complete identity of interest; it resembles a game that is partly distributive but also partly productive. The particular international activity which, on the Grotian view, best typifies international activity as a whole is neither war between states, nor horizontal conflict cutting across the boundaries of states, but trade—or, more generally, economic and social intercourse between one country and another.

The Grotian prescription for international conduct is that all states, in their dealings with one another, are bound by the rules and institutions of the society they form. As against the view of the Hobbesians, states in the Grotian view are bound not only by rules of prudence or expediency but also by imperatives of morality and law. But, as against the view of the universalists, what these imperatives enjoin is not the overthrow of the system of states and its replacement by a universal community of mankind, but rather acceptance of the requirements of coexistence and co-operation in a society of states.

Each of these traditions embodies a great variety of doctrines about international politics, among which there exists only a loose connection. In different periods each pattern of thought appears in a different idiom and in relation to different issues and preoccupations. This is not the place to explore further the connections and distinctions within each tradition. Here we have only to take account of the fact that the Grotian idea of international society has always been present in thought about the states system, and to indicate in broad terms the metamorphoses which, in the last three to four centuries, it has undergone. . . .

World International Society

In the twentieth century, as in the sixteenth and seventeenth centuries, the idea of international society has been on the defensive. On the one hand, the Hobbesian or realist interpretation of international politics has been fed by the two World Wars, and by the expansion of international society beyond its originally European confines. On the other hand, Kantian or universalist interpretations have been fed by a striving to transcend the states system so as to escape the conflict and disorder that have accompanied it in this century, and by the Russian and Chinese revolutions, which have given a new currency to doctrines of global transnational solidarity, both communist and anticommunist. Ideas of international society in the twentieth century may be said to be closer to those that were entertained in the early centuries of the states system than to those that prevailed in the eighteenth and nineteenth centuries.

In the twentieth century international society ceased to be regarded as specifically European and came to be considered as global or world wide. In the 1880s the Scottish natural lawyer James Lorimer expressed the orthodox doctrine of the time when he wrote that mankind was divided into civilised humanity, barbarous humanity and savage humanity. Civilised humanity comprised the nations of Europe and the Americas, which were entitled to full recognition as members of international society. Barbarous humanity comprised the independent states of Asia—Turkey, Persia, Siam, China and Japan—which were entitled to partial recognition. And savage humanity was the rest of mankind, which stood beyond the pale of the society of states, although it was entitled to 'natural or human recognition'. It is worth noting in passing that Lorimer's distinction is in fact the same one which is made by social scientists today when they distinguish between modern societies, traditional societies and primitive societies.

Today, when non-European states represent the great majority in international society and the United Nations is nearly universal in its membership, the doctrine that this society rests upon a specific culture or civilisation is generally rejected and even the echo of it that survives in the Statute of the International Court of Justice—which lists the law common to civilised states among the sources of international law it recognises—has become an embarrassment. It is important to bear in mind, however, that if contemporary international society does have any cultural basis, this is not any genuinely global culture, but is rather the culture of so-called 'modernity'. And if we ask what is modernity in culture, it

is not clear how we answer this except by saying that it is the culture of the dominant Western powers. . . .

In the twentieth century, also, there has been a retreat from the confident assertions, made in the age of Vattel, that the members of international society were states and nations, towards the ambiguity and imprecision on this point that characterised the era of Grotius. The state as a bearer of rights and duties, legal and moral, in international society today is widely thought to be joined by international organisations, by non-state groups of various kinds operating across frontiers, and—as implied by the Nuremberg and Tokyo War Crimes Tribunals, and by the Universal Declaration of Human Rights—by individuals. There is no agreement as to the relative importance of these different kinds of legal and moral agents, or on any general scheme of rules that would relate them one to another, but Vattel's conception of a society simply of states has been under attack from many different directions.

In this century, also, the theory of international society has moved away from the emphasis of eighteenth- and nineteenth-century legal and historical positivism on existing practice as the source of norms about international conduct, in favour of a return to natural law principles or to some contemporary equivalent of them; in political as in legal analysis of international relations the idea of international society has been rested less on the evidence of co-operation in the actual behaviour of states than on principles purporting to show how they should behave, such as those proclaimed in the League Covenant, the Kellogg-Briand Pact or the Charter of the United Nations.

Going along with this there has been a reappearance of universalist or solidarist assumptions in the way the rules of coexistence are formulated. The idea that the means states use in war should be limited has been qualified by the reappearance of the distinction between objectively just and unjust causes for which war is waged, as in the attempts to prohibit "aggressive" war. The idea that neutrals should behave impartially towards belligerent states has been qualified in the same way, as in the doctrine of 'collective security' embodied in the League of Nations Covenant and the United Nations Charter.

The twentieth-century emphasis upon ideas of a reformed or improved international society, as distinct from the elements of society in actual practice, has led to a treatment of the League of Nations, the United Nations and other general international organisations as the chief institutions of international society, to the neglect of those institutions whose role in the maintenance of international order is the central one. Thus there has developed the Wilsonian rejection of the balance of power, the denigration of diplomacy and the tendency to seek to replace it by international administration, and a return to the tendency that prevailed in the Grotian era to confuse international law with international morality or international improvement.

THE REALITY OF INTERNATIONAL SOCIETY

But does this idea of international society conform to reality? Do the theories of philosophers, international lawyers and historians in the Grotian tradition reflect the thought of statesmen? If statesmen pay lip-service to international society

and its rules, does this mean that the latter affect their decisions? If the idea of international society played some real part during periods of relative international harmony, as in Europe for long stretches of the eighteenth and nineteenth centuries, was it not extinguished during the wars of religion, the wars of the French Revolution and Napoleon, and the World Wars of the present century? What meaning can it have, for example, to say that Hitler's Germany and Stalin's Russia, locked in a struggle to the death during the Second World War, regarded each other as bound by common rules and co-operated in the working of common institutions? If the Christian and, later, European international system that existed from the sixteenth century to the nineteenth was also an international society, were not the bonds of this society stretched and ultimately broken as the system expanded and became worldwide? Is not the international politics of the present time best viewed as an international system that is not an international society?

The Element of Society

My contention is that the element of a society has always been present, and remains present, in the modern international system, although only as one of the elements in it, whose survival is sometimes precarious. The modern international system in fact reflects all three of the elements singled out, respectively, by the Hobbesian, the Kantian and the Grotian traditions: the element of war and struggle for power among states, the element of transnational solidarity and conflict, cutting across the divisions among states, and the element of co-operation and regulated intercourse among states.

In different historical phases of the states system, in different geographical theatres of its operation, and in the policies of different states and statesmen, one of these three elements may predominate over the others.

Thus one may say that in the trade and colonial wars fought in the late seventeenth and eighteenth centuries, chiefly by Holland, France and England, where the object was trading monopoly enforced by sea power and the political control of colonies, the element of a state of war was predominant. In the wars of religion that marked the first phase of the states system up till the Peace of Westphalia, in the European convulsion of the wars of the French Revolution and Napoleon, and in the ideological struggle of communist and anti-communist powers in our own times, the element of transnational solidarity and conflict has been uppermost—expressed not only in the revolutionist transnational solidarities of the Protestant parties, the democratic or republican forces favourable to the French Revolution, and the Communist Internationals, but also in the counter-revolutionist solidarities of the Society of Jesus, International Legitimism and Dullesian anti-communism. In nineteenth-century Europe, in the interval between the struggle of revolutionism and Legitimism that remained in the aftermath of the Napoleonic wars, and the re-emergence, late in the century, of the patterns of great power conflict that led to the First World War, one may say that the element of international society was predominant.

The element of international society has always been present in the modern international system because at no stage can it be said that the conception of the common interests of states, of common rules accepted and common institutions worked by them, has ceased to exert an influence. Most states at most times pay some respect to the basic rules of coexistence in international society, such as mutual respect for sovereignty, the rule that agreements should be kept, and rules limiting resort to violence. In the same way most states at most times take part in the working of common institutions: the forms and procedures of international law, the system of diplomatic representation, acceptance of the special position of great powers, and universal international organisations such as the functional organisations that grew up in the nineteenth century, the League of Nations and the United Nations.

The idea of "international society" has a basis in reality that is sometimes precarious but has at no stage disappeared. Great wars that engulf the states system as a whole strain the credibility of the idea, and cause thinkers and statesmen to turn to Hobbesian interpretations and solutions, but they are followed by periods of peace. Ideological conflicts in which states and factions within them are ranged on opposite sides sometimes lead to a denial of the idea of international society by both sides, and lend confirmation to Kantian interpretations, but they are followed by accommodations in which the idea reappears.

Even at the height of a great war or ideological conflict the idea of international society, while it may be denied by the pronouncements of the contending states—each side treating the other as outside the framework of any common society—does not disappear so much as go underground, where it continues to influence the practice of states. The Allied and Axis powers at the height of the Second World War did not accept each other as members of a common international society, and they did not cooperate with each other in the working of common institutions. But one could not say that the idea of international society ceased to affect the practice of international relations in that period. The Allied powers continued to respect the ordinary rules of international society in their relations among themselves and in their dealings with neutral countries; so did Germany, Italy and Japan. Within both groups of belligerent powers there were persons and movements who sought out the basis of a negotiated peace. The Allied and Axis states each insisted that the others were bound as members of international society to observe the Geneva conventions concerning prisoners of war, and in the case of the Western allies and Germany, in respect of one another's prisoners, in large measure actually did observe these conventions.

Similarly, when the Cold War was being prosecuted most vigorously, the United States and the Soviet Union were inclined to speak of each other as heretics or outcasts beyond the pale, rather than as member states of the same international society. However, they did not even then break off diplomatic relations, withdraw recognition of one another's sovereignty, repudiate the idea of a common international law or cause the breakup of the United Nations into rival organisations. In both the Western and communist blocs there were voices raised in favour of compromise, drawing attention to the common interests of the two sides in coexistence and restating, in secular form, the principle *cuijus regio, eijus religio* that had provided a basis for accommodation in the wars of religion. Thus, even in periods when international politics is best described in terms of a Hobbesian state of war or a Kantian condition of transnational solidarity, the idea of international society has survived as an important part of reality, and its survival in these times of stress lays the foundation for the reconstruction of international society when war gives place to peace or ideological conflict to *detente.*

It may help to make clear the persistent reality of the element of international society if we contrast the relations of states within that system with examples of relations between independent political communities in which the element of society is entirely absent. The relations of Chingis Khan's Mongol invaders, and the Asian and European peoples whom they subjugated, were not moderated by a belief on each side in common rules binding on both in their dealings with one another. Chingis Khan's conquests did have a basis in the moral ideas of the Mongols themselves: Chingis believed that he had the mandate of heaven to rule the world, that whatever peoples lay outside the *de facto* control of the Mongols were nevertheless *de jure* subjects of the Mongol empire, and that peoples who failed to submit to the Mongol court were therefore rebels against the divinely inspired order, against whom the waging of war was a right and a duty. But these ideas formed no part of the thinking of the peoples who were subjugated and in some cases annihilated by the Mongols.

When the Spanish Conquistadors confronted the Aztecs and the Incas, this similarly took place in the absence of any common notion of rules and institutions. The Spaniards debated among themselves what duties they had towards the Indians—whether their right to invade derived from the claim of the Pope to *imperium mundi,* the duty of a Christian prince to spread the faith, the failure of the Indians to extend rights of hospitality, and so on. But the rights which the Indians were acknowledged—by scholars such as Victoria—to have, were rights deriving from a system of rules recognised by the Spaniards; they did not derive from any system of rules acknowledged by the Indians also. The Spaniards and the Indians were able to recognise each other as human beings, to engage in negotiations and to conclude agreements. But these dealings took place in the absence of any common framework of rules and institutions.

The long history of relations between Europe and Islam provides a further illustration of this theme. As long as modern international society thought of itself as Christian or European, Islam in its successive embodiments was viewed as a barbarian power against which it was the duty of Christian princes to maintain a common front, even if they did not always do so in practice. Islamic thought reciprocated by dividing the world into *dar-al-Islam,* the region of submission to the will of God, and *dar-al-Harb,* the region of war which was yet to be converted. Coexistence with infidel states was possible; diplomatic exchanges, treaties and alliances could be and were concluded; and these relations were subject to rules—but only rules binding on Moslems. There was no conception of a common society in which Islamic and infidel states both had their place; the latter were regarded as having only a provisional existence, and coexistence with them as only a temporary phase in a process leading inexorably to their absorption.

It might be argued that while there is indeed a contrast between cases where a common idea of international society is shared by adversary communities, and

cases where no such idea exists, this is of no practical consequence; the language of a common international society spoken by states in the modern international system is mere lip-service. Thus, as Grotius notes, for some states which claim that they have a just cause for going to war with one another, this just cause is often simply a pretext, their real motives being quite otherwise. Grotius distinguishes between causes of war that are 'justifiable', that is to say which are undertaken in the belief that there is a just cause, from causes of war that are merely 'persuasive', that is in which allegation of a just cause is simply a pretext.

The question, however, is whether an international system in which it is necessary to have a pretext for beginning a war is not radically different from one in which it is not. The state which at least alleges a just cause, even where belief in the existence of a just cause has played no part in its decision, offers less of a threat to international order than one which does not. The state which alleges a just cause, even one it does not itself believe in, is at least acknowledging that it owes other states an explanation of its conduct, in terms of rules that they accept. There are, of course, differences of opinion as to the interpretation of the rules and their application to concrete situations; but such rules are not infinitely malleable and do circumscribe the range of choice of states which seek to give pretexts in terms of them. The giving of a pretext, moreover, means that the violence which the offending state does to the structure of commonly accepted rules by going to war in disregard of them is less than it would otherwise be; to make war without any explanation, or with an explanation stated only in terms of the recalcitrant state's own beliefs—

such as the Mongols' belief in the Mandate of Heaven, or the belief of the Conquistadors in the Pope's *imperium mundi*—is to hold all other states in contempt, and to place in jeopardy all the settled expectations that states have about one another's behavior.

Grotius recognises that while international society is threatened by states which wage war for merely "persuasive" causes, and not for "justifiable" ones, it is even more threatened by states which wage war without "persuasive" causes either; wars which lack causes of either sort he speaks of as "the wars of savages." Vattel speaks of those who wage war without pretext of any kind as 'monsters unworthy of the name of men', whom nations may unite to suppress.

The Anarchical Society

It is often maintained that the existence of international society is disproved by the fact of anarchy, in the sense of the absence of government or rule. It is obvious that sovereign states, unlike the individuals within them, are not subject to a common government, and that in this sense there is, in the phrase made famous by Goldsworthy Lowes Dickinson, an "international anarchy." A persistent theme in the modern discussion of international relations has been that, as a consequence of this anarchy, states do not form together any kind of society; and that if they were to do so it could only be by subordinating themselves to a common authority.

A chief intellectual support of this doctrine is what I have called the domestic analogy, the argument from the experience of individual men in domestic society to the experience of states, according to which states, like individuals, are capable of orderly social life only if, as in Hobbes's phrase, they stand in awe of a common power. In the case of Hobbes himself and his successors, the domestic analogy takes the form simply of the assertion that states or sovereign princes, like individual men who live without government, are in a state of nature which is a state of war. It is not the view of Hobbes, or other thinkers of his school, that a social contract of states that would bring international anarchy to an end either should or can take place. By contrast, in the thinking of those who look forward—or backward—to a universal or world government, the domestic analogy is taken further, to embrace not only the conception of a state of nature but also that of a social contract among states that will reproduce the conditions of order within the state on a universal scale.

There are three weaknesses in the argument that states do not form a society because they are in a condition of international anarchy. The first is that the modern international system does not entirely resemble a Hobbesian state of nature. Hobbes's account of relations between sovereign princes is a subordinate part of his explanation and justification of government among individual men. As evidence for his speculations as to how men would live were they to find themselves in a situation of anarchy, Hobbes mentions the experience of civil war, the life of certain American tribes and the facts of international relations:

> But though there had never been any time wherein particular men were in a condition of warre one against another; yet in all times Kings, and Persons of Soveraigne authority, because of their Independency, are in continual jealousies, and in the state and posture of Gladiators;

having their weapons pointing, and their eyes fixed on one another; that is, their Forts, Garrisons and Guns, upon the Frontiers of their Kingdomes; and continual Spyes upon their neighbours; which is a posture of warre.

In Hobbes's account the situation in which men live without a common power to keep them in awe has three principal characteristics. In this situation there can be no industry, agriculture, navigation, trade or other refinements of living because the strength and invention of men is absorbed in providing security against one another. There are no legal or moral rules: "The notions of Right and Wrong, Justice and Injustice have there no place. . . . It is consequent also to the same condition, that there can be no Propriety, no Dominion, no *Mine* and *Thine* distinct; but only that to be every mans, that he can get; and for so long as he can keep it." Finally, the state of nature is a state of war: war understood to consist "not in actual fighting; but in the known disposition thereto, during all the time there is no assurance to the contrary"; and to be "such a warre, as is of every man, against every man."

The first of these characteristics clearly does not obtain in international anarchy. The absence of a world government is no necessary bar to industry, trade and other refinements of living. States do not in fact so exhaust their strength and invention in providing security against one another that the lives of their inhabitants are solitary, poor, nasty, brutish and short; they do not as a rule invest resources in war and military preparations to such an extent that their economic fabric is ruined. On the contrary, the armed forces of states, by providing security against external attack and internal disorder, establish the conditions under which economic improvements may take place within their borders. The absence of a universal government has not been incompatible with international economic interdependence.

It is also clear that the second feature of Hobbes's state of nature, the absence in it of notions of right and wrong, including notions of property, does not apply to modern international relations. Within the system of states that grew up in Europe and spread around the world, notions of right and wrong in international behaviour have always held a central place.

Of the three principal features of Hobbes's state of nature the only one that might be held to apply to modern international relations is the third—the existence in it of a state of war, in the sense of a disposition on the part of every state to war with every other state. Sovereign states, even while they are at peace, nevertheless display a disposition to go to war with one another, inasmuch as they prepare for war and treat war as one of the options open to them.

The second weakness of the argument from international anarchy is that it is based on false premises about the conditions of order among individuals and groups other than the state. It is not, of course, the case that fear of a supreme government is the only source of order within a modern state: no account of the reasons why men are capable of orderly social coexistence within a modern state can be complete which does not give due weight to factors such as reciprocal interest, a sense of community or general will, and habit or inertia.

If, then, we are to compare international relations with an imagined, pre-contractual state of nature among individual men, we may well choose not Hobbes's description of that condition but Locke's. Locke's conception of the state of nature as a society without government does in fact provide us with a close analogy with the society of states. In modern international society, as in Locke's state of nature, there is no central authority able to interpret and enforce the law, and thus individual members of the society must themselves judge and enforce it. Because in such a society each member of it is a judge in his own cause, and because those who seek to enforce the law do not always prevail, justice in such a society is crude and uncertain. But there is nevertheless a great difference between such a rudimentary form of social life and none at all.

The third weakness of the argument from international anarchy is that it overlooks the limitations of the domestic analogy. States, after all, are very unlike human individuals. Even if it could be contended that government is a necessary condition of order among individual men, there are good reasons for holding that anarchy among states is tolerable to a degree to which among individuals it is not.

We have already noted that, unlike the individual in Hobbes's state of nature, the state does not find its energies so absorbed in the pursuit of security that the life of its members is that of mere brutes. Hobbes himself recognises this when, having observed that persons in sovereign authority are in "a posture of war," he goes on to say that "because they uphold thereby the industry of their subjects, there does not follow from it that misery which accompanies the liberty of particular men." The same sovereigns that find themselves in a state of nature in relation to one another have provided,

within their territories, the conditions in which refinements of life can flourish.

Moreover, states are not vulnerable to violent attack to the same degree that individuals are. Spinoza, echoing Hobbes in his assertion that 'two states are in the same relation to one another as two men in the condition of nature,' goes on to add, 'with this exception, that a commonwealth can guard itself against being subjugated by another, as a man in the state of nature cannot do. For, of course, a man is overcome by sleep every day, is often afflicted by disease of body or mind, and is finally prostrated by old age; in addition, he is subject to troubles against which a commonwealth can make itself secure.' One human being in the state of nature cannot make himself secure against violent attack; and this attack carries with it the prospect of sudden death. Groups of human beings organised as states, however, may provide themselves with a means of defence that exists independently of the frailties of any one of them. And armed attack by one state upon another has not brought with it a prospect comparable to the killing of one individual by another. For one man's death may be brought about suddenly in a single act; and once it has occurred it cannot be undone. But war has only occasionally resulted in the physical extinction of the vanquished people.

In modern history it has been possible to take Clausewitz's view that "war is never absolute in its results," and that defeat in it may be "a passing evil which can be remedied." Moreover, war in the past, even if it could in principle lead to the physical extermination of one or both of the belligerent peoples, could not be thought capable of doing so at once in the course of a single act. Clausewitz, in holding that war does not consist of a single instantaneous blow, but always of a succession of separate actions, was drawing attention to something that in the past has always held true and has rendered violence among independent political communities different from violence between individual persons. It is only in the context of nuclear weapons and other recent military technology that it has become pertinent to ask whether war could not now both be "absolute in its results" and "take the form of a single, instantaneous blow," in Clausewitz's understanding of these terms; and whether, therefore, violence does not now confront the state with the same sort of prospect it has always held for the individual.

This difference, that states have been less vulnerable to violent attack by one another than individual men, is reinforced by a further one: that in so far as states have been vulnerable to physical attack, they have not been equally so. Hobbes builds his account of the state of nature on the proposition that 'Nature hath made men so equal, in the faculties of body and mind, [that] the weakest has strength enough to kill the strongest.' It is this equal vulnerability of every man to every other that, in Hobbes's view, renders the condition of anarchy intolerable. But in modern international society there has been a persistent distinction between great powers and small. Great powers have not been vulnerable to violent attack by small powers to the same extent that small powers have been vulnerable to attack by great ones. Once again it is only the spread of nuclear weapons to small states, and the possibility of a world of many nuclear powers, that raises the question whether in international relations, also, a situation may come about in which 'the weakest has strength enough to kill the strongest.'

The argument, then, that because men cannot form a society without government, sovereign princes or states cannot, breaks down not only because some degree of order can in fact be achieved among individuals in the absence of government, but also because states are unlike individuals, and are more capable of forming an anarchical society. The domestic analogy is no more than an analogy; the fact that states form a society without government reflects features of their situation that are unique.

THE LIMITATIONS OF INTERNATIONAL SOCIETY

We have shown that the modern international system is also an international society, at least in the sense that international society has been one of the elements permanently at work in it; and that the existence of this international society is not as such disproved by the fact of international anarchy. It is important, however, to retain a sense of the limitations of the anarchical international society.

Because international society is no more than one of the basic elements at work in modern international politics, and is always in competition with the elements of a state of war and of transnational solidarity or conflict, it is always erroneous to interpret international events as if international society were the sole or the dominant element. This is the error committed by those who speak or write as if the Concert of Europe, the League of Nations or the United Nations were the principal factors in international politics in their respective times; as if international law were to be assessed only in relation to the function it has of binding states together, and not also in relation to its function as an instrument of state interest and as a vehicle of transnational purposes; as if attempts to maintain a balance of power were to be interpreted only as endeavours to preserve the system of states, and not also as manoeuvres on the part of particular powers to gain ascendancy; as if great powers were to be viewed only as 'great responsibles' or 'great indispensables,' and not also as great predators; as if wars were to be construed only as attempts to violate the law or to uphold it, and not also simply as attempts to advance the interests of particular states or of transnational groups. The element of international society is real, but the elements of a state of war and of transnational loyalties and divisions are real also, and to reify the first element, or to speak as if it annulled the second and third, is an illusion.

Moreover, the fact that international society provides some element of order in international politics should not be taken as justifying an attitude of complacency about it, or as showing that the arguments of those who are dissatisfied with the order provided by international society are without foundation. The order provided within modern international society is precarious and imperfect. To show that modern international society has provided some degree of order is not to have shown that order in world politics could not be provided more effectively by structures of a quite different kind.

QUESTIONS

1. How does Bull explain the possibility that an international system governed by law has always existed?

2. Is such a world society viable under current conditions? Explain.

---

14. Influence, Marginality, and Centrality in the International Legal System

Louis Henkin

In this article, Louis Henkin provides a broad overview of the role of international law in the global state system. He notes that international law is a "political instrument" that helps to regulate the interactions of states. Henkin concludes that the creation and enforcement of international law are political acts that are generally the result of negotiation and compromise between different groups of states and different regions of the world. This selection is from the *Jerusalem Journal of International Relations* (1989).

Louis Henkin is a professor at Columbia University and director of the university's Center for the Study of Human Rights. Other works include *Arms Control and Inspection in American Law* (1958), *Foreign Affairs and the Constitution* (1972), and *Constitutionalism, Democracy and Foreign Affairs* (1990), as well as numerous journal contributions.

International law is the law of the international state system, serving purposes and ends like those that law serves in national societies—order, predictability, efficiency, convenience, the promotion of common or dominant values (individual and common good and the general welfare? autonomy? equality? justice?). As in national societies, international law is made by political actors through political processes for political ends. Perspectives on the political influence of states and of regions, on equality or hierarchy, on marginality or centrality, apply to the legal dimension of the system as well. But international law also has its own laws, modifying those that govern international politics generally.

INTERNATIONAL LAW AND ORDER

International law aims at international order. International order—more precisely, interstate order—suggests order in a system of states, not the order that might be achieved by hegemony of a single power (such as a *Pax Romana*) or by world law under world government. Order in a system of states, moreover, is not a single, defined concept. From Westphalia (1648) to San Francisco (1945, the UN Conference), the order for which international law strove was that of a "liberal" system of states,[1] one that aimed at a maximum of liberty—sovereignty, being let alone—for each state, consistent with similar liberty for other states.[2] The

international liberal order was enhanced in our day by the law of the UN Charter, which prohibited the use of force by any state against the political independence or territorial integrity of any other state. Equal liberty for equal states was enhanced also by adopting into law the principle of self-determination, which in effect outlawed involuntary colonialism.

The liberal state system and its law are committed to peace and order, to respect for state autonomy and to *"pacta sunt servanda"* (agreements are to be kept); the state system is not a "welfare system" dedicated to ensuring that every state can meet its basic needs and those of its inhabitants, or to reducing inequalities among states. Since 1945 the system has taken small steps away from strict liberalism: the UN Charter dedicated the UN Organization, among other purposes, to promoting the welfare of states and the human rights of individuals, and during forty years the United Nations has established international human rights and promoted economic development. But the international system has remained essentially liberal and international law continues to reflect that liberalism. The system exerts influence for internal change and for interstate cooperation, but in principle states remain autonomous. Internal changes must come from internal forces; cooperation is voluntary. International law has little to say about constitutional government or democracy within a state. No state is required to adhere to any human rights covenant or convention.[3] No state is required to help another state meet the needs of its inhabitants. Foreign aid, development assistance, have remained voluntary.

International law promotes a liberal state system because international political forces are committed to that system. In the political system law is neither central nor marginal. International law has no ends of its own; it is a means and a dimension of politics. Law confirms, it does not lead; it cannot get ahead of politics; law is a result, not a cause of politics.[4]

The Law and Politics of International Law

International law is a particular political instrument for ordering interstate relations. Making and maintaining international law are political processes, and the axioms, norms, procedures, and institutions of the law reflect political forces effectively brought to bear within the system. But the politics of lawmaking has its own process and its own laws of continuity and change.

International law consists principally of customary law and treaties. Treaties are made by agreement and a treaty is binding only on states that are parties to it. Customary law is the result of state "practice," and is generally binding on all states.

It is useful to distinguish between two kinds of customary law. Traditional customary law was largely "constitutional," fundamental, consisting of the basic principles of the state system and the basic norms of any legal system. These included: the concept and definition of the state, the implications of state sovereignty (including territorial integrity and inviolability), the norms of diplomatic intercourse, principles of property, contract, tort (delict) in relations between states. It included also the law of "commonage," governing common domain and common resources, notably the law of the sea. But custom continues to be available also as a means of legislating new, contemporary norms—for example, some new customary law of human rights. The traditional customary law is binding on all states, including states that have become states (and entered the state system) recently, and such customary law has remained largely immune to contemporary political forces. New customary law, on the other hand, results only when contemporary political forces will it.

Treaties too may be subdivided along lines of political significance. Bilateral treaties serve the needs of the two state parties and respond to their bargaining interests and powers. Multilateral agreements—which are also binding only on states that adhere to them—are used for general (or regional, or other group) legislative purposes, and are the product of a complex of political forces brought to bear at a particular time, on a particular issue, often in a particular forum.

In the latter half of the twentieth century, the state system has resorted to treaties for codifying and developing customary law. Like other treaties, "codificatory" treaties, such as the Vienna Convention on the Law of Treaties or the Vienna Convention on Diplomatic Relations, are binding only on states that adhere to them, but since they largely correspond to customary law they serve also as an authoritative restatement of the obligations of all states under customary law.

Whether as customs or by treaty, international law is made by the states themselves; there has been no representative body to legislate for the system. By the "constitutional" theory of the system, all states are autonomous and equal in status and authority. In principle—sometimes called the principle of unanimity—no state can be compelled to accept law to which it objects before it becomes law; no state can impose law on any other, unwilling, state.[5] That principle does not prevent those who wish to make law for themselves from doing so; it does not give others a veto. But opposition by one or more important states can preclude general law, and abstention by one or more states may sometimes undermine law made by other states for themselves, as when a few states refrain from adhering to an anti-hijacking agreement and serve as a haven for hijackers. International law, therefore, is difficult to make and difficult to change, and the laws of lawmaking favor nonregulation, state autonomy, laissez-faire, reliance on market forces, the status quo.

Law is made by governments, by politicians (not by lawyers). Since law results from agreement of many states or from their practice in relation to each other, lawmaking is a complex of actions by political actors and of layers of negotiation. Subject to the principle of unanimity, the forces that exert influence in the political system generally do so as well in the complex process of lawmaking. In bilateral negotiations, in conferences convened for the purpose of developing and concluding international agreements, in international organizations, in special bodies established to promote lawmaking (such as the International Law Commission), states are subject to persuasion,

and political forces reflect political centrality, marginality, and other influences as in the system at large.[6] Group commitments may also have particular significance in law-making. Military allies, members of regional or economic groups, tend to seek law reflecting their common interests, and they will frequently support each other in promoting or resisting or shaping law on other issues as well. In recent decades, I shall suggest, the Third World has exhibited "solidarity" in the lawmaking process even on issues that do not involve their obvious common interests. Particular states have important, often dominant influence in resisting or shaping international norms that would regulate activities or interests in their possession or under their control.

Since the Second World War, international organizations have contributed to the development of international law. International (intergovernmental) organizations are generally established by treaty, and such treaties become part of international law. Some constitutive treaties also include normative principles of major significance, such as the UN Charter provisions prohibiting the use of force. In general, international organizations have no legislative authority, but resolutions of major organizations, such as the UN General Assembly, contribute to the development of international law: they may declare or clarify the state of the law on a particular matter; they may constitute state practice contributing to the development of customary law; they may encourage and promote the negotiation of treaties and help shape the content of such treaties.[7] The contribution of international organizations to lawmaking is shaped in part by political forces brought to bear in those organizations.

compensation if foreign properties or investments were nationalized. They sought to improve their situation in the financial markets and in international financial institutions. They pressed for "more equitable" terms in trade that would assure poor states higher prices for their exports and afford them technology and other manufactured goods at lower than "market" prices.

Since they had "possession" of their natural resources, since "gunboat diplomacy" and other military intervention were no longer acceptable in the international system, Third World states succeeded in ending many concessions to foreign investors and in renegotiating foreign investment on a new basis in various forms of "joint ventures," with greater governmental control and a larger share for the host state. Third World states also joined in the United Nations to adopt resolutions denying any international obligation to compensate for expropriation of foreign properties or investments.[16] But Third World states needed foreign investment and, as a condition of investment, Western states effectively compelled importing states to acquiesce in an obligation under international law to compensate for expropriation, or to conclude specific agreements assuring such compensation.[17] In time, states that had previously expropriated agreed to "lump-sum" settlements, sometimes in order to open the way to future investments and to improve relations generally.

Perhaps the greatest Third World failure and disappointment was in its effort to achieve a new order in trade. All the poor states together could not change the law of the free market, although the General Agreement on Tariffs and Trade (GATT) permits some special concessions to developing states.[18] Ar-guments based on "community" and interdependence, and claims for "reparation" against former colonial powers, invoked international morality, not law. Appeals to self-interest urging that development and new arrangements would benefit all did not persuade those who had to be persuaded. Foreign aid to developing countries has remained essentially voluntary; the UN Development Program has provided assistance to the extent that the rich states could be pressed or shamed into contributing; banks and governments and international institutions provided some debt relief, but those concessions granted from sympathy or prudence have not acquired normative character.

The Use of Force

Until 1945 war was not unlawful, but lesser uses of force required justification and were subject to principles of necessity and proportionality. In the UN Charter, the nations agreed to outlaw war and other uses of armed force, except in self-defense against armed attack. They also established institutions, notably the Security Council, to enforce the prohibitions of the Charter and maintain international peace and security. The major powers insisted on and obtained a veto in the Security Council.

The Security Council, all know, has been rendered largely ineffective to date by big-power conflict and the big-power veto, and the United Nations has exerted only marginal influence on enforcing the law of the Charter, principally through its peacekeeping activities. The law against war and other uses of force has suffered. To be sure, the big powers have been deterred from overt resort to war by mutual fear of terrible weapons, but recurrently they have been involved in surrogate wars or in interventions and counter-interventions—Korea, Czechoslovakia, Vietnam, Afghanistan, Nicaragua. Big-power hostility, and their competition for the favor of small powers, has limited big-power influence against war by smaller powers. The mass of nations in the United Nations, and smaller groups in regional organizations, have not been sufficiently committed to the law of the Charter, have not cared enough to attempt to prevent, deter, or terminate war, and some states have even resisted such efforts by others. As a result, some states (other than the big powers or their allies) have felt free to engage in war, regardless of law. The Middle East has seen several wars between the Arab states and Israel, the lengthy war between Iran and Iraq, and interventions and counterinterventions in Cyprus and Lebanon. There have been small wars and other illegal uses of force in Africa, in Asia, in Central America, and between Argentina and the United Kingdom. Law has not been irrelevant, but it has had insufficient effect.

For decades, the big powers have not seen it as in their common interest to support that law and to impose or strongly press for peace; they have not themselves been scrupulous to respect the law. The USSR has generally seen its interest in maintaining or spreading communism, or expanding Soviet influence, as greater than any interest in peace. The United States was firmly committed to the law of the Charter, but also to the containment of communism. In the Reagan years, the United States was seen as moving beyond its earlier insistence on the right to engage in collective self-defense against armed attack and against indirect aggression, and proclaiming the right to use force to prevent or undo

communist regimes (even if not externally imposed), to spread democracy, and to respond to terrorism (Libya). That policy has been attacked by other states and by many in the legal community; some of these actions have been declared illegal by the International Court of Justice.[19]

In 1988, the USSR began the process of fully withdrawing its forces from Afghanistan. The United States suspended arms assistance to the Contras fighting in Nicaragua. The big powers agreed on, and the United Nations helped achieve, a cease-fire between Iraq and Iran. It remains to be seen whether in the post-Reagan years the United States will revert to greater attention to the law of the Charter and to a renewed commitment to enforcing it against other states. It remains to be seen, too, whether the United States and the USSR might begin to cooperate to that end.

Most of the uses of force in the past decades have been internal—rebellions and civil wars—with interventions and counterinterventions by other states, notably by the big powers or their surrogates. International law has not attempted to and could not regulate internal uses of force, but it has attempted to regulate external interventions by force in such internal struggles. Some of these interventions of recent decades were illegal by international norms; the legality of other forms of support or intervention is uncertain.

Law is made by states through incumbent governments, all of which wish to be free to receive aid, including armed support against rebellion, even in civil war; all incumbent governments desire law forbidding intervention in support of rebellion or civil war. On the other hand, opposition forces seek support from other states, and some states have given such aid, including armed support.

There is a need to define and refine the law governing intervention in rebellion and civil wars. But the principal "would-be" intervenors and countervenors are the superpowers and their allies or surrogates, and no new law, or clarification of the existing law, is likely unless the superpowers agree to have it.

In the enforcement of the law against war, I regret to conclude, all states (and the United Nations) have been more or less marginal. One may hope that in the future, big-power cooperation will justify a different conclusion.

Human Rights

Human rights is a Western idea, but it has been universally accepted, at least nominally. The Universal Declaration is repeatedly invoked; the various covenants and conventions are adhered to by states from every region and of every ideological hue. More than half of the states have adhered to the International Covenant on Civil and Political Rights; the Genocide Convention and the Convention on the Elimination of All Forms of Radical Discrimination, in particular, have received overwhelming support.

The enforcement of universal standards has been less successful. The commitment to human rights has been insufficiently strong to mobilize effective (and sometimes costly) collective actions, though the determination of Black Africa to eradicate apartheid has moved other states, too, to take some measures against it. In international bodies, particular countries—for example, the Scandinavian states—have sometimes taken the lead to nudge the majority toward constructive action. But the United Nations

has been "politicized," and, except when directed against South Africa, Israel, or Chile, there have been only spasmodic efforts to address human rights violations. Politicization is particularly strong and rampant in larger political organs such as the UN General Assembly; increasingly, it has been possible to address egregious human rights violations in smaller, less prominent bodies, notably the Human Rights Commission. Regional organizations and other groupings sometimes provide inducements to comply with human rights law. European institutions, and increasingly those of the American states, have helped maintain universally accepted norms. It remains to be seen whether the African states will develop effective means to implement the African Charter of Human and People's Rights. The Commonwealth and the French Community have exerted some informal influence against egregious violations. Arab states have not yet moved effectively to adopt common standards and effective machinery to enforce them. Individual states—notably the United States—have sought to address "consistent patterns of gross violations" by refusing economic and arms assistance, but it is difficult to assess the deterrent effect of such sanctions, or of public condemnation or of "quiet diplomacy" by the United States, other countries, nongovernmental organizations, and international communications media.

POLITICAL-ECONOMIC MARGINALIZATION AND INTERNATIONAL LAW

In the international system, lawmaking and law enforcement are collective political acts. In the complex processes involved, no state or group of states and no particular region consistently wields extraordinary influence, and none has been wholly marginal. Political and economic power is persuasive in these political acts as in others, but general law requires general agreement. By its numbers and solidarity, the Third World has generally been an impressive force, but it is a negotiating bloc, not a legislative body.

The international system is not in perfect health, and its law reflects its weaknesses. The hopes of 1945 for a peaceful world are frayed, and the law on the use of force is in some disarray. The interdependence of states demands ecological and economic regulation, but there has been insufficient success in achieving it. Technology continues to aggravate inequalities, but there are no law and legal institutions to make the economic system more just and efficient, to reduce gross inequalities, or even to create a minimal "welfare system" that would assure that the basic human needs of all are met. One can expect some firm agreement on the law of the sea. One can hope for an emergence of political forces that would lead to law against terrorism. There is little basis for expecting radical change in the law generally: one cannot predict the unpredictable.

A basic order is in place, reflecting established customary law, confirmed and extended by contemporary multilateral treaties and by a network of bilateral arrangements. For the rest, the system—and the rules and the politics of lawmaking—favor state autonomy, laissez-faire. That leaves many needs of the system and of individual countries unmet. There is urgent need for new law, but law is an instrument of politics; there can be no effective law if politics does not will it. Political will to make law requires general agreement, which requires a will by some—the rich, the mighty, the wise, the brave—to lead, and by all—including the many poor—to join and help. Will it require world economic crisis, world environmental crisis, world nuclear catastrophe, to forge that will?

NOTES

1. As the word *liberal* is used in the term *liberal state,* i.e., a state that does not have its own conception of the good but whose purpose is to maximize the realization of every individual's conception

2. Hedley Bull described the state system as an "anarchical society."

3. The modest customary law of human rights has also come about by state consent, though the system has effectively outlawed apartheid over the resistance of the Republic of South Africa.

4. See generally L. Henkin, *How Nations Behave: Law and Foreign Policy,* 2nd ed. (New York: Columbia University Press, 1979).

5. But by the rules of the system, preexisting customary law is binding on new states entering the political system.

   Traditional international law did not refuse effect to unequal, even unconscionable bargains, even to treaties imposed by force; since World War II, treaties imposed by use or threat of armed force are illegal and not enforceable, but agreement is not vitiated because it results from economic coercion or unequal bargaining power.

6. Nongovernmental entities can influence the process of influencing states.

7. General Assembly resolutions have made notable contributions to the law of human rights and the law of the sea.

8. Issues of the law governing foreign nationals and foreign investment will be addressed below.

9. For a time there was uncertainty about succession to treaties, but decolonization provided its own rules: in large measure

the older states allowed the new states to choose among the treaties of their colonial predecessors, succeeding to the treaties they desired and rejecting the others. With decolonization virtually ended, the law of state succession has receded in significance.

10. See, e.g., Article 1 of the International Covenant on Economic, Social and Cultural Rights, and Article 1 of the International Covenant on Civil and Political Rights.

11. By the principle of unanimity no state is compelled to adhere to any international agreement, but generally the content of an international agreement is determined in organizations or conferences governed by majority or two-thirds vote.

12. In a real sense, peace within Eastern Europe is maintained by the USSR, peace within Western Europe by regional forces.

13. See UNGA Res. 2749 (1970).

14. Some observers think that "radical states" saw effective control of mining as a step toward Third World control of other uses of the oceans, and in turn a step toward establishing other powerful institutions with authority in other aspects of international life.

15. See Restatement, Third, Foreign Relations Law of the United States, Introduction to Part V (1987).

16. See the Charter of Economic Rights and Duties of States, GA Res. 3281 (1974).

17. Latin American states have resisted such agreements.

18. See Restatement, §810.

19. It is not clear that the United States itself is prepared to support generally the view that it is legal for any country to intervene or to counterintervene in other countries, or to attack states believed to be responsible for terrorism.

QUESTIONS

1. Explain how the success of the international legal system has been based almost exclusively on the cooperation of the world's most powerful nations.

2. Does international law actually modify the behavior of the most powerful states? Explain using an example from contemporary international politics.

15. The UN in a New World Order

Bruce Russett and James S. Sutterlin

In this article, Russett and Sutterlin offer their recommendations for possible United Nations responses to military aggression against member states. Drawing on the experiences of the Korean Conflict and the Persian Gulf War, the authors present various options that the United Nations—through a unified Security Council command— might use to counter military aggression in the future. This selection is from the journal *Foreign Affairs* (1991).

Bruce Russett is a professor of international relations and world politics at Yale University. He has written many books on international affairs including *Power and Community in World Politics* (1974), *Interest and Ideology* (1975), and *Prisoners of Insecurity* (1983).

The new world order envisioned by Presidents Bush and Gorbachev would be founded on the rule of law and on the principle of collective security. That principle necessarily entails the possibility of military enforcement measures by the United Nations. Twice in its history the Security Council has authorized such action. The first instance was in the Korean War in 1950; the second was in the Persian Gulf in 1990. More occasions are likely to follow.

The U.N. Charter gives the Security Council the authority ''to maintain or restore international peace and security,'' and to enforce the will of the council on a state that has broken the peace. Use of military force by the council for these purposes was foreseen by the founders of the United Nations. Indeed it was seen almost half a century ago as an essential element in the world order that the United Nations was intended to establish. Should the need arise, countries would be protected from aggression by forces provided to the Security Council by member states, serving as a U.N. army at the council's will. Military forces, however, have not been available to the council on this basis and improvisation has therefore been required. The action taken by the Security Council in response to the Iraqi invasion of Kuwait amounted to just that—an improvisation to permit enforcement of the council's will without the specific means provided in the charter for that purpose.

Military force has much more frequently been used by the United Nations

for the purpose of peacekeeping, something not foreseen in the charter at all. This improvisation was first devised in haste to facilitate an end to the 1956 hostilities in the Middle East. Since that beginning, which amply demonstrated the value of the technique, U.N. use of military and civilian personnel provided by member states for peacekeeping has become a well-established practice now supported by all the major powers.

The use of military force by the United Nations for both of these purposes—enforcement and peacekeeping—is surely essential to a world order in which international security is heavily dependent on the Security Council. The experience of the Gulf War and of the more distant past offers important lessons and raises trenchant questions as to how this can most effectively be done in the gulf (as action moves from military victory to the maintenance of peace in the region) and wherever else peace may be endangered.

II

Since the Suez crisis of 1956, the United Nations has developed a notable elasticity in using peacekeeping forces, to the point that it is now difficult to formulate a precise definition—or the limits—of what peacekeeping functions may be. The original role of standing between hostile forces has been expanded to encompass, among other functions, the maintenance of security or stability within a given area (as in southern

Lebanon), the monitoring of elections (Namibia, Haiti), the provision of humanitarian assistance (Cyprus) and the disarmament of insurgents (Nicaragua). This flexibility greatly increases the value of peacekeeping forces as an instrument available to the Security Council in dealing with potential or existing conflicts. For example, the permanent members of the Security Council have recently developed a plan to bring peace to Cambodia that would use peacekeeping forces—both military and civilian—for broad purposes of pacification, stabilization and administration.

Three limitations on the use of peacekeeping have been consistently honored: (1) peacekeeping has been interpreted, as originally articulated by United Nations Secretary General Dag Hammarskjöld, as a provisional measure under the U.N. Charter, that is, as a measure undertaken without prejudice to the rights, claims or positions of the parties concerned; (2) peacekeeping operations have been undertaken only with the consent of all the parties concerned; (3) peacekeeping forces may use arms only in self-defense. Again in accordance with the original decision by Hammarskjöld, U.S. and Soviet troops have never been included in peacekeeping forces.

In domestic conflicts the consent of all the parties is likely to remain a compelling requirement. It was clearly shown in non-U.N. peacekeeping undertakings, in Lebanon in 1983–84 and more recently in Liberia, that without the consent of the parties grave risks are involved and the results can be disastrous. This may not, however, be the case in interstate conflicts. When peacekeeping forces are deployed between hostile forces after a truce or ceasefire has been achieved, an essential purpose is to deter a renewal of hostilities. In this sense deterrence is already an accepted function of peacekeeping. Yet in interstate conflicts a situation could well arise in which peacekeeping forces are needed for deterrence purposes but the consent of one of the parties is not obtainable. This should not, a priori, preclude a Security Council decision to deploy them if the other characteristic limitations are maintained.

The situation in the gulf could present the council with precisely such a need, as a long-term settlement of hostilities is sought. Some sort of convincing deterrent force will be needed to prevent renewed threats against Kuwait and, conceivably, to monitor any demilitarized zones that may be established. For the near term, further military adventures are unlikely. But in the long run, neither Iraqi motives and potential for revenge nor the ambitions of one or more of its neighbors can be ignored. Whatever misgivings some parties may have about the U.S.-led gulf operation, they have excellent reasons to converge on some sort of substantial U.N. presence in the gulf in the future. The emergence of the United Nations as an important institution for promoting international security can moderate any revival of Soviet-American tensions that might stem from disagreements regarding the gulf or other regions.

U.S. and Soviet forces could be usefully included in such an operation to ensure, through its size and composition, maximum credibility. But to be acceptable to the majority of U.N. members such a force must retain an indisputable U.N. identity and must not be dominated by one member state. In other border disputes—of which many exist—a comparable need for deterrence may arise, preferably under circumstances that would permit deployment of peacekeeping forces before hostilities actually occur. Indeed, if at the request of Kuwait a peacekeeping force had been deployed on its border with Iraq in August 1990, the Gulf War might have been avoided.

It is worth emphasizing that nothing in the charter prohibits the Security Council from deploying peacekeeping forces without the consent of all the parties, or from including troop contingents from the permanent members of the council in such forces where the need for deterrence arises. (U.S. and Soviet military personnel already serve in U.N. military observer missions.) Such action would still fall under the definition of a provisional measure to be taken by the council "to prevent an aggravation of the situation" before deciding on enforcement action as foreseen in Articles 41 and 42 of the U.N. Charter. The provision of troops by member states for such deterrence operations would remain voluntary, as in other peacekeeping missions, with financing determined on an ad hoc basis by the council, either through assessment of all members or through payment of the cost by the countries requesting the deployment, as could be the case in a situation like the gulf where wealthy states are involved as parties.

The command structure need be no different from other peacekeeping operations: a commander of the U.N. force is appointed by the secretary general after the peacekeeping operation has been authorized by the Security Council for a defined mission. Troop contingents provided by member states serve under their national officers—a battalion commander, for example—who in turn receives orders from the U.N. force commander. The U.N. force commander reports to the secretary general from whom he receives operational guidance.

The secretary general reports to the Security Council and obtains its concurrence if any change in the mission of the peacekeeping force is contemplated.

One can question whether it will be logistically feasible for the United Nations to mount, and maintain over a period of time, peacekeeping operations of sufficient size to provide a credible deterrent. It can only be said that where the need for peacekeeping has been evident, as in Namibia, the magnitude of required support has not inhibited action.

A good number of countries might well oppose in principle the idea of deploying peacekeeping forces without the consent of all the parties concerned, fearing that it would open the way to action contrary to their own national interests. Unlike the United States and the other four permanent members of the Security Council, they would not enjoy the protection of the veto. When a similar idea was put forward some years ago, in the course of confidential consultations in the Security Council on how its effectiveness might be enhanced, there was little response. The Gulf War has served, however, to heighten interest in effective deterrence using multilateral means not under the domination of one or several U.N. members. There is certainly now a broad recognition that adequate means of deterrence will be essential to a peaceful world order.

III

The second broad purpose for the Security Council's use of military force falls largely under the heading of compellence, or coercion, rather than simply deterrence. In the context of the Security Council such action is best understood as enforcement action. Use of "air, sea or land forces" for enforcement is specifically foreseen in Chapter VII, Articles 39–46 of the U.N. Charter, in which all members undertake to make available to the Security Council "on its call and in accordance with a special agreement or agreements, armed forces, assistance and facilities, including rights of passage, necessary for the purpose of maintaining international peace and security."

Since no such special agreements have been concluded, no standing multilateral force has been available to the Security Council. Therefore the Security Council authorized the use of ad hoc forces to restore international peace in Korea and the Persian Gulf. When the North Korean attacks on South Korea were formally brought to the Security Council's attention, the council's resolution of July 7, 1950—adopted in the temporary absence of the Soviet Union—called on member states to assist South Korea in resisting the North Korean aggression. It recommended "that all members providing military forces and other assistance pursuant to the aforesaid Security Council resolutions make such forces and other assistance available to a unified command under the United States." It requested further that the United States designate the commander of such forces. The same resolution authorized use of the U.N. flag.

Thus in the case of Korea the Security Council requested one member state to lead a combined effort on behalf of the United Nations to resist aggression. Notwithstanding his designation as commander of U.N. forces in Korea, General Douglas MacArthur, the commander named by the United States, never reported directly to the Security Council. (Routine, unclassified status reports were provided by the United States.) Neither the Military Staff Committee—a body composed of military representatives of the five permanent members intended to advise the council on military matters—nor the council itself had any role in directing military operations of the unified command. The General Assembly did, however, establish a three-nation cease-fire committee that sought a formula to end the war, and the secretary general suggested the procedure of direct talks between the military commanders that was ultimately followed and through which an armistice was achieved.

The advantages offered by this procedure were:

- Expeditious action to resist aggression. Only the United States had troops deployed in South Korea capable of taking quick military action.
- The unambiguous command structure needed for large-scale field operations.
- A practical way to meet the responsibilities of the United Nations under the charter in the absence of a multilateral force under the Security Council for which the necessary agreements with member states had not been reached.
- Validation of the concept of collective security, since states acted jointly in response to Security Council (and subsequently General Assembly) decisions.

The disadvantages of this procedure (which became more evident in the course of time) were:

- The United Nations lacked control or influence over the course of military action or the precise purposes for which it was exercised (e.g., to repel and punish aggression, to reunify the country).
- The military operation became identified with the policy of the nation lead-

ing the effort rather than with the United Nations.

■ Divisive forces within the United Nations were encouraged by the dominant role of one member state pursuing goals not universally shared.

■ Opportunities were afforded the aggressor to identify the struggle with one country, the United States, rather than with the international community as a whole.

All of these disadvantages were intensified in the Korean case by the bitter disagreements that prevailed at the time between the Soviet Union and the United States. Under conditions of harmony among the permanent members of the Security Council, these various disadvantages could have considerably less force.

In the Persian Gulf crisis the Security Council authorized, albeit in oblique language, the use of force for enforcement in another interstate conflict. After imposing a comprehensive embargo in order to bring about Iraqi withdrawal from Kuwait and the restoration of its legitimate government, the council called upon "those member states cooperating with the government of Kuwait which are deploying maritime forces to the area to use such measures commensurate to the specific circumstances as may be necessary under the authority of the Security Council . . . to ensure strict implementation" of the provisions laid down in the resolution relating to economic sanctions. Then, in Resolution 678 of November 29, 1990, the Security Council authorized "member states cooperating with the government of Kuwait . . . to use all necessary means to uphold and implement Security Council Resolution 660 and all subsequent relevant resolutions and to restore international peace and se-

curity in the area." All states were requested to provide appropriate support for "the actions undertaken."

This action, with specific reference to Chapter VII of the charter, constituted a new approach to implementation of the collective security concept. As in the earlier enforcement action in Korea, when there was no reference to Chapter VII, a basis for the council to mobilize a U.N. force for military enforcement action did not exist. Therefore the council again turned to member states to act in its behalf through such measures as might be necessary. But this time no unified command was established, and the use of the U.N. flag was not authorized.

The gulf action became possible because the permanent members of the Security Council cooperated on a matter of peace and security in the way originally foreseen when the United Nations was founded. Representatives of the United States and the Soviet Union have repeatedly suggested that such action is an important element in a new world order; that is, a world in which nations will be secure because of the capacity of the United Nations to guarantee their security through collective measures. This fundamental goal of the United Nations is unquestionably brought closer through the sustained cooperation and a notably increased commonality of interests among the major powers, evident not only in the Gulf War but also in other conflicts such as Cambodia and Angola. Two questions nonetheless warrant careful examination: Is the approach that was taken to enforce the council's decisions with regard to the Iraq-Kuwait crisis necessarily a viable model for implementing collective security in the future? Is there a realistic alternative that would offer greater advantages?

IV

With regard to the first question, it is clear that the Security Council, in deciding on action to counter the Iraqi aggression, prescribed action for all member states. While it authorized individual states to take "the necessary action," it requested "all states to provide appropriate support for the actions undertaken." Thus all states were called on to assist in defending one state, Kuwait, from aggression. Actions to be taken for this purpose would seem clearly to constitute "effective collective measures for the prevention and removal of threats to the peace, and for the suppression of acts of aggression" as foreseen in Article 1 of the charter.

But the procedure adopted is not without its difficulties. The Security Council has no means of controlling when, how or in what degree the collective measures are applied. In the gulf case, the states concerned were only requested "to keep the council regularly informed"; some measures taken might not have had majority support in the Security Council or the General Assembly. The state that is in command may have from the outset an interpretation of U.N. goals different from that of other Security Council members, or its aims may become more expansive in the course of the operation. The latter happened in Korea with the U.S. decision to cross the 38th parallel and try to reunify the country by force. It would have been the case in the gulf had the United States pursued military action beyond the Kuwaiti theater of operations.

If the measures taken cease to have the endorsement of the majority of the Security Council, can they still be considered collective measures taken in the council's behalf? This problem is inherent in a procedure in which action is taken on behalf of the council but without any council control over the nature, timing or extent of the action. The major danger is that the entire undertaking will be identified with the country or countries actually involved in military action rather than with the United Nations. In any case, many U.N. members will not view the military action as an appropriate application of collective security if the action appears to conflict with the Security Council's goals.

The gulf operation and the terms for ending military action against Iraq offer a case in point. None of the 12 Security Council resolutions called for eliminating Iraq's war-making capability or deposing Saddam Hussein. But the former clearly became a goal of some coalition members, and the latter was widely suspected. President Bush and the coalition partners felt free to give their own interpretation to the Security Council resolutions. Those members, including the Soviet Union, that interpreted the resolutions more narrowly may be reluctant next time to give such unconstrained authority to member states acting on the council's behalf. In any operation, if the Security Council has asserted no control over the military action authorized, will it be possible for it to assert control over the terms of peace?

Such questions indicate the problems that can arise when a procedure such as that developed for the Gulf War is followed. Moreover the approach adopted in the gulf case is not likely to be viable unless vital interests of one or more major military powers are at risk. For example, the United States might not be interested in deploying substantial forces, even if authorized to do so by the

Security Council, to deter or repel an Egyptian attack on Libya.

V

There are alternative procedures that might in the future be followed by the Security Council, ones that would offer the prospect of effective enforcement action without the disadvantages and problems associated with according responsibility to individual member states.

One would be a variant of the procedure followed in Korea. National forces could be brought together in ad hoc fashion under a unified U.N. command, with the commander designated by whichever happened to be the major troop-contributing country. The problems that arose in the Korean case could conceivably be alleviated if the unified commander were required to consult with the Security Council, or with some form of military authority appointed by the council, on the mission of the military operation and the basic strategy to be followed in achieving it. The country supplying the major troop contingent can be expected to resist such a procedure as inhibiting unacceptably the freedom of action of the commander and subjecting its forces to perilous uncertainties. But if favorable relations among the permanent members of the Security Council persist, such a consultative, though not command, procedure might be feasible. It would have the distinct advantage of maintaining a close U.N. identification with all action taken and of giving the Security Council some influence, if not control, over any military action.

The other alternative is the procedure defined in Articles 42 and 43 of the U.N. Charter, according to which all members of the United Nations undertake "to make available to the Security Council on its call in accordance with a special agreement or agreements, armed forces, facilities and assistance." In the Korean War, the "uniting for peace" resolution of 1950 recommended that each member maintain within its armed forces earmarked units so trained that they could promptly be made available for service "as a United Nations unit or units."

The hostile relations between the United States and the Soviet Union were long perceived as the major obstacle to implementing such provisions. If after the Gulf War the two countries remain in accord on using the United Nations, that obstacle may be lifted. The willingness of member states to commit themselves in advance to provide troops and facilities at the request of the Security Council for enforcement purposes has never been tested. It can be argued that such commitment is inherent in U.N. membership, a condition for which is acceptance of the obligations contained in the charter and ability and willingness to carry out those obligations. For such a commitment to be reliable, however, it must be embodied in agreements between the Security Council and those member states prepared to assume the obligations. Such commitments will not be undertaken lightly.

The subject was discussed in detail in 1945 in the U.S. Senate when the U.N. Charter was under consideration. John Foster Dulles, a member of the U.S. delegation to the San Francisco conference at which the charter was signed, told the Senate Foreign Relations Committee that an agreement with the United Nations on the provision of troops should be regarded as a treaty requiring approval of a two-thirds majority of the Senate. The recorded comments of the senators indicate wide agreement with that interpretation. It was also discussed whether the president would need to obtain the consent of Congress to provide troops, when called upon by the United Nations after completion of an agreement. No consensus emerged on the question, but one senator suggested at the time that the size of the force requested could be decisive. Two or three thousand troops for "police action" would not need congressional approval, whereas a battle force would.

Soviet representatives have recently expressed a positive view of a U.N. agreement on the provision of troops for enforcement purposes, but they have emphasized that in no case could the troops be provided without the specific approval of the Soviet parliament.

Once agreements on the provision of troops were completed with a fair portion of member states, the Security Council would have the capacity to call into being a multilateral force (land, sea and air) under a U.N. commander "to maintain or restore international peace and security." In military operations the commander would presumably have full tactical authority but would operate under the guidance of the Security Council or a body established by the council to serve this purpose. Subsequent understandings would be required on command, intelligence, logistics and other more or less centralized functions. The Military Staff Committee could, as foreseen 46 years ago, "advise and assist the Security Council on all questions relating to military requirements." It could do this without acquiring any command authority, which would be inadvisable since it functions on the basis of consensus.

In some ways a U.N. force of this type would be quite similar to a peacekeeping force, since it would be made up of troops provided by member states and would have a U.N. commander. It would differ markedly, however, in mission, armament, composition and command.

A U.N. force of this nature would not entail the problems and disadvantages that the other identified approaches could present. Identification with the United Nations from initiation to end of any operation would be assured, and control could be clearly in the hands of the Security Council. The likelihood of sustained support among U.N. members for the action undertaken would be strong. Yet in this approach, too, likely problems can be identified.

First of all, it is not clear how many states will be willing to conclude the agreements foreseen in the U.N. Charter—or how long this will take. It can only be said that international circumstances, especially in the wake of the Gulf War, appear more favorable than at any time since 1945. It is also questionable whether a force as large and elaborately equipped as one needed to maintain peace in the gulf, for example, could have been organized quickly on this basis. Any very large operation is bound to depend heavily on a major contingent from one or more of the principal military powers; the larger and more sophisticated the contingent provided, the less likely the contributing country will be willing to place it under non-national command.

Organization and deployment of a multilateral force by the Security Council would likely require more time than if action were delegated to one or more member states, especially if a large-scale operation were foreseen. To shorten the lead time, the secretary general might be given authority, not subject to the veto, to send an unarmed observer corps to any international border at any time. According to Article 99 of the U.N. Charter, the secretary general "may bring to the attention of the Security Council any matter which in his opinion may threaten the maintenance of international peace and security." To do so he needs to be informed. An authorization to send observers without specific consent of the parties raises difficulties, but it would allow the Security Council to be forewarned and to make quick preparations if an enforcement action were required. The very presence of observers can have a deterrent effect, possibly avoiding the need for subsequent enforcement.

Then, too, there is a very basic question as to whether a military action can be successfully carried out under multilateral strategic command, or as successfully as under national command. Administrative aspects of managing the use of force by the Security Council have received little attention. Save for peacekeeping and the peculiar conditions permitting the Korean operation, the prospects of using U.N. forces were nil during the Cold War. Nonetheless important multinational dimensions characterized U.S. military plans during the Korean War, in the U.S. commitment to NATO and notably in the Persian Gulf.

The force of the NATO and Korea precedents must not be exaggerated. In both instances there was virtual consensus on the nature of the military threat, decades-long experience of close cooperation and, in Europe, a high degree of cultural and political homogeneity—far more than likely in most future

U.N.-sanctioned operations. If the United States should put its forces under another state's commander, one would have to expect a relatively much smaller contribution of U.S. troops and financing than in the gulf operations. By its treaty commitments and geographic deployment, however, the United States stood a great chance of being involved in any military operations in Europe and Korea. Any U.N. enforcement action would have to be authorized by the Security Council and would thus be subject to U.S. veto. This fact should reassure Congress.

One question inherent in any big multilateral action concerns the level at which integration of command of multinational forces would occur. The distinction in U.S. military terminology between command and operational control (OPCON) is useful in this respect. Command applies to such matters as discipline, pay, morale and logistics; most of these (perhaps not logistics) would be carried out at the level of the national military contingents. OPCON is likely to be different. If U.S. troops were involved there would probably have to be, under an overall U.N. commander from some country, a U.S. "component commander" operating with substantial independence. OPCON can be decentralized by confining each member's forces to a specific sector, physically dividing up the ground, as has been done in most U.N. peacekeeping operations.

Some other functions may be even harder to divide than OPCON. Intelligence gathering, for example, will be dominated by states with vast technological capacities for overhead and electronic surveillance. In the gulf operation other coalition members presumably accepted U.S. control of intelligence, but if there were substantial Soviet participation the Soviets would likely not accept it. Secure communications would be required among participating forces in the field, either through sharing encryption (politically very sensitive) or cumbersome procedures for transmission and delivery. It is likely that some states will be unable or unwilling to provide adequate logistical support for their troops, and that those with the motivation and ability to do so will have to provide for others. Some U.N. "headquarters" personnel and facilities will be required for these functions, probably drawing on the experience and capabilities of the secretary general's staff.

The problem of financing such military actions demands careful attention. The history of financing past peacekeeping efforts by voluntary contribution is, to say the least, not encouraging. The gulf operation was heavily dependent on the willingness and ability of the most deeply involved states—the United States, Saudi Arabia and Kuwait—to pay most of the immediate costs, and in turn their willingness depended upon their ability to control the means and ends of military operations. A future operation that less directly engaged the interests of such states would have to rely on broader support, probably through an assessment of all member governments. Reasonably complete and prompt payment of those assessments would have to be assured.

Such problems may be equally severe for the peacetime maintenance of standing earmarked forces. Unless any additional costs incurred can be covered by the United Nations, Third World states may be unable to participate. Certain central (non-state-specific) services, such as administration, intelligence, command and control, perhaps logistics and trans-port, must be prepared and institutionalized in advance. Provision in the regular budget of the United Nations might cover such ongoing costs of multilateral readiness, with special assessments made to cover the cost of any enforcement actions undertaken.

VI

The credibility of U.N. action to repel aggression and restore international peace and security, as foreseen in the U.N. Charter, has been profoundly affected by the response to the Iraqi invasion of Kuwait. The Security Council showed itself capable of taking decisive action. Its ability to impose comprehensive sanctions and see them enforced was clearly demonstrated, even though the ultimate effectiveness of the sanctions was not adequately tested. By authorizing the use of military force the council gained compliance with all of its relevant resolutions. The Security Council has shown that it has the capacity to initiate collective measures essential for the maintenance of peace in a new world order.

This development can enhance the United Nations' ability not just to restore the status quo as it existed prior to a breach of the peace, but also to change the parameters of the global order to something more favorable than existed under the prior status quo. In this it may even go beyond the vision of the U.N. founders. Furthermore knowledge that the United Nations has such a capability will also enhance its ability to deter breaches of the peace, and so make actual enforcement or later peacekeeping less necessary. Collective security may suppress incipient acts of aggression as well as defeat or punish those that do emerge.

Nevertheless it should not be assumed that any U.N. role in enforcement during the 1990s will be automatic. It will require a deliberate political judgment that can only be made by members of the Security Council acting collectively, and will depend on some continuing commonality of interests among the five permanent members of the council—the United States and the Soviet Union in particular. The effectiveness of the United Nations in dealing with international security problems, whether by enforcement measures, peacekeeping or mediation, will always be sensitive to the nature of relations between these two superpowers. A United Nations whose credibility in dealing with aggression and threats to peace has been restored, however, can serve to moderate any revival of tension between them by lessening the need for, or likelihood of, unilateral intervention in regional crises.

The manner in which the gulf military action was executed by the United States and its coalition partners will likely limit the willingness of council members to follow a similar procedure in the future—a procedure that leaves council members little control over the course of military operations and over the conclusion of hostilities. Neither the United States nor any other country will be ready to act under all circumstances to preserve or restore peace. Nor will other states always be ready to endorse unilateral actions. Some states may not wish to contribute to an operation, and the council may not always wish to depend disproportionately on a particular state's contribution.

Some U.N. capacity to carry out these functions on a permanent basis will therefore be desirable. For this reason, as well as others previously mentioned, the Security Council should be able to mobilize a force to serve under U.N. command for enforcement purposes. That capacity may be virtually indispensable in an emergent world order. The chance to achieve it should not be missed.

QUESTIONS

1. What are some disadvantages to a collective security force controlled under the auspices of the U.N. Security Council?

2. What were the primary differences between U.N. actions in the Korean Conflict and in the Persian Gulf War?

16. Interdependence and Power

Joseph S. Nye Jr.

In this excerpt, Joseph S. Nye Jr. presents the primary concepts of interdependence using the oil crisis of 1973 as a case in point. He suggests that interdependence is not simply cooperation among nations, but a relationship between states characterized by cooperation, dependence, and interaction in a number of different areas. States, as well as other transnational actors, are connected in a global network of cooperation and interdependence. This selection is from *Understanding International Conflicts: An Introduction to Theory* (1993).

Joseph S. Nye Jr. is a professor of international politics at Harvard University. His other works include *Nuclear Ethics* (1986) and *Understanding International Conflict* (1993).

Economic interdependence increased rapidly in the postwar period, but it was the 1973 oil crisis that brought economic conflict to center stage. Some people think that interdependence means peace and cooperation, but unfortunately it is not that simple. Conflict goes on, even in a world of interdependence. Because the coalitions are more complex and different forms of power are used, the conflicts are often like playing chess on several boards at the same time. Conflicts in the late twentieth century involve *both* guns and butter. China's Chairman Mao Tse-tung said that power grows out of the barrel of a gun. After the oil crisis of 1973, the world was reminded that power can also grow out of a barrel of oil. Some realists overreacted to the oil crisis of 1973, likening it to events in 1914 and 1939. Hans Morgenthau, a great thinker in the realist tradition, said that 1973 was historically unprecedented because it divorced military power from economic power based on raw materials.

The 1973 oil crisis presents an important question: Why did the most powerful countries in the world allow the transfer of hundreds of billions of dollars to weak states and not use force? Such an event would have been unthinkable in the eighteenth century. Or, in the nineteenth century, the rich countries would have used their superior military power,

colonized the troublesome era, and settled the situation on their own terms. What changed in 1973? It was neither a new era of power based on raw materials and cartels nor a total divorce of military and economic power. Rather, all these factors became intertwined in complex relationships. To understand the changes in world politics, we must consider how interdependence can be a source of power.

THE CONCEPT OF INTERDEPENDENCE

Interdependence is a fuzzy term used in a variety of conflicting ways like other political words such as nationalism or imperialism. Statesmen and analysts have different motives when they use political words. The statesman wants as many people marching behind his or her banner as possible. Political leaders blur meanings and try to create a connotation of a common good: "We are all in the same boat together, therefore we must cooperate, therefore follow me." The analyst, on the other hand, makes distinctions to understand the world better. She distinguishes questions of good and bad from more and less. The analyst may point out the boat we are all in may be heading for one person's port but not another's, or that one person is doing all the rowing while another steers or has a free ride. In other words, interdependence can be used both ideologically as well as analytically, and we should be aware of such different usage. As a political verb, interdependence is conjugated "I depend; you depend; we depend; they rule."

As an analytical word, interdependence refers to situations in which actors or events in different parts of a system affect each other. Simply put, interdependence means mutual dependence. Such a situation is neither good nor bad in itself, and there can be more or less of it. In personal relations, interdependence is summed up by the marriage vow in which each partner is interdependent with another "for richer, for poorer, for better, or for worse." And interdependence among nations sometimes means richer, sometimes poorer, sometimes for better, sometimes for worse. In the eighteenth century, Jean-Jacques Rousseau pointed out that along with interdependence comes friction and conflict. His "solution" was isolation and separation. But this is seldom possible in the modern world. When countries try isolation, like Albania or Myanmar (formerly Burma), it comes at enormous economic cost. It is not easy for nations to divorce the rest of the world.

Sources of Interdependence

Four distinctions illuminate the dimensions of interdependence: its sources, benefits, relative costs, and symmetry. Interdependence can originate in physical (i.e., in nature) or social (economic, political, or perceptual) phenomena. Both are usually present at the same time. The distinction helps to make clear the

degree of choice in situations of reciprocal or mutual dependence.

Military interdependence is the mutual dependence that arises from military competition. There is a physical aspect in the weaponry, especially dramatic since the development of nuclear weapons and the resulting possibility of mutually assured destruction. However, there is also an important element of perception involved in interdependence, and a change in perception or policy can reduce the intensity of the military interdependence. Americans lost little sleep over the existence of British or French nuclear weapons because there was no perception that those weapons would ever land on American soil. Similarly, Westerners slept a bit easier in the late 1980s after Gorbachev announced his "new thinking" in Soviet foreign policy. It was not so much the number of Soviet weapons that made the difference, but the change in the perception of Soviet hostility or intent.

Generally speaking, economic interdependence is similar to military interdependence, in that it is the stuff of traditional international politics and has a high degree of social, especially perceptual, origin. Economic interdependence involves policy choices about values and costs. For example, in the early 1970s, there was concern the world's population was outstripping global food supplies. Many countries were buying American grain, which in turn drove up the price of food in American supermarkets. A loaf of bread cost more in the United States because the Indian monsoons failed and because the Soviet Union had mishandled its harvest. In 1973, the United States, in an effort to prevent price rises at home, decided to stop exporting soybeans to Japan. As a result, Japan invested in soybean production in Brazil. A few years later, when supply and demand were better equilibrated, U.S. farmers greatly regretted that embargo because the Japanese were buying their soybeans from a cheaper source in Brazil. Social choices as well as physical shortages affect economic interdependence in the long run. It is always worth considering the long-term perspective when making short-term choices.

Benefits of Interdependence

The benefits of interdependence are sometimes expressed as zero sum and non-zero sum. In a zero-sum situation, your loss is my gain and vice versa. In a positive-sum situation, we both gain; in a negative-sum situation, we both lose. Dividing a pie is zero sum, baking a larger pie is positive sum, and dropping it on the floor is negative sum. Both zero-sum and non-zero-sum aspects are present in mutual dependence.

Some liberal economists tend to think of interdependence only in terms of joint gain, that is, positive-sum situations in which everyone benefits and everyone is better off. Failure to pay attention to the inequality of benefits and the conflicts that arise over the distribution of relative gains causes such analysts to miss the political aspects of interdependence. It is true that both sides can gain from trade, for example, if Japan and Korea trade textiles and television sets, but how will the gains from trade be divided? Even if Japan and Korea are both better off, is Japan a lot better off and Korea only a little better off, or vice versa? The distribution of benefits—who gets how much of the joint gain—is a zero-sum situation in which one side's gain is the other's loss. The result is that there is almost always some political conflict in economic interdependence. Even when there is a larger pie, people can fight over who gets the biggest slices. Even if interdependent countries enjoy a joint gain, there may be conflict over who gets more or less of the joint gain.

Some political analysts make the mistake of thinking that as the world becomes more interdependent, cooperation will replace competition. Their reason is that interdependence creates joint benefits, and those joint benefits encourage cooperation. But economic interdependence can also be used as a weapon—witness the oil crisis of 1973. Indeed, economic interdependence is more effective than force in some cases because it may have more subtle gradations and fewer collateral costs. And in some circumstances, states are less interested in their absolute gain from interdependence than how the relatively greater gains of their rivals might be used to hurt them.

Even ecological interdependence can be used as a weapon, as it was in 1991 when Iraq set fire to Kuwait's oil fields, and released oil into the Persian Gulf. There can also be conflicts over global ecological issues. For example, if global warming occurs, who will win and who will lose? If the temperature of the earth rises on average two degrees centigrade, Maldive Islanders at sea level or Africans who live at the edge of the Sahara would suffer terribly if the islands were submerged or the desert moved southward. But some Siberians or Canadians might be better off. If so, will Siberians or Canadians pay to slow global warming?

Some analysts believe that traditional world politics was always zero sum. But that is misleading about the past. Traditional international politics could be positive sum, depending on the actors' intentions. It made a difference whether Bismarck or Hitler was in charge of Germany. If one party sought aggrandizement, as Hitler did, then indeed politics was zero sum—one side's gain was another's loss. But if all parties wanted stability, there could be joint gain in the balance of power. Conversely, the new politics of economic interdependence has competitive zero-sum aspects as well as cooperative positive-sum aspects.

In the politics of interdependence, the distinction about what is domestic and what is foreign becomes blurred. For example, the soybean situation mentioned earlier involved the domestic issue of controlling inflation at home, as well as American relations with Japan and Brazil. Or to take another example, after Iran's 1979 revolution curtailed oil production, the American government urged citizens to cut their energy consumption by driving 55 mph and turning down thermostats; was that a domestic or a foreign policy issue? Should the United States allow strip mining of coal if the coal is to be exported? Do those who import that coal pay the additional costs that accompany the destruction of the countryside in West Virginia? Interdependence thoroughly mixes domestic and foreign issues, which gives rise to much more complex coalitions, more intricate patterns of conflict, and a different way of distribution of benefits than in the past.

Interdependence also affects domestic politics in a different way. In 1890, a French politician concerned with relative gains needed a policy of holding Germany back. Today a policy of slowing economic growth in Germany is not good for France. Economic interdependence between France and Germany means that the best predictor of whether France is better off economically is when Germany is growing economically. Now it is in the self-interest of the French politicians that Germany do well economically. The classical balance-of-power theory which predicts that one country will act only to keep the other down lest the other gain preponderance does not fit well. In economic interdependence, states are interested in absolute gains as well as gains relative to other states.

Costs of Interdependence

The costs of interdependence can involve short-run sensitivity or long-term vulnerability. *Sensitivity* refers to the amount and rapidity of the effects of dependence; that is, how quickly does change in one part of the system bring about change in another part? For example, in the 1970s, a rumor about a possible exchange rate change led to $2 billion flooding into Germany in one day. In 1987, the New York stock market crashed suddenly because of foreigners' anxieties about U.S. interest rates and what might happen to the price of bonds and stocks. It all happened very quickly; the market was very sensitive to the withdrawal of foreign funds.

A high level of sensitivity, however, is not the same as a high level of vulnerability. *Vulnerability* refers to the relative costs of changing the structure of a system of interdependence. It is the cost of escaping from the system or of changing the rules of the game. The less vulnerable of two countries is not necessarily the less sensitive, but rather the one that would incur lower costs from altering the situation. During the 1973 oil crisis, the United States depended on imported energy for only about 16 percent of its total energy uses. On the other hand, in 1973, Japan depended about 95 percent on imported energy. The United States was sensitive to the Arab oil boycott insofar as prices shot up in 1973, but it was not as vulnerable as Japan was.

Vulnerability involves degree. When the shah of Iran was overthrown in 1979, Iranian oil production was disrupted at a time when demand was high and markets were already tight. The loss of Iran's oil caused the total amount of oil on the world markets to drop by about 5 percent, but that led to a very large increase in oil prices. Markets were sensitive, and shortages of supply were rapidly transformed into higher prices. But Americans could save 5 percent of their energy use simply by turning down their thermostats and driving 55 mph. It appears that the United States was sensitive but not very vulnerable if it could avoid damage by such simple actions.

Vulnerability, however, depends on more than aggregate measures. It also depends on whether a society is capable of responding quickly to change. For example, the United States was less adept at responding to changes in the oil markets than Japan. Furthermore, private actors, large corporations, and speculators in the market may each look at a market situation and decide to hoard supplies because they think shortages are going to grow worse. Their actions will drive the price even higher, because it will make the shortages greater and put more demand on the market. Thus degrees of vul-

nerability are not quite so simple as they first look.

Vulnerability also depends on whether or not substitutes are available and whether there are diverse sources of supply. In 1970, Lester Brown of the World Watch Institute expressed alarm about the increasing dependence of the United States, and therefore its vulnerability, on imported raw materials. Of 13 basic industrial raw materials, the United States was dependent on imports for nearly 90 percent of aluminum, chromium, manganese, and nickel. By 1985, he predicted the United States would be dependent on imports in 10 of the basic 13. He felt this would lead to a dramatic increase in U.S. vulnerability as well as drastically increasing the strength of the less developed countries that produced those raw materials.

But in the 1980s, raw materials prices went down, not up. What happened to his prediction? In judging vulnerability, Brown failed to consider the alternative sources of raw materials and the diversity of sources of supply that prevented producers from jacking up prices artificially. Moreover, technology develops. Yesterday's waste may become a new resource. Companies now mine discarded tailings because new technology has made it possible to extract copper from ore that was considered depleted years ago. Today's reduced use of copper is also due to the introduction of fiber optic cables made from silicon whose basic origin is sand. Thus projections of U.S. vulnerability to shortages of raw materials went wrong because technology and alternatives were not adequately considered.

Symmetry of Interdependence

Symmetry refers to situations of relatively balanced versus unbalanced de-

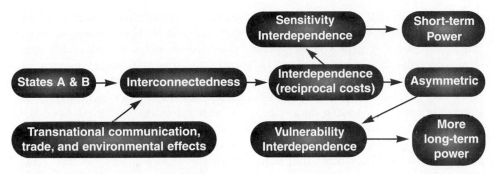

FIGURE 1 *The Dimensions of Interdependance*

pendence. Being less dependent can be a source of power. If two parties are interdependent but one is less dependent than the other, the less dependent party has a source of power as long as both value the interdependent relationship. Manipulating the asymmetries of interdependence can be a source of power in international politics. Analysts who say that interdependence occurs only in situations of equal dependence, define away the most interesting political behavior. Such perfect symmetry is quite rare; so are cases of complete imbalance in which one side is totally dependent and the other is not dependent at all. Asymmetry is at the heart of the politics of interdependence. (See Figure 1.)

Asymmetry often varies according to different issues. In the 1980s, when the United States cut taxes and raised expenditures, it became dependent on imported Japanese capital to balance its federal government budget. Some argued that this gave Japan tremendous power over the United States. But the other side of the coin was that Japan would hurt itself as well as the United States if it stopped lending to the United States. In addition, Japanese investors who already had large stakes in the United States would have found their investments devalued by the damage done to the American economy if Japan suddenly stopped lending to the United States. Japan's economy was a little over half the size of the American economy, and that meant the Japanese needed the American market for their exports more than vice versa, although both needed each other and both benefited from the interdependence.

Moreover, security was often linked to other issues in the U.S.-Japan relationship. After World War II, Japan followed the policy of a trading state and did not develop a large military capability or gain nuclear weapons. It relied on the American security guarantee to balance the power of the Soviet Union and China in the East Asian region. Thus when a dispute seemed to be developing between the United States and Japan over trade in 1990, the Japanese made concessions to prevent weakening the overall security relationship.

When there is asymmetry of interdependence in different issue areas, a state may try to link or unlink issues. If each issue could be thought of as a poker game, and all poker games were played simultaneously, one state might have most of the chips at one table and another state might have most of the chips at another table. Depending on a state's interests and position, it might want to keep the games separate or create linkages between the tables. Therefore, much of the politics of interdependence involves the creation or prevention of linkage. States want to manipulate interdependence in the areas where they are strong and avoid being manipulated in areas where they are relatively weak.

By setting agendas and defining issue areas, international institutions often set the rules for the trade-offs in interdependent relationships. States try to use international institutions to set the rules that affect the transfer of chips among tables. Ironically, international institutions can benefit the weaker players by keeping some of the issues where the poorer states are relatively better endowed separated from the military table where strong states dominate. The danger remains, however, that some players will be strong enough to overturn one or more of the tables. With separate institutions for money, shipping, pollution, and trade, if the militarily strong players are beaten too badly, there is a danger they may try to kick over the other tables. Yet when the United States and Europe were beaten at the oil table in 1973, they did not use their preponderant military force to kick over the oil table because, as we see later, a complex web of linkages held them back.

The largest state does not always win in the manipulation of economic interdependence. If a smaller or weaker state has a greater concern about an issue, it may do quite well. For instance, because the United States accounts for nearly three-quarters of Canada's foreign trade while Canada accounts for about one-quarter of the U.S. foreign trade, Canada is more dependent on the United States than vice versa. Nonetheless, Canada often prevailed in a number of disputes with the United States because Canada was willing to threaten retaliatory actions, such as tariffs and restrictions, that deterred the United States. The Canadians would have suffered much more than the United States if their actions had led to a full dispute, but Canada felt it was better to risk occasional retaliation than to agree to rules that would *always* make them lose. Deterrence via manipulation of economic interdependence is somewhat like nuclear deterrence, in that it rests on a capability for effective damage and credible intentions. Small states can often use their greater intensity and greater credibility to overcome their relative vulnerability in asymmetrical interdependence.

Leadership in the World Economy

By and large, the rules of international economy are set by the largest states. In the nineteenth century, Great Britain was the strongest of the major world economies. In the monetary area, the Bank of England adhered to the gold standard, which set a stable framework for world money. Britain also enforced freedom of the seas for navigation and commerce, and provided a large open market for world trade until 1932. After World War I, Britain was severely weakened by its fight against the kaiser's Germany. The United States became the world's largest economy, but it turned away from international affairs. The largest player in the world economy behaved as if it could still take a free ride rather than provide the leadership its size implied. Some economists believe that the Great Depression of the 1930s was aggravated by bad monetary policy and lack of American leadership. Britain was too weak to maintain an open international economy and the United States was not living up to its new responsibilities.

After World War II, the lessons of the 1930s were on the minds of American statesmen and they set up institutions to maintain an open, international economy. The International Monetary Fund (IMF) lends money, usually to developing countries, to help when they have difficulties with their balance of payments or with paying interest on their debts. The IMF generally conditions its loans on the recipient country reforming its economic policies, for example reducing budget deficits and price subsidies. The International Bank for Reconstruction and Development (the World Bank) lends money to poorer countries for development projects. (There are also regional development banks for Asia, Latin America, Africa, and Eastern Europe.) The General Agreement on Tariffs and Trade (GATT) established rules for liberal trade and has served as the locus for a series of rounds of multilateral negotiations that have lowered trade barriers. The Organization for Economic Cooperation and Development (OECD) serves as a forum for two dozen of the most developed countries to coordinate their international economic policies. Since the mid-1970s, the leaders of the seven largest economies that account for two-thirds of world production have met at annual summit conferences (the Group of Seven) to discuss conditions of the world economy. These institutions helped reinforce government policies that allow rapid growth of private transnational interactions. The result has been a rapid increase in economic interdependence. In most of the period after 1945, trade grew between 3 and 9 percent a year, faster even than the growth of world product. International trade, which represented 4 percent of the U.S. GNP in 1950, tripled to 13 percent of the U.S. GNP by 1990. Large multinational corporations with global strategies became more significant as international investments increased by nearly 10 percent per year.

Nonetheless, there are still problems in managing a transnational economy in a world of separate states. In the 1980s, the United States became a net debtor when it refused to tax itself to pay its bills at home and instead borrowed money from abroad. Some analysts believed that this was setting the scene for a repeat of the 1930s, that the United States would experience decline as Britain did, while Japan becomes the new world economic superpower. They feared the Japanese in the 1990s would have the same free-rider mentality that the Americans had in the 1930s, unwilling to open their markets or maintain international stability. But this need not be the case. The United States need not decline and turn inward. Much will depend on what happens in the relationships of the large economies and the willingness of their governments to cooperate to maintain stability in the international economic system. In any case, the international political and economic system is more complicated and complex. There will be more sectors, more states, more issues, and more private

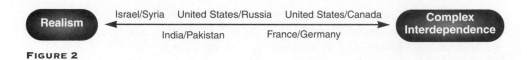

FIGURE 2

actors involved in the complexity of interdependent relationships.

Realism and Complex Interdependence

What would the world look like if the three key assumptions of realism were reversed? These assumptions are that states are the only significant actors, military force is the dominant instrument, and security is the dominant goal. Reversed, we postulate a different world politics: (1) states are not the only significant actors— transnational actors working across state boundaries are also major actors; (2) force is not the only significant instrument—economic manipulation and the use of international institutions is the dominant instrument; (3) security is not the dominant goal—welfare is the dominant goal. We can label this antirealist world *complex interdependence.* Social scientists call complex interdependence an "ideal type." It is an imaginary concept that does not exist in the real world, but neither does realism perfectly fit the real world. Complex interdependence is a thought experiment that allows us to imagine a different type of world politics.

Both realism and complex interdependence are simple models or ideal types. The real world lies somewhere between the two. We can ask where certain country relationships fit on a spectrum between realism and complex interdependence. The Middle East is closer to the realist end of the spectrum, but relations between the United States and Canada or relations between France and Germany today come much closer to the complex interdependence end of the spectrum. Different politics and different forms of the struggle for power occur depending on where on the spectrum a particular relationship between a set of countries is located. In fact, countries can change their position on the spectrum. In the Cold War the U.S.-Soviet relationship was clearly near the realist end of the spectrum, but with Gorbachev's changes the Soviet-U.S. relationship moved closer to the center between realism and complex interdependence. (See Figure 2.)

QUESTIONS

1. Provide a detailed description of the benefits and costs of interdependence as defined by Nye.

2. Explain the role of the multinational corporation in Nye's thesis, and compare this to Robert Tucker's view in "Realism and the New Consensus."

17.   Cooperation and International Regimes

Robert O. Keohane

In this selection, Robert Keohane examines the roles of harmony, cooperation, and discord in the international system and assesses their individual effects on the relationships of nation-states. In this selection, he argues that "cooperation is possible and that it is facilitated by international regimes." Keohane uses the example of trade relations to help explain the effect of interdependence, and how nations either cooperate or an atmosphere of discord is perpetuated. This selection is from his book *After Hegemony: Cooperation and Discord in the World Political Economy* (1984).

Robert Keohane is a professor of international relations at Harvard University. He has also written *Power and Interdependence: World Politics in Transition*.

Hegemonic leadership can help to create a pattern of order. Cooperation is not antithetical to hegemony; on the contrary, hegemony depends on a certain kind of asymmetrical cooperation, which successful hegemons support and maintain. . . . Contemporary international economic regimes were constructed under the aegis of the United States after World War II. In accounting for the creation of international regimes, hegemony often plays an important role, even a crucial one.

Yet the relevance of hegemonic cooperation for the future is questionable. . . . The United States is less preponderant in material resources now than it was in the 1950s and early 1960s. Equally important, the United States is less willing than formerly to define its interests in terms complementary to those of Europe and Japan. The Europeans, in particular, are less inclined to defer to American initiatives, nor do they believe so strongly that they must do so in order to obtain essential military protection against the Soviet Union. Thus the sub-

jective elements of American hegemony have been eroded as much as the tangible power resources upon which hegemonic systems rest. But neither the Europeans nor the Japanese are likely to have the capacity to become hegemonic powers themselves in the foreseeable future.[1]

This prospect raises the issue of cooperation "after hegemony." . . . It also leads back to a crucial tension between economics and politics: international coordination of policy seems highly beneficial in an interdependent world economy, but cooperation in world politics is particularly difficult. One way to relax this tension would be to deny the premise that international economic policy coordination is valuable by assuming that international markets will automatically yield optimal results (Corden, 1981). The decisive objection to this argument is that, in the absence of cooperation, governments will interfere in markets unilaterally in pursuit of what they regard as their own interests, whatever liberal economists may say. They will intervene in foreign exchange markets, impose various restrictions on imports, subsidize favored domestic industries, and set prices for commodities such as petroleum (Strange, 1979). Even if one accepted cooperation to maintain free markets, but no other form of policy coordination, the further objection could be raised that economic market failure would be likely to occur (Cooper, 1983, pp. 45-46). Suboptimal outcomes of transactions could result, for a variety of reasons including problems of collective action. It would take an ideological leap of faith to believe that free markets lead necessarily to optimal results.

Rejecting the illusion that cooperation is never valuable in the world political economy, we have to cope with the fact that it is very difficult to organize. One recourse would be to lapse into fatalism—acceptance of destructive economic conflict as a result of political fragmentation. Although this is a logically tenable position for those who believe in the theory of hegemonic stability, even its most powerful theoretical advocate shies away from its bleak normative implications (Gilpin, 1981). A fatalistic view is not taken here. Without ignoring the difficulties that beset attempts to coordinate policy in the absence of hegemony, this [writer] contends that nonhegemonic cooperation is possible, and that it can be facilitated by international regimes.

In making this argument, I will draw a distinction between the creation of international regimes and their maintenance. . . . When shared interests are sufficiently important and other key conditions are met, cooperation can emerge and regimes can be created without hegemony. Yet this does not imply that regimes can be created easily, much less that contemporary international economic regimes actually came about in this way. . . . I argue that international regimes are easier to maintain than to create, and that recognition of this fact is crucial to understanding why they are valued by governments. Regimes may be maintained, and may continue to foster cooperation, even under conditions that would not be sufficiently benign to bring about their creation. Cooperation is possible after hegemony not only because shared interests can lead to the creation of regimes, but also because the conditions for maintaining existing international regimes are less demanding than those required for creating them. Although hegemony helps to explain the creation of contemporary international regimes, the decline of hegemony does not necessarily lead symmetrically to their decay.

This chapter analyzes the meaning of two key terms: "cooperation" and "international regimes." It distinguishes cooperation from harmony as well as from discord, and it argues for the value of the concept of international regimes as a way of understanding both cooperation and discord. Together the concepts of cooperation and international regimes help us clarify what we want to explain: how do patterns of rule-guided policy coordination emerge, maintain themselves, and decay in world politics?

HARMONY, COOPERATION, AND DISCORD

Cooperation must be distinguished from harmony. Harmony refers to a situation in which actors' policies (pursued in their own self-interest without regard for others) *automatically* facilitate the attainment of others' goals. The classic example of harmony is the hypothetical competitive-market world of the classical economists, in which the Invisible Hand ensures that the pursuit of self-interest by each contributes to the interest of all. In this idealized, unreal world, no one's actions damage anyone else; there are no "negative externalities," in the economists' jargon. Where harmony reigns, cooperation is unnecessary. It may even be injurious, if it means that certain individuals conspire to exploit others. Adam Smith, for one, was very critical of guilds and other conspiracies against freedom of trade (1776/1976). Cooperation and harmony are by no means identical and ought not to be confused with one another.

Cooperation requires that the actions of separate individuals or organizations—which are not in pre-existent harmony—be brought into conformity with one another through a process of negotiation, which is often referred to as "policy coordination." Charles E. Lindblom has defined policy coordination as follows (1965, p. 227):

> A set of decisions is coordinated if adjustments have been made in them, such that the adverse consequences of any one decision for other decisions are to a degree and in some frequency avoided, reduced, or counterbalanced or overweighed.

Cooperation occurs when actors adjust their behavior to the actual or anticipated preferences of others, through a process of policy coordination. To summarize more formally, *intergovernmental cooperation takes place when the policies actually followed by one government are regarded by its partners as facilitating realization of their own objectives, as the result of a process of policy coordination.*

With this definition in mind, we can differentiate among cooperation, har-

mony, and discord, as illustrated by Figure 1. First, we ask whether actors' policies automatically facilitate the attainment of others' goals. If so, there is harmony: no adjustments need to take place. Yet harmony is rare in world politics. Rousseau sought to account for this rarity when he declared that even two countries guided by the General Will in their internal affairs would come into conflict if they had extensive contact with one another, since the General Will of each would not be general for both. Each would have a partial, self-interested perspective on their mutual interactions. Even for Adam Smith, efforts to ensure state security took precedence over measures to increase national prosperity. In defending the Navigation Acts, Smith declared: "As defence is of much more importance than opulence, the act of navigation is, perhaps, the wisest of all the commercial regulations of England" (1776/1976, p. 487). Waltz summarizes the point by saying that "in anarchy there is no automatic harmony" (1959, p. 182).

Yet this insight tells us nothing definitive about the prospects for cooperation. For this we need to ask a further question about situations in which harmony does not exist. Are attempts made by actors (governmental or nongovernmental) to adjust their policies to each others' objectives? If no such attempts are made, the result is discord: a situation in which governments regard each others' policies as hindering the attainment of their goals, and hold each other responsible for these constraints.

Discord often leads to efforts to induce others to change their policies; when these attempts meet resistance, policy conflict results. Insofar as these attempts at policy adjustment succeed in making policies more compatible,

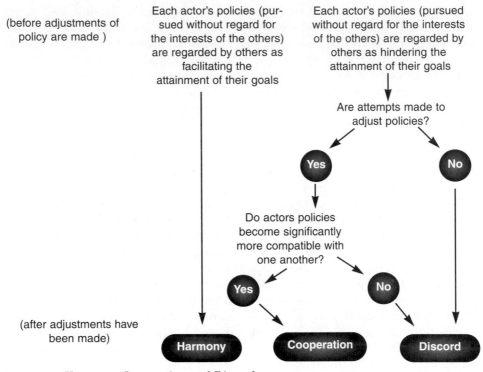

FIGURE 1 *Harmony, Cooperation and Discord*

however, cooperation ensues. The policy coordination that leads to cooperation need not involve bargaining or negotiation at all. What Lindblom calls "adaptive" as opposed to "manipulative" adjustment can take place: one country may shift its policy in the direction of another's preferences without regard for the effect of its action on the other state, defer to the other country, or partially shift its policy in order to avoid adverse consequences for its partner. Or nonbargained manipulation—such as one actor confronting another with a *fait accompli*—may occur (Lindblom, 1965, pp. 33–34 and ch. 4). Frequently, of course, negotiation and bargaining indeed take place, often accompanied by other ac-

tions that are designed to induce others to adjust their policies to one's own. Each government pursues what it perceives as its self-interest, but looks for bargains that can benefit all parties to the deal, though not necessarily equally.

Harmony and cooperation are not usually distinguished from one another so clearly. Yet, in the study of world politics, they should be. Harmony is apolitical. No communication is necessary, and no influence need be exercised. Cooperation, by contrast, is highly political: somehow, patterns of behavior must be altered. This change may be accomplished through negative as well as positive inducements. Indeed, studies of international crises, as well as game-theoretic experiments and simulations, have shown that under a variety of conditions strategies that involve threats and punishments as well as promises and rewards are more effective in attaining cooperative outcomes than those that rely entirely on persuasion and the force of good example (Axelrod, 1981, 1984; Lebow, 1981; Snyder and Diesing, 1977).

Cooperation therefore does not imply an absence of conflict. On the contrary, it is typically mixed with conflict and reflects partially successful efforts to overcome conflict, real or potential. Cooperation takes place only in situations in which actors perceive that their policies are actually or potentially in conflict, not where there is harmony. Cooperation should not be viewed as the absence of conflict, but rather as a reaction to conflict or potential conflict. Without the specter of conflict, there is no need to cooperate.

The example of trade relations among friendly countries in a liberal international political economy may help to illustrate this crucial point. A naive observer, trained only to appreciate the overall welfare benefits of trade, might assume that trade relations would be harmonious: consumers in importing countries benefit from cheap foreign goods and increased competition, and producers can increasingly take advantage of the division of labor as their export markets expand. But harmony does not normally ensue. Discord on trade issues may prevail because governments do not even seek to reduce the adverse consequences of their own policies for others, but rather strive in certain respects to increase the severity of those effects. Mercantilist governments have sought in the twentieth century as well as the seventeenth to manipulate foreign trade, in conjunction with warfare, to damage each other economically and to gain productive resources themselves (Wilson, 1957; Hirschman, 1945/1980). Governments may desire "positional goods," such as high status (Hirsch, 1976), and may therefore resist even mutually beneficial cooperation if it helps others more than themselves. Yet even when neither power nor positional motivations are present, and when all participants would benefit in the aggregate from liberal trade, discord tends to predominate over harmony as the initial result of independent governmental action.

This occurs even under otherwise benign conditions because some groups or industries are forced to incur adjustment costs as changes in comparative advantage take place. Governments often respond to the ensuing demands for protection by attempting, more or less effectively, to cushion the burdens of adjustment for groups and industries that are politically influential at home. Yet unilateral measures to this effect almost always impose adjustment costs abroad, and discord continually threatens. Governments enter into international negotiations in order to reduce the conflict that would otherwise result. Even substantial potential common benefits do not create harmony when state power can be exercised on behalf of certain interests and against others. In world politics, harmony tends to vanish: attainment of the gains from pursuing complementary policies depends on cooperation.

Observers of world politics who take power and conflict seriously should be attracted to this way of defining cooperation, since my definition does not relegate cooperation to the mythological world of relations among equals in power. Hegemonic cooperation is not a contradiction in terms. Defining cooperation in contrast to harmony should, I hope, lead readers with a Realist orientation to take cooperation in world politics seriously rather than to dismiss it out of hand. To Marxists who also believe in hegemonic power theories, however, even this definition of cooperation may not seem to make it relevant to the contemporary world political economy. From this perspective, mutual policy adjustments cannot possibly resolve the contradictions besetting the system because they are attributable to capitalism rather than to problems of coordination among egoistic actors lacking common government. Attempts to resolve these contradictions through international cooperation will merely transfer issues to a deeper and even more intractable level. Thus it is not surprising that Marxian analyses of the international political economy have, with few exceptions, avoided sustained examinations of the conditions under which cooperation among major capitalist countries can take place. Marxists see it as more important to expose relationships of exploitation and conflict between major capitalist powers on the one hand and the masses of people in the periphery of world capitalism on the other. And, from a Leninist standpoint, to examine the conditions for international cooperation without first analyzing the contradictions of capitalism, and recognizing the irreconcilability of conflicts among capitalist countries, is a bourgeois error.

This is less an argument than a statement of faith. Since sustained international coordination of macroeconomic policies has never been tried, the statement that it would merely worsen the contradictions facing the system is speculative. In view of the lack of evidence for it, such a claim could even be considered rash. Indeed, one of the most perceptive Marxian writers of recent years, Stephen Hymer (1972), recognized explicitly that capitalists face problems of collective action and argued that they were seeking, with at least temporary prospects of success, to overcome them. As he recognized, any success in internationalizing capital could pose grave threats to socialist aspirations and, at the very least, would shift contradictions to new points of tension. Thus even were we to agree that the fundamental issue is posed by the contradictions of capitalism rather than the tensions inherent in a state system, it would be worthwhile to study the conditions under which cooperation is likely to occur.

INTERNATIONAL REGIMES AND COOPERATION

One way to study cooperation and discord would be to focus on particular actions as the units of analysis. This would require the systematic compilation of a data set composed of acts that could be regarded as comparable and coded according to the degree of cooperation that they reflect. Such a strategy has some attractive features. The problem with it, however, is that instances of cooperation and discord could all too easily be isolated from the context of beliefs and behavior within which they are embedded. This [writer] does not view cooperation atomistically as a set of discrete, isolated acts, but rather seeks to understand patterns of cooperation in the world political economy. Accordingly, we need to examine actors' expectations about future patterns of interaction, their assumptions about the proper nature of economic arrangements, and the kinds of political activities they regard as legitimate. That is, we need to analyze cooperation within the context of international institutions, broadly defined . . . in terms of practices and expectations. Each act of cooperation or discord affects the beliefs, rules, and practices that form the context for future actions. Each act must therefore be interpreted as embedded within a chain of such acts and their successive cognitive and institutional residues.

This argument parallels Clifford Geertz's discussion of how anthropologists should use the concept of culture to interpret the societies they investigate. Geertz sees culture as the "webs of significance" that people have created for themselves. On their surface, they are enigmatical; the observer has to interpret them so that they make sense. Culture, for Geertz, "is a context, something within which [social events] can be intelligibly described" (1973, p. 14). It makes little sense to describe naturalistically what goes on at a Balinese cock-fight unless one understands the meaning of the event for Balinese culture. There is not a world culture in the fullest sense, but even in world politics, human beings spin webs of significance. They develop implicit standards for behavior, some of which emphasize the principle of sovereignty and legitimize the pursuit of self-interest, while others rely on quite different principles. Any act of cooperation or apparent cooperation needs to be interpreted within the context of related actions, and of prevailing expectations and shared beliefs, before its meaning can be properly understood. Fragments of political behavior become comprehensible when viewed as part of a larger mosaic.

The concept of international regime not only enables us to describe patterns of cooperation; it also helps to account for both cooperation and discord. Although regimes themselves depend on conditions that are conducive to interstate agreements, they may also facilitate further efforts to coordinate policies. . . . To understand international cooperation, it is necessary to comprehend how institutions and rules not only reflect, but also affect, the facts of world politics.

Defining and Identifying Regimes

When John Ruggie introduced the concept of international regimes into the international politics literature in 1975, he defined a regime as "a set of mutual expectations, rules and regulations, plans, organizational energies and financial commitments, which have been accepted by a group of states" (p. 570). More recently, a collective definition, worked out at a conference on the subject, defined international regimes as "sets of implicit or explicit principles, norms, rules and decision-making procedures around which actors' expectations converge in a given area of international relations. Principles are beliefs of fact, causation, and rectitude. Norms are standards of behavior defined in terms of rights and obligations. Rules are specific prescriptions or proscriptions for action. Decision-making procedures are prevailing practices for making and implementing collective choice" (Krasner, 1983, p. 2).

This definition provides a useful starting-point for analysis, since it begins with the general conception of regimes as social institutions and explicates it further. The concept of norms, however, is ambiguous. It is important that we understand norms in this definition simply as standards of behavior defined in terms of rights and obligations. Another usage would distinguish norms from rules and principles by stipulating that participants in a social system regard norms, but not rules and principles, as morally binding regardless of considerations of narrowly defined self-interest. But to include norms, thus defined, in a definition of necessary regime characteristics would be to make the conception of regimes based strictly on self-interest a contradiction in terms. Since this [writer] regards regimes as largely based on self-interest, I will maintain a definition of norms simply as standards of behavior, whether adopted on grounds of self-interest or otherwise. Only [later] will the possibility again be taken seriously that some regimes may contain norms and principles justified on the basis of values extending beyond self-interest, and regarded as obligatory on moral grounds by governments.

The principles of regimes define, in general, the purposes that their members are expected to pursue. For instance, the principles of the postwar trade and monetary regimes have emphasized the value of open, nondiscriminatory patterns of international economic transactions; the fundamental principle of the nonproliferation regime is that the spread of nuclear weapons is dangerous. Norms contain somewhat clearer injunctions to members about legitimate and illegitimate behavior, still defining responsibilities and obligations in relatively general terms. For instance, the norms of the General Agreement on Tariffs and Trade (GATT) do not require that members resort to free trade immediately, but incorporate injunctions to members to practice non-discrimination and reciprocity and to move toward increased liberalization. Fundamental to the nonproliferation regime is the norm that members of the regime should not act in ways that facilitate nuclear proliferation.

The rules of a regime are difficult to distinguish from its norms; at the margin, they merge into one another. Rules are, however, more specific: they indicate in more detail the specific rights and obligations of members. Rules can be altered more easily than principles or norms, since there may be more than one set of rules that can attain a given set of purposes. Finally, at the same level of specificity as rules, but referring to procedures rather than substances, the decisionmaking procedures of regimes provide ways of implementing their principles and altering their rules.

An example from the field of international monetary relations may be helpful. The most important principle of the international balance-of-payments regime since the end of World War II has been that of liberalization of trade and payments. A key norm of the regime has been the injunction to states not to manipulate their exchange rates unilaterally for national advantage. Between 1958 and 1971 this norm was realized through pegged exchange rates and procedures for consultation in the event of change, supplemented with a variety of devices to help governments avoid exchange-rate changes through a combination of borrowing and internal adjustment. After 1973 governments have subscribed to the same norm, although it has been implemented more informally and probably less effectively under a system of floating exchange rates. Ruggie (1983b) has argued that the abstract principle of liberalization, subject to constraints imposed by the acceptance of the welfare state, has been maintained throughout the postwar period: "embedded liberalism" continues, reflecting a fundamental element of continuity in the international balance-of-payments regime. The norm of nonmanipulation has also been maintained, even though the specific rules of the 1958–71 system having to do with adjustment have been swept away.

The concept of international regime is complex because it is defined in terms of four distinct components: principles, norms, rules, and decisionmaking procedures. It is tempting to select one of these levels of specificity—particularly, principles and norms or rules and procedures—as *the* defining characteristic of regimes (Krasner, 1983; Ruggie, 1983b). Such an approach, however, creates a false dichotomy between principles on the one hand and rules and procedures on the other. As we have noted, at the margin norms and rules cannot be sharply distinguished from each other. It is difficult if not impossible to tell the difference between an "implicit rule" of broad significance and a well-understood, relatively specific operating principle. Both rules and principles may affect expectations and even values. In a strong international regime, the linkages between principles and rules are likely to be tight. Indeed, it is precisely the linkages among principles, norms, and rules that give regimes their legitimacy. Since rules, norms, and principles are so closely intertwined, judgments about whether changes in rules constitute changes *of* regime or merely changes *within* regimes necessarily contain arbitrary elements.

Principles, norms, rules, and procedures all contain injunctions about behavior: they prescribe certain actions and proscribe others. They imply obligations, even though these obligations are not enforceable through a hierarchical legal system. It clarifies the definition of regime, therefore, to think of it in terms of injunctions of greater or lesser specificity. Some are far-reaching and extremely important. They may change only rarely. At the other extreme, injunctions may be merely technical, matters of convenience that can be altered without great political or economic impact. In-between are injunctions that are both specific enough that violations of them are in principle identifiable and that changes in them can be observed, and sufficiently significant that changes in them make a difference for the behavior of actors and the nature of the international political economy. It is these intermediate injunctions—politically consequential but specific enough that violations and changes can be identified—that I take as the essence of international regimes.[2]

A brief examination of international oil regimes, and their injunctions, may help us clarify this point. The pre-1939 international oil regime was dominated by a small number of international firms and contained explicit injunctions about where and under what conditions companies could produce oil, and where and how they should market it. The rules of the Red Line and Achnacarry or "As-Is" agreements of 1928 reflected an "anticompetitive ethos": that is, the basic principle that competition was destructive to the system and the norm that firms should not engage in it (Turner, 1978, p. 30). This principle and this norm both persisted after World War II, although an intergovernmental regime with explicit rules was not established, owing to the failure of the Anglo-American Petroleum Agreement. . . . Injunctions against price-cutting were reflected more in the practices of companies than in formal rules.

Yet expectations and practices of major actors were strongly affected by these injunctions, and in this sense the criteria for a regime—albeit a weak one—were met. As governments of producing countries became more assertive, however, and as formerly domestic independent companies entered international markets, these arrangements collapsed; after the mid-to-late 1960s, there was no regime for the issue-area as a whole, since no injunctions could be said to be accepted as obligatory by all influential actors. Rather, there was a "tug of war" (Hirschman, 1981) in which all sides resorted to self-help. The Organization of Petroleum Exporting Countries (OPEC) sought to create a producers' regime based on rules for prorationing oil production, and consumers established an emergency oil-sharing system in the new International Energy Agency to counteract the threat of selective embargoes.

If we were to have paid attention only to the principle of avoiding competition, we would have seen continuity: whatever the dominant actors, they have always sought to cartelize the industry one way or another. But to do so would be to miss the main point, which is that momentous changes have occurred. At the other extreme, we could have fixed our attention on very specific particular arrangements, such as the various joint ventures of the 1950s and 1960s or the specific provisions for controlling output tried by OPEC after 1973, in which case we would have observed a pattern of continual flux. The significance of the most important events—the demise of old cartel arrangements, the undermining of the international majors' positions in the 1960s, and the rise of producing governments to a position of influence in the 1970s—could have been missed. Only by focusing on the intermediate level of rel-

atively specific but politically consequential injunctions, whether we call them rules, norms, or principles, does the concept of regime help us identify major changes that require explanation.

As our examples of money and oil suggest, we regard the scope of international regimes as corresponding, in general, to the boundaries of issue-areas, since governments establish regimes to deal with problems that they regard as so closely linked that they should be dealt with together. Issue-areas are best defined as sets of issues that are in fact dealt with in common negotiations and by the same, or closely coordinated, bureaucracies, as opposed to issues that are dealt with separately and in uncoordinated fashion. Since issue-areas depend on actors' perceptions and behavior rather than on inherent qualities of the subject-matters, their boundaries change gradually over time. Fifty years ago, for instance, there was no oceans issue-area, since particular questions now grouped under that heading were dealt with separately; but there was an international monetary issue-area even then (Keohane and Nye, 1977, ch. 4). Twenty years ago trade in cotton textiles had an international regime of its own—the Long-Term Agreement on Cotton Textiles—and was treated separately from trade in synthetic fibers (Aggarwal, 1981). Issue-areas are defined and redefined by changing patterns of human intervention; so are international regimes.

Self-Help and International Regimes

The injunctions of international regimes rarely affect economic transactions directly: state institutions, rather than international organizations, impose tariffs and quotas, intervene in foreign exchange markets, and manipulate oil prices through taxes and subsidies. If we think about the impact of the principles, norms, rules, and decision-making procedures of regimes, it becomes clear that insofar as they have any effect at all, it must be exerted on national controls, and especially on the specific interstate agreements that affect the exercise of national controls (Aggarwal, 1981). International regimes must be distinguished from these specific agreements; . . . a major function of regimes is to facilitate the making of specific cooperative agreements among governments.

Superficially, it could seem that since international regimes affect national controls, the regimes are of superior importance—just as federal laws in the United States frequently override state and local legislation. Yet this would be a fundamentally misleading conclusion. In a well-ordered society, the units of action—individuals in classic liberal thought—live together within a framework of constitutional principles that define property rights, establish who may control the state, and specify the conditions under which subjects must obey governmental regulations. In the United States, these principles establish the supremacy of the federal government in a number of policy areas, though not in all. But world politics is decentralized rather than hierarchic: the prevailing principle of sovereignty means that states are subject to no superior government (Ruggie, 1983a). The resulting system is sometimes referred to as one of "self-help" (Waltz, 1979).

Sovereignty and self-help mean that the principles and rules of international regimes will necessarily be weaker than in domestic society. In a civil society, these rules "specify terms of exchange" within the framework of constitutional principles (North, 1981, p. 203). In world politics, the principles, norms, and rules

of regimes are necessarily fragile because they risk coming into conflict with the principle of sovereignty and the associated norm of self-help. They may promote cooperation, but the fundamental basis of order on which they would rest in a well-ordered society does not exist. They drift around without being tied to the solid anchor of the state.

Yet even if the principles of sovereignty and self-help limit the degree of confidence to be placed in international agreements, they do not render cooperation impossible. Orthodox theory itself relies on mutual interests to explain forms of cooperation that are used by states as instruments of competition. According to balance-of-power theory, cooperative endeavors such as political-military alliances necessarily form in self-help systems (Waltz, 1979). Acts of cooperation are accounted for on the grounds that mutual interests are sufficient to enable states to overcome their suspicions of one another. But since even orthodox theory relies on mutual interests, its advocates are on weak ground in objecting to interpretations of system-wide cooperation along these lines. There is no logical or empirical reason why mutual interests in world politics should be limited to interests in combining forces against adversaries. As economists emphasize, there can also be mutual interests in securing efficiency gains from voluntary exchange or oligopolistic rewards from the creation and division of rents resulting from the control and manipulation of markets.

International regimes should not be interpreted as elements of a new international order "beyond the nation-state." They should be comprehended chiefly as arrangements motivated by self-interest: as components of systems in which sovereignty remains a constitutive principle.

This means that, as Realists emphasize, they will be shaped largely by their most powerful members, pursuing their own interests. But regimes can also affect state interests, for the notion of self-interest is itself elastic and largely subjective. Perceptions of self-interest depend both on actors' expectations of the likely consequences that will follow from particular actions and on their fundamental values. Regimes can certainly affect expectations and may affect values as well. Far from being contradicted by the view that international behavior is shaped largely by power and interests, the concept of international regime is consistent both with the importance of differential power and with a sophisticated view of self-interest. Theories of regimes can incorporate Realist insights about the role of power and interest, while also indicating the inadequacy of theories that define interests so narrowly that they fail to take the role of institutions into account.

Regimes not only are consistent with self-interest but may under some conditions even be necessary to its effective pursuit. They facilitate the smooth operation of decentralized international political systems and therefore perform an important function for states. In a world political economy characterized by growing interdependence, they may become increasingly useful for governments that wish to solve common problems and pursue complementary purposes without subordinating themselves to hierarchical systems of control.

CONCLUSIONS

In this chapter international cooperation has been defined as a process through which policies actually followed by governments come to be regarded by their partners as facilitating realization of their own objectives, as the result of policy coordination. Cooperation involves mutual adjustment and can only arise from conflict or potential conflict. It must therefore be distinguished from harmony. Discord, which is the opposite of harmony, stimulates demands for policy adjustments, which can either lead to cooperation or to continued, perhaps intensified, discord.

Since international regimes reflect patterns of cooperation and discord over time, focusing on them leads us to examine long-term patterns of behavior, rather than treating acts of cooperation as isolated events. Regimes consist of injunctions at various levels of generality, ranging from principles to norms to highly specific rules and decisionmaking procedures. By investigating the evolution of the norms and rules of a regime over time, we can use the concept of international regime both to explore continuity and to investigate change in the world political economy.

From a theoretical standpoint, regimes can be viewed as intermediate factors, or "intervening variables," between fundamental characteristics of world politics such as the international distribution of power on the one hand and the behavior of states and nonstate actors such as multinational corporations on the other. The concept of international regime helps us account for cooperation and discord. To understand the impact of regimes, it is not necessary to posit idealism on the part of actors in world politics. On the contrary, the norms and rules of regimes can exert an effect on behavior even if they do not embody common ideals but are used by self-interested states and corporations engaging in a process of mutual adjustment.

NOTES

1. Historically hegemonies have usually arisen only after major wars. The two principal modern powers that could be considered hegemonic leaders—Britain after 1815 and the United States after 1945—both emerged victorious from world conflicts. I am assuming, in regarding hegemony as unlikely in the foreseeable future, that any world war would have such disastrous consequences that no country would emerge as hegemonic over a world economy resembling that of the present. For a discussion of the cycle of hegemony, see Gilpin (1981) and Modelski (1978 and 1982).

2. Some authors have defined "regime" as equivalent to the conventional concept of international system. For instance, Puchala and Hopkins (1983) claim that "a regime exists in every substantive issue-area in international relations where there is discernibly patterned behavior" (p. 63). To adopt this definition would be to make either "system" or "regime" a redundant term. At the opposite extreme, the concept of regime could be limited to situations with genuine normative content, in which governments followed regime rules *instead of* pursuing their own self-interests when the two conflicted. If this course were chosen, the concept of regime would be just another way of expressing ancient "idealist" sentiments in international relations. The category of regime would become virtually empty. This dichotomy poses a false choice between using "regime" as a new label for old patterns and defining regimes as utopias. Either strategy would make the term irrelevant.

QUESTIONS

1. Provide a detailed explanation of the effects of harmony, cooperation, and discord on the international system.

2. How does Keohane's view of interdependence differ from that of Robert Gilpin?

18.   Who is Us?

Robert B. Reich

In this article, Robert B. Reich examines the benefits offered by American owned multinational corporations and those offered by foreign owned corporations with factories located in the United States. Reich argues that the U.S. should reconsider its traditional support for American owned multinational corporations. Rather, in an increasingly global economy, the U.S. should encourage foreign owned corporations that employ and train American workers. This selection is from the *Harvard Business Review* (1990).

Robert B. Reich, currently serving as Secretary of Labor in the Clinton Administration, was professor of political economy and management with the John F. Kennedy School of Government at Harvard University. He is the author of many books on trade competitiveness, industrial policy, and government.

Across the United States, you can hear calls for us to revitalize our national competitiveness. But wait—who is "us"? Is it IBM, Motorola, Whirlpool, and General Motors? Or is it Sony, Thomson, Philips, and Honda?

Consider two successful corporations:

■ Corporation A is headquartered north of New York City. Most of its top managers are citizens of the United States. All of its directors are American citizens, and a majority of its shares are held by American investors. But most of Corporation A's employees are non-Americans. Indeed, the company undertakes much of its R&D and product design, and most of its complex manufacturing, outside the borders of the United States in Asia, Latin America, and Europe. Within the American market, an increasing amount of the company's product comes from its laboratories and factories abroad.

■ Corporation B is headquartered abroad, in another industrialized nation. Most of its top managers and directors are citizens of that nation, and a majority of its shares are held by citizens of that nation. But most of Corporation B's employees are Americans. Indeed, Corporation B undertakes much of its R&D and new product design in the United States. And it does most of its manufacturing in the U.S. The company exports an increasing proportion of its American-based production, some of it even back to the nation where Corporation B is headquartered.

Now, who is "us"? Between these two corporations, which is the American corporation, which the foreign corporation? Which is more important to the economic future of the United States?

As the American economy becomes more globalized, examples of both Corporation A and B are increasing. At the same time, American concern for the competitiveness of the United States is increasing. Typically, the assumed vehicle for improving the competitive performance of the United States is the American corporation—by which most people would mean Corporation A. But today, the competitiveness of American-owned corporations is no longer the same as American competitiveness. Indeed, American ownership of the corporation is profoundly less relevant to America's economic future than the skills, training, and knowledge commanded by American workers—workers who are increasingly employed within the United States by foreign-owned corporations.

So who is us? The answer is, the American work force, the American people, but not particularly the American corporation. The implications of this new answer are clear: if we hope to revitalize the competitive performance of the United States economy, we must invest in people, not in nationally defined corporations. We must open our borders to investors from around the world rather than favoring companies that may simply fly the U.S. flag. And government policies should promote human capital in this country rather than assuming that American corporations will invest on "our" behalf. The American corporation is simply no longer "us."

GLOBAL COMPANIES

American corporations have been abroad for years, even decades. So in one sense, the multinational identity of American companies is nothing new. What is new is that American-owned multinationals are beginning to employ large numbers of foreigners relative to their American work forces, are beginning to rely on foreign facilities to do many of their most technologically complex activities, and are beginning to export from their foreign facilities—including bringing products back to the United States.

Around the world, the numbers are already large—and still growing. Take IBM—often considered the thoroughbred of competitive American corporations. Forty percent of IBM's world employees are foreign, and the percentage is increasing. IBM Japan boasts 18,000 Japanese employees and annual sales of more than $6 billion, making it one of Japan's major exporters of computers.

Or consider Whirlpool. After cutting its American work force by 10% and buying Philips's appliance business, Whirlpool now employs 43,500 people around the world in 45 countries—most of them non-Americans. Another example is Texas Instruments, which now does most of its research, development, design, and manufacturing in East Asia. TI employs over 5,000 people in Japan alone, making advanced semiconductors—almost half of which are exported, many of them back to the United States.

American corporations now employ 11% of the industrial work force of Northern Ireland, making everything from cigarettes to computer software, much of which comes back to the United

States. More than 100,000 Singaporians work for more than 200 U.S. corporations, most of them fabricating and assembling electronic components for export to the United States. Singapore's largest private employer is General Electric, which also accounts for a big share of that nation's growing exports. Taiwan counts AT&T, RCA, and Texas Instruments among its largest exporters. In fact, more than one-third of Taiwan's notorious trade surplus with the United States comes from U.S. corporations making or buying things there, then selling or using them back in the United States. The same corporate sourcing practice accounts for a substantial share of the U.S. trade imbalance with Singapore, South Korea, and Mexico—raising a question as to whom complaints about trade imbalances should be directed.

The pattern is not confined to America's largest companies. Molex, a suburban Chicago maker of connectors used to link wires in cars and computer boards, with revenues of about $300 million in 1988, has 38 overseas factories, 5 in Japan. Loctite, a midsize company with sales in 1988 of $457 million, headquartered in Newington, Connecticut, makes and sells adhesives and sealants all over the world. It has 3,500 employees—only 1,200 of whom are Americans. These companies are just part of a much larger trend: according to a 1987 McKinsey & Company study, America's most profitable midsize companies increased their investments in overseas production at an annual rate of 20% between 1981 and 1986.

Overall, the evidence suggests that U.S. companies have not lost their competitive edge over the last 20 years—they've just moved their base of operations. In 1966, American-based multinationals accounted for about 17% of world exports; since then their share has remained almost unchanged. But over the same period, the share of exports from the United States in the world's total trade in manufactures fell from 16% to 14%. In other words, while Americans exported less, the overseas affiliates of U.S.-owned corporations exported more than enough to offset the drop.

The old trend of overseas capital investment is accelerating: U.S. companies increased foreign capital spending by 24% in 1988, 13% in 1989. But even more important, U.S. businesses are now putting substantial sums of money into foreign countries to do R&D work. According to National Science Foundation figures, American corporations increased their overseas R&D spending by 33% between 1986 and 1988, compared with a 6% increase in R&D spending in the United States. Since 1987, Eastman Kodak, W.R. Grace, Du Pont, Merck, and Upjohn have all opened new R&D facilities in Japan. At Du Pont's Yokohama laboratory, more than 180 Japanese scientists and technicians are working at developing new materials technologies. IBM's Tokyo Research Lab, tucked away behind the far side of the Imperial Palace in downtown Tokyo, houses a small army of Japanese engineers who are perfecting image-processing technology. Another IBM laboratory, the Kanagawa arm of its Yamato Development Laboratory, houses 1,500 researchers who are developing hardware and software. Nor does IBM confine its pioneering work to Japan: recently, two European researchers at IBM's Zurich laboratory announced major breakthroughs into superconductivity and microscopy—earning them both Nobel Prizes.

An even more dramatic development is the arrival of foreign corporations in the United States at a rapidly increasing pace. As recently as 1977, only about 3.5% of the value added and the employment of American manufacturing originated in companies controlled by foreign parents. By 1987, the number had grown to almost 8%. In just the last two years, with the faster pace of foreign acquisitions and investments, the figure is now almost 11%. Foreign-owned companies now employ 3 million Americans, roughly 10% of our manufacturing workers. In fact, in 1989, affiliates of foreign manufacturers created more jobs in the United States than American-owned manufacturing companies.

And these non-U.S. companies are vigorously exporting from the United States. Sony now exports audio- and videotapes to Europe from its Dothan, Alabama factory and ships audio recorders from its Fort Lauderdale, Florida plant. Sharp exports 100,000 microwave ovens a year from its factory in Memphis, Tennessee. Last year, Dutch-owned Philips Consumer Electronics Company exported 1,500 color televisions from its Greenville, Tennessee plant to Japan. Its 1990 target is 30,000 televisions; by 1991, it plans to export 50,000 sets. Toshiba America is sending projection televisions from its Wayne, New Jersey plant to Japan. And by the early 1990s, when Honda annually exports 50,000 cars to Japan from its Ohio production base, it will actually be making more cars in the United States than in Japan.

THE NEW AMERICAN CORPORATION

In an economy of increasing global investment, foreign-owned Corporation B, with its R&D and manufacturing presence in the United States and its reliance on American workers, is far more important to America's economic future than American-owned Corporation A, with its platoons of foreign workers. Corporation A may fly the American flag, but Corporation B invests in Americans. Increasingly, the competitiveness of American workers is a more important definition of "American competitiveness" than the competitiveness of American companies. Issues of ownership, control, and national origin are less important factors in thinking through the logic of "who is us" and the implications of the answer for national policy and direction.

Ownership is less important. Those who favor American-owned Corporation A (that produces overseas) over foreign-owned Corporation B (that produces here) might argue that American ownership generates a stream of earnings for the nation's citizens. This argument is correct, as far as it goes. American shareholders do, of course, benefit from the global successes of American corporations to the extent that such successes are reflected in higher share prices. And the entire U.S. economy benefits to the extent that the overseas profits of American companies are remitted to the United States.

But American investors also benefit from the successes of non-American companies in which Americans own a minority interest—just as foreign citizens benefit from the successes of American companies in which they own a minority interest, and such cross-ownership is on the increase as national restrictions on foreign ownership fall by the wayside. In 1989, cross-border equity investments by Americans, British, Japanese, and West Germans increased 20%, by value, over 1988.

The point is that in today's global economy, the total return to Americans from their equity investments is not solely a matter of the success of particular companies in which Americans happen to have a controlling interest. The return depends on the total amount of American savings invested in global portfolios comprising both American and foreign-owned companies—and on the care and wisdom with which American investors select such portfolios. Already Americans invest 10% of their portfolios in foreign securities; a recent study by Salomon Brothers predicts that it will be 15% in a few years. U.S. pension managers surveyed said that they predict 25% of their portfolios will be in foreign-owned companies within 10 years.

Control is less important. Another argument marshaled in favor of Corporation A might be that because Corporation A is controlled by Americans, it will act in the best interests of the United States. Corporation B, a foreign national, might not do so—indeed, it might act in the best interests of its nation of origin. The argument might go something like this: even if Corporation B is now hiring more Americans and giving them better jobs than Corporation A, we can't be assured that it will continue to do so. It might bias its strategy to reduce American competitiveness; it might even suddenly withdraw its investment from the United States and leave us stranded.

But this argument makes a false assumption about American companies—namely, that they are in a position to put national interests ahead of company or shareholder interests. To the contrary: managers of American-owned companies who sacrificed profits for the sake of national goals would make themselves vulnerable to a takeover or liable for a breach of fiduciary responsibility to their shareholders. American managers are among the loudest in the world to declare that their job is to maximize shareholder returns—not to advance national goals.

Apart from wartime or other national emergencies, American-owned companies are under no special obligation to serve national goals. Nor does our system alert American managers to the existence of such goals, impose on American managers unique requirements to meet them, offer special incentives to achieve them, or create measures to keep American managers accountable for accomplishing them. Were American managers knowingly to sacrifice profits for the sake of presumed national goals, they would be acting without authority, on the basis of their own views of what such goals might be, and without accountability to shareholders or to the public.

Obviously, this does not preclude American-owned companies from displaying their good corporate citizenship or having a sense of social responsibility. Sensible managers recognize that acting "in the public interest" can boost the company's image; charitable or patriotic acts can be good business if they promote long-term profitability. But in this regard, American companies have no particular edge over foreign-owned companies doing business in the United States. In fact, there is every reason to believe that a foreign-owned company would be even more eager to demonstrate to the American public its good citizenship in America than would the average American company. The American subsidiaries of Hitachi, Matsushita, Siemens, Thomson, and many other foreign-owned companies lose no opportunity to contribute funds to American charities, sponsor community events, and support public libraries, universities, schools, and other

institutions. (In 1988, for example, Japanese companies operating in the United States donated an estimated $200 million to American charities; by 1994, it is estimated that their contributions will total $1 billion.)[1]

By the same token, American-owned businesses operating abroad feel a similar compulsion to act as good citizens in their host countries. They cannot afford to be seen as promoting American interests; otherwise they would jeopardize their relationships with foreign workers, consumers, and governments. Some of America's top managers have been quite explicit on this point. "IBM cannot be a net exporter from every nation in which it does business," said Jack Kuehler, IBM's new president. "We have to be a good citizen everywhere." Robert W. Galvin, chairman of Motorola, is even more blunt: should it become necessary for Motorola to close some of its factories, it would not close its Southeast Asian plants before it closed its American ones. "We need our Far Eastern customers," says Galvin, "and we cannot alienate the Malaysians. We must treat our employees all over the world equally." In fact, when it becomes necessary to reduce global capacity, we might expect American-owned businesses to slash more jobs in the United States than in Europe (where labor laws often prohibit precipitous layoffs) or in Japan (where national norms discourage it).

Just as empty is the concern that a foreign-owned company might leave the United States stranded by suddenly abandoning its U.S. operation. The typical argument suggests that a foreign-owned company might withdraw for either profit or foreign policy motives. But either way, the bricks and mortar would still be here. So would the equipment. So too would be the accumulated learning among American workers. Under such circumstances, capital from another source would fill the void; an American (or other foreign) company would simply purchase the empty facilities. And most important, the American work force would remain, with the critical skills and capabilities, ready to go back to work.

After all, the American government and the American people maintain jurisdiction—political control—over assets within the United States. Unlike foreign assets held by American-owned companies that are subject to foreign political control and, occasionally, foreign expropriation, foreign-owned assets in the United States are secure against sudden changes in foreign governments' policies. This not only serves as an attraction for foreign capital looking for a secure haven; it also benefits the American work force.

Work force skills are critical. As every advanced economy becomes global, a nation's most important competitive asset becomes the skills and cumulative learning of its work force. Consequently, the most important issue with regard to global corporations is whether and to what extent they provide Americans with the training and experience that enable them to add greater value to the world economy. Whether the company happens to be headquartered in the United States or the United Kingdom is fundamentally unimportant. The company is a good "American" corporation if it equips its American work force to compete in the global economy.

Globalization, almost by definition, makes this true. Every factor of production other than work force skills can be duplicated anywhere around the world. Capital now sloshes freely across international boundaries, so much so that the cost of capital in different countries is rapidly converging. State-of-the-art factories can be erected anywhere. The latest technologies flow from computers in one nation, up to satellites parked in space, then back down to computers in another nation—all at the speed of electronic impulses. It is all fungible: capital, technology, raw materials, information—all, except for one thing, the most critical part, the one element that is unique about a nation: its work force.

In fact, because all of the other factors can move so easily any place on earth, a work force that is knowledgeable and skilled at doing complex things attracts foreign investment. The relationship forms a virtuous circle: well-trained workers attract global corporations, which invest and give the workers good jobs; the good jobs, in turn, generate additional training and experience. As skills move upward and experience accumulates, a nation's citizens add greater and greater value to the world—and command greater and greater compensation from the world, improving the country's standard of living.

Foreign-owned corporations help American workers add value. When foreign-owned companies come to the United States, they frequently bring with them approaches to doing business that improve American productivity and allow American workers to add more value to the world economy. In fact, they come here primarily because they can be more productive in the United States than can other American rivals. It is not solely America's mounting external indebtedness and relatively low dollar that account for the rising level of foreign investment in the United States. Actual growth of foreign investment in the United States dates from the mid-1970s rather than from the onset of the large current account deficit in 1982. Moreover, the two leading foreign investors in the United States are the British and the Dutch—not the Japanese and the West Germans, whose enormous surpluses are the counterparts of our current account deficit.

For example, after Japan's Bridgestone tire company took over Firestone, productivity increased dramatically. The joint venture between Toyota and General Motors at Fremont, California is a similar story: Toyota's managerial system took many of the same workers from what had been a deeply troubled GM plant and turned it into a model facility, with upgraded productivity and skill levels.

In case after case, foreign companies set up or buy up operations in the United States to utilize their corporate assets with the American work force. Foreign-owned businesses with better design capabilities, production techniques, or managerial skills are able to displace American companies on American soil precisely because those businesses are more productive. And in the process of supplanting the American company, the foreign-owned operation can transfer the superior know-how to its American work force—giving American workers the tools they need to be more productive, more skilled, and more competitive. Thus foreign companies create good jobs in the United States. In 1986 (the last date for which such data are available), the average American employee of a foreign-owned manufacturing company earned $32,887, while the average American employee of an American-owned manufacturer earned $28,954.[2]

This process is precisely what happened in Europe in the 1950s and 1960s. Europeans publicly fretted about the invasion of American-owned multinationals and the onset of "the American challenge." But the net result of these operations in Europe has been to make Europeans more productive, upgrade European skills, and thus enhance the standard of living of Europeans.

NOW WHO IS US?

American competitiveness can best be defined as the capacity of Americans to add value to the world economy and thereby gain a higher standard of living in the future without going into ever deeper debt. American competitiveness is not the profitability or market share of American-owned corporations. In fact, because the American-owned corporation is coming to have no special relationship with Americans, it makes no sense for Americans to entrust our national competitiveness to it. The interests of American-owned corporations may or may not coincide with those of the American people.

Does this mean that we should simply entrust our national competitiveness to any corporation that employs Americans, regardless of the nationality of corporate ownership? Not entirely. Some foreign-owned corporations are closely tied to their nation's economic development—either through direct public ownership (for example, Airbus Industrie, a joint product of Britain, France, West Germany, and Spain, created to compete in the commercial airline industry) or through financial intermediaries within the nation that, in turn, are tied to central banks and ministries of finance (in particular the model used by many Korean and Japanese corporations). The primary goals of such corporations are to enhance the wealth of their nations, and the standard of living of their nations' citizens, rather than to enrich their shareholders. Thus, even though they might employ American citizens in their worldwide operations, they may employ fewer Americans—or give Americans lower value-added jobs—than they would if these corporations were intent simply on maximizing their own profits.[3]

On the other hand, it seems doubtful that we could ever shift the goals and orientations of American-owned corporations in this same direction—away from profit maximization and toward the development of the American work force. There is no reason to suppose that American managers and shareholders would accept new regulations and oversight mechanisms that forced them to sacrifice profits for the sake of building human capital in the United States. Nor is it clear that the American system of government would be capable of such detailed oversight.

The only practical answer lies in developing national policies that reward *any* global corporation that invests in the American work force. In a whole set of public policy areas, involving trade, publicly supported R&D, antitrust, foreign direct investment, and public and private investment, the overriding goal should be to induce global corporations to build human capital in America.

Trade policy. We should be less interested in opening foreign markets to American-owned companies (which may in fact be doing much of their production overseas) than in opening those markets to companies that employ Americans— even if they happen to be foreign-owned. But so far, American trade policy experts have focused on representing the interests of companies that happen to carry the American flag—without regard to where the actual production is being done. For example, the United States recently accused Japan of excluding Motorola from the lucrative Tokyo market for cellular telephones and hinted at retaliation. But Motorola designs and makes many of its cellular telephones in Kuala Lumpur, while most of the Americans who make cellular telephone equipment in the United States for export to Japan happen to work for Japanese-owned companies. Thus we are wasting our scarce political capital pushing foreign governments to reduce barriers to American-owned companies that are seeking to sell or produce in their market.

Once we acknowledge that foreign-owned Corporation B may offer more to American competitiveness than American-owned Corporation A, it is easy to design a preferable trade policy—one that accords more directly with our true national interests. The highest priority for American trade policy should be to discourage other governments from invoking domestic content rules—which have the effect of forcing global corporations, American and foreign-owned alike, to locate production facilities in those countries rather than in the United States.

The objection here to local content rules is not that they may jeopardize the competitiveness of American companies operating abroad. Rather, it is that these requirements, by their very nature, deprive the American work force of the opportunity to compete for jobs, and with those jobs, for valuable skills, knowledge, and experience. Take, for example, the recently promulgated European Community nonbinding rule on television-program production, which urges European television stations to devote a majority of their air time to programs made in Europe. Or consider the European allegations of Japanese dumping of office machines containing semiconductors, which has forced Japan to put at least 45% European content into machines sold in Europe (and thus fewer American-made semiconductor chips).

Obviously, U.S.-owned companies are already inside the EC producing both semiconductors and television programs. So if we were to adopt American-owned Corporation A as the model for America's competitive self-interest, our trade policy might simply ignore these EC initiatives. But through the lens of a trade policy focused on the American work force, it is clear how the EC thwarts the abilities of Americans to excel in semiconductor fabrication and filmmaking—two areas where our work force already enjoys a substantial competitive advantage.

Lack of access by American-owned corporations to foreign markets is, of course, a problem. But it only becomes a crucial problem for America to the extent that both American and foreign-owned companies must make products within the foreign market—products that they otherwise would have made in the United States. Protection that acts as a domestic content requirement skews investment away from the United States— and away from U.S. workers. Fighting against that should be among the highest priorities of U.S. trade policy.

Publicly supported R&D. Increased global competition, the high costs of re-search, the rapid rate of change in science and technology, the model of Japan with its government-supported commercial technology investments—all of these factors have combined to make this area particularly critical for thoughtful public policy. But there is no reason why preference should be given to American-owned companies. Dominated by our preoccupation with American-owned Corporation A, current public policy in this area limits U.S. government-funded research grants, guaranteed loans, or access to the fruits of U.S. government-funded research to American-owned companies. For example, membership in Sematech, the research consortium started two years ago with $100 billion annual support payments by the Department of Defense to help American corporations fabricate complex memory chips, is limited to American-owned companies. More recently, a government effort to create a consortium of companies to catapult the United States into the HDTV competition has drawn a narrow circle of eligibility, ruling out companies such as Sony, Philips, and Thomson that do R&D and production in the United States but are foreign-owned. More generally, long-standing regulations covering the more than 600 government laboratories and research centers that are spread around the United States ban all but American-owned companies from licensing inventions developed at these sites.

Of course, the problem with this policy approach is that it ignores the reality of global American corporations. Most U.S.-owned companies are quite happy to receive special advantages from the U.S. government—and then spread the technological benefits to their affiliates all over the world. As Sematech gets under way, its members are busily going global: Texas Instruments is building a new $250 million semiconductor fabrication plant in Taiwan; by 1992, the facility will produce four-megabit memory chips and custom-made, application-specific integrated circuits—some of the most advanced chips made anywhere. TI has also joined with Hitachi to design and produce a super chip that will store 16 million bits of data. Motorola, meanwhile, has paired with Toshiba to research and produce a similar generation of futurist chips. Not to be outdone, AT&T has a commitment to build a state-of-the-art chip-making plant in Spain. So who will be making advanced chips in the United States? In June 1989, Japanese-owned

NEC announced plans to build a $400 million facility in Rosedale, California for making four-megabit memory chips and other advanced devices not yet in production anywhere.

The same situation applies to HDTV. Zenith Electronics is the only remaining American-owned television manufacturer, and thus the only one eligible for a government subsidy. Zenith employs 2,500 Americans. But there are over 15,000 Americans employed in the television industry who do not work for Zenith—undertaking R&D, engineering, and high-quality manufacturing. They work in the United States for foreign-owned companies: Sony, Philips, Thomson, and others (see the accompanying

U.S. TV Set Production, 1988

COMPANY NAME	PLANT TYPE	LOCATION	EMPLOYEES	ANNUAL PRODUCTION
Bang & Olufsen	Assembly	Compton, Calif.	n.a.†	n.a.
Goldstar	Total*	Huntsville, Ala.	400	1,000,000
Harvey Industries	Assembly	Athens, Tex.	900	600,000
Hitachi	Total	Anaheim, Calif.	900	360,000
JVC	Total	Elmwood Park, N.J.	100	480,000
Matsushita	Assembly	Franklin Park, Ill.	800	1,000,000
American Kotobuki (Matsushita)	Assembly	Vancouver, Wash.	200	n.a.
Mitsubishi	Assembly	Santa Ana, Calif.	550	400,000
Mitsubishi	Total	Braselton, Ga.	300	285,000
NEC	Assembly	McDonough, Ga.	400	240,000
Orion	Assembly	Princeton, Ind.	250	n.a.
Philips	Total	Greenville, Tenn.	3,200	2,000,000+
Samsung	Total	Saddle Brook, N.J.	250	1,000,000
Sanyo	Assembly	Forrest City, Ark.	400	1,000,000
Sharp	Assembly	Memphis, Tenn.	770	1,100,000
Sony	Total	San Diego, Calif.	1,500	1,000,000
Tatung	Assembly	Long Beach, Calif.	130	17,500
Thomson	Total	Bloomington, Ind.	1,766	3,000,000+
Thomson	Components	Indianapolis, Ind.	1,604	n.a.
Toshiba	Assembly	Lebanon, Tenn.	600	900,000
Zenith	Total	Springfield, Mo.	2,500	n.a.

† Not available.
* Total manufacturing involves more than the assembling of knocked-down kits. Plants that manufacture just the television cabinets are not included in this list. *Source:* Electronic Industries Association, HDTV Information Center, Washington, D.C.

table). Of course, none of these companies is presently eligible to participate in the United States's HDTV consortium—nor are their American employees.

Again, if we follow the logic of Corporation B as the more "American" company, it suggests a straightforward principle for publicly supported R&D: we should be less interested in helping *American-owned companies* become technologically sophisticated than in helping *Americans* become technologically sophisticated. Government-financed help for research and development should be available to any corporation, regardless of the nationality of its owners, as long as the company undertakes the R&D in the United States—using American scientists, engineers, and technicians. To make the link more explicit, there could even be a relationship between the number of Americans involved in the R&D and the amount of government aid forthcoming. It is important to note that this kind of public-private bargain is far different from protectionist domestic content requirements. In this case, the government is participating with direct funding and thus can legitimately exact a quid pro quo from the private sector.

Antitrust policy. The Justice Department is now in the process of responding to the inevitability of globalization; it recognizes that North American market share alone means less and less in a global economy. Consequently, the Justice Department is about to relax antitrust policy—for American-owned companies only. American-owned companies that previously kept each other at arm's length for fear of prompting an inquiry into whether they were colluding are now cozying up to one another. Current antitrust policy permits research joint ventures; the attorney general is on the verge of recommending that antitrust policy permit joint production agreements as well, when there may be significant economies of scale and where competition is global—again, among American-owned companies.

But here again, American policy seems myopic. We should be less interested in helping American-owned companies gain economies of scale in research, production, and other key areas, and more interested in helping corporations engaged in research or production within the United States achieve economies of scale—regardless of their nationality. U.S. antitrust policy should allow research or production joint ventures among any companies doing R&D or production within the United States, as long as they can meet three tests: they could not gain such scale efficiencies on their own, simply by enlarging their investment in the United States; such a combination of companies would allow higher levels of productivity within the United States; and the combination would not substantially diminish global competition. National origin should not be a factor.

Foreign direct investment. Foreign direct investment has been climbing dramatically in the United States: last year it reached $329 billion, exceeding total American investment abroad for the first time since World War I (but be careful with these figures, since investments are valued at cost and this substantially understates the worth of older investments). How should we respond to this influx of foreign capital?

Clearly, the choice between Corporation A and Corporation B has important implications. If we are most concerned about the viability of American-owned corporations, then we should put obstacles in the way of foreigners seeking to buy controlling shares in American-owned companies, or looking to build American production facilities that would compete with American-owned companies.

Indeed, current policies tilt in this direction. For example, under the so-called Exon-Florio Amendment of the Omnibus Trade and Competitiveness Act of 1988, foreign investors must get formal approval from the high-level Committee on Foreign Investments in the United States, comprising the heads of eight federal agencies and chaired by the secretary of the treasury, before they can purchase an American company. The expressed purpose of the law is to make sure that a careful check is done to keep "national security" industries from passing into the hands of foreigners. But the law does not define what "national security" means: thus it invites all sorts of potential delays and challenges. The actual effect is to send a message that we do not look with favor on the purchase of American-owned assets by foreigners. Other would-be pieces of legislation send the same signal. In July 1989, for instance, the House Ways and Means Committee voted to apply a withholding capital gains tax to foreigners who own more than 10% of a company's shares. Another provision of the committee would scrap tax deductibility for interest on loans made by foreign parents to their American subsidiaries. A third measure would limit R&D tax credits for foreign subsidiaries. More recently, Congress is becoming increasingly concerned about foreign takeovers of American airlines. A subcommittee of the House Commerce Committee has voted to give the Transportation Department authority to block foreign acquisitions.

These policies make little sense—in fact, they are counterproductive. Our primary concern should be the training and development of the American work force, not the protection of the American-owned corporation. Thus we should encourage, not discourage, foreign direct investment. Experience shows that foreign-owned companies usually displace American-owned companies in just those industries where the foreign businesses are simply more productive. No wonder America's governors spend a lot of time and energy promoting their states to foreign investors and offer big subsidies to foreign companies to locate in their states, even if they compete head-on with existing American-owned businesses.

Public and private investment. The current obsession with the federal budget deficit obscures a final, crucial aspect of the choice between Corporation A and Corporation B. Conventional wisdom holds that government expenditures "crowd out" private investment, making it more difficult and costly for American-owned companies to get the capital they need. According to this logic, we may have to cut back on public expenditures in order to provide American-owned companies with the necessary capital to make investments in plant and equipment.

But the reverse may actually be the case—particularly if Corporation B is really more in America's competitive interests than Corporation A. There are a number of reasons why this is true.

First, in the global economy, America's public expenditures don't reduce the amount of money left over for private investment in the United States. Today capital flows freely across national borders—including a disproportionately large inflow to the United States. Not only are foreign savings coming to the United States, but America's private savings are finding their way all over the world.

Sometimes the vehicle is the far-flung operations of a global American-owned company, sometimes a company in which foreigners own a majority stake. But the old notion of national boundaries is becoming obsolete. Moreover, as I have stressed, it is a mistake to associate these foreign investments by American-owned companies with any result that improves the competitiveness of the United States. There is simply no necessary connection between the two.

There is, however, a connection between the kinds of investments that the public sector makes and the competitiveness of the American work force. Remember: a work force that is knowledgeable and skilled at doing complex things attracts foreign investment in good jobs, which in turn generates additional training and experience. A good infrastructure of transporation and communication makes a skilled work force even more attractive. The public sector often is in the best position to make these sorts of "pump priming" investments—in education, training and retraining, research and development, and in all of the infrastructure that moves people and goods and facilitates communication. These are the investments that distinguish one nation from another—they are the relatively nonmobile factors in the global competition. Ironically, we do not ordinarily think of these expenditures as investments; the federal budget fails to distinguish between a capital and an operating budget, and the national income accounts treat all government expenditures as consumption. But without doubt, these are precisely the investments that most directly affect our future capacity to compete.

During the 1980s, we allowed the level of these public investments either to remain stable or, in some cases, to decline. As America enters the 1990s, if we hope to launch a new campaign for American competitiveness, we must substantially increase public funding in the following areas:

■ *Government spending on commercial R&D.* Current spending in this critical area has declined 95% from its level two decades ago. Even as late as 1980, it comprised .8% of gross national product; today it comprises only .4%—a much smaller percentage than in any other advanced economy.

■ *Government spending to upgrade and expand the nation's infrastructure.* Public investment in critical highways, roads, bridges, ports, airports, and waterways dropped from 2.3% of GNP two decades ago to 1.3% in the 1980s. Thus many of our bridges are unsafe, and our highways are crumbling.

■ *Expenditures on public elementary and secondary education.* These have increased, to be sure. But in inflation-adjusted terms, per pupil spending has shown little gain. Between 1959 and 1971, spending per student grew at a brisk 4.7% in real terms—more than a full percentage point above the increase in the GNP—and teachers' salaries increased almost 3% a year. But since then, growth has slowed. Worse, this has happened during an era when the demands on public education have significantly increased, due to the growing incidence of broken homes, unwed mothers, and a rising population of the poor. Teachers' salaries, adjusted for inflation, are only a bit higher than they were in 1971. Despite the rhetoric, the federal government has all but retreated from the field of education. In fact,

George Bush's 1990 education budget is actually smaller than Ronald Reagan's in 1989. States and municipalities, already staggering under the weight of social services that have been shifted onto them from the federal government, simply cannot carry this additional load. The result of this policy gap is a national education crisis: one out of five American 18-year-olds is illiterate, and in test after test, American schoolchildren rank at the bottom of international scores. Investing more money here may not be a cure-all—but money is at least necessary.

■ *College opportunity for all Americans.* Because of government cutbacks, many young people in the United States with enough talent to go to college cannot afford it. During the 1980s, college tuitions rose 26%; family incomes rose a scant 5%. Instead of filling the gap, the federal government created a vacuum: guaranteed student loans have fallen by 13% in real terms since 1980.

■ *Worker training and retraining.* Young people who cannot or do not wish to attend college need training for jobs that are becoming more complex. Older workers need retraining to keep up with the demands of a rapidly changing, technologically advanced workplace. But over the last eight years, federal investments in worker training have dropped by more than 50%.

These are the priorities of an American strategy for national competitiveness—a strategy based more on the value of human capital and less on the value of financial capital. The simple fact of American ownership has lost its relevance to America's economic future. Corporations that invest in the United States, that build the value of the American work force, are more critical to our future standard of living than are American-owned corporations investing abroad. To attract and keep them, we need public investments that make America a good place for any global corporation seeking talented workers to set up shop.

NOTES

1. Craig Smith, editor of *Corporate Philanthropy Report,* quoted in *Chronicle of Higher Education,* November 8, 1989, p. A-34.
2. Bureau of Economic Analysis, *Foreign Direct Investment in the U.S.: Operations of U.S. Affiliates, Preliminary 1986 Estimates* (Washington, D.C.: U.S. Department of Commerce, 1988) for data on foreign companies; Bureau of the Census, *Annual Survey of Manufactures: Statistics for Industry Groups and Industries,* 1986 (Washington, D.C., 1987) for U.S. companies.
3. Robert B. Reich and Eric D. Mankin, "Joint Ventures with Japan Give Away Our Future," HBR March-April 1986, p. 78.

QUESTIONS

1. According to Reich, what are the benefits to the United States economy of foreign-owned corporations operating within the country? Why?

2. Is this form of transnationalism consistent with the interdependence paradigm defined by Joseph S. Nye Jr.? Explain.

Chapter 4

CLASS SYSTEM THEORY

COMPONENTS OF CLASS SYSTEM THEORY

Focus of Analysis ········▶	• Capitalist world system
Major Actors ········▶	• States • Transnational class coalitions • Multinational corporations • International organizations
Behavior of States ········▶	• Class struggle • Accumulation of wealth for capitalist class
Goals of States ········▶	• Enhance wealth of capitalist class
View of Human Nature ········▶	• Selfish and dominating but reformable
Condition of International System ········▶	• Domination of capitalist world system • Cycle of exploitation/dependency
Key Concepts ········▶	• Capitalist world system; Class struggle; Dependency theory; Imperialism; Transnational class coalitions; Uneven development

INTRODUCTION

The final system-level theory is what we have termed *class system theory*. This paradigm is also known as the radical, globalist, or neo-Marxist theory. Class system seems a particularly good title, since advocates of this theory contend that it is classes, and the divisions between them, that define and determine the course of international politics.

Class system theory is based on four important concepts. First, proponents suggest economic factors are the driving force of international politics. Political and military power are the direct result of the underlying economic strength of the dominant class. Second, class system theory focuses on the development of the capitalist world economy and how it both creates and perpetuates uneven development between advanced capitalist states and poor, less developed states. Third, theorists point to an international class structure in which the advanced industrialized states in the center of the world capitalist system dominate and exploit poorer states, occupying the periphery of this system. Finally, transnational class coalitions represent the primary actors in international politics. States are important, but only as agents of the dominant class. Non-state actors, most notably multinational corporations, allow capitalist elites to maintain the exploitative economic links that bind core countries with those on the periphery.

Economic forces, then, are a key part of the framework of class system theory. Unlike economic transnationalists, however, class system theorists emphasize the exploitative nature of international economic ties between states. They believe there is a systemwide hierarchy of classes and states that is rooted in the unequal distribution of wealth. According to class system theory, the structure and process of international relations is largely the result of the struggle between rich and poor countries over the control and distribution of economic resources. The tension between rich and poor countries is often referred to as the **North-South conflict.** The North represents the wealthy industrialized states that lie primarily in the northern hemisphere, while the South is a term used to depict the less developed countries, generally located in the southern hemisphere.

When conflict arises among states, it is caused, according to class system theory, by the clash of opposing economic interests—namely the clash between capitalist and non-capitalist states. War is the result of capitalist states attempting to increase their wealth and power through imperialist foreign policies—policies in which strong capitalist states seek to exploit weaker non-capitalist states. Presumably, these conflicts will continue until the international status quo is radically altered, socialism replaces capitalism as the dominant socio-economic system, and a more equitable distribution of wealth among nations is attained. However, beneficiaries of the "capitalist world system," the dominant capitalist class, certainly have a stake in preventing such radical change and preserving the current arrangement: keeping the rich wealthy, while the poor remain poor.

Class system theorists acknowledge that states are important actors, but they also emphasize that the dominant class exerts significant influence and often controls government policymakers. Unlike realism, which holds that states pursue national security interests, class system theory argues that states act in accordance with the wishes of the dominant economic class within the state. If the dominant class is capitalist, a state's foreign policy will be oriented to enhance the wealth and influence of the capitalist class.

With the diminished position of individual states, or groups of states, and emphasis on class conflict, class system theory also attributes a greater role to non-state

V. I. Lenin, founder of the communist party of the Soviet Union, used Hobson's writings as the basis for his notion that imperialism is, in fact, "the highest stage of capitalism." He contended that international politics was simply the "internationalization of the class system." Lenin asserted that in order to survive, capitalism needed to expand constantly. Having exploited the workers in their own states, European capitalists sought new markets, cheap raw materials, and greater profits. The acquisition of colonies fulfilled these requirements.

The problem with this "scramble for colonies" was that, by the late nineteenth-century, most areas in the world were already colonized. Once this occurred, the expansion of one imperialist power could come only at the expense of other imperialist powers. This process, according to Lenin, led to world war between the great European imperialist states. World War I, he reasoned, was simply the final stage of capitalist imperialism.

This link, between imperialism and the inevitability of war *because* of imperialism, is one of Lenin's fundamental contributions to international relations theory. We now see that, although their explanations are quite different, both class system theorists and neo-realists view the causes of war as coming from the nature of and conditions in the international system itself. For neo-realists, the problem is anarchy; for class system theorists, it is imperialism and economic dependence.

DEPENDENCY THEORY

Dependency theory, as part of the class system paradigm, is discussed in the articles by Theotonio Dos Santos and Immanuel Wallerstein. They developed dependency theory to explain the uneven development in wealth between poor and rich countries. **Uneven development** is defined as the propensity of capitalism to create and perpetuate an unequal dispersal of global wealth and prosperity. **Dependency theory** asserts that trade, foreign investment, and even foreign aid between advanced, industrialized countries and poor, less developed states is inherently exploitative, works to the disadvantage of the poor nations, and perpetuates the dependency of these less developed countries.

With respect to dependency theory, both Dos Santos and Wallerstein suggest that relations between states in the international system can be classified as part of a system of dependency and exploitation. The term **neo-imperialism** is used to describe the less overt control now exercised by the North over exports and raw materials in developing nations. Though distinct from the imperialist practices of the European colonial empires, the economic and political influence exercised by advanced capitalist powers over less developed countries is simply a new, more subtle form of imperialism.

In conjunction with dependency theory, Wallerstein also developed the notion of a **capitalist world system,** dividing states into three categories: core (wealthy), periphery (poor), and semi-periphery (less developed). In many ways, the relationship between these three categories of countries parallels that between different classes within capitalist society. Dominant core nations are wealthy, with economies geared more toward technologically or economically advanced businesses—from high technology manufacturing to banking and global finance. These countries control, if you will, the global means of production. Machinery for manufacturing, tools for agricultural production, and world monetary systems are in the hands of these core nations.

To support their dominant position, core nations depend on the raw materials and cheap labor of periphery or poor states. Like the underclass or proletariat in a capitalist society, periphery states depend on the orders and work provided by core countries for their survival. Indeed, core countries exploit the cheap labor and raw materials to maintain a high profit margin and to sustain their own dominant position in the international system. Semi-periphery states, or less developed countries, are important when the cost of labor in core countries becomes too high, and they also serve as markets for excess production and investment capital.

Using Wallerstein's outline of the capitalist world system, let us look at the positions of core, periphery, and semi-periphery countries with respect to one another; this should help to explain why and how such a system is maintained. This theory not only describes the hierarchical international system in which the rich states continue to dominate poor, less developed states but also provides an explanation for the uneven rates of development between the North and the South.

Dominant core countries have a stake in preserving this cycle of dependency and exploitation that exists with periphery and semi-periphery states and pursue foreign and domestic policies to further that goal. Poor and less developed countries are virtually locked into a position of dependency. As we discussed earlier with regard to transnational class coalitions, class system theorists suggest that strong capitalist nations have allies in these poor nations. Small groups of capitalist elites in the peripheral states act as liaisons to and partners with leaders, policymakers, and business executives in the core countries. These elites have more in common with the capitalists of foreign nations than with the underclass of their own state. They too, then, have a stake in preserving the status quo—the dependency and exploitation—of their own country.

CLASS SYSTEM THEORY AND THE END OF THE COLD WAR

Finally, the selection by Fred Halliday provides us with an example of how the major assumptions of class system theory can be used to develop an innovative and provocative explanation for the collapse of the Soviet Union and the end of the Cold War. His analysis emphasizes the vitality of Western capitalism and the inability of the Soviet Union to compete effectively.

Realist theoreticians treated the Cold War as a continuation of traditional power politics, but Halliday focuses on the ideological and socio-economic aspects of superpower conflict. He argues that the structure of the international system is actually the result of specific historical conditions. The conditions that prevailed in the Cold War environment depended on the dominance of two contending political, economic, and ideological systems locked in a struggle for ascendancy.

Though Halliday's analysis of the Cold War acknowledges that the U.S. and Soviet Union were engaged in a broad bipolar conflict, that conflict was actually motivated and propelled by competition on three distinct levels. Two of these, socioeconomic and ideological, were at least as important, if not ultimately more important, than the third, traditional military competition. Despite his mistrust and criticism of capitalism, Halliday, unlike many class system theorists, at least acknowledges the vitality of capitalism as a dynamic economic and social system.

A CRITIQUE OF CLASS SYSTEM THEORY

Like the proponents of all our system level theories, class system theorists tend to emphasize the unique contributions of their own paradigm as a model to assess and interpret international relations. This theory does, indeed, have certain strengths. While both realism and transnationalism tend to focus primarily on the interaction of wealthy, powerful states, only class system theory examines the so-called pattern of dependence that distinguishes the relationship between rich and poor countries.

Perhaps, for this reason, class system theory, though out of favor in Western circles, remains popular and widely accepted by scholars in less developed nations. Today, many prominent class system theorists are, in fact, from Latin America. This theory, with its emphasis on the North-South conflict and problems of development, poverty, and other social-welfare issues, is one of the few paradigms that tries to provide an explanation for the disparities in wealth and development worldwide.

Class system theory must be credited with at least some success in providing an explanation for these and other problems facing less developed states. Certainly, poor countries are more vulnerable to shifts in the international marketplace, relying on exports of primary products—raw materials and natural resources—to sustain themselves economically.

Moreover, class system theory contains a valuable critique of the excesses of capitalism and its impact on less developed countries. It is difficult to deny that some vestiges of imperialism are still in place today. Many people living in third world countries resent not only the economic but also the cultural penetration of their countries. Capitalism, from their vantage point, is closely linked to Western—particularly American—culture and viewed as a potential threat to indigenous cultural traditions and ways of life.

Though there is merit to the arguments in favor of class system theory, critics are not without ammunition. Many critics argue that class system theory exaggerates the role that the world capitalist system plays in limiting development, and ignores the impact that policies adopted in the less developed states themselves have on their own economic development.

Specifically, class system theory fails to address the impact that different development strategies have had on various countries facing similar problems with economic development. Dependency theory can only account for those countries that have failed to develop. How could, for example, Dos Santos and Wallerstein explain the remarkable economic growth of many countries occupying what they describe as the semi-periphery? Rapid and successful industrial development in Taiwan, Singapore, Hong Kong, South Korea, and Brazil is difficult for class system theorists to explain or dismiss. These newly industrialized countries (NICs) are the rising economic powers of the late twentieth century and already compete successfully with major capitalist powers in the North. Clearly, these countries serve as examples that, contrary to the suppositions of class system theory, capitalism can be beneficial and bring prosperity to developing countries.

In addition to ignoring the progress of these economically vibrant nations, some class system theorists have been criticized for being ahistorical—a potential trap for any theorist of international relations. Critics point out that class system theorists rely on case studies that conform to and confirm their particular paradigm. Conversely, states that fall outside these parameters tend to be ignored.

This theoretical blind eye is especially true with respect to weaknesses of communist nations. While focusing on North-South relations, class system theorists fail to account for a significant percentage of the globe. The former Soviet Union and Eastern European states, even China, present some difficulties for the class system paradigm. Certainly, during the Cold War era, the Soviet Union maintained policies of imperialism in the subjugation and exploitation of Eastern Europe. Imperialist domination of other states is, evidently, not limited solely to capitalist powers.

Class system theory also falls short in explaining the failure of Marxist principles and communist doctrine in the former USSR and Eastern Bloc nations, as well as the capitalist reforms now underway in these countries. Though advocates might suggest that true Marxist doctrine was never fully implemented in the region, surely this cannot be considered true of communist China. Even in this most ideologically committed nation, the Chinese government has turned to free enterprise and open markets to stimulate its formerly stagnant socialized economy.

Despite these flaws, class system theory still provides important insights into the economic development process and remains a highly popular explanation of global politics, particularly among scholars in less developed countries. Like any theory, it is important for students to decide for themselves which explanation, if any, provides the most accurate description of international relations.

KEY CONCEPTS

Capitalist world system   is a concept of class system theory that focuses on the exploitative nature of the global spread of capitalism. This system divides states into three categories: core (wealthy), periphery (poor), and semi-periphery (less developed). Core nations are wealthy, advanced powers that control the global means of production and use their wealth and power to exploit and dominate those states residing in the semi-periphery and periphery of the global economic system.

Class struggle   is the Marxist theory that history is a story of struggle between economic classes in which the oppressed worker and peasant classes attempt to free themselves from the domination of the wealthy capitalist class.

Dependency theory   is a concept associated with class system theorists that asserts that trade, foreign investment, and even foreign aid between advanced industrialized countries and poor, lesser developed states is inherently exploitative and works to the disadvantage of the poor nations.

Dialectical materialism   is a theory developed by Karl Marx positing that history moves through stages—from feudalism to capitalism to socialism and, finally, to communism. The transition from one stage to the next is often prompted by the struggle between economic classes, as well as by the development and spread of technology.

Imperialism   is the policy of expanding a state's power and authority by conquering and controlling territories, called colonies.

(*continued*)

(continued from previous page)

Neo-imperialism is used to describe the process of the international system in which the advanced industrial states' control of exports and raw materials in developing nations are simply more subtle forms of domination than the previous imperialist practices of the European colonial empires. The economic and political influence exercised by the advanced capitalist powers over less developed countries is simply a new, more insidious form of imperialism.

North–South conflict is a phrase used to characterize the tension between rich and poor countries. *North* represents the wealthy, industrialized states that lie primarily in the Northern Hemisphere, while *South* is the term used for the less developed countries mainly located in the Southern Hemisphere.

Proletariat is a Marxist term that refers to industrial workers living in urban areas and working in capitalist-owned factories. Marx wrote that the workers are nothing more than "wage slaves," paid subsistence wages and exploited by capitalist factory owners, whose sole motivation is greed.

Transnational class coalitions is a concept of class system theory contending that economic classes form close ties across national boundaries. Unlike transnationalists, who focus on the positive aspects of increasing international economic linkages, class system theorists emphasize the exploitative nature of the global economic system and the role that transnational actors, like multinational corporations, play in this exploitation.

Uneven development is the propensity of capitalism to create and perpetuate an unequal dispersal of global wealth and prosperity.

19.   Manifesto of the Communist Party

Karl Marx and Friedrich Engels

In this excerpt Karl Marx and Fredrich Engels generate the framework for what we call class system theory. Marx and Engels argue that history is based largely on class struggle, that the capitalist economic system created a world situation in which wealth and the control of wealth is in the hands of a few, and that growing tension among the classes during various stages of development would finally be resolved by a transformation to political and economic socialism. This selection is from the *Manifesto of the Communist Party* (1848).

    Karl Marx (1818–1883) and Fredrich Engels (1820–1895) were two of the founders of the communist movement in Europe during the nineteenth century. Their other works include *The Capital, The German Ideology,* and *The Poverty of Philosophy.*

A spectre is haunting Europe—the spectre of Communism. All the Powers of old Europe have entered into a holy alliance to exorcise this spectre: Pope and Czar, Metternich and Guizot, French Radicals and German police-spies.

    Where is the party in opposition that has not been decried as Communistic by its opponents in power? Where the Opposition that has not hurled back the branding reproach of Communism, against the more advanced opposition parties, as well as against its reactionary adversaries?

    Two things result from this fact.

    I. Communism is already acknowledged by all European Powers to be itself a Power.

    II. It is high time that Communists should openly, in the face of the whole world, publish their views, their aims, their tendencies, and meet this nursery tale of the Spectre of Communism with a Manifesto of the party itself.

    To this end, Communists of various nationalities have assembled in London, and sketched the following Manifesto, to be published in the English, French, German, Italian, Flemish and Danish languages.

I. BOURGEOIS AND PROLETARIANS[1]

The history of all hitherto existing society[2] is the history of class struggles.

    Freeman and slave, patrician and plebeian, lord and serf, guild-master[3] and journeyman, in a word, oppressor and oppressed, stood in constant opposition to one another, carried on an uninterrupted, now hidden, now open fight, a fight that each time ended, either in a revolutionary re-constitution of society at large, or in the common ruin of the contending classes.

    In the earlier epochs of history, we find almost everywhere a complicated arrangement of society into various orders, a manifold gradation of social rank. In ancient Rome we have patricians, knights, plebeians, slaves; in the Middle Ages, feudal lords, vassals, guild-masters, journey-men, apprentices, serfs; in almost all of these classes, again, subordinate gradations.

The modern bourgeois society that has sprouted from the ruins of feudal society has not done away with clash antagonisms. It has but established new classes, new conditions of oppression, new forms of struggle in place of the old ones.

Our epoch, the epoch of the bourgeoisie, possesses, however, this distinctive feature: it has simplified the class antagonisms: Society as a whole is more and more splitting up into two great hostile camps, into two great classes directly facing each other: Bourgeoisie and Proletariat.

From the serfs of the Middle Ages sprang the chartered burghers of the earliest towns. From these burgesses the first elements of the bourgeoisie were developed.

The discovery of America, the rounding of the Cape, opened up fresh ground for the rising bourgeoisie. The East-Indian and Chinese markets, the colonisation of America, trade with the colonies, the increase in the means of exchange and in commodities generally, gave to commerce, to navigation, to industry, an impulse never before known, and thereby, to the revolutionary element in the tottering feudal society, a rapid development.

The feudal system of industry, under which industrial production was monopolised by closed guilds, now no longer sufficed for the growing wants of the new markets. The manufacturing system took its place. The guild-masters were pushed on one side by the manufacturing middle class; division of labour between the different corporate guilds vanished in the face of division of labour in each single workshop.

Meantime the markets kept ever growing, the demand ever rising. Even manufacture no longer sufficed. Thereupon, steam and machinery revolutionised industrial production. The place of manufacture was taken by the giant, Modern Industry, the place of the industrial middle class, by industrial millionaires, the leaders of whole industrial armies, the modern bourgeois.

Modern industry has established the world-market, for which the discovery of America paved the way. This market has given an immense development to commerce, to navigation, to communication by land. This development has, in its turn, reacted on the extension of industry; and in proportion as industry, commerce, navigation, railways extended, in the same proportion the bourgeoisie developed, increased its capital, and pushed into the background every class handed down from the Middle Ages.

We see, therefore, how the modern bourgeoisie is itself the product of a long course of development, of a series of revolutions in the modes of production and of exchange.

Each step in the development of the bourgeoisie was accompanied by a corresponding political advance of that class. An oppressed class under the sway of the feudal nobility, an armed and self-governing association in the mediaeval commune,[4] here independent urban republic (as in Italy and Germany), there taxable "third estate" of the monarchy (as in France), afterwards, in the period of manufacture proper, serving either the semi-feudal or the absolute monarchy as a counterpoise against the nobility, and, in fact, corner-stone of the great monarchies in general, the bourgeoisie has at last, since the establishment of Modern Industry and of the world-market, conquered for itself, in the modern representative State, exclusive political sway. The executive of the modern State is but a committee for managing the common affairs of the whole bourgeoisie.

The bourgeoisie, historically, has played a most revolutionary part.

The bourgeoisie, wherever it has got the upper hand, has put an end to all feudal, patriarchal, idyllic relations. It has pitilessly torn asunder the motley feudal ties that bound man to his "natural superiors," and has left remaining no other nexus between man and man than naked self-interest, than callous "cash payment." It has drowned the most heavenly ecstasies of religious fervour, of chivalrous enthusiasm, of philistine sentimentalism, in the icy water of egotistical calculation. It has resolved personal worth into exchange value, and in place of the numberless indefeasible chartered freedoms, has set up that single, unconscionable freedom—Free Trade. In one word, for exploitation, veiled by religious and political illusions, it has substituted naked, shameless, direct, brutal exploitation.

The bourgeoisie has stripped of its halo every occupation hitherto honoured and looked up to with reverent awe. It has converted the physician, the lawyer, the priest, the poet, the man of science, into its paid wage-labourers.

The bourgeoisie has torn away from the family its sentimental veil, and has reduced the family relation to a mere money relation.

The bourgeoisie has disclosed how it came to pass that the brutal display of vigour in the Middle Ages, which Reactionists so much admire, found its fitting complement in the most slothful indolence. It has been the first to show what man's activity can bring about. It has accomplished wonders far surpassing Egyptian pyramids, Roman aqueducts, and Gothic cathedrals; it has conducted expeditions that put in the shade all former Exoduses of nations and crusades.

The bourgeoisie cannot exist without constantly revolutionising the instruments of production, and thereby the relations of production, and with them the whole relations of society. Conservation of the old modes of production in unaltered form, was, on the contrary, the first condition of existence for all earlier industrial classes. Constant revolutionising of production, uninterrupted disturbance of all social conditions, everlasting uncertainty and agitation distinguish the bourgeois epoch from all earlier ones. All fixed, fast-frozen relations, with their train of ancient and venerable prejudices and opinions, are swept away, all newformed ones become antiquated before they can ossify. All that is solid melts into air, all that is holy is profaned, and man is at last compelled to face with sober senses, his real conditions of life, and his relations with his kind.

The need of a constantly expanding market for its products chases the bourgeoisie over the whole surface of the globe. It must nestle everywhere, settle everywhere, establish connexions everywhere.

The bourgeoisie has through its exploitation of the world-market given a cosmopolitan character to production and consumption in every country. To the great chagrin of Reactionists, it has drawn from under the feet of industry the national ground on which it stood. All old-established national industries have been destroyed or are daily being destroyed. They are dislodged by new industries, whose introduction becomes a life and death question for all civilised nations, by industries that no longer work up indigenous raw material, but raw material drawn from the remotest zones; industries whose products are consumed, not only at home, but in every quarter of the globe. In place of the old wants, satisfied by the productions of the country, we find new wants, requiring for their satisfaction the products of distant lands and climes. In place of the old local and national seclusion and self-sufficiency, we have intercourse in every direction, universal inter-dependence of nations. And as in material, so also in intellectual production. The intellectual creations of individual nations become common property. National one-sidedness and narrow-mindedness become more and more impossible, and from the numerous national and local literatures, there arises a world literature.

The bourgeoisie, by the rapid improvement of all instruments of production, by the immensely facilitated means of communication, draws all, even the most barbarian, nations into civilisation. The cheap prices of its commodities are the heavy artillery with which it batters down all Chinese walls, with which it forces the barbarians' intensely obstinate hatred of foreigners to capitulate. It compels all nations, on pain of extinction, to adopt the bourgeois mode of production; it compels them to introduce what it calls civilisation into their midst, *i.e.,* to become bourgeois themselves. In one word, it creates a world after its own image.

The bourgeoisie has subjected the country to the rule of the towns. It has created enormous cities, has greatly increased the urban population as compared with the rural, and has thus rescued a considerable part of the population from the idiocy of rural life. Just as it has made the country dependent on the towns, so it has made barbarian and semi-barbarian countries dependent on the civilised ones, nations of peasants on nations of bourgeois, the East on the West.

The bourgeoisie keeps more and more doing away with the scattered state of the population, of the means of production, and of property. It has agglomerated population, centralised means of production, and has concentrated property in a few hands. The necessary consequence of this was political centralisation. Independent, or but loosely connected provinces, with separate interests, laws, governments and systems of taxation, became lumped together into one nation, with one government, one code of laws, one national class-interest, one frontier and one customs-tariff.

The bourgeoisie, during its rule of scarce one hundred years, has created more massive and more colossal productive forces than have all preceding generations together. Subjection of Nature's forces to man, machinery, application of chemistry to industry and agriculture, steam-navigation, railways, electric telegraphs, clearing of whole continents for cultivation, canalisation of rivers, whole populations conjured out of the ground—what earlier century had even a presentiment that such productive forces slumbered in the lap of social labour?

We see then: the means of production and of exchange, on whose foundation the bourgeoisie built itself up, were generated in feudal society. At a certain stage in the development of these means of production and of exchange, the conditions under which feudal society produced and exchanged, the feudal organisation of agriculture and manufacturing industry, in one word, the feudal relations of property became no longer compatible with the already developed productive forces; they became so many fetters. They had to be burst asunder; they were burst asunder.

Into their place stepped free competition, accompanied by a social and political constitution adapted to it, and by the economical and political sway of the bourgeois class.

A similar movement is going on before our own eyes. Modern bourgeois society with its relations of production, of exchange and of property, a society that has conjured up such gigantic means of production and of exchange, is like the sorcerer, who is no longer able to control the powers of the nether world whom he has called up by his spells. For many a decade past the history of industry and commerce is but the history of the revolt of modern productive forces against modern conditions of production, against the property relations that are the conditions for the existence of the bourgeoisie and of its rule. It is enough to mention the commercial crises that by their periodical return put on its trial, each time more threateningly, the existence of the entire bourgeois society. In these crises a great part not only of the existing products, but also of the previously created productive forces, are periodically destroyed. In these crises there breaks out an epidemic that, in all earlier epochs, would have seemed an absurdity—the epidemic of over-production. Society suddenly finds itself put back into a state of momentary barbarism; it appears as if a famine, a universal war of devastation had cut off the supply of every means of subsistence; industry and commerce seem to be destroyed; and why? Because there is too much civilisation, too much means of subsistence, too much industry, too much commerce. The productive forces at the disposal of society no longer tend to further the development of the conditions of bourgeois property; on the contrary, they have become too powerful for these conditions, by which they are fettered, and so soon as they overcome these fetters, they bring disorder into the whole of bourgeois society, endanger the existence of bourgeois property. The conditions of bourgeois society are too narrow to comprise the wealth created by them. And how does the bourgeoisie get over these crises? On the one hand by enforced destruction of a mass of productive forces; on the other, by the conquest of new markets, and by the more thorough exploitation of the old ones. That is to say, by paving the way for more extensive and more destructive crises, and by diminishing the means whereby crises are prevented.

The weapons with which the bourgeoisie felled feudalism to the ground are now turned against the bourgeoisie itself.

But not only has the bourgeoisie forged the weapons that bring death to itself; it has also called into existence the men who are to wield those weapons—the modern working class—the proletarians.

In proportion as the bourgeoisie, *i.e.,* capital, is developed, in the same proportion is the proletariat, the modern working class, developed—a class of labourers, who live only so long as they find work, and who find work only so long as their labour increases capital. These labourers, who must sell themselves piece-meal, are a commodity, like every other article of commerce, and are consequently exposed to all the vicissitudes of competition, to all the fluctuations of the market.

Owing to the extensive use of machinery and to division of labour, the work of the proletarians has lost all individual character, and consequently, all charm for the workman. He becomes an appendage of the machine, and it is only the most simple, most monotonous, and most easily acquired knack, that is required of him. Hence, the cost of production of a workman is restricted, almost entirely, to the means of subsistence that he requires for his maintenance, and for the propagation of his race. But the price of a commodity, and therefore also of labour,[5] is equal to its cost of production. In proportion, therefore, as the repulsiveness of the work increases, the wage decreases. Nay more, in proportion as the use of machinery and division of labour increases, in the same proportion the burden of toil also increases, whether by prolongation of the working hours, by increase of the work exacted in a given time or by increased speed of the machinery, etc.

Modern industry has converted the little workshop of the patriarchal master into the great factory of the industrial capitalist. Masses of labourers, crowded into the factory, are organised like soldiers. As privates of the industrial army they are placed under the command of a perfect hierarchy of officers and sergeants. Not only are they slaves of the bourgeois class, and of the bourgeois State; they are daily and hourly enslaved by the machine, by the over-looker, and, above all, by the individual bourgeois manufacturer himself. The more openly this despotism proclaims gain to be its end and aim, the more petty, the more hateful and the more embittering it is.

The less the skill and exertion of strength implied in manual labour, in other words, the more modern industry becomes developed, the more is the labour of men superseded by that of women. Differences of age and sex have no longer any distinctive social validity for the working class. All are instruments of labour, more or less expensive to use, according to their age and sex.

No sooner is the exploitation of the labourer by the manufacturer, so far, at an end, that he receives his wages in cash, than he is set upon by the other portions of the bourgeoisie, the landlord, the shopkeeper, the pawnbroker, etc.

The lower strata of the middle class—the small tradespeople, shopkeepers, and retired tradesmen generally, the handicraftsmen and peasants—all these sink gradually into the proletariat, partly because their diminutive capital does not suffice for the scale on which Modern Industry is carried on, and is swamped in the competition with the large capitalists, partly because their specialised skill is rendered worthless by new methods of production. Thus the proletariat is recruited from all classes of the population.

The proletariat goes through various stages of development. With its birth begins its struggle with the bourgeoisie. At first the contest is carried on by individual labourers, then by the workpeople of a factory, then by the operatives of one trade, in one locality, against the individual bourgeois who directly exploits them. They direct their attacks not against the bourgeois conditions of production, but against the instruments of production themselves; they destroy imported wares that compete with their labour, they smash to pieces machinery, they set factories ablaze, they seek to restore by force the vanished status of the workman of the Middle Ages.

At this stage the labourers still form an incoherent mass scattered over the whole country, and broken up by their mutual competition. If anywhere they unite to form more compact bodies, this is not yet the consequence of their own active union, but of the union of the bourgeoisie, which class, in order to attain its own political ends, is compelled to set the whole proletariat in motion, and is moreover yet, for a time, able to do so. At this stage, therefore, the proletarians do not fight their enemies, but the enemies of their enemies, the remnants of absolute monarchy, the landowners, the non-industrial bourgeois, the petty bourgeoisie. Thus the whole historical movement is concentrated in the hands of the bourgeoisie; every victory so obtained is a victory for the bourgeoisie.

But with the development of industry the proletariat not only increases in number; it becomes concentrated in greater masses, its strength grows, and it feels that strength more. The various interests and conditions of life within the ranks of the proletariat are more and more equalised, in proportion as machinery obliterates all distinctions of labour, and nearly everywhere reduces wages to the same low level. The growing competition among the bourgeois, and the resulting commercial crises, make the wages of the workers ever more fluctuating. The unceasing improvement of machinery, ever more rapidly developing, makes their livelihood more and more precarious; the collisions between individual workmen and individual bourgeois take more and more the character of collisions between two classes. Thereupon the workers begin to form combinations (Trades Unions) against the bourgeois; they club together in order to keep up the rate of wages; they found permanent associations in order to make provision beforehand for these occasional revolts. Here and there the contest breaks out into riots.

Now and then the workers are victorious, but only for a time. The real fruit of their battles lies, not in the immediate result, but in the ever-expanding union of the workers. This union is helped on by the improved means of communication that are created by modern industry and that place the workers of different localities in contact with one another. It was just this contact that was needed to centralise the numerous local struggles, all of the same character, into one national struggle between classes. But every class struggle is a political struggle. And that union, to attain which the burghers of the Middle Ages, with their miserable highways, required centuries, the modern proletarians, thanks to railways, achieve in a few years.

This organisation of the proletarians into a class, and consequently into a political party, is continually being upset again by the competition between the workers themselves. But it ever rises up again, stronger, firmer, mightier. It compels legislative recognition of particular interests of the workers, by taking advantage of the divisions among the bourgeoisie itself. Thus the ten-hours' bill in England was carried.

Although collisions between the classes of the old society further, in many ways, the course of development of the proletariat. The bourgeoisie finds itself involved in a constant battle. At first with the aristocracy; later on, with those portions of the bourgeoisie itself, whose interests have become antagonistic to the progress of industry; at all times, with the bourgeoisie of foreign countries. In all these battles it sees itself compelled to appeal to the proletariat, to ask for its help, and thus, to drag it into the political arena. The bourgeoisie itself, therefore, supplies the proletariat with its own elements of political and general education, in other words, it furnishes the proletariat with weapons for fighting the bourgeoisie.

Further, as we have already seen, entire sections of the ruling classes are, by the advance of industry, precipitated into the proletariat, or are at least threatened in their conditions of existence. These also supply the proletariat with fresh elements of enlightenment and progress.

Finally, in times when the class struggle nears the decisive hour, the process of dissolution going on within the ruling class, in fact within the whole range of society, assumes such a violent, glaring character, that a small section of the ruling class cuts itself adrift, and joins the revolutionary class, the class that holds the future in its hands. Just as, therefore, at an earlier period, a section of the nobility went over to the bourgeoisie, so now a portion of the bourgeoisie goes over to the proletariat, and in particular, a portion of the bourgeois ideologists, who have raised themselves to the level of comprehending theoretically the historical movement as a whole.

Of all the classes that stand face to face with the bourgeoisie today, the proletariat alone is a really revolutionary class. The other classes decay and finally disappear in the face of Modern Industry;

the proletariat is its special and essential product.

The lower middle class, the small manufacturer, the shopkeeper, the artisan, the peasant, all these fight against the bourgeoisie, to save from extinction their existence as fractions of the middle class. They are therefore not revolutionary, but conservative. Nay more, they are reactionary, for they try to roll back the wheel of history. If by chance they are revolutionary, they are so only in view of their impending transfer into the proletariat, they thus defend not their present, but their future interests, they desert their own standpoint to place themselves at that of the proletariat.

The "dangerous class," the social scum, that passively rotting mass thrown off by the lowest layers of old society, may, here and there, be swept into the movement by a proletarian revolution; its conditions of life, however, prepare it far more for the part of a bribed tool of reactionary intrigue.

In the conditions of the proletariat, those of old society at large are already virtually swamped. The proletarian is without property; his relation to his wife and children has no longer anything in common with the bourgeois family-relations; modern industrial labour, modern subjection to capital, the same in England as in France, in America as in Germany, has stripped him of every trace of national character. Law, morality, religion, are to him so many bourgeois prejudices, behind which lurk in ambush just as many bourgeois interests.

All the preceding classes that got the upper hand, sought to fortify their already acquired status by subjecting society at large to their conditions of appropriation. The proletarians cannot become masters of the productive forces of society, except by abolishing their own previous mode of appropriation, and thereby also every other previous mode of appropriation. They have nothing of their own to secure and to fortify; their mission is to destroy all previous securities for, and insurances of, individual property.

All previous historical movements were movements of minorities, or in the interests of minorities. The proletarian movement is the self-conscious, independent movement of the immense majority, in the interests of the immense majority. The proletariat, the lowest stratum of our present society, cannot stir, cannot raise itself up, without the whole superincumbent strata of official society being sprung into the air.

Though not in substance, yet in form, the struggle of the proletariat with the bourgeoisie is at first a national struggle. The proletariat of each country must, of course, first of all settle matters with its own bourgeoisie.

In depicting the most general phases of the development of the proletariat, we traced the more or less veiled civil war, raging within existing society, up to the point where that war breaks out into open revolution, and where the violent overthrow of the bourgeoisie lays the foundation for the sway of the proletariat.

Hitherto, every form of society has been based, as we have already seen, on the antagonism of oppressing and oppressed classes. But in order to oppress a class, certain conditions must be assured to it under which it can, at least, continue its slavish existence. The serf, in the period of serfdom, raised himself to membership in the commune, just as the petty bourgeois, under the yoke of feudal absolutism, managed to develop into a bourgeois. The modern labourer, on the contrary, instead of rising with the progress of industry, sinks deeper and deeper below the conditions of existence of his own class. He becomes a pauper, and pauperism develops more rapidly than population and wealth. And here it becomes evident, that the bourgeoisie is unfit any longer to be the ruling class in society, and to impose its conditions of existence upon society as an over-riding law. It is unfit to rule because it is incompetent to assure an existence to its slave within his slavery, because it cannot help letting him sink into such a state, that it has to feed him, instead of being fed by him. Society can no longer live under this bourgeoisie, in other words, its existence is no longer compatible with society.

The essential condition for the existence, and for the sway of the bourgeois class, is the formation and augmentation of capital; the condition for capital is wage-labour. Wage-labour rests exclusively on competition between the labourers. The advance of industry, whose involuntary promoter is the bourgeoisie, replaces the isolation of the labourers, due to competition, by their revolutionary combination, due to association. The development of Modern Industry, therefore, cuts from under its feet the very foundation on which the bourgeoisie produces and appropriates products. What the bourgeoisie, therefore, produces, above all, is its own grave-diggers. Its fall and the victory of the proletariat are equally inevitable.

NOTES

1. By bourgeoisie is meant the class of modern Capitalists, owners of the means of social production and employers of

wage-labour. By proletariat, the class of modern wage-labourers who, having no means of production of their own, are reduced to selling their labour-power in order to live. [*Engels, English edition of 1888*]

2. That is, all *written* history. In 1847, the pre-history of society, the social organisation existing previous to recorded history, was all but unknown. Since then, Haxthausen discovered common ownership of land in Russia, Maurer proved it to be the social foundation from which all Teutonic races started in history, and by and by village communities were found to be, or to have been the primitive form of society everywhere from India to Ireland. The inner organisation of this primitive Communistic society was laid bare, in its typical form, by Morgan's crowning discovery of the true nature of the *gens* and its relation to the *tribe*. With the dissolution of these primaeval communities society begins to be differentiated into separate and finally antagonistic classes. I have attempted to retrace this process of dissolution in: "Der Ursprung der Familie, des Privateigenthums und des Staats" [*The Origin of the Family, Private Property and the State*], 2nd edition, Stuttgart 1886. [*Engels, English edition of 1888*]

3. Guild-master, that is, a full member of a guild, a master within, not a head of a guild. [*Engels, English edition of 1888*]

4. "Commune" was the name taken, in France, by the nascent towns even before they had conquered from their feudal lords and masters local self-government and political rights as the "Third Estate." Generally speaking, for the economical development of the bourgeoisie, England is here taken as the typical country; for its political development, France. [*Engels, English edition of 1888*]

   This was the name given their urban communities by the townsmen of Italy and France, after they had purchased or wrested their initial rights of self-government from their feudal lords. [*Engels, German edition of 1890*]

5. Subsequently Marx pointed out that the worker sells not his labour but his labour power

QUESTIONS

1. Describe in detail the various stages of development in Marx's and Engels' discussion of class struggle.

2. Can a link be made on the basis of security between class struggle and the anarchic nature of the international system described by Hans Morgenthau? Explain.

20.   Imperialism

John A. Hobson

In this excerpt, John A. Hobson explains the importance of economics in understanding imperialism. Indeed, he explains that imperialism is rooted in economics. Both surplus capital and over-production of goods grow at a much faster rate than consumption. This disproportion of growth forces industrialists and manufacturers to secure foreign markets in the Third World for the distribution of surplus capital. This selection is from *Imperialism: A Study* (1938).

John A. Hobson was an English economist and social reformer during the late nineteenth and early twentieth centuries. His writings profoundly influenced V.I. Lenin.

THE ECONOMIC TAPROOT OF IMPERIALISM

No mere array of facts and figures adduced to illustrate the economic nature of the new Imperialism will suffice to dispel the popular delusion that the use of national force to secure new markets by annexing fresh tracts of territory is a sound and a necessary policy for an advanced industrial country like Great Britain.[1] It has indeed been proved that recent annexations of tropical countries, procured at great expense, have furnished poor and precarious markets, that our aggregate trade with our colonial possessions is virtually stationary, and that our most profitable and progressive trade is with rival industrial nations, whose territories we have no desire to annex, whose markets we cannot force, and whose active antagonism we are provoking by our expansive policy.

But these arguments are not conclusive. It is open to Imperialists to argue thus: "We must have markets for our growing manufactures, we must have new outlets for the investment of our surplus capital and for the energies of the adventurous surplus of our population: such expansion is a necessity of life to a nation with our great and growing powers of production. An ever larger share of our population is devoted to the manufactures and commerce of towns, and is thus dependent for life and work upon food and raw materials from foreign lands. In order to buy and pay for these things we must sell our goods abroad. During the first three-quarters of the nineteenth century we could do so without difficulty by a natural expansion of commerce with continental nations and our colonies, all of which were far behind us in the main arts of manufacture and the carrying trades. So long as England held a virtual monopoly of the world markets for certain important classes of manufactured goods, Imperialism was unnecessary. After 1870 this manufacturing and trading supremacy was greatly impaired: other nations, especially Germany, the United States, and Belgium, advanced with great rapidity, and while they have not crushed or even stayed the increase of our external trade, their competition made it more and more difficult to dispose of the full surplus of our manufactures at a profit. The encroachments made by these nations upon our old markets, even in our own possessions, made it most urgent that we should take energetic means to secure new markets. These new markets had to lie in hitherto undeveloped countries, chiefly in the tropics, where vast populations lived capable of growing economic needs which our manufacturers and merchants could supply. Our rivals were seizing and annexing territories for similar purposes, and when they had annexed them closed them to our trade. The diplomacy and the arms of Great Britain had to be used in order to compel the owners of the new markets to deal with us: and experience showed that the safest means of securing and developing such markets is by establishing 'protectorates' or by annexation. The value in 1905 of these markets must not be taken as a final test of the economy of such a policy; the process of educating civilized needs which we can supply is of necessity a gradual one, and the cost of such Imperialism must be regarded as a capital outlay, the fruits of which posterity would reap. The new markets might not be large, but they formed serviceable outlets for the overflow of our great textile and metal industries, and, when the vast Asiatic and African populations of the interior were reached, a rapid expansion of trade was expected to result.

"Far larger and more important is the pressure of capital for external fields of investment. Moreover, while the manufacturer and trader are well content to trade with foreign nations, the tendency for investors to work towards the political annexation of countries which contain their more speculative investments is very powerful. Of the fact of this pressure of capital there can be no question. Large savings are made which cannot find any profitable investment in this country; they must find employment elsewhere, and it is to the advantage of the nation that they should be employed as largely as possible in lands where they can be utilized in opening up markets for British trade and employment for British enterprise.

"However costly, however perilous, this process of imperial expansion may be, it is necessary to the continued existence and progress of our nation;[2] if we abandoned it we must be content to leave the development of the world to other nations, who will everywhere cut into

our trade, and even impair our means of securing the food and raw materials we require to support our population. Imperialism is thus seen to be, not a choice, but a necessity."

The practical force of this economic argument in politics is strikingly illustrated by the later history of the United States. Here is a country which suddenly broke through a conservative policy, strongly held by both political parties, bound up with every popular instinct and tradition, and flung itself into a rapid imperial career for which it possessed neither the material nor the moral equipment, risking the principles and practices of liberty and equality by the establishment of militarism and the forcible subjugation of peoples which it could not safely admit to the condition of American citizenship.

Was this a mere wild freak of spread-eaglism, a burst of political ambition on the part of a nation coming to a sudden realization of its destiny? Not at all. The spirit of adventure, the American "mission of civilization," were as forces making for Imperialism, clearly subordinate to the driving force of the economic factor. The dramatic character of the change is due to the unprecedented rapidity of the industrial revolution in the United States from the eighties onwards. During that period the United States, with her unrivalled natural resources, her immense resources of skilled and unskilled labour, and her genius for invention and organization, developed the best equipped and most productive manufacturing economy the world has yet seen. Fostered by rigid protective tariffs, her metal, textile, tool, clothing, furniture, and other manufactures shot up in a single generation from infancy to full maturity, and, having passed through a period of intense competition, attained, under the able control of great trust-makers, a power of production greater than has been attained in the most advanced industrial countries of Europe.

An era of cut-throat competition, followed by a rapid process of amalgamation, threw an enormous quantity of wealth into the hands of a small number of captains of industry. No luxury of living to which this class could attain kept pace with its rise of income, and a process of automatic saving set in upon an unprecedented scale. The investment of these savings in other industries helped to bring these under the same concentrative forces. Thus a great increase of savings seeking profitable investment is synchronous with a stricter economy of the use of existing capital. No doubt the rapid growth of a population, accustomed to a high and an always ascending standard of comfort, absorbs in the satisfaction of its wants a large quantity of new capital. But the actual rate of saving, conjoined with a more economical application of forms of existing capital, exceeded considerably the rise of the national consumption of manufactures. The power of production far outstripped the actual rate of consumption, and, contrary to the older economic theory, was unable to force a corresponding increase of consumption by lowering prices.

This is no mere theory. The history of any of the numerous trusts or combinations in the United States sets out the facts with complete distinctness. In the free competition of manufactures preceding combination the chronic condition is one of "over-production," in the sense that all the mills or factories can only be kept at work by cutting prices down towards a point where the weaker competitors are forced to close down,

because they cannot sell their goods at a price which covers the true cost of production. The first result of the successful formation of a trust or combine is to close down the worse equipped or worse placed mills, and supply the entire market from the better equipped and better placed ones. This course may or may not be attended by a rise of price and some restriction of consumption: in some cases trusts take most of their profits by raising prices, in other cases by reducing the costs of production through employing only the best mills and stopping the waste of competition.

For the present argument it matters not which course is taken; the point is that this concentration of industry in "trusts," "combines," etc., at once limits the quantity of capital which can be effectively employed and increases the share of profits out of which fresh savings and fresh capital will spring. It is quite evident that a trust which is motived by cut-throat competition, due to an excess of capital, cannot normally find inside the "trusted" industry employment for that portion of the profits which the trust-makers desire to save and to invest. New inventions and other economies of production or distribution within the trade may absorb some of the new capital, but there are rigid limits to this absorption. The trust-maker in oil or sugar must find other investments for his savings: if he is early in the application of the combination principles to his trade, he will naturally apply his surplus capital to establish similar combinations in other industries, economising capital still further, and rendering it ever harder for ordinary saving men to find investments for their savings.

Indeed, the conditions alike of cut-throat competition and of combination attest the congestion of capital in the manufacturing industries which have entered the machine economy. We are not here concerned with any theoretic question as to the possibility of producing by modern machine methods more goods than can find a market. It is sufficient to point out that the manufacturing power of a country like the United States would grow so fast as to exceed the demands of the home market. No one acquainted with trade will deny a fact which all American economists assert, that this is the condition which the United States reached at the end of the century, so far, as the more developed industries are concerned. Her manufactures were saturated with capital and could absorb no more. One after another they sought refuge from the waste of competition in "combines" which secure a measure of profitable peace by restricting the quantity of operative capital. Industrial and financial princes in oil, steel, sugar, railroads, banking, etc., were faced with the dilemma of either spending more than they knew how to spend, or forcing markets outside the home area. Two economic courses were open to them, both leading towards an abandonment of the political isolation of the past and the adoption of imperialist methods in the future. Instead of shutting down inferior mills and rigidly restricting output to correspond with profitable sales in the home markets, they might employ their full productive power, applying their savings to increase their business capital, and, while still regulating output and prices for the home market, may "hustle" for foreign markets, dumping down their surplus goods at prices which would not be possible save for the profitable nature of their home market. So likewise they might employ their savings in seeking investments outside their country, first repaying the capital borrowed from Great Britain and other countries for the early development of their railroads, mines and manufactures, and afterwards becoming themselves a creditor class to foreign countries.

It was this sudden demand for foreign markets for manufactures and for investments which was avowedly responsible for the adoption of Imperialism as a political policy and practice by the Republican party to which the great industrial and financial chiefs belonged, and which belonged to them. The adventurous enthusiasm of President Theodore Roosevelt and his "manifest destiny" and "mission of civilization" party must not deceive us. It was Messrs. Rockefeller, Pierpont Morgan, and their associates who needed Imperialism and who fastened it upon the shoulders of the great Republic of the West. They needed Imperialism because they desired to use the public resources of their country to find profitable employment for their capital which otherwise would be superfluous.

It is not indeed necessary to own a country in order to do trade with it or to invest capital in it, and doubtless the United States could find some vent for their surplus goods, and capital in European countries. But these countries were for the most part able to make provision for themselves: most of them erected tariffs against manufacturing imports, and even Great Britain was urged to defend herself by reverting to Protection. The big American manufacturers and financiers were compelled to look to China and the Pacific and to South America for their most profitable chances; Protectionists by principle and practice, they would insist upon getting as close a monopoly of these markets as they can secure, and the competition of Germany,

Export Trade of United States, 1890–1900.

YEAR	AGRICULTURE	MANUFACTURERS	MISCELLANEOUS
	£	£	£
1890	125,756,000	31,435,000	13,019,000
1891	146,617,000	33,720,000	11,731,000
1892	142,508,000	30,479,000	11,660,000
1893	123,810,000	35,484,000	11,653,000
1894	114,737,000	35,557,000	11,168,000
1895	104,143,000	40,230,000	12,174,000
1896	132,992,000	50,738,000	13,639,000
1897	146,059,000	55,923,000	13,984,000
1898	170,383,000	61,585,000	14,743,000
1899	156,427,000	76,157,000	18,002,000
1900	180,931,000	88,281,000	21,389,000

England, and other trading nations would drive them to the establishment of special political relations with the markets they most prize. Cuba, the Philippines, and Hawaii were but the *hors d'œuvre* to whet an appetite for an ampler banquet. Moreover, the powerful hold upon politics which these industrial and financial magnates possessed formed a separate stimulus, which, as we have shown, was operative in Great Britain and elsewhere; the public expenditure in pursuit of an imperial career would be a separate immense source of profit to these men, as financiers negotiating loans, shipbuilders and owners handling subsidies, contractors and manufacturers of armaments and other imperialist appliances.

The suddenness of this political revolution is due to the rapid manifestation of the need. In the last years of the nineteenth century the United States nearly trebled the value of its manufacturing export trade, and it was to be expected that, if the rate of progress of those years continued, within a decade it would overtake our more slowly advancing export trade,

and stand first in the list of manufacture-exporting nations.[3]

This was the avowed ambition, and no idle one, of the keenest business men of America; and with the natural resources, the labour and the administrative talents at their disposal, it was quite likely they would achieve their object.[4] The stronger and more direct control over politics exercised in America by business men enabled them to drive more quickly and more straightly along the line of their economic interests than in Great Britain. American Imperialism was the natural product of the economic pressure of a sudden advance of capitalism which could not find occupation at home and needed foreign markets for goods and for investments.

The same needs existed in European countries, and, as is admitted, drove Governments along the same path. Overproduction in the sense of an excessive manufacturing plant, and surplus capital which could not find sound investments within the country, forced Great Britain, Germany, Holland, France to place larger and larger portions of their economic resources outside the area of their present political domain, and then stimulate a policy of political expansion so as to take in the new areas. The economic sources of this movement are laid bare by periodic trade-depressions due to an inability of producers to find adequate and profitable markets for what they can produce. The Majority Report of the Commission upon the Depression of Trade in 1885 put the matter in a nutshell. "That, owing to the nature of the times, the demand for our commodities does not increase at the same rate as formerly; that our capacity for production is consequently in excess of our requirements, and could be considerably increased at short notice; that this is due partly to the competition of the capital which is being steadily accumulated in the country." The Minority Report straightly imputed the condition of affairs to "over-production." Germany was in the early 1900's suffering severely from what is called a glut of capital and of manufacturing power: she had to have new markets; her Consuls all over the world were "hustling" for trade; trading settlements were forced upon Asia Minor; in East and West Africa, in China and elsewhere the German Empire was impelled to a policy of colonization and protectorates as outlets for German commercial energy.

Every improvement of methods of production, every concentration of ownership and control, seems to accentuate the tendency. As one nation after another enters the machine economy and adopts advanced industrial methods, it becomes more difficult for its manufacturers, merchants, and financiers to dispose profitably of their economic resources, and they are tempted more and more to use their Governments in order to secure for their particular use some distant undeveloped country by annexation and protection.

The process, we may be told, is inevitable, and so it seems upon a superficial inspection. Everywhere appear excessive powers of production, excessive capital in search of investment. It is admitted by all business men that the growth of the powers of production in their country exceeds the growth in consumption, that more goods can be produced than can be sold at a profit, and that more capital exists than can find remunerative investment.

It is this economic condition of affairs that forms the taproot of Imperialism. If the consuming public in this country raised its standard of consumption to keep pace with every rise of productive powers, there could be no excess of goods or capital clamorous to use Imperialism in order to find markets: foreign trade would indeed exist, but there would be no difficulty in exchanging a small surplus of our manufacturers for the food and raw material we annually absorbed, and all the savings that we made could find employment, if we chose, in home industries.

There is nothing inherently irrational in such a supposition. Whatever is, or can be, produced, can be consumed, for a claim upon it, as rent, profit, or wages, forms part of the real income of some member of the community, and he can consume it, or else exchange it for some other consumable with some one else who will consume it. With everything that is produced a consuming power is born. If then there are goods which cannot get consumed, or which cannot even get produced because it is evident they cannot get consumed, and if there is a quantity of capital and labour which cannot get full employment because its products cannot get consumed, the only possible explanation of this paradox is the refusal of owners of consuming power to apply that power in effective demand for commodities.

It is, of course, possible that an excess of producing power might exist in particular industries by misdirection, being engaged in certain manufactures, whereas it ought to have been engaged in agriculture or some other use. But no one can seriously contend that such misdirection explains the recurrent gluts and consequent depressions of modern industry, or that, when over-production is manifest in the leading manufactures, ample avenues are open for the surplus capital and labour in other industries. The general character of the excess of producing power is proved by the existence at such times of large bank stocks of idle money seeking any sort of profitable investment and finding none.

The root questions underlying the phenomena are clearly these: "Why is it that consumption fails to keep pace automatically in a community with power of production?" "Why does under-consumption or over-saving occur?" For it is evident that the consuming power, which, if exercised, would keep tense the reins of production, is in part withheld, or in other words is "saved" and stored up for investment. All saving for investment does not imply slackness of production; quite the contrary. Saving is economically justified, from the social standpoint, when the capital in which it takes material shape finds full employment in helping to produce commodities which, when produced, will be consumed. It is saving in excess of this amount that causes mischief, taking

shape in surplus capital which is not needed to assist current consumption, and which either lies idle, or tries to oust existing capital from its employment, or else seeks speculative use abroad under the protection of the Government.

But it may be asked, "Why should there be any tendency to over-saving? Why should the owners of consuming power withhold a larger quantity for savings than can be serviceably employed?" Another way of putting the same question is this, "Why should not the pressure of present wants keep pace with every possibility of satisfying them?" The answer to these pertinent questions carries us to the broadest issue of the distribution of wealth. If a tendency to distribute income or consuming power according to needs were operative, it is evident that consumption would rise with every rise of producing power, for human needs are illimitable, and there could be no excess of saving. But it is quite otherwise in a state of economic society where distribution has no fixed relation to needs, but is determined by other conditions which assign to some people a consuming power vastly in excess of needs or possible uses, while others are destitute of consuming power enough to satisfy even the full demands of physical efficiency. The following illustration may serve to make the issue clear. "The volume of production has been constantly rising owing to the development of modern machinery. There are two main channels to carry off these products—one channel carrying off the product destined to be consumed by the workers, and the other channel carrying off the remainder to the rich. The workers' channel is in rock-bound banks that cannot enlarge, owing to the competitive wage system preventing wages rising *pro rata* with increased efficiency. Wages are based upon cost of living, and not upon efficiency of labour. The miner in the poor mine gets the same wages per day as the miner in the adjoining rich mine. The owner of the rich mine gets the advantage—not his labourer. The channel which conveys the goods destined to supply the rich is itself divided into two streams. One stream carries off what the rich 'spend' on themselves for the necessities and luxuries of life. The other is simply an 'overflow' stream carrying off their 'savings.' The channel for spending, i.e. the amount wasted by the rich in luxuries, may broaden somewhat, but owing to the small number of those rich enough to indulge in whims it can never be greatly enlarged, and at any rate it bears such a small proportion to the other channel that in no event can much hope of avoiding a flood of capital be hoped for from this division. The rich will never be so ingenious as to spend enough to prevent over-production. The great safety overflow channel which has been continuously more and more widened and deepened to carry off the ever-increasing flood of new capital is that division of the stream which carried the savings of the rich, and this is not only suddenly found to be incapable of further enlargement, but actually seems to be in the process of being dammed up."[5]

Though this presentation over-accentuates the cleavage between rich and poor and over-states the weakness of the workers, it gives forcible and sound expression to a most important and ill-recognised economic truth. The "overflow" stream of savings is of course fed not exclusively from the surplus income of "the rich"; the professional and industrial middle classes, and to some slight extent the workers, contribute. But the "flooding" is distinctly due to the automatic saving of the surplus income of rich men. This is of course particularly true of America, where multi-millionaires rise quickly and find themselves in possession of incomes far exceeding the demands of any craving that is known to them. To make the metaphor complete, the overflow stream must be represented as reentering the stream of production and seeking to empty there all the "savings" that it carries. Where competition remains free, the result is a chronic congestion of productive power and of production, forcing down home prices, wasting large sums in advertising and in pushing for orders, and periodically causing a crisis followed by a collapse, during which quantities of capital and labour lie unemployed and unremunerated. The prime object of the trust or other combine is to remedy this waste and loss by substituting regulation of output for reckless over-production. In achieving this it actually narrows or even dams up the old channels of investment, limiting the overflow stream to the exact amount required to maintain the normal current of output. But this rigid limitation of trade, though required for the separate economy of each trust, does not suit the trust-maker, who is driven to compensate for strictly regulated industry at home by cutting new foreign channels as outlets for his productive power and his excessive savings. Thus we reach the conclusion that Imperialism is the endeavour of the great controllers of industry to broaden the channel for the flow of their surplus wealth by seeking foreign markets and foreign investments to take off the goods and capital they cannot sell or use at home.

The fallacy of the supposed inevitability of imperial expansion as a necessary outlet for progressive industry is now manifest. It is not industrial progress that demands the opening up of new markets and areas of investment, but maldistribution of consuming power which prevents the absorption of commodities and capital within the country. The oversaving which is the economic root of Imperialism is found by analysis to consist of rents, monopoly profits, and other unearned or excessive elements of income, which, not being earned by labour of head or hand, have no legitimate *raison d'être*. Having no natural relation to effort of production, they impel their recipients to no corresponding satisfaction of consumption: they form a surplus wealth, which, having no proper place in the normal economy of production and consumption, tends to accumulate as excessive savings. Let any turn in the tide of politico-economic forces divert from these owners their excess of income and make it flow, either to the workers in higher wages, or to the community in taxes, so that it will be spent instead of being saved, serving in either of these ways to swell the tide of consumption—there will be no need to fight for foreign markets or foreign areas of investment.

Many have carried their analysis so far as to realise the absurdity of spending half our financial resources in fighting to secure foreign markets at times when hungry mouths, ill-clad backs, ill-furnished houses indicate countless unsatisfied material wants among our own population. If we may take the careful statistics of Mr. Rowntree[6] for our guide, we shall be aware that more than one-fourth of the population of our towns is living at a standard which is below bare physical efficiency. If, by some economic readjustment, the products which flow from the surplus saving of the rich to swell the overflow streams could be diverted so as to raise the incomes and the standard of consumption of this inefficient fourth, there would be no need for pushful Imperialism, and the cause of social reform would have won its greatest victory.

It is not inherent in the nature of things that we should spend our natural resources on militarism, war, and risky, unscrupulous diplomacy, in order to find markets for our goods and surplus capital. An intelligent progressive community, based upon substantial equality of economic and educational opportunities, will raise its standard of consumption to correspond with every increased power of production, and can find full employment for an unlimited quantity of capital and labour within the limits of the country which it occupies. Where the distribution of incomes is such as to enable all classes of the nation to convert their felt wants into an effective demand for commodities, there can be no overproduction, no under-employment of capital and labour, and no necessity to fight for foreign markets.

The most convincing condemnation of the current economy is conveyed in the difficulty which producers everywhere experience in finding consumers for their products: a fact attested by the prodigious growth of classes of agents and middlemen, the multiplication of every sort of advertising, and the general increase of the distributive classes. Under a sound economy the pressure would be reversed: the growing wants of progressive societies would be a constant stimulus to the inventive and operative energies of producers, and would form a constant strain upon the powers of production. The simultaneous excess of all the factors of production, attested by frequently recurring periods of trade depression, is a most dramatic exhibition of the false economy of distribution. It does not imply a mere miscalculation in the application of productive power, or a brief temporary excess of that power; it manifests in an acute form an economic waste which is chronic and general throughout the advanced industrial nations, a waste contained in the divorcement of the desire to consume and the power to consume.

If the apportionment of income were such as to evoke no excessive saving, full constant employment for capital and labour would be furnished at home. This, of course, does not imply that there would be no foreign trade. Goods that could not be produced at home, or produced as well or as cheaply, would still be purchased by ordinary process of international exchange, but here again the pressure would be the wholesome pressure of the consumer anxious to buy abroad what he could not buy at home, not the blind eagerness of the producer to use every force or trick of trade or politics to find markets for his "surplus" goods.

The struggle for markets, the greater eagerness of producers to sell than of consumers to buy, is the crowning proof of a false economy of distribution. Imperialism is the fruit of this false economy; "social reform" is its remedy. The primary purpose of "social reform," using the term in its economic signification, is to raise the wholesome standard of private and public consumption for a nation, so as to enable the nation to live up to its highest standard of production. Even those social reformers who aim directly at abolishing or reducing some bad form of consumption, as in the Temperance movement, generally recognise the necessity of substituting some better form of current consumption which is more educative and stimulative of other tastes, and will assist to raise the general standard of consumption.

There is no necessity to open up new foreign markets; the home markets are capable of indefinite expansion. Whatever is produced in England can be consumed in England, provided that the "income" or power to demand commodities, is properly distributed. This only appears untrue because of the unnatural and unwholesome specialisation to which this country has been subjected, based upon a bad distribution of economic resources, which has induced an overgrowth of certain manufacturing trades for the express purpose of effecting foreign sales. If the industrial revolution had taken place in an England founded upon equal access by all classes to land, education and legislation, specialisation in manufactures would not have gone so far (though more intelligent progress would have been made, by reason of a widening of the area of selection of inventive and organising talents); foreign trade would have been less important, though more steady; the standard of life for all portions of the population would have been high, and the present rate of national consumption would probably have given full, constant, remunerative employment to a far larger quantity of private and public capital than is now employed.[7] For the over-saving or wider consumption that is traced to excessive incomes of the rich is a suicidal economy, even from the exclusive standpoint of capital; for consumption alone vitalises capital and makes it capable of yielding profits. An economy that assigns to the "possessing" classes an excess of consuming power which they cannot use, and cannot convert into really serviceable capital, is a dog-in-the-manger policy. The social reforms which deprive the possessing classes of their surplus will not, therefore, inflict upon them the real injury they dread; they can only use this surplus by forcing on their country a wrecking policy of Imperialism. The only safety of nations lies in removing the unearned increments of income from the possessing classes, and adding them to the wage-income of the working classes or to the public income, in order that they may be spent in raising the standard of consumption.

Social reform bifurcates, according as reformers seek to achieve this end by raising wages or by increasing public taxation and expenditure. These courses are not essentially contradictory, but are rather complementary. Working-class movements aim, either by private co-operation or by political pressure on legislative and administrative government, at increasing the proportion of the national income which accrues to labour in the form of wages, pensions, compensation for injuries, etc. State Socialism aims at getting for the direct use of the whole society an increased share of the "social values" which arise from the closely and essentially co-operative work of an industrial society, taxing property and incomes so as to draw into the public exchequer for public expenditure the "unearned elements" of income, leaving to individual producers those incomes which are necessary to induce them to apply in the best way their economic energies, and to private enterprises those businesses which do not breed monopoly, and which the public need not or cannot undertake. These are not, indeed, the sole or perhaps the best avowed objects of social reform movements. But for the purposes of this analysis they form the kernel.

Trade Unionism and Socialism are thus the natural enemies of Imperialism, for they take away from the "imperialist" classes the surplus incomes which form the economic stimulus of Imperialism.

This does not pretend to be a final statement of the full relations of these forces. When we come to political analysis we shall perceive that the tendency of Imperialism is to crush Trade Unionism and to "nibble" at or parasitically exploit State Socialism. But, confining ourselves for the present to the narrowly economic setting, Trade Unionism and State Socialism may be regarded as complementary forces arrayed against Imperialism, in as far as, by diverting to working-class or public expenditure elements of income which would otherwise be surplus savings, they raise the general standard of home consumption and abate the pressure for foreign markets. Of course, if the increase of working-class income were wholly or chiefly "saved," not spent, or if the taxation of unearned incomes were utilised for the relief of other taxes borne by the possessing classes, no such result as we have described would follow. There is, however, no reason to anticipate this result from trade-union or socialistic measures. Though no sufficient natural stimulus exists to force the well-to-do classes to spend in further luxuries the surplus incomes which they save, every working-class family is subject to powerful stimuli of economic needs, and a reasonably governed State would regard as its prime duty the relief of the present poverty of public life by new forms of socially useful expenditure.

But we are not here concerned with what belongs to the practical issues of political and economic policy. It is the economic theory for which we claim acceptance—a theory which, if accurate, dispels the delusion that expansion of foreign trade, and therefore of empire, is a necessity of national life.

Regarded from the standpoint of economy of energy, the same "choice of life" confronts the nation as the individual. An individual may expend all his energy in acquiring external possessions, adding field to field, barn to barn, factory to factory—may "spread himself" over the widest area of property, amassing material wealth which is in some sense "himself" as containing the impress of his power and interest. He does this by specialising upon the lower acquisitive plane of interest at the cost of neglecting the cultivation of the higher qualities and interests of his nature. The antagonism is not indeed absolute. Aristotle has said, "We must first secure a livelihood and then practise virtue." Hence the pursuit of material property as a reasonable basis of physical comfort would be held true economy by the wisest men; but the absorption of time, energy, and interest upon such quantitative expansion at the necessary cost of starving the higher tastes and faculties is condemned as false economy. The same issue comes up in the business life of the individual: it is the question of intensive *versus* extensive cultivation. A rude or ignorant farmer, where land is plentiful, is apt to spread his capital and labour over a large area, taking in new tracts and cultivating them poorly. A skilled, scientific farmer will study a smaller patch of land, cultivate it thoroughly, and utilise its diverse properties, adapting it to the special needs of his most remunerative markets. The same is true of other businesses; even where the economy of large-scale production is greatest there exists some limit beyond which the wise business man will not go, aware that in doing so he will risk by enfeebled management what he seems to gain by mechanical economies of production and market.

Everywhere the issue of quantitative *versus* qualitative growth comes up. This is the entire issue of empire. A people limited in number and energy and in the land they occupy have the choice of improving to the utmost the political and economic management of their own land, confining themselves to such accessions of territory as are justified by the most economical disposition of a growing population; or they may proceed, like the slovenly farmer, to spread their power and energy over the whole earth, tempted by the speculative value or the quick profits of some new market, or else by mere greed of territorial acquisition, and ignoring the political and economic wastes and risks involved by this imperial career. It must be clearly understood that this is essentially a choice of alternatives; a full simultaneous application of intensive and extensive cultivation is impossible. A nation may either, following the example of Denmark or Switzerland, put brains into agriculture, develop a finely varied system of public education, general and technical, apply the ripest science to its special manufacturing industries, and so support in progressive comfort and character a considerable population upon a strictly limited area; or it may, like Great Britain, neglect its agriculture, allowing its lands to go out of cultivation and its population to grow up in towns, fall behind other nations in its methods of education and in the capacity of adapting to its uses the latest scientific knowledge, in order that it may squander its pecuniary and military resources in forcing bad markets and finding speculative fields of investment in distant corners of the earth, adding millions of square miles and of unassimilable population to the area of the Empire.

The driving forces of class interest which stimulate and support this false economy we have explained. No remedy will serve which permits the future operation of these forces. It is idle to attack Imperialism or Militarism as political expedients or policies unless the axe is laid at the economic root of the tree, and the classes for whose interest Imperialism works are shorn of the surplus revenues which seek this outlet.

NOTES

1. Written in 1905.
2. "And why, indeed, are wars undertaken, if not to conquer colonies which permit the employment of fresh capital, to acquire commercial monopolies, or to obtain the exclusive use of certain highways of commerce?" (Loria, *Economic Foundations of Society,* p. 267).
3. Post-war conditions, with the immense opportunities afforded for exports of American goods and capital brought a pause and a temporary withdrawal from imperialist policy.
4. "We hold now three of the winning cards in the game for commercial greatness, to wit—iron, steel and coal. We have long been the granary of the world, we now aspire to be its workshop, then we want to be its clearing-house." (The President of the American Bankers' Association at Denver, 1898.)
5. *The Significance of the Trust,* by H. G. Wilshire.
6. *Poverty: A Study of Town Life.*
7. The classical economists of England, forbidden by their theories of parsimony and of the growth of capital to entertain the notion of an indefinite expansion of home markets by reason of a constantly rising standard of national comfort, were early driven to countenance a doctrine of the necessity of finding external markets for the investment of capital. So J. S. Mill: "The expansion of capital would soon reach its ultimate boundary if the boundary itself did not continually open and leave more space" (*Political Economy*). And before him Ricardo (in a letter to Malthus): "If with every accumulation of capital we could take a piece of fresh fertile land to our island, profits would never fall."

QUESTIONS

1. According to Hobson, why is it important to understand the relationship between production and consumption? Explain.

2. Define what Hobson meant by "social reform." How can it be brought about?

---

21.   Imperialism: The Highest Stage of Capitalism

Vladimir I. Lenin

In this excerpt, Lenin explains how imperialism is the inevitable by-product of capitalism. According to Lenin, the colonial empires of Western capitalist nations can only be maintained by the extention of boundaries and exploitation of outlying territories. Since the number of new territories was limited, the struggle to attain more colonies ultimately caused capitalist states to war with one another. This selection is from *Imperialism, The Highest Stage of Capitalism* (1952).

Vladmir Illyich Lenin (1870–1924) was leader of the Bolshevik Revolution that brought an end to czarist Russia in 1917. He subsequently ruled the Soviet Union until his death.

IMPERIALISM, AS A SPECIAL STAGE OF CAPITALISM

Imperialism emerged as the development and direct continuation of the fundamental characteristics of capitalism in general. But capitalism only became capitalist imperialism at a definite and very high stage of its development, when certain of its fundamental characteristics began to change into their opposites, when the features of the epoch of transition from capitalism to a higher social and economic system had taken shape and revealed themselves all along the line. Economically, the main thing in this process is the displacement of capitalist free competition by capitalist monopoly. Free competition is the fundamental characteristic of capitalism, and of commodity production generally; monopoly is the exact opposite of free competition, but we have seen the latter being transformed into monopoly before our eyes, creating large-scale industry and forcing out small industry, replacing large-scale by still larger-scale industry, and carrying concentration of production and capital to the point where out of it has grown and is growing monopoly: cartels, syndicates and trusts, and merging with them, the capital of a dozen or so banks, which manipulate thousands of millions. At the same time the monopolies, which have grown out of free competition, do not eliminate the latter, but exist over it and alongside of it, and thereby give rise

to a number of very acute, intense antagonisms, frictions and conflicts. Monopoly is the transition from capitalism to a higher system.

If it were necessary to give the briefest possible definition of imperialism we should have to say that imperialism is the monopoly stage of capitalism. Such a definition would include what is most important, for, on the one hand, finance capital is the bank capital of a few very big monopolist banks, merged with the capital of the monopolist combines of industrialists; and, on the other hand, the division of the world is the transition from a colonial policy which has extended without hindrance to territories unseized by any capitalist power, to a colonial policy of monopolistic possession of the territory of the world which has been completely divided up.

But very brief definitions, although convenient, for they sum up the main points, are nevertheless inadequate, since very important features of the phenomenon that has to be defined have to be especially deduced. And so, without forgetting the conditional and relative value of all definitions in general, which can never embrace all the concatenations of a phenomenon in its complete development, we must give a definition of imperialism that will include the following five of its basic features: 1) the concentration of production and capital has developed to such a high stage that it has created monopolies which play a decisive role in economic life; 2) the merging of bank capital with industrial capital, and the creation, on the basis of this "finance capital," of a financial oligarchy; 3) the export of capital as distinguished from the export of commodities acquires exceptional importance; 4) the formation of international monopolist capitalist combines which share the world among themselves, and 5) the territorial division of the whole world among the biggest capitalist powers is completed. Imperialism is capitalism in that stage of development in which the dominance of monopolies and finance capital has established itself; in which the export of capital has acquired pronounced importance; in which the division of the world among the international trusts has begun; in which the division of all territories of the globe among the biggest capitalist powers has been completed. . . .

THE PLACE OF IMPERIALISM IN HISTORY

We have seen that in its economic essence imperialism is monopoly capitalism. This in itself determines its place in history, for monopoly that grows out of the soil of free competition, and precisely out of free competition, is the transition from the capitalist system to a higher social-economic order. We must take special note of the four principal types of monopoly, or principal manifestations of monopoly capitalism, which are characteristic of the epoch we are examining.

Firstly, monopoly arose out of a very high stage of development of the concentration of production. This refers to the monopolist capitalist combines, cartels, syndicates and trusts. We have seen the important part these play in present-day economic life. At the beginning of the twentieth century, monopolies had acquired complete supremacy in the advanced countries, and although the first steps towards the formation of the cartels were first taken by countries enjoying the protection of high tariffs (Germany, America), Great Britain, with her system of free trade, revealed the same basic phenomenon, only a little later, namely, the birth of monopoly out of the concentration of production.

Secondly, monopolies have stimulated the seizure of the most important sources of raw materials, especially for the basic and most highly cartelized industries in capitalist society: the coal and iron industries. The monopoly of the most important sources of raw materials has enormously increased the power of big capital, and has sharpened the antagonism between cartelized and noncartelized industry.

Thirdly, monopoly has sprung from the banks. The banks have developed from humble middlemen enterprises into the monopolists of finance capital. Some three to five of the biggest banks in each of the foremost capitalist countries have achieved the "personal union" of industrial and bank capital, and have concentrated in their hands the control of thousands upon thousands of millions which form the greater part of the capital and income of entire countries. A financial oligarchy, which throws a close network of dependence relationships over all the economic and political institutions of present-day bourgeois society without exception—such is the most striking manifestation of this monopoly.

Fourthly, monopoly has grown out of colonial policy. To the numerous "old" motives of colonial policy, finance capital has added the struggle for the sources of raw materials, for the export of capital, for "spheres of influence," i.e., for spheres for profitable deals, concessions, monopolist profits and so on, and finally, for economic territory in general. When the colonies of the European powers in Africa, for instance, comprised only one-tenth of that territory (as was the case in 1876), colonial policy was able to develop by methods other than those of monopoly—by the "free grabbing" of territories, so to speak. But when nine-tenths of Africa had been seized (by 1900), when the whole world had been divided up, there was inevitably ushered in the era of monopoly ownership of colonies and, consequently, of particularly intense struggle for the division and the redivision of the world.

The extent to which monopolist capital has intensified all the contradictions of capitalism is generally known. It is sufficient to mention the high cost of living and the tyranny of the cartels. This intensification of contradictions constitutes the most powerful driving force of the transitional period of history, which began from the time of the final victory of world finance capital.

Monopolies, oligarchy, the striving for domination instead of striving for liberty, the exploitation of an increasing number of small or weak nations by a handful of the richest or most powerful nations—all these have given birth to those distinctive characteristics of imperialism which compel us to define it as parasitic or decaying capitalism. More and more prominently there emerges, as one of the tendencies of imperialism, the creation of the "rentier state," the usurer state, in which the bourgeoisie to an ever increasing degree lives on the proceeds of capital exports and by "clipping coupons." It would be a mistake to believe that this tendency to decay precludes the rapid growth of capitalism. It does not. In the epoch of imperialism, certain branches of industry, certain strata of the bourgeoisie and certain countries betray, to a greater or lesser degree, now one and now another of these tendencies. On the whole, capitalism is growing far more rapidly than before; but this growth is not only becoming more and more uneven in general, its unevenness also manifests itself, in particular, in the decay of the countries which are richest in capital (England).

QUESTIONS

1. How does Lenin explain the evolution of imperialism from capitalism?

2. According to Lenin, there are four principle manifestations of monopoly capitalism. Explain them.

22.   The Structure of Dependence

Theotonio Dos Santos

In this article, Theotonio Dos Santos identifies three types of dependence: colonial, financial-industrial, and technological-industrial. He focuses particular attention on technological-industrial dependence and its effect on Latin America. Dos Santos also evaluates the internal structures of the dependent nation and the international system. He concludes that lesser developed countries (LDCs) will remain dependent under the current international capitalist system. This selection is from the *American Economic Review* (1970).

Theotonio Dos Santos is a professor at the Center for Socio-Economic Studies of the Faculty of Economic Science of the University of Chile.

This paper attempts to demonstrate that the dependence of Latin American countries on other countries cannot be overcome without a qualitative change in their internal structures and external relations. We shall attempt to show that the relations of dependence to which these countries are subjected conform to a type of international and internal structure which leads them to underdevelopment or more precisely to a dependent structure that deepens and aggravates the fundamental problems of their peoples.

I. WHAT IS DEPENDENCE?

By dependence we mean a situation in which the economy of certain countries is conditioned by the development and expansion of another economy to which the former is subjected. The relation of interdependence between two or more economies, and between these and world trade, assumes the form of dependence when some countries (the dominant ones) can expand and can be self-sustaining, while other countries (the dependent ones) can do this only as a reflection of that expansion, which can have either a positive or a negative effect on their immediate development [7, p. 6].

The concept of dependence permits us to see the internal situation of these countries as part of world economy. In the Marxian tradition, the theory of imperialism has been developed as a study of the process of expansion of the imperialist centers and of their world domination. In the epoch of the revolutionary movement of the Third World, we have to develop the theory of laws of internal development in those countries that are the object of such expansion and are governed by them. This theoretical step transcends the theory of development which seeks to explain the situation of the underdeveloped countries as a product of their slowness or failure to adopt the patterns of efficiency characteristic of developed countries (or to "modernize" or "develop" themselves). Although capitalist development theory admits the existence of an "external" dependence, it is unable to perceive underdevelopment in the way our present theory perceives it, as a consequence and part of the process of the world expansion of capitalism—a part that is necessary to and integrally linked with it.

In analyzing the process of constituting a world economy that integrates the so-called "national economies" in a world market of commodities, capital, and even of labor power, we see that the relations produced by this market are unequal and combined—unequal because development of parts of the system occurs at the expense of other parts. Trade relations are based on monopolistic control of the market, which leads to the transfer of surplus generated in the dependent countries to the dominant countries; financial relations are, from the viewpoint of the dominant powers, based on loans and the export of capital, which permit them to receive interest and profits; thus increasing their domestic surplus and strengthening their control over the economies of the other countries. For the dependent countries these relations represent an export of profits and interest which carries off part of the surplus generated domestically and leads to a loss of control over their productive resources. In order to permit these disadvantageous relations, the dependent countries must generate large surpluses, not in such a way as to create higher levels of technology but rather superexploited manpower. The result is to limit the development of their internal market and their technical and cultural capacity, as well as the moral and physical health of their people. We call this combined development because it is the combination of these inequalities and the transfer of resources from the most backward and dependent sectors to the most advanced and dominant ones which explains the inequality, deepens it, and

transforms it into a necessary and structural element of the world economy.

II. HISTORIC FORMS OF DEPENDENCE

Historic forms of dependence are conditioned by: (1) the basic forms of this world economy which has its own laws of development; (2) the type of economic relations dominant in the capitalist centers and the ways in which the latter expand outward; and (3) the types of economic relations existing inside the peripheral countries which are incorporated into the situation of dependence within the network of international economic relations generated by capitalist expansion. It is not within the purview of this paper to study these forms in detail but only to distinguish broad characteristics of development.

Drawing on an earlier study, we may distinguish: (1) Colonial dependence, trade export in nature, in which commercial and financial capital in alliance with the colonialist state dominated the economic relations of the Europeans and the colonies, by means of a trade monopoly complemented by a colonial monopoly of land, mines, and manpower (serf or slave) in the colonized countries. (2) Financial-industrial dependence which consolidated itself at the end of the nineteenth century, characterized by the domination of big capital in the hegemonic centers, and its expansion abroad through investment in the production of raw materials and agricultural products for consumption in the hegemonic centers. A productive structure grew up in the dependent countries devoted to the export of these products (which Levin labeled export economies [11]; other analysis in other regions [12] [13]), producing what ECLA has called "foreign-oriented development" (*desarrollo hacia afuera*) [4]. (3) In the postwar period a new type of dependence has been consolidated, based on multinational corporations which began to invest in industries geared to the internal market of underdeveloped countries. This form of dependence is basically technological-industrial dependence [6].

Each of these forms of dependence corresponds to a situation which conditioned not only the international relations of these countries but also their internal structures: the orientation of production, the forms of capital accumulation, the reproduction of the economy, and, simultaneously, their social and political structure.

III. THE EXPORT ECONOMIES

In forms (1) and (2) of dependence, production is geared to those products destined for export (gold, silver, and tropical products in the colonial epoch; raw materials and agricultural products in the epoch of industrial-financial dependence); i.e., production is determined by demand from the hegemonic centers. The internal productive structure is characterized by rigid specialization and monoculture in entire regions (the Caribbean, the Brazilian Northeast, etc.). Alongside these export sectors there grew up certain complementary economic activities (cattle-raising and some manufacturing, for example) which were dependent, in general, on the export sector to which they sell their products. There was a third, subsistence economy which provided manpower for the export sector under favorable conditions and toward which excess population shifted during periods unfavorable to international trade.

Under these conditions, the existing internal market was restricted by four factors: (1) Most of the national income was derived from export, which was used to purchase the inputs required by export production (slaves, for example) or luxury goods consumed by the hacienda- and mine-owners, and by the more prosperous employees. (2) The available manpower was subject to very arduous forms of superexploitation, which limited its consumption. (3) Part of the consumption of these workers was provided by the subsistence economy, which served as a complement to their income and as a refuge during periods of depression. (4) A fourth factor was to be found in those countries in which land and mines were in the hands of foreigners (cases of an enclave economy): a great part of the accumulated surplus was destined to be sent abroad in the form of profits, limiting not only internal consumption but also possibilities of reinvestment [1]. In the case of enclave economies the relations of the foreign companies with the hegemonic center were even more exploitative and were complemented by the fact that purchases by the enclave were made directly abroad.

IV. THE NEW DEPENDENCE

The new form of dependence, (3) above, is in process of developing and is conditioned by the exigencies of the international commodity and capital markets. The possibility of generating new investments depends on the existence of financial resources in foreign currency for the purchase of machinery and processed raw materials not produced domestically.

Such purchases are subject to two limitations: the limit of resources generated by the export sector (reflected in the balance of payments, which includes not only trade but also service relations); and the limitations of monopoly on patents which leads monopolistic firms to prefer to transfer their machines in the form of capital rather than as commodities for sale. It is necessary to analyze these relations of dependence if we are to understand the fundamental structural limits they place on the development of these economies.

1. Industrial development is dependent on an export sector for the foreign currency to buy the inputs utilized by the industrial sector. The first consequence of this dependence is the need to preserve the traditional export sector, which limits economically the development of the internal market by the conservation of backward relations of production and signifies, politically, the maintenance of power by traditional decadent oligarchies. In the countries where these sectors are controlled by foreign capital, it signifies the remittance abroad of high profits, and political dependence on those interests. Only in rare instances does foreign capital not control at least the marketing of these products. In response to these limitations, dependent countries in the 1930s and 1940s developed a policy of exchange restrictions and taxes on the national and foreign export sector; today they tend toward the gradual nationalization of production and toward the imposition of certain timid limitations on foreign control of the marketing of exported products. Furthermore, they seek, still somewhat timidly, to obtain better terms for the sale of their products. In recent decades, they have created mechanisms for international price agreements, and today UNCTAD and ECLA press to obtain more favorable tariff conditions for these products on the part of the hegemonic centers. It is important to point out that the industrial development of these countries is dependent on the situation of the export sector, the continued existence of which they are obliged to accept.

2. Industrial development is, then, strongly conditioned by fluctuations in the balance of payments. This leads toward deficit due to the relations of dependence themselves. The causes of the deficit are three:

a) Trade relations take place in a highly monopolized international market, which tends to lower the price of raw materials and to raise the prices of industrial products, particularly inputs. In the second place, there is a tendency in modern technology to replace various primary products with synthetic raw materials. Consequently the balance of trade in these countries tends to be less favorable (even though they show a general surplus). The overall Latin American balance of trade from 1946 to 1968 shows a surplus for each of those years. The same thing happens in almost every underdeveloped country. However, the losses due to deterioration of the terms of trade (on the basis of data from ECLA and the International Monetary Fund), excluding Cuba, were $26,383 million for the 1951–66 period, taking 1950 prices as a base. If Cuba and Venezuela are excluded, the total is $15,925 million.

b) For the reasons already given, foreign capital retains control over the most dynamic sectors of the economy and repatriates a high volume of profit; consequently, capital accounts are highly unfavorable to dependent countries. The data show that the amount of capital leaving the country is much greater than the amount entering; this produces an enslaving deficit in capital accounts. To this must be added the deficit in certain services which are virtually under total foreign control—such as freight transport, royalty payments, technical aid, etc. Consequently, an important deficit is produced in the total balance of payments; thus limiting the possibility of importation of inputs for industrialization.

c) The result is that "foreign financing" becomes necessary, in two forms: to cover the existing deficit, and to "finance" development by means of loans for the stimulation of investments and to "supply" an internal economic surplus which was decapitalized to a large extent by the remittance of part of the surplus generated domestically and sent abroad as profits.

Foreign capital and foreign "aid" thus fill up the holes that they themselves created. The real value of this aid, however, is doubtful. If overcharges resulting from the restrictive terms of the aid are subtracted from the total amount of the grants, the average net flow, according to calculations of the Inter-American Economic and Social Council, is approximately 54 percent of the gross flow [5].

If we take account of certain further facts—that a high proportion of aid is paid in local currencies, that Latin American countries make contributions to international financial institutions, and that credits are often "tied"—we find a "real component of foreign aid" of 42.2 percent on a very favorable hypothesis and of 38.3 percent on a more realistic one [5, II-33]. The gravity of the situation becomes even clearer if we consider that these credits are used in large part to finance North American investments, to subsidize foreign imports which compete with national products, to introduce technology not adapted to the needs of underdeveloped countries, and to invest in low-priority sectors of the national economies. The hard truth is that the underdeveloped countries have to pay for all of the "aid" they receive. This situation is generating an enormous protest movement by Latin American governments seeking at least partial relief from such negative relations.

3. Finally, industrial development is strongly conditioned by the technological monopoly exercised by imperialist centers. We have seen that the underdeveloped countries depend on the importation of machinery and raw materials for the development of their industries. However, these goods are not freely available in the international market; they are patented and usually belong to the big companies. The big companies do not sell machinery and processed raw materials as simple merchandise: they demand either the payment of royalties, etc., for their utilization or, in most cases, they convert these goods into capital and introduce them in the form of their own investments. This is how machinery which is replaced in the hegemonic centers by more advanced technology is sent to dependent countries as capital for the installation of affiliates. Let us pause and examine these relations, in order to understand their oppressive and exploitative character.

The dependent countries do not have sufficient foreign currency, for the reasons given. Local businessmen have financing difficulties, and they must pay for the utilization of certain patented techniques. These factors oblige the national bourgeois governments to facilitate the entry of foreign capital in order to supply the restricted national market, which is strongly protected by high tariffs in order to promote industrialization. Thus, foreign capital enters with all the advantages: in many cases, it is given exemption from exchange controls for the importation of machinery; financing of sites for installation of industries is provided; government financing agencies facilitate industrialization; loans are available from foreign and domestic banks, which prefer such clients; foreign aid often subsidizes such investments and finances complementary public investments; after installation, high profits obtained in such favorable circumstances can be reinvested freely. Thus it is not surprising that the data of the U.S. Department of Commerce reveal that the percentage of capital brought in from abroad by these companies is but a part of the total amount of invested capital. These data show that in the period from 1946 to 1967 the new entries of capital into Latin America for direct investment amounted to $5,415 million, while the sum of reinvested profits was $4,424 million. On the other hand, the transfers of profits from Latin America to the United States amounted to $14,775 million. If we estimate total profits as approximately equal to transfers plus reinvestments we have the sum of $18,983 million. In spite of enormous transfers of profits to the United States, the book value of the United States's direct investment in Latin America went from $3,045 million in 1946 to $10,213 million in 1967. From these data it is clear that: (1) Of the new investments made by U.S. companies in Latin America for the period 1946-67, 55 percent corresponds to new entries of capital and 45 percent to reinvestment of profits; in recent years, the trend is more marked, with reinvestments between 1960 and 1966 repre-senting more than 60 percent of new investments. (2) Remittances remained at about 10 percent of book value throughout the period. (3) The ratio of remitted capital to new flow is around 2.7 for the period 1946-67; that is, for each dollar that enters $2.70 leaves. In the 1960s this ratio roughly doubled, and in some years was considerably higher.

The *Survey of Current Business* data on sources and uses of funds for direct North American investment in Latin America in the period 1957-64 show that, of the total sources of direct investment in Latin America, only 11.8 percent came from the United States. The remainder is in large part, the result of the activities of North American firms in Latin America (46.4 percent net income, 27.7 percent under the heading of depreciation), and from "sources located abroad" (14.1 percent). It is significant that the funds obtained abroad that are external to the companies are greater than the funds originating in the United States.

V. EFFECTS ON THE PRODUCTIVE STRUCTURE

It is easy to grasp, even if only superficially, the effects that this dependent structure has on the productive system itself in these countries and the role of this structure in determining a specified type of development, characterized by its dependent nature.

The productive system in the underdeveloped countries is essentially determined by these international relations. In the first place, the need to conserve the agrarian or mining export structure generates a combination between more advanced economic centers that extract surplus value from the more backward sectors, and also between internal "metropolitan" centers and internal interdependent "colonial" centers [10]. The unequal and combined character of capitalist development at the international level is reproduced internally in an acute form. In the second place the industrial and technological structure responds more closely to the interests of the multinational corporations than to internal developmental needs (conceived of not only in terms of the overall interests of the population, but also from the point of view of the interests of a national capitalist development). In the third place, the same technological and economic-financial concentration of the hegemonic economies is transferred without substantial alteration to very different economies and societies, giving rise to a highly unequal productive structure, a high concentration of incomes, underutilization of installed capacity, intensive exploitation of existing markets concentrated in large cities, etc.

The accumulation of capital in such circumstances assumes its own characteristics. In the first place, it is characterized by profound differences among domestic wage-levels, in the context of a local cheap labor market, combined with a capital-intensive technology. The result, from the point of view of relative surplus value, is a high rate of exploitation of labor power. (On measurements of forms of exploitation, see [3].)

This exploitation is further aggravated by the high prices of industrial products enforced by protectionism, exemptions and subsidies given by the national governments, and "aid" from hegemonic centers. Furthermore, since dependent accumulation is necessarily tied into the international economy, it is profoundly conditioned by the unequal and combined character of international capitalist economic relations, by the technological and financial control of the imperialist centers by the realities of the balance of payments, by the economic policies of the state, etc. The role of the state in the growth of national and foreign capital merits a much fuller analysis than can be made here.

Using the analysis offered here as a point of departure, it is possible to understand the limits that this productive system imposes on the growth of the internal markets of these countries. The survival of traditional relations in the countryside is a serious limitation on the size of the market, since industrialization does not offer hopeful prospects. The productive structure created by dependent industrialization limits the growth of the internal market.

First, it subjects the labor force to highly exploitative relations which limit its purchasing power. Second, in adopting a technology of intensive capital use, it creates very few jobs in comparison with population growth, and limits the generation of new sources of income. These two limitations affect the growth of the consumer goods market. Third, the remittance abroad of profits carries away part of the economic surplus generated within the country. In all these ways limits are put on the possible creation of basic national industries which could provide a market for the capital goods this surplus would make possible if it were not remitted abroad.

From this cursory analysis we see that the alleged backwardness of these economies is not due to a lack of integration with capitalism but that, on the contrary, the most powerful obstacles to their full development come from the way in which they are joined to this international system and its laws of development.

VI. SOME CONCLUSIONS: DEPENDENT REPRODUCTION

In order to understand the system of dependent reproduction and the socioeconomic institutions created by it, we must see it as part of a system of world economic relations based on monopolistic control of large-scale capital, on control of certain economic and financial centers over others, on a monopoly of a complex technology that leads to unequal and combined development at a national and international level. Attempts to analyze backwardness as a failure to assimilate more advanced models of production or to modernize are nothing more than ideology disguised as science. The same is true of the attempts to analyze this international economy in terms of relations among elements in free competition, such as the theory of comparative costs which seeks to justify the inequalities of the world economic system and to conceal the relations of exploitation on which it is based [14].

In reality we can understand what is happening in the underdeveloped countries only when we see that they develop within the framework of a process of dependent production and reproduction. This system is a dependent one because it reproduces a productive system whose development is limited by those world relations which necessarily lead to the development of only certain economic sectors, to trade under unequal conditions [9], to domestic competition with international capital under unequal conditions, to the imposition of relations of superexploitation of the domestic labor force with a view of dividing the economic surplus thus generated between internal and external forces of domination. (On economic surplus and its utilization in the dependent countries, see [1].)

In reproducing such a productive system and such international relations, the development of dependent capitalism reproduces the factors that prevent it from reaching a nationally and internationally advantageous situation; and it thus reproduces backwardness, misery, and social marginalization within its borders. The development that it produces benefits very narrow sectors, encounters unyielding domestic obstacles to its continued economic growth (with respect to both internal and foreign markets), and leads to the progressive accumulation of balance-of-payments deficits, which in turn generate more dependence and more superexploitation.

The political measures proposed by the developmentalists of ECLA, UNCTAD, BID, etc., do not appear to permit destruction of these terrible chains imposed by dependent development. We have examined the alternative forms of development presented for Latin America and the dependent countries under such conditions elsewhere [8]. Everything now indicates that what can be expected is a long process of sharp political and military confrontations and of profound social radicalization which will lead these countries to a dilemma: governments of force which open the way to facism, or popular revolutionary governments, which open the way to socialism. Intermediate solutions have proved to be, in such a contradictory reality, empty and utopian.

REFERENCES

1. PAUL BARAN, *Political Economy of Growth* (Monthly Review Press, 1967).
2. THOMAS BALOGH, *Unequal Partners* (Basil Blackwell, 1963).
3. PABLO GONZALEZ CASANOVA, *Sociologia de la explotación,* Siglo XXI (México, 1969).
4. CEPAL, *La CEPAL y el Análisis del Desarrollo Latinoamericano* (1968, Santiago, Chile).
5. Consejo Interamericano Economico Social (CIES) O.A.S., Interamerican Economic and Social Council, External Financing for Development in L.A. *El Financiamiento Externo para el Desarrollo de América Latina* (Pan-American Union, Washington, 1969).
6. THEOTONIO DOS SANTOS, *El neuvo carácter de la dependencia,* CESO (Santiago de Chile, 1968).
7. ———, *La crisis de la teoria del desarrollo y las relaciones de dependencia en América Latina.* Boletín del CESO, 3 (Santiago, Chile, 1968).
8. ———, *La dependencia económica y las alternativas de cambio en América Latina,* Ponencia a IX Congreso Latinoamericano de Sociologia (México, Nov., 1969).
9. A. EMMANUEL, *L'Echange Inégal* (Maspero, Paris, 1969).
10. ANDRE G. FRANK, *Development and Underdevelopment in Latin America* (Monthly Review Press, 1968).
11. I. V. LEVIN, *The Export Economies* (Harvard Univ. Press, 1964).
12. GUNNAR MYRDAL, *Asian Drama* (Pantheon, 1968).
13. K. NKRUMAH, *Neocolonialismo, última etapa del imperialismo,* Siglo XXI (México, 1966).
14. CRISTIAN PALLOIX, *Problemes de la Croissance en Economie Ouverte* (Maspero, Paris, 1969).

QUESTIONS

1. Define the three forms of dependence discussed in the essay.

2. According to Dos Santos, what role do industrial development and deficits play in technological-industrial dependence?

23. The Capitalist World Economy

Immanuel Wallerstein

In this article, Immanuel Wallerstein presents the key elements of the capitalist world economy. Concepts such as the core and periphery zones of goods and services and socialization of the productive process are also discussed. This selection is from the journal *Contemporary Marxism* (1984).

Immanuel Wallerstein is a professor at the Fernand Braudel Center at the State University of New York, Binghamton. His works include *World Inequality* (1975) and *Historic Capitalism* (1983), as well as contributions to various professional journals.

1. THE NATURE OF THE WORLD-ECONOMY

1.1. The concept world-economy (*économie-monde* in French) should be distinguished from that of world economy (*économie mondiale*) or international economy. The latter concept presumes there are a series of separate "economies" which are "national" in scope, and that under certain circumstances these "national economies" trade with each other, the sum of these (limited) contacts being called the international economy. Those who use this latter concept argue that the limited contacts have been expanding in the 20th century. It is thus asserted that the world has become "one world" in a sense it wasn't prior to the 20th century.

By contrast, the concept "world-economy" assumes that there exists an "economy" wherever (and if but only if) there is an ongoing extensive and relatively complete social division of labor with an integrated set of production processes which relate to each other through a "market" which has been "instituted" or "created" in some complex way. Using such a concept, the world-economy is not new in the 20th century, nor is it a coming together of "national economies," none of the latter constituting complete divisions of labor. Rather, a world-economy, capitalist in form, has been in existence in at least part of the globe since the 16th century. Today, the entire globe is operating within the framework of this singular social division of labor we are calling the capitalist world-economy.

1.2. The capitalist world-economy has, and has had since its coming into existence, boundaries far larger than that of any political unit. Indeed, it seems to be one of the basic defining features of a capitalist world-economy that there exists no political entity with ultimate authority in all its zones.

Rather, the political superstructure of the capitalist world-economy is an interstate system within which and through which political structures called "sovereign states" are legitimized and constrained. Far from meaning the total autonomy of decision-making, the term "sovereignty" in reality implies a formal autonomy combined with real limitations on this autonomy, which are implemented both via the explicit and implicit rules of the interstate system and via the power of other states in the interstate system. No state in the interstate system, even the single most powerful one at any given time, is totally autonomous—but obviously some enjoy far greater autonomy than others.

1.3. The world-economy is a complex of cultures—in the sense of languages, religions, ideologies—but this complex is not haphazard. There exists a *Weltanschauung* of imperium, albeit one with several variants, and there exist cultures of resistance to this imperium.

1.4. The major social institutions of the capitalist world-economy—the states, the classes, the "peoples," and the households—are all shaped (even created) by the ongoing workings of the world-economy. None of them are primordial, in the sense of permanent, pre-existing, relatively fixed structures to which the workings of the capitalist world-economy are exogenous.

1.5. The capitalist world-economy is a *historical* social system. It came into existence, and its genesis must be explained. Its existence is defined by certain patterns—both cyclical rhythms and secular trends—which must be explicated. It is highly probable that it will one day go out of existence (become transformed into another type of historical social system), and we can therefore assess the historical alternatives that are before us.

2. THE PATTERNS OF THE WORLD-ECONOMY

All historical structures constantly evolve. However, the use of any concept is a capturing in fixed form of some continuing pattern. We could not discern the world, interpret it, or consciously change it unless we used concepts, with all the limitations that any reification, however slight, implies.

2.1. The world-economy has a capitalist mode of production. This is an empirical statement. Although there have been other world-economies (as defined above) known in history, the modern one of which we are speaking is the only one which has survived over a long period of time without either disintegrating or being transformed into a world-empire (with a singular political structure). This modern one has had a capitalist mode of production—that is, its economy has been dominated by those who operate on the primacy of endless accumulation, such entrepreneurs (or controllers of production units) driving from the arena those who seek to operate on other premises. Since only one world-economy has survived over a long period of time, and since this one has been capitalist in form, we may suspect that the two phenomena are theoretically linked: that a world-economy to survive must have a capitalist mode of production, and inversely that capitalism cannot be the mode of production except in a system that has the form of a world-economy (a division of labor more extensive than any one political entity).

2.2. The capitalist world-economy has operated via a social relationship called capital/labor, in which the surplus created by direct producers has been appropriated by others either at the point of production or at the most immediate market place, in either case by virtue of the fact that the appropriators control the "capital" and that their "rights" to the surplus are legally guaranteed. The extractors of surplus-value may in many cases be individuals, but they have tended increasingly to be collective entities (private or state corporations).

2.3. Once surplus-value has been extracted, it has yet to be "distributed" among a network of beneficiaries. The exchange processes of the "market" are one mode through which this redistribution occurs. In particular, the structure of the world-economy permits an unequal exchange of goods and services (primarily trans-state), such that much of the surplus-value extracted in the peripheral zones of the world-economy is transferred to the core zones.

2.4. The exchange of products containing unequal amounts of social labor we may call the core/periphery relationship. This is pervasive, continuing, and constant. There tend to be geographical localizations of productive activities such that core-like production activities and periphery-like production activities tend each to be spatially grouped together. We can thus, for shorthand purposes, refer to some states as core states and others as peripheral states.

2.5. Insofar as some states function as loci of mixed kinds of production activities (some core-like, some periphery-like), we can speak of such states as semi-peripheral. There always exist semi-peripheral zones.

2.6. While the pattern of a spatial hierarchy of production processes within the capitalist world-economy is a constant, the position of any given state is not, since there have been regular partial relocations of core-like and periphery-like economic activities.

2.7. Since what makes a production process core-like or periphery-like is the degree to which it incorporates labor-value, is mechanized, and is highly profitable, and all these characteristics shift over time for any given product because of "product cycles," it follows that no product is inherently core-like or periphery-like, but has that characteristic for a given time. Nonetheless, there are always some products which are core-like and others which are periphery-like at any given time.

2.8. Because the imperatives of accumulation operate via the individual decisions of entrepreneurs, each seeking to maximize his profit—the so-called anarchy of production—there is an inherent tendency to the expansion of absolute volume of production in the world-economy. Profit can, however, only be realized if there is effective demand for the global product. World effective demand, however, is a function of the sum of political arrangements in the various states (the result of prior class struggles), which determine the real distribution of the global surplus. These arrangements are stable for intermediate periods of time. Consequently, world supply expands at a steady rate while world demand remains relatively fixed for intermediate periods. Such a system must result, and historically has resulted, in recurring bottlenecks of accumulation, which are translated into periods of economic stagnation. The A-phases of expansion and the B-phases of stagnation seem to have occurred historically in cycles of 40–55 years (sometimes called "Kondratieff cycles").

2.9. Each period of stagnation has created pressures to restructure the network of production processes and the social relations that underlie them in ways that would overcome the bottlenecks to accumulation. Among the mechanisms that have operated to renew expansion are:

a. reduction of production costs of former core-like products by further mechanization and/or relocation of these activities in lower-wage zones;

b. creation of new core-like activities ("innovation"), which promise high initial rates of profit, thus encouraging new loci of investment;

c. an intensified class struggle both within the core states and between groups located in different states such that there may occur at the end of the process some political redistribution of world surplus to workers in core zones (often by means of fully proletarianizing hitherto semi-proletarian households) and to bourgeois in semi-peripheral and peripheral zones, thereby augmenting world effective demand;

d. expansion of the outer boundaries of the world-economy, thereby creating new pools of direct producers who can be involved in world production as semi-proletarianized workers receiving wages below the cost of reproduction.

2.10. States in which core-like activities occur develop relatively strong state apparatuses which can advance the interests of their bourgeoisies, less by protection (a mechanism of the medium-strong seeking to be stronger) than by preventing other states from erecting political barriers to the profitability of these activities. In general, states seek to shape the world market in ways that will advance the interests of some entrepreneurs against that of others.

2.11. There seem to be cycles as well, within the interstate system. On three separate occasions, one state has been able to achieve what may be called a hegemonic position in the world-economy: the United Provinces, 1620–1650; the United Kingdom, 1815–1873; the United States, 1945–1967. When producers located within a given state can undersell producers located in other core states in the latter's "home market," they can over time transform this production advantage into one in the commercial arena and then into one in the financial arena. The combined advantages may be said to constitute hegemony and are reflected as well in a political-military advantage in the interstate system. Such hegemonies are relatively short-lived, since the production advantages cannot be sustained indefinitely and mechanisms

of the balance of power intrude to reduce the political advantage of the single most powerful state.

2.12. The core states in general, and the hegemonic state when one exists in particular, seek to reinforce the advantages of their producers and to legitimize their role in the interstate system by imposing their cultural dominance on the world. To some extent, this occurs in the easily visible form of language, religion, and mores, but more importantly this occurs in the form of seeking to impose modes of thought and analysis, including in particular the paradigms that inform philosophy and the sciences/social sciences.

3. THE SECULAR TRENDS OF THE WORLD-ECONOMY

The patterns of the world-economy may be at first glance cyclical in form, but they are not perfectly cyclical. The world-economy has a historical development which is structural and can be analyzed in terms of its secular trends.

3.1. The drive to accumulate leads to the constant deepening of the capitalist development. The search to reduce long-term costs of production leads to a steady increase in the degree to which production is mechanized. The search for the least expensive source of factors of production (including as an expense delays in time in acquiring access) leads to a steady increase in the degree to which these factors (land, labor, and goods) are commodified. The desire to reduce barriers to the process of accumulation leads to a steady increase in the degree to which economic transactions are contractualized. It is important to recognize two things about these processes of mechanization, commodification, and contractualization.

3.1.1. While there are regular increases in the world-economy taken as a whole of the degree of mechanization, commodification, and contractualization, the pattern is not linear but stepwise, each significant advance leading to overall expansion, and each overall stagnation leading to a restructuring of the world-economy such that there is further advance.

3.1.2. The capitalist development of the world-economy at the world level is far from complete in the 20th century. These processes are still in full operation.

3.2. The recurring stagnations of the world-economy, which have led to the regular restructuring of this world-economy, have involved as part of restructuring the expansion of the "outer" boundaries of the world-economy, a process which, however, has been nearly completed as of now. This expansion, which was central to world history of the past several hundred years, gradually eliminated from the globe other kinds of historical social systems, creating the historically unique situation of there being, for all effects and purposes, a single social division of labor on the earth.

3.3. The steady but still incomplete commodification of labor, side by side with the now largely completed expansion of the outer boundaries of the world-economy, accounts for the shape of two of the major institutional structures of the capitalist world-economy: the classes and the households.

3.3.1. The commodification of labor ultimately means a structure in which direct producers have no access to the means of production except by selling their labor-power on a market; that is, they become proletarians. Although the percentage of direct producers who are full-lifetime proletarians has been growing worldwide over time, nonetheless, even today such proletarians are still probably no more than half of the world's work force.

3.3.2. The commodification of land and capital ultimately means a structure in which controllers of land or capital (including "human capital") have no access to the maintenance and reproduction of land and capital except by pursuing an active policy of maximizing the accumulation of capital; that is, they become bourgeois. In the 20th century, there are very few who control land or capital—directly (individually) or indirectly (collectively)—who are not bourgeois, that is, persons whose economic raison d'être is the accumulation of capital.

3.3.3. Hence, we have a situation in which *a part but not all* of the direct producers are (full-lifetime) proletarians (the other part we may designate as "semi-proletarians"), but *most* of the controllers of land and capital are bourgeois.

3.3.4. The creation of two large worldwide classes has led to the molding of appropriate household structures as the member-units of these classes. We mean by household the unit which, over a longish (30–50 year) period, pools the income of all its members, from whatever source and in whatever form is this income.

3.3.5. The "semi-proletarian" household, so extensive in peripheral zones of the world-economy, permits the wage-employment of some of its members for parts of their lives at wages below the proportionate cost of reproduction by pooling this wage-income with that received from subsistence, petty commodity, rental, and transfer income. This is what is meant by "super-exploitation" (since in this case the employer of the wage-laborer is receiving not merely the surplus-value created by the wage-laborer, but that which other members of the household are creating).

3.3.6. The proletarian household, tending to receive wage-income approximating the real costs of reproduction (no less but also not much more) tends to move in the direction of more "nucleated" households, sloughing off *affines* and others not defined as pulling their full weight.

3.3.7. The bourgeois household, seeking to maximize the use of capital, the direct control of which tends to increase by age, and utilizing the family structure as the primary mechanism of avoiding social redistribution, tends to take the form of extended, multilocal households.

3.4. The steady (now largely completed) expansion of the outer boundaries of the world-economy, combined with the continuing competition among bourgeois for advantage in the capitalist world-economy, accounts for the shape of the other two major institutional structures of the capitalist world-economy: the states and the peoples.

3.4.1. The drive of bourgeois for competitive advantage has led to increasing definition ("power") of the states as political structures and increasing emphasis on their constraint by the inter-state system. This push for a "strong" state (strong vis-à-vis both other internal loci of power and vis-à-vis other states and external nonstate forces) has been greatest and therefore most efficacious in those states with core-like production ac-

tivities. The strong state has been the principal mechanism by which the bourgeois controlling these core-like production activities have been able a) to limit and moderate the economic demands of their national work forces, b) to shape the world market so as to compete effectively with bourgeoisies located in other states, and c) to incorporate new zones into the world-economy, thus constantly re-creating new centers of peripheral production activities.

3.4.2. The increasing definition of state structures has led to the shaping, re-shaping, creation, destruction, revival of "people." To the extent that these "peoples" are defined by themselves (and by others) as controlling or having the "moral" right to control state structures, these "peoples" become "nations." To the extent that they are not defined as having the right to control a state structure, these people become "minorities" or "ethnic groups." Defining given states as nation-states is an aid in strengthening the state. Such a definition requires emphasizing one "people" and deemphasizing, even destroying (conceptually or literally), others. This is particularly important for semi-peripheral states seeking to transform their structural role in the world-economy. Various groups have interests supporting and opposing any particular nation-state definition. "Nationalism" is a mechanism both of imperium/integration and of resistance/liberation. The people are not haphazardly defined but neither are they simple and unfixed derivations from a historical past. They are solidarity groupings whose boundaries are a matter of constant social transmittal/redefinition.

3.5. As the classes come to be defined vis-à-vis the developing division of labor in the world-economy and the peoples come to be defined vis-à-vis the increasing rationalized interstate system, the locational concentration of various oppressed groups gives rise over time to anti-systemic movements. These movements have organized in two main forms around two main themes: the social movement around "class" and the national movement around "nation" or people.

3.5.1. The seriously anti-systemic (or revolutionary) forms of such movements first emerged in *organized* form in the 19th century. Their general objective, human equality, was by definition incompatible with the functioning of the capitalist world-economy, a hierarchical system based on uneven development, unequal exchange, and the appropriation of surplus-value. However, the political structure of the capitalist world-economy—the fact that it was not a single unit but a series of sovereign states—pressed the movements to seek the transformation of the world-system via the achievement of political power within separate states. The organization of these anti-systemic movements at the state level had contradictory effects.

3.5.2. Organization at the state level for the social movement was ideologically confusing from the beginning, as it counterposed the logical and ideological necessity of worldwide struggle (proletarian internationalism) against the immediate political need of achieving power within one state. Either the social movement resisted "nationalism" and was rendered inefficacious or it utilized nationalism and then faced ambiguously the so-called "national question"—that is, the "nationalisms" of the "minorities" within the boundaries of the state. Whatever the tactic of a given social movement, the achievement of partial or total state power involved power in a structure constrained by the interstate system, hence unable by itself to transform the system entirely (that is, to withdraw totally from the capitalist world-economy).

3.5.3. Organization at the state level created dilemmas for the national movements as well. The smaller the zone within which the national movement defined itself, the easier the access to state power but the less consequential. Hence, all national movements have oscillated in terms of the unit of definition, and the various "pan-" movements have had limited success. But defeats of "pan-" movements have tended to dilute the anti-systemic thrust of particular national movements.

3.5.4. In general, both social and national movements have had a difficult time reconciling long-run anti-systemic objectives and short-run "developmentalist" or "catching-up" objectives, which tend to reinforce rather than undermine the world-system. Nonetheless, the collective momentum of the social and national movements over time has been anti-systemic in effect, despite the "reformism" or "revisionism" of the various movements taken separately. Furthermore, the collective momentum of these movements has been such as to confound increasingly the social and national movements, which has in fact been a source of additional strength.

3.6. The unfolding of the institutional structures of the world-system—the classes, the states, the peoples, the households—has been reflected in the cultural mosaic of the world-system, whose pattern has been increasingly that of the tension between imperium and resistance.

3.6.1. As the axial division of labor became more pronounced and more unequal, the need to facilitate its operation through the allocation of work forces and the justification of inequality led to an ideology of racism that became the central organizing cultural theme of the world bourgeoisie. The existence of superior groups (whether in particular instances these groups were defined as Caucasians or Anglosaxons or other variants on this theme) became a method of simple *triage* in job and income allocation.

3.6.2. Whereas racism has served as a mechanism of worldwide control of direct producers, the bourgeoisie of strong core states (and particularly of the hegemonic power) sought also to direct the activities of the bourgeois of other states and various middle strata worldwide into channels that would maximize the close integration of production processes and the smooth operation of the interstate system such that the accumulation of capital was facilitated. This required the creation of a world bourgeois cultural framework that could be grafted onto "national" variations. This was particularly important in terms of science and technology, but quite important too in the realm of political ideas and of the social sciences.

3.6.3. The concept of a neutral "universal" culture to which the cadres of the world division of labor would be "assimilated" (the passive tense being important here) hence came to serve as one of the pillars of the world-system as it historically evolved. The exaltation of progress, and later of "modernization," summarized this set of ideas, which served less as true norms of social action than as status-symbols of obeisance and of participation in the world's upper strata.

3.6.4. Resistance to this cultural assimilationism was to be found among competitive bourgeois in semi-peripheral and nonhegemonic core states and took the form of asserting the autonomy of "national" traditions and/or antipathy to structural generalizations in the domain of ideas. It also took the form of reinforcing alternative world linguistic groupings to the hegemonic one (in practice, of English).

3.6.5. More fundamental cultural resistance on the part of anti-systemic movements has come slowly to take the form of positing civilizational alternatives to dominant cultural forms. In particular, it has counterdistinguished civilizations (plural) to civilization (singular and imperial).

4. THE SYSTEM IN CRISIS

4.1. A system that has cyclical patterns has recurring downturns, whatever we wish to call them. We have argued the regularity of world economic stagnations as one of the patterns of the capitalist world-economy. But insofar as there are also mechanisms that regularly bring these stagnations to an end and relaunch world economic expansion, we cannot count these cyclical downturns as crises, however much they are perceived as such by the individuals living through them.

4.2. Rather, a "crisis" is a situation in which the restitutive mechanisms of the system are no longer functioning well, and therefore the system will either be transformed fundamentally or disintegrate. It is in this sense that we could talk for example of the "crisis of feudalism" in Europe in the period 1300–1450, a crisis whose resolution was the historic emergence of a capitalist world-economy located in that particular geographic arena. We may say that this capitalist world-economy in turn entered into a long "crisis" of a comparable nature in the 20th century, a crisis in the midst of which we are living.

4.3. The causes of the crisis are internal to the system, the result of the contradictions built into the processes.

4.3.1. One of the mechanisms whereby the world-economy has overcome its downturn phases has been the expansion of the outer boundaries of the world-economy, but this is a process which has inbuilt limits which are nearly reached.

4.3.2. Another of the mechanisms whereby the world-economy has overcome its downturn phases has been the expansion of world effective demand, in part through proletarianization of the direct producers, in part by redistribution of the surplus among the world bourgeoisie.

4.3.2.1. Proletarianization is also a process that has inbuilt limits. While they have hardly yet been reached, the process has been speeding up, and one can foresee it reaching its asymptote within the coming century.

4.3.2.2. Redistribution of the surplus among the bourgeoisie is itself the result of bourgeoisification, which has entailed an increase of the total percentage of the world population who are bourgeois. If one distinguishes between the small group of bourgeois who control most of the fixed capital and the much larger group of bourgeois who control principally human capital, the growth and social concentration of the latter group have resulted in their acquisition of considerable political power in core states.

They have been able, as the price of their political support for the world-system as a system, to ensure that an increasing proportion of the appropriated surplus will be redistributed to them, reducing over the long run the rate of profit to the holders of fixed capital.

4.4. Increasing proletarianization and the increasing constraint on individual mobility because of the degree to which definitions of peoples have been linked to position in the world-economy have led to the rise of the anti-systemic movements. These movements have a cumulative effect which may be said to draw a logarithmic curve. We have entered into the phase of acute escalation.

4.5. The fact that we are in a systemic crisis and have been in one at least since the Russian Revolution—which was its symbolic detonator and has always been seen as such—does not mean that the capitalist development of the world-economy has come to an end. Quite the contrary. It is as vigorous as ever, perhaps more so. This is indeed the prime cause of the crisis. The very vigor of capitalist development has been and will continue to be the main factor that exacerbates the contradictions of the system.

4.6. It is therefore not the case that the crisis will be imminently resolved. A crisis of a system is a long, slow, difficult process, and for it to play itself out over a 150-year period is scarcely surprising. We have little perspective on it as we are amidst it, and we therefore tend to exaggerate each minor fork in the road. There is some constructive value in being overly optimistic in a short run, but the negative side of such exaggeration is the disillusionments it breeds. A crisis is best navigated by a cool, long-run strategy. It cannot however be totally planned, as the crisis itself gives rise to new possibilities of human action.

5. PROSPECTIVES

There are three different logics which are playing themselves out in the present world crisis. The outcome will be the result of their interaction.

5.1. There is the logic of socialism.

5.1.1. The capitalist development of the world-economy itself moves toward the socialization of the productive process. There is an *organizational* (as opposed to a political) imperative in which the full achievement of capitalist relations of production—through its emphasis on the increase of relative surplus-value and the maximum efficiency (free flow) of the factors of production—pushes toward a fully planned single productive organizational network in the world-economy.

5.1.2. Furthermore, the political logic of the appropriation of surplus by the few leads to the growth of the antisystemic movements and therefore toward the spread of socialist values among the world's direct producers.

5.1.3. Finally, the structure of the world-economy (multiple states within the division of labor) has created the possibility of socialist political movements coming to power in individual states, seeking to "construct socialism." Despite the fact that their continued location in the capitalist world-economy and the interstate system seriously constrains the kinds of transformations they can effectuate within boundaries of a given state, their attempts to approximate in various ways a socialist order create additional institutional pressures on the world-system to move in the direction of socialism.

5.2. There is also the logic of domination.

5.2.1. Insofar as the powerful have, by definition, more power than the mass of the world population, and insofar as the process of transformation is slow and contradictory, it creates much opportunity for the ruling strata (the world bourgeoisie) to invent modes of continuity of power and privilege. The adoption of new social roles and new ideological clothing may be a route for existing dominant strata to perpetuate themselves in a new system. It is certainly the logic of domination that dominant groups seek to survive even a "crisis." As the landowning hero of di Lampedusa's *Il Gattopardo* says: "We must change everything in order that everything remain the same."

5.2.2. In the process of the world bourgeoisie seeking to retain their power, they may engage in policies which lead to a nuclear world war. This could bring about a demise of the present system in a manner that would destroy much of the forces of production and thereby make a socialist world order far less structurally feasible.

5.3. There is a logic of the civilizational project.

5.3.1. While the capitalist world-economy has been the first and only social system that has managed to eliminate from the earth all contemporaneous social systems, this has been historically true only for a very recent period of time. We could regard it as simply the conquest by Western Europeans of the globe. In this case, in the long run of history, the political and technological supremacy of the West constitutes a short interval and, from the perspective of alternative "civilizational" centers, might be thought of as a transitory and aberrant interlude. There is thus a drive for a restituted civilizational balance, which the very process of capitalist development of the world-economy makes more urgent and more realizable.

5.3.2. How a restituted civilizational balance fits in, however, with world socialism on the one hand and the drive of world ruling strata to survive on the other is not at all clear.

5.4. We live facing real historical alternatives. It is clear that the capitalist world-economy cannot survive, and that as a historical social system it is in the process of being superseded. The forces at play are also clear, as are the secular trends. We can struggle for our preferences. We can analyze probabilities. But we cannot foretell, because we cannot yet know for certain how the conjuncture of forces at play will constrain the directions of change and even less can we know what new possibilities of human liberation they will afford. The only thing of which we may be certain is that our present activity will be a major factor in the outcome of the crisis.

QUESTIONS

1. Explain how Wallerstein defines the development of the core and periphery zone in the capitalist world economy.

2. Discuss how Morgenthau and Waltz might respond to Wallerstein's thesis.

---

24. A Singular Collapse: The Soviet Union, Market Pressure and Inter-State Competition

Fred Halliday

In this article, Fred Halliday examines "how far and in what ways" the ideological and economic competition between the United States and the Soviet Union contributed to the final collapse of the communist system. Halliday concludes that the Soviet Union collapsed because it was ultimately unable to compete with the consumerism and capitalist policies of the West. This selection is from the journal *Contention* (1991).

Fred Halliday is a professor in the Department of International Relations at the London School of Economics.

INTRODUCTION: NEW LIGHT ON OLD QUESTIONS

The collapse of the Soviet system within the U.S.S.R. and internationally in the late 1980s, in addition to its manifold implications for global politics and policy, has raised a range of important and unresolved issues, analytically and within social and international theory. The first question is that of explanation, of providing why a political and socio-economic system that was broadly equal to its rival in military terms should have collapsed rapidly and unequivocally, and in the absence of significant international military conflict.[1] No explanation in terms of a single factor is possible, and there is much that will only become clearer with the passage of time. What is being attempted here is a provisional analysis of the causes of the collapse of the communist system, focusing on the international dimensions of this process. The internal weaknesses of the system played a major role in its demise, not least the paralysis at both economic and political levels that characterized it,[2] but an analysis of the international factors is of relevance for several reasons—first, because so much has been said and written about how international competition did contribute to the failure of communism and it is worth now assessing these claims; second, because, despite talk of its "failure," this system did not fall because of internal pressures alone; third, because a discussion of the historical question, why communism collapsed, may cast light on underlying theoretical issues pertaining to interstate and intersystemic competition.

The communist leaderships were engaged in a project that was both national and international: it was international as a result of systemic pressure from other states, but it was also ideologically international, an attempt to constitute a model society on an international scale, and to promote similar movements in other countries. Yet if the overall failure of communism includes its failure to spread worldwide, a better starting point to analyze why the regimes collapsed is the record of internal, top-down transformation which the regimes promoted. The elites in the central committees and politbureaus of the ruling parties sought to transform the societies in accordance with a theoretical blueprint of where socialist society should be going. This project was a failure, not only in reaching its goal, but also because much of what had apparently been achieved was impermanent and superficial. The claims that "developed socialism" or some sort of more perfect society had been reached were false, and so too were the apparently less apologetic claims that these societies were in some implicitly teleological sense "in transition" to a new socio-economic model and represented a permanent advance beyond what capitalism could provide.

This failure is as true for attempts to create a viable and self-sustaining planned economy as it is for those to forge politically viable one-party systems, and for attempts to reform attitudes regarding major areas of ideological importance, notably work, gender, religion, and ethnicity. The simplest explanation of the collapse is to say that such a project was, in an absolute sense, a "failure": this is the conclusion that many in the communist countries now draw, as those who deny the efficacy of "social engineering" have always done. There are, however, reasons to resist this conclusion. In terms of the capacities of states to transform society from above, the record is not so absolute.

First, it is far too early to say how much of the legacy of communist rule will endure and whether some of it may not in fact survive. Second, it is wrong to take as evidence of the failure of communism the emergence of forces that appear to mark a return to pre-communist forms of behavior, since many of these have a character that has been shaped by the very impact of communist transformation—ethnic conflict being an obvious case. Similarly, as many who have analyzed the emergence of Gorbachev have shown, the change in Soviet society is in some respects a product of the achievements of communism—expansion in education and urbanization being obvious contributory factors.[3] Third, even if much or all of what is associated with communist rule does disappear, say in a decade or two, the historical fact of the communist achievement over some decades will remain: this was evident in socioeconomic transformation, the raising of living standards and the implementation of a widespread social welfare system, the sustenance and reproduction of a political system and, not least, a considerable success in the most testing area of all, inter-state competition. It may be that the success of the latter—Soviet victory in World War II, plus four decades of rivalry with the West thereafter—provided part of the illusion of communism's overall efficacy, at home and abroad. However, the record of interstate competition alone would suggest that the characterization of the communist record as a "failure" is simplistic. Such a verdict would have come as rather a surprise to, for example, the 250,000 Germans captured at Stalingrad as it would have to military planners in the Pentagon during the 1970s and early 1980s. The achievement was substantial, even if temporary.

THE NATURE OF COLD WAR

If the events of 1989 signal the end of the Cold War, they make it more possible to address the question of what the Cold War was, and how as one specific instance it pertains to broader conceptions of interstate competition. Despite its apparent distinctiveness, the Cold War has been treated by most writers as merely another chapter in a longer history of international competition. The term "cold war" tended to be used in two ways: one to denote particular periods of intense East-West rivalry, 1947-53, the classic original "Cold War" and, though this is more disputed, the period 1979-84, the "Second Cold War." The other usage denotes not specific periods but the more protracted rivalry of the two systems, capitalist and communist, as it developed after 1945 and originated in 1917.[4]

The academic literature has tended to focus on historical questions pertaining to the first, narrower sense of cold war, of who originated the intensified conflict in 1947 or 1979 and why, and this is the basis of the debate between orthodox, revisionist and post-revisionist historians on the origins of the cold war. Less articulated has been the theoretical debate, on what kind of conflict this cold war in the broader sense was, and what its implications are for international and other social theory. In one view, there was no problem: the Cold War was a strategic rivalry between great powers like any other and susceptible to conventional "realist" analysis. This explanation had several things to recommend it: it had considerable explanatory power; it drew attention to what were undoubtedly points of comparison between historic great power conflicts and the Soviet-American one, most obviously competition for spheres of influence and military power; it provided a way of creating academic distance from the rival ideological claims of both sides to be representing one or other set of universal values; it distinguished itself from the orthodox Marxist view that in some way the Cold War represented an internationalized political conflict, class struggle on a world scale.

Yet it can be questioned how far this conventional description of the Cold War did accord with reality and, not least, how far it can be seen to provide a basis for understanding communism's collapse. One initial novelty about East-West rivalry in the postwar epoch was the role of nuclear weapons, the limits these placed upon direct territorial competition between the core blocs and the peculiarly intense but controlled competition of the arms race. While the two blocs were involved in wars in the Third World to challenge hegemony or take territory in core states of the other bloc, it was not possible. More important, if often overstated by the two competitors themselves, was the fact that the Cold War involved not just relative degrees of power and strategic advantage, but also competition about the way in which society and political systems were to be organized. It involved a drive by both sides to produce a homogeneous world, not just in the conventional International Relations sense of states that performed in roughly similar ways on the international stage, but in terms of internal political and socioeconomic organization. It was heterogeneity in this latter domain that lay at the core of the Cold War and which, for all its strategic and other similarities with great power conflicts of the past, made it distinctive.

What was involved in the Cold War was the confrontation of two societies, including but not solely involving, the United States. Both U.S.-led capitalism and Soviet-led communism sought nothing less than to create worlds in their own image: although, for four decades both were checked by the military and political strength of the other, the endurance of this universalizing drive was evident. Soviet communism gave up its global political aspirations at some point after the mid-1970s—with the collapse of Eurocommunism and the paralysis of Third World socialist and socialist-oriented regimes. Western capitalism did not give up and, with greater resources and determination, sustained its pressure, and in the end prevailed. Nothing bore this underlying nature of the conflict out more clearly than the manner in which it ended. Had the Cold War been a traditional great power conflict alone it could have ended with a truce, negotiated distribution of power and military strength. This was what had existed in Europe after 1945 and what was attempted, without success, in the Third World. Ultimately, the denouement came in the apparently paralyzed, "balanced" core, namely Europe, and as a result of a change of policy at the core. It came because one system was no longer able to sustain itself in the face of the other, and it was as a result of this, of one side in effect collapsing, that the Cold War could be said to have ended.

THE ROLE OF EXTERNAL COMPETITION

It is now possible to address the main question of this analysis, one of both historical and theoretical importance, namely how far and in what ways external competition contributed to the evolution and final collapse of the communist system.[5] As already noted, that system was not destroyed by war, nor was its collapse solely exogenous. Internal factors, most importantly the paralysis of the economies and political systems, played a major part. But external forces, including economic ones, did contribute to the final collapse of 1989. Two kinds of factors conventionally evolved in analysis of interstate competition—"traditional" and contemporary—can be examined: the conclusion will be that, above all, it was neither of these but competition in the fields of perceived economic and ideological performance that determined the outcome.

The cold war was not the first case of international competition between heterogeneous states. The fate of the Ottoman and Chinese empires in the latter half of the nineteenth centuries up to their final disappearances during World War I are two classic earlier instances of this. Here too military competition, administrative reform as a response to interstate competition, and rising dissension within all contributed to the collapse of the weaker system. As in the cold war, the erosion was gradual, not cataclysmic, and involved military, economic and diplomatic dimensions. Yet for all the similarities, the differences between these earlier cases of intersystemic competition and the later cold war are rather greater. At the military level, the Soviet system was far more an equal of its rival than were the Ottoman and Qing (Manchu) empires, and there was no equivalent of the incursions and annexations that preceded the collapse of the latter. Indeed, in the postwar period the

Soviet system survived the military challenges at the margin—Korea, Vietnam, even Afghanistan—comparatively well. Economically, the contest was even more different: whereas the Ottoman and Qing (Manchu) empires had been eroded by foreign trade, capitulations, debt and so forth, the Soviet system used interaction with the western economies as a means of retaining power. Loans to, trade with, and investment in these countries did not weaken, but rather strengthened, the power of the communist states. It was not the "market," in any direct sense of intervention within these societies and economies, that contributed to their ultimate demise.[6]

INTERNATIONAL FACTORS IN COLD WAR

The other set of international factors often cited are more recent and more singular, those which are commonly held to be responsible for the collapse of the communist regimes, and in particular for the crisis of the U.S.S.R., in the late 1980s. These revolve around the argument that in one way or another the pressure that the West placed upon the communist system for the mid-1970s onwards, embodied in the policies of the Second Cold War, was such that the Soviet system could not endure. Breaking this general argument down, three specific factors are often cited: the burden of the arms race, the economic and CoCom technological embargoes, and the anti-communist guerrilla movements in the Third World Soviet allies. On their own, or in some kind of combination, these were, it is frequently argued, the forms of international competition and pressure that brought the U.S.S.R. to its knees.

(I) The Arms Race

Enough is now known for us to be able to outline the history and significance of the East-West arms race. In summary form, its record was as follows: (A) from the late 1940s onwards, the U.S.S.R. and the U.S.A. were engaged in an arms race, conventional and nuclear, involving growing expenditures, and a technological race, in which, for all major dimensions except space in the late 1950s, the U.S.A. was in the lead in the technological field, and remained, in most dimensions, in the lead in the quantitative domain;[7] (B) despite this U.S. lead, the relative burden on the U.S.A. was significantly less, representing between 5% and 10% of GNP, whereas for the U.S.S.R. arms expenditure represented between 10% and 20% throughout this period—some Soviet officials now say it was as high as 25%; (C) despite the lack of a direct U.S.-Soviet military confrontation, conventional or nuclear, this arms race represented, in a Clausewitzian sense, a continuation of politics by other means: it reflected a search for an elusive but strategically meaningful measure of "superiority" over the other, it embodied a pursuit by both sides of prestige and status in the international arena, and it constituted a means of pressure on the budget and hence on the state-society relationship within the other bloc.[8]

Given the burden on the U.S.S.R. and its evident inability to compete with the U.S.A., it is frequently argued that it was this which forced the U.S.S.R. into strategic retreat in the mid-1980s. At least three variants of this argument can be noted: an economic one, that the level of expenditure on arms and the diversion of resources to the military sector were such that the U.S.S.R. could not continue to compete, and needed a drastic reduction in military expenditure in order to divert resources for domestic economic reorganization; a technological argument, that it was the continued U.S. lead, acutely represented in the early 1980s by two developments, the strategic defense initiative ("Star Wars") and cruise missiles, which forced the Soviet leadership to realize that it could not continue to compete; and a political argument, that the dangers of nuclear war and the costs involved forced the Soviets to abandon the idea of the world as one divided between two camps, locked in social conflict, in favor of a stress on the common interests of human kind. All three are, in varying degrees, found in the writings of Soviet and Western writers and each must have played a role. Gorbachev himself has consistently evoked the third, political argument. The power of nuclear weapons and the accident of Chernobyl in 1986 certainly served to reinforce this awareness of the dangers of nuclear energy and, by extension, nuclear weapons.

Important as it is, there are reasons to qualify the import of the arms race explanation as the major factor behind the Soviet collapse. Certainly, the economic argument must have considerable force: indeed, the very quantitative figure of 10% or 20% of Soviet GNP being spent on defense understates the qualitative and distorting impact, with the allocation of the best administrative and scientific personnel and of key material resources to this sector. On the other hand, military expenditure at 10% or more of GNP is far from being an adequate explanation for the failings of the Soviet economy. The very high rate of military expenditure as a percentage of GNP is but another way of saying that GNP itself was rather low—the figures for overall expenditure as between the U.S. and the U.S.S.R. show that in absolute terms the U.S.A. was out-spending the U.S.S.R.[9] The focus must, therefore, be as much on the efficiency and allocative mechanisms of the civilian sector as on the claim of the military on GNP: had the Soviet GNP been rather higher and the remaining 80% of the Soviet economy been more efficiently organized, the "burden" of military expenditure would have been less and would, given reasonable efficiency and growth rates, have represented a lower percentage of GNP anyway.

Similar problems arise with the technological argument: the assumption of much analysis of the arms race and of the conventional Soviet approach prior to this was that, more or less, the U.S.S.R. was compelled by the necessities of interstate competition to match the U.S.A. in qualitative and quantitative terms. Previously, the U.S.S.R. had imitated U.S. advances—as in the MIRVing of missiles after 1972 and the development of a submarine-launched intercontinental capacity. By the late 1970s this was no longer possible: the challenges of SDI and of cruise missiles were that the U.S.S.R. had no comparable riposte antidote. In particular, it could not compete in the technology of the third industrial revolution. Yet the U.S.S.R. could have produced some countermeasures to these U.S. challenges—a few low flying missiles plus decoys would have done much to invalidate SDI. A policy of what is termed "minimum deterrence" could have made a substantial difference and enabled the U.S.S.R. to escape from its self-defeating pursuit of "rough parity." It was perhaps not so much at the military level as such, but what the new technologies symbolized about the overall retardation of the system, that forced the Soviet leaders into retreat. The third argument relevant to the arms race, the political argument

about the threat to humanity of nuclear weapons, has much validity and it is to the credit of Gorbachev that he articulated it more clearly than anyone else: but it does not entail the overall process of political and social change within the U.S.S.R. that has accompanied the adoption of these universal values associated with "new thinking." It is conceivable that the U.S.S.R. would have opted out of the nuclear arms race as previously pursued but insisted on preserving its distinctive political and socio-economic system. To explain the latter involves looking beyond the realm of the arms race and its economic, technical, and political costs.

(II) Economic Pressures

The second set of factors commonly adduced to explain the Soviet retreat is the economic, and in particular the impact on the U.S.S.R. of Western embargoes and restrictions in the field of high technology. Most postwar discussion of the relationship between trade and security in the East-West context has operated with the assumption that increased commercial interaction between the two blocs would contribute to the stability of the Soviet bloc: the argument, as it developed in the 1970s, was between those who believed that greater trade, by making the Soviet Union more secure, would reduce areas of conflict between it and the West, and those who thought it would encourage combative behavior. If the former view, drawing on theories of "interdependence," was dominant in the early 1970s, it was the latter view that prevailed in the period of the Second Cold War.

On the basis of the partial evidence available, it would appear that economic interaction and pressure of various kinds were a factor in the collapse of the communist system, but that the most important factor was the inability of the centrally planned regimes to make use of the advantages that trade with the capitalist world brought. In the case of certain Eastern European countries—Poland is the most striking example—the opening up to the West in the early 1970s had short-term gains, in terms of availability of consumer goods and investment, but led to a longer-run crisis, with foreign debt and increased pressure on domestic earnings once debt repayment became necessary. The centrally planned economic system could not make use of such external support adequately to develop its own economy, and ended up being trapped by its international commitments. In the case of the U.S.S.R., all the evidence suggests that straightforward commercial interaction with the capitalist world had the effect of strengthening the existing system in the short run: most obviously, wheat imports provided a means of offsetting failures in agriculture. The rise in the price of oil in the 1970s gave the U.S.S.R. a windfall profit for much of the decade: however, as Soviet writers have recently pointed out, the longer-run consequences of these profits were inhibiting, since they enabled the central planners and managers to postpone changes that might otherwise have had to be introduced more rapidly.

The same applied in the field of technology: the record of technological innovation in the U.S.S.R. is by no means as bleak as is often suggested, but there is no doubt that most of the major technological innovations of recent decades originated in the West. Here the U.S.S.R. was at a disadvantage in two respects. It did not make any major innovations itself and was therefore compelled, in the civilian and military spheres, to copy or simply steal new technologies from the capitalist world. The degree of Soviet insulation from the international market was never as great as conventional images suggest: the industrialization of the 1930s relied heavily on capital goods imports from Britain and Germany; the history of Soviet aerospace is one of reproduction of Western planes and technologies. Yet in this pursuit of technological development, the U.S.S.R. was always behind. Even more important, however, it was unable to make proper use of the technologies it did have: there was little interaction between the military and civilian sectors; the system of central planning contained built-in disincentives for innovation and encouraged the use of inefficient and traditional methods of production; political and ideological constraints inhibited the use of information technology throughout the system. The pattern of ''conservative modernization'' identified as endemic to the centrally planned economies operated in this regard.[10] Hence the third industrial revolution, which began in the early 1970s, outstripped it more than ever.

The factor of economic pressure and its political impact is important even when it comes to the embargoes. Here it has been argued that Soviet behavior in the international arena was affected by Western restrictions, both those of a strictly national security kind, through CoCom, and broader political embargoes announced in the wake of Afghanistan. The former, it was said, would make it more difficult for the U.S.S.R. to compete in the arms race, the latter would act as disincentives for unwelcome Soviet foreign policy actions. Given the degree to which the U.S.S.R. protested about these restrictions, it would seem that their impact was considerable.[11] Yet these pressures in themselves can hardly explain the change in Soviet orientation from the mid-1980s onwards: the U.S.S.R., faced with a dire technological lag in the military sphere, could have made substantial concessions without placing their overall strategy in question; in the short run at least, they did not respond to Western political sanctions by making major foreign policy concessions and were indeed more intransigent up to 1985 than had hitherto been the case. The very same factors that diminished the import of Western commercial and technological impact served to lessen the impact of their withdrawal: the centralized political and economic system could absorb the denial, just as it could inhibit the diffusion, of the new technologies.

(III) Erosion of the Bloc

A third major factor adduced to explain the retreat of Soviet power is the cost of supporting its Third World allies, at both the economic and military levels. Soviet writers themselves now complain openly about the costs, economic and diplomatic, of backing Third World allies and have reversed the earlier Khrushchevite view that national liberation and Third World revolutionary movements made a positive contribution to the power of the U.S.S.R.;[12] the concept of "imperial overstretch" would seem to apply here and provide a comparative perspective on the Soviet retreat. The character of Soviet relations with Third World allies, resting on substantial economic subsidies in return for political and strategic rewards, made this set of relationships especially burdensome. For U.S. strategic planners in the early 1980s the weakest link of the Soviet system lay in the Third World, which is why there evolved the doctrine of support for anti-communist guerrilla movements.

On closer examination, however, the pressure of Third World commitments seems different and in some ways smaller than at first sight appeared. The greatest cost to the U.S.S.R. of its Third World commitments was in the diplomatic field, e.g., Soviet support for revolutionary allies and movements worsened U.S.-Soviet relations, and the invasion of Afghanistan provided a means by which the West could for the first time weaken the U.S.S.R.'s relationship with the Third World as a whole. The other factors normally adduced, economic and military, may have been less significant. First, the figures for Soviet "aid" to the Third World comprise a variety of forms of support, including, in the case of the largest commitment, Cuba, major long-term trading agreements: though these gave Cuba far better terms of trade than it could have gotten on the world market (high prices for sugar, low for oil), they were not net transfers in the ordinary sense. There were benefits to the U.S.S.R.—getting sugar and nickel that were paid for in rubles, rather than having to pay in hard currency. In other cases, the Third World ally was able to provide the U.S.S.R. with valuable imports—Afghan gas being one example. Second, despite Soviet over-stated claims, the amount of aid was in comparative terms very low—0.25% of GNP, roughly equivalent to the U.S. record.[13] Politically convenient as it may now be within the U.S.S.R. to blame Third World allies, who certainly were also mismanaging their economies, for the economic woes of the U.S.S.R., this was not a major factor in the economic crisis of the Soviet system.

As with military expenditure within the U.S.S.R. itself, the focus of criticism must go back to the overall system of planning and production and the inefficiencies it contained, which were, incidentally, reproduced by Soviet aid programs within Third World states themselves. The strategic cost of sustaining Third World allies in the 1980s was certainly rising, but if the purpose of U.S. support to Third World anti-communist movements was to weaken the U.S.S.R. at its weakest point this did not happen. One of the major reasons for Soviet and Western involvement in Afghanistan was the demonstration effect of a ruling communist party being overthrown: the impact on Eastern Europe of Kabul's falling was, both sides believed, potentially enormous. Yet in the end it was not in Nicaragua or Afghanistan that Soviet allies were first overthrown, but in Eastern Europe. It was what happened in Warsaw, Berlin, and Prague that affected developments in Managua, Aden, and Kabul and not the other way around.

COMPETITION: THE EXTERNAL IN PERSPECTIVE

The argument so far has identified two categories of external factors, the traditional-imperial ones and the East-West Cold War ones, which can be considered to have played a role in eroding and undermining Soviet power. While both categories have some explanatory power, we have argued that they alone are inadequate. If this is true, it encourages a reexamination of the reasons for the collapse of Soviet power, at both the historical and the theoretical levels: i.e., a reexamination both of what actually happened, and of how our conception of interstate competition may need modifying in the light of the Soviet case.

What needs explanation is that an international system of states collapsed in the absence of the most evident forms of threat: it was not defeated in war; it did not face overwhelming political challenges from below (Poland being the only, partial, exception); it was not, despite its manifold economic and social problems, unable to meet the basic economic demands of its citizenry. It did not, therefore, "collapse," "fail," "break down" in any absolute sense. What occurred, rather, was that the leadership of the most powerful state in the system decided to introduce a radically new set of policies, within the U.S.S.R. and within the system as a whole: it was not that the ruled could not go on being ruled in the old way so much as that the rulers could not go on ruling in the old way. The question is what it was that led these rulers, who cannot be accused of lacking a desire to retain power or of being covert supporters of the West, to introduce the changes they did.

Two kinds of reason, one endogenous and the other exogenous, seem to have been responsible. They can be termed, in summary form, socioeconomic paralysis and lack of international competitiveness. The internal paralysis was evident in a wide range of spheres: falling growth rates, rising social problems, growing corruption and disillusionment, ecological crises. Not only could the system not go on reproducing the rates of growth and improvement in welfare provision characteristic of earlier phases—the 1930s, the 1950s—but it seemed to have run out of steam in a comprehensive manner. This was increasingly clear not just to the leadership but to the growing body of educated people produced by the system. These phenomena are often referred to in the Soviet literature as "stagnation," yet in many ways this is a simplistic term:[14] it understates the degree to which there was continued progress in some spheres, not least the lessening of political repression; it still contains within it the teleological assumption that the system could, under other circumstances, have continued to grow and develop.

Most important, however, "stagnation" leaves out what was also a major factor in forcing the Soviet leadership, faced with this trend, to introduce change, namely the awareness of the system's *comparative* failure vis-a-vis the West. It is here, in the perceived inability of the Soviet system to catch up, let alone overtake, the West that a central aspect of the Soviet collapse must be seen. It was a failure to compete internationally that, on top of the internal crisis, led to the post-1985 changes in the U.S.S.R.: once begun, an attempt to reform the system the better to survive and compete quickly capsized into an attempt to save the state as such.

The awareness of the system's inability to compete in the 1980s was the final in several stages of such loss of hope. The first, historical, disappointment was that immediately after 1917 when the Bolsheviks realized that their revolution would not be reproduced in Germany. This realization led to a double redefinition of strategy—temporary abandonment of the idea of world revolution, proclamation of the idea that a socialist regime *could* be built in the U.S.S.R. With the victories in World War II and the increase in the number of Third World pro-Soviet allies, it appeared for the 1950s and 1960s as if the initial encirclement of the U.S.S.R. could be overcome concomitant with the development of socialism within the U.S.S.R. itself. The successes of post-war reconstruction and space technology in the 1950s seemed to confirm this: hence the new, secularly optimistic, program of Khrushchev which combined continued rivalry with the West in the Third World with a policy of socio-economic development designed

to "catch up with and overtake" the West in two decades. It would seem, difficult as it is to believe now, that this perspective, modified by Brezhnev, dominated Soviet thinking until the early 1980s: there were continued advances in the Third World, the U.S.S.R. attained "rough parity" with the U.S.A. in the arms race, and at home it was official policy to state that the U.S.S.R. was now at a new stage, one of "developed socialism."

The reality was, however, rather different, as each of the major areas of interstate and interbloc competition showed. In the most public and privileged area of competition, the military, the U.S.S.R. was always inferior in numbers and quality, except for its conventional strength in Eastern Europe. If this was the area where the Soviet Union was to compete the most, it was evidently not doing anything like well enough.

The international system created by the U.S.S.R. was also markedly weaker quantitatively and qualitatively than that created by the West. Not only was the international capitalist market far stronger in terms of economic output, technological change, and number of countries included within it, but its degree of integration was greater: despite all the talk of a new socialist "system," one of the paradoxes of planning within the U.S.S.R. and the Soviet international system more generally was its inability to integrate sectors beyond giving them separate, if supposedly coordinated, production targets. In many respects, not least innovation and pricing, it remained dependent on the capitalist system, and ineffectually imitative of it. In the military sphere a similar disparity and qualitative inferiority prevailed in the comparison between NATO and the Warsaw

Pact. For all the talk of constituting an alternative world order, the Soviet one was less integrated and much weaker overall.[15]

This failure to compete in international terms would, in itself, have been a major problem, given the fact that underlying East-West rivalry and Cold War was an attempt by both sides to provide a basis for a new international "order," to demonstrate the superiority of the one over the other. But this external blockage, one going right back to 1917 and only obscured by subsequent international triumphs, was compounded by the internal limits of the system in many spheres: the failure to match levels of output in the West, the growing gap in living standards between developed socialist and developed capitalist states and, obscured by rhetoric about "socialist" democracy, the contrast between a substantial degree of democratic success in the West and continuing if less brutal centralized political control in the East. Had the U.S.S.R. been able to rival the West successfully in other spheres, these internal deficiencies, those denoted by "stagnation," might have been concealed the longer: but it was the failure at the international level combined with that at home that forced the leadership to face up to them.

Here we come to a central feature of the collapse: almost impossible to believe as it may now be, it would seem that up to the early 1980s this contrast in internal achievement was hidden from, or at least not recognized by, most Soviet observers, in the leadership or elsewhere. The underlying self-confidence of the Soviet system, a product of the revolution's historic claims and of victory in World War II, seemed to have lasted up to that time; but at some point in the early 1980s it began to erode, first amongst the leadership and

then within the population as a whole. The awareness of how people lived in the West and of the enormous gap in living standards produced a situation in which the self-confidence that had lasted from 1917 evaporated in the space of a few short years. The lack of political freedom played its part through Helsinki and Western pressure: but the evidence suggests that it was the economic which played the major role in getting this process going. Once the living standards gap became evident then the residual legitimacy of the communist political system was swept away and that of the alternative system, the Western variant of pluralism, was enhanced.

Here it is worth looking at the mechanism by which this change of attitude occurred. The insulation of Soviet society was both physical—lack of communication, radio jamming, absence of travel, punishment of those who sought contact with the outside world—and psychological—a belief that whatever went wrong, "*u nas lushche*"—"things are better with us."[16] Those who traveled abroad or had access to comparative data were condemned to silence, even when they realized the truth. Here the change of heart of the leadership, one encouraged by broader awareness in the society, was of pivotal importance and opened the floodgates to popular discontent: the breaking of the secular self-confidence of the top leadership must certainly have been encouraged by the failures of international competition in the military and economic spheres, but it would appear that the very perception of the contrast in living standards, highlighting the reality of internal paralysis in the late 1970s, and the growing military gap associated with the third industrial revolution, played the crucial part. In Gorbachev's case, for example, it would seem that his visits to Canada provided such an occasion: it would only take five minutes in an average Canadian supermarket for the point to become clear, and for the specific experience of shortages and administrative problems he experienced in running the Stavropol region to be set in its decisive, internationalized, context.

Once this change had occurred, then the process of broader awareness followed inexorably. The liberalization of the political system within the U.S.S.R. allowed of greater information about the capitalist world, almost all of it favorable when not uncritical, and for a more negative assessment of the record of the U.S.S.R. It is noticeable too how, in speeches made after 1985, Gorbachev himself would make telling comparisons with the capitalist world, in the field of social indicators—infant mortality, hospital conditions, alcoholism, availability of basic foods—as well as in broader macro-economic and political terms.[17] His own process of self-education seems to have followed such a path: already dissatisfied with socialist performance, he came into office in 1985 apparently believing that the socialist system could reform itself by applying technology in a more intense way, the better to "accelerate" production; but by 1989 he had moved much further on both the economic and political fronts, in the face of the evident inability of the system to reform itself within orthodox socialist political and economic parameters. In other words, the international comparison that had brought him to the point of initiating major reform in 1985 pushed him after 1985 to envisage a much more radical reform of the system. The fact that, through forcing the comparison onto the Soviet public, he had unleashed widespread additional dissatisfaction, only served to confirm this trend.

THREE LEVELS OF INTERNATIONAL COMPETITION

This analysis of East-West competition up to the late 1980s has a number of implications for theories of interstate and intersociety competition in particular. No one analyzing East-West conflict can deny the relevance within it of conventional, interstate, forms of competition—at the military, economic, and political levels. The rivalry of the Soviet and U.S. systems in the postwar period involved a comprehensive competition in which the innovation was not the role of states but rather the way in which this interstate competition developed into new domains—the arms race, on the one hand, the comprehensive mobilization of ideological resources on the other. Given its strong position in the economic field, it was natural that the West should seek to use its economic strength to place pressure on the U.S.S.R. for security reasons: the international political economy of East-West relations was, in essence, one of the uses of economic instruments by the stronger bloc, that of Western states, for political and military ends.

This interstate competition, comprehensive as it was, is not sufficient to explain how, why, and when the communist system collapsed, how the West succeeded in prevailing over the East. We have seen how earlier cases of intersystemic conflict—the Ottoman and Manchu cases—provide at best partial points of comparison: despite some similarities, theirs was fundamentally a very different story. The specifically Cold War instruments of interstate competition—arms race, embargoes, Third World harassment—do not, in themselves, explain why the Soviet leadership took the decisions it did after 1985. To analyze this rivalry it is necessary to take a broader look at East-West conflict as a whole, one that encompasses the competition of systems, i.e. capitalism and "communism," within which state competition plays an important, but not exclusive, role.

In this perspective, it becomes possible to distinguish three dimensions of competition which are interrelated but analytically distinct: the level of activities of states; that of social and economic entities, most notably businesses; and what can, in the broadest sense, be termed the "ideological," the perception of and belief about the political, economic levels and culture of another society. In addressing the question of "how" the West put pressure on the East this tripartite distinction may be helpful. Operating on the first level, Western state action had effects, but it was not the only story. Paradoxically, the ability of Western states directly to put such pressure is now greater than ever before as the linking of economic assistance to socioeconomic change within the U.S.S.R. and Eastern Europe show: *perestroika* has created the conditions for such a socioeconomic intervention by the Group of 7, not resulted from it. In the case of Eastern Europe, Western firms—industrial enterprises, banks—also played a role, especially in dealings with Poland in the early 1970s and in the handling of the Soviet oil output. In the opening up that took place from late 1989 onwards, West German business enterprises have taken a lead, somewhat coordinated with but separate from, that of the Bonn government itself. It would be analytically misleading either to reduce state policy in East-West relations to the wishes of multinational corporations, or to see the latter as acting simply within parameters laid down by or at the behest of Western states. Their actions are parallel and usu-

ally—though not always—convergent: the generally negative response of sectors of the business community to political embargoes was evidence enough of divergence in this regard.

The ideological dimension is, perhaps, of even greater importance: its role in the collapse of communism and in the East-West rivalry that preceded it was in some ways decisive. Here capitalism operated not just through states or firms, but through the society as a whole. What above all forced the leadership of the CPSU to change course, and what destroyed the support or acquiescence of the peoples of Eastern Europe and the U.S.S.R. to communism, was, on top of the difference in political achievement, the perceived contrast in political and economic standards and in living conditions between East and West. This ideological dimension is certainly something that states help to promote and regulate, and which their information and propaganda organs disseminate; it is something that rests upon political record and on economic performance, on the output and sales policies of business corporations. But it is something distinct, encompassing as it does the perception of political system, popular culture, the media, fashion, and, in broad terms the image of what constitutes a good life, in the eyes of the leadership and population of the rival system. Moreover, the dissemination of images pertaining to this is not simply the result of state or business enterprise decisions: it takes place in an uncoordinated but pervasive way, through television and film, through popular music, through impressions gained from travel and personal encounter. It is informal and diffuse, but constitutes the most potent interface between two societies. The abandonment by the majority of the inhabitants of East Germany of any belief in a separate socialist way or entity was above all a product of this encounter: years of exposure to West German images on television, followed by the direct encounter itself, the *Reiseshock.*

Insofar as this distinction is valid, and the importance of ideological and perceptual factors in international relations is accepted, then it suggests another interpretation of the Cold War and its end, and of international relations more generally. Relations between states retain their importance, and the particular mechanisms of conflict and resource mobilization at any one time are open to analysis on a contingent basis. The denial of state efficacy and the premature reduction of its role are as misleading as the insistence that all international relations can be seen, or deemed, to be ones between states. At the same time, international competition involves two other major dimensions: the unofficial and the ideological. The latter has always operated—it would be impossible to follow the history of Christianity, its diffusion and division, without it. But the ideological has a special salience in a world where material well-being, fashion and consumerism together with political freedoms occupy a special role in the constitution of specific societies, and in an international situation characterized by immediate transmission of sound and images. There is clearly a relationship between power in one domain and power in the ideological domain—through control of images and their means of diffusion. Never was Gramsci's conception of hegemony, in the sense of ideological and cultural factors as instruments of domination, so relevant as in analyzing the international system today. If communism surrendered without firing a shot, it was because the instrument of international competition in the late twentieth century was as much the T-shirt as the gunboat.

POSTSCRIPT: THE END OF THE SOVIET UNION

The denouncement of the August crisis in the U.S.S.R. has unexpectedly accelerated the process analysed here. A last-ditch attempt to save the old regime only brought forward the collapse of the traditional centers of power, and of the Soviet Union itself: it showed how discredited, and divided, the old centers were and, through their implication in the coup attempt, confirmed that discrediting. Leaders and led no longer believed in the system. The goal of those brought to office by the coup is both to complete the abandonment of the U.S.S.R.'s pre-existing international role and to integrate the remnants, as far as possible, into the political and economic structures of the capitalist West. The victory of the West, promoted at all three levels analyzed above, has now been reinforced.

NOTES

An earlier version of this paper was given at the Economic and Social Research Council conference, "Structural Change in the West," held at Emmanuel College, Cambridge, September 1990. I am grateful to Jeff Frieden, Michael Mann, Perry Anderson and Nikki Keddie for their most helpful comments on the text.

1. See my "The Ends of Cold War," *New Left Review,* 180(March–April 1990): 5–23; George Schopflin, "Why Communism Collapsed," *International Affairs,* 66, 1(1990): 3–16.

2. For the argument as to why, on economic grounds, the state socialist model could not work, despite initial successes and a margin for reform, see Wlodzimierz Brus and Kazimierz Laski, *From Marx to Market* (Oxford: The Clarendon Press, 1989).

3. Moshe Lewin, *The Gorbachev Phenomenon* (Berkeley: University of California Press, 1988), is a lucid overview of the social and economic preconditions for the breakdown of the Brezhnevite order in the 1980s.

4. Fred Halliday, *The Making of the Second Cold War* (London: Verso, 1983), chapter 1, on the different meanings of "cold war."

5. Theda Skoepol, *States and Social Revolutions,* (Princeton: Princeton University Press, 1979), remains a classic discussion of this question.

6. On the Ottoman background see Roger Owen, *The Middle East in the World Economy, 1800–1914* (Oxford: Oxford University Press, 1981): Caglar Keyder, *State and Class in Turkey, A Study in Capitalist Development* (London: Verso, 1987).

7. On the arms race see my *The Making of the Second Cold War,* chapter 3.

8. This was conventionally known as the "arms race theory of arms control."

9. U.S. expenditure in 1971 was $120 billions, as against Soviet $94 billions, in 1980 $111 billions as against $107. Total Soviet plus allies expenditure was only half that of its opponents, NATO plus Far Eastern allies (China, Japan) expenditure: in 1980 $120 billions for the WTO as against $243 billions. All data from *SIPRI Yearbook* (Stockholm: SIPRI, 1981), figures in constant 1978 prices. U.S. expenditure was conventionally understated by a number of accounting devices: one calculation was that the 1980 figure of $127 billions should be adjusted upwards to $223 billions, i.e., from 5.2% to 9.5% of GNP: James Cypher, "Rearing America," *Monthly Review,* 33, 6(November 1981): 11–27.

10. See Brus-Laski.

11. For a Soviet view of the Western embargo see Igor Artemiev "International Economic Security," in Igor Artemiev and Fred Halliday *International Economic Security: Soviet and British Approaches,* (London: Chatham House Discussion Paper, no. 7, 1988).

12. Fred Halliday, *From Kabul to Managua,* (New York: Pantheon, 1989). (UK title *Cold War, Third World.* London: Hutchinson/Radius, 1989), chapter 4, for the rethinking of Soviet policy towards the Third World.

13. According to OECD DAC figures.

14. On "stagnation" see Mikhail Gorbachev, *Perestroika, New Thinking for Our Country and the World* (London: Collins, 1987), chapter 1.

15. On the NATO-WTO comparison see note 14 above. The degree of economic integration between the Eastern European Comecon members was far less than that within the EEC: most trade was on a bilateral, Soviet-East European, basis.

16. Hedrick Smith, *The Russians* (London: Sphere, 1976), gives a powerful evocation of this attitude in the period prior to the collapse of Soviet confidence.

17. Gorbachev's *Perestroika* is replete with calls for the Soviet economy to rise to "world standards," i.e., those of the West.

QUESTIONS

1. What are the three levels of international competition identified by Halliday?

2. Does Halliday's conclusion about the collapse of the Soviet Union prove or disprove George Kennan's policy on containment? Explain.

State Level International Relations Theories

In Part I, we discussed system level theories of international relations, focusing on the nature of the global system and how it shapes the behavior of states within it. Now, we turn our attention to the theories that fall under Waltz's second level of analysis—the state level. State level theories, as noted in Chapter 1, concentrate on the individual attributes of states, rather than the overall system in which they operate. The primary concern here is with the domestic, political and cultural characteristics of a state. The key assumption is that the internal character and institutions of a state have a direct bearing on its foreign policy.

There are two primary state level theories presented in this book, focusing on the role of the state and its impact on international relations—political culture theory and decision-making process theory. In the first chapter, we examine the tenets of political culture theory, as well as its strengths and weaknesses. Some political culture theorists argue that the type of government is a broad determining factor in the behavior and foreign policy of a state. On a basic level, these theorists suggest that, generally, democracies tend to be inherently peaceful, while authoritarian regimes are likely to pursue more aggressive policies.

A second group of political culture theorists acknowledge that these differences between regimes can be important, but it is the cultural and civilizing aspects of a society that shape and guide foreign policy. For them, the traditions, customs, values, and beliefs that characterize a particular group of people also have an influence on the political behavior of that group or its governing body.

The theory presented in the following chapter, decision-making process theory, emphasizes the importance of how decisions are made and the impact of the bureaucracy itself on the government's decision-making process. The implication is that the structure of the government—with its different departments and competing interests—can have substantial sway over not just the policy-making process but the policies themselves.

In the next two chapters, we take a closer look at one of the primary actors on the world stage—the state. From this level of analysis, we examine how states and governments can influence the course of events in international relations. Types of political systems, bureaucratic structure, and unique characteristics of different cultures and civilizations are just some of the important features we will discuss as part of the second, state level of analysis.

Chapter 5

POLITICAL CULTURE THEORY

COMPONENTS OF POLITICAL CULTURE THEORY

Focus of Analysis ········▶	• Domestic political and cultural characteristics of states or civilizations
Major Influences ········▶	• Type of government or civilization
Behavior of States ········▶	• (Regimists) Behavior based on type of government • (Civilizationists) Competitive, based on cultural values
Basis of a State's Foreign Policy ········▶	• Assumes that a state's foreign policy reflects the dominant values, attitudes, and beliefs of society/civilizations
Key Concepts ········▶	• Authoritarian regimes; Civilizationist perspective; Cultural fault lines; Culture; Elitism; End of history; Liberal democracies; Political culture; Regimist perspective

INTRODUCTION

Before we begin our discussion of political culture theory, it might be helpful to answer a few fundamental questions about states and how they operate, as well as to define some commonly used terms. Though it may seem fairly basic, let us first ask, What is a state, and how does a state differ from a government?

We can all list the names of any number of states throughout the world—France, Singapore, the United States, Kenya, etc. All are very different, yet all are considered states. A **state** or country (these terms are synonymous) is a political, legal, and territorial entity. A state consists of an internationally recognized territory, a permanent population, and a government that has control over the people within its acknowledged boundaries. In theory, states are **sovereign.** That is, the government is the supreme authority within the state and does not answer to any outside power. This sovereignty is recognized by international law and by other states through diplomatic relations, and often by membership in the United Nations. Though this definition may sound complex, if we refer back to our examples, we see they all fit this description. Each state has specific borders recognized by other states in the international community, and also has specific and unique political, economic, and military structures and goals.

On a broad level, the interaction of states is guided by each state's government. **Government** is a public institution that has the authority to create, implement, and enforce rules, laws, and decisions within a state's territorial borders. These rules, laws, and decisions maintain order within society as well as project and protect the state's interests abroad. The number of branches within any particular system of government can vary but commonly consists of at least a leadership wing, a bureaucratic or administrative structure, and a judicial branch.

Governments present themselves and their interests to the international community using foreign policy. **Foreign policy** consists of the decisions and strategies used by governments to guide their interaction with other states in the international system. Typically, foreign policy promotes the political, economic, and military interests of the state. The way foreign policy is made depends, in large part, on the type of government that exists in any given country.

Returning to our discussion of political culture theory, this paradigm actually contains two distinct aspects. One emphasizes the type of government—democratic or authoritarian—of a country in the formulation and implementation of its foreign policy and, therefore, its behavior within the world community. The second category focuses on the broader features of culture or civilization as determining factors for a state's behavior in the international system.

In this section of political culture theory, we will look at the **regimist perspective,** which, as noted above, emphasizes the nature of a state's government as a vital factor in its foreign policy and behavior within the global system. The second category, termed here the **civilizationist perspective** of political culture theory, acknowledges some points made by proponents of the regime category, but stresses the importance of culture and civilization in determining the future of world politics.

Before we begin our discussion of either the regimists or civilizationists, as we will call them, it might be helpful to take a look at several fundamental terms. First, **culture** refers to a particular social group's commonly shared behavior patterns, including language, traditions, values, customs, institutions, and beliefs. **Political culture** points specifically to the dominant values, attitudes, and beliefs that affect the politics and behavior of individual governments. This set of common attitudes and values about politics is fostered by the collective history of the political system and becomes embedded in the national character. It is important to remember that political culture reflects the *dominant* values and beliefs of a society, which is not necessarily representative of the beliefs of all people within that society.

Political culture can be shaped by a wide array of factors—ideological, religious, social, and economic—that may influence a country's behavior. Political culture often varies dramatically from state to state, with each reflecting its own unique approach to politics and the role of government. The political culture of the United States, for example, reflects a common belief in democracy, individual rights, capitalism, and the separation of church and state, among many other things. On the other hand, the political culture of North Korea emphasizes order, obedience, deference to authority, and the sacrifice of individual rights in favor of the community as a whole.

Political culture theorists—emphasizing either the type of regime or civilization— argue that a state's political culture has a substantial influence over its foreign policy. It establishes broad guidelines within which leaders make foreign policy, and creates an attitudinal environment in which every political system operates. While not normally responsible for specific policies, political culture broadly affects the range of policy options available to individual leaders.

THE REGIMISTS

Political culture theorists who emphasize the importance of regimes argue that it is the inherent differences between various types of government that can, indeed, influence both their behavior on the world stage and, consequently, international politics. Unlike system level theorists—who point to the characteristics of the system as a whole as the central force in international politics—this group of political culture theorists suggests that the domestic characteristics of state governments are key determinants of world politics.

Let's look at the two primary types of governments and how their differences affect both their respective foreign policies and foreign policy-making processes. **Liberal democracies** (or "open" societies), in which the citizenry has a voice in government through duly elected representatives from two or more political parties, generally take a more pluralistic approach to foreign policy-making. **Pluralism** describes a political system in which decisions and policies are formulated on the basis of many different viewpoints or interests. Not just political parties but other special interest groups (business, labor, or environmental groups, or even certain factions within the bureaucracy) can make their opinions known by contacting leaders directly or through more indirect means (media campaigns, etc.). Though the ultimate decisions on these matters do rest with a fairly small leadership circle, the people can, and often do, influence the course and content of the policy-making process.

Conversely, in **authoritarian regimes** (or "closed" societies), decisions and policies are made by an individual or small group of leaders. The people in these states generally have no meaningful impact on the political agenda or foreign policy of the country. Under this system of decision making, sometimes called **elitism,** the policies that control the actions of the state and those who live within it are created and directed by a small ruling elite. This group formulates both the domestic and foreign policy agendas. The decisions are not completely without parameters—limitations of political, economic, or military power, bureaucratic inertia or resistance, etc.—but these are minor when compared with the variety of interests represented in a liberal democracy.

The selection taken from Bruce Russett's book, *Controlling the Sword,* makes the case for proponents of the regime aspect of political culture theory, emphasizing the differences between these two types of governments. Liberal democracies, Russet suggests, are less "warlike" than authoritarian or totalitarian regimes. He looks at not only empirical evidence about whether democracies go to war less often, but also at domestic factors that might make democratic states more or less reticent to engage in conflict.

Studies and empirical research into what types of nations (democratic or authoritarian) go to war and how often they go to war have shown that democracies are just as likely to engage in conflict as any other type of regime. The important difference to note here, however, is that liberal democracies rarely, if ever, make war with one another. They actually tend to bond together, forming protective, generally defensive, political-military alliances. According to Russett, the specific structure, nature, and characteristics common to democratic governments all contribute to promote a more peaceful, less aggressive foreign policy.[1]

Political culture regimists point to a number of other broader political and social ideals associated with liberal democracies that contribute to a less warlike foreign policy. Respect for human rights and the rule of law (international law, in this case), as well as the tradition of resolution through negotiation, tend to promote both peace and greater stability.

In the next selection, Francis Fukuyama agrees with the points made by Russett about the impact of a state's regime on the course of its foreign policy and behavior in the world community. Fukuyama contends that ideological competition has been the driving force of conflict between the major powers in the twentieth-century. These wars have been fought largely to secure a dominant position for what one might call the great "isms" of the day. Clashes occurred between western political and economic liberalism and its two ideological antagonists, fascism and communism. Fascism was defeated and discredited at the end of World War II with the victory over Nazi Germany by the allied powers and, forty-five years later, communism was dealt a severe blow with the collapse of the Soviet empire.

The success of western liberalism over its two ideological opponents led Fukuyama to take the regimist position on political culture theory a step further,

---

[1] Many institutional transnationalists introduced in our analysis of system level theories, such as Immanuel Kant and Woodrow Wilson, have been strong advocates of the positive contribution made to the stability of the international system by liberal democratic regimes. Kant, in his work *Perpetual Peace,* published in 1795, argued that the accountability of democratic leaders to the people for their decisions makes them more cautious about taking steps that could lead to armed conflict. Understandably, the people tend to be equally cautious in supporting a bellicose foreign policy, since they would be called upon to do any fighting should the need arise.

concluding that "what we may be witnessing is not just the end of the Cold War, or the passing of a particular period in postwar history, but the **end of history** as such: that is, the end point of mankind's ideological evolution and the universalization of western liberal democracy as the final form of human government."[2] Western liberal democracy has triumphed over its ideological rivals and—since history is marked by the clash of ideas—history, according to Fukuyama, has come to an end.

While this victory is "incomplete" and many nations, particularly in the third world, have not yet or not fully adopted western economic and political liberalism, Fukuyama believes the course of history will inevitably lead to the expansion and broad acceptance of these ideals. Prior to this point, the world can be divided into two major categories based on levels of liberal democratic development. Relations among liberal democratic countries in the "post-historical" stage are characterized by cooperation and stability. While the non-democratic nations, classified as "still in history," continue to struggle with ethnic and nationalist conflicts. International conflict, Fukuyama argues, will revolve around these states, while relations among post-historical states—largely in the West—will be limited primarily to peaceful economic and technological competition.

Fukuyama's thesis about the triumph of liberal democracy and what this means for the future of international relations has been hotly debated. In the article, "No Exit: The Errors of Endism," Samuel Huntington disagrees with Fukuyama on a number of issues. He argues that the end of the Cold War does not necessarily represent the end of political rivalries among states—either post-historical or still in history. Indeed, as we will discuss in more detail later, Huntington believes that the post–Cold War period may well lead to greater instability and conflict in world politics.

Though Fukuyama himself concedes that war will continue to occur among developing "still in history" states, Huntington doubts that conflict among the industrialized nations has ended despite the spread of liberal democratic values. He is also skeptical of the contention by political regime theorists that democracies are inherently more peaceful than authoritarian regimes. At the very least, Huntington believes this notion needs to be qualified.

For example, Huntington asks whether peaceful relations among democracies result more from mutual convenience than shared values. The democratic "zone of peace" may be a "historical phenomenon" linked with the limited number of democracies and their numerous common enemies. The lack of conflict among democracies, Huntington asserts, may have more to do with the dominant position of the United States and the formal alliances it established with other major democratic powers as a safeguard against non-democratic states. The end of the Cold War and inevitable weakening of the western alliance may signal the return of the relatively non-ideological conflicts that characterized balance-of-power politics of eighteenth- and nineteenth-century Europe.

In addition to the post–Cold War weakening of the Western alliance, the conversion of many Eastern Bloc countries from communism to liberal democracy is far

---

[2] Francis Fukuyama, "The End of History?" *The National Interest*, Number 16/Summer 1989, p. 4.

from assured. Many of these new democracies face enormous economic problems and strident ethnic rivalries. Harsh social and economic conditions could weaken or even destroy the fragile political institutions that hold these new democracies together. The trend toward democracy might then ultimately be reversed, with these nations returning to familiar patterns or even adopting a new ideology altogether.

Overall, Huntington concludes that Fukuyama's thesis is not only overly optimistic and naive, but potentially dangerous. History is neither predictable nor guaranteed to move in a progressive fashion. Indeed, history is marked by periods of enlightenment and progress, as well as conflict and inhumanity. Today's hope and optimism could easily be marred by tomorrow's tragedy. History simply reflects the contradictions and unpredictability of human nature.

THE CIVILIZATIONISTS

The second perspective on political culture theory examines the impact of broad cultural factors on the behavior of individual states, or even groups of states that share a common culture. Samuel P. Huntington is, once again, a primary participant in this debate. With the civilizationist view of political culture theory, however, he has developed his own variation, stressing the importance of culture in international relations. Joining the debate first with his 1993 *Foreign Affairs* article "The Clash of Civilizations?," Huntington outlined this new theory of international politics for the post–Cold War world. Unlike proponents of the regimist position who are concerned primarily with the differences between democratic and authoritarian governments, Huntington focuses on the broader cultural attributes that both unite and divide people, states, and the world.

His view of civilization is a key component of this thesis. Huntington defines **civilization** as the "highest cultural grouping of people and the broadest level of cultural identity people have, short of that which distinguishes them from other species." Civilization, then, is composed of those elements that bind people together, such as common language, religion, customs, institutions, and identification with a particular culture. According to these criteria, states can be grouped together into eight major civilizations: Western, Confucian, Japanese, Islamic, Hindu, Slavic-Orthodox, Latin American, and African.

Now, let us see how Huntington applies the concept of civilization to his political culture theory of international relations. To begin, Huntington agrees with two points regarding the end of the Cold War in Fukuyama's article "The End of History?" First, Huntington accepts that the end of the Cold War was a turning point in global politics, setting the stage for new theories to explain recent developments in international relations. Second, he agrees, too, that this event also signaled the diminished relevance of ideology as a source of conflict between western countries. Though, as we noted in the preceding section, Huntington draws the line well before Fukuyama, stating that conflicts themselves have not ended, and we are by no means at an end of history.

"The Clash of Civilizations?" lays out a theoretical framework that suggests cultural differences have supplanted ideological differences as the most important source of conflict among peoples and states. Conflicts, Huntington contends, are most likely to develop between groups that are part of different civilizations. Likewise, cooperation occurs more frequently within civilizations rather than between them.

This argument centers on the idea that cultural differences between the eight civilizations—Western, Confucian, Japanese, Islamic, Hindu, Slavic-Orthodox, Latin American, and African—are more serious and could even be more dangerous than the traditional ideological and economic clashes characterizing past wars. Huntington asserts that advances in global communication and increasing economic and social interaction between people in different regions of the world have enhanced the awareness and importance of "civilization." In addition, modernization has eroded the relevance of local and national cultural identifications while magnifying the significance of this broader grouping.

As we noted, Huntington believes increasing "civilization consciousness" implies that cooperation will occur with greatest frequency among states within a particular civilization. Conflict is more likely to occur between groups in different civilizations. This is because cultural issues like religion and social traditions are more fundamental and less easily resolved through compromise and negotiation. Conflict will likewise most often occur along "**cultural fault lines.**" A cultural fault line is found where different civilizations share a common border; this includes both borders between different states, as well as the more tenuous ones found within states. According to Huntington, cultural fault lines now represent the most probable new "flash points for crisis and bloodshed."[3]

To support his theory, Huntington points to several contemporary ethnic and religious conflicts in the world. Among those flash points are the current warfare in the former Yugoslavia, where Western and Islamic civilizations meet within a confined geographic area. Christian and Muslim factions now battle for control over territory they once shared peacefully under a communist regime that successfully suppressed these ethnic tensions. Also, the continued unrest between Israel and its Arab neighbors emphasizes not only the vehemence with which civilizations can clash, but also serves as a testament to the prolonged nature of these feuds. One other example might be found in India and Pakistan; both countries have been plagued by violence between Hindu and Muslim peoples within each state's own borders.

Clearly, there is no shortage of examples worldwide where one might find Huntington's clash of civilizations. But, what do these clashes mean for the West and for western civilization? Taking a fairly dim view of the future, Huntington fears that conflict on a global scale—what he refers to as the "West versus the Rest"—is a possibility. Western political, economic, and cultural dominance is increasingly challenged by Confucian and Islamic states. These particular civilizations are increasingly more willing and able to assert their own economic, political, and military power against western-oriented institutions and ideals. Huntington believes that the West will have to learn to "accommodate" these rising non-western civilizations and

---

[3] Samuel Huntington, "The Clash of Civilizations?" *Foreign Affairs,* Summer 1993, p. 29.

KEY CONCEPTS

Authoritarian regimes are societies in which dominant political authority and power resides in an individual or small group of leaders who are not responsible to the people under their control.

Civilization is composed of those elements that bind people together such as common language, religion, customs, institutions, and identification with a particular culture. Samuel P. Huntington defines civilization as the "highest cultural grouping of people and the broadest level of cultural identity people have short of that which distinguishes them from other species."

Civilizationist perspective, as used in this book, is one of two major divisions of political culture theory and is based on the theory set forth by Samuel P. Huntington in his article, "The Clash of Civilizations?" The civilizationist perspective stresses that the "principle conflicts of global politics will occur between nations and groups of different civilizations."

Cultural fault line is found where different civilizations share a common border; this includes both borders between different states as well as the more tenuous ones found within states. This term was coined by Samuel P. Huntington.

Culture refers to commonly shared behavior patterns, including language, traditions, values, customs, institutions, and religious beliefs of a particular social group.

Elitism exists where a small group of people control, rule, or dominate the actions of a state. This group formulates both the domestic and foreign policy agendas.

End of history is a phrase used by Francis Fukuyama to describe the triumph of western economic and political liberalism over its ideological alternatives, such as fascism and Marxism-Leninism, and the coming universalization of western liberal democracy.

(continued)

"coexist" with countries "whose values and interests differ significantly from those of the West."[4]

The "Clash of Civilizations?" thesis has been subjected to a remarkable amount of criticism from a variety of sources. Here, we offer a selection by Fouad Ajami that

---

[4] Huntington, p. 49.

(continued from previous page)

Foreign policy is the strategy used by a government to make decisions and guide its interaction with other states in the international system. Typically, foreign policy promotes the political, economic, and military interests of the state.

Government is a public institution that has the authority to create, implement, and enforce rules, laws, and decisions within a state's territorial borders. These rules, laws, and decisions maintain order within society, as well as project and protect the state's interests abroad.

Liberal democracies are states in which the citizenry has a voice in government through duly elected representatives from two or more political parties.

Pluralism is a political system in which decisions and policies are formulated on the basis of many different viewpoints or interests.

Political culture refers to the dominant values, attitudes, and beliefs that affect the politics and behavior of individual governments.

Regimist perspective, as used in this text, is one of two major divisions of political culture theory. Regimists argue that democracies and authoritarian regimes behave differently in foreign affairs. Their analysis focuses on regime type as a vital factor in determining a state's foreign policy and behavior within the global system.

Sovereignty exists when the domestic government is the supreme authority within the state and does not answer to any outside power. This sovereignty is recognized by international law and by other states through diplomatic relations and often by membership in the United Nations.

State is a political, legal, and territorial entity. A state consists of an internationally recognized territory, a permanent population, and a government that has control over the people within its acknowledged boundaries.

provides a forceful critique of Huntington's civilizationist theory. Ajami questions the emphasis on civilizations as a source of either unity among or division between peoples. He contests Huntington's notion that civilizations are cohesive groupings, united in purpose. Huntington, according to Ajami, glosses over significant economic, social, and political cleavages that exist within all of what he has called civilizations. Similarly, examples of cooperation between states representing different civilizations are largely ignored.

But we might ask why Ajami sees cooperation between civilizations, whereas Huntington sees conflict. In a fashion reminiscent of realism, Ajami argues that, even in the post–Cold War environment, states remain the primary actors on the international political stage. The individual geopolitical and economic self-interests of the state supersede any fidelity toward a particular civilization. In addition, Ajami suggests that economic and technological modernization and secularism actually enhance, rather than prohibit cooperation between states. The recent Gulf War, uniting western and Arab countries in an alliance against the Arab state of Iraq, serves as a case in point. Political and economic interests brought these two civilizations together in a common purpose—the defeat of Sadam Hussein.

In the end, Ajami's argument echoes the realist view that international politics will continue to be dominated by states vying for geopolitical and economic position. Though we see many cases of this competition coming along the fault lines of Huntington's civilizations, contemporary history has also shown that when circumstances warrant cooperation between states and peoples, the differences of civilizations can be set aside in the interests of *realpolitic.*

A CRITIQUE OF POLITICAL CULTURE THEORY

Certainly, the article by Fouad Ajami provides a thorough critique of the "civilizationist" perspective of political culture theory offered by Samuel Huntington. It might be useful, however, to review here the major points both for and against what we call the regimist viewpoint of political culture theory.

There is little doubt that the type of government and the larger cultural attributes of a country have an impact on the course of international politics. As Bruce Russet and Francis Fukuyama indicated, considerable evidence is available showing that democracies do behave differently than authoritarian regimes. The virtual absence of war between democratic regimes speaks volumes about the cooperative nature of these governments. Critics have argued, though, that peace among democracies may be the result of particular geopolitical factors, rather than the influence of shared common values. Regimists do, however, provide substantial evidence—both quantitative and qualitative—that democracies more commonly resort to negotiation than do authoritarian regimes as a means of conflict resolution.

The civilizationist perspective of political culture theory outlined in Samuel P. Huntington's "The Clash of Civilizations?" article is perhaps the most innovative and ambitious attempt to codify international relations theory in the post–Cold War era. His idea that conflict between civilizations will supplant ideological conflict as the dominant force in international politics offers a unique look into the domestic-level explanations of what drives the actions of states and groups of states.

The question remains, however, whether civilization consciousness is truly a uniting or dividing force among states. Are cultural, religious, and ethnic factors vitally important sources of states' actions? Can the principles of liberal democracy bring states and peoples together? Or could the actions of states be shaped more by systemic factors, compelling all governments—irrespective of regime or civilization—to act in similar manner? Or might it be some combination?

25.   Controlling the Sword

Bruce Russett

In this excerpt, Bruce Russett discusses the reasons why democracies are not likely to go to war with each other. He lays out the causes, limitations, and implications of a democratic world system. Russett also criticizes the realist view that states are motivated primarily by a quest for power. This selection is from *Controlling the Sword: The Democratic Governance of National Security* (1990).

Bruce Russett is a professor of international relations and world politics at Yale University. He has authored many books on international relations, including *Power and Community in World Politics* (1974), *Interest and Ideology* (1975), and *Prisoners of Insecurity* (1983).

Two apparent facts about contemporary international patterns of war and peace stare us in the face. The first is that some states expect, prepare for, and fight wars against other states. The second is that some states do *not* expect, prepare for, or fight wars *at least against each other*. The first is obvious to everyone. The second is widely ignored, yet it is now true on a historically unprecedented scale, encompassing wide areas of the earth. In a real if still partial sense, peace is already among us. We need only recognize it, and try to learn from it.

An understanding of why some states do not engage in hostility may lead us to an attainable basis for an alternative system of security, one that does not depend on acceptance of a world state to enforce peace or on a particular configuration of strategy and weaponry to provide a peace of sorts through some form of stable deterrence. . . .

PEACE AMONG DEMOCRACIES

I refer to the peace among the industrialized and democratically governed states, primarily in the northern hemisphere. These states—members of the Organization for Economic Cooperation and Development (OECD: Western Europe, North America, Japan, Australia, and New Zealand), plus a few scattered less-industrialized democratic states—constitute a vast zone of peace, with more than three quarters of a billion people. Not only has there been no war among them for 45 years (see table on page 310), there has been little expectation of or preparation for war among them either. By war I mean large-scale organized international violence with, by a conventional social science definition, at least 1,000 battle deaths. In fact, even much smaller-scale violence between these countries has been virtually absent. The nearest exception is Greece and Turkey, with their brief and limited violent clashes over Cyprus; they are, however, among the poorest countries of this group, and only sporadically democratic.

In the years before 1945 many of these states fought often and bitterly—but always when at least one of the states in any warring pair was ruled by an authoritarian or totalitarian regime. Despite that past, war among them is now

Distribution of International Wars, 1945–1989.

FOUGHT BY	FOUGHT IN		
	OECD COUNTRIES	COMMUNIST COUNTRIES	LDCs
OECD countries	0	1	7
Communist countries	0	3	3
LDCs (less developed countries)	0	1	19

Source: Small and Singer, 1982, updated to 1989. Includes all interstate and colonial wars (not civil wars) with more than 1000 battle deaths.

virtually unthinkable. What had been seemingly the most permanent enmities—for instance, between France and Germany—have for the past two or three decades appeared well buried. Individual citizens may not love each other across national boundaries, but neither do they expect the other's state to attack, or wish to mount an attack on it. Expectations of peace are thus equally important; these peoples make few preparations for violence between them; peace for them means more than just the prevention of war through threat and deterrence. This condition has been characterized as a "security community," or as "stable peace" (Deutsch et al., 1957; Boulding, 1979). In duration and expectation it differs from the simple absence of war that may prevail between some other states, including nondemocratic ones in the third world. By the standards of world history this is an extraordinary achievement.

It is not easy to explain just why this peace has occurred. Partly it is due to the network of *international law and institutions* deliberately put into place in order to make a repetition of the previous world wars both unthinkable and impossible. But that network is strongest in Western Europe, often excluding the

countries in North America and the Far East; even in the strongest instance the institutions typically lack full powers to police and coerce would-be breakers of the peace; and, as we shall see below, even powerful institutions cannot guarantee peace if the underlying preconditions of peace are lacking.

In part it is due to favorable *economic conditions* associated with advanced capitalism. Fairly steady economic growth, a high absolute level of prosperity, relative equality of incomes within and across the industrial states, and a dense network of trade and investment across national borders all make the resort to violence dubious on cost-benefit grounds; a potential aggressor who already is wealthy risks much from the large-scale destructiveness of modern war, for only moderate gain (Mueller, 1989). But the condition of peace among these rich states has not been endangered by such periods of postwar recession and stagnation as have occurred, and in other parts of the world, especially Latin America, there are democratic states that are not wealthy but are still at peace with one another.

Partly, too, peace is the result of a perceived *"external" threat* faced by the industrialized democracies; they maintain peace among themselves in order not to invite intervention by the communist powers. Where peace among them is threatened, it may be enforced by the dominant "hegemonic" power of the United States (Weede, 1984). But the external threat also has waxed and waned without affecting the peace among these states; indeed, their peace became even more stable during the very time, over the past two decades, when the cold war abated and Europeans, especially, ceased to have much fear of Soviet attack. All these explanations, therefore, are at best only partial ones, and we are driven back to observing that the period of peace among the highly industrialized states essentially coincides with the period when they all have been under democratic rule.[1]

Conceptually and empirically the competing explanations overlap somewhat and reinforce one another, especially for the post-World War II era. International law has served to legitimate widely many of the domestic legal principles of human rights associated with liberal democracy; all advanced capitalist industrial states have been, since World War II, democratic (though not all democratic states are economically advanced); most of them have also been part of the American "hegemonic" alliance system (which has also included nondemocratic and economically less-developed countries). While this overlap prevents a definitive test, all the alternative hypotheses find their predictions falsified by at least one warring pair: the British-Argentine war in 1982, between two capitalist (Argentina only moderately advanced) states allied with the United States. World Wars I and II of course included many industrial capitalist countries as warring pairs. Analysts as different

as Joseph Schumpeter and Karl Kautsky predicted peace among advanced capitalist states; Lenin did not. Nor is it simply part of a general statement that politically or culturally similar countries do not fight one another (Russett, 1968, ch. 12; Wilkinson, 1980, ch. 9). An empirical correlation between cultural similarity and relative absence of war exists, but it is a weak one. There are several examples of wars or threats of war within Eastern Europe and Latin America in recent decades; by contrast, a reduction in regional enmities is associated with parallel democratization (for example, Argentina and Brazil). . . .

By a democratic state I mean one with the conditions of public contestation and participation, essentially as identified by Robert Dahl (1971), with a voting franchise for a substantial fraction of male citizens (in the nineteenth and early twentieth centuries; wider thereafter), contested elections, and an executive either popularly elected or responsible to an elected legislature. While scholars who have found this pattern differ slightly in their definitions, agreement on the condition of virtual absence of war among democracies ("liberal," "libertarian," or "polyarchic" states) is now overwhelming (Wallensteen, 1973; Small and Singer, 1976; Rummel, 1983, 1985; Chan, 1984; Weede, 1984; Doyle, 1986; Maoz and Abdolali, 1989). This simple fact cries out for explanation: What is there about democratic governments that so inhibits their people from fighting one another?

In exploring that question we should be clear about what is not implied. The condition of peace *between* democratic states does not mean that democratic states are ipso facto peaceful with *all* countries. . . .

INTERNAL PEACE AND INTERNATIONAL PEACE

There are powerful norms against the use of lethal force both within democratic states and between them. Within them is of course the basic norm of liberal democratic theory—that disputes can be resolved without force through democratic political processes which in some balance are to ensure both majority rule and minority rights. A norm of equality operates both as voting equality and certain egalitarian rights to human dignity. Democratic government rests on the consent of the governed, but justice demands that consent not be abused. Resort to organized lethal violence, or the threat of it, is considered illegitimate, and unnecessary to secure one's "legitimate" rights. Dissent within broad limits by a loyal opposition is expected and even needed for enlightened policymaking, and the opposition's basic loyalty to the system is to be assumed in the absence of evidence to the contrary.

All participants in the political process are expected to share these norms. In practice the norms do sometimes break down, but the normative restraints on violent behavior—by state and citizens—are fully as important as the state's monopoly on the legitimate use of force in keeping incidents of the organized use of force rare. Democracy is a set of institutions and norms for peaceful resolution of conflict. The norms are probably more important than any particular institutional characteristic (two-party/multiparty, republican/parliamentary) or formal constitutional provision. Institutions may precede the development of norms. If they do, the basis for restraint is likely to be less secure.

Democracy did not suddenly emerge full-blown in the West, nor by any linear progression. Only over time did it come to mean the extension of a universal voting franchise, formal protection for the rights of ethnic, racial, and religious minorities, and the rights of groups to organize for economic and social action. The rights to organize came to imply the right to carry on conflict—but nonviolently, as by strikes, under the principle that each side in the conflict had to recognize the right of the other to struggle, so long as that struggle was constrained by law, mutual self-interest, and mutual respect. The implicit or explicit contract in the extension of such rights was that the beneficiaries of those rights would in turn extend them to their adversaries.

To observe this is not to accept democratic theory uncritically, or to deny that it is part of a belief structure that, in Gramsci's view of cultural hegemony, may serve to legitimate dominant-class interests and provide subordinate classes with a spurious sense of their own political efficacy.[2] As such, it may exaggerate belief in the "reasonableness" of both the demands of one's own state in international politics and those of other democratic states. But it is precisely beliefs and perceptions that are primarily at issue here; insofar as the other state's demands are considered ipso facto reasonable according to a view of one's own system that extends to theirs, popular sentiment for war or resistance to compromise is undermined.

Politics within a democracy is seen as a largely nonzero-sum enterprise: by cooperating, all can gain something even if all do not gain equally, and the winners today are restrained from crushing the losers; indeed, the winners may, with shifting coalitions, wish tomorrow to ally with today's losers. If the conflicts degenerate to physical violence, either by those in control of the state or by insurgents, all can lose. In international politics—the anarchy of a self-help system with no superordinate governing authority—these norms are not the same. "Realists" remind us of the powerful norms of legitimate self-defense and the acceptability of military deterrence, norms much more extensive internationally than within democratic states. Politics between nations takes on a more zero-sum hue. True, we know we all can lose in nuclear war or in a collapse of international commerce, but we worry much more about comparative gains and losses. The essence of "realist" politics is that even when two states both become more wealthy, if one gains much more wealth than the other it also gains more power, more potential to coerce the other, thus the one which is lagging economically only in relative terms may be an absolute loser in the power contest.

The principles of anarchy and self-help in a zero-sum world are seen most acutely in "structural realist" theories of international relations. Specifically, a bipolar system of two great states or alliances, each much more powerful than any others in the international system, is seen as inherently antagonistic. The nature of the great powers' internal systems of government is irrelevant; whatever they may work out with or impose on some of their smaller allies, their overall behavior with other great powers is basically determined by the structure of the international system and their position in that structure. Athens and Sparta, or the United States and the Soviet Union, are doomed to compete and to resist any substantial accretion to the other's power. To fail to compete is to risk the death of sovereignty, or death itself. Through prudence and self-interest they may avoid a full-scale war that might destroy or cripple both of them (the metaphor of two scorpions in a bottle), but the threat of war is never absent, and can never be absent. "Peace," such as it is, can come only from deterrence, eternal vigilance, and probably violent competition between their "proxies" elsewhere in the world. By this structural realist understanding, the kind of stable peace that exists between the democratic countries can never exist on a global scale (Waltz, 1979).

Efforts to establish norms against the use of lethal violence internationally have been effective only to a limited degree. The Kellogg-Briand Pact of 1928 to outlaw war was a failure from the outset, as have been efforts to outlaw "aggressive" war. Despite its expression of norms and some procedures for the pacific settlement of disputes, the United Nations Charter fully acknowledges "the inherent right of individual or collective self-defense if an armed attack occurs" (Article 51). It could hardly do otherwise in the absence of superordinate authority. The norm of national self-defense—including collective self-defense on behalf of allies, and defense of broadly conceived "vital" interests even when national survival is not at stake—remains fully legitimate to all but tiny pacifist minorities. While there is some cross-cultural variation in the readiness of different peoples to use lethal force in different modes of self-defense, these differences are not strongly linked to form of government. Citizens of small democracies who perceive themselves as beleaguered (such as Israel), or citizens of large powerful democracies with imperial histories or a sense of global responsibilities for the welfare of others (such as Britain or the United States) are apt to interpret national or collective interest quite broadly. Especially across international cultural barriers, perversions of the "right" of self-defense come easily.

Yet democratic peoples exercise that right within a sense that somehow they and other peoples *ought* to be able to satisfy common interests and work out compromise solutions to their problems, without recourse to violence or threat of it. After all, that is the norm for behavior to which they aspire within democratic systems. Since other people living in democratic states are presumed to share those norms of live and let live, they can be presumed to moderate their behavior in international affairs as well. That is, they can be respected as self-governing peoples, and expected to offer the same respect to other democratic countries in turn. The habits and predispositions they show in their behavior in internal politics can be presumed to apply when they deal with like-minded outsiders. If one claims the principle of self-determination for oneself, normatively one must accord it to others perceived as self-governing. Norms do matter. Within a transnational democratic culture, as within a democratic nation, others are seen as possessing rights and exercising those rights in a spirit of enlightened self-interest. Acknowledgment of those rights both prevents us from wishing to dominate them and allows us to mitigate our fears that they will try to dominate us.

Realism has no explanation for the fact that certain kinds of states—namely, democratic ones—do not fight or prepare to fight one another. One must look instead to the liberal idealist vision of Immanuel Kant's *Perpetual Peace,* embodied also in Woodrow Wilson's vision of a peaceful world of democratic states. This same vision inspired American determination to root out fascism and establish the basis for democratic governments in West Germany and Japan after World War II (and partly also explains and was used to justify interventions in Vietnam, Grenada, Nicaragua, and so on).

Democratic states, with their wide variety of active interest groups in shifting coalitions, also present the opportunity for the formation of transnational coalitions in alliance with groups in other democracies. This may seem a form of "meddling"; it also provides another channel for resolution of international conflict. International anarchy is not supplanted by institutions of common government, but conflicts of interest within the anarchy can be moderated fairly peacefully on the principle of self-determination within an international society.

How much importance should we attribute to perceptions among the public in general, and how much to those of the elites including, in particular, the leaders of the state? Decisions for war, and indeed most major decisions in national security matters, are taken by the leaders and debated largely among the elites. They have some ability to mold mass opinion. Nevertheless, the elites in a democracy know that the expenditure of blood and treasure in any extended or costly international conflict will not be popular, and can be sustained only with the support of the general public. Whereas there may be leads and lags either way, . . . long-term serious differences between public opinion and official foreign policy are rare. Hence the elites will be somewhat constrained by popular views of the reasonableness of engaging in violent conflict with a particular foreign country. . . .

RELATIONS WITH NONDEMOCRATIC STATES

When we look within the construct of democratic ideology, it is apparent that the restraints on behavior that operate between separately governed democratic peoples do not apply to their relations with nondemocratic states. If other self-governing (democratic) peoples can be presumed to be worthy of being treated in a spirit of compromise and as in turn acting in that spirit, the same presumption does not apply to authoritarian states. According to democratic norms, authoritarian states do not rest on the proper consent of the governed, and thus they cannot properly represent the will of their peoples—if they did, they would not need to rule through undemocratic, authoritarian institutions. Rulers who control their own people by such means, who do not behave in a just way that respects their own people's right to self-determination, cannot be expected to behave better toward peoples outside their states. "Because non-liberal governments are in a state of aggression with their own people, their foreign relations become for liberal governments deeply suspect. In short, fellow liberals benefit from a presumption of amity; nonliberals suffer from a presumption of enmity" (Doyle, 1986, p. 1161). Authoritarian governments are expected to aggress against others if given the power and the opportunity. By this reasoning, democracies must be eternally vigilant against them, and may even sometimes feel the need to engage in preemptive or preventive (defensively motivated) war against them.

Whereas wars against other democratic states are neither expected nor considered legitimate, wars against authoritarian states may often be expected and "legitimated" by the principles outlined above. Thus an international system composed of both democratic and authoritarian states will include both zones of peace (actual and expected, among the democracies) and zones of war or at best deterrence between democratic states and authoritarian ones and, of course, between authoritarian states. Two states may avoid war even if one of them is not a democracy, but chiefly because of the power of one or both states to deter the other from the use of lethal force: the one-sided deterrence of dominance, or mutual deterrence between those more or less equally powerful. If the democratic state is strong, its "forbearance" may permit war to be avoided.

Of course, democracies have not fought wars only out of motivations of self-defense, however broadly one may define self-defense to include "extended deterrence" for the defense of allies and other interests or to include anticipation of others' aggression. Many of them have also fought imperialist wars to acquire or hold colonies (like the French in Vietnam) or, since World War II, to retain control of states formally independent but within their spheres of influence (like the Americans in Vietnam). In these cases they have fought against people who on one ground or another could be identified as not self-governing.[3] . . .

HUMAN RIGHTS AND INFORMATION

Whatever the faults of Western liberal (bourgeois) democracy, a world of spreading democratic ideology and practice offers some significant possibilities also for spreading peace. Those possibilities can be enhanced by attention to implementing a broad definition of human rights and institutionalizing a freer flow of information.[4] Human rights and information are elements both of greater global democratization and of direct and indirect contributions to international peace. In a world of imperfect democratization, such elements can help reduce those imperfections, and can compensate for some of them in the avoidance of war.

1. Recent American governments have tended, in different ways, to emphasize a commitment to human rights. In the Carter administration this began with an emphasis on political rights and civil liberties throughout the world; American standards were applied both to communist countries and to Third World states. Those governments found wanting did not appreciate the criticism. American attention to human rights in the Soviet Union reflected and perhaps hastened the decline of détente; despite some successes in the Third World, American pressures often angered allies thought to be strategically important, and the pressures were lessened. During the early years of the Reagan administration, official policy on human rights seemed to be turned most critically toward the Soviet Union and its allies, with abuses by American allies typically overlooked, tolerated, or even abetted. American allies were said to be merely authoritarian states, not totalitarian ones. The frequent ineffectiveness or hypocrisy of American policy on human rights has given the whole concept a bad name to some otherwise sympathetic and liberal-minded people. But the forces strengthening human rights can at least be assisted by low-key persuasion and good example.

Efforts to promote human rights internationally have not been uniformly ineffective or hypocritical. Third world states sometimes do relax the worst of their oppression in response to external pressures, whether those pressures come from governments, international organizations, or private transnational organizations like Amnesty International and Americas Watch. External pressures can contribute to the legitimacy of internal opposition. Some of the rhetoric and liberalizing action of Gorbachev owes a great debt to the power and attractiveness of Western concepts of human rights. Western efforts to reiterate those concepts and their implications—for Eastern Europe as well as for the Soviet Union itself—can hardly be abandoned. An image of the Soviet government as willing to grant a fairly high degree of autonomy to its own citizens but not to its neighbors would hardly fit the image of a state with the "liberal," "live-and-let-live" policy essential to the basis of international peace being discussed in these pages.

Yet political concessions in the form of domestic human rights policies cannot be *demanded* of another great power. The principle of noninterference in the internal governance of other states (in international law, statist and positivist norms), dating from the end of the Thirty Years War, does help to defuse one major source of interstate conflict and cannot lightly be cast aside. Hectoring or badgering the leaders of another great power is likely to poison political relations and exacerbate other conflicts; linkage of human rights concessions to important arms control measures is likely to hobble efforts to reduce real dangers of inadvertent escalation of conflict. The failure to reach human rights goals should not become a reason to forgo arms control agreements or, worse, used as an excuse to prevent arms control agreements.

International discussions on human rights are properly a dialogue, wherein the normatively persuasive elements are not solely those of Western advocates. A broad conception of human rights most certainly requires great emphasis on the kind of political rights stressed in American statements. Movement toward a more democratic world requires continued repetition of that message. It also requires a recognition of the legitimacy of some of the rights stressed by others: economic rights, to employment, housing, and some basic standard of material life (Beitz, 1979; Kim, 1984.) Justice demands political liberty, and it also demands a decent level of economic well-being. Political and social peace within democratic countries has been bought in part by this recognition; severe dismantlement of the welfare state would inflame class and ethnic conflict, and most elected political leaders know it. Internationally, recognition of the multifaceted nature of human rights is essential if the dialogue is to be one of mutual comprehension and persuasion. This is a way in which political rights, economic rights, and international peace are bound inextricably together.

Increasing worldwide adherence to democratic political norms and practices cannot alone bear all the weight of sustaining peace. Greater prosperity and economic justice, especially in the Third World, must also bear a major part. This conviction has often been expressed (for example, Brandt, 1980; Shue, 1980); cynics often dismiss it. But it is unlikely to be merely a coincidence that, as noted earlier, the industrial democracies are rich as well as democratic. The distribution of material rewards within them, while hardly ideal, is nevertheless far more egalitarian than that within many Third World countries, or between First and Third World peoples. That relatively just distribution does affect the cost-benefit analysis of those who would drastically alter it by violence; both rich and poor know they could lose badly. Some such calculation, including but not limited to the normative demands of justice, must apply to cement peace between nations. The broader human rights dialogue, incorporating political, cultural, and economic rights, constitutes a key element of global democratization where the domestic institutions of democracy are imperfect.

2. Another aspect of a stable international peace—reinforcing but not fully contained in concepts of political democracy and human rights—concerns practices and institutions for international communication and cooperation. This has several elements.

One is *economic:* a freer flow of goods and services between communist and capitalist countries, especially including the Soviet Union. Henry Kissinger's détente policy envisaged such a network of interdependence, giving the Soviet Union a greater material stake in peaceful relations with the capitalist world, and increased Soviet interest in Western products and markets makes the vision all the more plausible. The vision is consistent with traditional liberal prescriptions for trade and international cooperation (Rosecrance, 1986). While it is not a sufficient condition for peace, and possibly not even a necessary one, it certainly can make an important contribution.

Economic exchange is also a medium and an occasion for the exchange of *information*. Facilitation of a freer flow of information is a second major element. Without a free flow of information outward there can be no confidence in the outside world that democratic practices are really being followed within a country, and sharp restrictions on the flow of information into one's own country are incompatible with the full democratic competition of ideas inside it. Cultural exchanges and free travel across state boundaries can help ease misunderstandings of the other's reasoning, goals, and intent. Across the spectrum from academic game theory to concrete social experience, we know that the prospects for cooperation are much enhanced if the relevant actors can communicate their preferences and actions clearly. This too is not a sufficient condition, and it is easy to trivialize or ridicule the idea by imagining that communication alone can solve international problems. But without the dependable exchange of information, meaningful cooperation is virtually impossible in a world of complex problems and complex national governing systems.[5]

It is in this sense that *institutions*—especially what Keohane (1984) calls "information rich" institutions—are valuable as a means to discover and help achieve shared and complementary interests. Global organizations such as UN agencies are important purveyors of relevant information. Regional organizations, especially among culturally similar countries, may be much less important as instruments of coercion or enforcement than as a means of spotlighting major human rights violations and upholding the moral force of higher norms. The European Commission on Human Rights and the European Court of Human Rights have done this effectively, the Inter-American Commission on Human Rights and the Inter-American Court of Human Rights to a lesser degree (Weston et al., 1987). Transnational and populist legal norms serve to counter statist ones, and principles of democratic rights become incorporated, often through treaties, into international law and thereby into other states' domestic law (see MacDougal et al., 1980; Falk, 1981; Boyle, 1985).

The element of information exchange relates directly to progress on *security* issues. Arms control and disarmament agreements require confidence that compliance with the agreements can be verified. Arrangements for ensuring verification must be established on a long-term, reliable basis. Without verification the agreements are continually hostage both to real fears that the agreements are being violated and to pernicious charges by those who are opposed to the agreements whether or not they are being violated. An authoritarian government can more easily, if it wishes, pursue long-term strategies of aggressive expansion than can a pluralistic democracy with many power centers and voices. "Democratic governments can also have their military buildups, of course, but cannot mask them because a public atmosphere of fear or hostility will have to be created to justify the sacrifices; they can threaten other countries, but only after their action has been justified in the open." (Luttwak, 1987, p. 235). Liberalization of the Soviet Union allows its external partners and adversaries to feel less apprehensive, and to feel more confident that they will have early warning of any newly aggressive policy.

A dense, informal network of information exchange which extends across a wide range of issues and is beyond the control of any government will help, as will some formal institutions for information-sharing. Just as substantial freedom of information is essential to democratic processes within a country, it is essential to peaceful collaboration between autonomous, self-determining peoples organized as nation-states.

Certain specific kinds of multilateral institutions can be important in controlling crises. One possibility is to create crisis management centers, of the kind already established by the United States and the Soviet Union but extended to include other nuclear powers whose actions might cascade a crisis. Another is to strengthen the information and communications base—now sadly inadequate—of the United Nations, and especially of the Secretary General, so that in some future event like the Cuban missile crisis he could act as an informed and timely mediator. Yet another possibility is to have observation satellites operated by third parties (other countries, or international organizations) to monitor military activities and arms control compliance by a variety of electronic means (Boudreau, 1984; Florini, 1988). As long as nuclear weapons exist, even in a world of substantial political liberalization, reliable means of information exchange will be essential. . . .

THE COMING TEST?

Realist theories about the inherently antagonistic structure of international relations have never been tested in a world where all the major states were governed more or less democratically. Thus we never have had a proper test of some realist propositions against liberal idealist ones.[6] Perhaps we are about to see one. Even if liberal idealist theories are correct, it is not clear whether some threshold of democratic norms and practices must be crossed to achieve peace, or whether (Rummel, 1983, 1985) it is merely a matter of greater *degree* of democratization bringing a greater *likelihood* of peace between states. . . .

NOTES

1. These attempted explanations are considered at greater length in Russett and Starr, 1989, ch. 14. For the European states, Duroselle, 1988, credits democracy and also the demise of colonialism and therefore the end of colonial rivalries. Small and Singer, 1976, p. 67, noted that in their data—ending in 1965—relatively few democracies were contiguous and therefore had much opportunity to fight. Many more contiguous democracies have emerged since then—but no wars.

2. If one or both governments is not broadly representative despite the cultural belief that it is, the possibility of irreconcilable conflicts of interest between them is increased.

3. There also have been cases of covert intervention (rather than overt attack) against some radical but elected Third World governments (Guatemala, Chile) justified by a cold war ideology and public belief that the government in question was allying itself with the major nondemocratic adversary.

4. Any discussion of human rights, as of democracy, is inevitably colored by one's historical context, including mine as a privileged member of society in a powerful capitalist country, governed by democratic procedures as understood in the Western

liberal tradition. My perspective on these matters is nevertheless one of the moderate historicism: that whereas all are in some sense conventions, they can be substantially grounded across ages and cultures. See Bernstein, 1983, and Haskell, 1987.

5. A balanced assessment of functionalist benefits in the range of Soviet-American exchanges is Jangotch, 1985. In a very different context, see Russett, 1963. Specifically on the conflict-reducing effects of East-West trade, see Gasiorowski and Polachek, 1982.

6. Neither realist nor liberal idealist theories are fully adequate, but the dominance of realist thinking in contemporary academic as well as government circles has tended to diminish attention to realism's analytical and empirical weaknesses. See Nye, 1988; Vasquez, 1988. Note that the theoretical perspective of this chapter attends neither to the international-system level of analysis nor to the individual nation-state, but rather to the nature of *relations* between two states. For the distinction, see Russett and Starr, 1989, ch. 1. The whole analysis of this book, that domestic politics importantly influence foreign policy, is outside the mainstream of realist thinking.

QUESTIONS

1. Are democracies more or less prone to war than other systems of government?

2. How could realists respond to this essay?

26.   The End of History?

Francis Fukuyama

In this article, Francis Fukuyama presents his view on the "end of history," in which ideological conflict is no longer the driving force behind relations among major powers. He suggests that the two ideologies that most threatened liberalism—fascism and Marxist-Leninist doctrine—are no longer viable alternatives. Written in 1989, Fukuyama notes broad-base democratic capitalist reform programs in both the Soviet Union and China, though both nations maintained the ideological trappings of communism. He also discusses the role of nationalism and religious fundamentalism in this global ideological shift. This selection is from the journal *The National Interest* (1989).

Francis Fukuyama is a former deputy director of the United States Department of State policy planning staff. He is currently a resident consultant at the RAND Corporation in Washington, D.C.

In watching the flow of events over the past decade or so, it is hard to avoid the feeling that something very fundamental has happened in world history. The past year has seen a flood of articles commemorating the end of the Cold War, and the fact that "peace" seems to be breaking out in many regions of the world. Most of these analyses lack any larger conceptual framework for distinguishing between what is essential and what is contingent or accidental in world history, and are predictably superficial. If Mr. Gorbachev were ousted from the Kremlin or a new Ayatollah proclaimed the millennium from a desolate Middle Eastern capital, these same commentators would scramble to announce the rebirth of a new era of conflict.

And yet, all of these people sense dimly that there is some larger process at work, a process that gives coherence and order to the daily headlines. The twentieth century saw the developed world descend into a paroxysm of ideological violence, as liberalism contended first with the remnants of absolutism, then bolshevism and fascism, and finally an updated Marxism that threatened to lead to the ultimate apocalypse of nuclear war. But the century that began full of self-confidence in the ultimate triumph of Western liberal democracy seems at its close to be returning full circle to where it started: not to an "end of ideology" or a convergence between capitalism and socialism, as earlier predicted, but to an unabashed victory of economic and political liberalism.

The triumph of the West, of the Western *idea,* is evident first of all in the total exhaustion of viable systematic alternatives to Western liberalism. In the past decade, there have been unmistakable changes in the intellectual climate of the world's two largest communist countries, and the beginnings of significant reform movements in both. But this phenomenon extends beyond high politics and it can be seen also in the ineluctable spread of consumerist Western culture in such diverse contexts as the peasants' markets and color television sets now omnipresent throughout China, the cooperative restaurants and clothing stores opened in the past year in Moscow, the Beethoven piped into Japanese department stores, and the rock music enjoyed alike in Prague, Rangoon, and Tehran.

What we may be witnessing is not just the end of the Cold War, or the passing of a particular period of postwar history, but the end of history as such: that is, the end point of mankind's ideological evolution and the universalization of Western liberal democracy as the final form of human government. This is not to say that there will no longer be events to fill the pages of *Foreign Affairs's* yearly summaries of international relations, for the victory of liberalism has occurred primarily in the realm of ideas or consciousness and is as yet incomplete in the real or material world. But there are powerful reasons for believing that it is the ideal that will govern the material world *in the long run.* To understand how this is so, we must first consider some theoretical issues concerning the nature of historical change.

I

The notion of the end of history is not an original one. Its best known propagator was Karl Marx, who believed that the direction of historical development was a purposeful one determined by the interplay of material forces, and would come to an end only with the achievement of a communist utopia that would finally resolve all prior contradictions. But the concept of history as a dialectical process with a beginning, a middle, and an end was borrowed by Marx from his great German predecessor, Georg Wilhelm Friedrich Hegel.

For better or worse, much of Hegel's historicism has become part of our contemporary intellectual baggage. The notion that mankind has progressed through a series of primitive stages of consciousness on his path to the present, and that these stages corresponded to concrete forms of social organization, such as tribal, slave-owing, theocratic, and finally democratic-egalitarian societies, has become inseparable from the modern understanding of man. Hegel was the first philosopher to speak the language of modern social science, insofar as man for him was the product of his concrete historical and social environment and not, as earlier natural right theorists would have it, a collection of more or less fixed "natural" attributes. The mastery and transformation of man's natural environment through the application of science and technology was originally not a Marxist concept, but a Hegelian one. Unlike later historicists whose historical relativism degenerated into relativism *tout court,* however, Hegel believed that history culminated in an absolute moment—a moment in which a final, rational form of society and state became victorious.

It is Hegel's misfortune to be known now primarily as Marx's precursor, and it is our misfortune that few of us are familiar with Hegel's work from direct study, but only as it has been filtered through the distorting lens of Marxism. In France, however, there has been an effort to save Hegel from his Marxist interpreters and to resurrect him as the philosopher who most correctly speaks to our time. Among those modern French interpreters of Hegel, the greatest was certainly Alexandre Kojève, a brilliant Russian emigre who taught a highly influential series of seminars in Paris in the 1930s at the *Ecole Practique des Hautes Etudes.*[1] While largely unknown in the United States, Kojève had a major impact on the intellectual life of the continent. Among his students ranged such future luminaries as Jean-Paul Sartre on the Left and Raymond Aron on the Right; postwar existentialism borrowed many of its basic categories from Hegel via Kojève.

Kojève sought to resurrect the Hegel of the *Phenomenology of Mind,* the Hegel who proclaimed history to be at an end in 1806. For as early as this Hegel saw in Napoleon's defeat of the Prussian monarchy at the Battle of Jena the victory of the ideals of the French Revolution, and the imminent universalization of the state incorporating the principles of liberty and equality. Kojève, far from rejecting Hegel in light of the turbulent events of the next century and a half, insisted that the latter had been essentially correct.[2] The Battle of Jena marked the end of history because it was at that point that the *vanguard* of humanity (a term quite familiar to Marxists) actualized the principles of the French Revolution. While there was considerable work to be done after 1806—abolishing slavery and the slave trade, extending the franchise to workers, women, blacks, and other racial minorities, etc.—the basic *principles* of the liberal democratic state could not be improved upon. The two world wars in this century and their attendant revolutions and upheavals simply had the effect of extending those principles spatially, such that the various provinces of human civilization were brought up to the level of its most advanced outposts, and of forcing those societies in Europe and

North America at the vanguard of civilization to implement their liberalism more fully.

The state that emerges at the end of history is liberal insofar as it recognizes and protects through a system of law man's universal right to freedom, and democratic insofar as it exists only with the consent of the governed. For Kojève, this so-called "universal homogenous state" found real-life embodiment in the countries of postwar Western Europe— precisely those flabby, prosperous, self-satisfied, inward-looking, weak-willed states whose grandest project was nothing more heroic than the creation of the Common Market.[3] But this was only to be expected. For human history and the conflict that characterized it was based on the existence of "contradictions": primitive man's quest for mutual recognition, the dialectic of the master and slave, the transformation and mastery of nature, the struggle for the universal recognition of rights, and the dichotomy between proletarian and capitalist. But in the universal homogenous state, all prior contradictions are resolved and all human needs are satisfied. There is no struggle or conflict over "large" issues, and consequently no need for generals or statesmen; what remains is primarily economic activity. And indeed, Kojève's life was consistent with his teaching. Believing that there was no more work for philosophers as well, since Hegel (correctly understood) had already achieved absolute knowledge, Kojève left teaching after the war and spent the remainder of his life working as a bureaucrat in the European Economic Community, until his death in 1968.

To his contemporaries at mid-century, Kojève's proclamation of the end of history must have seemed like the typical eccentric solipsism of a French intellectual, coming as it did on the heels of World War II and at the very height of the Cold War. To comprehend how Kojève could have been so audacious as to assert that history has ended, we must first of all understand the meaning of Hegelian idealism.

II

For Hegel, the contradictions that drive history exist first of all in the realm of human consciousness, i.e. on the level of ideas[4]—not the trivial election year proposals of American politicians, but ideas in the sense of large unifying world views that might best be understood under the rubric of ideology. Ideology in this sense is not restricted to the secular and explicit political doctrines we usually associate with the term, but can include religion, culture, and the complex of moral values underlying any society as well.

Hegel's view of the relationship between the ideal and the real or material worlds was an extremely complicated one, beginning with the fact that for him the distinction between the two was only apparent.[5] He did not believe that the real world conformed or could be made to conform to ideological preconceptions of philosophy professors in any simple-minded way, or that the "material" world could not impinge on the ideal. Indeed, Hegel the professor was temporarily thrown out of work as a result of a very material event, the Battle of Jena. But while Hegel's writing and thinking could be stopped by a bullet from the material world, the hand on the trigger of the gun was motivated in turn by the ideas of liberty and equality that had driven the French Revolution.

For Hegel, all human behavior in the material world, and hence all human history, is rooted in a prior state of consciousness—an idea similar to the one expressed by John Maynard Keynes when he said that the views of men of affairs were usually derived from defunct economists and academic scribblers of earlier generations. This consciousness may not be explicit and self-aware, as are modern political doctrines, but may rather take the form of religion or simple cultural or moral habits. And yet this realm of consciousness *in the long run* necessarily becomes manifest in the material world, indeed creates the material world in its own image. Consciousness is cause and not effect, and can develop autonomously from the material world; hence the real subtext underlying the apparent jumble of current events is the history of ideology.

Hegel's idealism has fared poorly at the hands of later thinkers. Marx reversed the priority of the real and the ideal completely, relegating the entire realm of consciousness—religion, art, culture, philosophy itself—to a "superstructure" that was determined entirely by the prevailing material mode of production. Yet another unfortunate legacy of Marxism is our tendency to retreat into materialist or utilitarian explanations of political or historical phenomena, and our disinclination to believe in the autonomous power of ideas. A recent example of this is Paul Kennedy's hugely successful *The Rise and Fall of the Great Powers,* which ascribes the decline of great powers to simple economic overextension. Obviously, this is true on some level: an empire whose economy is barely above the level of subsistence cannot bankrupt its treasury indefinitely. But whether a highly productive modern industrial society

chooses to spend 3 or 7 percent of its GNP on defense rather than consumption is entirely a matter of that society's political priorities, which are in turn determined in the realm of consciousness.

The materialist bias of modern thought is characteristic not only of people on the Left who may be sympathetic to Marxism, but of many passionate anti-Marxists as well. Indeed, there is on the Right what one might label the *Wall Street Journal* school of deterministic materialism that discounts the importance of ideology and culture and sees man as essentially a rational, profit-maximizing individual. It is precisely this kind of individual and his pursuit of material incentives that is posited as the basis for economic life as such in economic textbooks.[6] One small example will illustrate the problematic character of such materialist views.

Max Weber begins his famous book, *The Protestant Ethic and the Spirit of Capitalism,* by noting the different economic performance of Protestant and Catholic communities throughout Europe and America, summed up in the proverb that Protestants eat well while Catholics sleep well. Weber notes that according to any economic theory that posited man as a rational profit-maximizer, raising the piece-work rate should increase labor productivity. But in fact, in many traditional peasant communities, raising the piece-work rate actually had the opposite effect of *lowering* labor productivity: at the higher rate, a peasant accustomed to earning two and one-half marks per day found he could earn the same amount by working less, and did so because he valued leisure more than income. The choices of leisure over income, or of the militaristic life of the Spartan hoplite over the wealth of the Athenian trader, or even the ascetic life of the early capitalist entrepreneur over that of a traditional leisured aristocrat, cannot possibly be explained by the impersonal working of material forces, but come preeminently out of the sphere of consciousness—what we have labeled here broadly as ideology. And indeed, a central theme of Weber's work was to prove that contrary to Marx, the material mode of production, far from being the "base," was itself a "superstructure" with roots in religion and culture, and that to understand the emergence of modern capitalism and the profit motive one had to study their antecedents in the realm of the spirit.

As we look around the contemporary world, the poverty of materialist theories of economic development is all too apparent. The *Wall Street Journal* school of deterministic materialism habitually points to the stunning economic success of Asia in the past few decades as evidence of the viability of free market economics, with the implication that all societies would see similar development were they simply to allow their populations to pursue their material self-interest freely. Surely free markets and stable political systems are a necessary precondition to capitalist economic growth. But just as surely the cultural heritage of those Far Eastern societies, the ethic of work and saving and family, a religious heritage that does not, like Islam, place restrictions on certain forms of economic behavior, and other deeply ingrained moral qualities, are equally important in explaining their economic performance.[7] And yet the intellectual weight of materialism is such that not a single respectable contemporary theory of economic development addresses consciousness

and culture seriously as the matrix within which economic behavior is formed.

Failure to understand that the roots of economic behavior lie in the realm of consciousness and culture leads to the common mistake of attributing material causes to phenomena that are essentially ideal in nature. For example, it is commonplace in the West to interpret the reform movements first in China and most recently in the Soviet Union as the victory of the material over the ideal—that is, a recognition that ideological incentives could not replace material ones in stimulating a highly productive modern economy, and that if one wanted to prosper one had to appeal to baser forms of self-interest. But the deep defects of socialist economies were evident thirty or forty years ago to anyone who chose to look. Why was it that these countries moved away from central planning only in the 1980s? The answer must be found in the consciousness of the elites and leaders ruling them, who decided to opt for the "Protestant" life of wealth and risk over the "Catholic" path of poverty and security.[8] That change was in no way made inevitable by the material conditions in which either country found itself on the eve of the reform, but instead came about as the result of the victory of one idea over another.[9]

For Kojève, as for all good Hegelians, understanding the underlying processes of history requires understanding developments in the realm of consciousness or ideas, since consciousness will ultimately remake the material world in its own image. To say that history ended in 1806 meant that mankind's ideological evolution ended in the ideals of the French or American Revolutions: while particular regimes in the real world might not implement these ideals fully, their theoretical truth is absolute and could not be improved upon. Hence it did not matter to Kojève that the consciousness of the postwar generation of Europeans had not been universalized throughout the world; if ideological development had in fact ended, the homogenous state would eventually become victorious throughout the material world.

I have neither the space nor, frankly, the ability to defend in depth Hegel's radical idealist perspective. The issue is not whether Hegel's system was right, but whether his perspective might uncover the problematic nature of many materialist explanations we often take for granted. This is not to deny the role of material factors as such. To a literal-minded idealist, human society can be built around any arbitrary set of principles regardless of their relationship to the material world. And in fact men have proven themselves able to endure the most extreme material hardships in the name of ideas that exist in the realm of the spirit alone, be it the divinity of cows or the nature of the Holy Trinity.[10]

But while man's very perception of the material world is shaped by his historical consciousness of it, the material world can clearly affect in return the viability of a particular state of consciousness. In particular, the spectacular abundance of advanced liberal economies and the infinitely diverse consumer culture made possible by them seem to both foster and preserve liberalism in the political sphere. I want to avoid the materialist determinism that says that liberal economics inevitably produces liberal politics, because I believe that both economics and politics presuppose an autonomous prior state of consciousness that makes them possible. But that state of consciousness that permits the growth of liberalism seems to stabilize in the way one would expect at the end of history if it is underwritten by the abundance of a modern free market economy. We might summarize the content of the universal homogenous state as liberal democracy in the political sphere combined with easy access to VCRs and stereos in the economic.

III

Have we in fact reached the end of history? Are there, in other words, any fundamental "contradictions" in human life that cannot be resolved in the context of modern liberalism, that would be resolvable by an alternative political-economic structure? If we accept the idealist premises laid out above, we must seek an answer to this question in the realm of ideology and consciousness. Our task is not to answer exhaustively the challenges to liberalism promoted by every crackpot messiah around the world, but only those that are embodied in important social or political forces and movements, and which are therefore part of world history. For our purposes, it matters very little what strange thoughts occur to people in Albania or Burkina Faso, for we are interested in what one could in some sense call the common ideological heritage of mankind.

In the past century, there have been two major challenges to liberalism, those of fascism and of communism. The former[11] saw the political weakness, materialism, anomie, and lack of community of the West as fundamental contradictions in liberal societies that could only be resolved by a strong state that forged a new "people" on the basis of national exclusiveness. Fascism was destroyed as a living ideology by World War II. This was a defeat, of course, on a very material level, but it amounted to a defeat of the idea as well. What destroyed fascism as an idea was not universal moral revulsion against it, since plenty of people were willing to endorse the idea as long as it seemed the wave of the future, but its lack of success. After the war, it seemed to most people that German fascism as well as its other European and Asian variants were bound to self-destruct. There was no material reason why new fascist movements could not have sprung up again after the war in other locales, but for the fact that expansionist ultranationalism, with its promise of unending conflict leading to disastrous military defeat, had completely lost its appeal. The ruins of the Reich chancellory as well as the atomic bombs dropped on Hiroshima and Nagasaki killed this ideology on the level of consciousness as well as materially, and all of the proto-fascist movements spawned by the German and Japanese examples like the Peronist movement in Argentina or Subhas Chandra Bose's Indian National Army withered after the war.

The ideological challenge mounted by the other great alternative to liberalism, communism, was far more serious. Marx, speaking Hegel's language, asserted that liberal society contained a fundamental contradiction that could not be resolved within its context, that between capital and labor, and this contradiction has constituted the chief accusation against liberalism ever since. But surely, the class issue has actually been successfully resolved in the West. As Kojève (among others) noted, the egalitarianism of modern America represents the essential achievement of the classless society envisioned by Marx. This is not to say that there are not rich people and poor people in the United States, or that the gap between them has not grown in recent years. But the root causes of economic inequality do not have to do with the underlying legal and social structure of our society, which remains fundamentally egalitarian and moderately redistributionist, so much as with the cultural and social characteristics of the groups that make it up, which are in turn the historical legacy of premodern conditions. Thus black poverty in the United States is not the inherent product of liberalism, but is rather the "legacy of slavery and racism" which persisted long after the formal abolition of slavery.

As a result of the receding of the class issue, the appeal of communism in the developed Western world, it is safe to say, is lower today than any time since the end of the First World War. This can be measured in any number of ways: in the declining membership and electoral pull of the major European communist parties, and their overtly revisionist programs; in the corresponding electoral success of conservative parties from Britain and Germany to the United States and Japan, which are unabashedly pro-market and anti-statist; and in an intellectual climate whose most "advanced" members no longer believe that bourgeois society is something that ultimately needs to be overcome. This is not to say that the opinions of progressive intellectuals in Western countries are not deeply pathological in any number of ways. But those who believe that the future must inevitably be socialist tend to be very old, or very marginal to the real political discourse of their societies.

One may argue that the socialist alternative was never terribly plausible for the North Atlantic world, and was sustained for the last several decades primarily by its success outside of this region. But it is precisely in the non-European world that one is most struck by the occurrence of major ideological transformations. Surely the most remarkable changes have occurred in Asia. Due to the strength and adaptability of the indigenous cultures there, Asia became a battleground for a variety of imported Western ideologies early in this century. Liberalism in Asia was a very weak reed in the period after World War I; it is easy today to forget how gloomy Asia's political future looked as recently as ten or fifteen years ago. It is easy to forget as well how momentous the outcome of Asian ideological struggles seemed for world political development as a whole.

The first Asian alternative to liberalism to be decisively defeated was the fascist one represented by Imperial Japan. Japanese fascism (like its German version) was defeated by the force of American arms in the Pacific war, and liberal democracy was imposed on Japan by a victorious United States. Western capitalism and political liberalism when transplanted to Japan were adapted and transformed by the Japanese in such a way as to be scarcely recognizable.[12] Many Americans are now aware that Japanese industrial organization is very different from that prevailing in the United States or Europe, and it is questionable what relationship the factional maneuvering that takes place with the governing Liberal Democratic Party bears to

democracy. Nonetheless, the very fact that the essential elements of economic and political liberalism have been so successfully grafted onto uniquely Japanese traditions and institutions guarantees their survival in the long run. More important is the contribution that Japan has made in turn to world history by following in the footsteps of the United States to create a truly universal consumer culture that has become both a symbol and an underpinning of the universal homogeneous state. V. S. Naipaul travelling in Khomeini's Iran shortly after the revolution noted the omnipresent signs advertising the products of Sony, Hitachi, and JVC, whose appeal remained virtually irresistible and gave the lie to the regime's pretensions of restoring a state based on the rule of the *Shariah*. Desire for access to the consumer culture, created in large measure by Japan, has played a crucial role in fostering the spread of economic liberalism throughout Asia, and hence in promoting political liberalism as well.

The economic success of the other newly industrializing countries (NICS) in Asia following on the example of Japan is by now a familiar story. What is important from a Hegelian standpoint is that political liberalism has been following economic liberalism, more slowly than many had hoped but with seeming inevitability. Here again we see the victory of the idea of the universal homogenous state. South Korea had developed into a modern, urbanized society with an increasingly large and well-educated middle class that could not possibly be isolated from the larger democratic trends around them. Under these circumstances it seemed intolerable to a large part of this population that it should be ruled by an anachronistic military regime while Japan, only a decade or so ahead in economic terms, had parliamentary institutions for over forty years. Even the former socialist regime in Burma, which for so many decades existed in dismal isolation from the larger trends dominating Asia, was buffeted in the past year by pressures to liberalize both its economy and political system. It is said that unhappiness with strongman Ne Win began when a senior Burmese officer went to Singapore for medical treatment and broke down crying when he saw how far socialist Burma had been left behind by its ASEAN neighbors.

But the power of the liberal idea would seem much less impressive if it had not infected the largest and oldest culture in Asia, China. The simple existence of communist China created an alternative pole of ideological attraction, and as such constituted a threat to liberalism. But the past fifteen years have seen an almost total discrediting of Marxism-Leninism as an economic system. Beginning with the famous third plenum of the Tenth Central Committee in 1978, the Chinese Communist party set about decollectivizing agriculture for the 800 million Chinese who still lived in the countryside. The role of the state in agriculture was reduced to that of a tax collector, while production of consumer goods was sharply increased in order to give peasants a taste of the universal homogeneous state and thereby an incentive to work. The reform doubled Chinese grain output in only five years, and in the process created for Deng Xiao-ping a solid political base from which he was able to extend the reform to other parts of the economy. Economic statistics do not begin to describe the dynamism, initiative, and openness evident in China since the reform began.

China could not now be described in any way as a liberal democracy. At present, no more than 20 percent of its economy has been marketized, and most importantly it continues to be ruled by a self-appointed Communist party which has given no hint of wanting to devolve power. Deng has made none of Gorbachev's promises regarding democratization of the political system and there is no Chinese equivalent of *glasnost*. The Chinese leadership has in fact been much more circumspect in criticizing Mao and Maoism than Gorbachev with respect to Brezhnev and Stalin, and the regime continues to pay lip service to Marxism-Leninism as its ideological underpinning. But anyone familiar with the outlook and behavior of the new technocratic elite now governing China knows that Marxism and ideological principle have become virtually irrelevant as guides to policy, and that bourgeois consumerism has a real meaning in that country for the first time since the revolution. The various slowdowns in the pace of reform, the campaigns against "spiritual pollution" and crackdowns on political dissent are more properly seen as tactical adjustments made in the process of managing what is an extraordinarily difficult political transition. By ducking the question of political reform while putting the economy on a new footing, Deng has managed to avoid the breakdown of authority that has accompanied Gorbachev's *perestroika*. Yet the pull of the liberal idea continues to be very strong as economic power devolves and the economy becomes more open to the outside world. There are currently over 20,000 Chinese students studying in the U.S. and other Western countries, almost all of them the children of the Chinese elite. It is hard to believe that when they return home to run the country they will be content for China to be the only country in Asia unaffected by the larger democratizing trend. The student demonstrations in Beijing that broke out first in December 1986 and recurred recently on the occasion of Hu Yao-bang's death were only the beginning of what will inevitably be mounting pressure for change in the political system as well.

What is important about China from the standpoint of world history is not the present state of the reform or even its future prospects. The central issue is the fact that the People's Republic of China can no longer act as a beacon for illiberal forces around the world, whether they be guerrillas in some Asian jungle or middle class students in Paris. Maoism, rather than being the pattern for Asia's future, became an anachronism, and it was the mainland Chinese who in fact were decisively influenced by the prosperity and dynamism of their overseas co-ethnics—the ironic ultimate victory of Taiwan.

Important as these changes in China have been, however, it is developments in the Soviet Union—the original "homeland of the world proletariat"—that have put the final nail in the coffin of the Marxist-Leninist alternative to liberal democracy. It should be clear that in terms of formal institutions, not much has changed in the four years since Gorbachev has come to power: free markets and the cooperative movement represent only a small part of the Soviet economy, which remains centrally planned; the political system is still dominated by the Communist party, which has only begun to democratize internally and to share power with other groups; the regime continues to assert that it is seeking only to modernize socialism and that its ideological basis remains

Marxism-Leninism; and, finally, Gorbachev faces a potentially powerful conservative opposition that could undo many of the changes that have taken place to date. Moreover, it is hard to be too sanguine about the chances for success of Gorbachev's proposed reforms, either in the sphere of economics or politics. But my purpose here is not to analyze events in the short-term, or to make predictions for policy purposes, but to look at underlying trends in the sphere of ideology and consciousness. And in that respect, it is clear that an astounding transformation has occurred.

Emigres from the Soviet Union have been reporting for at least the last generation now that virtually nobody in that country truly believed in Marxism-Leninism any longer, and that this was nowhere more true than in the Soviet elite, which continued to mouth Marxist slogans out of sheer cynicism. The corruption and decadence of the late Brezhnev-era Soviet state seemed to matter little, however, for as long as the state itself refused to throw into question any of the fundamental principles underlying Soviet society, the system was capable of functioning adequately out of sheer inertia and could even muster some dynamism in the realm of foreign and defense policy. Marxism-Leninism was like a magical incantation which, however absurd and devoid of meaning, was the only common basis on which the elite could agree to rule Soviet society.

What has happened in the four years since Gorbachev's coming to power is a revolutionary assault on the most fundamental institutions and principles of Stalinism, and their replacement by other principles which do not amount to liberalism *per se* but whose only connecting thread is liberalism. This is most evident in the economic sphere, where the reform economists around Gorbachev have become steadily more radical in their support for free markets, to the point where some like Nikolai Shmelev do not mind being compared in public to Milton Friedman. There is a virtual consensus among the currently dominant school of Soviet economists now that central planning and the command system of allocation are the root cause of economic inefficiency, and that if the Soviet system is ever to heal itself, it must permit free and decentralized decision-making with respect to investment, labor, and prices. After a couple of initial years of ideological confusion, these principles have finally been incorporated into policy with the promulgation of new laws on enterprise autonomy, cooperatives, and finally in 1988 on lease arrangements and family farming. There are, of course, a number of fatal flaws in the current implementation of the reform, most notably the absence of a thoroughgoing price reform. But the problem is no longer a *conceptual* one: Gorbachev and his lieutenants seem to understand the economic logic of marketization well enough, but like the leaders of a Third World country facing the IMF, are afraid of the social consequences of ending consumer subsidies and other forms of dependence on the state sector.

In the political sphere, the proposed changes to the Soviet constitution, legal system, and party rules amount to much less than the establishment of a liberal state. Gorbachev has spoken of democratization primarily in the sphere of internal party affairs, and has shown little intention of ending the Communist party's monopoly of power; indeed, the political reform seeks to legitimize and therefore strengthen the CPSU's rule.[13] Nonetheless, the general principles underlying many of the reforms—that the "people" should be truly responsible for their own affairs, that higher political bodies should be answerable to lower ones, and not vice versa, that the rule of law should prevail over arbitrary police actions, with separation of powers and an independent judiciary, that there should be legal protection for property rights, the need for open discussion of public issues and the right of public dissent, the empowering of the Soviets as a forum in which the whole Soviet people can participate, and of a political culture that is more tolerant and pluralistic—come from a source fundamentally alien to the USSR's Marxist-Leninist tradition, even if they are incompletely articulated and poorly implemented in practice.

Gorbachev's repeated assertions that he is doing no more than trying to restore the original meaning of Leninism are themselves a kind of Orwellian doublespeak. Gorbachev and his allies have consistently maintained that intraparty democracy was somehow the essence of Leninism, and that the various liberal practices of open debate, secret ballot elections, and rule of law were all part of the Leninist heritage, corrupted only later by Stalin. While almost anyone would look good compared to Stalin, drawing so sharp a line between Lenin and his successor is questionable. The essence of Lenin's democratic centralism was centralism, not democracy; that is, the absolutely rigid, monolithic, and disciplined dictatorship of a hierarchically organized vanguard Communist party, speaking in the name of the *demos*. All of Lenin's vicious polemics against Karl Kautsky, Rosa Luxemburg, and various other Menshevik and Social Democratic rivals, not to mention his contempt for "bourgeois legality" and freedoms, centered around his profound conviction that a revolution could not be successfully made by a democratically run organization.

Gorbachev's claim that he is seeking to return to the true Lenin is perfectly easy to understand: having fostered a thorough denunciation of Stalinism and Brezhnevism as the root of the USSR's present predicament, he needs some point in Soviet history on which to anchor the legitimacy of the CPSU's continued rule. But Gorbachev's tactical requirements should not blind us to the fact that the democratizing and decentralizing principles which he has enunciated in both the economic and political spheres are highly subversive of some of the most fundamental precepts of both Marxism and Leninism. Indeed, if the bulk of the present economic reform proposals were put into effect, it is hard to know how the Soviet economy would be more socialist than those of other Western countries with large public sectors.

The Soviet Union could in no way be described as a liberal or democratic country now, nor do I think that it is terribly likely that *perestroika* will succeed such that the label will be thinkable any time in the near future. But at the end of history it is not necessary that all societies become successful liberal societies, merely that they end their ideological pretensions of representing different and higher forms of human society. And in this respect I believe that something very important has happened in the Soviet Union in the past few years: the criticisms of the Soviet system sanctioned by Gorbachev have been so thorough and devastating that there is very little chance of going back to either Stalinism or Brezhnevism in any simple way. Gorbachev has finally permitted people to say what they had privately understood for many years, namely, that

the magical incantations of Marxism-Leninism were nonsense, that Soviet socialism was not superior to the West in any respect but was in fact a monumental failure. The conservative opposition in the USSR, consisting both of simple workers afraid of unemployment and inflation and of party officials fearful of losing their jobs and privileges, is outspoken and may be strong enough to force Gorbachev's ouster in the next few years. But what both groups desire is tradition, order, and authority; they manifest no deep commitment to Marxism-Leninism, except insofar as they have invested much of their own lives in it.[14] For authority to be restored in the Soviet Union after Gorbachev's demolition work, it must be on the basis of some new and vigorous ideology which has not yet appeared on the horizon.

If we admit for the moment that the fascist and communist challenges to liberalism are dead, are there any other ideological competitors left? Or put another way, are there contradictions in liberal society beyond that of class that are not resolvable? Two possibilities suggest themselves, those of religion and nationalism.

The rise of religious fundamentalism in recent years within the Christian, Jewish, and Muslim traditions has been widely noted. One is inclined to say that the revival of religion in some way attests to a broad unhappiness with the impersonality and spiritual vacuity of liberal consumerist societies. Yet while the emptiness at the core of liberalism is most certainly a defect in the ideology— indeed, a flaw that one does not need the perspective of religion to recognize[15]—it is not at all clear that it is remediable through politics. Modern liberalism itself was historically a consequence of the weakness of religiously-based societies which, failing to agree on the nature of the good life, could not provide even the minimal preconditions of peace and stability. In the contemporary world only Islam has offered a theocratic state as a political alternative to both liberalism and communism. But the doctrine has little appeal for non-Muslims, and it is hard to believe that the movement will take on any universal significance. Other less organized religious impulses have been successfully satisfied within the sphere of personal life that is permitted in liberal societies.

The other major "contradiction" potentially unresolvable by liberalism is the one posed by nationalism and other forms of racial and ethnic consciousness. It is certainly true that a very large degree of conflict since the Battle of Jena has had its roots in nationalism. Two cataclysmic world wars in this century have been spawned by the nationalism of the developed world in various guises, and if those passions have been muted to a certain extent in postwar Europe, they are still extremely powerful in the Third World. Nationalism has been a threat to liberalism historically in Germany, and continues to be one in isolated parts of "post-historical" Europe like Northern Ireland.

But it is not clear that nationalism represents an irreconcilable contradiction in the heart of liberalism. In the first place, nationalism is not one single phenomenon but several, ranging from mild cultural nostalgia to the highly organized and elaborately articulated doctrine of National Socialism. Only systematic nationalisms of the latter sort can qualify as a formal ideology on the level of liberalism or communism. The vast majority of the world's nationalist movements do not have a political program beyond the negative desire of independence *from* some other group or people, and do not offer anything like a comprehensive agenda for socio-economic organization. As such, they are compatible with doctrines and ideologies that do offer such agendas. While they may constitute a source of conflict for liberal societies, this conflict does not arise from liberalism itself so much as from the fact that the liberalism in question is incomplete. Certainly a great deal of the world's ethnic and nationalist tension can be explained in terms of peoples who are forced to live in unrepresentative political systems that they have not chosen.

While it is impossible to rule out the sudden appearance of new ideologies or previously unrecognized contradictions in liberal societies, then, the present world seems to confirm that the fundamental principles of socio-political organization have not advanced terribly far since 1806. Many of the wars and revolutions fought since that time have been undertaken in the name of ideologies which claimed to be more advanced than liberalism, but whose pretensions were ultimately unmasked by history. In the meantime, they have helped to spread the universal homogenous state to the point where it could have a significant effect on the overall character of international relations.

IV

What are the implications of the end of history for international relations? Clearly, the vast bulk of the Third World remains very much mired in history, and will be a terrain of conflict for many years to come. But let us focus for the time being on the larger and more developed states of the world who after all account for the greater part of world politics. Russia and China are not likely to join the developed nations of the West as liberal societies any time in the foreseeable future, but suppose for a moment that Marxism-Leninism ceases to be a factor driving the foreign policies of these states—a prospect which, if not yet here, the last few years have made a real possibility. How will the overall characteristics of a de-ideologized world differ from those of the one with which we are familiar at such a hypothetical juncture?

The most common answer is—not very much. For there is a very widespread belief among many observers of international relations that underneath the skin of ideology is a hard core of great power national interest that guarantees a fairly high level of competition and conflict between nations. Indeed, according to one academically popular school of international relations theory, conflict inheres in the international system as such, and to understand the prospects for conflict one must look at the shape of the system— for example, whether it is bipolar or multipolar—rather than at the specific character of the nations and regimes that constitute it. This school in effect applies a Hobbesian view of politics to international relations, and assumes that aggression and insecurity are universal characteristics of human societies rather than the product of specific historical circumstances.

Believers in this line of thought take the relations that existed between the participants in the classical nineteenth century European balance of power as a model for what a de-ideologized contemporary world would look like. Charles Krauthammer, for example, recently explained that if as a result of Gorbachev's reforms the USSR is shorn of Marxist-Leninist ideology, its behavior will revert to that of nineteenth century imperial Russia.[16] While he finds this more reassuring than the threat posed by a communist Russia, he implies that there will still be a substantial degree of competition and conflict in the international system, just as there was say between Russia and Britain or Wilhelmine Germany in the last century. This is, of course, a convenient point of view for people who want to admit that something major is changing in the Soviet Union, but do not want to accept responsibility for recommending the radical policy redirection implicit in such a view. But is it true?

In fact, the notion that ideology is a superstructure imposed on a substratum of permanent great power interest is a highly questionable proposition. For the way in which any state defines its national interest is not universal but rests on some kind of prior ideological basis, just as we saw that economic behavior is determined by a prior state of consciousness. In this century, states have adopted highly articulated doctrines with explicit foreign policy agendas legitimizing expansionism, like Marxism-Leninism or National Socialism.

The expansionist and competitive behavior of nineteenth-century European states rested on no less ideal a basis; it just so happened that the ideology driving it was less explicit than the doctrines of the twentieth century. For one thing, most ''liberal'' European societies were illiberal insofar as they believed in the legitimacy of imperialism, that is, the right of one nation to rule over other nations without regard for the wishes of the ruled. The justifications for imperialism varied from nation to nation, from a crude belief in the legitimacy of force, particularly when applied to non-Europeans, to the White Man's Burden and Europe's Christianizing mission, to the desire to give people of color access to the culture of Rabelais and Molière. But whatever the particular ideological basis, every "developed" country believed in the acceptability of higher civilizations ruling lower ones—including, incidentally, the United States with regard to the Philippines. This led to a drive for pure territorial aggrandizement in the latter half of the century and played no small role in causing the Great War.

The radical and deformed outgrowth of nineteenth-century imperialism was German fascism, an ideology which justified Germany's right not only to rule over non-European peoples, but over *all* non-German ones. But in retrospect it seems that Hitler represented a diseased bypath in the general course of European development, and since his fiery defeat, the legitimacy of any kind of territorial aggrandizement has been thoroughly discredited.[17] Since the Second World War, European nationalism has been defanged and shorn of any real relevance to foreign policy, with the consequence that the nineteenth-century model of great power behavior has become a serious anachronism. The most extreme form of nationalism that any Western European state has mustered since 1945 has been Gaullism, whose self-assertion has been confined largely to the realm of nuisance politics and culture. International life for the part of the world that has reached the end of history is far more preoccupied with economics than with politics or strategy.

The developed states of the West do maintain defense establishments and in the post-war period have competed vigorously for influence to meet a worldwide communist threat. This behavior has been driven, however, by an external threat from states that possess overtly expansionist ideologies, and would not exist in their absence. To take the "neorealist" theory seriously, one would have to believe that "natural" competitive behavior would reassert itself among the OECD states were Russia and China to disappear from the face of the earth. That is, West Germany and France would arm themselves against each other as they did in the 1930s, Australia and New Zealand would send military advisers to block each others' advances in Africa, and the U.S.-Canadian border would become fortified. Such a prospect is, of course, ludicrous: minus Marxist-Leninist ideology, we are far more likely to see the "Common Marketization" of world politics than the disintegration of the EEC into nineteenth-century competitiveness. Indeed, as our experience in dealing with Europe on matters such as terrorism or Libya prove, they are much further gone than we down the road that denies the legitimacy of the use of force in international politics, even in self-defense.

The automatic assumption that Russia shorn of its expansionist communist ideology should pick up where the czars left off just prior to the Bolshevik Revolution is therefore a curious one. It assumes that the evolution of human consciousness has stood still in the meantime, and that the Soviets, while picking up currently fashionable ideas in the realm of economics, will return to foreign policy views a century out of date in the rest of Europe. This is certainly not what happened to China after it began its reform process. Chinese competitiveness and expansionism on the world scene have virtually disappeared: Beijing no longer sponsors Maoist insurgencies or tries to cultivate influence in distant African countries as it did in the 1960s. This is not to say that there are not trouble-some aspects to contemporary Chinese foreign policy, such as the reckless sale of ballistic missile technology in the Middle East; and the PRC continues to manifest traditional great power behavior in its sponsorship of the Khmer Rouge against Vietnam. But the former is explained by commercial motives and the latter is a vestige of earlier ideologically-based rivalries. The new China far more resembles Gaullist France than pre-World War I Germany.

The real question for the future, however, is the degree to which Soviet elites have assimilated the consciousness of the universal homogenous state that is post-Hitler Europe. From their writings and from my own personal contacts with them, there is no question in my mind that the liberal Soviet intelligentsia rallying around Gorbachev has arrived at the end-of-history view in a remarkably short time, due in no small measure to the contacts they have had since the Brezhnev era with the larger European civilization around them. "New political thinking," the general rubric for their views, describes a world dominated by economic concerns, in which there are no ideological grounds for major conflict between nations, and in which, consequently, the use of military force becomes less legitimate. As Foreign Minister Shevardnadze put it in mid-1988:

> The struggle between two opposing systems is no longer a determining tendency of the present-day era. At the modern stage, the ability to build up material wealth at an accelerated rate on the basis of front-ranking science and high-level techniques and technology, and to distribute it fairly, and through joint efforts to restore and protect the resources necessary for mankind's survival acquires decisive importance.[18]

The post-historical consciousness represented by "new thinking" is only one possible future for the Soviet Union, however. There has always been a very strong current of great Russian chauvinism in the Soviet Union, which has found freer expression since the advent of *glasnost.* It may be possible to return to traditional Marxism-Leninism for a while as a simple rallying point for those who want to restore the authority that Gorbachev has dissipated. But as in Poland, Marxism-Leninism is dead as a mobilizing ideology: under its banner people cannot be made to work harder, and its adherents have lost confidence in themselves. Unlike the propagators of traditional Marxism-Leninism, however, ultra-nationalists in the USSR believe in their Slavophile cause passionately, and one gets the sense that the fascist alternative is not one that has played itself out entirely there.

The Soviet Union, then, is at a fork in the road: it can start down the path that was staked out by Western Europe forty-five years ago, a path that most of Asia has followed, or it can realize its own uniqueness and remain stuck in history. The choice it makes will be highly important for us, given the Soviet Union's size and military strength, for that power will continue to preoccupy us and slow our realization that we have already emerged on the other side of history.

V

The passing of Marxism-Leninism first from China and then from the Soviet Union will mean its death as a living ideology of world historical significance. For while there may be some isolated true believers left in places like Managua, Pyongyang, or Cambridge, Massachusetts, the fact that there is not a single large state in which it is a going concern undermines completely its pretensions to being in the vanguard of human history. And the death of this ideology means the growing "Common Marketization" of international relations, and the diminution of the likelihood of large-scale conflict between states.

This does not by any means imply the end of international conflict *per se*. For the world at that point would be divided between a part that was historical and a part that was post-historical. Conflict between states still in history, and between those states and those at the end of history, would still be possible. There would still be a high and perhaps rising level of ethnic and nationalist violence, since those are impulses incompletely played out, even in parts of the post-historical world. Palestinians and Kurds, Sikhs and Tamils, Irish Catholics and Walloons, Armenians and Azeris, will continue to have their unresolved grievances. This implies that terrorism and wars of national liberation will continue to be an important item on the international agenda. But large-scale conflict must involve large states still caught in the grip of history, and they are what appear to be passing from the scene.

The end of history will be a very sad time. The struggle for recognition, the willingness to risk one's life for a purely abstract goal, the worldwide ideological struggle that called forth daring, courage, imagination, and idealism, will be replaced by economic calculation, the endless solving of technical problems, environmental concerns, and the satisfaction of sophisticated consumer demands. In the post-historical period there will be neither art nor philosophy, just the perpetual caretaking of the museum of human history. I can feel in myself, and see in others around me, a powerful nostalgia for the time when history existed. Such nostalgia, in fact, will continue to fuel competition and conflict even in the post-historical world for some time to come. Even though I recognize its inevitability, I have the most ambivalent feelings for the civilization that has been created in Europe since 1945, with its north Atlantic and Asian offshoots. Perhaps this very prospect of centuries of boredom at the end of history will serve to get history started once again.

NOTES

1. Kojève's best-known work is his *Introduction à la lecture de Hegel* (Paris: Editions Gallimard, 1947), which is a transcript of the *Ecole Practique* lectures from the 1930s. This book is available in English entitled *Introduction to the Reading of Hegel* arranged by Raymond Queneau, edited by Allan Bloom, and translated by James Nichols (New York: Basic Books, 1969).

2. In this respect Kojève stands in sharp contrast to contemporary German interpreters of Hegel like Herbert Marcuse who, being more sympathetic to Marx, regarded Hegel ultimately as an historically bound and incomplete philosopher.

3. Kojève alternatively identified the end of history with the postwar "American way of life," toward which he thought the Soviet Union was moving as well.

4. This notion was expressed in the famous aphorism from the preface to the *Philosophy of History* to the effect that "everything that is rational is real, and everything that is real is rational."

5. Indeed, for Hegel the very dichotomy between the ideal and material worlds was itself only an apparent one that was ultimately overcome by the self-conscious

subject; in his system, the material world is itself only an aspect of mind.

6. In fact, modern economists, recognizing that man does not always behave as a *profit* maximizer, posit a "utility" function, utility being either income or some other good that can be maximized: leisure, sexual satisfaction, or the pleasure of philosophizing. That profit must be replaced with a value like utility indicates the cogency of the idealist perspective.

7. One need look no further than the recent performance of Vietnamese immigrants in the U.S. school system when compared to their black or Hispanic classmates to realize that culture and consciousness are absolutely crucial to explain not only economic behavior but virtually every other important aspect of life as well.

8. I understand that a full explanation of the origins of the reform movements in China and Russia is a good deal more complicated than this simple formula would suggest. The Soviet reform, for example, was motivated in good measure by Moscow's sense of *insecurity* in the technological-military realm. Nonetheless, neither country on the eve of its reforms was in such a state of *material* crisis that one could have predicted the surprising reform paths ultimately taken.

9. It is still not clear whether the Soviet peoples are as "Protestant" as Gorbachev and will follow him down that path.

10. The internal politics of the Byzantine Empire at the time of Justinian revolved around a conflict between the so-called monophysites and monothelites, who believed that the unity of the Holy Trinity was alternatively one of nature or of will. This conflict corresponded to some extent to one between proponents of different racing teams in the Hippodrome in Byzantium and led to a not insignificant level of political violence. Modern historians would tend to seek the roots of such conflicts in antagonisms between social classes or some other modern economic category, being unwilling to believe that men would kill each other over the nature of the Trinity.

11. I am not using the term "fascism" here in its most precise sense, fully aware of the frequent misuse of this term to denounce anyone to the right of the user. "Fascism" here denotes any organized ultra-nationalist movement with universalistic pretensions—not universalistic with regard to its nationalism, of course, since the latter is exclusive by definition, but with regard to the movement's belief in its right to rule other people. Hence Imperial Japan would qualify as fascist while former strongman Stoessner's Paraguay or Pinochet's Chile would not. Obviously fascist ideologies cannot be universalistic in the sense of Marxism or liberalism, but the structure of the doctrine can be transferred from country to country.

12. I use the example of Japan with some caution, since Kojève late in his life came to conclude that Japan, with its culture based on purely formal arts, proved that the universal homogeneous state was not victorious and that history had perhaps not ended. See the long note at the end of the second edition of *Introduction à la Lecture de Hegel,* 462–3.

13. This is not true in Poland and Hungary, however, whose Communist parties have taken moves toward true power-sharing and pluralism.

14. This is particularly true of the leading Soviet conservative, former Second Secretary Yegor Ligachev, who has publicly recognized many of the deep defects of the Brezhnev period.

15. I am thinking particularly of Rousseau and the Western philosophical tradition that flows from him that was highly critical of Lockean or Hobbesian liberalism, though one could criticize liberalism from the standpoint of classical political philosophy as well.

16. See his article, "Beyond the Cold War," *New Republic,* December 19, 1988.

17. It took European colonial powers like France several years after the war to admit the illegitimacy of their empires, but

decolonialization was an inevitable consequence of the Allied victory which had been based on the promise of a restoration of democratic freedoms.

18. *Vestnik Ministerstva Inostrannikb Del SSSR* no. 15 (August 1988), 27–46. "New

thinking" does of course serve a propagandistic purpose in persuading Western audiences of Soviet good intentions. But the fact that it is good propaganda does not mean that its formulators do not take many of its ideas seriously.

QUESTIONS

1. According to Fukuyama, what are the major factors promoting the end of history?

2. Compare and contrast Fred Halliday's article with Francis Fukuyama's. Specifically, do Fukuyama and Halliday agree on the role and importance of ideology in international politics?

27.   No Exit: The Errors of Endism

Samuel P. Huntington

In this article, Samuel P. Huntington responds to Fukuyama's article "The End of History?" by presenting critical analysis of this "endist theory" and warns against the overly optimistic view that wars among the great powers will not occur again. By reminding the reader that the Cold War was also the "Long Peace," Huntington offers a valuable theoretical critique on the end-of-history perspective. This selection is from *The National Interest* (1989).

Samuel P. Huntington is Eaton Professor of the Science of Government and director of the John M. Olin Institute for Strategic Studies at Harvard University. He has written many books, including *The Soldier and the State* (1975), *Political Order in Changing Societies* (1968), *The Third Wave: Democratization in the Late Twentieth Century* (1991), and has contributed to numerous political science and international studies journals.

For a second year serious discussion of international affairs has been dominated by a major theoretical and academic issue. In 1988 the issue was American decline. The theory of declinism, articulated by many thinkers, but most notably by Paul Kennedy, became the focus of extended and intense debate. Was the

United States following in the path of Great Britain and declining as a great power? To what extent was its economic base being undermined by spending too much on defense and/or too much on consumption?

The major issue in 1989 is very different. The theory of declinism has been displaced by the theory of endism. Its central element is that bad things are coming to an end.[1] Endism manifests itself in at least three ways. At its most specific level, endism hails the end of the Cold War. In the spring of 1989 the *New York Times* and the International Institute for Strategic Studies, George Kennan and George Bush, all set forth this proposition in one form or another. The end of the Cold War became the Foreign Policy Establishment's Established Truth.

At a second level, endism manifested itself in the more academic and more general proposition that wars among nation states, or at least among some types of nation states, were coming to an end. Many scholars pointed to the historical absence of wars between democratic countries and saw the multiplication of democratic regimes since 1974 as evidence that the probability of war was declining. In a related but somewhat different version of this proposition, Michael Doyle argued that wars were impossible between liberal states. In a still more sweeping formulation, John Mueller contended that the advance of civilization was making war obsolescent and that it would disappear the same way that slavery and duelling had disappeared in advanced societies.[2] Wars still might occur among backward Third World countries, but among developed countries, communist or capitalist, war was unthinkable.

The third and most extreme formulation of endism was advanced by Francis Fukuyama in a brilliant essay called ''The End of History?'' in the summer issue of this journal. Fukuyama celebrates not just the end of the Cold War or the end of wars among developed nation states, but instead ''the end of history as such.'' This results from the ''unabashed victory of

economic and political liberalism'' and the ''exhaustion of viable systematic alternatives.'' Like Mueller, Fukuyama concedes that wars may occur among Third World states still caught up in the historical process. But for the developed countries, the Soviet Union, and China, history is at an end.

Endism—the intellectual fad of 1989—contrasts rather dramatically with declinism—the intellectual fad of 1988. Declinism is conditionally pessimistic. It is rooted in the study of history and draws on the parallels between the United States in the late twentieth century, Britain in the late nineteenth century, and France, Spain, and other powers in earlier centuries. Its proponents and its critics debate the relevance of these parallels and argue over detailed, historical data concerning economic growth, productivity, defense spending, savings, and investment.[3] Endism, on the other hand, is oriented to the future rather than the past and is unabashedly optimistic. In its most developed form, as with Fukuyama, it is rooted in philosophical speculation rather than historical analysis. It is based not so much on evidence from history as on assumptions about history. In its extreme form, declinism is historically deterministic: nations naturally, and perhaps inevitably, evolve through phases of rise, expansion, and decline. They are caught in the inexorable grip of history. In the extreme form of endism, in contrast, nations escape from history.

The message of declinism for Americans is ''We're losing''; the message of endism is ''We've won!'' Despite or perhaps even because of its deterministic strand, declinism performs a useful historical function. It provides a warning and a goad to action in order to head off and reverse the decline that it says is taking place. It serves that purpose now as it did in its earlier manifestations in the 1950s, 1960s, and 1970s. Endism, in contrast, provides not a warning of danger but an illusion of well-being. It invites not corrective action but relaxed complacency. The consequences of its thesis being in error, hence, are far more dangerous and subversive than those that would result if the declinist thesis should be wrong.

THE END OF THE COLD WAR

"The cold war is over" was the prevailing cry in the spring of 1989. What does this mean? It typically referred to two related developments: the changes usually referred to as glasnost and perestroika in the Soviet Union and the improvements that were occurring in Soviet-American relations. "The cold war," as the *New York Times* put it, "of poisonous Soviet-American feelings, of domestic political hysteria, of events enlarged and distorted by East-West confrontation, of almost perpetual diplomatic deadlock is over."[4] Several questions can be raised about this proposition.

First, is it really true? The easing in Soviet-American relations in the late 1950s was followed by the Berlin and Cuban crises; detente in the early 1970s was followed by Angola and Afghanistan. How do we know that the current relaxation is not simply another swing of the cycle? One answer is that the changes occurring within the Soviet Union are far more fundamental than those that have occurred in the past, and this is certainly the case. The opening up of political debate, limited but real competition in elections, the formation of political groups outside the Party, the virtual abandonment, indeed, of the idea of a monolithic

party, the assertion of power by the Supreme Soviet—all these will, if continued, lead to a drastically different Soviet political system. The price of attempting to reverse them increases daily, but it would be rash to conclude that they are as yet irreversible, and the costs of reversing them could decline in the future.

On the international level, the Soviets have cooperated in resolving regional conflicts in the Persian Gulf, southern Africa, and Indochina. They have promised to reduce their overall military forces and their deployments in Eastern Europe. As yet, however, no perceptible changes have taken place in Soviet force structure, Soviet deployments, or Soviet output of military equipment. Even if these do occur, the competition between the United States and the Soviet Union for influence and power in world affairs will still go on. It has been continuing as President Bush and President Gorbachev attempt to woo Eastern and Western European publics. Europe, it is well to remember, is where the Cold War started. It is the overwhelmingly preeminent stake in the Cold War, and Gorbachev's public relations can be as much a threat to American interests in Europe as were Brezhnev's tanks (which, for the moment at any rate, Gorbachev also has).

Let us, however, concede that in some meaningful and not transitory sense the Cold War is over and that a real change has occurred in Soviet-American relations. How do the proponents of this thesis see the post-Cold War world? The "we-they world" that has existed, the editors of the *New York Times* assure us, is giving way "to the more traditional struggles of great powers." In a similar vein, George Kennan alleges that the Soviet Union "should now be regarded essentially as another great power, like other great powers.'' Its interests may differ from ours but these differences can be ''adjusted by the normal means of compromise and accommodation.''[5]

Russia was, however, just ''another great power'' for several centuries before it became a communist state. As a great power, Russia frequently deployed its armies into Europe and repeatedly crushed popular uprisings in central Europe. Soviet troops bloodily suppressed the Hungarian Revolution in 1956 and trampled the embryonic Czech democracy in 1968. Russian troops bloodily suppressed the Hungarian revolution of 1848–49 and violently put down uprisings in Poland in 1831 and again in 1863–64. Soviet forces occupied Berlin in 1945; Russian troops occupied and burnt Berlin in 1760. In pursuit of Russia's interests as a great power, Russian troops appeared many places where as yet Soviet troops have not. In 1799 Russian troops occupied Milan and Turin and fought a battle on the outskirts of Zurich. The same year, they occupied the Ionian islands off Greece and stayed there until 1807. These excursions preceded Napoleon's invasion of Russia. As a great power, Russia regularly participated in the partitions of Poland. In 1914 Nicholas II directly ruled more of Europe (including most of Poland) than Gorbachev does today.

The past record of Russia as a ''normal'' great power, therefore, is not reassuring for either the liberty of Eastern Europe or the security of Western Europe. Some suggest that the liberalizing and democratizing trends in the Soviet Union will prevent that country from bludgeoning other countries in the manner of the tsars. One cannot assume, Fukuyama argues, that ''the evolution of human consciousness has stood still'' and that ''the Soviets will return to foreign

policy views a century out of date in the rest of Europe.'' Fukuyama is right: one cannot assume that the Soviets will revert to the bad old ways of the past. One also cannot assume that they will not. Gorbachev may be able to discard communism but he cannot discard geography and the geopolitical imperatives that have shaped Russian and Soviet behavior for centuries. And, as any Latin American will quickly point out, even a truly democratic superpower is capable of intervening militarily in the affairs of its smaller neighbors.

The era of the Cold War, John Lewis Gaddis reminds us, has also been the era of the Long Peace, the longest period in history without hot war between major powers. Does the end of the Cold War mean the end of the Long Peace? Two central elements of both have been bipolarity and nuclear weapons: they have in considerable measure defined both the Soviet-American rivalry and its limits. The end of the Cold War will mean a loosening of bipolarity even if it does not mean, as some declinists predict, a world of five or more roughly equal major powers. The delegitimation of nuclear weapons and the increasing constraints on their deployment and potential use could increase the probability of conventional war.

Active American involvement in world affairs has been substantially limited to two world wars and one prolonged and ideologically-driven cold war. In the absence of the Kaiser, Hitler, Stalin, and Brezhnev, the American inclination may well be to relax and to assume that peace, goodwill, and international cooperation will prevail: that if the Cold War is over, American relations with the Soviet Union will be similar to its relations with Canada, France, or Japan. Americans tend to see competition and conflict as normal and even desirable features of their domestic economy and politics and yet perversely assume them to be abnormal and undesirable in relations among states. In fact, however, the history of the relations among great powers, when it has not been the history of hot wars, has usually been the history of cold wars.

The end of the Cold War does not mean the end of political, ideological, diplomatic, economic, technological, or even military rivalry among nations. It does not mean the end of the struggle for power and influence. It very probably does mean increased instability, unpredictability, and violence in international affairs. It could mean the end of the Long Peace.

THE END OF WAR

A second manifestation of endism postulates the end of war between certain types of nation states. A number of authors, including Dean V. Babst, R.J. Rummel, and Bruce Russett, have pointed to the fact that no significant interstate wars have occurred between democratic regimes since the emergence of such regimes in the early nineteenth century. Michael Doyle has similarly argued that a "pacific union" exists among liberal regimes (which includes and is slightly broader than the class of democratic regimes, as defined by most scholars). "*[C]onstitutionally secure liberal states,*" he says, "*have yet to engage in war with each other. Even threats of war have been regarded as illegitimate.*"

Given the large number of wars between non-democratic regimes and

between democratic regimes and non-democratic regimes, the almost total absence of armed conflict between democratic regimes is indeed striking. It is, as Bruce Russett says, "perhaps the strongest non-trivial or non-tautological statement that can be made about international relations." It is also plausible to believe that this absence of war may stem from the nature of the regime. Democracy is a means for the peaceful resolution of disputes, involving negotiation and compromise as well as elections and voting. The leaders of democracies may well expect that they ought to be able to resolve through peaceful means their differences with the leaders of other democracies. In the years since World War II, for instance, several conflicts which could or did lead to war between countries tended to moderate when the countries became democratic. The controversies between Britain and Argentina, Guatemala, and Spain over the remnants of empire (one of which did lead to war and one of which produced significant military deployment) moderated considerably when those three countries became democratic. The conflict between Greece and Turkey similarly seemed to ease in the 1980s after both countries had democratically-elected regimes.

The democratic "zone of peace" is a dramatic historical phenomenon. If that relationship continues to hold and if democracy continues to spread, wars should become less frequent in the future than they have been in the past. This is one endist argument that has a strong empirical base. Three qualifications have to be noted, however, to its implications for the end of war.

First, democracies are still a minority among the world's regimes. The 1989

Freedom House survey classified 60 out of 167 sovereign states as "free" according to its rather generous definition of freedom. Multiple possibilities for war thus continue to exist among the 107 states that are not free, and between those states and the democratic states.

Second, the number of democratic states has been growing, but it tends to grow irregularly in a two-step forward, one-step backward pattern. A major wave of democratization occurred in the nineteenth century, but then significant reversals to authoritarianism took place in the 1920s and 1930s. A second wave of democratization after World War II was followed by several reversals in the 1960s and 1970s. A third wave of democratization began in 1974, with fifteen to twenty countries shifting in a democratic direction since then. If the previous pattern prevails, some of these new democracies are likely to revert to authoritarianism. Hence the possibility of war could increase rather than decrease in the immediate future, although still remaining less than it was prior to 1974.

Finally, peace among democratic states could be related to extraneous accidental factors and not to the nature of democracy. In the nineteenth century, for instance, wars tended to occur between geographical neighbors. Democratic states were few in number and seldom bordered on each other. Hence the absence of war could be caused by the absence of propinquity.[6] Since World War II most democratic countries have been members of the alliance system led by the United States, which has been directed against an alliance of nondemocratic regimes and within which the hegemonic position of the U.S. has precluded war between other alliance members (e.g., between Greece and Turkey). If American leadership weakens and the alliance system loosens, the probability of war between its erstwhile members, democratic or otherwise, could well increase.

The "democratic zone of peace" argument is thus valid as far as it goes, but it may not go all that far.

In his book, *Retreat from Doomsday,* John Mueller argues for the growing obsolescence of war on more general grounds. He sees the Long Peace since 1945 not as the result of bipolarity or nuclear weapons but rather as the result of a learning experience that wars do not pay and that there are few conflicts of interest among countries where it would be reasonable for either side to resort to war to achieve its goals. World War II was an aberration from the twentieth-century trend away from war due largely to the idiosyncratic and irrational personality of Hitler. As countries become more developed and civilized, they will become more peaceful. Denmark is the future model for individual countries, U.S.-Canadian relations the future model for relations between countries.

Mueller makes much of the argument that war will become "obsolete, subrationally unthinkable," and unacceptable in civilized society in the way slavery and duelling have become. Why, however, are those social practices the appropriate parallels to war? Why not murder? Murder has been unacceptable in civilized societies for millennia, and yet it seems unlikely that the murder rate in twentieth-century New York is less than it was in fifth-century Athens. While major wars between developed countries have not occurred since World War II, interstate and intrastate violence has been widespread with the casualties numbering in the tens of millions.

Mueller himself substantially qualifies his case. He agrees that wars will continue among less developed countries. He also concedes that irrational leaders on the Hitler model could involve their countries in future wars. Economic considerations motivate strongly against war, he says, but economic prosperity "is not always an overriding goal even now." Territorial issues exist even in the developed world that "could lead to wars of expansion or territorial readjustment." The Cold War is being resolved peacefully, "but there is no firm guarantee that this trend will continue."

A more general problem may also exist with the end-of-war or even a decline-in-war thesis. As Michimi Muranushi of Yale has pointed out, peace can be self-limiting rather than cumulative. If relations between two countries become more peaceful, this may, in some circumstances, increase the probability that either or both of those countries will go to war with a third country. The Hitler-Stalin pact paves the way for the attacks on Poland; normalization of U.S.-China relations precipitates China's war with Vietnam. If the Soviet threat disappears, so also does an inhibitor of Greek-Turkish war.

In addition, if more countries become like Denmark, forswearing war and committing themselves to material comfort, that in itself may produce a situation which other countries will wish to exploit. History is full of examples of leaner, meaner societies overrunning richer, less martial ones.

THE END OF HISTORY

"The end of history" is a sweeping, dramatic, and provocative phrase. What does Fukuyama mean by it? The heart of Fukuyama's argument is an alleged change in political consciousness throughout the principal societies in the world and the emergence of a pervasive consensus on liberal-democratic principles. It posits the triumph of one ideology and the consequent end of ideology and ideological conflict as significant factors in human existence. His choice of language suggests, however, that he may have something more sweeping in mind than simply the obsolescence of war highlighted by Mueller or the end of ideology predicted by Daniel Bell twenty-five years ago.

Insofar as it is focused on war, Fukuyama's argument suffers all the weaknesses that Mueller's does. He admits that "conflict between states still in history, and between those states and those at the end of history, would still be possible." At the same time he includes China and the Soviet Union among those states that are out of history. Current Soviet leaders, he says, have arrived at the "end-of-history view" and "assimilated the consciousness of the universal homogenous state that is post-Hitler Europe"; yet he also admits that the Soviet Union could turn to Slavophile Russian chauvinism and thus remain stuck in history.

Fukuyama ridicules the idea that Germany and France might fight each other again. That is a valid but irrelevant point. A hundred years ago one could have validly made the point that Pennsylvania and Virginia would not fight each other again. That did not prevent the United States, of which each was a part, from engaging in world wars in the subsequent century. One trend in history is the amalgamation of smaller units into larger ones. The probability of war between the smaller units declines but the probability of war between the larger amalgamated units does not necessarily change. A united European community may end the possibility of Franco-German war; it does not end the possibility of war between that community and other political units.

With respect to China, Fukuyama argues that "Chinese competitiveness and expansionism on the world scene have virtually disappeared" and, he implies strongly, will not reappear. A more persuasive argument, however, could be made for exactly the opposite proposition that Chinese expansionism has yet to appear on the world scene. Britain and France, Germany and Japan, the United States and the Soviet Union, all became expansionist and imperialist powers in the course of industrialization. China is just beginning seriously to develop its industrial strength. Maybe China will be different from all the other major powers and not attempt to expand its influence and control as it industrializes. But how can one be confident that it will pursue this deviant course? And if it follows the more familiar pattern, a billion Chinese engaged in imperial expansion are likely to impose a lot of history on the rest of the world.

Fukuyama quite appropriately emphasizes the role of consciousness, ideas, and ideology in motivating and shaping the actions of men and nations. He is also right in pointing to the virtual end of the appeal of communism as an ideology. Ideologically, communism has been "the grand failure" that Brzezinski labels it. It is erroneous, however, to jump from the decline of communism to the global triumph of liberalism and the disappearance of ideology as a force in world affairs.

First, revivals are possible. A set of ideas or an ideology may fade from the scene in one generation only to reappear with renewed strength a generation or two later. From the 1940s to the 1960s, dominant currents in economic thinking were Keynesianism, welfare statism, social democracy, and planning. It was hard to find much support for classical economic liberalism. By the late 1970s, however, the latter had staged an amazing comeback: economists and economic institutions were devoted to The Plan in the 1950s; they have been devoted to The Market in the 1980s. Somewhat similarly, social scientists in the decades immediately after World War II argued that religion, ethnic consciousness, and nationalism would all be done in by economic development and modernization. But in the 1980s these have been the dominant bases of political action in most societies. The revival of religion is now a global phenomenon. Communism may be down for the moment, but it is rash to assume that it is out for all time.

Second, the universal acceptance of liberal democracy does not preclude conflicts within liberalism. The history of ideology is the history of schism. Struggles between those who profess different versions of a common ideology are often more intense and vicious than struggles between those espousing entirely different ideologies. To a believer the heretic is worse than the nonbeliever. An ideological consensus on Christianity existed in Europe in 1500 but that did not prevent Protestants and Catholics from slaughtering each other for the next century and a half. Socialists and communists, Trotskyites and Leninists, Shi'ites and Sunnis have treated each other in similar fashion.

Third, the triumph of one ideology does not preclude the emergence of new ideologies. Nations and societies presumably will continue to evolve. New challenges to human well-being will emerge, and people will develop new concepts, theories, and ideologies as to how those challenges should be met. Unless all social, economic, and political distinctions disappear, people will also develop belief systems that legitimate what they have and justify their getting more. Among its other functions, for instance, communism historically legitimized the power of intellectuals and bureaucrats. If it is gone for good, it seems highly likely that intellectuals and bureaucrats will develop new sets of ideas to rationalize their claims to power and wealth.

Fourth, has liberal democracy really triumphed? Fukuyama admits that it has not won out in the Third World. To what extent, however, has it really been accepted in the Soviet Union and China? Between them these societies encompass well over one-quarter of the world's population. If any one trend is operative in the world today it is for societies to turn back toward their traditional cultures, values, and patterns of behavior. This trend is manifest in the revival of traditional identities and characters of Eastern European countries, escaping from the deadly uniformity of Soviet-imposed communism, and also in the increasing differentiation among the republics within the Soviet Union itself. Russia and China do not lack elements of liberalism and democracy in their histories. These are, however, minor chords, and their subordinate importance is underlined by the contemporary problems facing economic liberalism in the Soviet Union and political democracy in communist China.

More generally, Fukuyama's thesis itself reflects not the disappearance of Marxism but its pervasiveness. His image of the end of history is straight from Marx. Fukuyama speaks of the "universal homogeneous state," in which "all prior contradictions are resolved and all human needs are satisfied." What is this but the Marxist image of a society without class conflict or other contradictions organized on the basis of from each according to his abilities and to each according to his needs? The struggles of history, Fukuyama says, "will be replaced by economic calculation, the endless solving of technical problems, environmental concerns, and the satisfaction of sophisticated consumer demands." Engels said it even more succinctly: "The government of persons is replaced by the administration of things and the direction of the process of production." Fukuyama says liberalism is the end of history. Marx says communism "is the solution to the riddle of history." They are basically saying the same thing and, most importantly, they are thinking the same way. Marxist ideology is alive and well in Fukuyama's arguments to refute it.

TWO FALLACIES

The Soviet Union is increasingly preoccupied with its own problems and a significant political loosening has occurred in that country. The ideological intensity of the early Cold War has virtually disappeared, and the probability of hot war between the two superpowers is as low as it has ever been. War is even more unlikely between any of the advanced industrialized democracies. On these points, endist propositions are accurate. The more extensive formulations of the endist argument, however, suffer from two basic fallacies.

First, endism overemphasizes the predictability of history and the permanence of the moment. Current trends may or may not continue into the future. Past experience certainly suggests that they are unlikely to do so. The record of past predictions by social scientists is not a happy one. Fifteen years ago, just as the democratic wave was beginning, political analysts were elaborating fundamental reasons why authoritarianism had to prevail in the Third World. Ten years ago foreign policy journals were filled with warnings of the rise of Soviet military power and political influence throughout the world. Five years ago what analyst of the Soviet Union predicted the extent of the political changes that have occurred in that country? Given the limitations of human foresight, endist predictions of the end of war and ideological conflict deserve a heavy dose of skepticism. Indeed, in the benign atmosphere of the moment, it is sobering to speculate on the possible future horrors that social analysts are now failing to predict.

Second, endism tends to ignore the weakness and irrationality of human nature. Endist arguments often assume that because it would be rational for human beings to focus on their economic well-being, they will act in that way, and therefore they will not engage in wars that do not meet the tests of cost-benefit analysis or in ideological conflicts that are much ado about nothing. Human beings are at times rational, generous, creative, and wise, but they are also often stupid, selfish, cruel, and sinful. The struggle that is history began with the eating of the forbidden fruit and is rooted in human nature. In history there may be total defeats, but there are no final solutions. So long as human beings exist, there is no exit from the traumas of history.

To hope for the benign end of history is human. To expect it to happen is un-realistic. To plan on it happening is disastrous.

NOTES

1. Some have raised the question as to what extent endist writers are really serious in their arguments. The time and intellectual effort they have devoted to elaborating those arguments suggest that they are, and I will assume this to be the case. The arguments also deserve to be taken seriously because of their widespread popularity.

2. Michael W. Doyle, "Kant, Liberal Legacies, and Foreign Affairs," *Philosophy and Public Affairs,* vol. 12 (Summer, Fall 1983), pp. 205-235, 323-353, and "Liberalism and World Politics," *American Political Science Review,* vol. 80 (December 1986), pp. 1151-1169; John Mueller, *Retreat from Doomsday: The Obsolescence of Major War* (New York: Basic Books, 1989). Also see Dean V. Babst, "A Force for Peace," *Industrial Research,* vol. 14 (April 1972), pp. 55-58; R.J. Rummel, "Libertarianism and International Violence," *Journal of Conflict Resolution,* vol. 27 (March 1983), pp. 27-71; Ze'ev Maoz and Nasrin Abdolali, "Regime Types and International Conflict, 1816-1976," *Journal of Conflict Resolution,* vol. 33 (March 1989), pp. 3-35; Bruce Russett, "The Politics of an Alternative Security System: Toward a More Democratic and Therefore More Peaceful World," in Burns Weston, ed., *Alternatives to Nuclear Deterrence* (Boulder: Westview Press, forthcoming 1989).

3. For a careful analysis of the evidence and arguments on this issue, see Joseph S. Nye, Jr.'s forthcoming book, *American Power: Past and Future* (New York: Basic Books).

4. "The Cold War Is Over," *New York Times,* April 2, 1989, p. E30.

5. "Just Another Great Power," *New York Times,* April 9, 1989, p. E25.

6. See J. David Singer and Melvin Small, "The War-Proneness of Democratic Regimes, 1815-1965," *Jerusalem Journal of International Relations,* vol. 1 (Summer 1976), p. 67.

QUESTIONS

1. What are Huntington's primary criticisms of Fukuyama's essay "The End of History?"

2. Does Huntington underestimate the importance of ideology in international relations?

28.   The Clash of Civilizations?

Samuel P. Huntington

In this article, Samuel P. Huntington argues that world politics is entering a new phase in which the great divisions among humankind and the dominating source of international conflict will be cultural. Civilizations—the highest cultural groupings of people—are differentiated from each other by religion, history, language, and tradition. These divisions are deep and increasing in importance. From Yugoslavia to the Middle East to Central Asia, the fault lines of civilizations are the battle lines of the future. In this emerging era of cultural conflict, the United States must forge alliances with similar cultures to spread its values wherever possible. In the final analysis, all civilizations will have to learn to tolerate each other. This selection is from the journal *Foreign Affairs* (1993).

Samuel P. Huntington is Eaton Professor of the Science of Government and director of the John M. Olin Institute for Strategic Studies at Harvard University. He has written many books, including *The Soldier and the State* (1975), *Political Order in Changing Societies* (1968), *The Third Wave: Democratization in the Late Twentieth Century* (1991), and has contributed to numerous political science and international studies journals.

THE NEXT PATTERN OF CONFLICT

World politics is entering a new phase, and intellectuals have not hesitated to proliferate visions of what it will be—the end of history, the return of traditional rivalries between nation states, and the decline of the nation state from the conflicting pulls of tribalism and globalism, among others. Each of these visions catches aspects of the emerging reality.

Yet they all miss a crucial, indeed a central, aspect of what global politics is likely to be in the coming years.

It is my hypothesis that the fundamental source of conflict in this new world will not be primarily ideological or primarily economic. The great divisions among humankind and the dominating source of conflict will be cultural. Nation states will remain the most powerful actors in world affairs, but the principal conflicts of global politics will occur between nations and groups of different civilizations. The clash of civilizations will dominate global politics. The fault lines between civilizations will be the battle lines of the future.

Conflict between civilizations will be the latest phase in the evolution of conflict in the modern world. For a century and a half after the emergence of the modern international system with the Peace of Westphalia, the conflicts of the Western world were largely among princes—emperors, absolute monarchs and constitutional monarchs attempting to expand their bureaucracies, their armies, their mercantilist economic strength and, most important, the territory they ruled. In the process they created nation states, and beginning with the French Revolution the principal lines of conflict were between nations rather than princes. In 1793, as R. R. Palmer put it, "The wars of kings were over; the wars of peoples had begun." This nineteenth-century pattern lasted until the end of World War I. Then, as a result of the Russian Revolution and the reaction against it, the conflict of nations yielded to the conflict of ideologies, first among communism, fascism-Nazism and liberal democracy, and then between communism and liberal democracy. During the Cold War, this latter conflict became embodied in the struggle between the two superpowers, neither of which was a nation state in the classical European sense and each of which defined its identity in terms of its ideology.

These conflicts between princes, nation states and ideologies were primarily conflicts within Western civilization, "Western civil wars," as William Lind has labeled them. This was as true of the Cold War as it was of the world wars and the earlier wars of the seventeenth, eighteenth and nineteenth centuries. With the end of the Cold War, international politics moves out of its Western phase, and its centerpiece becomes the interaction between the West and non-Western civilizations and among non-Western civilizations. In the politics of civilizations, the peoples and governments of non-Western civilizations no longer remain the objects of history as targets of Western colonialism but join the West as movers and shapers of history.

THE NATURE OF CIVILIZATIONS

During the cold war the world was divided into the First, Second and Third Worlds. Those divisions are no longer relevant. It is far more meaningful now to group countries not in terms of their political or economic systems or in terms of their level of economic development but rather in terms of their culture and civilization.

What do we mean when we talk of a civilization? A civilization is a cultural entity. Villages, regions, ethnic groups, nationalities, religious groups, all have distinct cultures at different levels of cultural heterogeneity. The culture of a village in southern Italy may be different from that of a village in northern Italy, but both will share in a common Italian culture that distinguishes them from German villages. European communities, in turn, will share cultural features that distinguish them from Arab or Chinese communities. Arabs, Chinese and Westerners, however, are not part of any broader cultural entity. They constitute civilizations. A civilization is thus the highest cultural grouping of people and the broadest level of cultural identity people have short of that which distinguishes humans from other species. It is defined both by common objective elements, such as language, history, religion, customs, institutions, and by the subjective self-identification of people. People have levels of identity: a resident of Rome may define himself with varying degrees of intensity as a Roman, an Italian, a Catholic, a Christian, a European, a Westerner. The civilization to which he belongs is the broadest level of identification with which he intensely identifies. People can and do redefine their identities and, as a result, the composition and boundaries of civilizations change.

Civilizations may involve a large number of people, as with China ("a civilization pretending to be a state," as Lucian Pye put it), or a very small number of people, such as the Anglophone Caribbean. A civilization may include several nation states, as is the case with Western, Latin American and Arab civilizations, or only one, as is the case with Japanese civilization. Civilizations obviously blend and overlap, and may include subcivilizations. Western civilization has two major variants, European and North American, and Islam has its Arab, Turkic and Malay subdivisions. Civilizations are nonetheless meaningful entities, and while the lines between them are seldom sharp, they are real. Civilizations are dynamic; they rise and fall; they divide and merge. And, as any student of history knows, civilizations disappear and are buried in the sands of time.

Westerners tend to think of nation states as the principal actors in global affairs. They have been that, however, for only a few centuries. The broader reaches of human history have been the history of civilizations. In *A Study of History,* Arnold Toynbee identified 21 major civilizations; only six of them exist in the contemporary world.

WHY CIVILIZATIONS WILL CLASH

Civilization identity will be increasingly important in the future, and the world will be shaped in large measure by the interactions among seven or eight major civilizations. These include Western, Confucian, Japanese, Islamic, Hindu, Slavic-Orthodox, Latin American and possibly African civilization. The most important conflicts of the future will occur along the cultural fault lines separating these civilizations from one another.

Why will this be the case?

First, differences among civilizations are not only real; they are basic. Civilizations are differentiated from each other by history, language, culture, tradition and, most important, religion. The people of different civilizations have different views on the relations between God and man, the individual and the group, the citizen and the state, parents and children, husband and wife, as well as differing views of the relative importance of rights and responsibilities, liberty and authority, equality and hierarchy. These differences are the product of centuries. They will not soon disappear. They are far more fundamental than differences among political ideologies and political regimes. Differences do not necessarily mean conflict, and conflict does not necessarily mean violence. Over the centuries, however, differences among civilizations have generated the most prolonged and the most violent conflicts.

Second, the world is becoming a smaller place. The interactions between peoples of different civilizations are increasing; these increasing interactions intensify civilization consciousness and awareness of differences between civilizations and commonalities within civilizations. North African immigration to France generates hostility among Frenchmen and at the same time increased receptivity to immigration by "good" European Catholic Poles. Americans react far more negatively to Japanese investment than to larger investments from Canada and European countries. Similarly, as Donald Horowitz has pointed out, "An Ibo may be . . . an Owerri Ibo or an Onitsha Ibo in what was the Eastern region of Nigeria. In Lagos, he is simply an Ibo. In London, he is a Nigerian. In New York, he is an African." The interactions among peoples of different civilizations enhance the civilization-consciousness of people that, in turn, invigorates differences and animosities stretching or thought to stretch back deep into history.

Third, the processes of economic modernization and social change throughout the world are separating people from longstanding local identities. They also weaken the nation state as a source of identity. In much of the world religion has moved in to fill this gap, often in the form of movements that are labeled "fundamentalist." Such movements are found in Western Christianity, Judaism, Buddhism and Hinduism, as well as in Islam. In most countries and most religions the people active in fundamentalist movements are young, college-educated, middle-class technicians, professionals and business persons. The "unsecularization of the world," George Weigel has remarked, "is one of the dominant social facts of life in the late twentieth century." The revival of religion, "la revanche de Dieu," as Gilles Kepel

labeled it, provides a basis for identity and commitment that transcends national boundaries and unites civilizations.

Fourth, the growth of civilization-consciousness is enhanced by the dual role of the West. On the one hand, the West is at a peak of power. At the same time, however, and perhaps as a result, a return to the roots phenomenon is occurring among non-Western civilizations. Increasingly one hears references to trends toward a turning inward and "Asianization" in Japan, the end of the Nehru legacy and the "Hinduization" of India, the failure of Western ideas of socialism and nationalism and hence "re-Islamization" of the Middle East, and now a debate over Westernization versus Russianization in Boris Yeltsin's country. A West at the peak of its power confronts non-Wests that increasingly have the desire, the will and the resources to shape the world in non-Western ways.

In the past, the elites of non-Western societies were usually the people who were most involved with the West, had been educated at Oxford, the Sorbonne or Sandhurst, and had absorbed Western attitudes and values. At the same time, the populace in non-Western countries often remained deeply imbued with the indigenous culture. Now, however, these relationships are being reversed. A de-Westernization and indigenization of elites is occurring in many non-Western countries at the same time that Western, usually American, cultures, styles and habits become more popular among the mass of the people.

Fifth, cultural characteristics and differences are less mutable and hence less easily compromised and resolved than political and economic ones. In the former Soviet Union, communists can become democrats, the rich can become poor and the poor rich, but Russians cannot become Estonians and Azeris cannot become Armenians. In class and ideological conflicts, the key question was "Which side are you on?" and people could and did choose sides and change sides. In conflicts between civilizations, the question is "What are you?" That is a given that cannot be changed. And as we know, from Bosnia to the Caucasus to the Sudan, the wrong answer to that question can mean a bullet in the head. Even more than ethnicity, religion discriminates sharply and exclusively among people. A person can be half-French and half-Arab and simultaneously even a citizen of two countries. It is more difficult to be half-Catholic and half-Muslim.

Finally, economic regionalism is increasing. The proportions of total trade that were intraregional rose between 1980 and 1989 from 51 percent to 59 percent in Europe, 33 percent to 37 percent in East Asia, and 32 percent to 36 percent in North America. The importance of regional economic blocs is likely to continue to increase in the future. On the one hand, successful economic regionalism will reinforce civilization-consciousness. On the other hand, economic regionalism may succeed only when it is rooted in a common civilization. The European Community rests on the shared foundation of European culture and Western Christianity. The success of the North American Free Trade Area depends on the convergence now underway of Mexican, Canadian and American cultures. Japan, in contrast, faces difficulties in creating a comparable economic entity in East Asia because Japan is a society and civilization unique to itself. However strong the trade and investment links Japan may develop with other East Asian countries, its cultural differences with those countries inhibit and perhaps preclude its promoting regional economic integration like that in Europe and North America.

Common culture, in contrast, is clearly facilitating the rapid expansion of the economic relations between the People's Republic of China and Hong Kong, Taiwan, Singapore and the overseas Chinese communities in other Asian countries. With the Cold War over, cultural commonalities increasingly overcome ideological differences, and mainland China and Taiwan move closer together. If cultural commonality is a prerequisite for economic integration, the principal East Asian economic bloc of the future is likely to be centered on China. This bloc is, in fact, already coming into existence. As Murray Weidenbaum has observed,

> Despite the current Japanese dominance of the region, the Chinese-based economy of Asia is rapidly emerging as a new epicenter for industry, commerce and finance. This strategic area contains substantial amounts of technology and manufacturing capability (Taiwan), outstanding entrepreneurial, marketing and services acumen (Hong Kong), a fine communications network (Singapore), a tremendous pool of financial capital (all three), and very large endowments of land, resources and labor (mainland China) . . . . From Guangzhou to Singapore, from Kuala Lumpur to Manila, this influential network—often based on extensions of the traditional clans—has been described as the backbone of the East Asian economy.[1]

Culture and religion also form the basis of the Economic Cooperation Organization, which brings together ten non-Arab Muslim countries: Iran, Pakistan, Turkey, Azerbaijan, Kazakhstan, Kyrgyzstan, Turkmenistan, Tadjikistan,

Uzbekistan and Afghanistan. One impetus to the revival and expansion of this organization, founded originally in the 1960s by Turkey, Pakistan and Iran, is the realization by the leaders of several of these countries that they had no chance of admission to the European Community. Similarly, Caricom, the Central American Common Market and Mercosur rest on common cultural foundations. Efforts to build a broader Caribbean-Central American economic entity bridging the Anglo-Latin divide, however, have to date failed.

As people define their identity in ethnic and religious terms, they are likely to see an "us" versus "them" relation existing between themselves and people of different ethnicity or religion. The end of ideologically defined states in Eastern Europe and the former Soviet Union permits traditional ethnic identities and animosities to come to the fore. Differences in culture and religion create differences over policy issues, ranging from human rights to immigration to trade and commerce to the environment. Geographical propinquity give rise to conflicting territorial claims from Bosnia to Mindanao. Most important, the efforts of the West to promote its values of democracy and liberalism as universal values, to maintain its military predominance and to advance its economic interests engender countering responses from other civilizations. Decreasingly able to mobilize support and form coalitions on the basis of ideology, governments and groups will increasingly attempt to mobilize support by appealing to common religion and civilization identity.

The clash of civilizations thus occurs at two levels. At the micro-level, adjacent groups along the fault lines between civilizations struggle, often violently, over the control of territory and each other. At the macro-level, states from different civilizations compete for relative military and economic power, struggle over the control of international institutions and third parties, and competitively promote their particular political and religious values. . . .

CIVILIZATION RALLYING: THE KIN-COUNTRY SYNDROME

Groups or states belonging to one civilization that become involved in war with people from a different civilization naturally try to rally support from other members of their own civilization. As the post-Cold War world evolves, civilization commonality, what H.D.S. Greenway has termed the "kin-country" syndrome, is replacing political ideology and traditional balance of power considerations as the principal basis for cooperation and coalitions. It can be seen gradually emerging in the post-Cold War conflicts in the Persian Gulf, the Caucasus and Bosnia. None of these was a full-scale war between civilizations, but each involved some elements of civilizational rallying, which seemed to become more important as the conflict continued and which may provide a foretaste of the future.

. . . In the Gulf War one Arab state invaded another and then fought a coalition of Arab, Western and other states: While only a few Muslim governments overtly supported Saddam Hussein, many Arab elites privately cheered him on, and he was highly popular among large sections of the Arab publics. Islamic fundamentalist movements universally supported Iraq rather than the Western-backed governments of Kuwait and Saudi

Arabia. Forswearing Arab nationalism, Saddam Hussein explicitly invoked an Islamic appeal. He and his supporters attempted to define the war as a war between civilizations. "It is not the world against Iraq," as Safar Al-Hawali, dean of Islamic Studies at the Umm Al-Qura University in Mecca, put it in a widely circulated tape. "It is the West against Islam." Ignoring the rivalry between Iran and Iraq, the chief Iranian religious leader, Ayatollah Ali Khamenei, called for a holy war against the West: "The struggle against American aggression, greed, plans and policies will be counted as a jihad, and anybody who is killed on that path is a martyr." "This is a war," King Hussein of Jordan argued, "against all Arabs and all Muslims and not against Iraq alone."

The rallying of substantial sections of Arab elites and publics behind Saddam Hussein caused those Arab governments in the anti-Iraq coalition to moderate their activities and temper their public statements. Arab governments opposed or distanced themselves from subsequent Western efforts to apply pressure on Iraq, including enforcement of a no-fly zone in the summer of 1992 and the bombing of Iraq in January 1993. The Western-Soviet-Turkish-Arab anti-Iraq coalition of 1990 had by 1993 become a coalition of almost only the West and Kuwait against Iraq.

Muslims contrasted Western actions against Iraq with the West's failure to protect Bosnians against Serbs and to impose sanctions on Israel for violating U.N. resolutions. The West, they alleged, was using a double standard. A world of clashing civilizations, however, is inevitably a world of double standards: people apply one standard to their kin-countries and a different standard to others. . . .

Civilization rallying to date has been limited, but it has been growing, and it clearly has the potential to spread much further. As the conflict . . . in the Persian Gulf . . . continued, the positions of nations and the cleavages between them increasingly were along civilizational lines. Populist politicians, religious leaders and the media have found it a potent means of arousing mass support and of pressuring hesitant governments. In the coming years, the local conflicts most likely to escalate into major wars will be those, as in Bosnia and the Caucasus, along the fault lines between civilizations. The next world war, if there is one, will be a war between civilizations.

THE WEST VERSUS THE REST

The West is now at an extraordinary peak of power in relation to other civilizations. Its superpower opponent has disappeared from the map. Military conflict among Western states is unthinkable, and Western military power is unrivaled. Apart from Japan, the West faces no economic challenge. It dominates international political and security institutions and with Japan international economic institutions. Global political and security issues are effectively settled by a directorate of the United States, Britain and France, world economic issues by a directorate of the United States, Germany and Japan, all of which maintain extraordinarily close relations with each other to the exclusion of lesser and largely non-Western countries. Decisions made at the U.N. Security Council or in the International Monetary Fund that reflect the interests of the West are presented to the world as reflecting the desires of the world community. The very phrase "the world community" has become the euphemistic collective noun (replacing "the Free World") to give global legitimacy to actions reflecting the interests of the United States and other Western powers.[2] Through the IMF and other international economic institutions, the West promotes its economic interests and imposes on other nations the economic policies it thinks appropriate. In any poll of non-Western peoples, the IMF undoubtedly would win the support of finance ministers and a few others, but get an overwhelmingly unfavorable rating from just about everyone else, who would agree with Georgy Arbatov's characterization of IMF officials as "neo-Bolsheviks who love expropriating other people's money, imposing undemocratic and alien rules of economic and political conduct and stifling economic freedom."

Western domination of the U.N. Security Council and its decisions, tempered only by occasional abstention by China, produced U.N. legitimation of the West's use of force to drive Iraq out of Kuwait and its elimination of Iraq's sophisticated weapons and capacity to produce such weapons. It also produced the quite unprecedented action by the United States, Britain and France in getting the Security Council to demand that Libya hand over the Pan Am 103 bombing suspects and then to impose sanctions when Libya refused. After defeating the largest Arab army, the West did not hesitate to throw its weight around in the Arab world. The West in effect is using international institutions, military power and economic resources to run the world in ways that will maintain Western predominance, protect Western interests and promote Western political and economic values.

That at least is the way in which non-Westerners see the new world, and there is a significant element of truth in their view. Differences in power and struggles for military, economic and institutional power are thus one source of conflict between the West and other civilizations. Differences in culture, that is basic values and beliefs, are a second source of conflict. V. S. Naipaul has argued that Western civilization is the "universal civilization" that "fits all men." At a superficial level much of Western culture has indeed permeated the rest of the world. At a more basic level, however, Western concepts differ fundamentally from those prevalent in other civilizations. Western ideas of individualism, liberalism, constitutionalism, human rights, equality, liberty, the rule of law, democracy, free markets, the separation of church and state, often have little resonance in Islamic, Confucian, Japanese, Hindu, Buddhist or Orthodox cultures. Western efforts to propagate such ideas produce instead a reaction against "human rights imperialism" and a reaffirmation of indigenous values, as can be seen in the support for religious fundamentalism by the younger generation in non-Western cultures. The very notion that there could be a "universal civilization" is a Western idea, directly at odds with the particularism of most Asian societies and their emphasis on what distinguishes one people from another. Indeed, the author of a review of 100 comparative studies of values in different societies concluded that "the values that are most important in the West are least important worldwide."[3] In the political realm, of course, these differences are most manifest in the efforts of the United States and other Western powers to induce other peoples to adopt Western ideas concerning democracy and human rights. Modern democratic government originated in the West. When it has developed in non-Western societies it has usually been the product of Western colonialism or imposition.

The central axis of world politics in the future is likely to be, in Kishore Mahbubani's phrase, the conflict between "the West and the Rest" and the responses of non-Western civilizations to Western power and values.[4] Those responses generally take one or a combination of three forms. At one extreme, non-Western states can, like Burma and North Korea, attempt to pursue a course of isolation, to insulate their societies from penetration or "corruption" by the West, and, in effect, to opt out of participation in the Western-dominated global community. The costs of this course, however, are high, and few states have pursued it exclusively. A second alternative, the equivalent of "band-wagoning" in international relations theory, is to attempt to join the West and accept its values and institutions. The third alternative is to attempt to "balance" the West by developing economic and military power and cooperating with other nonWestern societies against the West, while preserving indigenous values and institutions; in short, to modernize but not to Westernize.

THE TORN COUNTRIES

In the future, as people differentiate themselves by civilization, countries with large numbers of peoples of different civilizations, such as the Soviet Union and Yugoslavia, are candidates for dismemberment. Some other countries have a fair degree of cultural homogeneity but are divided over whether their society belongs to one civilization or another. These are torn countries. Their leaders typically wish to pursue a bandwagoning strategy and to make their countries members of the West, but the history, culture and traditions of their countries are non-Western. The most obvious and prototypical torn country is Turkey. The late twentieth-century leaders of Turkey have followed in the Attatürk tradition and defined Turkey as a modern, secular, Western nation state. They allied Turkey with the West in NATO and in the Gulf War; they applied for membership in the European Community. At the same time, however, elements in Turkish society have supported an Islamic revival and have argued that Turkey is basically a Middle Eastern Muslim society. In addition, while the elite of Turkey has defined Turkey as a Western society, the elite of the West refuses to accept Turkey as such. Turkey will not become a member of the European Community, and the real reason, as President Özal said, "is that we are Muslim and they are Christian and they don't say that." Having rejected Mecca, and then being rejected by Brussels, where does Turkey look? Tashkent may be the answer. The end of the Soviet Union gives Turkey the opportunity to become the leader of a revived Turkic civilization involving seven countries from the borders of Greece to those of China. Encouraged by the West, Turkey is making strenuous efforts to carve out this new identity for itself. . . .

To redefine its civilization identity, a torn country must meet three requirements. First, its political and economic elite has to be generally supportive of and enthusiastic about this move. Second, its public has to be willing to acquiesce in the redefinition. Third, the dominant groups in the recipient civilization have to be willing to embrace the convert. . . .

THE CONFUCIAN-ISLAMIC CONNECTION

The obstacles to non-Western countries joining the West vary considerably. They are least for Latin American and East European countries. They are greater for the Orthodox countries of the former Soviet Union. They are still greater for Muslim, Confucian, Hindu and Buddhist societies. Japan has established a unique position for itself as an associate member of the West: it is in the West in some respects but clearly not of the West in important dimensions. Those countries that for reason of culture and power do not wish to, or cannot, join the West compete with the West by developing their own economic, military and political power. They do this by promoting their internal development and by cooperating with other non-Western countries. The most prominent form of this cooperation is the Confucian-Islamic connection that has emerged to challenge Western interests, values and power.

Almost without exception, Western countries are reducing their military power; under Yeltsin's leadership so also is Russia. China, North Korea and several Middle Eastern states, however, are significantly expanding their military capabilities. They are doing this by the import of arms from Western and non-Western sources and by the development of indigenous arms industries. One result is the emergence of what Charles Krauthammer has called ''Weapon States,'' and the

Weapon States are not Western states. Another result is the redefinition of arms control, which is a Western concept and a Western goal. During the Cold War the primary purpose of arms control was to establish a stable military balance between the United States and its allies and the Soviet Union and its allies. In the post-Cold War world the primary objective of arms control is to prevent the development by non-Western societies of military capabilities that could threaten Western interests. The West attempts to do this through international agreements, economic pressure and controls on the transfer of arms and weapons technologies.

The conflict between the West and the Confucian-Islamic states focuses largely, although not exclusively, on nuclear, chemical and biological weapons, ballistic missiles and other sophisticated means for delivering them, and the guidance, intelligence and other electronic capabilities for achieving that goal. The West promotes nonproliferation as a universal norm and nonproliferation treaties and inspections as means of realizing that norm. It also threatens a variety of sanctions against those who promote the spread of sophisticated weapons and proposes some benefits for those who do not. The attention of the West focuses, naturally, on nations that are actually or potentially hostile to the West.

The non-Western nations, on the other hand, assert their right to acquire and to deploy whatever weapons they think necessary for their security. They also have absorbed, to the full, the truth of the response of the Indian defense minister when asked what lesson he learned from the Gulf War: ''Don't fight the United States unless you have nuclear weapons.'' Nuclear weapons, chemical weapons and missiles are viewed, probably erroneously, as the potential equalizer of superior Western conventional power. China, of course, already has nuclear weapons; Pakistan and India have the capability to deploy them. North Korea, Iran, Iraq, Libya and Algeria appear to be attempting to acquire them. A top Iranian official has declared that all Muslim states should acquire nuclear weapons, and in 1988 the president of Iran reportedly issued a directive calling for development of "offensive and defensive chemical, biological and radiological weapons." . . .

A Confucian-Islamic military connection has thus come into being, designed to promote acquisition by its members of the weapons and weapons technologies needed to counter the military power of the West. It may or may not last. At present, however, it is, as Dave McCurdy has said, "a renegades' mutual support pact, run by the proliferators and their hackers." A new form of arms competition is thus occurring between Islamic-Confucian states and the West. In an old-fashioned arms race, each side developed its own arms to balance or to achieve superiority against the other side. In this new form of arms competition, one side is developing its arms and the other side is attempting not to balance but to limit and prevent that arms build-up while at the same time reducing its own military capabilities.

IMPLICATIONS FOR THE WEST

This article does not argue that civilization identities will replace all other identities, that nation states will disappear, that each civilization will become a single coherent political entity, that groups within a civilization will not conflict with and even fight each other. This paper does set forth the hypotheses that differences between civilizations are real and important; civilization-consciousness is increasing; conflict between civilizations will supplant ideological and other forms of conflict as the dominant global form of conflict; international relations, historically a game played out within Western civilization, will increasingly be de-Westernized and become a game in which non-Western civilizations are actors and not simply objects; successful political, security and economic international institutions are more likely to develop within civilizations than across civilizations; conflicts between groups in different civilizations will be more frequent, more sustained and more violent than conflicts between groups in the same civilization; violent conflicts between groups in different civilizations are the most likely and most dangerous source of escalation that could lead to global wars; the paramount axis of world politics will be the relations between "the West and the Rest"; the elites in some torn non-Western countries will try to make their countries part of the West, but in most cases face major obstacles to accomplishing this; a central focus of conflict for the immediate future will be between the West and several Islamic-Confucian states.

This is not to advocate the desirability of conflicts between civilizations. It is to set forth descriptive hypotheses as to what the future may be like. If these are plausible hypotheses, however, it is necessary to consider their implications for Western policy. These implications should be divided between short-term advantage and long-term accommodation. In the short term it is clearly in the interest of the West to promote greater cooperation and unity within its own civilization, particularly between its European and North American components; to incorporate into the West societies in Eastern Europe and Latin America whose cultures are close to those of the West; to promote and maintain cooperative relations with Russia and Japan; to prevent escalation of local inter-civilization conflicts into major inter-civilization wars; to limit the expansion of the military strength of Confucian and Islamic states; to moderate the reduction of Western military capabilities and maintain military superiority in East and Southwest Asia; to exploit differences and conflicts among Confucian and Islamic states; to support in other civilizations groups sympathetic to Western values and interests; to strengthen international institutions that reflect and legitimate Western interests and values and to promote the involvement of non-Western states in those institutions.

In the longer term other measures would be called for. Western civilization is both Western and modern. Non-Western civilizations have attempted to become modern without becoming Western. To date only Japan has fully succeeded in this quest. Non-Western civilizations will continue to attempt to acquire the wealth, technology, skills, machines and weapons that are part of being modern. They will also attempt to reconcile this modernity with their traditional culture and values. Their economic and military strength relative to the West will increase. Hence the West will increasingly have to accommodate these non-Western modern civilizations whose power approaches that of the West but whose values and interests differ significantly from those of the West. This will require the West to maintain the economic and military power necessary to protect its interests in relation to these civilizations. It will also, however, require the West to develop a more profound understanding of the basic religious and philosophical assumptions underlying other civilizations and the ways in which people in those civilizations see their interests. It will require an effort to identify elements of commonality between Western and other civilizations. For the relevant future, there will be no universal civilization, but instead a world of different civilizations, each of which will have to learn to coexist with the others.

NOTES

1. Murray Weidenbaum, *Greater China: The Next Economic Superpower?*, St. Louis: Washington University Center for the Study of American Business, Contemporary Issues, Series 57, February 1993, pp. 2–3.
2. Almost invariably Western leaders claim they are acting on behalf of "the world community." One minor lapse occurred during the run-up to the Gulf War. In an interview on "Good Morning America," Dec. 21, 1990, British Prime Minister John Major referred to the actions "the West" was taking against Saddam Hussein. He quickly corrected himself and subsequently referred to "the world community." He was, however, right when he erred.
3. Harry C. Triandis, *The New York Times,* Dec. 25, 1990, p. 41, and "Cross-Cultural Studies of Individualism and Collectivism," Nebraska Symposium on Motivation, vol. 37, 1989, pp. 41–133.
4. Kishore Mahbubani, "The West and the Rest," *The National Interest,* Summer 1992, pp. 3–13.

QUESTIONS

1. Explain what Huntington means by "the clash of civilizations."

2. Do you think the current the ethnic conflicts in Bosnia, Somalia, and Rwanda strengthen or weaken Huntington's argument?

29. The Summoning

Fouad Ajami

In this article, Fouad Ajami responds to Huntington's essay "The Clash of Civilizations?" which maintains that the conflicts of the future will be based upon civilizations or cultures against each other. He argues, rather, that states will continue to be the primary actors in the international system and, thus, will act in their best interests. Ajami provides examples of states forsaking their traditional civilizations in favor of military, economic, and political gains. This selection is from the journal *Foreign Affairs* (1993).

Fouad Ajami is Jajid Khadduir Professor of Middle Eastern Studies with the School of Advanced International Studies at Johns Hopkins University.

In Joseph Conrad's *Youth,* a novella published at the turn of the century, Marlowe, the narrator, remembers when he first encountered "the East":

> And then, before I could open my lips, the East spoke to me, but it was in a Western voice. A torrent of words was poured into the enigmatical, the fateful silence; outlandish, angry words mixed with words and even whole sentences of good English, less strange but even more surprising. The voice swore and cursed violently; it riddled the solemn peace of the bay by a volley of abuse. It began by calling me Pig, and from that went crescendo into unmentionable adjectives—in English.

The young Marlowe knew that even the most remote civilization had been made and remade by the West, and taught new ways.

Not so Samuel P. Huntington. In a curious essay, "The Clash of Civilizations," Huntington has found his civilizations whole and intact, watertight under an eternal sky. Buried alive, as it were, during the years of the Cold War, these civilizations (Islamic, Slavic-Orthodox, Western, Confucian, Japanese, Hindu, etc.) rose as soon as the stone was rolled off, dusted themselves off, and proceeded to claim the loyalty of their adherents. For this student of history and culture, civilizations have always seemed messy creatures. Furrows run across whole civilizations, across individuals themselves—that was modernity's verdict. But Huntington looks past all that.

The crooked and meandering alleyways of the world are straightened out. With a sharp pencil and a steady hand Huntington marks out where one civilization ends and the wilderness of "the other" begins.

More surprising still is Huntington's attitude toward states, and their place in his scheme of things. From one of the most influential and brilliant students of the state and its national interest there now comes an essay that misses the slyness of states, the unsentimental and cold-blooded nature of so much of what they do as they pick their way through chaos. Despite the obligatory passage that states will remain "the most powerful actors in world affairs," states are written off, their place given over to clashing civilizations. In Huntington's words, "The next world war, if there is one, will be a war between civilizations."

THE POWER OF MODERNITY

Huntington's meditation is occasioned by his concern about the state of the West, its power and the terms of its engagement with "the rest."[1] "He who gives, dominates," the great historian Fernand Braudel observed of the traffic of civilizations. In making itself over the centuries, the West helped make the others as well. We have come to the end of this trail, Huntington is sure. He is impressed by the "de-Westernization" of societies, their "indigenization" and apparent willingness to go their own way. In his view of things such phenomena as the "Hinduization" of India and Islamic fundamentalism are ascendant. To these detours into "tradition" Huntington has assigned great force and power.

But Huntington is wrong. He has underestimated the tenacity of modernity and secularism in places that acquired these ways against great odds, always perilously close to the abyss, the darkness never far. India will not become a Hindu state. The inheritance of Indian secularism will hold. The vast middle class will defend it, keep the order intact to maintain India's—and its own—place in the modern world of nations. There exists in that anarchic polity an instinctive dread of playing with fires that might consume it. Hindu chauvinism may coarsen the public life of the country, but the state and the middle class that sustains it know that a detour into religious fanaticism is a fling with ruin. A resourceful middle class partakes of global culture and norms. A century has passed since the Indian bourgeoisie, through its political vehicle the Indian National Congress, set out to claim for itself and India a place among nations. Out of that long struggle to overturn British rule and the parallel struggle against "communalism," the advocates of the national idea built a large and durable state. They will not cede all this for a political kingdom of Hindu purity.

We have been hearing from the traditionalists, but we should not exaggerate their power, for traditions are often most insistent and loud when they rupture, when people no longer really believe and when age-old customs lose their ability to keep men and women at home. The phenomenon we have dubbed as Islamic fundamentalism is less a sign of resurgence than of panic and bewilderment and guilt that the border with "the other" has been crossed. Those young urban poor, half-educated in the cities of the Arab world, and their Sorbonne-educated lay preachers, can they be evidence of a genuine return to tradition? They crash Europe's and America's gates in search of liberty and work, and they rail against the sins of the West. It is easy to understand Huntington's frustration with this kind of complexity, with the strange mixture of attraction and repulsion that the West breeds, and his need to simplify matters, to mark out the borders of civilizations.

Tradition-mongering is no proof, though, that these civilizations outside the West are intact, or that their thrashing about is an indication of their vitality, or that they present a conventional threat of arms. Even so thorough and far-reaching an attack against Western hegemony as Iran's theocratic revolution could yet fail to wean that society from the culture of the West. That country's cruel revolution was born of the realization of the "armed Imam" that his people were being seduced by America's ways. The gates had been thrown wide open in the 1970s, and the high walls Ayatollah Khomeini built around his polity were a response to that cultural seduction. Swamped, Iran was "rescued" by men claiming authenticity as their banner. One extreme led to another.

"We prayed for the rain of mercy and received floods," was the way Mehdi Bazargan, the decent modernist who was Khomeini's first prime minister, put it. But the millennium has been brought down to earth, and the dream of a pan-Islamic revolt in Iran's image has vanished into the wind. The terror and the shabbiness have caught up with the utopia. Sudan could emulate the Iranian "revolutionary example." But this will only mean the further pauperization and ruin of a desperate land. There is no rehabilitation of the Iranian example.

A battle rages in Algeria, a society of the Mediterranean, close to Europe—a wine-producing country for that matter—and in Egypt between the secular powers that be and an Islamic alternative.

But we should not rush to print with obituaries of these states. In Algeria the nomenklatura of the National Liberation Front failed and triggered a revolt of the young, the underclass and the excluded. The revolt raised an Islamic banner. Caught between a regime they despised and a reign of virtue they feared, the professionals and the women and the modernists of the middle class threw their support to the forces of "order." They hailed the army's crackdown on the Islamicists; they allowed the interruption of a democratic process sure to bring the Islamicists to power; they accepted the "liberties" protected by the repression, the devil you know rather than the one you don't.

The Algerian themes repeat in the Egyptian case, although Egypt's dilemma over its Islamicist opposition is not as acute. The Islamicists continue to hound the state, but they cannot bring it down. There is no likelihood that the Egyptian state—now riddled with enough complacency and corruption to try the celebrated patience and good humor of the Egyptians—will go under. This is an old and skeptical country. It knows better than to trust its fate to enforcers of radical religious dogma. These are not deep and secure structures of order that the national middle classes have put in place. But they will not be blown away overnight.

Nor will Turkey lose its way, turn its back on Europe and chase after some imperial temptation in the scorched domains of Central Asia. Huntington sells that country's modernity and secularism short when he writes that the Turks—rejecting Mecca and rejected by Brussels—are likely to head to Tashkent in search of a Pan-Turkic role. There is no journey to that imperial past. Ataturk severed that link with fury, pointed his country westward, embraced the civilization of Europe and did it without qualms or second thoughts. It is on Frankfurt and Bonn—and Washington—not on Baku and Tashkent that the attention of the Turks is fixed. The inheritors of Ataturk's legacy are too shrewd to go chasing after imperial glory, gathering about them the scattered domains of the Turkish peoples. After their European possessions were lost, the Turks clung to Thrace and to all that this link to Europe represents.

Huntington would have nations battle for civilizational ties and fidelities when they would rather scramble for their market shares, learn how to compete in a merciless world economy, provide jobs, move out of poverty. For their part, the "management gurus" and those who believe that the interests have vanquished the passions in today's world tell us that men want Sony, not soil.[2] There is a good deal of truth in what they say, a terrible exhaustion with utopias, a reluctance to set out on expeditions of principle or belief. It is hard to think of Russia, ravaged as it is by inflation, taking up the grand cause of a "second Byzantium," the bearer of the orthodox-Slavic torch.

And where is the Confucian world Huntington speaks of? In the busy and booming lands of the Pacific Rim, so much of politics and ideology has been sublimated into finance that the nations of East Asia have turned into veritable workshops. The civilization of Cathay is dead; the Indonesian archipelago is deaf to the call of the religious radicals in Tehran as it tries to catch up with Malaysia and Singapore. A different wind blows in the lands of the Pacific. In that world economics, not politics, is in command. The world is far less antiseptic than Lee

Kuan Yew, the sage of Singapore, would want it to be. A nemesis could lie in wait for all the prosperity that the 1980s brought to the Pacific. But the lands of the Pacific Rim—protected, to be sure, by an American security umbrella—are not ready for a great falling out among the nations. And were troubles to visit that world they would erupt within its boundaries, not across civilizational lines.

The things and ways that the West took to "the rest"—those whole sentences of good English that Marlowe heard a century ago—have become the ways of the world. The secular idea, the state system and the balance of power, pop culture jumping tariff walls and barriers, the state as an instrument of welfare, all these have been internalized in the remotest places. We have stirred up the very storms into which we now ride.

THE WEAKNESS OF TRADITION

Nations "cheat": they juggle identities and interests. Their ways meander. One would think that the traffic of arms from North Korea and China to Libya and Iran and Syria shows this—that states will consort with any civilization, however alien, as long as the price is right and the goods are ready. Huntington turns this routine act of selfishness into a sinister "Confucian-Islamic connection." There are better explanations: the commerce of renegades, plain piracy, an "underground economy" that picks up the slack left by the great arms suppliers (the United States, Russia, Britain and France).

Contrast the way Huntington sees things with Braudel's depiction of the traffic between Christendom and Islam across the Mediterranean in the sixteenth century—and this was in a religious age, after the fall of Constantinople to the Turks and of Granada to the Spanish:

"Men passed to and fro, indifferent to frontiers, states and creeds. They were more aware of the necessities for shipping and trade, the hazards of war and piracy, the opportunities for complicity or betrayal provided by circumstances."[3]

Those kinds of "complicities" and ambiguities are missing in Huntington's analysis. Civilizations are crammed into the nooks and crannies—and checkpoints—of the Balkans. Huntington goes where only the brave would venture, into that belt of mixed populations stretching from the Adriatic to the Baltic. Countless nationalisms make their home there, all aggrieved, all possessed of memories of a fabled past and equally ready for the demagogues vowing to straighten a messy map. In the thicket of these pan-movements he finds the line that marked "the eastern boundary of Western Christianity in the year 1500." The scramble for turf between Croatian nationalism and its Serbian counterpart, their "joint venture" in carving up Bosnia, are made into a fight of the inheritors of Rome, Byzantium and Islam.

But why should we fall for this kind of determinism? "An outsider who travels the highway between Zagreb and Belgrade is struck not by the decisive historical fault line which falls across the lush Slavonian plain but by the opposite. Serbs and Croats speak the same language, give or take a few hundred words, have shared the same village way of life for centuries."[4] The cruel genius of Slobodan Milosevic and Franjo Tudjman, men on horseback familiar in lands and situations of distress, was to make their bids for power into grand civilizational undertakings—the ramparts of the Enlightenment defended against Islam or, in Tudjman's case, against the heirs of the Slavic-Orthodox faith. Differences had to be magnified. Once Tito, an equal opportu-

nity oppressor, had passed from the scene, the balancing act among the nationalities was bound to come apart. Serbia had had a measure of hegemony in the old system. But of the world that loomed over the horizon—privatization and economic reform—the Serbs were less confident. The citizens of Sarajevo and the Croats and the Slovenes had a head start on the rural Serbs. And so the Serbs hacked at the new order of things with desperate abandon.

Some Muslim volunteers came to Bosnia, driven by faith and zeal. Huntington sees in these few stragglers the sweeping power of "civilizational rallying," proof of the hold of what he calls the "kin-country syndrome." This is delusion. No Muslim cavalry was ever going to ride to the rescue. The Iranians may have railed about holy warfare, but the Chetniks went on with their work. The work of order and mercy would have had to be done by the United States if the cruel utopia of the Serbs was to be contested.

It should have taken no powers of prophecy to foretell where the fight in the Balkans would end. The abandonment of Bosnia was of a piece with the ways of the world. No one wanted to die for Srebrenica. The Europeans averted their gaze, as has been their habit. The Americans hesitated for a moment as the urge to stay out of the Balkans did battle with the scenes of horror. Then "prudence" won out. Milosevic and Tudjman may need civilizational legends, but there is no need to invest their projects of conquest with this kind of meaning.

In his urge to find that relentless war across Islam's "bloody borders," Huntington buys Saddam Hussein's interpretation of the Gulf War. It was, for Saddam and Huntington, a civilizational battle. But the Gulf War's verdict was entirely different. For if there was a campaign that laid bare the interests of states, the lengths to which they will go to restore a tolerable balance of power in a place that matters, this was it. A local despot had risen close to the wealth of the Persian Gulf, and a Great Power from afar had come to the rescue. The posse assembled by the Americans had Saudi, Turkish, Egyptian, Syrian, French, British and other riders.

True, when Saddam Hussein's dream of hegemony was shattered, the avowed secularist who had devastated the *ulama,* the men of religion in his country, fell back on Ayatollah Khomeini's language of fire and brimstone and borrowed the symbolism and battle cry of his old Iranian nemesis. But few, if any, were fooled by this sudden conversion to the faith. They knew the predator for what he was: he had a Christian foreign minister (Tariq Aziz); he had warred against the Iranian revolution for nearly a decade and had prided himself on the secularism of his regime. Prudent men of the social and political order, the *ulama* got out of the way and gave their state the room it needed to check the predator at the Saudi/Kuwaiti border.[5] They knew this was one of those moments when purity bows to necessity. Ten days after Saddam swept into Kuwait, Saudi Arabia's most authoritative religious body, the Council of Higher Ulama, issued a *fatwa,* or a ruling opinion, supporting the presence of Arab and Islamic and "other friendly forces." All means of defense, the *ulama* ruled, were legitimate to guarantee the people "the safety of their religion, their wealth, and their honor and their blood, to protect what they enjoy of safety and stability." At some remove, in Egypt, that country's leading religious figure, the Shaykh of Al Ashar, Shaykh Jadd al Haqq,

denounced Saddam as a tyrant and brushed aside his Islamic pretensions as a cover for tyranny.

Nor can the chief Iranian religious leader Ayatollah Ali Khamenei's rhetoric against the Americans during the Gulf War be taken as evidence of Iran's disposition toward that campaign. Crafty men, Iran's rulers sat out that war. They stood to emerge as the principal beneficiaries of Iraq's defeat. The American-led campaign against Iraq held out the promise of tilting the regional balance in their favor. No tears were shed in Iran for what befell Saddam Hussein's regime.

It is the mixed gift of living in hard places that men and women know how to distinguish between what they hear and what there is: no illusions were thus entertained in vast stretches of the Arab Muslim world about Saddam, or about the campaign to thwart him for that matter. The fight in the gulf was seen for what it was: a bid for primacy met by an imperial expedition that laid it to waste. A circle was closed in the gulf: where once the order in the region "east of Suez" had been the work of the British, it was now provided by Pax Americana. The new power standing sentry in the gulf belonged to the civilization of the West, as did the prior one. But the American presence had the anxious consent of the Arab lands of the Persian Gulf. The stranger coming in to check the kinsmen.

The world of Islam divides and subdivides. The battle lines in the Caucasus, too, are not coextensive with civilizational fault lines. The lines follow the interests of states. Where Huntington sees a civilizational duel between Armenia and Azerbaijan, the Iranian state has cast religious zeal and fidelity to the wind. Indeed, in that battle the Iranians have tilted toward Christian Armenia.

THE WRIT OF STATES

We have been delivered into a new world, to be sure. But it is not a world where the writ of civilizations runs. Civilizations and civilizational fidelities remain. There is to them an astonishing measure of permanence. But let us be clear: civilizations do not control states, states control civilizations. States avert their gaze from blood ties when they need to; they see brotherhood and faith and kin when it is in their interest to do so.

We remain in a world of self-help. The solitude of states continues; the disorder in the contemporary world has rendered that solitude more pronounced. No way has yet been found to reconcile France to Pax Americana's hegemony, or to convince it to trust its security or cede its judgment to the preeminent Western power. And no Azeri has come up with a way the lands of Islam could be rallied to the fight over Nagorno Karabakh. The sky has not fallen in Kuala Lumpur or in Tunis over the setbacks of Azerbaijan in its fight with Armenia.

The lesson bequeathed us by Thucydides in his celebrated dialogue between the Melians and the Athenians remains. The Melians, it will be recalled, were a colony of the Lacedaemonians. Besieged by Athens, they held out and were sure that the Lacedaemonians were "bound, if only for very shame, to come to the aid of their kindred." The Melians never wavered in their confidence in their "civilizational" allies: "Our common blood insures our fidelity."[6] We know what became of the Melians. Their allies did not turn up, their island was sacked, their world laid to waste.

NOTES

1. The West itself is unexamined in Huntington's essay. No fissures run through it. No multiculturalists are heard from. It is orderly within its ramparts. What doubts Huntington has about the will within the walls, he has kept within himself. He has assumed that his call to unity will be answered, for outside flutter the banners of the Saracens and the Confucians.
2. Kenichi Ohmae, "Global Consumers Want Sony, Not Soil," *New Perspectives Quarterly,* Fall 1991.
3. Ferdinand Braudel, *The Mediterranean and the Mediterranean World in the Age of Philip II,* Vol. II, New York: Harper & Row, 1976, p. 759.
4. Michael Ignatieff, "The Balkan Tragedy," *New York Review of Books,* May 13, 1993.
5. Huntington quotes one Safar al Hawali, a religious radical at Umm al Qura University in Mecca, to the effect that the campaign against Iraq was another Western campaign against Islam. But this can't do as evidence. Safar al Hawali was a crank. Among the *ulama* class and the religious scholars in Saudi Arabia he was, for all practical purposes, a loner.
6. Thucydides, *The Peloponnesian War,* New York: The Modern American Library, 1951, pp. 334-335.

QUESTIONS

1. What weaknesses does Ajami identify in "The Clash of Civilizations?"

2. How do you think Huntington would respond to Ajami's criticism?

Chapter 6

DECISION-MAKING PROCESS THEORY

COMPONENTS OF DECISION-MAKING THEORY

Focus of Analysis ········▶	• Internal decision-making process of governments
Major Actors ········▶	• Bureaucracies, agencies, and organizations within government
Behavior of States ········▶	• States not necessarily rational actors • Complex interplay of internal and external factors
Basis of a State's Foreign Policy ········▶	• Compromise/competition between government agencies • Adherence to standard operating procedures • Incrementalism
Key Concepts ········▶	• Bureaucracy; Bureaucratic politics model; Incrementalism; Decision-making organizational process model; Rational actor model; Standard operating procedures

INTRODUCTION

In the introduction to Part II, we discussed how state level theories examine the impact of domestic factors on the course and conduct of foreign policy. This chapter focuses on decision-making process theory; a state level theory that emphasizes the role of bureaucratic organizations, and how the process of decision-making within these organizations, and within a government as a whole, can affect its foreign policy and international relations.

As this notion suggests, decision-making process theory disassembles the state bureaucratic structure, taking a targeted look at specific component parts to understand how decisions are made. The idea here is that different factions of a large bureaucracy are likely to approach problems or issues from different perspectives and with different preconceptions and priorities. These different perspectives result from the fact that each faction or department has unique responsibilities. A pattern of decision-making is established based on the priorities that stem from these individualized responsibilities. Thus, bureaucratic agencies address issues from different points of view, or, as the saying goes, "Where you stand is largely determined by where you sit." Certainly, international conditions and forces surrounding an event or crisis have an impact, but, according to decision-making process theorists, the inner workings of the bureaucracy—bargaining strategies, departmental priorities, etc.—cannot be disassociated from an assessment of foreign policy or international relations.

BUREAUCRACIES AND DECISION-MAKING

Before we proceed in our discussion of decision-making process theory, it might be helpful to answer two important questions. First, what is a bureaucracy, and, second, what do we mean by decision-making? A **bureaucracy** could be defined as a network of interconnected departments and organizations designed to manage and administrate the operations of a state. Authority for different aspects of this administration and management is diffused throughout the various offices. That is, a single department generally takes the lead over a unique and specific area of policy or governance, though several departments usually have input into any given decision.

Decision-making theorists believe the manner in which government bureaucracies arrive at these decisions is a critical part of both foreign policy and relations between states. The method that a state or bureaucracy uses to reach decisions is called **decision-making.** Decision-making is the process by which government officials select a policy to pursue from among a range of different options. A key part of this process and a defining feature of large bureaucracies is their dependence on **standard operating procedures (SOPs).** SOPs are accepted routines or patterns used by bureaucracies to organize and simplify the decision-making process. Standard operating procedures are utilized to handle problems or make decisions on a wide array of issues that confront governments on a daily basis—from internal personnel decisions to matters of international trade and diplomacy. Bureaucracies use SOPs because time, resources, and information in the decision-making process can be in short supply. Presumably, these standardized procedures simplify the decision-making process and help preserve the orderly functioning of government.

While standard operating procedures are aimed at making government more efficient and methodical, they have a profound impact on the type and quality of decisions made, as well as the policies adopted by governments. By relying on a set of specific procedures, a bureaucracy can limit the range and variety of policy options available to decision-makers. Hence, both bureaucracies and leaders tend to depend on past policies or procedures in handling new problems. New policy decisions generally conform to those made in the past. A new, non-conforming policy would not only send a mixed message about a government's foreign policy platform and complicate the implementation process but would also disrupt the orderly workings of bureaucratic policy formulation. Therefore, if it is impossible to find a policy that is compatible with established SOPs, bureaucracies conduct a narrow search for alternatives and solutions that will require minimum change from accepted practices.

New policies, then, are often the result of what is called **incrementalism.** That is, a bureaucracy allows only incremental or marginal alterations in existing policy to prevent major changes from established norms. This "new" policy may not be the best available alternative but is, instead, a broadly palatable option resulting from bargains and compromises between competing individuals and bureaucratic organs or factions. To a certain extent, the nature of a bureaucracy—with its competing departments jostling for position—creates a measure of rivalry, territoriality, and one-up-manship among the various offices. This translates into a cautious pattern of decision-making, designed to avoid risk-taking both in the process itself and with respect to the final decision or policy.

STATES AND FOREIGN POLICY

Decision-making process theorists view foreign policy and international relations largely as a by-product of these inner-workings and the interaction of various state bureaucracies. The development of the decision-making approach to the study of foreign policy and international relations actually began in the 1950s as scholars became interested in applying the methodology of the traditional "hard" sciences to the study of human behavior. The "behavioralist school" of political science emerged as scholars began to rely more on the use of empirical research and quantitative analysis in developing and testing theories of international politics. Emphasizing the decision-making process of governments fit in quite well with this new, more scientific approach to the study of international relations and incorporated a number of features that had, up to that point, been largely overlooked.

The excerpt from Snyder, Brock, and Sapin's book, *Foreign Policy Decision-Making,* represents one of the first systematic approaches to the study of the decision-making process. Snyder and his colleagues developed a method for examining various components that influence the decisions taken by governments. The authors set up diagrams of "relevant factors" that might influence a state's behavior in a given situation. The premise here is that once the situation is defined, the path or policy a state chooses can be predicted by determining the factors that are relevant to the choice.

The diversity of viewpoints and responsibilities within a bureaucracy almost inevitably leads to conflict. Making a decision is not merely a progression of selecting goals, accumulating information, analyzing the various choices, and selecting a policy that most optimizes those goals. Policies are the result of diplomatic bargaining and compromise that take place within and between government agencies and bureaucracies. Also, being part of a bureaucracy can affect an individual's perceptions of the decision-making process and their role within it. The structure, purpose, and objectives or duties of these organizations can influence the decisions made by individuals working within them. These conditions tend to direct their attention away from purely international objectives and toward internal, domestic, and intra-bureaucratic concerns.

There is a subtle but crucial distinction between this notion and the premise of the theories in the following chapter that specifically addresses the role of individuals. It might be said, without oversimplifying the difference between these ideas, that the discussion here revolves around how bureaucratic organizations affect individuals. The next section presents theories on how individuals affect government decisions.

According to decision-making process theorists, then, there are a number of factors that influence a state's foreign policy and international relations. First, individuals operating within a large bureaucratic organization are constrained by position, loyalties, and duties within their individual departments and the bureaucracy as a whole. Second, the standard operating procedures used to guide the functions and decisions of the bureaucracy can limit the range of policy options. Decisions or policies are made largely to conform to existing SOPs and are often the result of compromise between various factions (usually competing) within the bureaucratic organization. Finally, as a result, policy follows a fairly pedantic, incremental course that can be predicted based on precedent and on an analysis of the decision-making mechanism itself.

One of the classic works of theory using this framework is the study of the Cuban missile crisis by Graham Allison. In the excerpt, taken from Allison's article "Conceptual Models and the Cuban Missile Crisis," the author isolates three distinct models for explaining foreign policy decisions: the rational actor model, the organizational process model, and the bureaucratic politics model. According to the **rational actor model,** decision-makers carefully define and identify foreign policy problems, gather all available information about the foreign policy options, weigh all possible alternatives, and select policies that are most likely to promote the state's national interests.

By contrast, the **organizational process model** focuses on the routines, standard patterns of behavior, and institutional perspectives of particular agencies and their impact on foreign policy decisions. It assumes that all governments generally rely on standard operating procedures, are relatively predictable, and favor only marginal changes in existing policy. The **bureaucratic politics model** emphasizes the struggle between various agencies of the government and its impact on the decision-making process. This model contends that the formulation of policy is largely the result of the competition among government agencies, representing diverse views. Such a competitive process means that foreign policy is often based more on domestic political struggles than on objective calculations of the national interest.

The point of Allison's highly regarded study is that each of the three models produce different explanations and each provides its own unique insights into the foreign policy decision-making process. While each model has particular strengths and weaknesses, Allison concludes that a complete understanding of any foreign policy situation must take into account several different institutional, political, and international factors.

The final article by Jack Levy illustrates the importance of the bureaucratic process and its impact on decision-making in a military context. Levy discusses how the inflexible nature of standard operating procedures that characterize the military and its operations may contribute to the outbreak of war. Using the events and processes leading to World War I as a case study, Levy points to the confining nature of these organizational routines and how placing limitations or parameters on the exploration of ideas and possibilities may contribute to both political misunderstandings and military missteps.

A CRITIQUE OF DECISION-MAKING PROCESS THEORY

Certainly, it would be difficult to criticize proponents of decision-making process theory for overlooking the details and minutiae of government that are a part of how decisions might be made. The inclusive approach of decision-making process theory to how states interact has actually been the subject of criticism from realists for just this reason. In a classic forest-through-the-trees argument, some scholars have suggested that the decision-making framework focuses too much on the details of the foreign policy-making process, thus losing the broader analytical and theoretical implications of history and events. By attempting to incorporate such a broad range of factors into their analysis, decision-making process theorists are often accused of describing the interaction of states, as opposed to providing a true theory of international relations.

In response, Allison and other decision-making theorists actually challenge the realist assumption that assumes states base their foreign policy decisions on a rational cost-benefit analysis of the relative risks and potential gains associated with particular policy options as too narrow. They argue that while the rational actor model is valuable, it is also limited on its own and fails to provide an adequate explanation of international relations.

For example, the rational actor model suggests decision makers behave in a similar fashion, seeking to maximize strategic goals and objectives. The implication here is that governments use the best information available and select the policy that is most likely to maximize the national interests. Decision-making theory proceeds several steps farther, suggesting that all decisions must be analyzed and understood within the context of how governments really operate. Government bureaucracies function under conditions that often involve limited time, resources, and information—all of which are incompatible with the realist's rational-actor model. If we wish to understand why particular policies were selected over others, then decision-making theorists insist we must first understand the process by which these choices were made. In short, process affects outcome.

Decision-making theory has also been attacked for being western-centric. Critics contend that decision-making theory is useful primarily for explaining the pluralistic foreign policy process of western democratic governments. It does not, however, present an accurate model for studying the more centralized, hierarchic decision-making process of non-western, non-democratic states. Decision-making theorists counter that every type of government, from the most rigid authoritarian regime to pluralistic democracies, have large bureaucratic structures with competing interests. Bureaucratic politics and adherence to standard operating procedures are not limited to democratic regimes but represent vital parts of the decision-making process in any type of government.

In the end, the manner in which governments make decisions about relations with other nations, particularly regarding decisions on war and peace, are basic to the study of international politics. It is critical, therefore, to understand how those decisions are reached and how they are actually implemented. In order to do this, you must examine the relationship between the process and the decisions that are produced from it. Decision-making theory focuses on the complex policy-making process and the governmental and bureaucratic settings in which those decisions are made.

KEY CONCEPTS

Bureaucratic politics model is one of three conceptual models devised by Graham Allison to explain and predict the foreign policy behavior of states. The bureaucratic model focuses on the struggle between various agencies of the government and its impact on the decision-making process. This model contends that the formulation of policy is largely the result of the competition among government agencies, representing diverse views. Such a competitive process means that foreign policy is often based more on domestic political struggles than on objective calculations of the national interest.

Bureaucracy is a network of interconnected departments and organizations designed to manage and administrate the operations of a state.

Decision-making is the process of identifying problems, devising alternative policy options, and selecting which one of the alternatives to pursue.

Incrementalism is a tendency of decision-makers to make only incremental or marginal alterations in existing policy in order to prevent major changes from established norms.

Organizational process model is the second of the three models devised by Graham Allison to explain and predict the foreign policy behavior of states. The organizational process model focuses on the routines, standard patterns of behavior, and institutional perspectives of particular agencies and their impact on foreign policy decisions. It assumes that all governments generally rely on standard operating procedures, are relatively predictable, and favor only marginal changes in existing policy.

Rational actor model is associated with the realist theory of decision-making and the first of three models used by Graham Allison to explain and predict the foreign policy behavior of states. According to the rational actor model, decision-makers carefully define and identify foreign policy problems, gather all available information about the foreign policy options, weigh all possible alternatives, and select policies that are most likely to promote the state's national interests.

Standard operating procedures (SOPs) are accepted routines or patterns used by bureaucracies to organize and simplify the decision-making process. Standard operating procedures are utilized to handle problems or make decisions on a wide array of issues that confront governments on a daily basis—from internal personnel decisions to matters of international trade and diplomacy.

30.   Foreign Policy Decision-Making

Richard Snyder, H. W. Bruck, and Burton Sapin

In this except, Richard Snyder, H. W. Bruck, and Burton Sapin examine the various interrelationships between nation-states. The authors provide a typology of nations that includes "basic political organizations, range of decision-making systems, strengths and weaknesses of decision-making systems, and types of foreign policy strategies employed." This selection is from *Foreign Policy Decision-Making* (1962).

Richard Snyder is a professor of political science at the Mershon Center at Ohio State University. His other works include *American Foreign Policy* (1948), *Theory and Research on the Causes of War* (1969), and contributions to political science journals. Burton Sapin is a professor at George Washington University. His other major work is *The Making of U.S. Foreign Policy.*

H. W. Bruck was affiliated with the Foreign Policy Analysis Project when this article was written. He later held a position with the Department of Commerce.

DEFINITION OF INTERNATIONAL POLITICS

Definition of phenomena to be observed and explained is not, of course, identical with definition of methods of observation and explanation. Both will be spelled out as this essay proceeds. Suffice it to say here, we believe that those who study international politics are mainly concerned with the actions, reactions, and interactions among political entities called national states. Emphasis on action suggests *process* analysis, that is, the passage of time plus continuous changes in relationships—including the conditions underlying change and its consequences. Since there is a multiplicity of actions, reactions, and interactions, analysis must be concerned with a *number of processes.*

Action arises from the necessity to establish, to maintain, and to regulate sat-isfying, optional contacts between states and to exert some control over unwanted yet inescapable contacts. Action is planful in the sense that it represents an attempt to achieve certain aims, and to prevent or minimize the achievement of the incompatible or menacing aims of other states.

The action-reaction-interaction formulation suggests that sequences of action and interaction are always closed or symmetrical. This may be diagrammed State A $\leftrightarrow$ State B which implies a reciprocal relationship. Such is clearly not always the case. Many sequences are asymmetrical, that is, State A $\rightarrow$ State B $\rightarrow$ in which case State A acts, State B reacts, but there is no immediate further action by A in response to B's action. With more than two states involved, of course, there are other possibilities—as suggested by:

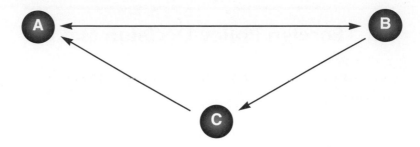

Given the fact that relationships may be symmetrical or asymmetrical and given the fact that action sequences though initiated at different times are nonetheless carried on simultaneously, there will be both the appearance and the possibility of *discontinuity* (that is, discontinuous processes) within the total set of processes which link any one state with all others. The process of state interaction is not, to repeat, always a sequence of action and *counteraction,* of attempt and frustration, of will opposing will. Nor should it be assumed that the process *necessarily* has an automatic chess-game quality or that reactions to action are necessarily immediate or self-evident. Not all national purposes are mutually incompatible, that is, it is not necessary that one nation's purposes be accomplished at the expense of another set of national purposes. One state may respond to the action of another without opposing that action per se; it may or may not be able to block that action effectively; it may or may not want to do so. The response may be in the form of inaction (calculated inaction we shall regard analytically as a form of action), or it may be in the form of action quite unrelated to the purposes of the state which acted first. Much diplomacy consists in probing the limits of tolerance for a proposed course of action and in discovering common purposes. As action unfolds, purposes may change due to resistances or altered circumstances and hence, often, head-on conflicts are avoided or reduced in impact. For these reasons the processes of state interaction are much less orderly than—hopefully—the analysis of these processes.

State action and therefore interaction obviously takes many forms—a declaration, a formal agreement, regulation of relationships, discussion, a gift or loan, armed conflict, and so on. Reactions take the same forms only they are viewed as responses. Since we are dealing with planful actions (rather than random behavior), interaction is characterized by *patterns,* that is, recognizable *repetitions* of action and reaction. Aims *persist.* Kinds of action become *typical.* Reactions become *uniform.* Relationships become *regularized.* Further comment on the identification and characterization of patterns will be made below.

Thus far, there would probably be few disagreements except relatively minor ones on specific terminology. Now the question is: how is the political process (remembering always that this connotes multiple processes and *kinds* of processes) at the international level to be analyzed? Clearly there are *what, how,* and *why* questions with respect to state interaction. In order to be true to our previously stated philosophy, we should recognize that there is more than one

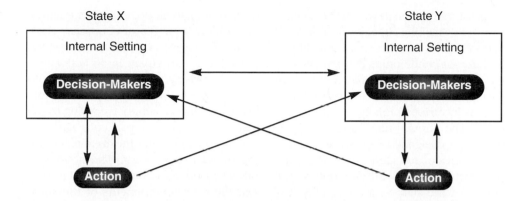

possible approach, depending on the purposes of the observer and on the kinds of questions which interest him most.

Commentary

1. The first aspect of this diagrammatic presentation of an analytical scheme is the *assumption* that the most effective way to gain perspective on international politics and to find ways of grasping the complex determinants of state behavior is to pitch the analysis on the level of *any state.* An understanding of *all* states is to be founded on an understanding of *any one* state through the use of a scheme which will permit the analytical construction of properties of action which will be shared in common by all specific states. That is, the model is a fictional state whose characteristics are such as to enable us to say certain things about all real states regardless of how different they may appear to be in some ways. Therefore, if the scheme is moderately successful, we should be able to lay the foundation for analyzing the impact of cultural values on British foreign policy and on Soviet foreign policy even though the values are different in each case and produce quite different consequences. "State X," then, stands for all states or for any one state. We have rejected the assumption that two different analytical schemes are required simply because two states behave differently.

It should be added immediately that theoretical progress in the study of international politics will require eventually a *typology* of states based on basic political organization, range of decision-making systems, strengths and weaknesses of decision-making systems, and types of foreign policy strategies employed. This will facilitate comparison, of course, but it will also make it possible to take into account certain significant differences among states while at the same time analyzing the behavior of all states in essentially the same way.

2. We are also assuming that the nation-state is going to be the significant unit of political action for many years to come. Strategies of action and commitment of resources will continue to be decided at the national level. This assumption is made on grounds of analytical convenience and is not an expression of preference by the authors. Nor does it blind us to the development or existence of supranational forces and organizations. The basic question is solely how the latter are to be treated. We prefer to view the United Nations as a special

mode of interaction in which the identity and policy-making capacity of individual national states are preserved but subject to different conditioning factors. The collective action of the United Nations can hardly be explained without reference to actions in various capitals.

3. The phrase "state as actor in a situation" is designed primarily as a short-hand device to alert us to certain perspectives while still adhering to the notion of the state as a collectivity. Explicit mention must be made of our employment of action analysis and (both here and in the detailed treatment of decision-making) *of some of the vocabulary* of the now well-known Parsons-Shils scheme. We emphasize vocabulary for two reasons. First, as new schemes of social analysis are developed (mostly outside of political science), there is a great temptation to apply such schemes quickly, one result being the use of new words without comprehension of the theoretical system of which they are a part. Second, we have rejected a general application of the Parsons-Shils approach as an organizing concept—for reasons which will emerge later. At this point we may simply note that our intellectual borrowings regarding fundamental questions of method owe much more to the works of Alfred Schuetz.

Basically, action exists (analytically) when the following components can be ascertained: actor (or actors), goals, means, and situation. The situation is defined by the actor (or actors) in terms of the way the actor (or actors) relates himself to other actors, to possible goals, and to possible means, and in terms of the way means and ends are formed into strategies of action subject to relevant factors in the situation. These ways of relating himself to the situation (and thus of defining it) will depend on the nature of the actor—or his orientations. Thus, "state X" mentioned above may be regarded as a participant in an action system comprising other actors; state X is the focus of the observer's attention. State X orients to action according to the manner in which the particular situation is viewed by certain officials and according to what they want. The actions of other actors, the actor's goals and means, and the other components of the situation are related meaningfully by the actor. His action flows from his definition of the situation.

4. We need to carry the actor-situation scheme one step further in an effort to rid ourselves of the troublesome abstraction "state." It is one of our basic methodological choices to define the state as its official decision-makers—those whose authoritative acts are, to all intents and purposes, the acts of the state. *State action is the action taken by those acting in the name of the state.* Hence, the state is its decision-makers. State X as *actor* is translated into its decision-makers as actors. It is also one of our basic choices to take as our prime analytical objective the re-creation of the "world" of the decision-makers as *they* view it. The manner in which *they* define situations becomes another way of saying how the state oriented to action and why. This is a quite different approach from trying to recreate the situation and interpretation of it *objectively,* that is, by the observer's judgment rather than that of the actors themselves.

To focus on the individual actors who are the state's decision-makers and to reconstruct the situation as defined by the decision-makers requires, of course, that a central place be given to the analysis of the behavior of these officials.

One major significance of the diagram is that it calls attention to the sources of state action and to the essentially subjective (that is, from the standpoint of the decision-makers) nature of our perspective.

5. Now let us try to clarify a little further. We have said that the key to the explanation of why the state behaves the way it does lies in the way its decision-makers as actors define their situation. *The definition of the situation* is built around the projected action as well as the reasons for the action. Therefore, it is necessary to analyze the actors (the official decision-makers) in the following terms: (a) their *discrimination* and *relating* of objects, conditions, and other actors—various things are perceived or expected in a relational context; (b) the existence, establishment, or definition of *goals*—various things are wanted from the situation; (c) attachment of *significance* to various courses of action suggested by the situation according to some criteria of estimation; and (d) application of *"standards of acceptability"* which (1) narrow the range of perceptions, (2) narrow the range of objects wanted, and (3) narrow the number of alternatives.

Three features of all orientations emerge: *perception, choice,* and *expectation.*

Perhaps a translation of the vocabulary of action theory will be useful. We are saying that the actors' orientations to action are reconstructed when the following kinds of questions are answered: what did the decision-makers think was relevant in a particular situation? how did they determine this? how were the relevant factors related to each other—what connections did the decision-makers see between diverse elements in the situation? how did they establish the connec-

tions? what wants and needs were deemed involved in or affected by the situation? what were the sources of these wants and needs? how were they related to the situation? what specific or general goals were considered and selected? what courses of action were deemed fitting and effective? how were fitness and effectiveness decided?

6. We have defined international politics as processes of state interaction at the governmental level. However, there are nongovernmental factors and relationships which must be taken into account by any system of analysis, and there are obviously nongovernmental effects of state action. Domestic politics, the non-human environment, cross-cultural and social relationships are important in this connection. We have chosen to group such factors under the concept of *setting.* This is an analytic term which reminds us that the decision-makers act upon and respond to conditions and factors which exist outside themselves and the governmental organization of which they are a part. Setting has two aspects: *external* and *internal.* We have deliberately chosen setting instead of environment because the latter term is either too inclusive or has a technical meaning in other sciences. Setting is really a set of categories of *potentially relevant factors and conditions* which may affect the action of any state.

External setting refers, in general, to such factors and conditions beyond the territorial boundaries of the state—the actions and reactions of other states (their decision-makers), the societies for which they act, and the physical world. Relevance of particular factors and conditions *in general* and *in particular situations* will depend on the attitudes, perceptions, judgments, and purpose of state X's decision-makers, that is, on how they react to various stimuli. It should be noted that our conception of setting does *not* exclude certain so-called environmental limitations such as the state of technology, morbidity ratio, and so on, which *may* limit the achievement of objectives or which *may* otherwise become part of the conditions of action *irrespective* of *whether* and *how* the decision-makers perceive them. However—and this is important—this does not in our scheme imply the substitution of an omniscient observer's judgment for that of the decision-maker. Setting is an analytical device to suggest certain enduring kinds of relevances and to limit the number of non-governmental factors with which the student of international politics must be concerned. The external setting is constantly changing and will be composed of *what the decision-makers decide is important.* This "deciding" can mean simply that certain lacks—such as minerals or guns—not imposed on them, that is, must be *accepted.* A serious native revolt in South Africa in 1900 was not a feature of the external setting of United States decision-makers; it would be in 1963. Compare, too, the relatively minor impact of Soviet foreign activities on the United States decision-makers in the period of 1927 to 1933 with the present impact.

Usually the factors and conditions referred to by the term *internal setting* are loosely labeled "domestic politics," "public opinion," or "geographical position." A somewhat more adequate formulation might be: some clues to the way any state behaves toward the world must be sought in the way its society is organized and functions, in the character and behavior of its people, and in its physical habitat. The list of categories under B (see p. 72) may be somewhat unfamiliar. There are two reasons for insisting that the analysis of the society for which state X acts be pushed to this fundamental level. First, the list invites attention to a much wider range of potentially relevant factors than the more familiar terms like morale, attitudes, national power, party politics, and so on. For example, the problem of vulnerability to subversive attack is rarely discussed by political scientists in terms of the basic social structure of a particular nation, that is, in terms of B3. Nor is recruitment of manpower often connected with the way the roles of the sexes are differentiated in a society. Second, if one is interested in the fundamental "why" of state behavior, the search for reliable answers must go beyond the *derived* conditions and factors (morale, pressure groups, production, attitudes, and so on) which are normally the focus of attention.

7. The diagram suggests another important point. Line BC is a two-way arrow connoting rightly an interaction between social organization and behavior on the one hand and decision-making on the other. Among other things this arrow represents the impact of domestic social forces on the formulation and execution of foreign policy. BC implies that the influence of conditions and factors in the society is felt through the decision-making process. But line DB is also important because it indicates that a nation experiences its own external actions. State action is designed primarily to alter factors and behavior or to otherwise affect conditions in the external setting, yet it may have equally serious consequences for the society itself. We need only suggest the range of possibilities here. Extensive foreign relations may enhance the power of the central government relative

to other regulatory institutions. Particular programs may contribute to the redistribution of resources, income, and social power. For example, the outpouring of billions in foreign aid by the United States since 1945 has contributed to the increased power and influence of scientists, military leaders, engineers, and the managerial group. The people of a state experience foreign policy in other ways—they may feel satisfaction, alarm, guilt, exhilaration, or doubt about it. There will be nongovernmental *interpretations*—perhaps several major ones—shared by various members or groups of the society. Such interpretations may or may not be identical with the prevailing official interpretation. There will also be nongovernmental expectations concerning state action which, again, may or may not correspond to official expectations. Discrepancies between nongovernmental and governmental interpretations and expectations may have important ramifications. For one thing, public support and confidence may be undermined if state action produces consequences which fundamentally violate public expectations.

The point to be made here is that the diagrammatic expression of our scheme shows that the impact of domestic social factors (line BCD) must be viewed also as a part of a larger feedback process as indicated by line BCDBC.

8. Another significant set of relationships emerges from the diagram in line ABE. The external and internal settings are related to each other. Among others, two implications may be stressed here. First, because we have defined international politics as interaction process at the governmental level, it may appear that we are making the focus unduly narrow, thus ignoring a whole host of private, nongovernmental interactions. Nothing could be further from the truth. Societies interact with each other in a wide range of ways through an intricate network of communications—trade, family ties, professional associations, shared values, cultural exchanges, travel, mass media, and migration. While all of these patterns may be subject to governmental regulation (in some form), they *may* have very little to do with the origins and forms of state action. At any rate, the question of the political significance of intersocietal, intercultural, nongovernmental interactions requires an analytical scheme which will make possible some understanding of how such interactions condition official action. This in turn requires a much more systematic description of interactions than we now have, plus a way of accounting for their connection with state action.

One can, however, study the interactions connoted by line ABE for their own sake with only a slight interest in their political aspects. In this case, it seems proper to say that the focus is international relations rather than international politics.

Nongovernmental international relations do not enter the analysis of state behavior *unless* it can be shown that the behavior of the decision-makers is in some manner determined by or directed toward such relations. For example, assume a bitter, hostile campaign against a foreign government by powerful United States newspapers and assume the campaign is well publicized in the other nation. By itself this would constitute an asymmetrical interaction between two societies. It would not become a matter of state interaction unless or until the following happened: (a) an official protest to the U.S. State Department by the for-

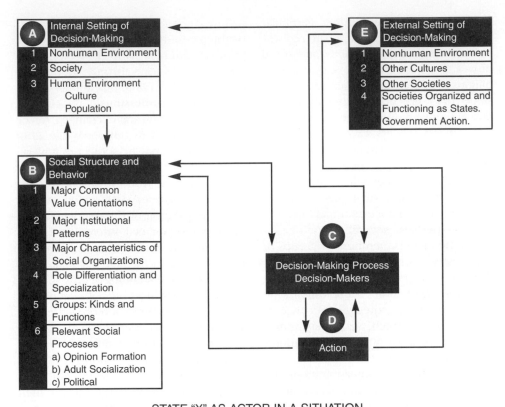

STATE "X" AS ACTOR IN A SITUATION
(Situation is comprised of a combination of selectively relevant factors in the external and internal setting as interpreted by the decision-makers.)

eign government; (b) retaliation against United States citizens in the foreign country; (c) disturbance of negotiations between the two governments on quite another issue; (d) arousal of public opinion in the foreign country to the point where the effectiveness of United States policies toward that country was seriously affected; (e) the pressure generated by the campaign in the United States caused the decision-makers to modify their actions and reactions vis-à-vis the other state; (f) the United States government officially repudiated the criticism and apologized to the other government. This same *kind* of argument would hold for all types of nongovernmental rela-

tions except that there would be varying degrees of directness (that is, change in intersocietal relations → change in state action) and indirectness (that is, change in intersocietal relations → change in social organization and behavior → derived condition or factor → change in state action) and therefore different time-sequences.

Second, while the most obvious consequences of state action are to be looked for in the reactions of other states along the lines CDE4C in the diagram, changes in the external setting can influence state action along the lines CDE3A3BC, that is, indirectly through changes in nongovernmental relations which ultimately are recognized and taken into account by the decision-makers.

9. To get back to the center of the diagram, it should be noted that CD is a two-way arrow. The rest of this essay is concerned with the nature of decision-making, but it can be said here that in addition to the feedback relationships CDBC and CDE3A3, DC connotes a direct feedback from an awareness by the decision-makers of their own action and from assessments of the progress of action. This is to say that state action has an impact on decision-making apart from subsequent reactions of other states and apart from effects mediated through the state's social organization and behavior.

10. So far as this diagram is concerned, most attention in the field of international politics is paid to interactions CDE4CD. CD represents action(s); DE (particularly DE4) represents consequences for, or impact upon, the external setting; EC represents new conditions or stimuli—reactions or new actions (E4C). Therefore, CDECD represents the action-reaction-interaction sequence.

Obviously these lines stand for a wide range of relationships and kinds of action. What should be emphasized here is that interactions can be really understood fully only in terms of the decision-making responses of states to situations, problems, and the actions of other states. The combination of interaction and decision-making can be diagrammed as shown on page 382.

Naturally if one thinks of all the separate actions and reactions, and all the combinations involved in the governmental relationships between one state and all others, it seems unrealistic and somewhat absurd to let a few lines on a diagram represent so much. Indeed, all

would be lost unless one could speak of *patterns* and *systems*. Patterns refer to *uniformities* and *persistence* of actions and sets of relationships. "Nationalism," "imperialism," "internationalism," "aggression," "isolationism," "peace," "war," "conflict," and "cooperation" are familiar ways of characterizing kinds of actions and reactions as well as patterned relationships among states. These terms are, of course, both descriptive and judgmental—they are shorthand expressions covering complicated phenomena and also may imply approval or disapproval, goodness or badness.

System in this context refers to the modes, rules, and nature of reciprocal influence which structure the interaction between states. Five kinds of system—there are others—may be mentioned: *coalitions* (temporary and permanent); *supranational organization; bilateral; multilateral* (unorganized); and *ordination-subordination* (imperial relationships and satellites). Once again, the way these interactions and relationships arise and the particular form or substance they take would seem to be explainable in terms of the way the decision-makers in the participating political organisms "define their situation." As we have said elsewhere, there seem to be only two ways of scientifically studying international politics: (1) the description and measurement of interaction; and (2) decision-making—the formulation and execution of policy. Interaction patterns can be studied by themselves without reference to decision-making except that the "why" of the patterns cannot be answered.

Summary

To conclude this brief commentary, it may be said that the diagram presented

. . . is designed in the first instance to portray graphically the basic perspectives of our frame of reference: *any* state as a way of saying something about *all* states; the central position of the decision-making focus; and the integration of a wide range of factors which may explain state action, reaction, and interaction.

The lines of the diagram carry *two* suggestive functions. First, they alert the observer to possible (known and hypothetical) relationships among empirical factors. Thus, the diagram simultaneously invites attention to three interrelated, intersecting empirical processes—state interaction (CDEC) at the governmental level, intersocietal interaction (ABE) at the nongovernmental level, and intrasocietal interaction (BCDB) at both the governmental and nongovernmental level. These processes arise, to put the matter another way, from decision-makers interacting with factors which constitute the dual setting, from state interaction as normally conceived, and from the factors which constitute internal and external settings acting upon each other.

Second, the diagram is intended to suggest possible analytic and theoretical relationships as well. The boxes indicate ways of specifying the relevant factors in state behavior through the employment of certain concepts—decision-making, action, setting, situation, society, culture, and so on—which provide, if they are successfully developed, criteria of relevance and ways of handling the empirical phenomena and their interrelationships. There are in existence a large number of tested and untested hypotheses, general and "middle range" theories, applicable within each of the categories comprising the diagram. The central concept of decision-making may provide a basis for linking a group of theories which hitherto have been applicable only to a segment of international politics or have not been susceptible of application at all. We may cite two examples. The concept of culture is clearly suggested by A2, B2, and E2 which specify empirical phenomena branded analytically as cultural in the technical sense. Based on this important social science concept is the derived concept of National Character—typical behavior patterns uniquely (or allegedly so) characteristic of one nation. Suggestive as national character analysis has been, it has been thus far impossible to bridge the analytic gap between behavior patterns at the cultural level and state action on the governmental level. Communication theory (really a cluster of related theories) has been applied almost exclusively to mass media (B6) and to techniques of state action (D). Only recently has an attempt been made to apply recent developments in communication theory to intersocietal interaction and to decision-making.

QUESTIONS

1. Describe the various interrelationships that affect decision-making by the nation-state.

2. What conclusions can be drawn from this except regarding foreign policy decision-making?

31.   Essence of Decision

Graham T. Allison

In this article, Allison provides three models of the decision-making process in foreign affairs. The rational actor model is the traditional realist paradigm. The organizational process and bureaucratic politics models are also examined in this essay. This study provides important questions about the coherency of the rational actor model (realism) to explain foreign policy decision-making and assesses the strength and weaknesses of the three models. This selection is from the *American Political Science Review* (1967).

Graham T. Allison is Douglas Dillon Professor of Government at Harvard's John F. Kennedy School of Government and author of many books and articles on American foreign policy and the decision-making process.

The Cuban missile crisis is a seminal event. For thirteen days of October 1962, there was a higher probability that more human lives would end suddenly than ever before in history. Had the worst occurred, the death of 100 million Americans, over 100 million Russians, and millions of Europeans as well would make previous natural calamities and inhumanities appear insignificant. Given the probability of disaster—which President Kennedy estimated as "between 1 out of 3 and even"—our escape seems awesome.[1] This event symbolizes a central, if only partially thinkable, fact about our existence. That such consequences could follow from the choices and actions of national governments obliges students of government as well as participants in governance to think hard about these problems.

Improved understanding of this crisis depends in part on more information and more probing analyses of available evidence. To contribute to these efforts is part of the purpose of this study. But here the missile crisis serves primarily as grist for a more general investigation. This study proceeds from the premise that marked improvement in our understanding of such events depends critically on more self-consciousness about what observers bring to the analysis. What each analyst sees and judges to be important is a function not only of the evidence about what happened but also of the "conceptual lenses" through which he looks at the evidence. The principal purpose of this essay is to explore some of the fundamental assumptions and categories employed by analysts in thinking about problems of governmental behavior, especially in foreign and military affairs.

The general argument can be summarized in three propositions:

1. Analysts think about problems of foreign and military policy in terms of largely implicit conceptual models that have significant consequences for the content of their thought.[2]

Though the present product of foreign policy analysis is neither systematic nor powerful, if one carefully examines explanations produced by analysts, a number of fundamental similarities emerge. Explanations produced by particular analysts display quite regular, predictable features. This predictability suggests a substructure. These regularities reflect an analyst's assumptions about the character of puzzles, the categories in which problems should be considered, the types of evidence that are relevant, and the determinants of occurrences. The first proposition is that clusters of such related assumptions constitute basic frames of reference or conceptual models in terms of which analysts both ask and answer the questions: What happened? Why did the event happen? What will happen?[3] Such assumptions are central to the activities of explanation and prediction, for in attempting to explain a particular event, the analyst cannot simply describe the full state of the world leading up to that event. The logic of explanation requires that he single out the relevant, important determinants of the occurrence.[4] Moreover, as the logic of prediction underscores, the analyst must summarize the various determinants as they bear on the event in question. Conceptual models both fix the mesh of the nets that the analyst drags through the material in order to explain a particular action or decision and direct him to cast his net in select ponds, at certain depths, in order to catch the fish he is after.

2. Most analysts explain (and predict) the behavior of national governments in terms of various forms of one basic conceptual model, here entitled the Rational Policy Model (Model I).[5]

In terms of this conceptual model, analysts attempt to understand happenings as the more or less purposive acts of unified national governments. For these analysts, the point of an explanation is to show how the nation or government could have chosen the action in question, given the strategic problem that it faced. For example, in confronting the problem posed by the Soviet installation of missiles in Cuba, rational policy model analysts attempt to show how this was a reasonable act from the point of view of the Soviet Union, given Soviet strategic objectives.

3. Two "alternative" conceptual models, here labeled an Organizational Process Model (Model II) and a Bureaucratic Politics Model (Model III) provide a base for improved explanation and prediction. . . .

MODEL I: RATIONAL POLICY

Rational Policy Model Illustrated

Where is the pinch of the puzzle raised by the *New York Times* over Soviet deployment of an antiballistic missile system?[6] The question, as the *Times* states it, concerns the Soviet Union's objective in allocating such large sums of money for this weapon system while at the same time seeming to pursue a policy of increasing détente. In former President Johnson's words, "the paradox is that this [Soviet deployment of an antiballistic missile system] should be happening at a time when there is abundant evidence that our mutual antagonism is beginning to ease."[7] This question troubles people primarily because Soviet antiballistic missile deployment, and evidence of Soviet actions towards détente, when juxtaposed in our implicit model, produce a question. With reference to what objective could the Soviet government have rationally chosen the simultaneous pursuit of these two courses of actions? This question arises only when the analyst attempts to structure events as purposive choices of consistent actors. . . .

How do analysts attempt to explain the Soviet emplacement of missiles in Cuba? The most widely cited explanation of this occurrence has been produced by two RAND Sovietologists, Arnold Horelick and Myron Rush.[8] They conclude that "the introduction of strategic missiles into Cuba was motivated chiefly by the Soviet leaders' desire to overcome . . . the existing large margin of U.S. strategic superiority."[9] How do they reach this conclusion? In Sherlock Holmes style, they seize several salient characteristics of this action and use these features as criteria against which to test alternative hypotheses about Soviet objectives. For example, the size of the Soviet deployment, and the simultaneous emplacement of more expensive, more visible intermediate range missiles as well as medium range missiles, it is argued, exclude an explanation of the action in terms of Cuban defense—since that objective could have been secured with a much smaller number of medium range missiles alone. Their explanation presents an argument for one objective that permits interpretation of the details of Soviet behavior as a value-maximizing choice.

How do analysts account for the coming of the First World War? According to Hans Morgenthau, "the first World War had its origin exclusively in the fear of a disturbance of the European balance of power."[10] In the period preceding World War I, the Triple Alliance precariously balanced the Triple Entente. If either power combination could gain a decisive advantage in the Balkans, it would achieve a decisive advantage in the balance of power. "It was this fear," Morgenthau asserts, "that motivated Austria in July 1914 to settle its accounts with Serbia once and for all, and that induced Germany to support Austria unconditionally. It was the same fear that brought Russia to the support of Serbia, and France to the support of Russia."[11] How is Morgenthau able to resolve this problem so confidently? By imposing on the data a "rational outline."[12] The value of this method, according to Morgenthau, is that "it provides for rational discipline in action and creates astounding continuity in foreign policy which makes American, British, or Russian foreign policy appear as an intelligent, rational continuum . . . regardless of the different motives, preferences, and intellectual and moral qualities of successive statesmen."[13] . . .

Most contemporary analysts (as well as laymen) proceed predominantly—albeit most often implicitly—in terms of this model when attempting to explain happenings in foreign affairs. Indeed, that occurrences in foreign affairs are the *acts* of *nations* seems so fundamental to thinking about such problems that this underlying model has rarely been recognized: to explain an occurrence in foreign policy simply means to show how the government could have rationally chosen that action.[14] These brief examples illustrate five uses of the model. To prove that most analysts think largely in terms of the rational policy model is not possible. In this limited space it is not even possible to illustrate the range of employment of the framework. Rather, my purpose is to convey to the reader a grasp of the model and a challenge: let the reader examine the literature with which he is most familiar and make his judgment.

The general characterization can be sharpened by articulating the rational policy model as an "analytic paradigm" in the technical sense developed by Robert K. Merton for sociological analyses.[15] Systematic statement of basic assumptions, concepts, and propositions employed by Model I analysts highlights the distinctive thrust of this style of analysis. To articulate a largely implicit framework is of necessity to caricature. But caricature can be instructive.

Rational Policy Paradigm

I. Basic Unit of Analysis: Policy as National Choice

Happenings in foreign affairs are conceived as actions chosen by the nation or national government.[16] Governments select the action that will maximize strategic goals and objectives. These "solutions" to strategic problems are the fundamental categories in terms of which the analyst perceives what is to be explained.

II. Organizing Concepts

A. *National Actor.* The nation or government, conceived as a rational, unitary decision-maker, is the agent. This actor has one set of specified goals (the equivalent of a consistent utility function), one set of perceived options, and a single estimate of the consequences that follow from each alternative.

B. *The Problem.* Action is chosen in response to the strategic problem which the nation faces. Threats and opportunities arising in the "international strategic market place" move the nation to act.

C. *Static Selection.* The sum of activity of representatives of the government relevant to a problem constitutes what the nation has chosen as its "solution." Thus the action is conceived as a steady-state choice among alternative outcomes (rather than, for example, a large number of partial choices in a dynamic stream).

D. *Action as Rational Choice.* The components include:

1. *Goals and Objectives.* National security and national interests are the principal categories in which strategic goals are conceived. Nations seek security and a range of further objectives. (Analysts rarely translate strategic goals and objectives into an explicit utility function; nevertheless, analysts do focus on major goals and objectives and trade off side effects in an intuitive fashion.)

2. *Options.* Various courses of action relevant to a strategic problem provide the spectrum of options.

3. *Consequences.* Enactment of each alternative course of action will produce a series of consequences. The relevant consequences constitute benefits and costs in terms of strategic goals and objectives.

4. *Choice.* Rational choice is value-maximizing. The rational agent selects the alternative whose consequences rank highest in terms of his goals and objectives.

III. Dominant Inference Pattern

This paradigm leads analysts to rely on the following pattern of inference: if a nation performed a particular action, that nation must have had ends towards which the action constituted an optimal means. The rational policy model's explanatory power stems from this inference pattern. Puzzlement is relieved by revealing the purposive pattern within which the occurrence can be located as a value-maximizing means.

IV. General Propositions

The disgrace of political science is the infrequency with which propositions of any generality are formulated and tested. "Paradigmatic analysis" argues for explicitness about the terms in which analysis proceeds, and seriousness about the logic of explanation. Simply to illustrate the kind of propositions on which analysts who employ this model rely, the formulation includes several.

The basic assumption of value-maximizing behavior produces propositions central to most explanations. The general principle can be formulated as follows: the likelihood of any particular action results from a combination of the nation's (1) relevant values and objectives, (2) perceived alternative courses of action, (3) estimates of various sets of consequences (which will follow from each alternative), and (4) net valuation of each set of consequences. This yields two propositions.

A. An increase in the cost of an alternative, i.e., a reduction in the value of the set of consequences which will follow from that action, or a reduction in the probability of attaining fixed consequences, reduces the likelihood of that alternative being chosen.

B. A decrease in the costs of an alternative, i.e., an increase in the value of the set of consequences which will follow from that alternative, or an increase in the probability of attaining fixed consequences, increases the likelihood of that action being chosen.[17]

V. Specific Propositions

A. *Deterrence.* The likelihood of any particular attack results from the factors specified in the general proposition. Combined with factual assertions, this general proposition yields the propositions of the sub-theory of deterrence.

(1) A stable nuclear balance reduces the likelihood of nuclear attack. This proposition is derived from the general proposition plus the asserted fact that a second-strike capability affects the potential attacker's calculations by increasing the likelihood and the costs of one particular set of consequences which might follow from attack—namely, retaliation.

(2) A stable nuclear balance increases the probability of limited war. This proposition is derived from the general proposition plus the asserted fact that though increasing the costs of a nuclear exchange, a stable nuclear balance nevertheless produces a more significant reduction in the probability that such consequences would be chosen in response to a limited war. Thus this set of consequences weighs less heavily in the calculus.

B. *Soviet Force Posture.* The Soviet Union chooses its force posture (i.e., its weapons and their deployment) as a value-maximizing means of implementing Soviet strategic objectives and military doctrine. A proposition of this sort underlies Secretary of Defense Laird's inference from the fact of 200 SS-9s (large intercontinental missiles) to the assertion that, "the Soviets are going for a first-strike capability, and there's no question about it."[18]

Variants of the Rational Policy Model

This paradigm exhibits the characteristics of the most refined version of the rational model. The modern literature of strategy employs a model of this sort. Problems and pressures in the "international strategic marketplace" yield probabilities of occurrence. The international actor, which could be any national actor, is simply a value-maximizing mechanism for getting from the strategic problem to the logical solution. But the explanations and predictions produced by most analysts of foreign affairs depend primarily on variants of this "pure" model. The point of each is the same: to place the action within a value-maximizing framework, given certain constraints. Nevertheless, it may be helpful to identify several variants, each of which might be exhibited similarly as a paradigm. The first focuses upon the national actor and his choice in a particular situation, leading analysts to further constrain the goals, alternatives, and consequences considered. Thus, (1) national propensities or personality traits reflected in an "operational code," (2) concern with certain objectives, or (3) special principles of action, narrow the "goals" or "alternatives" or "consequences" of the paradigm. For example, the Soviet deployment of ABMs is sometimes explained by reference to the Soviet's "defense-mindedness." Or a particular Soviet action is explained as an instance of a special rule of action in the Bolshevik operational code.[19] A second, related, cluster of variants focuses on the individual leader or leadership group as the actor whose preference function is maximized and whose personal (or group) characteristics are allowed to modify the alternatives, consequences, and rules of choice. Explanations of the U.S. involvement in Vietnam as a natural consequence of the Kennedy-Johnson Administration's axioms of foreign policy rely on this variant. A third, more complex variant of the basic model recognizes the existence of several actors within a government, for example, Hawks and Doves or military and civilians, but attempts to explain (or predict) an occurrence by reference to the objectives of the victorious actor. Thus, for example, some revisionist histories of the Cold War recognize the forces of light and the forces of darkness within the U.S. government, but explain American actions as a result of goals and perceptions of the victorious forces of darkness.

Each of these forms of the basic paradigm constitutes a formalization of what analysts typically rely upon implicitly. In the transition from implicit conceptual model to explicit paradigm much of the richness of the best employments of this model has been lost. But the purpose in raising loose, implicit conceptual models to an explicit level is to reveal the basic logic of analysts' activity. Perhaps some of the remaining artificiality that surrounds the statement of the paradigm can be erased by noting a number of the standard additions and modifications employed by analysts who proceed *predominantly* within the rational policy model. First, in the course of a document, analysts shift from one variant of the basic model to another, occasionally appropriating in an *ad hoc* fashion aspects of a situation which are logically incompatible with the basic model. Second, in the course of explaining a number of occurrences, analysts sometimes pause over a particular event about which they have a great deal of information and unfold it in such detail that an impression of randomness is created. Third, having employed other assumptions and categories in deriving an explanation or prediction, analysts will present their product in a neat, convincing rational policy model package. (This accommodation is a favorite of members of the intelligence community whose association with the details of a process is considerable, but who feel that by putting an occurrence in a larger rational framework, it will be more comprehensible to their audience.) Fourth, in attempting to offer an explanation—particularly in cases where a prediction derived from the basic model has failed—the notion of a "mistake" is invoked. Thus, the failure in the prediction of a "missile gap" is written off as a Soviet mistake in not taking advantage of their opportunity. Both these and other modifications permit Model I analysts considerably more variety than the paradigm might suggest. But such accommodations are essentially appendages to the basic logic of these analyses. . . .

MODEL II: ORGANIZATIONAL PROCESS

For some purposes, governmental behavior can be usefully summarized as action chosen by a unitary, rational decision-maker: centrally controlled, completely informed, and value maximizing. But this simplification must not be allowed to conceal the fact that a "government" consists of a conglomerate of semi-feudal, loosely allied organizations, each with a substantial life of its own. Government leaders do sit formally, and to some extent in fact, on top of this conglomerate. But governments perceive problems through organizational sensors. Governments define alternatives and estimate consequences as organizations process information. Governments act as these organizations enact routines. Government behavior can therefore be understood according to a second conceptual model, less as deliberate choices of leaders and more as *outputs* of large organizations functioning according to standard patterns of behavior.

To be responsive to a broad spectrum of problems, governments consist of large organizations among which primary responsibility for particular areas is divided. Each organization attends to a special set of problems and acts in quasi-independence on these problems. But few important problems fall exclusively within the domain of a single organization. Thus government behavior relevant to any important problem reflects the independent output of several organizations, partially coordinated by government leaders. Government leaders can substantially disturb, but not substantially control, the behavior of these organizations.

To perform complex routines, the behavior of large numbers of individuals must be coordinated. Coordination requires standard operating procedures: rules according to which things are done. Assured capability for reliable performance of action that depends upon the behavior of hundreds of persons requires established "programs." Indeed, if the eleven members of a football team are to perform adequately on any particular down, each player must not "do what he thinks needs to be done" or "do what the quarterback tells him to do." Rather, each player must perform the maneuvers specified by a previously established play which the quarterback has simply called in this situation.

At any given time, a government consists of *existing* organizations, each with a *fixed* set of standard operating procedures and programs. The behavior of these organizations—and consequently of the government—relevant to an issue in any particular instance is, therefore, determined primarily by routines established in these organizations prior to that instance. But organizations do change. Learning occurs gradually, over time. Dramatic organizational change occurs in response to major crises. Both learning and change are influenced by existing organizational capabilities.

Borrowed from studies of organizations, these loosely formulated propositions amount simply to *tendencies.* Each must be hedged by modifiers like "other things being equal" and "under certain conditions." In particular instances, tendencies hold—more or less. In specific situations, the relevant question is: more or less? But this is as it should be. For, on the one hand, "organizations" are no more homogeneous a class than "solids." When scientists tried to generalize about "solids," they achieved similar results. Solids tend to expand when heated, but some do and some don't. More adequate categorization of the various elements now lumped under the rubric "organizations" is thus required. On the other hand, the behavior of particular organizations seems considerably more complex than the behavior of solids. Additional information about a particular organization is required for further specification of the tendency statements. In spite of these two caveats, the characterization of government action as organizational output differs distinctly from Model I. Attempts to understand problems of foreign affairs in terms of this frame of reference should produce quite different explanations.[20]

Organizational Process Paradigm[21]

I. Basic Unit of Analysis: Policy as Organizational Output

The happenings of international politics are, in three critical senses, outputs of organizational processes. First, the actual occurrences are organizational outputs. For example, Chinese entry into the Korean War—that is, the fact that Chinese soldiers were firing at U.N. soldiers south of the Yalu in 1950—is an organizational action: the action of men who are soldiers in platoons which are in companies, which in turn are in armies, responding as privates to lieutenants who are responsible to captains and so on to the commander, moving into Korea, advancing against enemy troops, and firing according to fixed routines of the Chinese Army. Government leaders' decisions trigger organizational routines. Government leaders can trim the edges of this output and exercise some choice in combining outputs. But the mass of behavior is determined by previously established procedures. Second, existing organizational routines for employing present physical capabilities constitute the effective options open to government leaders confronted with any problem. Only the existence of men, equipped and trained as armies and capable of being transported to North Korea, made entry into the Korean War a live option for the Chinese leaders. The fact that fixed programs (equipment, men, and routines which exist at the particular time) exhaust the range of buttons that leaders can push is not always perceived by these leaders. But in every case it is critical for an understanding of what is actually done. Third, organizational outputs structure the situation within the narrow constraints of which leaders must contribute their "decision" concerning an issue. Outputs raise the problem, provide the information, and make the initial moves that color the face of the issue that is turned to the leaders. As Theodore Sorensen has observed: "Presidents rarely, if ever, make decisions—particularly in foreign affairs—in the sense of writing their conclusions on a clean slate . . . The basic decisions, which confine their choices, have all too often been previously made."[22] If one understands the structure of the situation and the face of the issue—which are determined by the organizational outputs—the formal choice of the leaders is frequently anticlimactic.

II. Organizing Concepts

A. *Organizational Actors.* The actor is not a monolithic "nation" or "government" but rather a constellation of loosely allied organizations on top of which government leaders sit: This constellation acts only as component organizations perform routines.[23]

B. *Factored Problems and Fractionated Power.* Surveillance of the multiple facets of foreign affairs requires that problems be cut up and parcelled out to various organizations. To avoid paralysis, primary power must accompany primary responsibility. But if organizations are permitted to do anything, a large part of what they do will be determined within the organization. Thus each organization perceives problems, processes information, and performs a range of actions in quasi-independence (within broad guidelines of national policy). Factored problems and fractionated power are two edges of the same sword. Factoring permits more specialized attention to particular facets of problems than would be possible if government leaders tried to cope with these problems by themselves. But this additional attention must be paid for in the coin of discretion for *what* an organization attends to, and *how* organizational responses are programmed.

C. *Parochial Priorities, Perceptions, and Issues.* Primary responsibility for a narrow set of problems encourages organizational parochialism. These tendencies are enhanced by a number of additional factors: (1) selective information available to the organization, (2) recruitment of personnel into the organization, (3) tenure of individuals in the organization, (4) small group pressures within the organization, and (5) distribution of rewards by the organization. Clients (e.g., interest groups), government allies (e.g., Congressional committees), and extra-national counterparts (e.g., the British Ministry of Defense for the Department of Defense, ISA, or the British Foreign Office for the Department of State, EUR) galvanize this parochialism. Thus organizations develop relatively stable propensities concerning operational priorities, perceptions, and issues.

D. *Action as Organizational Output.* The preeminent feature of organizational activity is its programmed character: the extent to which behavior in any particular case is an enactment of preestablished routines. In producing outputs, the activity of each organization is characterized by:

1. *Goals: Constraints Defining Acceptable Performance.* The operational goals of an organization are seldom revealed by formal mandates. Rather, each organization's operational goals emerge as a set of constraints defining acceptable performance. Central among these constraints is organizational health, defined usually in terms of bodies assigned and dollars appropriated. The set of constraints emerges from a mix of expectations and demands of other organizations in the government, statutory authority, demands from citizens and special interest groups, and bargaining within the organization. These constraints represent a quasi-resolution of conflict—the constraints are relatively stable, so there is some resolution. But conflict among

alternative goals is always latent; hence, it is a quasi-resolution. Typically, the constraints are formulated as imperatives to avoid roughly specified discomforts and disasters.[24]

2. *Sequential Attention to Goals.* The existence of conflict among operational constraints is resolved by the device of sequential attention. As a problem arises, the subunits of the organization most concerned with that problem deal with it in terms of the constraints they take to be most important. When the next problem arises, another cluster of subunits deals with it, focusing on a different set of constraints.

3. *Standard Operating Procedures.* Organizations perform their "higher" functions, such as attending to problem areas, monitoring information, and preparing relevant responses for likely contingencies, by doing "lower" tasks, for example, preparing budgets, producing reports, and developing hardware. Reliable performance of these tasks requires standard operating procedures (hereafter SOPs). Since procedures are "standard" they do not change quickly or easily. Without these standard procedures, it would not be possible to perform certain concerted tasks. But because of standard procedures, organizational behavior in particular instances often appears unduly formalized, sluggish, or inappropriate.

4. *Programs and Repertoires.* Organizations must be capable of performing actions in which the behavior of large numbers of individuals is carefully coordinated. Assured performance requires clusters of rehearsed SOPs for producing specific actions, e.g., fighting enemy units or answering an embassy's cable. Each cluster comprises a "program" (in the terms both of drama and computers) which the organization has available for dealing with a situation. The list of programs relevant to a type of activity, e.g., fighting, constitutes an organizational repertoire. The number of programs in a repertoire is always quite limited. When properly triggered, organizations execute programs; programs cannot be substantially changed in a particular situation. The more complex the action and the greater the number of individuals involved, the more important are programs and repertoires as determinants of organizational behavior.

5. *Uncertainty Avoidance.* Organizations do not attempt to estimate the probability distribution of future occurrences. Rather, organizations avoid uncertainty. By arranging a *negotiated environment,* organizations regularize the reactions of other actors with whom they have to deal. The primary environment, relations with other organizations that comprise the government, is stabilized by such arrangements as agreed budgetary splits, accepted areas of responsibility, and established conventional practices. The secondary environment, relations with the international world, is stabilized between allies by the establishment of contracts (alliances) and "club relations" (U.S. State and U.K. Foreign Office or U.S. Treasury and U.K. Treasury). Between enemies, contracts and accepted conventional practices perform a similar function, for example, the rules of the "precarious status quo" which President Kennedy referred to in the missile crisis. Where the international environment cannot be negotiated, organizations deal with remaining uncertainties by establishing a set of *standard scenarios* that constitute the contingencies for which they prepare. For example, the standard scenario for Tactical Air

Command of the U.S. Air Force involves combat with enemy aircraft. Planes are designed and pilots trained to meet this problem. That these preparations are less relevant to more probable contingencies, e.g., provision of close-in ground support in limited wars like Vietnam, has had little impact on the scenario.

6. *Problem-directed Search.* Where situations cannot be construed as standard, organizations engage in search. The style of search and the solution are largely determined by existing routines. Organizational search for alternative courses of action is problem-oriented: it focuses on the atypical discomfort that must be avoided. It is simple-minded: the neighborhood of the symptom is searched first; then, the neighborhood of the current alternative. Patterns of search reveal biases which in turn reflect such factors as specialized training or experience and patterns of communication.

7. *Organizational Learning and Change.* The parameters of organizational behavior mostly persist. In response to non-standard problems, organizations search and routines evolve, assimilating new situations. Thus learning and change follow in large part from existing procedures. But marked changes in organizations do sometimes occur. Conditions in which dramatic changes are more likely include: (1) Periods of budgetary feast. Typically, organizations devour budgetary feasts by purchasing additional items on the existing shopping list. Nevertheless, if committed to change, leaders who control the budget can use extra funds to effect changes. (2) Periods of prolonged budgetary famine. Though a single year's famine typically results in few changes in organizational structure but a loss of effectiveness in performing some programs, prolonged famine forces major retrenchment. (3) Dramatic performance failures. Dramatic change occurs (mostly) in response to major disasters. Confronted with an undeniable failure of procedures and repertoires, authorities outside the organization demand change, existing personnel are less resistant to change, and critical members of the organization are replaced by individuals committed to change.

E. *Central Coordination and Control.* Action requires decentralization of responsibility and power. But problems lap over the jurisdictions of several organizations. Thus the necessity for decentralization runs headlong into the requirement for coordination. (Advocates of one horn or the other of this dilemma—responsive action entails decentralized power vs. coordinated action requires central control—account for a considerable part of the persistent demand for government reorganization.) Both the necessity for coordination and the centrality of foreign policy to national welfare guarantee the involvement of government leaders in the procedures of the organizations among which problems are divided and power shared. Each organization's propensities and routines can be disturbed by government leaders' intervention. Central direction and persistent control of organizational activity however, is not possible. The relation among organizations, and between organizations and the government leaders depends critically on a number of structural variables including: (1) the nature of the job, (2) the measures and information available to government leaders, (3) the system of rewards and punishments for organizational members, and (4) the procedures by which human and material resources get committed. For example, to the extent that rewards and punishments for the members of an organization are distributed by higher authorities, these authorities can exercise some control by specifying criteria in terms of which organizational output is to be evaluated. These criteria become constraints within which organizational activity proceeds. But constraint is a crude instrument of control.

Intervention by government leaders does sometimes change the activity of an organization in an intended direction. But instances are fewer than might be expected. As Franklin Roosevelt, the master manipulator of government organizations, remarked:

> The Treasury is so large and far-flung and ingrained in its practices that I find it is almost impossible to get the action and results I want. . . . But the Treasury is not to be compared with the State Department. You should go through the experience of trying to get any changes in the thinking, policy, and action of the career diplomats and then you'd know what a real problem was. But the Treasury and the State Department put together are nothing compared with the Na-a-vy . . . To change anything in the Na-a-vy is like punching a feather bed. You punch it with your right and you punch it with your left until you are finally exhausted, and then you find the damn bed just as it was before you started punching.[25]

John Kennedy's experience seems to have been similar: "The State Department," he asserted, "is a bowl full of jelly."[26] And lest the McNamara revolution in the Defense Department seem too striking a counter-example, the Navy's recent rejection of McNamara's major intervention in Naval weapons procurement, the F-111B, should be studied as an antidote.

F. *Decisions of Government Leaders.* Organizational persistence does not exclude shifts in governmental behavior. For government leaders sit atop the conglomerate of organizations. Many important issues of governmental action require that these leaders decide what organizations will play out which programs where. Thus stability in the parochialisms and SOPs of individual organizations is consistent with some important shifts in the behavior of governments. The range of these shifts is defined by existing organizational programs.

III. Dominant Inference Pattern

If a nation performs an action of this type today, its organizational components must yesterday have been performing (or have had established routines for performing) an action only marginally different from this action. At any specific point in time, a government consists of an established conglomerate of organizations, each with existing goals, programs, and repertoires. The characteristics of a government's action in any instance follows from those established routines, and from the choice of government leaders—on the basis of information and estimates provided by existing routines—among existing programs. The best explanation of an organization's behavior at t is $t - 1$; the prediction of $t + 1$ is t. Model II's explanatory power is achieved by uncovering the organizational routines and repertoires that produced the outputs that comprise the puzzling occurrence.

IV. General Propositions

A number of general propositions have been stated above. In order to illustrate clearly the type of proposition employed by Model II analysts, this section formulates several more precisely.

A. *Organizational Action.* Activity according to SOPs and programs does not constitute far-sighted, flexible adaptation to "the issue" (as it is conceived by the analyst). Detail and nuance of actions by organizations are determined predominantly by organizational routines, not government leaders' directions.

1. SOPs constitute routines for dealing with *standard* situations. Routines allow large numbers of ordinary individuals to deal with numerous instances, day after day, without considerable thought, by responding to basic stimuli. But this regularized capability for adequate performance is purchased at the price of standardization. If the SOPs are appropriate, average performance, i.e., performance averaged over the range of cases, is better than it would be if each instance were approached individually (given fixed talent, timing, and resource constraints). But specific instances, particularly critical instances that typically do not have "standard" characteristics, are often handled sluggishly or inappropriately.

2. A program, i.e., a complex action chosen from a short list of programs in a repertoire, is rarely tailored to the specific situation in which it is executed. Rather, the program is (at best) the most appropriate of the programs in a previously developed repertoire.

3. Since repertoires are developed by parochial organizations for standard scenarios defined by that organization, programs available for dealing with a particular situation are often ill-suited.

B. *Limited Flexibility and Incremental Change.* Major lines of organizational action are straight, i.e., behavior at one time is marginally different from that behavior at $t - 1$. Simpleminded predictions work best: Behavior at $t + 1$ will be marginally different from behavior at the present time.

1. Organizational budgets change incrementally—both with respect to totals and with respect to intra-organizational splits. Though organizations could divide the money available each year by carving up the pie anew (in the light of changes in objectives or environment), in practice, organizations take last year's budget as a base and adjust incrementally. Predictions that require large budgetary shifts in a single year between organizations or between units within an organization should be hedged.

2. Once undertaken, an organizational investment is not dropped at the point where "objective" costs outweigh benefits. Organizational stakes in adopted projects carry them quite beyond the loss point.

C. *Administrative Feasibility.* Adequate explanation, analysis, and prediction must include administrative feasibility as a major dimension. A considerable gap separates what leaders choose (or might rationally have chosen) and what organizations implement.

1. Organizations are blunt instruments. Projects that require several organizations to act with high degrees of precision and coordination are not likely to succeed.

2. Projects that demand that existing organizational units depart from their accustomed functions and perform previously unprogrammed tasks are rarely accomplished in their designed form.

3. Government leaders can expect that each organization will do its "part" in terms of what the organization knows how to do.

4. Government leaders can expect incomplete and distorted information from each organization concerning its part of the problem.

5. Where an assigned piece of a problem is contrary to the existing goals of an organization, resistance to implementation of that piece will be encountered.

V. Specific Propositions.

1. *Deterrence.* The probability of nuclear attack is less sensitive to balance and imbalance, or stability and instability (as these concepts are employed by Model I strategists) than it is to a number of organizational factors. Except for the special case in which the Soviet Union acquires a credible capability to destroy the U.S. with a disarming blow, U.S. superiority or inferiority affects the probability of a nuclear attack less than do a number of organizational factors.

First, if a nuclear attack occurs, it will result from organizational activity: the firing of rockets by members of a missile group. The enemy's *control system,* i.e., physical mechanisms and standard procedures which determine who can launch rockets when, is critical. Second, the enemy's programs for bringing his strategic forces to *alert status* determine probabilities of accidental firing and momentum. At the outbreak of World War I, if the Russian Tsar had understood the organizational processes which his order of full mobilization triggered, he would have realized that he had chosen war. Third, organizational repertoires fix the range of effective choice open to enemy leaders. The menu available to Tsar Nicholas in 1914 has two entrees: full mobilization and no mobilization. Partial mobilization was not an organizational option. Fourth, since organizational routines set the chessboard, the training and deployment of troops and nuclear weapons is crucial. Given that the outbreak of hostilities in Berlin is more probable than most scenarios for nuclear war, facts about deployment, training, and tactical nuclear equipment of Soviet troops stationed in East Germany—which will influence the face of the issue seen by Soviet leaders at the outbreak of hostilities and the manner in which choice is implemented—are as critical as the question of "balance."

2. *Soviet Force Posture.* Soviet force posture, i.e., the fact that certain weapons rather than others are procured and deployed, is determined by organizational factors such as the goals and procedures of existing military services and the goals and processes of research and design labs, within budgetary constraints that emerge from the government leader's choices. The frailty of the Soviet Air Force within the Soviet military establishment seems to have been a crucial element in the Soviet failure to acquire a large bomber force in the 1950s (thereby faulting American intelligence predictions of a "bomber gap"). The fact that missiles were controlled until 1960 in the Soviet Union by the Soviet Ground Forces, whose goals and procedures reflected no interest in an intercontinental mission, was not irrelevant to the slow Soviet buildup of ICBMs (thereby faulting U.S. intelligence predictions of a "missile gap"). These organizational factors (Soviet Ground Forces' control of missiles and that service's fixation with European scenarios) make the Soviet deployment of so many MRBMs that European targets could be destroyed three times over, more understandable. Recent weapon developments, e.g., the testing of a Fractional Orbital Bombardment System (FOBS) and multiple warheads for the SS-9, very likely reflect the activity and interests of a cluster of Soviet research and development organizations, rather than a decision by Soviet leaders to acquire a first strike weapon system. Care-

ful attention to the organizational components of the Soviet military establishment (Strategic Rocket Forces, Navy, Air Force, Ground Forces, and National Air Defense), the missions and weapons systems to which each component is wedded (an independent weapon system assists survival as an independent service), and existing budgetary splits (which probably are relatively stable in the Soviet Union as they tend to be everywhere) offer potential improvements in medium and longer term predictions. . . .

Model III: Bureaucratic Politics

The leaders who sit on top of organizations are not a monolithic group. Rather, each is, in his own right, a player in a central, competitive game. The name of the game is bureaucratic politics: bargaining along regularized channels among players positioned hierarchically within the government. Government behavior can thus be understood according to a third conceptual model not as organizational outputs, but as outcomes of bargaining games. In contrast with Model I, the bureaucratic politics model sees no unitary actor but rather many actors as players, who focus not on a single strategic issue but on many diverse intranational problems as well, in terms of no consistent set of strategic objectives but rather according to various conceptions of national, organizational, and personal goals, making government decisions not by rational choice but by the pulling and hauling that is politics.

The apparatus of each national government constitutes a complex arena for the intra-national game. Political leaders at the top of this apparatus plus the men who occupy positions on top of the critical organizations form the circle of central players. Ascendancy to this circle assures some independent standing. The necessary decentralization of decisions required for action on the broad range of foreign policy problems guarantees that each player has considerable discretion. Thus power is shared.

The nature of problems of foreign policy permits fundamental disagreement among reasonable men concerning what ought to be done. Analyses yield conflicting recommendations. Separate responsibilities laid on the shoulders of individual personalities encourage differences in perceptions and priorities. But the issues are of first order importance. What the nation does really matters. A wrong choice could mean irreparable damage. Thus responsible men are obliged to fight for what they are convinced is right.

Men share power. Men differ concerning what must be done. The differences matter. This milieu necessitates that policy be resolved by politics. What the nation does is sometimes the result of the triumph of one group over others. More often, however, different groups pulling in different directions yield a resultant distinct from what anyone intended. What moves the chess pieces is not simply the reasons which support a course of action, nor the routines of organizations which enact an alternative, but the power and skill of proponents and opponents of the action in question.

This characterization captures the thrust of the bureaucratic politics orientation. If problems of foreign policy arose as discreet issues, and decisions were determined one game at a time, this account would suffice. But most "issues," e.g., Vietnam or the proliferation of nuclear weapons, emerge piecemeal, over time, one lump in one context, a second in another. Hundreds of issues compete for players' attention every day. Each player is forced to fix upon his issues for that day, fight them on their own terms, and rush on to the next. Thus the character of emerging issues and the pace at which the game is played converge to yield government "decisions" and "actions" as collages. Choices by one player, outcomes of minor games, outcomes of central games, and "foul-ups"—these pieces, when stuck to the same canvas, constitute government behavior relevant to an issue.

The concept of national security policy as political outcome contradicts both public imagery and academic orthodoxy. Issues vital to national security, it is said, are too important to be settled by political games. They must be "above" politics. To accuse someone of "playing politics with national security" is a most serious charge. What public conviction demands, the academic penchant for intellectual elegance reinforces. Internal politics is messy; moreover, according to prevailing doctrine, politicking lacks intellectual content. As such, it constitutes gossip for journalists rather than a subject for serious investigation. Occasional memoirs, anecdotes in historical accounts, and several detailed case studies to the contrary, most of the literature of foreign policy avoids bureaucratic politics. The gap between academic literature and the experience of participants in government is nowhere wider than at this point.

Bureaucratic Politics Paradigm[27]

I. Basic Unit of Analysis: Policy as Political Outcome

The decisions and actions of governments are essentially intra-national political outcomes: outcomes in the sense that what happens is not chosen as a solution to a problem but rather results from compromise, coalition, competition, and confusion among government officials who see different faces of an issue; political in the sense that the activity from which the outcomes emerge is best characterized as bargaining. Following Wittgenstein's use of the concept of a "game," national behavior in international affairs can be conceived as outcomes of intricate and subtle, simultaneous, overlapping games among players located in positions, the hierarchical arrangement of which constitutes the government.[28] These games proceed neither at random nor at leisure. Regular channels structure the game. Deadlines force issues to the attention of busy players. The moves in the chess game are thus to be explained in terms of the bargaining among players with separate and unequal power over particular pieces and with separable objectives in distinguishable subgames.

II. Organizing Concepts

A. *Players in Positions.* The actor is neither a unitary nation, nor a conglomerate of organizations, but rather a number of individual players.

C. *Interests, Stakes, and Power.* Games are played to determine outcomes. But outcomes advance and impede each player's conception of the national interest, specific programs to which he is committed, the welfare of his friends, and his personal interests. These overlapping interests constitute the stakes for which games are played. Each player's ability to play successfully depends upon his power. Power, i.e., effective influence on policy outcomes, is an elusive blend of at least three elements: bargaining advantages (drawn from formal authority and obligations, institutional backing, constituents, expertise, and status), skill and will in using bargaining advantages, and other players' perceptions of the first two ingredients. Power wisely invested yields an enhanced reputation for effectiveness. Unsuccessful investment depletes both the stock of capital and the reputation. Thus each player must pick the issues on which he can play with a reasonable probability of success. But no player's power is sufficient to guarantee satisfactory outcomes. Each player's needs and fears run to many other players. What ensues is the most intricate and subtle of games known to man.

D. *The Problem and the Problems.* "Solutions" to strategic problems are not derived by detached analysts focusing coolly on *the* problem. Instead, deadlines and events raise issues in games, and demand decisions of busy players in contexts that influence the face the issue wears. The problems for the players are both narrower and broader than *the* strategic problem. For each player focuses not on the total strategic problem but rather on the decision that must be made now. But each decision has critical consequences not only for the strategic problem but for each player's organizational, reputational, and personal stakes. Thus the gap between the problems the player was solving and the problem upon which the analyst focuses is often very wide.

E. *Action-Channels.* Bargaining games do not proceed randomly. Action-channels, i.e., regularized ways of producing action concerning types of issues, structure the game by pre-selecting the major players, determining their points of entrance into the game, and distributing particular advantages and disadvantages for each game. Most critically, channels determine "who's got the action," that is,

which department's Indians actually do whatever is chosen. Weapon procurement decisions are made within the annual budgeting process; embassies' demands for action cables are answered according to routines of consultation and clearance from State to Defense and White House; requests for instructions from military groups (concerning assistance all the time, concerning operations during war) are composed by the military in consultation with the Office of the Secretary of Defense, State, and White House; crisis responses are debated among White House, State, Defense, CIA, and Ad Hoc players; major political speeches, especially by the President but also by other Chiefs, are cleared through established channels.

F. *Action as Politics.* Government decisions are made and government actions emerge neither as the calculated choice of a unified group, nor as a formal summary of leaders' preferences. Rather the context of shared power but separate judgments concerning important choices, determines that politics is the mechanism of choice. Note the *environment* in which the game is played: inordinate uncertainty about what must be done, the necessity that something be done, and crucial consequences of whatever is done. These features force responsible men to become active players. The *pace of the game*—hundreds of issues, numerous games, and multiple channels—compels players to fight to "get other's attention," to make them "see the facts," to assure that they "take the time to think seriously about the broader issue." The *structure of the game*—power shared by individuals with separate responsibilities—validates each player's feeling that "others don't see my problem," and "others must be persuaded to look at the issue from a less parochial perspective." The *rules of the game*—he who hesitates loses his chance to play at that point, and he who is uncertain about his recommendation is overpowered by others who are sure—pressures players to come down on one side of a 51-49 issue and play. The *rewards of the game*—effectiveness, i.e., impact on outcomes, as the immediate measure of performance—encourages hard play. Thus, most players come to fight to "make the government do what is right." The strategies and tactics employed are quite similar to those formalized by theorists of international relations.

G. *Streams of Outcomes.* Important government decisions or actions emerge as collages composed of individual acts, outcomes of minor and major games, and foul-ups. Outcomes which could never have been chosen by an actor and would never have emerged from bargaining in a single game over the issue are fabricated piece by piece. Understanding of the outcome requires that it be disaggregated.

III. Dominant Inference Pattern

If a nation performed an action, that action was the *outcome* of bargaining among individuals and groups within the government. That outcome included *results* achieved by groups committed to a decision or action, *resultants* which emerged from bargaining among groups with quite different positions and *foul-ups.* Model III's explanatory power is achieved by revealing the pulling and hauling of various players, with different perceptions and priorities, focusing on separate problems, which yielded the outcomes that constitute the action in question.

IV. General Propositions

1. *Action and Intention.* Action does not presuppose intention. The sum of behavior of representatives of a government relevant to an issue was rarely intended by any individual or group. Rather separate individuals with different intentions contributed pieces which compose an outcome distinct from what anyone would have chosen.

2. *Where you stand depends on where you sit.*[29] Horizontally, the diverse demands upon each player shape his priorities, perceptions, and issues. For large classes of issues, e.g., budgets and procurement decisions, the stance of a particular player can be predicted with high reliability, from information concerning his seat. In the notorious B-36 controversy, no one was surprised by Admiral Radford's testimony that "the B-36 under any theory of war, is a bad gamble with national security," as opposed to Air Force Secretary Symington's claim that "a B-36 with an A-bomb can destroy distant objectives which might require ground armies years to take."[30]

3. *Chiefs and Indians.* The aphorism "where you stand depends on where you sit" has vertical as well as horizontal application. Vertically, the demands upon the President, Chiefs, Staffers, and Indians are quite distinct.

The foreign policy issues with which the President can deal are limited primarily by his crowded schedule: the necessity of dealing first with what comes next. His problem is to probe the special face worn by issues that come to his attention, to preserve his leeway until time has clarified the uncertainties, and to assess the relevant risks.

Foreign policy Chiefs deal most often with the hottest issue *de jour,* though they can get the attention of the President and other members of the government for other issues which they judge important. What they cannot guarantee is that "the President will pay the price" or that "the others will get on board." They must build a coalition of the relevant powers that be. They must "give the President confidence" in the right course of action.

Most problems are framed, alternatives specified, and proposals pushed, however, by Indians. Indians fight with Indians of other departments; for example, struggles between International Security Affairs of the Department of Defense and Political-Military of the State Department are a microcosm of the action at higher levels. But the Indian's major problem is how to get the *attention* of Chiefs, how to get an issue decided how to get the government "to do what is right."

In policy making then, the issue looking *down* is options: how to preserve my leeway until time clarifies uncertainties. The issue looking *sideways* is commitment: how to get others committed to my coalition. The issue looking *upwards* is confidence: how to give the boss confidence in doing what must be done. To paraphrase one of Neustadt's assertions which can be applied down the length of the ladder, the essence of a responsible official's task is to induce others to see that what needs to be done is what their own appraisal of their own responsibilities requires them to do in their own interests.

V. Specific Propositions

1. *Deterrence.* The probability of nuclear attack depends primarily on the probability of attack emerging as an outcome of the bureaucratic politics of the attacking government. First, which players can decide to launch an attack? Whether the effective power over action is controlled by an individual, a minor game, or the central game is critical. Second, though Model I's confidence in nuclear deterrence stems from an assertion that, in the end, governments will not commit suicide, Model III recalls historical precedents. Admiral Yamamoto, who designed the Japanese attack on Pearl Harbor, estimated accurately: "In the first six months to a year of war against the U.S. and England I will run wild, and I will show you an uninterrupted succession of victories; I must also tell you that, should the war be prolonged for two or three years, I have no confidence in our ultimate victory."[31] But Japan attacked. Thus, three questions might be considered. One: could any member of the government solve his problem by attack? What patterns of bargaining could yield attack as an outcome? The major difference between a stable balance of terror and a questionable balance may simply be that in the first case most members of the government appreciate fully the consequences of attack and are thus on guard against the emergence of this outcome. Two: what stream of outcomes might lead to an attack? At what point in the stream is the potential attacker's politics? If members of the U.S. government had been sensitive to the stream of decisions from which the Japanese attack on Pearl Harbor emerged, they would have been aware of a considerable probability of that attack. Three: how might miscalculation and confusion generate foul-ups that yield attack as an outcome? For example, in a crisis or after the beginning of conventional war, what happens to

the information available to, and the effective power of, members of the central game. . . .

CONCLUSION

This essay has obviously bitten off more than it has chewed. For further developments and synthesis of these arguments the reader is referred to the larger study.[32] In spite of the limits of space, however, it would be inappropriate to stop without spelling out several implications of the argument and addressing the question of relations among the models and extensions of them to activity beyond explanation.

At a minimum, the intended implications of the argument presented here are four. First, formulation of alternative frames of reference and demonstration that different analysts, relying predominantly on different models, produce quite different explanations should encourage the analyst's self-consciousness about the nets he employs. The effect of these "spectacles" in sensitizing him to particular aspects of what is going on—framing the puzzle in one way rather than another, encouraging him to examine the problem in terms of certain categories rather than others, directing him to particular kinds of evidence, and relieving puzzlement by one procedure rather than another—must be recognized and explored.

Second, the argument implies a position on the problem of "the state of the art." While accepting the commonplace characterization of the present condition of foreign policy analysis—personalistic, non-cumulative, and sometimes insightful—this essay rejects both the counsel of despair's justification of this condition as a consequence of the character of the enterprise, and the "new frontiersmen's" demand for *a priori* theorizing on the frontiers and *ad hoc* appropriation of "new techniques."[33] What is required as a first step is non-casual examination of the present product: inspection of existing explanations, articulation of the conceptual models employed in producing them, formulation of the propositions relied upon, specification of the logic of the various intellectual enterprises, and reflection on the questions being asked. Though it is difficult to overemphasize the need for more systematic processing of more data, these preliminary matters of formulating questions with clarity and sensitivity to categories and assumptions so that fruitful acquisition of large quantities of data is possible are still a major hurdle in considering most important problems.

Third, the preliminary, partial paradigms presented here provide a basis for serious reexamination of many problems of foreign and military policy. Model II and Model III cuts at problems typically treated in Model I terms can permit significant improvements in explanation and prediction.[34] Full Model II and III analyses require large amounts of information. But even in cases where the information base is severely limited, improvements are possible. Consider the problem of predicting Soviet strategic forces. In the mid-1950s, Model I style calculations led to predictions that the Soviets would rapidly deploy large numbers of long-range bombers. From a Model II perspective, both the frailty of the Air Force within the Soviet military establishment and the budgetary implications of such a buildup, would have led analysts to hedge this prediction. Moreover, Model II would have pointed to a sure, visible indicator of such a buildup:

noisy struggles among the Services over major budgetary shifts. In the late 1950s and early 1960s, Model I calculations led to the prediction of immediate, massive Soviet deployment of ICBMs. Again, a Model II cut would have reduced this number because, in the earlier period, strategic rockets were controlled by the Soviet Ground Forces rather than an independent Service, and in the later period, this would have necessitated massive shifts in budgetary splits. Today, Model I considerations lead many analysts both to recommend that an agreement not to deploy ABMs be a major American objective in upcoming strategic negotiations with the USSR, and to predict success. From a Model II vantage point, the existence of an ongoing Soviet ABM program, the strength of the organization (National Air Defense) that controls ABMs, and the fact that an agreement to stop ABM deployment would force the virtual dismantling of this organization, make a viable agreement of this sort much less likely. A Model III cut suggests that (a) there must be significant differences among perceptions and priorities of Soviet leaders over strategic negotiations, (b) any agreement will affect some players' power bases, and (c) agreements that do not require extensive cuts in the sources of some major players' power will prove easier to negotiate and more viable.

Fourth, the present formulation of paradigms is simply an initial step. As such it leaves a long list of critical questions unanswered. Given any action, an imaginative analyst should always be able to construct some rationale for the government's choice. By imposing, and relaxing, constraints on the parameters of rational choice (as in variants of Model I) analysts can construct a large number of

accounts of any act as a rational choice. But does a statement of reasons why a rational actor would choose an action constitute an explanation of the *occurrence* of that action? How can Model I analysis be forced to make more systematic contributions to the question of the determinants of occurrences? Model II's explanation of t in terms of $t − 1$ is explanation. The world is contiguous. But governments sometimes make sharp departures. Can an organizational process model be modified to suggest where change is likely? Attention to organizational change should afford greater understanding of why particular programs and SOPs are maintained by identifiable types of organizations and also how a manager can improve organizational performance. Model III tells a fascinating "story." But its complexity is enormous, the information requirements are often overwhelming, and many of the details of the bargaining may be superfluous. How can such a model be made parsimonious? The three models are obviously not exclusive alternatives. Indeed, the paradigms highlight the partial emphasis of the framework—what each emphasizes and what it leaves out. Each concentrates on one class of variables, in effect, relegating other important factors to a *ceteris parabus* clause. Model I concentrates on "market factors:" pressures and incentives created by the "international strategic marketplace." Models II and III focus on the internal mechanism of the government that chooses in this environment. But can these relations be more fully specified? Adequate synthesis would require a typology of decisions and actions, some of which are more amenable to treatment in terms of one model and some to another. Government behavior is but one cluster of factors relevant to occurrences in foreign affairs. Most students of foreign policy adopt this focus (at least when explaining and predicting). Nevertheless, the dimensions of the chess board, the character of the pieces, and the rules of the game—factors considered by international systems theorists—constitute the context in which the pieces are moved. Can the major variables in the full function of determinants of foreign policy outcomes be identified?

Both the outline of a partial, *ad hoc* working synthesis of the models, and a sketch of their uses in activities other than explanation can be suggested by generating predictions in terms of each. Strategic surrender is an important problem of international relations and diplomatic history. War termination is a new, developing area of the strategic literature. Both of these interests lead scholars to address a central question: *Why* do nations surrender *when?* Whether implicit in explanations or more explicit in analysis, diplomatic historians and strategists rely upon propositions which can be turned forward to produce predictions. Thus at the risk of being timely—and in error—the present situation (August, 1968) offers an interesting test case: Why will North Vietnam surrender when?[35]

In a nutshell, analysis according to Model I asserts: nations quit when costs outweigh the benefits. North Vietnam will surrender when she realizes "that continued fighting can only generate additional costs without hope of compensating gains, this expectation being largely the consequence of the previous application of force by the dominant side."[36] U.S. actions can increase or decrease Hanoi's strategic costs. Bombing North Vietnam increases the pain and thus increases the probability of surrender. This proposition and prediction are not without meaning. That—"other things being equal"—nations are more likely to surrender when the strategic cost-benefit balance is negative, is true. Nations rarely surrender when they are winning. The proposition specifies a range within which nations surrender. But over this broad range, the relevant question is: why do nations surrender?

Models II and III focus upon the government machine through which this fact about the international strategic marketplace must be filtered to produce a surrender. These analysts are considerably less sanguine about the possibility of surrender *at the point* that the cost-benefit calculus turns negative. Never in history (i.e., in none of the five cases I have examined) have nations surrendered at that point. Surrender occurs sometime thereafter. *When* depends on process of organizations and politics of players within these governments—as they are affected by the opposing government. Moreover, the effects of the victorious power's action upon the surrendering nation cannot be adequately summarized as increasing or decreasing strategic costs. Imposing additional costs by bombing a nation may increase the probability of surrender. But it also may reduce it. An appreciation of the impact of the acts of one nation upon another thus requires some understanding of the machine which is being influenced. For more precise prediction, Models II and III require considerably more information about the organizations and politics of North Vietnam than is publicly available. On the basis of the limited public information, however, these models can be suggestive.

Model II examines two sub-problems. First, to have lost is not sufficient. The government must know that the strategic cost-benefit calculus is negative. But neither the categories, nor the indicators, of strategic costs and benefits are clear. And the sources of information about both are organizations whose parochial priorities and perceptions do not facilitate accurate information or estimation. Military evaluation of military performance, military estimates of factors like "enemy morale," and military predictions concerning when "the tide will turn" or "the corner will have been turned" are typically distorted. In cases of highly decentralized guerrilla operations, like Vietnam, these problems are exacerbated. Thus strategic costs will be underestimated. Only highly *visible* costs can have direct impact on leaders without being filtered through organizational channels. Second, since organizations define the details of options and execute actions, surrender (and negotiation) is likely to entail considerable bungling in the early stages. No organization can define options or prepare programs for this treasonous act. Thus, early overtures will be uncoordinated with the acts of other organizations, e.g., the fighting forces, creating contradictory "signals" to the victor.

Model III suggests that surrender will not come at the point that strategic costs outweigh benefits, but that it will not wait until the leadership group concludes that the war is lost. Rather the problem is better understood in terms of four additional propositions. First, strong advocates of the war effort, whose careers are closely identified with the war, rarely come to the conclusion that costs outweigh benefits. Second, quite often from the outset of a war, a number of members of the government (particularly those whose responsibilities sensitize them to problems other than war, e.g., economic planners or intelligence experts) are convinced that the war effort is futile. Third, surrender is likely to come as the result of a political shift that enhances the effective power of the latter group (and adds swing members to it). Fourth, the course of the war, particularly actions of the victor, can influence the advantages and disadvantages of players in the loser's government. Thus, North Vietnam will surrender not when its leaders have a change of heart, but when Hanoi has a change of leaders (or a change of effective power within the central circle). How U.S. bombing (or pause), threats, promises, or action in the South affect the game in Hanoi is subtle but nonetheless crucial.

That these three models could be applied to the surrender of governments other than North Vietnam should be obvious. But that exercise is left for the reader.

NOTES

1. Theodore Sorensen, *Kennedy* (New York, 1965), p. 705.
2. In attempting to understand problems of foreign affairs, analysts engage in a number of related, but logically separable enterprises: (a) description, (b) explanation, (c) prediction, (d) evaluation, and (e) recommendation. This essay focuses primarily on explanation (and by implication, prediction).
3. In arguing that explanations proceed in terms of implicit conceptual models, this essay makes no claim that foreign policy analysts have developed any satisfactory, empirically tested theory. In this essay,

the use of the term "model" without qualifiers should be read "conceptual scheme."

4. For the purpose of this argument we shall accept Carl G. Hempel's characterization of the logic of explanation: an explanation "answers the question, '*Why* did the explanadum-phenomenon occur?' by showing that the phenomenon resulted from particular circumstances, specified in C_2, C_2, . . . C_k, in accordance with laws L_1, L_2, . . . L_r. By pointing this out, the argument shows that, given the particular circumstances and the laws in question, the occurrence of the phenomenon was to be *expected;* and it is in this sense that the explanation enables us to understand why the phenomenon occurred." *Aspects of Scientific Explanation* (New York, 1965), p. 337. While various patterns of explanation can be distinguished, *viz.,* Ernest Nagel, *The Structure of Science: Problems in the Logic of Scientific Explanation,* New York, 1961), satisfactory scientific explanations exhibit this basic logic. Consequently prediction is the converse of explanation.

5. Earlier drafts of this argument have aroused heated arguments concerning proper names for these models. To choose names from ordinary language is to court confusion, as well as familiarity. Perhaps it is best to think of these models as I, II, and III.

6. *New York Times,* February 18, 1967.

7. *Ibid.*

8. Arnold Horelick and Myron Rush, *Strategic Power and Soviet Foreign Policy* (Chicago, 1965). Based on A. Horelick, "The Cuban Missile Crisis: An Analysis of Soviet Calculations and Behavior," *World Politics* (April, 1964).

9. Horelick and Rush, *Strategic Power and Soviet Foreign Policy,* p. 154.

10. Hans Morgenthau, *Politics Among Nations* (3rd ed.; New York, 1960), p. 191.

11. *Ibid.,* p. 192.

12. *Ibid.,* p. 5.

13. *Ibid.,* pp. 5–6.

14. The larger study examines several exceptions to this generalization. Sidney Verba's excellent essay "Assumptions of Rationality and Non-Rationality in Models of the International System" is less an exception than it is an approach to a somewhat different problem. Verba focuses upon models of rationality and irrationality of *individual* statesmen: in Knorr and Verba, *The International System.*

15. Robert K. Merton, *Social Theory and Social Structures* (Revised and Enlarged Edition; New York, 1957), pp. 12–16. Considerably weaker than a satisfactory theoretical model, paradigms nevertheless represent a short step in that direction from looser, implicit conceptual models. Neither the concepts nor the relations among the variables are sufficiently specified to yield propositions deductively. "Paradigmatic Analysis" nevertheless has considerable promise for clarifying and codifying styles of analysis in political science. Each of the paradigms stated here can be represented rigorously in mathematical terms. For example, Model I lends itself to mathematical formulation along the lines of Herbert Simon's "Behavioral Theory of Rationality," *Models of Man* (New York, 1957). But this does not solve the most difficult problem of "measurement and estimation."

16. Though a variant of this model could easily be stochastic, this paradigm is stated in non-probabilistic terms. In contemporary strategy, a stochastic version of this model is sometimes used for predictions; but it is almost impossible to find an explanation of an occurrence in foreign affairs that is consistently probabilistic.

Analogies between Model I and the concept of explanation developed by R. G. Collingwood, William Dray, and other "revisionists" among philosophers concerned with the critical philosophy of history are not accidental. For a summary of the "revisionist position" see Maurice Mandelbaum, "Historical Explanation: The Problem of Covering Laws," *History and Theory* (1960).

17. This model is an analogue of the theory of the rational entrepreneur which has been developed extensively in economic theories of the firm and the consumer. These two propositions specify the "substitution effect." Refinement of this model and specification of additional general propositions by translating from the economic theory is straight-forward.

18. *New York Times,* March 22, 1969.

19. See Nathan Leites, *A Study of Bolshevism* (Glencoe, Illinois, 1953).

20. The influence of organizational studies upon the present literature of foreign affairs is minimal. Specialists in international politics are not students of organization theory. Organization theory has only recently begun to study organizations as decisionmakers and has not yet produced behavioral studies of national security organizations from a decisionmaking perspective. It seems unlikely, however, that these gaps will remain unfilled much longer. Considerable progress has been made in the study of the business firm as an organization. Scholars have begun applying these insights to government organizations, and interest in an organizational perspective is spreading among institutions and individuals concerned with actual government operations. The "decisionmaking" approach represented by Richard Snyder, R. Bruck, and B. Sapin, *Foreign Policy Decision-Making* (Glencoe, Illinois, 1962), incorporates a number of insights from organization theory.

21. The formulation of this paradigm is indebted both to the orientation and insights of Herbert Simon and to the behavioral model of the firm stated by Richard Cyert and James March, *A Behavioral Theory of the Firm* (Englewood Cliffs, 1963). Here, however, one is forced to grapple with the less routine, less quantified functions of the less differentiated elements in government organizations.

22. Theodore Sorensen, "You Get to Walk to Work," *New York Times Magazine,* March 19, 1967.

23. Organizations are not monolithic. The proper level of disaggregation depends upon the objectives of a piece of analysis. This paradigm is formulated with reference to the major organizations that constitute the U.S. government. Generalization to the major components of each department and agency should be relatively straightforward.

24. The stability of these constraints is dependent on such factors as rules for promotion and reward budgeting and accounting procedures, and mundane operating procedures.

25. Marriner Eccles, *Beckoning Frontiers* (New York, 1951), p. 336.

26. Arthur Schlesinger, *A Thousand Days* (Boston, 1965), p. 406.

27. This paradigm relies upon the small group of analysts who have begun to fill the gap. My primary source is the model implicit in the work of Richard E. Neustadt, though his concentration on presidential action has been generalized to a concern with policy as the outcome of political bargaining among a number of independent players, the President amounting to no more than a "superpower" among many lesser but considerable powers. As Warner Schilling argues, the substantive problems are of such inordinate difficulty that uncertainties and differences with regard to goals, alternatives, and consequences are inevitable. This necessitates what Roger Hilsman describes as the process of conflict and consensus building. The techniques employed in this process often resemble those used in legislative assemblies, though Samuel Huntington's

characterization of the process as "legislative" overemphasizes the equality of participants as opposed to the hierarchy which structures the game. Moreover, whereas for Huntington, foreign policy (in contrast to military policy) is set by the executive, this paradigm maintains that the activities which he describes as legislative are characteristic of the process by which foreign policy is made.

28. The theatrical metaphor of stage, roles, and actors is more common than this metaphor of games, positions, and players. Nevertheless, the rigidity connotated by the concept of "role" both in the theatrical sense of actors reciting fixed lines and in the sociological sense of fixed responses to specified social situations makes the concept of games, positions, and players more useful for this analysis of active participants in the determination of national policy. Objections to the terminology on the grounds that "game" connotes non-serious play overlook the concept's application to most serious problems both in Wittgenstein's philosophy and in contemporary game theory. Game theory typically treats more precisely structured games, but Wittgenstein's examination of the "language game" wherein men use words to communicate is quite analogous to this analysis of the less specified game of bureaucratic politics. See Ludwig Wittgenstein, *Philosophical Investigations,* and Thomas Schelling, "What is Game Theory?" in James Charlesworth, *Contemporary Political Analysis.*

29. This aphorism was stated first, I think, by Don K. Price.

30. Paul Y. Hammond, "Super Carriers and B-36 Bombers," in Harold Stein (ed.), *American Civil-Military Decisions* (Birmingham, 1963).

31. Roberta Wohlstetter, *Pearl Harbor* (Stanford, 1962), p. 350.

32. *Bureaucracy and Policy* (forthcoming, 1969).

33. Thus my position is quite distinct from both poles in the recent "great debate" about international relations. While many "traditionalists" of the sort Kaplan attacks adopt the first posture and many "scientists" of the sort attacked by Bull adopt the second, this third posture is relatively neutral with respect to whatever is in substantive dispute. See Hedly Bull, "International Theory: The Case for a Classical Approach," *World Politics* (April, 1966); and Morton Kaplan, "The New Great Debate: Traditionalism vs. Science in International Relations," *World Politics* (October, 1966).

34. A number of problems are now being examined in these terms both in the Bureaucracy Study Group on Bureaucracy and Policy of the Institute of Politics at Harvard University and at the Rand Corporation.

35. In response to several readers' recommendations, what follows is reproduced *verbatim* from the paper delivered at the September, 1968 Association meetings (Rand P-3919). The discussion is heavily indebted to Ernest R. May.

36. Richard Snyder, *Deterrence and Defense* (Princeton, 1961), p. 11. For a more general presentation of this position see Paul Kecskemeti, *Strategic Surrender* (New York, 1964).

QUESTIONS

1. Compare and contrast the organizational process model and the bureaucratic politics model.

2. How do these models differ from realism?

32. Organizational Routines and the Causes of War

Jack S. Levy

In this article, Jack S. Levy discusses how the organizational routines, or standard operating procedures, of a nation are an influential factor in determining a state's foreign policy. By analyzing the mobilization plans of the major European powers at the outbreak of World War I, Levy demonstrates the impact of the institutional makeup of a nation on its foreign policy decisions. The author introduces the idea that organizational routines are also affected by political, bureaucratic, technological, and psychological factors. This selection is from the *International Studies Quarterly* (1986).

Jack S. Levy is a professor at the University of Texas at Austin. His other works include *War in the Modern Great Power System, 1495-1975* (1983), as well as contributions to many international studies and political science journals.

One of the central concepts in the organizational process or cybernetic model of foreign policy decisionmaking is standard operating procedures or SOPs (Allison, 1971; Steinbruner, 1974). Although it is commonly believed that the model in general and SOPs in particular have more explanatory power in non-crisis as opposed to crisis decisions, and although most case studies dealing with the subject have focused on non-crisis issues, organizational processes and routines may also be important for the question of the causes of war . . .

In spite of the importance of the question of how organizational processes might contribute to the outbreak of war, it has never been studied systematically, either in the case of World War I or more generally.[1] The aim of this study is to identify the specific theoretical linkages by which organizational processes in general and military routines in particular may lead to the outbreak of war under certain conditions, and in doing so dis-cuss the analytical problems involved in making such causal inferences. My argument is that the theoretical linkages between military routines and the outbreak of war are logically incomplete without the inclusion of other systemic, institutional, and psychological variables. Military routines can never 'cause' war by themselves, but they can contribute to the outbreak of war under certain conditions and in conjunction with certain other variables. I illustrate the causal relationships through an examination of the World War I mobilization plans, and then briefly consider their relevance in the nuclear age.[2] . . .

MILITARY ROUTINES AND THE OUTBREAK OF WAR: THE CONVENTIONAL ARGUMENT

"Mobilization Means War"

Probably the most common explanation of how military routines contribute to the outbreak of war focuses on the momentum generated by the mobilization plans themselves. Each action in this process of incremental escalation leads logically to the next, locking in current policy and contributing to a mechanistic and practically irreversible process of escalation to war. Let us examine the common argument that in 1914 the military preparations of the great powers acquired a momentum of their own, that because of rigid military plans each step led inevitably to the next, that the serious threat of mobilization of one great power essentially forces certain other powers to mobilize, and that mobilization itself led inevitably to war.[3]

The World War I mobilization plans were based on the assumption that the advantage lay with the offense (Hart, 1932: 72; Taylor, 1969: 15; Levy, 1984: 233; Snyder, 1984a, b; Van Evera, 1984a, b) and that speed was of the essence. European leaders believed that a one- to three-day lead in mobilization would be militarily significant for the course of the war, leaving those who delayed vulnerable against their better-prepared adversaries (Van Evera, 1984a: 72–74). These perceptions created enormous incentives to strike first (Van Evera, 1984a: 71–79; Snyder, 1985a), which placed a premium on rapid mobilization plans, and which in turn required detailed advance planning. The entire process would be conducted by rail, and general staffs had been working for years to perfect their timetables. Thus, the railroad timetables became exceedingly complex and left little margin for error. . . .

The direct link between mobilization and war was particularly compelling in the German case. The German Schlieffen Plan, devised in response to the threat of a two-front war, called for a holding action against Russia in the East while the bulk of German forces were directed against France in the West. It was based on the assumptions that the numerical inferiority of the Austro-German forces could be overcome by the presumed advantages of internal lines of communication, that Russia could not be defeated quickly because of her size, and that the slowness of Russian mobilization made it feasible to defeat France first.[4] This had to be done quickly, however, so the German armies could be shifted to the East in time to meet the Russian onslaught. Chief of Staff von Schlieffen, recognizing the strength of the French forces along the Alsace–Lorraine frontier and entranced by Hannibal's double envelopment of the Romans at Cannae (Albertini, 1957: 3/237; Turner, 1979: 202–203), concluded that the French could be quickly defeated only by an enveloping movement through Belgium. But any advance into Belgium required the seizure of Liège, an absolutely vital railway junction. As Chief of Staff Moltke wrote, before the war, "the possession of Liège is the *sine qua non* of our advance" (Turner, 1979: 212). But the seizure of Liège had to be quick and surgical, so as not to destroy its vital tunnels and bridges. This would require "meticulous preparation and surprise" and had to be accomplished before Liège could be reinforced, and thus immediately after a declaration of war if not before. Complicating this was the fact that the railway lines required that four German armies, over 840,000 men, had to be routed through a single junction at Aachen. To allow them to pile up at the frontier and wait for a declaration of war would permit the reinforcement of Liège, make its surgical seizure much more problematical, and delay the completion of mobilization. The defense of Liège would prevent the rapid defeat of France and thus potentially ruin the entire German war effort (Van Evera, 1984a: 74). Thus the Schlieffen Plan required an advance into neutral Belgium as an integral part of mobilization itself. Thus Taylor (1969: 25) argues that, for Germany, "there is no breathing space between mobilization and war"; Albertini (1957: 2/480) argues that, for Germany, "mobilization . . . was identical with going to war"; Churchill concludes that "Mobilization therefore spelt war" (Turner, 1970: 63).

A German advance into Belgium would not only initiate hostilities but it would also undoubtedly bring Britain into the war (Albertini, 1957: 2/508; Taylor, 1969: 104).[5] It would also lead inevitably to an expansion of the war in the East, for because of the alliance systems and Russia's commitment to France, Russia would have to mobilize rapidly and invade Germany to relieve pressure on France, while Austria would have to aid her German ally by moving against Russia (Turner, 1970: 77). In this way, German mobilization itself made a general war virtually inevitable. . . .

The Difficulty of Improvising or Switching Plans

Because mobilization was a tightly coupled system in which many discrete elements had to mesh with perfect timing, no change or improvisation was perceived as possible during mobilization. Any deviation from the plan would bring only chaos, for given the interdependence of the elements of the system, a change in one of them would necessarily

affect all the rest. As Taylor (1974: 444) argues, 'The time-tables were rigid and could not be altered without months of preparation'. It is true that while Germany and France each had only one plan for mobilization, Russia and Austria each had multiple plans. Russia could initiate a general mobilization against both Germany and Austria-Hungary, or a partial mobilization against Austria-Hungary alone. Austria-Hungary could mobilize against either Serbia, Italy, or Russia. But these options were exclusive. The initiation of one of these plans "would make the switch to an alternative plan impossible. The time-tables could not be changed overnight" (Taylor, 1974: 444). The fact that the mobilization plans had never been rehearsed only added to their rigidity, for the general staffs had no experience improvising plans during their implementation (Taylor, 1969: 16; 1974: 444; Holsti, 1972: 157). A closer examination of last-minute attempts to alter or modify the plan (Germany and Austria) or switch from one plan to another (Russia) in a desperate effort to maintain the peace will illustrate the practical impossibility of improvisation.

As the crisis escalated, the Kaiser became increasingly fearful of the prospect of a two-front war, and on July 29 Bethmann sent a telegram to London requesting their neutrality. Immediately after the Kaiser's order for general mobilization on August 1, Berlin received a telegram from Lichnowsky, the German Ambassador in London, reporting that if Germany refrained from attacking France, 'England would remain neutral and guarantee the passivity of France' (Albertini, 1957: 3/380). The German Chancellor, Foreign Minister, and Kaiser were elated by this opportunity to localize the war in the East. The Kaiser summoned Moltke and announced, "Now we can go to war against Russia only. We simply march the whole of our army to the East" (Tuchman, 1962: 98).

Moltke refused. He had been planning this moment for a decade, and the thought of having his precision-tuned mobilization plans involving a million men wrenched into reverse was more than Moltke could bear. . . .

The Kaiser agreed not to reverse the plans but sought to delay their implementation by stopping the trains from crossing into Luxembourg. But the railways of Luxembourg were essential to the offensive through Belgium into France, and Moltke refused to sign the order countermanding the advance into Luxembourg. Before the issue could be resolved, however, a telegram arrived saying that the earlier suggestion of English neutrality had been based on a "misunderstanding" and was not possible (Albertini, 1957: 3/381–386). The point here, however, is that in the eyes of Moltke and others the prospect of English neutrality was not enough to alter the plans (Albertini, 1957: 3/381–386; Tuchman, 1962: 97–103; Stoessinger, 1978: 33–25).[6]

The German experience in 1914 demonstrates the practical difficulty of altering an existing plan. It also illustrates the complications introduced if an existing plan or plans provide policymakers with no limited military options between inaction and full mobilization. That may leave them with no means of preserving vital interests without a major war, no way of demonstrating resolve without automatically escalating the war, no possibility for a strategy of coercive diplomacy employing limited threats in pursuit of limited interests. The rigidity of the pre-ferred plan, in conjunction with the non-availability of existing alternatives, may preclude policymakers from adopting certain alternatives which might conceivably be sufficient to head off an impending war. Given the costs of inaction and the tendency toward worst-case analysis among the military (Betts, 1977: 160–162; Van Evera, 1984b: ch. 7), there is a strong tendency toward overreaction. Thus, the Kaiser perceived that he had no means of deterring Russian intervention against Austria in the Balkans without taking action that risked bringing Britain into the war and escalation to a general European war. Because of the importance of his only great power ally and the magnitude of the Russian threat, and denied the means of supporting a serious effort to gain British neutrality, the Kaiser chose to implement the Schlieffen Plan rather than stand idle.[7] . . .

The Timing of Mobilization

Military routines may also contribute to the outbreak of war by affecting the timing of mobilization, although this causal link is not generally given as much attention as the others. Plans which require a lengthy period of mobilization may contribute to war by inducing an early mobilization, intensifying the conflict spiral before all diplomatic means of reaching a settlement have been exhausted.[8] The slowness of the Russian mobilization in 1914 is a classic example. Because of its size and uneven population density, Russia did not have a mobilization plan in which each of its military districts recruited exclusively from within its own area (Fay, 1928: 2/450–451). The resulting delays in her mobilization plans generated enormous pressures for early mobilization, which helped bring on the war (Albertini, 1957: 2/543).[9] The slow rate of the Russian mobilization also led Germany to believe that she had time to conduct an offensive against France in the West and hence contributed to the expansion of the war.

The nature of mobilization plans can also work to delay rather than speed up their implementation. While under most circumstances this would decrease the likelihood of war, under some conditions it might actually make war more likely. It has been argued, for example, that Austria-Hungary's two-week delay in her ultimatum to Serbia and subsequent mobilization after the "blank check" from Germany on July 6 actually contributed to a general European war (Schmitt, 1930: 1/393; Williamson, 1979: 151). Taylor (1954: 522–523) asserts that 'The one chance of success for Austria-Hungary [to localize the war] would have been rapid action', for a fait accompli in immediate response to the assassination would have been perceived as having some legitimacy in the eyes of Europe, though whether this would have been sufficient to avert a general war is unclear. Williamson (1979: 152–154) explains the delay in terms of organizational routines involving the military. Because of the importance of harvests for the economy, Conrad, the Chief of the Austrian General Staff, had agreed to agrarian demands and instituted a policy of regular and routinized harvest leaves, allowing troops on active duty to return home to help with the harvests and then rejoin their units for the usual summer maneuvers. On July 6, Conrad learned that half of the corps manpower at Agram, Innsbruck, Kaschau, Temesvar, Budapest, Pressburg, and Graz were away on harvest leave and scheduled to return between July 19 and 25. Conrad and

Foreign Minister Berchtold had planned to act quickly against Serbia after receiving the German go-ahead, but to do that would have required them to recall the troops on harvest leave. This would not only disrupt the harvests and possibly confuse the mobilization, but it would also destroy any chance of a diplomatic or military surprise. Instead of recalling the troops, Vienna simply cancelled the remaining leaves and delayed the ultimatum to Serbia, ignorant at the time of the risks that this postponement would entail.[10]

Because of the perception that "mobilization meant war," because of the absence of alternatives between partial mobilization and full mobilization and the difficulties of switching from the former to the latter, and because of the difficulty of modifying an existing plan, World War I is often cited as the classic case of rigid organizational routines leading to war. The preceding analysis suggests strongly that organizational routines played an important role, but the reader will have noticed that other explanatory variables have implicitly been introduced into the analysis. The question of the causal impact of military routines on the outbreak of war cannot avoid some interesting analytical problems and interaction effects involving other variables. These have been given inadequate attention in the literature and need to be examined.

ANALYTICAL PROBLEMS AND THE ROLE OF OTHER VARIABLES

Analyses of the mobilization plans of 1914 have convincingly demonstrated that the rigid adherence to existing plans contributed to the outbreak of war. They have not convincingly determined the relative importance of this causal effect compared to that of other variables, but that is a different question and one which will not be examined here. More important for our purposes, they have not dealt with the critical question of *what explains the rigid adherence to existing plans.* The inherent rigidity of the plans themselves is just one of several variables which can lead to their rigid implementation, and one which rarely acts alone; other organizational, bureaucratic-political, psychological, and systemic variables may also be involved. . . .

Although organizational routines clearly impose constraints on decision-makers, and although the deviation from an existing plan undoubtedly involves costs, so does the adherence to an existing routine. In many cases, perhaps including 1914, the costs of implementing an existing military routine appear to outweigh the costs of adopting some alternative. The question in these cases is why decisionmakers still choose to adhere to an existing military contingency plan rather than adopt an alternative plan or devise a new plan. This choice cannot be fully explained in the absence of an understanding of why the preferred plan was initially developed (though other factors must also be included).

"Military Necessity" and the Problem of Spurious Inference

Let us assume for the moment that the primary determinant of a military contingency plan is "military necessity," as determined by a rational strategic calculus involving a state's relative military power, diplomatic alignments, geographical constraints, existing logistical and technological capabilities, and other relevant external variables. If the strategic situa-

tion in which the plans are implemented is the same as that for which the contingency plans were initially developed, then the same considerations of military necessity would apply. If political decisionmakers adhere to the original plan for those reasons, then the explanation for the rigid adherence to the original plan lies with military necessity, rather than with the nature of the routines themselves. The imputation of a causal relationship between military routines and the outbreak of war would then involve a spurious inference.[11]

One particularly important systemic-level phenomenon contributing to military necessity and illustrating the problem of causal inference is the "security dilemma," a situation structured in such a way that a state can increase its security only at the expense of another's security (Jervis, 1978). This problem is particularly acute if military technology creates an incentive to strike first. Even states with no aggressive intentions and a genuine commitment to peace may feel compelled by the logic of the situation to take actions which they recognize may contribute to war.[12]

The July crisis posed an intense security dilemma for many of the European powers, and many factors contributed to the perceived incentive to strike first.[13] These include: the perception that existing military technology favored the offense, 'the "offensive" character of the war plans of all of the great powers' (Snyder, 1984b; Van Evera, 1984a); the belief that the early stages of mobilization could be conducted secretly (Van Evera, 1984a: 75–79); the expectation that even short delays in mobilization could be disastrous (Van Evera, 1984a: 72–74);[14] mobilization systems which permitted full mobilization in two weeks (Van Evera, 1984a:

79); and the traditional proclivity of the military toward worst-case analysis, their perception (in July 1914 and for at least the previous year) that war was inevitable (Lebow, 1981: 254–257), and their tendency to place greater importance on winning such a war than on deterring its occurrence. Any delay in German mobilization might jeopardize the rapid defeat of France that was perceived to be essential in a two-front war, and thus many have argued that it would have been too risky for Germany to abandon the Schlieffen Plan and turn to the east (Wegerer, 1928). If decisionmakers acted on these grounds, then it was not the mobilization plans themselves, but instead perceived military necessity and the security dilemma that determined the critical decision that led to war. If it is true, as Albertini (1957: 2/543) argues, that Russia really had no choice but to adopt a general mobilization against both Germany and Austria-Hungary unless she was willing to put herself at a very serious military disadvantage, then it was the security dilemma and the conditions contributing to it that have the primary causal impact. Similarly, if it is true that even a Russian partial mobilization against Austria-Hungary would have led to a German mobilization and war, then any inference that the rigidity of the Russian plans themselves helped cause war would be spurious (Snyder, 1984a: 88).

This discussion leads us to the critical question of whether decisionmakers *perceive* that they are acting on the basis of military necessity. Since regardless of motivations routines are likely to be publicly justified in terms of military necessity, the problem is the methodological one of distinguishing true motivation from public rationalization. This leads us to evaluate whether the *process* of decisionmaking

appears to conform to a rational strategic calculus. Is there a deliberate effort to consider alternative plans, and to make subjective probability judgments as to their feasibility, and to compare their costs and benefits with those of existing plans with respect to the attainment of well-defined foreign policy objectives? If there is a reasonable search process for the time available, and if alternative plans or improvisations seem to be rejected on their merits, then it can be concluded that military necessity is the determining factor. Any inference that rigid military plans caused war would then be spurious. But if existing contingency plans and their underlying assumptions are blindly accepted in a crisis, with no attempt to evaluate the merits of possible alternatives, then it could be concluded that the inherent rigidity of the plans was a contributing cause of the war. . . .

Although the debate about the viability of the Schlieffen Plan and its various alternatives (Ritter, 1958, 1973; Turner, 1979: 212–217; Snyder, 1984b: 116–122) will perhaps never be resolved, this is not really important here. The critical question is how Moltke and others on the General Staff *perceived* military necessity in 1914. Though Moltke did have reservations about the political advisability and operational feasibility of the Schlieffen Plan (Ritter, 1973: 2/216–219; Snyder, 1984b: 116, 147–157), he believed that all of the alternatives were worse (Snyder, 1984b: 112–116). There is no evidence, however, that an eastern offensive was ever given serious consideration in 1914. Von Staab was never consulted regarding its feasibility (Lebow, 1981: 236), and it is not at all clear that the relative advantages and disadvantages of various alternatives were carefully weighed (Snyder, 1984b: ch. 6). This does not appear to be consistent with a rational decision process (Steinbruner, 1974: ch. 2). Thus the rigid implementation of existing routines in 1914 cannot be explained solely by a rational strategic calculus, and we can conclude that the routines themselves, in conjunction with other variables, had an important causal effect.[15] . . .

If the character of the military plans and the rigid implementation are not both the product of antecedent variables, the question is then what other variables might interact with military routines to produce their rigid implementation. These factors include: (1) systemic variables such as prestige and alliance commitments; (2) organizational and bureaucratic variables such as organizational autonomy, factored problems, parochial interests, and military-civilian and intra-military conflict; and (3) the psychology of individual decisionmakers and small-group dynamics. These variables are generally given inadequate attention in the literature, resulting in an incomplete explanation for rigid adherence to existing organizational routines during a crisis and the attribution of excessive causal significance to the nature of the routines themselves.

Systemic Variables

One systemic variable which may independently inhibit any modification of existing military contingency plans is prestige (or reputational interests). This may be particularly true of any proposed interruption or reversal of plans which is already in the early stages of implementation, for decisionmakers may fear that any interruption might be perceived as weakness by the adversary.[16] This effect may be intensified by the multiplicative interaction of reputational considerations and alliances. If specific military plans are designed to help support an ally, the importance for one's reputation of fulfilling an alliance commitment may lead to the rigid implementation of military plans, even if the strategic objectives for which the alliance was formed are no longer threatened. Thus Russia moved to a general mobilization in part because of the pressure from her French ally (Turner, 1968).[17] Thus, the alliance/reputation effect would add to that of the routines themselves.

Other Organizational and Bureaucratic Variables

There are other dimensions of organizational behavior which interact (multiplicatively) with military doctrine and routines to make them more rigid and unresponsive to changing political circumstances, and which may also have an independent and hence additive effect on rigidity. Posen (1984: 54–57) suggests several organizational factors which tend to impede innovation in military doctrine, and by implication changes in military plans deriving from that doctrine. The organization as a whole and individuals within it develop vested interests in existing organizational goals and routines, so any changes that would inevitably affect the existing status quo tend to be resisted. The inherent organizational tendency to minimize uncertainty (Allison, 1971: 76–77) also generates inhibitions against change from familiar routines to untested alternatives. The pattern of doctrinal stagnation persists in spite of technological change because of the tendency for new technologies to be assimilated into old doctrine, rather than stimulate change to a new one, and also because of the tendency not to learn about the operational implications of new technologies from the wars of others (Katzenbach, 1971; Posen, 1984: 55). Resistance to change is further enhanced by the inherent difficulties in achieving an integration of political ends and military means. One problem here is the priority given to autonomy by an organization and its interest in achieving total operational control over the means necessary to perform a given task (Halperin, 1974: 51–54). This is particularly true of the military, given the different professional socialization, skills, and roles of military and civilians (Huntington, 1957: ch. 3; Posen, 1984: 52).[18] In order to maintain their autonomy military organizations are also often unwilling to provide civilian policymakers with information, particularly information regarding doctrine and operational tactics, and this only increases policy-makers' unfamiliarity with military issues.[19]

Related to organizational autonomy is the tendency toward factored problems—the division of complex problems and their delegation to various sub-units within the organization (Allison, 1971: 71–72). There is little coordination among these distinct organizational sub-units, and solutions to the factored problems are generated independently and may be mutually contradictory. This may leave top decisionmakers unaware of the details of particular organizational routines and unaware of the extent to which these repertoires may constrain their behavior, and make it difficult for them to integrate these independent solutions into coherent national policy. Political leaders may devise policies without realizing the full extent to which existing military contingency plans either preclude the implementation of those poli-

cies or actually require other policies. This is particularly serious given the military tendency to elevate narrow operational requirements above the needs of state policy (Posen, 1984: 53). Numerous aspects of the July 1914 crisis fit this pattern of organizational behavior.

First of all, the military plans, particularly in Germany, were constructed without consultation with political decisionmakers and with total disregard for political considerations.[20] The war plans were regarded as the autonomous sphere of the military. As Holstein, a leading official in the German Foreign Office, remarked (in 1990), "If the Chief of Staff, especially a strategic authority such as Schlieffen, believes such a measure [the Schlieffen Plan] to be necessary, then it is the obligation of diplomacy to adjust to it and prepare for it in every possible way" (Ritter, 1958: 91). Whereas in France all operational plans had to be submitted to the government's supreme war council for the consideration and approval of top political decisionmakers (Kennedy, 1979: 7; Keiger, 1983), and whereas in Britain also civilian decisionmakers had the upper hand (Steiner, 1977: 220), the military were ascendant in Berlin. In contrast to the French civilians' rejection of the military's pressures for the violation of Belgian neutrality, Schlieffen's technical military plan was promptly accepted by the top political leadership in Germany without any real discussion of the grave countervailing political arguments. Foreign Secretary Jagow's request in 1912 that the need to violate Belgian territory be re-evaluated was rejected by Moltke (Snyder, 1984b: 121). Until 1913, at least, there was not even an inquiry into the feasibility of alternative operational plans that might hold fewer political dangers (Ritter,

1973: 2/205). As Snyder (1984b: 121) concludes: "Civilians had . . . little if any impact on the shape of German war plans."

As a result, European war plans in general and those of Germany in particular were based exclusively on military considerations (Ritter, 1958, 1973: vol. 2, ch. 9; Turner, 1979: 205).[21] They reflected the traditional military priority placed on winning any war that might occur, rather than deterring its occurrence. They were not particularly concerned with the specific political conditions that might make a war necessary or with how the mobilization plans themselves might make war more likely. More generally, the military plans were devised without regard for the specific national political interests that might be at stake in various conflicts. . . .

The development of German military plans without regard for political considerations had enormous consequences. By preventing her from mobilizing without going to war, it precluded a strategy of coercive diplomacy based on demonstrations of force and the control of risks through the fine-tuning of threats. In addition, the Schlieffen Plan made it inevitable that any war would be a two-front war and that England would intervene against her, so that a single spark would trigger a general war. Moreover, in demanding an early and rapid invasion and an early military offensive, the plan would force Germany to incur the diplomatic and moral costs of striking first, which no doubt contributed to the neutrality of Italy and Romania. Thus Ritter (1958: 90) argues that "The outbreak of war in 1914 is the most tragic example of a government's helpless dependence on the planning of strategists that history has ever seen," and Albertini (1957: 3/253)

concludes that the primary reason why Germany was led to "set fire to the powder cask" was "the requirements of the Schlieffen Plan, which no doubt was a masterpiece of military science, but also a monument of that utter lack of political horse-sense which is the main cause of European disorders and upheavals."

It was not just the apolitical nature of the military plans that had such serious consequences, but also the ignorance of those plans by top political decisionmakers until it was too late. Whereas the military tended to perceive mobilization as a means of preparing for a certain and immediate war, political leaders tended to perceive it as an instrument of deterrence or coercive diplomacy. They had little conception of how few options they had, of the extent to which their room to maneuver was limited, of the mismatch between their foreign policy objectives and the military instruments available to support them. They did not realize that certain actions which they took in all sincerity to avoid war only made war more likely, or that coercive actions, the risks of which they believed to be limited or at least manageable, would only push them beyond the point of no return. Adequate knowledge of the rigidity of the military plans might have been enough to preclude them from taking the risks that led to a general war that none of the statesmen really wanted.[22] . . .

The problem of civilian lack of understanding of military matters is compounded if the military are unaware of this ignorance. Admiral Tirpitz tells of how "horror-stricken" he and Moltke were to discover (at an 11 p.m. meeting on August 1) that political authorities had been unaware of the plan to seize Liège, and observed that the "political leadership had completely lost its head"

(Albertini, 1957: 3/195). Thus, the separation of military planning from political leadership, and the politicians' ignorance of the mobilization plans and their political requirements led to actions designed to maintain the peace, but which in actuality only accelerated the descent into war.

Another set of variables which interact (multiplicatively) with military routines, leading to their inflexible implementation and possibly to war, is bureaucratic politics.[23] Organizational routines play a critical role in the political bargaining process by setting the terms of the political debate (Barnet, 1972: 79–80). The policy preferences of the leading actors and their definition of the situation may be greatly influenced by the information and options provided by lower-level bureaucracies. The ignorance of military routines by political decisionmakers is one example of this. In addition, advocates of an existing military contingency plan have an advantage in persuading or bargaining with rival actors who lack such a plan (Betts, 1977: 155). The burden of proof is placed on those who propose to depart from an existing routine, particularly in a crisis where time constraints are severe. Gaining acceptance for an alternative plan is all the more difficult if the military is united behind a single plan, for any alternative lacking the expertise and political support of the military lacks credibility. Thus, political decisionmakers preparing to alter the mobilization plans in a last-ditch effort to maintain the peace in 1914 lacked not only a systemic plan to implement their policies; they also lacked the bargaining advantages that such a plan would provide and which were necessary to overcome the expertise and influence of the military. A related political advantage of existing contingency plans is that they create the illusion of precision and success, for most military contingency plans are accompanied by exceedingly optimistic forecasts (Barnet, 1972: 80).

Not only do existing routines help structure the political debate, but the key actors in the decisionmaking process can themselves use or manipulate the routines to advance their own policy preferences. All organizations have parochial interests which shape their perceptions of the national interest (Halperin, 1974: ch. 3). The organizational parochialism of the military is particularly distinctive (Huntington, 1957; Vagts, 1959). Military influence on crisis decisionmaking derives from its perceived legitimacy with respect to national security issues, the size of the resources which it controls in society, its ability to mobilize public support for its preferred policies, and the dependence of civilians upon the information which it controls. Military influence also depends greatly on the receptivity of key political decisionmakers, and this may vary. Bethmann-Hollweg admits in his memoirs, for example, that he deferred to military advice whenever questions of German security were being considered (Craig, 1955: 291). The military may exaggerate the rigidity of existing contingency plans or otherwise use their monopoly over critical information to exaggerate the feasibility of one plan or downgrade the prospects of another. Betts (1977: 155), for example, argues that Moltke exaggerated the rigidity of the Schlieffen Plan in order to prevent the shift in strategy to the East.[24] Kennedy (1979: 17) argues that in both Vienna and St. Petersburg "the soldiers were using false arguments" to influence political authorities. As we have seen, the military can also refuse to implement a decision by political authorities,[25] and whether the politicians back down or attempt to override the military is itself an interesting question in bureaucratic politics and psychology. There are other ploys at the military's disposal. For example, Russian Chief of Staff Ianushkevich told the Foreign Minister that he wanted to be informed as soon as the Tsar had been persuaded to change his mind and order the general mobilization he had cancelled on July 29. The Chief of Staff said that he would immediately take action and then "retire from sight, smash my telephone, and generally take all measures so that I cannot be found to give any contrary orders for a new postponement of general mobilization." After the Tsar had reversed his decision, Sasonov notified Ianushkevich and said, "Now you can smash the telephone. Give your orders, General, and then—disappear for the rest of the day" (Schilling, 1925: 64–66; Fay, 1928: 2/470, 472).

Thus although the inherent rigidity of military plans might by itself have very little influence on decisions regarding war and peace, in conjunction with the political influence of the military it can have an important impact. Statesmen may also use the rigidity of their military plans as bargaining leverage with an ally, in an attempt to influence their ally's military policy. Conrad, for example, informed the Germans on numerous occasions that his mobilization against Serbia would necessarily delay a major effort against Russia. Stone (1979: 235–242) concludes, however, that this was a deliberate exaggeration designed to serve his own primary interests of completely destroying Serbia before aiding Germany in the east, and that Conrad had "pleaded

technical difficulties for a decision already determined by his political views." In this case the basic determinant of policy is Conrad's predetermined preferences, and the link between routines and their rigid implementation would be spurious.

Psychological Variables

A more complete explanation for the rigid adherence to existing military routines can be constructed by incorporating psychological as well as organizational and bureaucratic variables. There is extensive psychological literature suggesting that years of work in developing, revising, and perfecting a plan or policy generates a psychological commitment to it. This commitment has what Kurt Lewin (1964) calls a "freezing effect": persons who are committed to a plan or a decision tend to be highly resistant to pressures for change (Kiesler, 1971; Lebow, 1981: 236). Cognitive theory suggests that individuals are more responsive to new information which supports their preexisting beliefs than to information which contradicts it (Jervis, 1976: 143–154), and consequently there is a tendency to discount warnings that existing military plans are inadequate. This "irrational consistency" also leads policymakers to fail to recognize the existence of conflicting objectives and the need to make value trade offs among them (Jervis, 1976: 128–141), resulting in a tendency to inflate both the value of the objectives a policy aims to achieve and the probability of its success. At the same time both the likelihood of negative outcomes and their costs are minimized. There is also a tendency for policymakers to become convinced not only that their plan is on balance superior to alternatives, but that it is preferable in every possible respect (Jervis, 1976: 130–132; Lebow, 1981: 106). This is perhaps one explanation for German insensitivity in 1914 to the likelihood and cost of British intervention, given the perceived necessity of the rapid defeat of France through an invasion of Belgium. Even more important in reinforcing commitment to existing plans is the cognitive phenomenon of post-decision rationalization or bolstering, which Festinger (1957) attempts to explain his theory of cognitive dissonance. To satisfy a cognitive need to justify their actions, individuals tend subsequently to modify their perceptions and beliefs and "spread apart" the earlier alternatives—upgrading the perceived benefits and diminishing the perceived costs of the alternative they have chosen, while doing the opposite for those they rejected. This increases the threshold of new information required to trigger a change in preference and hence increases the resistance to policy change (Jervis, 1976: ch. 11; Lebow, 1981: 106–107). These tendencies undoubtedly solidified the rigid commitments to the Schlieffen Plan and other military plans in 1914.

This problem is particularly serious because the degree of dissonance and the strength of efforts to reduce it may be the greatest under conditions where there is the greatest need for change. Experimental research indicates that the psychological need for post-decision rationalization is positively related to the importance of the initial decision, the attractiveness of alternative options, and the costs (political as well as economic) involved in making and implementing that decision (Jervis, 1976: 392–406; Lebow, 1981: 107). As Dixon (1976: 66) notes, "an inability to admit one has been in the wrong will be greater the more wrong

one has been, and the more wrong one has been, the more bizarre will be subsequent attempts to justify the unjustifiable." Moreover, any new information that the initial decision might have been wrong might, under certain conditions, make the individuals involved even *more* resistant to any reversal of that decision. As Jervis (1976: 404) argues, "If contradictory evidence arouses sufficient discomfort to trigger dissonance reduction but is not convincing enough to change the person's mind, he may end up holding his views even more strongly than before." This is the basis for Snyder's (1984b: 200) argument that the motivated biases of decisionmakers are greatest when their core beliefs are threatened, so that they tend to see the "necessary" as possible. Thus Snyder (1984b: 139) asserts that Schlieffen defended his central beliefs with an a priori reasoning that was virtually impervious to evidence, while freely adjusting views on peripheral issues in a way consistent with the concept of unconflicted change. Similarly, Snyder (1984b: 153) argues that "Moltke's General Staff confronted operational difficulties in a forthright manner only insofar as such problems did not directly challenge the essential features of the preferred strategy." . . .

The inability of decisionmakers to cope with extremely high levels of stress in a crisis may lead to extreme anxiety reactions involving dysfunctional physiological responses as well as additional defense mechanisms such as projection and denial. This generally reduces the willingness and capacity of individuals to perform tasks related to the source of anxiety, and may result in indecision, paralysis, and a freezing effect on policy (Lebow, 1981: 115–119), as individuals seek the familiarity, certainty, and security of known routines. Although considerable evidence would be necessary to demonstrate the existence of this behavior, it is interesting to hypothesize about the behavior of Moltke and others in this regard, for there is no doubt that decisionmakers were under extreme stress in July 1914. Moltke had little confidence in his own abilities and had told Bulow, "I lack the power of rapid decision; I am too reflective, too scrupulous" (Turner, 1979: 210). Lebow (1981: 237) refers to evidence of Moltke's feelings of inadequacy and physical and mental exhaustion. When the Kaiser told Moltke "Your uncle would have given me a different answer" in response to Moltke's insistence that the trains could not be shifted to the east, Moltke later said that it had "wounded me deeply. I never pretended to be the equal of the old Field Marshal" (Tuchman, 1962: 100). Moltke states in his memoirs that when the Kaiser called to cancel the movement of the trains into Luxembourg, " 'I thought my heart would break' and 'burst into bitter tears of abject despair.' " Handed the written order, Moltke "threw my pen down on the table and refused to sign." The hope of English neutrality was soon dashed, however, and the trains moved to the west. But the entire episode had a major impact on Moltke, who later wrote: "I never recovered from the shock of this incident. Something in me broke and I was never the same thereafter . . ." (Tuchman, 1962: 101–102; Albertini, 1957: 3/178). Moltke's behavior seems far more consistent with the psychological hypotheses suggested above than with Betts' (1977: 155) characterization of cool and deliberate political calculation.[26]

This tendency for acute stress to increase perpetual rigidity in individuals may be reinforced by similar mechanisms operating at other levels of analysis. At the small-group level, stress-induced ingroup pressures can under certain conditions generate "groupthink" (Janis, 1972), a concurrence-seeking tendency which can increase resistance to policy change through illusions of unanimity and invulnerability, moral certainty, self-censorship, and collective rationalization. At the organizational level, although crisis stress can improve performance,[27] under certain conditions it can lead decisionmakers to perceive that their own already limited options are narrowing, while those of the adversary are both larger in number and expanding (Holsti, 1972: ch. 6). There is also a tendency for decisionmakers to perceive the policy-making processes of other states as more centralized than they actually are (Jervis, 1976: ch. 8), and thus to assume that an adversary's policies are freely chosen to achieve certain goals rather than forced by bureaucratic or domestic pressures. This tendency is reinforced by a parallel psychological tendency for individuals to perceive that the actions of others are intentional rather than constrained, and to perceive that one's own actions are limited and forced by circumstances, as emphasized by attribution psychology (Kelley, 1972). These factors, acting independently and also interactively with military routines, further impede the likelihood of change.

Organizational routines may also interact with psychological variables to generate misperceptions, which may in turn lead to war (Levy, 1983). An adversary's rigid adherence to existing plans or policies may easily be perceived as an indicator of hostile intent, rather than rigid organizational constraints. At the same time, decisionmakers will misjudge the impact of their own behavior by failing to recognize that the adversary may perceive their actions as reflecting hostile intent, rather than as rigid organizational constraints.[28] In this way, organizational and psychological variables interact with the security dilemma to escalate the conflict spiral (Jervis, 1976: ch. 3). There is some evidence that in 1914 decisionmakers attributed to the adversary a flexibility which they knew they did not possess themselves (Holsti, 1972: ch. 6; Taylor, 1974: 444). Alternatively, rigid organizational routines may generate actions which are perceived as conciliatory, rather than hostile. While under certain conditions this perception may generate reciprocity, it may sometimes be taken as a sign of weakness or lack of commitment and thereby lead to war by undermining deterrence (Levy, 1983).[29]

Organizational Determinants of Military Doctrine and Plans

The preceding analysis has been based on the assumption that military contingency plans are formulated primarily on the basis of military necessity, as determined by a rational strategic calculus. The aim has been to identify those variables which interact with military routines to help explain why these plans are often so rigidly implemented even when they may no longer be appropriate. Having examined how several variables combine to produce the inflexible implementation of established military plans in a way that may contribute to war, let us now analyze how organizational interests and routines can affect the outbreak of war indirectly through their impact on the formation of the initial military plans and the military doctrine from which they derive.

One important set of causal linkages here is for organizational interests and routines to help generate "offensive" doctrines and war plans,[30] which in-

crease the likelihood of war in several ways.[31] They usually increase the incentives to strike first and seize the initiative,[32] which is perhaps the single most destabilizing factor in any crisis (Jervis, 1978; Wagner, 1983). This increases the need for secrecy, which increases mistrust, fuels the conflict spiral, and also increases the incentives to preempt. Offensive strategies, since their general character is usually known, increase the threat perceived by other states, which increases mistrust and misperceptions and intensifies the conflict spiral and arms races, which in turn may contribute to war. Offensive doctrines may also encourage the adoption of more aggressive policies, brinkmanship, fait accomplis and perhaps even the notion of preventive war (Van Evera, 1984a: 63–65). Because they increase the costs of delay, offensive doctrines also increase the need for reliable allies who are willing and able to respond immediately after the outbreak of war. This need may generate incentives for permanent alliances in peacetime (Osgood and Tucker, 1967: 78–88), as opposed to ad hoc alliances secured during periods of escalating tensions which often results in fairly rigid systems of opposing alliances which themselves are destabilizing (Fay, 1928: 1/34–38; Levy, 1981: 582–583). Offensive doctrines also encourage alliances for which the *causus belli* is unconditional, rather than an unprovoked attack, which reduces some incentives for caution. Finally, offensive doctrines generally require rapid mobilization and detailed advanced planning, which increase the costs of improvization and hence the rigidity of military plans (Van Evera, 1984a: 86).

There is no doubt that the military doctrines of 1914 were offensive in character or that they had some of the hypothesized effects. Thus Snyder (1984a: 108) argues that the war plans of 1914 and the offensive doctrines behind them "were in themselves an important and perhaps decisive cause of the war," and Van Evera (1984a: 58) argues that "the cult of the offensive was a principal cause of the First World War." If these offensive doctrines are generated from a rational strategic calculus, however, then the causal impact of military routines in the processes leading to war would be relatively small, though this varies with the particular causal path from offensive doctrine. For most of the sequences described above (e.g., doctrine → policy → war), the linkage between the routines and war is spurious, for military plans and war are independently determined by doctrine. If, however, offensive doctrines generate rigid mobilization plans, which in turn contribute to war through various paths discussed above (e.g., by preventing last-minute compromises), then doctrine and routines form a causal chain contributing to war, and both variables have some causal effect. . . .

One can derive from organizational theory several reasons why military organizations might prefer offensive doctrines and war plans.[33] Offensive doctrines and plans facilitate—or at least provide the illusion of facilitating—seizing the initiative, structuring the battle, and allowing one to fight the war on one's own terms, which serve a central organizational goal of uncertainty avoidance. Offensive plans also serve to increase organizational size and wealth, since offensive operations require greater manpower and larger budgets than more static defenses. Furthermore, the organizational autonomy of the military is greatest when its operational goal is to disarm

the adversary quickly and decisively by offensive means (Snyder, 1984b: 25). The prospect of dramatic victory also enhances military prestige and morale. These institutional interests and internal organizational needs are reinforced by perceptual biases which result in the tendency to "see the necessary as the possible," and by the tendency toward doctrinal simplification and dogmatism (Snyder, 1984b: 24–32, 200–201). Biased evaluations of the "lessons of history," and the tendency for current doctrine to determine the lessons rather than the reverse (Jervis, 1976: ch. 6), are particularly important, as is militarism and the infusion into society of the values, myths, and perceptions of the military.[34] These perceptual biases are most extreme and most unhinged from strategic reality whenever strategic doctrine can be used as a rationalization to protect a military organization from threats to its institutional interests. The more serious the threat and the more vital the institutional interests being threatened, and the greater the extent to which institutional interests deviate from objective strategic reality, the greater the motivated and doctrinal bias (Snyder, 1984a: 132; 1984b: 25).

This discussion of the relationship between organizational interests and needs, offensive doctrines and war plans, and the outbreak of war has revealed several implicit causal models (Snyder, 1985b). In one, organizational interests and needs generate offensive doctrines and plans, which contribute to war; in another, the causal relationship may be reversed: offensive doctrines and plans generate rigid routines, which contribute to war; or, there may be a more complex chain involving reciprocal causation: military organizations generate offensive doctrines and plans, which become routinized and in turn reinforce offensive tendency and increase the likelihood of war.[35]

Many of these considerations applied in 1914. In the case of France (Snyder, 1984b: ch. 3), the military adopted an organizational ideology emphasizing the need for offensive operations carried out by a standing army. This was motivated primarily by the concern to protect the parochial interests and "organizational essence" of the military from the threat posed by the left-leaning Third Republic after the Dreyfus affair. The terms of conscription had been reduced and greater use was to be made of reservists at the expense of the standing army, and some Radicals called for further civilian intervention in military affairs. The adoption of an offensive doctrine provided the military with a rationalization for resisting reservists and demanding a large standing army, since offensive operations could only be carried out by a standing army at a high degree of readiness. Thus the doctrine served generally to increase the autonomy and size of the army and preserve its traditional values. This organizational explanation is reinforced by a cognitive one. Snyder (1984b: 65) documents some of the "motivated biases" of the French military and argues that "doctrine ruled history, not vice versa."[36]

In the German case, Snyder (1984b: chs. 4–5) argues that the Schlieffen Plan was the product of several organizational and cognitive variables. The German military shared the common preference of military organizations for offensive doctrines to enhance autonomy and facilitate precision in planning. They also had a narrow and dogmatic organizational ideology which emphasized the zero-sum nature of international politics; the belief

that war was natural and in fact inevitable; and the belief that war was beneficial only if it was short and decisive. In addition, motivational biases, bolstering, and the need for doctrinal simplification led to distorted evaluations of military options and the failure to consider plausible alternatives. Snyder (1984b: 156) argues that the German military leadership "saw what they had to see if what they felt they had to do stood any chance to work." The problem was exacerbated by a pathological civil–military relationship which permitted the formulation of doctrine without civilian input. I would conclude that although the original Schlieffen Plan may have been a reasonable response to strategic realities, these organizational and cognitive variables help explain the Germans' lack of receptivity to new information, unwillingness to consider seriously any alternative contingency plans, and inflexible implementation of the plan under conditions in which it was no longer optimal.

The Russian case was somewhat different. As Snyder (1984a: 133–137; 1984b: chs. 6–7) points out, the Russian war plan of 1914 involved offensives against both Germany and Austria that entailed insufficient forces to permit either to succeed. The explanation for this can be traced to bureaucratic conflict and compromise. General Danilov and the General Staff in St Petersburg wanted to use the bulk of Russia's forces to conduct an offensive against Germany while maintaining a defensive shield against Austria. General Alekseev and the military district commanders, who would have to implement any plans and who were more concerned with operational tactics than grand strategy, preferred the opposite.[37] In the absence of strong civilian control, the result was a bureaucratic compromise involving dual offensives. The problem was that the outcome of this bureaucratic logrolling was that neither operation had sufficient forces to succeed. Snyder (1984a: 136–137) explains this suboptimal outcome in terms of organizational and cognitive variables and their multiplicative interaction effects. He generalizes that bureaucratic logrolling is likely to exacerbate the normal offensive bias for the military, and that military decisionmakers tend to overestimate the feasibility of an operational plan if a realistic assessment would conflict with fundamental beliefs or an organizational ideology.

SUMMARY AND CONCLUSIONS

This study has attempted to identify the theoretical linkages by which the organizational routines of the military may contribute to the outbreak of war. The key intervening variable between military plans and the outbreak of war is the inflexible implementation of an existing plan (under conditions where it is no longer optimal). This can increase the likelihood of war by requiring an early mobilization, which generates a momentum of its own and triggers a nearly irreversible action-reaction cycle. The absence of flexible options may deprive political authorities of the flexibility they need to demonstrate their resolve without unnecessarily threatening the adversary, to manage the escalating crisis without sacrificing vital national interests. This limited availability of options combines with the tendency toward worst-case analysis to generate the more escalatory option. In this way rigidity may preclude certain compromise solutions that might otherwise be acceptable.

The key question is how to explain this rigid implementation of the existing plan. I have argued that these organizational routines rarely act alone, but only in complex combinations with other systemic, organizational, bureaucratic, and psychological variables. There is often a failure to recognize the independent role of other variables in contributing to the rigid implementation of an existing military plan, which results in the exaggeration of the causal importance of the inherent rigidity of the plans themselves. There is also the danger of spurious inferences deriving from the failure to recognize that another variable determines both the nature of the military plan and its rigid implementation in a crisis. The greater the extent to which systemic variables determine—through a rational strategic calculus and "military necessity"—both the original military mobilization plans and the rigid adherence to those plans in a crisis, the less the causal impact of the plans themselves.

Often, however, the rigid adherence to preexisting plans cannot be explained by a rational strategic calculus. In these situations the rigid implementation of existing plans can be explained by complex interaction, in multiplicative relationships and in causal chains, of several variables: the inherent characteristics of the routines themselves, the organizational needs and interests of the military, cognitive and affective psychological constraints on rational decisionmaking, and bureaucratic political variables which explain why the preferences of the military may prevail in the political process. The organizational interests and routines of the military may also contribute to the outbreak of war through their effect on the formation of offensive military doctrines and war plans. These can contribute to war by increasing the incentives for preemption, by intensifying the perceived threat and exacerbating a conflict spiral, and by further crystallizing the rigidity of the routines.

The importance of this question of the relationship between military routines and the causes of war is not restricted to the classic case of World War I or to historical conditions in which a certain set of military or transport technologies prevailed.[38] Nor is it restricted to the theorist interested in decisionmaking and the causes of war. It also has enormous importance for national policy and crisis stability in the contemporary age. There has been increasing attention to the question of crisis management. Alexander George suggests, in addition to the limitation of one's political objectives, several behavioral norms that facilitate effective crisis management: presidential control of military options, pauses in military operations, availability of discriminating military options, coordination of military movements with political-diplomatic actions and with limited objectives, selection of military options that avoid motivating the opponent to escalate, avoidance of the impression of the intention to escalate to large-scale warfare, and provision of a non-humiliating way out of the crisis for the adversary (George, 1984: 226). The reader will recognize that the organizational routines of the military in 1914, in conjunction with other factors discussed above, violated every one of these basic requirements for effective crisis management.[39]

Rigid organizational routines may also affect crisis management in the contemporary age through their impact on the command and control of nuclear forces, as some recent literature emphasizes. Bracken (1983) argues that the institutions and procedures for the command and control of US nuclear forces share much in common with the rigid institutional arrangements of 1914. He points to the absence of tight central control over nuclear arsenals and decisionmaking procedures by political leaders in the US, and the gradual evolution from direct political control to more military control of nuclear arsenals in both the US and USSR since the 1960s; to the devolution of important intelligence and warning systems and decisionmaking authority to the military in a crisis; to the tightly coupled nature of complex command and control systems, in which a series of compound, highly correlated events can reverberate throughout the system and produce an unpredictable sequence of individual, bureaucratic, and technical reactions; to the limited capacity of highly centralized and tightly coupled systems to respond to unanticipated events; to various ways in which the readiness and alerting procedures work to impede a progression of finely tuned and tightly directed political actions; and to the concept of alert instability, and the implication that moderately high levels of nuclear alerts may generate dynamics similar to those of World War I mobilization plans (Bracken, 1983: 8, 23–29, 53–54, 73, 222–223, 243). Similarly, George (1984: 227–228) argues that 'the ability of top level political authority to maintain control over military moves . . . is jeopardized by the exceedingly large number and complexity of standing orders comprising the rules of engagement that will come into effect at the onset of a crisis and as it intensifies'. He notes, along with Sagan (1985), that because military rules of engagement and delegations of authority must be preplanned, they often do not fit the specific diplomatic and strategic needs of a particular crisis, and cannot be quickly reconsidered and revised. The problem is compounded by the fact that important changes in authorized rules of engagement may automatically go into effect as higher levels of alert are declared, and that these processes may be poorly understood by political leaders (George, 1984: 228). Many political leaders are insufficiently aware of the extent to which alert authority rests in the hands of individual military commanders, allowing them—in the absence of specific orders to the contrary—to place their forces on a higher state of alert if necessary to deal with an increased threat (George, 1984: 227; Sagan, 1985: 132–133).[40] Sagan (1985: 135) concludes that "any policy-maker's belief that he can 'fine-tune' alerts, intricately controlling the level of American responses to increases in Soviet commend readiness . . . [is] quite naive."[41]

Although there are important limitations on the validity of the 1914 analogy for the contemporary era, unsettling parallels do exist (Kahler, 1979/80). These are all the more disturbing because one undeniable difference between 1914 and the contemporary age is that the potential consequences for mankind are far greater today.

NOTES

1. The mobilization plans of 1914 have been studied extensively by historians, but more theoretically oriented efforts to generalize about their connection with the outbreak of war are rare. Political scientists occasionally generalize from the 1914 case, but usually only on the basis of superficial evidence, although Snyder (1984a,b) and Van Evera (1984a) are ex-

ceptions here. There have been some attempts to apply organizational concepts to questions involving the *conduct* of war (Jenkins, 1970; Gallucci, 1975), but the causal linkages are often different from those involved in the outbreak of war.

2. It should be emphasized that my focus is more theoretical than empirical, and that the World War I case should be regarded as illustrative rather than as evidentiary. No attempt will be made to evaluate empirically the causal importance of military routines relative to that of other variables in the 1914 case; that would require a sophisticated research design and extensive historical investigation. A theoretical analysis of the causal mechanisms by which military routines *could* lead to war is a prerequisite for any empirical analysis of whether they do in a particular case or the frequency with which this occurs.

3. It would be useful at this point to recall the chronological sequence of mobilizations and war declarations in 1914:

July 28   Austrian declaration of war against Serbia

German "Halt in Belgrade" proposal

July 29   Russian partial mobilization against Austria

German proposal for British neutrality

July 30   Russian general mobilization

July 31   German ultimatum to Russia

Austrian general mobilization

Aug. 1   French mobilization (3:55 p.m.)

German mobilization (4:00 p.m.)

German declaration of war against Russia (7:00 p.m.)

Aug. 2   German invasion of Luxemburg

Aug. 3   German declaration of war against France

German invasion of Belgium

Aug. 4   British declaration of war against Germany

Aug. 6   Austrian declaration of war against Russia

4. Forty days were required for full Russian mobilization, as compared to only two weeks for Germany or France (Snyder, 1984b: 107). The buildup of Russian strategic railways, however, was rapidly rendering this assumption obsolete (Stone, 1975: 41–42).

5. This was true because of domestic political as well as strategic considerations for Britain (Steiner, 1977: 236–238).

6. A comparable example of the difficulty of implementing even small changes in a mobilization plan can be found in the opposition of the French military to Premier Viviani's order for a "ten kilometer withdrawal" of forces from the German frontier (Fay, 1928: 2/482–492; Albertini, 1957: 2/627–632).

7. Although some have argued that Germany did have some viable strategic alternatives to the Schlieffen Plan (Snyder, 1984b: 116–122), what is critical here is that the Kaiser and other German decisionmakers *perceived* no better option (Turner, 1979: 214; Snyder, 1984b: 155).

8. Time-consuming mobilization plans will generate the greatest pressure for early mobilization when it is believed that mobilization can be conducted secretly (Van Evera, 1984b: 50).

9. Austrian mobilization plans of 1866 had similar consequences on the eve of the Austro-Prussian War (see Friedjung, 1966: 103, 126–128, 135–140).

10. There are, of course, other possible explanations for Vienna's delay. These center on Hungarian Premier Tisza's opposition to a military showdown and Vienna's need for a prolonged crisis to mobilize political support in Hungary, and on Vienna's domestic as well as diplomatic need to establish Serbian complicity in the assassination. These alternative explanations are rejected by Williamson (1979: 152).

11. Since in this case the nature of the military plan helps describe the process by which military necessity causes the rigid implementation of that plan, military routines provide an "interpretation" of the causal relationship. An interpretative relationship exists when a variable has no independent causal effect (i.e., it does not increase the amount of variance explained) but instead merely describes *how* another antecedent variable causes the dependent variable to change (Blalock, 1961: 84–87). If, however, perceptions of military necessity are themselves determined by military routines and interests, a more complex causal chain would be involved. It is possible, of course, for both military necessity and organizational rigidity to combine in an additive fashion to increase the likelihood of implementing an existing plan.

12. This use of the security dilemma concept is accepted in most of the literature. One exception is Wagner (1983: 339), who defines it to include the incentive to strike first. The compellingness of the security dilemma from the perspective of a key decisionmaker is illustrated by Sazonov. In his efforts to persuade the Tsar to reverse his position and order a general mobilization, Sazonov argued that was inevitable and that they must prepare to fight it under the most favorable conditions. "It is better without fear to call forth a war by our preparations for it, and to continue these preparations for it, and to continue these preparations carefully, rather than out of fear to give an inducement for war and be taken unawares" (Schilling, 1925: 65; Fay, 1928: 1/472).

13. On the assumptions of the security dilemma, see Wagner (1983). Here I am dealing with the actors' perceptions of the situation rather than with the 'objective' situation itself. This is more comparable to Snyder's (1985a) concept of a "perceptual security dilemma" than a structural security dilemma.

14. Joffre, for example, calculated that each day of delay in mobilization would cost

France 10–12 miles of territory, and other European military leaders shared similar views (Van Evera, 1984a: 72–73).

15. This conclusion is tentative. My primary concern here is not to provide a definitive answer to the historical question, but to suggest that kind of evidence that would be relevant to resolve the theoretical question of causality. A complete analysis of this question would have to include the role of future expectations in the strategic calculations of 1914. This would involve the question of the impact of the German military's pressure for preventive war (Levy, 1985).

16. As the Prussian Minister of War, von Roon, stated on the eve of the Austro-Prussian War: "When armaments are once in train, the outward thrust will either be followed by the beginning of a fight or, what is worse, by being ridiculed, if the sharpened sword is returned to the sheath without results" (Vagts, 1959: 338).

17. If, on the other hand, helping her French ally were necessary to secure those Russian strategic interests for which the alliance was initially formed, then the interaction of strategic interests and alliances would explain both the formation of military plans and their rigid implementation, so that the routine-war linkage would be spurious.

18. Thus the elder Moltke (Chief of the Prussian General Staff from 1857 to 1888, the job inherited by his nephew) once declared: "The politician should fall silent the moment mobilization begins" (Brodie, 1973: 11).

19. In fact, the complexity of military plans might in some cases be deliberately intended by the military as a means of limiting politicians' understanding of and hence influence over military matters (see Sagan, 1985: 138).

20. Fischer (1961: 1975) argues that there was considerable cooperation between German military and political leaders in 1914, but this debate has been exten-sively discussed elsewhere (e.g., Koch, 1972).

21. Even military considerations were defined rather narrowly. Snyder (1984b: 197) generalizes from the Russian case that "military decisionmakers are swayed less by their view of the comparative military balance, which is difficult to calculate, than by their own absolute level of organizational or administrative preparedness." On the autonomy of the military in Russia see Lieven (1983: ch. 3).

22. I'm accepting for now the arguments of Fay (1928: 2/ch. XII), Albertini (1957: 3/252–253), Ritter (1973: 2/275), and others, that none of the major European powers in 1914 wanted a general war and that each of them, perhaps excepting Austria, took sincere steps to avoid one. The major argument to the contrary is presented by Fischer (1961, 1975) and his followers.

23. Bureaucratic politics may also affect the likelihood of war through other causal sequences.

24. I have found little in Fay, Albertini, or Ritter to support this. Moltke was psychologically committed to the plan, as is argued in the next section.

25. For more on the question of faithful implementation and resistance, see Halperin (1974: ch. 13).

26. It is true, however, that organizational variables are critical in explaining Moltke's motivated biases and some of the psychological pressure on him (Snyder, 1985b).

27. Current organizational theory emphasizes that stress is often functional for most decisionmaking tasks (Holsti and George, 1975: 288–300).

28. This is one aspect of the more general phenomenon of misperception induced by a misunderstanding of another's decisionmaking process (Jervis, 1976; Levy, 1983).

29. The British announcement of the withdrawal of the *HMS Endurance* from the

South Atlantic in 1981 provides an example. The decision can be explained by budgetary constraints, factored problems, and the outcome of a bureaucratic struggle between the Defense Minister and Foreign Secretary. It was perceived by the Argentines as a deliberate strategic decision and interpreted as an indication of British unwillingness to use force to defend the Falklands/Malvinas. This was a critical misperception contributing to the outbreak of war (Franks, 1983: para. 44, 114–116).

30. The distinction between offensive and defensive doctrines and strategies is often not explicitly defined in the literature, and this has generated considerable confusion. By offensive strategies I mean those emphasizing attack and territorial penetration rather than the static defense of existing positions. They usually involve seizing the initiative and striking first, but this is not always the case. Offensive strategies are analytically distinct from the offensive/defensive balance (real or perceived) of military technology (Levy, 1984).

31. The following analysis borrows from Van Evera (1984a: 63–66, 70–79; 1984b: ch. 3). His otherwise excellent discussion is marred by his occasional confusion between offensive strategies and a military technology favoring the offense, though he does in principle recognize the difference.

32. A policy of not striking first *and* a strategy of 'active' defense and territorial penetration (or counter-offensive) in the event that war breaks out (Levy, 1984: 229), however, would *not* increase the likelihood of war.

33. This discussion borrows from Posen (1984: 47–58), Van Evera (1984b), and Snyder (1984b). Note, however, that Posen (1984) concludes from his study of British, French, and German doctrine between the two world wars that rational strategic calculation in the form of balance of power theory provides a better explanation of the sources of military doctrine.

34. Van Evera (1984b: ch. 7) argues that the military infuses society with a world view that contributes to war, not because military organizations prefer war, but rather because their institutional interests are served by these values and perceptions.

35. It appears that Van Evera (1984a,b) implicitly adopts the reciprocal model but emphasizes the offense → organizational routine linkage (as well as the direct offense → war linkage). Snyder (1984a,b) also recognizes reciprocal causation but seems to emphasize the primacy of organizational interests and needs, as does Posen (1984: ch. 1–2) but with less emphasis on reciprocal causation. I would emphasize the routines → doctrine linkage and recognize the independent effects of each (together with other variables) on war. Needless to say, these implicit models are not easily amendable to a critical empirical test. The nature of the relationship *between* these variables is probably less important, however, than the relative magnitude of their *combined* impact on war, compared to that of other variables.

36. For an alternative interpretation of the French army and military doctrine prior to 1914, see Porch (1981).

37. Snyder (1984b: 134–137) argues, however, that the preferences of Danilov and Alekseev were determined more by intellectual differences than by bureaucratic role. Different views regarding the feasibility of expansion in the Balkans and in Asia and of the extent of the German danger, reinforced by certain motivational biases, were particularly important.

38. We might expect, however, that this question is less relevant for periods before the late 19th century, for that was the first time that states in peacetime developed war plans in any systematic way (Kennedy, 1979: 1; Osgood and Tucker, 1967: 53–56).

39. The parallels between contemporary Soviet military doctrine for the European theater and the German Schlieffen Plan, especially their offensive character (Lebow, 1985b), are particularly disturbing in light of several of George's requirements for crisis management.

40. Defense Secretary Gates, for example, was unaware that his order for "a quiet increase in command readiness" in May 1960 would lead to a Defcon 3 alert (Sagan, 1985: 102–106).

41. This problem is compounded by the tendency of political leaders to believe—often erroneously, as Sagan demonstrates—that a military alert can be conducted secretly, leaving them unprepared for serious domestic effects that could conceivably generate enormous pressures for escalation or descalation (Sagan, 1985: 137).

REFERENCES

Albertini, L. (1957) *The Origins of the War of 1914,* 3 vols. Trans. by I. M. Massey. London: Oxford University Press.

Allison, G. T. (1971) *Essence of Decision.* New York: Little Brown.

Allison, G. T. (1977) "Questions about the Arms Race: Who's Racing Whom? A Bureaucratic Perspective". In *American Defense Policy,* 4th ed., edited by J. E. Endicott and R. W. Stafford, Jr. pp. 424–441. Baltimore: Johns Hopkins.

Allison, G. T., and M. Halperin. (1972) "Bureaucratic Politics: A Paradigm and Some Policy Implications." In *Theory and Policy in International Relations,* edited by R. Tanter and R. H. Ullman, pp. 40–79. Princeton: Princeton University Press.

Barnet, R. J. (1972) *Roots of War.* Baltimore, Md: Penguin.

Betts, P. K. (1977) *Soldiers, Statesmen, and Cold War Crisis.* Cambridge, Mass: Harvard University Press.

Bracken, P. (1983) *The Command and Control of Nuclear Forces.* New Haven: Yale University Press.

Blalock, H. M., Jr. (1961) *Causal Inferences in Non-Experimental Research.* New York: Norton.

Brodie, B. (1973) *War and Politics.* New York: Macmillan.

Craig, G. A. (1955) *The Politics of the Prussian Army, 1940–1945.* Oxford: Oxford University Press.

Dixon, N. (1976) *On the Psychology of Military Incompetence.* London: Jonathan Cape.

Fay, S. B. (1928) *The Origins of the World War,* 2 vols. New York: Free Press, 1966.

Festinger, L. (1957) *A Theory of Cognitive Dissonance.* Stanford: Stanford University Press.

Fischer, F. (1961) *Germany's Aims in the First World War.* New York: Norton.

Fischer, F. (1975) *War of Illusions.* New York: Norton.

Fiske, S. T. (1981) "Social Cognition and Affect." In *Cognition, Social Behavior, and the Environment,* edited by J. H. Harvey. Hillsdale, NJ: Lawrence Erlbaum.

Franks, L. (1983) *Falkland Islands Review: Report of a Committee of Privy Counsellors.* London: Her Majesty's Stationery Office.

Friedjung, H. (1966) *The Struggle for Supremacy in Germany, 1859–1966.* Trans. by A. J. P. Taylor and W. L. McElwee. New York: Russell and Russell.

Fuller, J. F. C. (1961) *The Conduct of War, 1789–1961.* New Jersey: Rutgers University Press.

Gallucci, R. L. (1975) *Neither Peace Nor Honor.* Baltimore: Johns Hopkins University Press.

George, A. (1984) Crisis Management: The Interaction of Political and Military Considerations. *Survival* (Sept./Oct.): 323–334.

Halperin, M. H. (1974) *Bureaucratic Politics and Foreign Policy.* Washington, DC: Brookings.

Hart, B. H. L. (1932) Aggression and the Problem of Weapons. *English Review* 55 (July): 71-78.

Holsti, O. R. (1972) *Crisis, Escalation, War.* Montreal: McGill-Queens University Press.

Holsti, O. R., and A. L. George. (1975) "The Effects of Stress on the Performance of Foreign Policy-Makers". In *Political Science Annual,* vol. 6, edited by C. P. Cotter, pp. 255-271. Indianapolis: BobbMerrill.

Howard, M. (1976) *War in European History.* Oxford: Oxford University Press.

Huntington, S. P. (1957) *The Soldier and the State.* New York: Vintage.

Janis, I. L. (1972) *Groupthink,* 2nd ed. Boston: Houghton Mifflin.

Janis, I. L., and L. Mann. (1977) *Decision Making; A Psychological Analysis of Conflict, Choice and Commitment.* New York: Free Press.

Jenkins, B. M. (1970) The Unchangeable War. Santa Monica, Calif: Rand.

Jervis, R. (1976) *Perception and Misperception in International Politics.* Princeton: Princeton University Press.

Jervis, R. (1978) Cooperation Under the Security Dilemma. *World Politics* 30 (January): 167-214.

Kahler, M. (1979/80) Rumors of War: The 1914 Analogy. *Foreign Affairs* 58 (Winter): 374-396.

Katzenbach, E. L., Jr. (1971) "The Horse Cavalry in the Twentieth Century". In *The Use of Force,* edited by R. J. Art and K. N. Waltz, pp. 277-297. Boston: Little Brown.

Keiger, J. F. V. (1983) *France on the Origins of the First World War.* New York: St Martin's Press.

Kelley, H. (1972) *Causal Schemata and the Attribution Process.* Morristown, NJ: General Learning Press.

Kennedy, P. M., Ed. (1979) *The War Plans of the Great Powers 1880-1914.* Boston, Mass: George Allen and Unwin.

Kiesler, C. A., Ed. (1971) *The Psychology of Commitment.* New York: Academic Press.

Koch, H. W., Ed. (1972) *The Origins of the First World War.* London: Macmillan.

Lebow, R. N. (1981) *Between Peace and War.* Baltimore: Johns Hopkins University Press.

Lebow, R. N. (1985a) Windows of Opportunity: Do States Jump through Them? *International Security* 9 (Summer): 147-186.

Lebow, R. N. (1985b) The Soviet Offensive in Europe: The Schlieffen Plan Revisited? *International Security* 9 (Spring): 44-78.

Levy, J. S. (1981) Alliance Formation and War Behavior. *Journal of Conflict Resolution* 25 (December): 581-613.

Levy, J. S. (1983) Misperception and the Causes of War. *World Politics* 35 (October): 76-99.

Levy, J. S. (1984) The Offensive/Defensive Balance of Military Technology: A Theoretical and Historical Analysis. *International Studies Quarterly* 28 (June): 219-238.

Levy, J. S. (1985) Declining Power and the Preventive Motivation. University of Texas at Austin, mimeo.

Lewin, K. (1964) *Field Theory in Social Science,* edited by D. Cartwright. New York: Harper and Row.

Lieven, D. C. B. (1983) *Russia and the Origins of the First World War.* New York: St Martin's Press.

Osgood, R. E., and R. W. Tucker. (1967) *Force, Order, and Justice.* Baltimore: Johns Hopkins.

Ostrom, C. W., Jr. (1977) Evaluating Alternative Foreign Policy Decision-Making Models: An Empirical Test Between an Arms Race Model and an Organizational Politics Model. *Journal of Conflict Resolution* 21: 235-266.

Paige, G. D. (1968) *The Korean Decision.* New York: Free Press.

Porch, D. (1981) *The March to the Marne: The French Army, 1871-1914.* Cambridge: Cambridge University Press.

Posen, B. R. (1984) *The Sources of Military Doctrine: France, Britain, and Germany Between the World Wars.* Ithaca, NY: Cornell University Press.

Renouvin, P. (1928) *The Immediate Origins of the War.* Trans. by T. C. Hulme. New Haven: Yale University Press.

Ritter, G. (1958) *The Schlieffen Plan.* Trans. by A. Wilson and E. Wilson. New York: Praeger.

Ritter, G. (1973) *The Sword and the Scepter: The Problem of Militarism in Germany,* 4 vols. Trans. by H. Norden. Coral Gables, Fla: University of Miami Press.

Sagan, S. D. (1985) Nuclear Alerts and Crisis Management. *International Security* 9 (Spring): 99-139.

Schilling, B. (1925) *How the War Began in 1914: The Diary of the Russian Foreign Office* London: George Allen and Unwin.

Schmitt, B. E. (1930) *The Coming of the War,* 2 vols. New York: Scribners.

Snyder, J. (1984a) Civil Military Relations and the Cult of the Offensive, 1914 and 1984. *International Security* 9 (Summer): 108-146.

Snyder, J. (1984b) *The Ideology of the Offensive: Military Decision Making and the Disasters of 1914.* Ithaca, NY: Cornell University Press.

Snyder, J. (1985a) "Perceptions of the Security Dilemma in 1914". In *Psychology and Deterrence,* edited by R. Jervis, R. N. Lebow and J. G. Stein. Baltimore: Johns Hopkins.

Snyder, J. (1985b) Private correspondence.

Steinbruner, J. D. (1974) *The Cybernetic Theory of Decision.* Princeton: Princeton University Press.

Steiner, Z. S. (1977) *Britain and the Origins of the First World War.* New York: St Martin's Press.

Stoessinger, J. G. (1978) *Why Nations Go to War,* 2nd ed. New York: St Martin's Press.

Stone, N. (1975) *The Eastern Front,* 1914-1917. New York: Scribner's.

Stone, N. (1979) "Moltke and Conrad: Relations between the Austro-Hungarian and German General Staffs, 1909-1914." In *The War Plans of the Great Powers,* 1880-1914, edited by P. M. Kennedy. Boston: George Allen and Unwin.

Taylor, A. J. P. (1954) *The Struggle for Mastery in Europe, 1848-1918.* New York: Oxford University Press.

Taylor, A. J. P. (1969) *War by Time-table.* London: Macdonald.

Taylor, A. J. P. (1974) "War by Time-table." In Purnell's *History of the 20th Century,* vol. 2, pp. 442-448. New York: Purnell.

Taylor, A. J. P. (1979) *How Wars Begin.* New York: Atheneum.

Tuchman, B. W. (1962) *The Guns of August.* New York: Dell.

Turner, L. C. F. (1968) The Russian Mobilization of 1914. *Journal of Contemporary History* 3 (January): 65-88.

Turner, L. C. F. (1970) *Origins of the First World War.* New York: W. W. Norton.

Turner, L. C. F. (1979) "The Significance of the Schlieffen Plan". In *The War Plans of the Great Powers, 1880-1914,* edited by P. M. Kennedy. Boston: George Allen and Unwin.

Vagts, A. (1959) *A History of Militarism.* New York: Free Press.

Van Evera, S. (1984a) The Cult of the Offensive and the Origins of the First World War. *International Security* 9 (Summer): 58-107.

Van Evera, S. (1984b) Causes of War. PhD dissertation, University of California, Berkeley.

Vyvyan, J. M. K. (1968) "The Approach of the War of 1914." In *The New Cambridge Modern History,* vol. XII: *The Shifting Balance of World Forces, 1898-1945,* ch. VI. Cambridge: Cambridge University Press.

Wagner, R. H. (1983) The Theory of Games and the Problem of International Cooperation. *American Political Science Review* 77 (June): 330–346.

Wegerer, A. Von. (1928) The Russian Mobilization of 1914. *Political Science Quarterly* 43.

Williamson, S. R., Jr. (1979) Theories of Organizational Process and Foreign Policy Outcomes. In *Diplomacy,* edited by P. Lauren, pp. 137–161. New York: Free Press.

QUESTIONS

1. What factors does Levy identify as being influential on the mobilization plan of the European powers in World War I?

2. How does Levy's view of state-level decision-making differ from Graham Allison's perspective? Explain.

Individual Level International Relations Theories

INTRODUCTION

We have now reached the third and final of our levels of analysis for international relations theory—the individual level. This section includes theories who view the foreign policy and interaction of states as a result of the nature, characteristics, and values of either people in general or individuals in leadership roles. Proponents of these theories emphasize that systems, countries, and governments don't necessarily dictate the behavior of states—people do.

Each theory differs significantly, however, in its approach to the role of the individual. The first theory presented in this section, human nature theory, and the last theory, peace studies theory, both focus on the broad characteristics of humans as a race, but from vastly different perspectives. Human nature theorists view the more violent tendencies of the human race as unavoidable and, therefore, an essential and integral part of our relationships with one another. Scholars dedicated to the theory of peace studies suggest that people can overcome this kind of aggression and learn to live and work together peacefully.

If we look at the individual level of analysis as a spectrum, with human nature theory and peace studies theory emphasizing a broad, all-encompassing look at the human race in general, then the second theory presented in this section, cognitive theory, stands at the opposite end of that spectrum. Cognitive theorists believe that the personalities of specific leaders and the personality traits characteristic of those individuals in leadership positions often have a significant impact on the course and implementation of a state's foreign policy. Certainly in the first instance, Adolph Hitler played a key role in the rise of Nazi Germany and is often used as a glaring historic example of the power of one individual to dictate, quite literally, the policies of a nation. In the second instance, we might view the pursuit and attainment of leadership positions as somewhat self-selecting. For example, not everyone wants to be president, and those individuals who aspire to that level usually have certain personality traits in common: drive, ambition, willingness to lead, ability to compromise, etc. Whether a specific person or simply "a leader," cognitive theorists argue that when it comes to making a decision that could affect the course of a nation and the course of history, the key component in the equation is the man or woman facing that decision.

Feminist theorists of international relations see the role of gender in world politics as a defining point in understanding both the course and analysis of human events. Articles in this section take two different approaches. First, feminist theorists critique traditional theories of international relations for failing to incorporate gender issues and perspectives into their evaluation of global politics. Feminist theory explains how the study of international relations has been shaped by male conceptions of politics, power, and competition. The second approach is a more direct theoretical application of gender to the study of international relations. This includes, among other issues, the feminist perspective of global gender inequality and its impact on the course and conduct of global affairs.

So, we see that the individual level of analysis looks at the distinctive characteristics of people, from the nature of humans as a species to the nature of specific individuals and gender groups within our society. We will begin with the fairly pessimistic view of human nature theorists, then take a look at the cognitive and gender perspectives, and end with perhaps a more optimistic analysis by the proponents of peace studies.

Chapter 7

HUMAN NATURE THEORY

COMPONENTS OF HUMAN NATURE THEORY

Focus of Analysis ••••••••▶	• Human nature • Innate patterns of human behavior • Instinct
Major Actors ••••••••▶	• Individual
Behavior of States ••••••••▶	• Guided by fundamental human characteristics
Basis of a State's Foreign Policy ••••••••▶	• Collective protection of individual against more violent tendencies of human nature
Key Concepts ••••••••▶	• Competition; Diffidence; Glory; Human nature; Instinct; State of nature

INTRODUCTION

In looking at the individual level of international relations theory, we begin with the fairly broad interpretation of "individual" that actually encompasses all of humanity—human nature theory. **Human nature** refers to the qualities and traits shared by all people, regardless of ethnicity, gender, culture, etc. Human nature theorists assert that the behavior of states is fundamentally patterned after the behavior of humans themselves. Human nature, then, can provide clues about when and why states might behave in a particular fashion.

Human nature theorists argue that, on a basic level, human nature—and, indeed, the nature of other species as well—is often guided by instinct. **Instinct** could be defined as an innate impulse that is prompted in response to specific environmental conditions. It is almost as if humans and other species are preprogrammed to respond in a certain manner when confronted with a particular set of circumstances. Just as the antelope of the African plains have an instinctive fear of lions and other predators, these scholars suggest it is basic human nature that makes states fearful of a neighboring country's perceived military strength and defensive of their territorial rights.

In the excerpt included here by the Greek scholar and philosopher Aristotle, he indicates that the nature of man is essentially divided into two parts (good and evil) and, therefore, life and the relations between people are also divided. That is, one cannot know or understand the bounty and tranquillity of peace without having experienced the hardship and terror of war. Although the human race can, according to Aristotle, emphasize one facet over the other (presumably peace over war), this exercise does not negate the presence of the less desirable side of existence. He also extends this theory of human nature to the nature of governments formed by humans, asserting that the government of "freemen" is nobler than that of authoritarian rule. Here we might go so far as to say that what is good for individuals (citizenry) is also good for the state.

In the excerpt taken from Thomas Hobbes' classic work *Leviathan,* the author asks us to imagine the wretchedness of human existence in a **"state of nature"** when there was a no central government able to control the baser instincts of humans and to provide order. Hobbes points to three specific causes of conflict that are endemic to human nature: competition, diffidence, and glory. It is important to understand the context in which he uses these terms. **Competition,** as Hobbes views it, represents the perpetual struggle between humans for resources, power, or anything else that might represent some sort of gain. We might presume that at some point relative parity is achieved between individuals or that a person could be content with the fruits of his or her individual labors in a civilized world.

This path, however, leads to diffidence in Hobbes' estimation. **Diffidence** arises from a perception of equality or a sense of self-satisfaction that occurs when individuals attain a particular set of goals or ends. Hobbes suggests conflict arises from the need to protect these gains from other humans who, because of their very nature, cannot help but try to subdue, conquer, and master another's holdings. So, whether you look at the individual attempting to seize another's possessions or the individual protecting his or her assets, both will likely be moved to violent means.

The quest for glory in human nature is the third portion of Hobbes' trilogy about the unavoidable violence of existence. He defines **glory** as the quest for and preservation of honor, respect, or reputation as it refers to the individual or, indeed, as it reflects on the family, friends, name, etc., associated with that individual. Under these conditions, Hobbes appears far less certain than Aristotle of man's capacity to avoid conflict. It is, in essence, impossible for an individual to be a pacifist, content with the status quo, because others will strive to change this balance. Humans seek to master others who present, may present, or are perceived as presenting a threat. It is not surprising, given this overall perception of human nature, that Hobbes declares that, in the state of nature, the "life of man was solitary, poore, nasty, brutish, and short." Later in his book, Hobbes concludes that life becomes bearable only when humans subjugate themselves to the control of a strong central authority that can enforce law and order.

Though we might hypothesize that these base traits are inevitably passed from the nature of humans to the nature of the states and other institutions that humans create, the last article by twentieth-century psychologist Sigmund Freud suggests otherwise. Freud argues that the natural violence of the human animal can actually be "overcome by the transference of power to a larger unity" or group. The group comes together and is linked by the emotional ties (belief in democracy and freedom, protection from a common threat, etc.) of its members. In his letter to Albert Einstein addressing the scientist's query about how future wars could be avoided, Freud states that transferring power to a central authority mitigates the possibility of violence. He suggests further that, although humans have an instinct for hatred and destruction, this is only half of the essential dichotomy of human instincts. In pairings of seemingly opposite characteristics, humans also have instincts for love and cooperation, which might be promoted and enhanced by such an overarching group authority.

Despite this more hopeful acknowledgment, the enduring theme linking the three articles in this section is that humans are by nature—and can generally be counted upon to be—violent and aggressive. Human nature theorists suggest that these traits, so instinctive to men and women, are thereby carried over to our relations on an international level. Just as the saying suggests that an apple doesn't fall far from the tree, the behavior of states does not stray far from the behavior of the people within them.

A Critique of Human Nature Theory

The use of psychology and examination of human behavioral patterns that characterize human nature theory have made some insightful contributions to the study of states and international relations. Classical realist theory is itself based in part on the assumption that man is inherently aggressive, and, as we noted earlier, represents a popular and widely accepted theory among contemporary scholars.

The critics of human nature theory argue, however, that it does not delve deeply enough into the driving forces of foreign policy and global politics. Proceeding on the assumption that the human animal is by nature competitive and prone to violence leads to a number of questions. First, does human nature theory provide a sufficient explanation of the complex character of international relations? We might also wonder whether this theory has the analytic depth necessary to understand international relations in our world today. The disintegration of the Soviet Union and its communist ideology, the integrated world economic structure, and the ever-expanding global communications network are just three of the many significant events and processes that have changed and are changing our planet. Can we assume that human beings' natural aggression and lust for power or even Aristotle's notion of the conflict between good and evil in individuals, represent the driving forces behind not only the behavior of states but behind all of these other events, as well?

KEY CONCEPTS

Competition   is a term used to represent the perpetual struggle between humans for resources, power, or anything else that might represent some sort of gain. According to Thomas Hobbes, competition is one of the three specific causes of conflict that are endemic to human nature. The other two causes are diffidence and glory.

Diffidence   According to Thomas Hobbes, diffidence is one of the three causes of conflict that are endemic to human nature. Diffidence arises from a human's perception of equality or a sense of self-satisfaction and occurs when individuals attain a particular set of goals or ends.

Glory   is defined by Thomas Hobbes as the quest for and preservation of honor, respect, or reputation as it refers to the individual or as it reflects on the family, friends, name, etc., associated with that individual. According to Hobbes, glory is one of the three causes of conflict that are endemic to human nature.

Human nature   refers to the qualities and traits shared by all people, regardless of ethnicity, gender, culture, etc. Human nature theorists assert that the behavior of states is fundamentally patterned after the behavior of humans themselves. Human nature, then, can provide clues about when and why states might behave in a particular fashion.

Instinct   is an innate pattern of behavior characteristic of species, including humans. To varying degrees, humans and other species are preprogrammed to respond in a certain manner when confronted with a particular set of circumstances.

State of nature   refers to Thomas Hobbes' pessimistic view of life prior to the creation of a central government or authority to control the baser instincts of humans and provide order. Under these conditions the life of humans would be "solitary, poor, nasty, brutish, and short."

It appears that human nature theory alone does not offer a sufficiently detailed framework to address these issues. Certainly, however, proponents of this theory can point to a number of instances throughout history where human instincts toward aggression and domination affected the course of international relations. Nazi Germany of the 1930s and 1940s, Iraq's invasion of Kuwait in 1990, and the rampage of the Mongols across the Asian continent in the thirteenth century are examples that come readily to mind. But, staying with an individual level perspective in our examination of the behavior of states, is the driving force actually human nature as we have defined it here? or should we take a closer look at individual leaders, their particular features, and unique ambitions?

33.   The Politics

Aristotle

In this except, Aristotle suggests that states reflect the nature of the individuals living within them. Thus, just as some individuals are more prone to violence than others, some nations are more inclined to peace and others more inclined to war. Aristotle argues that people conditioned exclusively for war will never enjoy the virtues and values of peace. This selection is from *The Politics.*

Aristotle (*c.* 384–322 B.C.) was a Greek philosopher and teacher, who studied under Plato and later tutored Alexander the Great. Although he laid out many empirical formulations in the study of the natural sciences, his greatest work was in the field of philosophy. Aristotle's other writings include *Nichomachean Ethics* and *On Philosophy,* each of which analyzes the use of logic in the field.

Now the soul of man is divided into two parts, one of which has a rational principle in itself, and the other, not having a rational principle in itself, is able to obey such a principle. And we call a man in any way good because he has the excellences of these two parts. In which of them the end is more likely to be found is no matter of doubt to those who adopt our division; for in the world both of nature and of art the inferior always exists for the sake of the superior, and the superior is that which has a rational principle. This principle, too, in our ordinary way of making the division, is divided into two kinds, for there is a practical and a speculative principle. This part, then, must evidently be similarly divided. And there must be a corresponding division of actions; the actions of the naturally better part are to be preferred by those who have it in their power to attain to two out of the three or to all, for that is always to everyone the most desirable which is the highest attainable by him. The whole of life is further divided into two parts, business and leisure, war and peace, and of actions some aim at what is necessary and useful, and some at what is honorable. And the preference given to one or the other class of actions must necessarily be like the preference given to one or other part of the soul and its actions over the other; there must be war for the sake of peace, business for the sake of leisure, things useful and necessary for the sake of things honourable. All these points the statesman should keep in view when he frames his laws; he should consider the parts of the soul and their functions, and above all the better and the end; he should also remember the diversities of human lives and actions. For men must be able to engage in business and to go to war, but leisure and peace are better; they must do what is necessary and indeed what is useful, but what is honourable is better. On such principles children and persons of every age which requires education should be trained. Whereas even the Greeks of the present day who are reputed to be best governed, and the legislators who gave them their constitutions, do not appear to have framed their governments with a regard to the best end, or to have given them laws and education with a view to all the excellences, but in a vulgar spirit have fallen back on those which promised to be more useful and profitable. Many modern writers have taken a similar view: they commend the Lacedaemonian constitution, and praise the legislator for making conquest and war his sole aim, a doctrine which may be refuted by argument and has long ago been refuted by facts. For most men desire empire in the hope of accumulating the goods of fortune; and on this ground Thibron and all those who have written about the Lacedaemonian constitution have praised their legislator, because the Lacedaemonians, by being trained to meet dangers, gained great power. But surely they are not a happy people now that their empire has passed away, nor was their legislator right. How ridiculous is the result, if, while they are continuing in the observance of his laws and no one interferes with them, they have lost the better part of life! These writers further err about the sort of government which the legislator should approve, for the government of freemen is nobler and implies more excellence than despotic government. Neither is a city to be deemed happy or a legislator to be praised because he trains his citizens to conquer and obtain dominion over their neighbours, for there is great harm in this. On a similar principle any citizen who could, should obviously try to obtain the power in his own state— the crime which the Lacedaemonians accuse king Pausanias of attempting, although he had such great honour already. No such principle and no law having this object is either statesmanlike or useful or right. For the same things are best both for individuals and for states, and these are the things which the legislator ought to implant in the minds of his citizens. Neither should men study war with a view to the enslavement of those who do not deserve to be enslaved; but first of all they should provide against their own enslavement, and in the second place obtain empire for the good of the governed, and not for the sake of exercising a general despotism, and in the third place they should seek to be masters only over those who deserve to be the slaves. Facts, as well as arguments, prove that the legislator should direct all his military and other measures to the provision of leisure and the establishment of peace. For most of these military states are safe only while they are at war, but fall when they have acquired their empire; like unused iron they lose their edge in time of peace. And for this the legislator is to blame, he never having taught them how to lead the life of peace.

Since the end of individuals and of states is the same, the end of the best man and of the best constitution must also be the same; it is therefore evident that there ought to exist in both of them the excellences of leisure; for peace, as has been often repeated, is the end of war, and leisure of toil. But leisure and cultivation may be promoted not only by those excellences which are practised in leisure, but also by some of those which are useful to business. For many necessaries of life have to be supplied before we can have leisure. Therefore a city must be temperate and brave, and able to endure: for truly, as the proverb says, 'There is no leisure for slaves,' and those who cannot face danger like men are the slaves of any invader. Courage and endurance are required for business and philosophy for leisure, temperance and justice for both, and more especially in times of peace and leisure, for war compels men to be just and temperate, whereas the enjoyment of good fortune and the leisure which comes with peace tend to make them insolent. Those then who seem to be the best-off and to be in the possession of every good, have special need of justice and temperance—for example, those (if such there be, as the poets say) who dwell in the Islands of the Blest; they above all will need philosophy and temperance and justice, and all the more the more leisure they have, living in the midst of abundance. There is no difficulty in seeing why the state that would be happy and good ought to have these excellences. If it is disgraceful in men not to be able to use the goods of life, it is peculiarly disgraceful not to be able to use them in time of leisure—to show excellent qualities in action and war, and when they have peace and leisure to be no better than slaves. That is why we should not practise excellence after the manner of the Lacedaemonians. For they, while agreeing with other men in their conception of the highest goods, differ from the rest of mankind in thinking that they are to be obtained by the practice of a single excellence. And since these goods and the enjoyment of them are greater than the enjoyment derived from the excellences . . . and that for its own sake, is evident from what has been said; we must now consider how and by what means it is to be attained.

QUESTIONS

1. How does Aristotle view war? Does he recognize the need for war?

2. How does Aristotle's view of human nature differ from that of Hobbes?

34. Leviathan

Thomas Hobbes

In this excerpt, Thomas Hobbes presents a pessimistic view of human nature. He suggests that human existence, without benefit of a strong central authority to enforce order, can be characterized as "solitary, poor, nasty, brutish, and short." Hobbes argues that this darker side of human nature guides not only individuals but nations and relations between states as well. This selection is from *Leviathan* (1651).

Thomas Hobbes (1603–1679) began his writing career in 1628 with a translation of Thucydides. One of the leading English political philosophers of the seventeenth century, his other writings include *The Elements of Law, Natural and Politic* (1640) and *De Cive* (1642).

Nature hath made men so equall, in the faculties of body, and mind; as that though there bee found one man sometimes manifestly stronger in body, or of quicker mind then another; yet when all is reckoned together, the difference between man, and man, is not so considerable, as that one man can thereupon claim to himselfe any benefit, to which another may not pretend, as well as he. For as to the strength of body, the weakest has strength enough to kill the strongest, either by secret machination, or by confederacy with others, that are in the same danger with himselfe.

And as to the faculties of the mind, (setting aside the arts grounded upon words, and especially that skill of proceeding upon generall, and infallible rules, called Science; which very few have, and but in few things; as being not a native faculty, born with us; nor attained, (as Prudence,) while we look after somewhat els,) I find yet a greater equality amongst men, than that of strength. For Prudence, is but Experience; which equall time, equally bestowes on all men, in those things they equally apply themselves unto. That which may perhaps make such equality incredible, is but a vain conceipt of ones owne wisdome, which almost all men think they have in a greater degree, than the Vulgar; that is, than all men but themselves, and a few others, whom by Fame, or for concurring with themselves, they approve. For such is the nature of men, that howsoever they may acknowledge many others to be more witty, or more eloquent, or more learned; Yet they will hardly believe there be many so wise as themselves: For

they see their own wit at hand, and other mens at a distance. But this proveth rather than men are in that point equall, than unequall. For there is not ordinarily a greater signe of the equall distribution of any thing, than that every man is contented with his share.

From this equality of ability, ariseth equality of hope in the attaining of our Ends. And therefore if any two men desire the same thing, which neverthelesse they cannot both enjoy, they become enemies; and in the way to their End, (which is principally their owne conservation, and sometimes their delectation only,) endeavour to destroy, or subdue one an other. And from hence it comes to passe, that where an Invader hath no more to feare, than an other mans single power; if one plant, sow, build, or possesse a convenient Seat, others may probably be expected to come prepared with forces united, to dispossesse, and deprive him, not only of the fruit of his labour, but also of his life, or liberty. And the Invader again is in the like danger of another.

And from this diffidence of one another, there is no way for any man to secure himselfe, so reasonable, as Anticipation; that is, by force, or wiles, to master the persons of all men he can, so long, till he see no other power great enough to endanger him: And this is no more than his own conservation requireth, and is generally allowed. Also because there be some, that taking pleasure in contemplating their own power in the acts of conquest, which they pursue farther than their security requires; if others, that otherwise would be glad to be at ease within modest bounds, should not by invasion increase their power, they would not be able, long time, by standing only on their defence, to subsist. And by consequence, such augmentation of dominion over men, being necessary to a mans conservation, it ought to be allowed him.

Againe, men have no pleasure, (but on the contrary a great deale of griefe) in keeping company, where there is no power able to over-awe them all. For every man looketh that his companion should value him, at the same rate he sets upon himself: And upon all signes of contempt, or undervaluing, naturally endeavours, as far as he dares (which amongst them that have no common power to keep them in quiet, is far enough to make them destroy each other,) to extort a greater value from his contemners, by dommage; and from others, by the example.

So that in the nature of man, we find three principall causes of quarrell. First, Competition; Secondly, Diffidence; Thirdly, Glory.

The first, maketh men invade for Gain; the second, for Safety; and the third, for Reputation. The first use Violence, to make themselves Masters of other mens persons, wives, children, and cattell; the second, to defend them; the third, for trifles, as a word, a smile, a different opinion, and any other signe of undervalue, either direct in their Persons, or by reflexion in their Kindred, their Friends, their Nation, their Profession, or their Name.

Hereby it is manifest, that during the time men live without a common Power to keep them all in awe, they are in that condition which is called Warre; and such a warre, as is of every man, against every man. For WARRE, consisteth not in Battell onely, or the act of fighting; but in a tract of time, wherein the Will to contend by Battell is sufficiently known: and therefore the notion of *Time,* is to be considered in the nature of Warre; as it is in the nature of Weather. For as the nature of Foule weather, lyeth not in a showre or two of rain; but in an inclination thereto of many dayes together: So the nature of War, consisteth not in actuall fighting; but in the known disposition thereto, during all the time there is no assurance to the contrary. All other time is PEACE.

Whatsoever therefore is consequent to a time of Warre, where every man is Enemy to every man; the same is consequent to the time, wherein men live without other security, than what their own strength, and their own invention shall furnish them withall. In such condition, there is no place for Industry; because the fruit thereof is uncertain: and consequently no Culture of the Earth; no Navigation, nor use of the commodities that may be imported by Sea; no commodious Building; no Instruments of moving, and removing such things as require much force; no Knowledge of the face of the Earth; no account of Time; no Arts; no Letters; no Society; and which is worst of all, continuall feare, and danger of violent death; And the life of man, solitary, poore, nasty, brutish, and short.

It may seem strange to some man, that has not well weighed these things; that Nature should thus dissociate, and render men apt to invade, and destroy one another: and he may therefore, not trusting to this Inference, made from the Passions, desire perhaps to have the same confirmed by Experience. Let him therefore consider with himselfe, when taking a journey, he armes himselfe, and seeks to go well accompanied; when going to sleep, he locks his dores; when even in his house he locks his chests; and this when he knowes there bee Lawes, and publike Officers, armed, to revenge all injuries shall bee done him; what opinion he has of his fellow subjects, when he rides armed; of his fellow Citizens, when he locks his dores; and of his children, and servants, when he locks his chests. Does he not there as much accuse mankind by his actions, as I do by my words? But neither of us accuse mans nature in it. The Desires, and other Passions of man, are in themselves no Sin. No more are the Actions, that proceed from those Passions, till they know a Law that forbids them: which till Lawes be made they cannot know: nor can any Law be made, till they have agreed upon the Person that shall make it.

It may peradventure be thought, there was never such a time, nor condition of warre as this; and I believe it was never generally so, over all the world: but there are many places, where they live so now. For the savage people in many places of *America,* except the government of small Families, the concord whereof dependeth on naturall lust, have no government at all; and live at this day in that brutish manner, as I said before. Howsoever, it may be perceived what manner of life there would be, where there were no common Power to feare; by the manner of life, which men that have formerly lived under a peaceful government, use to degenerate into, in a civil Warre.

But though there had never been any time, wherein particular men were in a condition of warre one against another; yet in all times, Kings, and Persons of Soveraigne authority, because of their Independency, are in continuall jealousies, and in the state and posture of Gladiators; having their weapons pointing, and their eyes fixed on one another; that is, their Forts, Garrisons, and Guns upon the Frontiers of their Kingdomes; and continuall Spyes upon their neighbours, which is a posture of War. But because they uphold thereby, the Industry of their Subjects; there does not follow from it, that misery, which accompanies the Liberty of particular men.

To this warre of every man against every man, this also is consequent; that nothing can be Unjust. The notions of Right and Wrong, Justice and Injustice have there no place. Where there is no common Power, there is no Law: where no Law, no Injustice. Force, and Fraud, are in warre the two Cardinall vertues. Justice, and Injustice are none of the Faculties neither of the Body, nor Mind. If they were, they might be in a man that were alone in the world, as well as his Senses, and Passions. They are Qualities, that relate to men in Society, not in Solitude. It is consequent also to the same condition, that there be no Propriety, no Dominion, no *Mine* and *Thine* distinct; but onely that to be every mans, that he can get; and for so long, as he can keep it. And thus much for the ill condition, which man by meer Nature is actually placed in; though with a possibility to come out of it, consisting partly in the Passions, partly in his Reason.

The Passions that encline men to Peace, are Feare of Death; Desire of such things as are necessary to commodious living; and a Hope by their Industry to obtain them. And Reason suggesteth convenient Articles of Peace, upon which men may be drawn to agreement. These Articles, are they, which otherwise are called the Lawes of Nature: . . .

QUESTIONS

1. What are the conditions of man in the state of nature described by Hobbes? Do you agree with his characterization? Explain.

2. According to Hobbes, why do individuals sacrifice their liberty to the Leviathan?

---

35.   Why War?[1]

Sigmond Freud

In this letter, a response to Albert Einstein, Sigmond Freud examines why war exists and concludes that humans have a tendency toward violence. He argues, though, that man has propensities for both war and peace, and suggests that war may be a natural part of human existence. This excerpt was part of a debate with Albert Einstein on the future of the League of Nations (1932).

Sigmond Freud (1856–1939), considered the father of modern psychoanalysis, wrote many books on human psychology.

VIENNA, *September,* 1932.
DEAR PROFESSOR EINSTEIN,

When I heard that you intended to invite me to an exchange of views on some subject that interested you and that seemed to deserve the interest of others besides yourself, I readily agreed. I expected you to choose a problem on the frontiers of what is knowable to-day, a problem to which each of us, a physicist and a psychologist, might have our own particular angle of approach and where we might come together from different directions upon the same ground. You have taken me by surprise, however, by posing the question of what can be done to protect mankind from the curse of war. . . .

You begin with the relation between Right and Might.[2] There can be no doubt that that is the correct starting-point for our investigation. But may I replace the word "might" by the balder and harsher word "violence"? To-day right and violence appear to us as antitheses. It can easily be shown, however, that the one has developed out of the other; and if we go back to the earliest beginnings and see how that first came about, the problem is easily solved. . . .

It is a general principle, then, that conflicts of interest between men are settled by the use of violence. This is true of the whole animal kingdom, from which men have no business to exclude themselves. In the case of men, no doubt, conflicts of *opinion* occur as well which may reach the highest pitch of abstraction and which seem to demand some other technique for their settlement. That, however, is a later complication. To begin with, in a small human horde,[3] it was superior muscular strength which decided who owned things or whose will should prevail. Muscular strength was soon supplemented and replaced by the use of tools: the winner was the one who had the better weapons or who used them the more skilfully. From the moment at which weapons were introduced, intellectual superiority already began to replace brute muscular strength; but the final purpose of the fight remained the same—one side or the other was to be compelled to abandon his claim or his objection by the damage inflicted on him and by the crippling of his strength. That purpose was most completely achieved if the victor's violence eliminated his opponent permanently, that is to say, killed him. This had two advantages: he could not renew his opposition and his fate deterred others from following his example. In addition to this, killing an enemy satisfied an instinctual inclination which I shall have to mention later. The intention to kill might be countered by a reflection that the enemy could be employed in performing useful services if he were left alive in an intimidated condition. In that case the victor's violence was content to subjugate him instead of killing him. This was a first beginning of the idea of sparing an enemy's life, but thereafter the victor had to reckon with his defeated opponent's lurking thirst for revenge and sacrificed some of his own security.

Such, then, was the original state of things: domination by whoever had the greater might—domination by brute violence or by violence supported by intellect. As we know, this régime was altered in the course of evolution. There

was a path that led from violence to right or law. What was that path? It is my belief that there was only one: the path which led by way of the fact that the superior strength of a single individual could be rivalled by the union of several weak ones. *'L'union fait la force.'* Violence could be broken by union, and the power of those who were united now represented law in contrast to the violence of the single individual. Thus we see that right is the might of a community. It is still violence, ready to be directed against any individual who resists it; it works by the same methods and follows the same purposes. The only real difference lies in the fact that what prevails is no longer the violence of an individual but that of a community. But in order that the transition from violence to this new right or justice may be effected, one psychological condition must be fulfilled. The union of the majority must be a stable and lasting one. If it were only brought about for the purpose of combating a single domineering individual and were dissolved after his defeat, nothing would have been accomplished. The next person who found himself superior in strength would once more seek to set up a dominion by violence and the game would be repeated *ad infinitum*. The community must be maintained permanently, must be organized, must draw up regulations to anticipate the risk of rebellion and must institute authorities to see that those regulations—the laws—are respected and to superintend the execution of legal acts of violence. The recognition of a community of interests such as these leads to the growth of emotional ties between the members of a united group of people—feelings of unity which are the true source of its strength.

Here, I believe, we already have all the essentials: violence overcome by the transference of power to a larger unity, which is held together by emotional ties between its members. What remains to be said is no more than an expansion and a repetition of this.

The situation is simple so long as the community consists only of a number of equally strong individuals. The laws of such an association will determine the extent to which, if the security of communal life is to be guaranteed, each individual must surrender his personal liberty to turn his strength to violent uses. But a state of rest of that kind is only theoretically conceivable. In actuality the position is complicated by the fact that from its very beginning the community comprises elements of unequal strength—men and women, parents and children—and soon, as a result of war and conquest, it also comes to include victors and vanquished, who turn into masters and slaves. The justice of the community then becomes an expression of the unequal degrees of power obtaining within it; the laws are made by and for the ruling members and find little room for the rights of those in subjection. From that time forward there are two factors at work in the community which are sources of unrest over matters of law but tend at the same time to a further growth of law. First, attempts are made by certain of the rulers to set themselves above the prohibitions which apply to everyone—they seek, that is, to go back from a dominion of law to a dominion of violence. Secondly, the oppressed members of the group make constant efforts to obtain more power and to have any changes that are brought about in that direction recognized in the laws—they press forward, that is, from unequal justice to equal justice for all. This second tendency becomes especially important if a real shift of power occurs within a community, as may happen as a result of a number of historical factors. In that case right may gradually adapt itself to the new distribution of power or, as is more frequent, the ruling class is unwilling to recognize the change, and rebellion and civil war follow, with a temporary suspension of law and new attempts at a solution by violence, ending in the establishment of a fresh rule of law. There is yet another source from which modifications of law may arise, and one of which the expression is invariably peaceful; it lies in the cultural transformation of the members of the community. This, however, belongs properly in another connection and must be considered later.

Thus we see that the violent solution of conflicts of interest is not avoided even inside a community. But the everyday necessities and common concerns that are inevitable where people live together in one place tend to bring such struggles to a swift conclusion and under such conditions there is an increasing probability that a peaceful solution will be found. But a glance at the history of the human race reveals an endless series of conflicts between one community and another or several others, between larger and smaller units—between cities, provinces, races, nations, empires—which have almost always been settled by force of arms. Wars of this kind end either in the spoliation or in the complete overthrow and conquest of one of the parties. It is impossible to make any sweeping judgement upon wars of conquest. Some, such as those waged by the Mongols and Turks, have brought nothing but evil.

Others, on the contrary, have contributed to the transformation of violence into law by establishing larger units within which the use of violence was made impossible and in which a fresh system of law led to the solution of conflicts. In this way the conquests of the Romans gave the countries round the Mediterranean the priceless *pax Romana,* and the greed of the French kings to extend their dominions created a peacefully united and flourishing France. Paradoxical as it may sound, it must be admitted that war might be a far from inappropriate means of establishing the eagerly desired reign of 'everlasting' peace, since it is in a position to create the large units within which a powerful central government makes further wars impossible. Nevertheless it fails in this purpose, for the results of conquest are as a rule short-lived: the newly created units fall apart once again, usually owing to a lack of cohesion between the portions that have been united by violence. Hitherto, moreover, the unifications created by conquest, though of considerable extent, have only been *partial,* and the conflicts between these have cried out for violent solution. Thus the result of all these warlike efforts has only been that the human race has exchanged numerous, and indeed unending, minor wars for wars on a grand scale that are rare but all the more destructive.

If we turn to our own times, we arrive at the same conclusion which you have reached by a shorter path. Wars will only be prevented with certainty if mankind unites in setting up a central authority to which the right of giving judgement upon all conflicts of interest shall be handed over. There are clearly two separate requirements involved in this: the creation of a supreme authority and its endowment with the necessary power. One without the other would be useless. The League of Nations is designed as an authority of this kind, but the second condition has not been fulfilled: the League of Nations has no power of its own and can only acquire it if the members of the new union, the separate States, are ready to resign it. And at the moment there seems very little prospect of this. The institution of the League of Nations would, however, be wholly unintelligible if one ignored the fact that here was a bold attempt such as has seldom (perhaps, indeed, never on such a scale) been made before. It is an attempt to base upon an appeal to certain idealistic attitudes of mind the authority (that is, the coercive influence) which otherwise rests on the possession of power. We have heard that a community is held together by two things: the compelling force of violence and the emotional ties (identifications is the technical name) between its members. If one of the factors is absent, the community may possibly be held together by the other. The ideas that are appealed to can, of course, only have any significance if they give expression to important concerns that are common to the members, and the question arises of how much strength they can exert. . . . Indeed it is all too clear that the national ideals by which nations are at present swayed operate in a contrary direction. Some people are inclined to prophesy that it will not be possible to make an end of war until Communist ways of thinking have found universal acceptance. But that aim is in any case a very remote one to-day, and perhaps it could only be reached after the most fearful civil wars. Thus the attempt to replace actual force by the force of ideas seems at present to be doomed to failure. We shall be making a false calculation if we disregard the fact that law was originally brute violence and that even to-day it cannot do without the support of violence.

I can now proceed to add a gloss to another of your remarks. You express astonishment at the fact that it is so easy to make men enthusiastic about a war and add your suspicion that there is something at work in them—an instinct for hatred and destruction—which goes halfway to meet the efforts of the war-mongers. Once again, I can only express my entire agreement. We believe in the existence of an instinct of that kind and have in fact been occupied during the last few years in studying its manifestations. Will you allow me to take this opportunity of putting before you a portion of the theory of the instincts which, after much tentative groping and many fluctuations of opinion, has been reached by workers in the field of psycho-analysis?

According to our hypothesis human instincts are of only two kinds: those which seek to preserve and unite—which we call "erotic," exactly in the sense in which Plato uses the word 'Eros' in his *Symposium,* or "sexual," with a deliberate extension of the popular conception of 'sexuality'—and those which seek to destroy and kill and which we class together as the aggressive or destructive instinct. As you see, this is in fact no more than a theoretical clarification of the universally familiar opposition between Love and Hate which may perhaps have some fundamental relation to the polarity of attraction and repulsion that plays a part in your own field of knowledge. We must not be too hasty in introducing ethical judgements of good and evil. Neither of these instincts is any less essential than the other; the phe-

nomena of life arise from the operation of both together, whether acting in concert or in opposition. It seems as though an instinct of the one sort can scarcely ever operate in isolation; it is always accompanied—or, as we say, alloyed—with an element from the other side, which modifies its aim or is, in some cases, what enables it to achieve that aim. Thus, for instance, the instinct of self-preservation is certainly of an erotic kind, but it must nevertheless have aggressiveness at its disposal if it is to fulfil its purpose. So, too, the instinct of love, when it is directed towards an object, stands in need of some contribution from the instinct of mastery if it is in any way to possess that object. The difficulty of isolating the two classes of instinct in their actual manifestations is indeed what has so long prevented us from recognizing them.

If you will follow me a little further, you will see that human actions are subject to another complication of a different kind. It is very rarely that an action is the work of a *single* instinctual impulse (which must in itself be compounded of Eros and destructiveness). In order to make an action possible there must be as a rule a *combination* of such compounded motives. . . . So that when human beings are incited to war they may have a whole number of motives for assenting—some noble and some base, some of which they speak openly and others on which they are silent. There is no need to enumerate them all. A lust for aggression and destruction is certainly among them: the countless cruelties in history and in our everyday lives vouch for its existence and its strength. The gratification of these destructive impulses is of course facilitated by their admixture with others of an erotic and idealistic kind. When we read of the atrocities of the past, it sometimes seems as though the idealistic motives served only as an excuse for the destructive appetites; and sometimes—in the case, for instance, of the cruelties of the Inquisition—it seems as though the idealistic motives had pushed themselves forward in consciousness, while the destructive ones lent them an unconscious reinforcement. Both may be true.

I fear I may be abusing your interest, which is after all concerned with the prevention of war and not with our theories. Nevertheless I should like to linger for a moment over our destructive instinct, whose popularity is by no means equal to its importance. As a result of a little speculation, we have come to suppose that this instinct is at work in every living being and is striving to bring it to ruin and to reduce life to its original condition of inanimate matter. Thus it quite seriously deserves to be called a death instinct, while the erotic instincts represent the effort to live. The death instinct turns into the destructive instinct if, with the help of special organs, it is directed outwards, on to objects. The living creature preserves its own life, so to say, by destroying an extraneous one. Some portion of the death instinct, however, remains operative *within* the living being, and we have sought to trace quite a number of normal and pathological phenomena to this internalization of the destructive instinct. We have even been guilty of the heresy of attributing the origin of conscience to this diversion inwards of aggressiveness. You will notice that it is by no means a trivial matter if this process is carried too far: it is positively unhealthy. On the other hand if these forces are turned to destruction in the external world, the living creature will be relieved and the effect must be beneficial. This would serve as a biological justification for all the ugly and dangerous impulses against which we are struggling. It must be admitted that they stand nearer to Nature than does our resistance to them, for which an explanation also needs to be found. It may perhaps seem to you as though our theories are a kind of mythology and, in the present case, not even an agreeable one. But does not every science come in the end to a kind of mythology like this? Cannot the same be said to-day of your own Physics?

For our immediate purpose then, this much follows from what has been said: there is no use in trying to get rid of men's aggressive inclinations. We are told that in certain happy regions of the earth, where nature provides in abundance everything that man requires, there are races whose life is passed in tranquillity and who know neither compulsion nor aggressiveness. I can scarcely believe it and I should be glad to hear more of these fortunate beings. The Russian Communists, too, hope to be able to cause human aggressiveness to disappear by guaranteeing the satisfaction of all material needs and by establishing equality in other respects among all the members of the community. That, in my opinion, is an illusion. They themselves are armed to-day with the most scrupulous care and not the least important of the methods by which they keep their supporters together is hatred of everyone beyond their frontiers. In any case, as you yourself have remarked, there is no question of getting rid entirely of human aggressive impulses; it is enough to try to divert them to such an extent that they need not find expression in war.

Our mythological theory of instincts makes it easy for us to find a formula for *indirect* methods of combating war. If willingness to engage in war is an effect of the destructive instinct, the most obvious plan will be to bring Eros, its antagonist, into play against it. Anything that encourages the growth of emotional ties between men must operate against war. These ties may be of two kinds. In the first place they may be relations resembling those towards a loved object, though without having a sexual aim. There is no need for psycho-analysis to be ashamed to speak of love in this connection, for religion itself uses the same words: 'Thou shalt love thy neighbour as thyself.' This, however, is more easily said than done. The second kind of emotional tie is by means of identification. Whatever leads men to share important interests produces this community of feeling, these identifications. And the structure of human society is to a large extent based on them.

A complaint which you make about the abuse of authority brings me to another suggestion for the indirect combating of the propensity to war. One instance of the innate and ineradicable inequality of men is their tendency to fall into the two classes of leaders and followers. The latter constitute the vast majority; they stand in need of an authority which will make decisions for them and to which they for the most part offer an unqualified submission. This suggests that more care should be taken than hitherto to educate an upper stratum of men with independent minds, not open to intimidation and eager in the pursuit of truth, whose business it would be to give direction to the dependent masses. It goes without saying that the encroachments made by the executive power of the State and the prohibition laid by the Church upon freedom of thought are far from propitious for the production of a class of this kind. The ideal condition of things would of course be a community of men who had subordinated their instinctual life to the dictatorship of reason. Nothing else could unite men so completely and so tenaciously, even if there were no emotional ties between them. But in all probability that is a Utopian expectation. No doubt the other indirect methods of preventing war are more practicable, though they promise no rapid success.An unpleasant picture comes to one's mind of mills that grind so slowly that people may starve before they get their flour.

The result, as you see, is not very fruitful when an unworldly theoretician is called in to advise on an urgent practical problem. It is a better plan to devote oneself in every particular case to meeting the danger with whatever weapons lie to hand. I should like, however, to discuss one more question, which you do not mention in your letter but which specially interests me. Why do you and I and so many other people rebel so violently against war? Why do we not accept it as another of the many painful calamities of life? After all, it seems quite a natural thing, no doubt it has a good biological basis and in practice it is scarcely avoidable. There is no need to be shocked at my raising this question. For the purpose of an investigation such as this, one may perhaps be allowed to wear a mask of assumed detachment. The answer to my question will be that we react to war in this way because everyone has a right to his own life, because war puts an end to human lives that are full of hope, because it brings individual men into humiliating situations, because it compels them against their will to murder other men, and because it destroys precious material objects which have been produced by the labours of humanity. Other reasons besides might be given, such as that in its present-day form war is no longer an opportunity for achieving the old ideals of heroism and that owing to the perfection of instruments of destruction a future war might involve the extermination of one or perhaps both of the antagonists. All this is true, and so incontestably true that one can only feel astonished that the waging of war has not yet been unanimously repudiated. No doubt debate is possible upon one or two of these points. It may be questioned whether a community ought not to have a right to dispose of individual lives; every war is not open to condemnation to an equal degree; so long as there exist countries and nations that are prepared for the ruthless destruction of others, those others must be armed for war. But I will not linger over any of these issues; they are not what you want to discuss with me, and I have something different in mind. It is my opinion that the main reason why we rebel against war is that we cannot help doing so. We are pacifists because we are obliged to be for organic reasons. And we then find no difficulty in producing arguments to justify our attitude.

No doubt this requires some explanation. My belief is this. For incalculable ages mankind has been passing through a process of evolution of culture. (Some people, I know, prefer to use the term "civilization.") We owe to that process the best of what we have become, as well as a good part of what we suffer from. Though its causes and beginnings are obscure and its outcome uncertain, some of its characteristics are easy to perceive. It may perhaps be leading to the extinction of the human race, for in more than one

way it impairs the sexual function; uncultivated races and backward strata of the population are already multiplying more rapidly than highly cultivated ones. The process is perhaps comparable to the domestication of certain species of animals and it is undoubtedly accompanied by physical alterations; but we are still unfamiliar with the notion that the evolution of culture is an organic process of this kind. The psychical modifications that go along with the cultural process are striking and unambiguous. They consist in a progressive displacement of instinctual aims and a restriction of instinctual impulses. Sensations which were pleasurable to our ancestors have become indifferent or even intolerable to ourselves; there are organic grounds for the changes in our ethical and aesthetic ideals. Of the psychological characteristics of culture two appear to be the most important: a strengthening of the intellect, which is beginning to govern instinctual life, and an internalization of the aggressive impulses, with all its consequent advantages and perils. Now war is in the crassest opposition to the psychical attitude imposed on us by the cultural process, and for that reason we are bound to rebel against it; we simply cannot any longer put up with it. This is not merely an intellectual and emotional repudiation; we pacifists have a constitutional intolerance of war, an idiosyncracy magnified, as it were, to the highest degree. It seems, indeed, as though the lowering of aesthetic standards in war plays a scarcely smaller part in our rebellion than do its cruelties.

And how long shall we have to wait before the rest of mankind become pacifists too? There is no telling. But it may not be Utopian to hope that these two factors, the cultural attitude and the justified dread of the consequences of a future war, may result within a measurable time in putting an end to the waging of war. By what paths or by what side-tracks this will come about we cannot guess. But one thing we *can* say: whatever fosters the growth of culture works at the same time against war.

I trust you will forgive me if what I have said has disappointed you, and I remain, with kindest regards,

Yours sincerely,

SIGM. FREUD

NOTES

1. *Warum Krieg?* was the title of an interchange of open letters between Professor Albert Einstein and Freud. This formed one of a series of similar interchanges arranged by the International Institute of Intellectual Co-operation under the auspices of the League of Nations, and was first published simultaneously in German, French and English in Paris in 1933. Freud's letter was reprinted *Ges. Schr.,* **12,** 347, and *Ges. W.,* **16.** Professor Einstein's, which preceded it, was a short one setting out the problems to be discussed. Present translation by James Strachey.

2. In the original the words "*Recht*" and "*Macht*" are used throughout the essay. It has unfortunately been necessary to sacrifice this stylistic unity in the translation. "*Recht*" has been rendered indifferently by "right," "law" and "justice"; and "*Macht*" by "might," "force" and "power."

3. Freud uses the word "horde" to denote a comparatively small group.

QUESTIONS

1. How does Freud explain the existence of war and peace?

2. According to Freud, what factor that might prevent war is absent in the structure of the League of Nations?

Chapter 8

COGNITIVE THEORY

COMPONENTS OF COGNITIVE THEORY

Focus of Analysis ········▶	• Personality and cognitive experience of leaders
Major Actors ········▶	• Individual
Behavior of States ········▶	• Guided by experience, preconceptions, background, and personality of leader(s)
Basis of a State's Foreign Policy ········▶	• Driven by operational reality of elites
Key Concepts ········▶	• Cognition; Elites; Independent leader; Operational reality; Participatory leader; Personality

INTRODUCTION

In the course of growing up and learning to live with others, we have all probably heard the phrase, "imagine how dull the world would be if everyone were the same." Dull, certainly, but such uniformity would make it easier for political scientists to predict people's behavior and put together theories of international relations. Doubtless, however, even most political scientists would thankfully acknowledge—along with the rest of us—that we are all unique individuals, with different personalities, beliefs, ambitions, skills, etc. The theory presented in this chapter, which we will call cognitive theory, suggests that a leader's specific personality guides not only his or her own actions but the destiny of the state and its relations with other countries.

We can define the term **personality** as the package of behavior, temperament, and other individualistic qualities that uniquely identifies each of us. Cognition is one element of this personality package. **Cognition** is what an individual comes to know as a result of learning and reasoning or, on a more instinctual level, intuition and perception. All of these components combine to form a person's cognitive facility. In our daily lives, we are perhaps more familiar with the term *recognize*. When you recognize a person or place, for example, you identify him, her, or it using accumulated knowledge or experience.

Cognitive theorists believe that the personality traits of leaders can often define both the agenda and specific features of a state's foreign policy. In his article "World Politics and Personal Insecurity," Harold Lasswell suggests that, unconsciously, leaders actually superimpose their own sense of self over that of the state. That is, the line separating the leader from the state becomes blurred, with the personality of the leader—complete with flaws and insecurities—shaping the policy and perceptions of the state.

A leader's individual perception of reality is naturally conditioned by emotional attachments and aversions that he or she formed in life. In putting together a worldview, Lasswell asserts, people tend to displace emotions of those close to us onto symbols that are more removed, such as nations, classes, and rulers. For example, the frustration of a peasant in pre-revolutionary France was not solely directed at a single aristocrat, but at the entire aristocracy. Or, a neighbor's dispute with one who is from a foreign country might prejudice his view toward that country as a whole. According to Lasswell, in political personalities, these associations—however loose—are likely to have some conditioning affect on performance and, hence, policy.

Margaret Hermann provides a structure for analyzing the individual traits that might affect a leader's decisions and policy-making. In "Explaining Foreign Policy Behavior Using the Personal Characteristics of Political Leaders," Hermann isolates four broad types of personal characteristics: beliefs, motives, decision style, and interpersonal style. Although other factors do come into play (interest in foreign affairs, diplomatic and foreign policy training), these can be combined with an assessment of a leader's basic characteristics to form a fairly complete profile.

From her analysis, Hermann reached the conclusion that leaders generally have two orientations toward foreign affairs: independent and participatory. An **independent leader** tends to be aggressive, with a limited capacity to consider different alternatives, and, not surprisingly, is willing to be the first to take action over a perceived threat. In regard to foreign policy, independent leaders seek to preserve a state's individual identity and tend to be somewhat isolationist, viewing contact with other nations as a slippery slope toward dependence and viable only under their own specific terms or conditions.

By contrast, Hermann defines a **participatory leader** as generally conciliatory, with an inclusive nature that encourages relationships with other countries, considers various alternatives in problem solving, and rarely seeks to initiate action. Participatory leaders also have a different approach to foreign policy. They promote contact and ventures with other nations and are likely to be quite sensitive and responsive to the international environment.

Whether independent or participatory, cognitive theorists view leaders' perceptions of other states and other heads of state as key components of foreign policy. Robert Jervis' well-respected work, *Perception and Misperception in International*

Politics, discusses how decision-makers perceive others' behavior and form judgments about their intentions. He actually focuses on several vital misperceptions that are common among people and often lead to disputes or even war. These misperceptions might be compared to the stereotype images of "good guys" versus "bad guys" in an old Hollywood western. First, we tend to view the people of other nations as more hostile than we are. That is, we might represent ourselves as the peace-loving townspeople and the other side as a band of aggressive marauders. Second, we also view other countries as better organized and integrated, behaving according to a coherent strategic plan. Returning to our old western movie analogy, the "bad guys" always seemed to operate within an accepted and rigid hierarchy and to have some sort of a plan to get what they wanted, whether it was robbing the town bank, getting control of the town, or capturing rights to the local water supply.

Finally, just as it is difficult to envision the gentle townspeople in this image intimidating the fierce band of marauders, we too find it difficult to believe that others might be afraid of or intimidated by us. But it is these kinds of misperceptions that can foster errors in judgment about the motives and aims behind the actions of other countries. We see, then, that the perceptions (and misperceptions) of leaders could affect the foreign policy of states and the international system as a whole.

If we take for granted that leaders are, in fact, conditioned by the unique features of their own personality, cognitive theorists would argue that we must also acknowledge that a leader's perception of policy, the state, and the system will be conditioned by these same features. **Operational reality** refers to the picture of the environment held by an individual (usually a leader), as it is modified by his or her personality, perceptions, and misperceptions. Essentially, we all live and work within our own operational reality, but in a leader, it has an impact on policies and decisions that influence millions of people and could well affect the course of history.

At this point, we need to acknowledge that often these policies and decisions are made by an influential collective or group. Although this chapter and the other chapters in this section focus on individual level of analysis theories, we might expand the image somewhat to include such groups of like-minded individuals. These individuals' beliefs about, ideology of, and approach to foreign policy fall within sufficiently narrow confines as to be considered a single voice.

The final contribution in this chapter, "The Beliefs of Leaders: Perceptual and Ideological Sources of Foreign Policy After the Cold War," by Mark P. Lagon suggests that elites might be considered such a group and actually represent a major determinant in American foreign policy. **Elites,** in this case, can be described as a group of leaders, decision-makers, and persons in positions of authority who have influence over the course and conduct of government policy. These elites are found both within the upper echelons of government or outside of government but with strong contacts and connections to it. Working from this notion that elites, or categories of elites, tend to function with a degree of commonality, Lagon traces a realignment of consensus, or beliefs, that took place among this group, resulting from the end of the Cold War. Just as Jervis suggested that we are susceptible as individuals to certain group perceptions and misperceptions, Lagon here isolates six specific ideological stands with various political, economic, and military viewpoints that are now emerging among the elite political leadership. With the waning of ideological conflict that characterized our beliefs and United States foreign policy for four decades, it is certainly important to analyze the shifts that are now taking place in our perceptions of both ourselves and the world.

Cognitive theory is really about individual personalities and perceptions and how they can affect the behavior of states in the international system. These unique qualities are based on both a person's innate, instinctive reactions and learned or reasoned patterns that come from knowledge and experience. Cognitive theorists suggest a leader's personality conditions how he or she makes decisions, implements those decisions, and judges the outcome within a global context. It would seem that the distinctions that make us who we are would quite likely have an impact on how we try to shape or control the world around us. But, should personality be the defining feature in an analysis of international relations?

A CRITIQUE OF COGNITIVE THEORY

The notion that individuals make foreign policy and can shape the international system in which they exist is the most important contribution of the individual level of analysis. Cognitive theory, with its emphasis on studying the values, beliefs, and personal characteristics of leaders, forces us to recognize that all explanations of political behavior must take into account the role of the individual. Only by narrowing our focus to the level of the individual can we understand fully the actions of states.

Critics of cognitive theory might argue that focusing on personality profiles of individual leaders to determine an analytical framework for studying international relations is, indeed, limiting. In addition, one's assessment of any leader should be based on a sophisticated and complete psychoanalysis. Such a scenario is improbable, at best, since most leaders have not and would not subject themselves to this type of scrutiny. Thus, it is left to the scholar to examine the background and behavior patterns of leaders or potential leaders, which would tend to produce both vague and problematic results.

Other criticisms of congnitive theory revolve around its limited scope. The emphasis of the theory (personality/cognition) is so narrow that it seems inappropriate to attempt a broad, all-encompassing application to international relations as a whole. The price of focusing on specific individuals is the danger of getting bogged down in a detailed analysis of the subject's idiosyncractic characteristics and losing sight of the broader picture. In addition, the principles of cognitive theory might lead us to believe that all wars are simply the result of misperceptions or misunderstandings between individual leaders. Cognitive theorists ignore the fact that wars often result from fundamental conflicting interests between states on larger issues, such as national security, competition over scarce resources, or dozens of other factors that affect global politics.

One final comment is similar to the critique used against human nature theory. Can cognitive theory provide a framework substantial enough to analyze contemporary issues of foreign policy in a contemporary context? Do personality,

KEY CONCEPTS

Cognition   is an individual's knowing as a result of learning and reasoning or, on a more instinctual level, intuiting and perceiving. All of these components combine to form a person's cognitive facility.

Elites   refers to leaders, decision-makers, and persons in positions of authority that have influence over the course and conduct of government policy.

Independent leader,   according to Margaret Hermann, is one of the two major orientations of leaders. Independent leaders tend to be aggressive, have a limited capacity to consider different alternatives, and are willing to be the first to take action over a perceived threat. Independent leaders seek to preserve a state's individual identity and tend to be somewhat isolationist, viewing contact with other nations as a slippery slope toward dependence and viable only under their own specific terms or conditions.

Operational reality   refers to the picture of the environment held by an individual (usually a leader) as it is modified by his or her personality, perceptions, and misperceptions.

Participatory leader   is a term used by Margaret Hermann to characterize a type of leader who is generally conciliatory and encourages relationships with other countries, considers various alternatives in problem solving, and rarely seeks to initiate action. Participatory leaders are likely to be quite sensitive and responsive to the international environment.

Personality   is the package of behavior, temperament, and other individualistic qualities that uniquely identifies each of us. Cognition is one element of this personality package.

perceptions, and beliefs hold the key to understanding international monetary policy, the formation of interdependent trading blocs, or the changing nature of collective security? We would have to say under these circumstances that cognitive theory—though important and useful in understanding how and in what way individual leaders do play a role in the formulation and conduct of foreign policy—may not offer a complete understanding of the patterns and process for international relations today and in the future.

36. World Politics and Personal Insecurity

Harold D. Lasswell

In this exerpt, Harold Laswell analyzes the impact of the "ego symbol" and "collective emblem" on the foreign policy of a nation-state. He argues that a leader will use these tools when confronted by pressure from the international community. Lasswell also investigates the use of symbols to enhance a leader's personal ambitions. This selection is from *World Politics and Personal Insecurity* (1965).

Harold Lasswell (1902–1978) was best known for his use of psychological theory in political study. His other book, *Politics: Who Gets What, When, How,* was accepted first by psychiatrists and only later, in the 1950s, by political scientists.

Owing to the assumption of violence in international and interclass relations, collective symbols are presented at the focus of attention under circumstances which are particularly prone to precipitate all manner of anxiety reactions. The meaning of these symbols is a function of the total personalities in which they occur, and they necessarily derive much of their significance from deeper and earlier sources than those connected with the immediate political situation.

Insecurities which are induced by threats of loss may be abated by direct acts of counterassertion. But in a world of limited opportunities the impulses toward boundless counteraggression which are elicited under such circumstances must submit to incessant chastening. Impulsive counterassertions are rarely consummated, and the most direct means by which the underlying anxieties may be removed are therefore unavailable. The continuing necessity of suppressing hostility, or of giving it indirect expression, means that a substantial measure of anxiety remains related to the secondary symbols. There are many ways of disposing of accumulated insecurities in relation to political symbols without directly implicating political symbols. Hence anxieties which arise from the rumors of foreign conspiracies may be effectively abolished by displacing hostilities upon wives, secretaries, or chauffeurs; or by orgiastic and diffuse release in orgasm, alcoholism, or pugilism. The routes to release are very numerous; they may be classified into acts which involve object orientations, reflective thinking, autism (moods and irrelevant fantasies), and somatic reactions (headaches and other bodily changes in which functional factors are important). Despite the rich variety of insecurity-abolishing alternatives, several circumstances conspire to connect world political symbols with anxiety reactions. The expectation of violence sustains an organization of communication which pays attention to what the various key participants in the balancing process are doing. Their names are continually before the population as targets for affective displacements of all kinds, and they are reported in connection with many events which directly expose the local symbol to the possibility of losing its independence, its material claims, or its prestige. Vested interests arise in connection with the special function of transmitting symbols in the press and elsewhere; and many of these vested interests extract direct advantages from emphasizing the threatening aspects of the world situation.

Although insecurities arising within the personality in its political aspects may be removed by nonpolitical acts, many of the reactions to insecurity are immediately relevant to politics. We have seen how the suppression of vigorous counterassertion in a world of many limitations sustains insecurities arising from the balancing process. Some of the aggressions which are mobilized and denied direct expression against the foreign environment are directed against the self. This is one of the most important dynamisms of our intrapsychic life, displaying itself in extreme form as suicide.

One of the chief immediate results of subjecting an ego symbol to external danger and of inhibiting counteraggression is thus the preoccupation of the ego with its own relations to the world. This represents a partial withdrawal of libido (affective interest) from the symbols of the surrounding environment. This growing absorption in the more central self-symbols reactivates the earlier, more primitive, less disciplined attitudes of the personality. The result is the elaboration of narcissistically gratifying fantasies of the self. A personality so reacting may create symbols to which he exposes others, boasting of the high moral worth and ultimate omnipotence of the collective symbol; or in the absence of autonomous elaboration, he may respond positively to such symbols when they are supplied by others in conversation or in print. A particular value is attached to acts of ceremonial deference to the collective emblem, since to personalities in such a condition each small detail seems to involve the fate of the whole collective symbol, and of national or class or race "honor.". . .

The ego symbol of any selected personality within a class or nation is a highly complicated structure which includes symbols of all degrees of differentiation. The ego sentiments which are organized with reference to brothers, sisters, friends, professional associates, and neighbors are much fuller of nuance than those which refer to such secondary objects as nations or classes. The personality-in-relation-to-partner is controlled by many reflective considerations, since there is much tested knowledge available about the capacities and proclivities of the partner.

That part of the ego symbol which is organized in relation to the ambiguous "we" called our nation, or class, or race, is in most instances but slightly modified by knowledge. In view of the undeveloped character of such a "we" symbol, it may properly be called a *rudimentary* sentiment or symbol. The ambiguity of reference of these secondary terms and the residues of early emotional attachments and aversions combine to minimize the "reality critique." The resulting instability of judgment is displayed in the ease with which uncorrected swings occur between extremes of hostility and of admiration in relation to secondary symbols. A study by E. S. Bogardus of the attitudes of Californians toward various national and racial groups showed that it was not the Japanese who were the most hated nation, but the Turks, whom the subjects had never seen.[1] The absence of information about Belgium made it easier to build up a vast idealization of the Belgian people than of the British or the Germans.

It should be explicitly stated that persons who are well integrated in their immediate personal relationships may be poorly developed toward remote objects and, reversely, that people who are poorly organized toward primary situations may have acquired the special knowledge which chastens reactions in dealing with remote objects. Indeed one of the principal functions of symbols of remote objects, like nations and classes, is to serve as targets for the relief of many of the tensions which might discharge disastrously in face-to-face relations. The hatred of the physical father may be displaced upon the symbol of the monarch, enabling the person to keep on good terms with the person toward whom the early animosities were mainly directed.

From this analysis it follows that the rudimentary self-symbols which are related to world politics may function in loose association with other aspects of the personality and, like all partly dissociated systems, may predominate in shaping overt conduct in situations which call them up.

The elaboration of regressive and fantastic processes in connection with the rudimentary self-symbols of world politics is favored by the weak superego formations which arise in consequence of the comparative absence of world mores. The assumption that the resort to violence is the ultimate appeal in world politics indicates the weakness of moral imperatives in this sphere of human relations. Impulses are permitted to discharge in elementary form owing to the fragmentary nature of world culture.

Strictly speaking, it is not legitimate to refer to rudimentary self-symbols as pathological expressions of the individual. Nor is it correct to oppose a sick society to a basically healthy person. Pathology is neither social in contrast with individual, nor individual in contrast with social; pathology is configurational. If the word is used at all, it may be defined as referring to events destructive of certain patterns defined as "normal" or "supernormal."

We have seen that one of the principal consequences of the expectation of violence in world politics is to build up insecurities which arise from the curbing of counteraggressive tendencies which are initially elicited by the dangers connected with the we-symbol in the balancing process. This prolonged indulgence of the reality-testing, cautious, self-controlling features of culture and personality favors the drastic redefinition of the situation in directions gratifying to the underindulged, unreflecting, incautious, and spontaneous patterns of culture and personality.

NOTES

1. See the articles on "Social Distance" by E. S. Bogardus in the *Journal of Applied Sociology* since 1925.

QUESTIONS

1. What role does the "ego" identified by Laswell play in shaping a nation's actions in the international system?

2. Provide an example in which a leader promoted the use of symbolism to achieve particular international aims.

37. Explaining Foreign Policy Behavior Using the Personal Characteristics of Political Leaders

Margaret G. Hermann

In this article Margaret G. Hermann moves a step closer than the implications on international relations of human nature in general and studies the impact of personality on foreign policy. Hermann examines whether the characteristics of individual heads of state can influence the behavior of that state in the international system. Dividing individual interests into two broad foreign policy orientations, the author uses a number of examples in her analysis.

Margaret G. Hermann is a professor with the Mershon Center at Ohio State University. She has written extensively on the impact of personality and ideology on American foreign policy.

INTRODUCTION

Parties to the continuing debate concerning whether the personal characteristics of political leaders can affect policy have increasingly turned to empirical research to seek resolution to the controversy. . . . Emerging from this research are portraits of national political leaders who influence their governments toward aggressive or toward conciliatory relations with other nations. The data suggest that aggressive leaders are high in need for power, low in conceptual complexity, distrustful of others, nationalistic, and likely to believe that they have some control over the events in which they are involved. In contrast, the data suggest that conciliatory leaders are high in need for affiliation, high in conceptual complexity, trusting of others, low in nationalism, and likely to exhibit little belief in their own ability to control the events in which they are involved.

The present article has as its purpose a further examination of how these 6 per-

sonal characteristics relate to foreign policy behavior for some 45 heads of government. The study is unique in several ways. (1) To date, researchers have not examined all 6 characteristics in the same study. (2) A conceptual scheme is presented to link these characteristics to foreign policy behavior. (3) An attempt is made to broaden the foreign policy behaviors that are examined beyond specifically aggressive (i.e., entry into war, arms increases) and conciliatory (i.e., entry into international agreements) behaviors.

CONCEPTUAL SCHEME[1]

The six personal characteristics we are examining in this research were selected because they have been found to relate to foreign policy behavior in several studies. The characteristics represent four broad types of personal characteristics that journalists and scholars alike suggest have an impact on the content as well as the means of making political decisions.

These four types of personal characteristics are beliefs, motives, decision style, and interpersonal style.

Beliefs refer to a political leader's fundamental assumptions about the world. Are events predictable, is conflict basic to human interaction, can one have some control over events, is the maintenance of national sovereignty and superiority the most important objective of a nation? Answers to questions such as these suggest some of a political leader's beliefs. Beliefs are proposed by many (e.g., Axelrod, 1976; DeRivera, 1968; Frank, 1968; Holsti, 1967; Jervis, 1976; Verba, 1969) to affect a political leader's interpretation of his environment and, in turn, the strategies that the leader employs. Two of the personal characteristics examined in the present study fall under the category of beliefs—nationalism and belief in one's own ability to control events. Nationalism is often used by journalists and policy makers as a reason for a specific political leader's actions, particularly in discussions of leaders of Third World countries. Ascertaining a political leader's belief in the controllability of events is thought to be fundamental in developing his/her operational code— the way a political leader defines the basic rules that govern political behavior (see George, 1969; Holsti, 1977).

It is hard to find journalistic political analysis that does not consider at some point the reasons why a political leader is doing what he/she is doing—in effect, the political leader's motives. Need for power is probably the most discussed motive with reference to political leaders. But others, such as need for affiliation and need for approval, also appear regularly in such writings. Motives appear to affect political leaders' interpretations of their environment and the strategies they

use (see Barber, 1965; Hermann, 1977, 1978). In the present research we will look at need for power and need for affiliation. . . . These two motives appeared to influence the type of foreign behavior the presidents urged on their governments.

By decision style is meant preferred methods of making decisions. How does the political leader go about making decisions? Are there certain ways of approaching a policy-making task which characterize the leader? Possible components of decision style are openness to new information, preference for certain levels of risk, complexity in structuring and processing information, and ability to tolerate ambiguity. . . .

The last type of personal characteristic—interpersonal style—deals with the characteristic ways in which a policy maker deals with other policy makers. Two interpersonal style characteristics— paranoia (excessive suspiciousness) and Machiavellianism (unscrupulous, manipulative behavior)—are often noted as particularly pronounced in political leaders (see Christie and Geis, 1970; Guterman, 1970; Hofstadter, 1965; Rutherford, 1966). Tucker (1965) has proposed that these two traits are related in a type of political leader having a "warfare personality," for example, Stalin and Hitler. The political behavior of such a leader is combative in nature. Suspiciousness or distrust of others is the interpersonal style variable examined in the present research.

These four types of personal characteristics are expected to affect both the style and content of foreign policy. Because beliefs and motives suggest ways of interpreting the environment, political leaders are likely to urge their governments to act in ways consistent with such images. Specifically, political leaders' beliefs and motives provide them with a map for charting their course. . . .

With regard to decision style and interpersonal style, we make an assumption that a political leader will generally engage in similar stylistic behavior regardless of arena. Thus, political leaders' preferred methods of making personal decisions and interacting with others will carry over to their political behavior. Style is probably one of the first differences, for example, noted when heads of government change as the new leader tries to make himself comfortable in his role. One head of state may focus foreign policy-making within his own office, while his predecessor may have been willing to let the bureaucracy handle all but problems of crisis proportions. One head of state may be given to rhetoric in the foreign policy arena; his predecessor may have wanted action. Moreover, the bureaucracy tends to adjust to changes in style from one chief executive to the next hoping to minimize differences between itself and the chief executive. The result may be to accentuate the stylistic predilections of high level decision makers. In turn, the policy begins to reflect the stylistic preferences of these high level policy makers.

Given this description of the types of personal characteristics that will affect foreign policy and how they will affect it, what kinds of foreign policy would we expect from political leaders with the six characteristics under study here? In addition to aggressive and conciliatory behavior, what foreign policy behaviors will such leaders urge that their governments consider? If we examine the dynamics of the traits associated with the aggressive leader, we find a need to manipulate and control others, little ability to consider a range of alternatives, suspiciousness of others' motives, a high interest in maintaining national identity and sovereignty, and a distinct willingness to initiate action. Extrapolating from these dynamics to foreign policy behavior, the characteristics are suggestive of a foreign policy which is independent in style and content. Such leaders will seek to maintain their nation's individuality, to keep their nations as much as possible apart from the other nations in the international system, since extensive contact with other nations may lead to dependence on these nations. They will urge their governments to be suspicious of the motives of leaders of other nations. When interaction is necessary, they expect it to be on their nations' terms.

Contrast the personal dynamics for the aggressive leader with those for the leader who has been found to be generally conciliatory. The personal characteristics of the conciliatory leader indicate a need to establish and maintain friendly relationships with others, an ability to consider a wide range of alternatives, little suspiciousness of others' motives, no overriding concern with the maintenance of national identity and sovereignty, and little interest in initiating action. These dynamics suggest a more participatory foreign policy. Such leaders are likely to be interested in having their nations interact with other nations, in learning what other nations have of value for their nation and find valuable about their nation, and in seeking a wide range of alternative solutions to problems jointly plaguing their nation and other nations. They will probably keep attuned to what is going on in international relations, being sensitive and responsive to this environment. In effect, these leaders will attempt to facilitate their nations' participation in the international system.

What we are suggesting by this discussion is that the personal characteristics under study interrelate to form a personal orientation to behavior or a general way of responding to one's environment. This personal orientation is transformed by the head of government into a general orientation to foreign affairs. By knowing a head of government's orientation to foreign affairs, one knows his predispositions when faced with a foreign policy-making task—how he will define the situation and the style of behavior he will be likely to emphasize. Heads of government with the personal characteristics in the present study are thought to be predisposed toward either an independent or participatory orientation to foreign affairs depending on how the characteristics interrelate. Traits that have characterized the aggressive political leader in previous research are expected to interrelate to form an independent orientation to foreign affairs and to lead to foreign policy behaviors which emphasize an independent foreign policy in style and content. On the other hand, traits that have characterized the conciliatory political leader in previous research are expected to interrelate to form a participatory orientation to foreign affairs and to lead to foreign policy behaviors which emphasize participation with other governments in style and content.

As the writer has proposed elsewhere (Hermann, 1976, 1978, 1979; Hermann and Hermann, 1979), the personal characteristics and orientations of heads of government examined in this research

are likely to have more impact on a government's foreign policy under some circumstances than under others. We will explore two such conditions in this study—one that is hypothesized to enhance the effect of leader personality on foreign policy behavior and one that is thought to diminish such effects. The two variables we will study here are interest in foreign affairs and training in foreign affairs. Interest in foreign affairs will enhance the effect of a political leader's characteristics on government policy, whereas training in foreign affairs will diminish such an effect.

Interest in foreign affairs acts as a motivating force. An important consequence of interest in foreign policy will be increased participation in the making of foreign policy. The head of government will want to be consulted on decisions and to be kept informed about what is happening in foreign affairs. Moreover, the reasons behind a head of government's interest in foreign policy—he places value on good external relations, he fears an enemy takeover, he sees it as a way of gaining re-election—may predetermine the course of action he will seek to implement. With little interest in foreign affairs, the head of government is likely to delegate authority to other people, negating the effect of his personality on the resultant policy except as his spokesman's personality is similar to his own.

With regard to training in foreign affairs, the head of government with little or no training has no expertise on which to call. He has no previous experience to suggest possible alternatives or plans of action. As a result, his natural predispositions come into play. The head of government with training, on the other hand, has some knowledge about what will succeed and fail in the international arena. As a consequence of his experience, he has very likely developed certain styles and strategies for dealing with a foreign policy situation that are particular to the issue and/or target nation involved. There is less dependence on his underlying predispositions.

MEASUREMENT OF PERSONAL CHARACTERISTICS . . .

Determining Orientations to Foreign Affairs

In the conceptual scheme presented earlier, we hypothesized that . . . personal characteristics . . . interrelate to form two orientations to foreign affairs that affect the content and style of foreign policy behavior. To test this hypothesis most directly, two composite measures were created. The first, which we call characteristic of the independent leader, consisted of being high in nationalism, high in belief in one's own ability to control events, high in need for power, low in conceptual complexity, and high in distrust of others. The second, which is characteristic of the participatory leader, consisted of being low in nationalism, low in belief in one's own ability to control events, high in need for affiliation, high in conceptual complexity, and low in distrust of others.[2] To determine these two composites, the heads of governments' scores on each of the six personal characteristics were ranked. For the independent composite, ranks for nationalism, belief in one's own ability to control events, need for power, conceptual complexity, and distrust in others were summed. For the participatory composite, ranks for nationalism, belief

in one's own ability to control events, need for affiliation, conceptual complexity, and distrust in others were summed. . . .

Interest in Foreign Affairs

Interest in foreign affairs refers to the amount of concern or attention which a head of government directs toward foreign policy-making. Is foreign policy a "passion"? Or does the head of government only become a participant in foreign policy-making on specific issues? Perhaps the head of government only deals with foreign affairs when forced to by circumstances.

Interest in foreign affairs was operationalized in this study by noting the percentage of foreign policy events in which a head of government participated while in office. Higher interest was indicated by a higher rate of participation. One of the variables in the CREON foreign policy events data set on which each event is coded notes if the head of government participated in the event or if his/her approval was probably needed for the action to take place (see Hermann et al., 1973: 102). The number of foreign policy events falling into these two categories for each head of government during his/her tenure in office formed the numerator for calculating rate of participation. Total number of foreign policy events during a head of government's term in office was the denominator. For most of the analyses in which we will examine interest, the variable will be dichotomized at the median denoting heads of government with high and low interest in foreign affairs.

Training in Foreign Affairs

By training in foreign affairs is meant having held some political or governmental position that would give one knowledge about foreign affairs and foreign policy-making. To determine amount of training for the heads of government in the present sample, a search was made of reference sources such as *Statesman's Year-Book* as well as autobiographies and biographies. All past political and governmental positions were noted. From this biographical record on the heads of government, the number of years each had held positions involving foreign affairs (e.g., foreign or defense minister, ambassador, in foreign or defense ministry, representative to UNESCO or the Common Market) was determined. The number of years the head of government had held his/her present office was also counted in the measure of training on the assumption that such a position was a good training ground in foreign affairs. A training score was calculated by finding what percentage of the years a head of government had been in politics involved positions in foreign affairs and foreign policy making. . . .

Relationships among Personal Characteristics, Orientations, Interest, and Training

. . . The correlations . . . indicate that the two orientations are significantly inversely related as would be expected from the nature of their construction. All five of the personal characteristics that were used in determining the independent orientation are significantly related to this composite measure in the directions suggested by the conceptual framework. Such is not the case for the participatory orientation. Nationalism, belief in one's own ability to control events, and distrust of others contribute

more to this orientation than conceptual complexity and need for affiliation. The reason why conceptual complexity and need for affiliation make a smaller contribution may lie in the significant inverse relationship between these two personal characteristics, contrary to the conceptual framework.

Several other correlations among the personal characteristics included in the orientations are noteworthy. Nationalism, need for power, and distrust of others are all three significantly interrelated. At least for this sample of heads of government, the nationalist appears to be high in need for power and distrust of others.

. . . The significant correlations with the interest variable suggest that the head of government with an independent orientation was more interested in foreign affairs than the head of government with the participatory orientation. Moreover, the more conceptually complex the leader was, the lower his interest in foreign affairs. For training, only the correlation with belief in one's own ability to control events is significant. The more highly trained the head of government was, the lower his/her belief in the ability to control events. Experience may lead to a realization of the range of variables which affect foreign policy over which one can have little control.

RELATIONSHIPS BETWEEN PERSONAL CHARACTERISTICS AND FOREIGN POLICY BEHAVIOR

Having suggested how the personal characteristics are expected to affect foreign policy behavior and having operationalized the personal characteristics employed in this research, let us examine how the personal characteristics do, in fact, relate to foreign policy behavior. The specific foreign policy behaviors included in this study are professed orientation to change, independence/interdependence of action, commitment, affect, and environmental feedback. . . . In what follows, we will focus on each foreign policy behavior by itself, further explicating conceptually how the personal characteristics are expected to affect it and showing the relationships between it and the personal characteristics that were found.

Professed Orientation to Change

By professed orientation to change we mean a government's public posture regarding the need for change in the international environment. Do the policy-makers of a nation express little or no need for change in the international arena, or do they argue that short-term and/or long-term changes are in order? Professed orientation to change is measured by noting what percentage of the time goal statements are present in the foreign policy events of a nation during a head of government's tenure in office. Goal refers here to a desired future condition. If goal statements are generally absent, the policy-makers of a nation are considered as professing little or no need for change in the international environment, i.e., as affirming the status quo. If goal statements are generally present, the policy-makers of a nation are viewed as professing a need for change in the international environment.

How is professed orientation to change probably affected by the independent and participatory orientations to

foreign affairs examined in the present study? In describing the independent orientation, we noted the importance of maintaining the status quo, that is, the importance of maintaining national individuality and the power base the head of government now has. Change is anathema to such leaders, since there is always the chance of losing what has already been gained in power and position. In some sense, heads of government with independent orientations are present or "now" oriented rather than future-oriented. They are concerned with the realities of day-to-day politics as opposed to future states or conditions. Moreover, independent leaders are secretive. Such leaders cannot be held to what they have not stated publicly; they maintain a certain maneuverability because their positions are not a matter of public record. Thus, heads of government with independent orientations are unlikely to urge their governments publicly to propose changes in the international arena.

On the other hand, heads of government with participatory orientations are likely publicly to advocate change in the international environment. One way for such heads of government to participate in the international arena is to make public their goals. Through such public goal statements, they can solicit support from and initiate relations with other nations. In effect, they signal the direction in which they are moving and their intentions to other nations through public goal statements. . . .

The correlations . . . are in the predicted direction for the participatory orientation for all but heads of government with much training. For the independent orientation, the correlations are only in the predicted direction for heads of government with low interest and heads of government with little training. The correlations are significant for both orientations for heads of government with little training. For the independent orientation, the correlation for heads of government with much training is significant but in the reverse direction from that predicted. In effect, the results . . . suggest support for the hypotheses for heads of government with little training in foreign affairs and the opposite of the hypotheses for heads of government with much training in foreign affairs. Training may afford the heads of government with a participatory orientation a wider variety of ways of signaling intent than the use of goal statements; it may teach the heads of government with an independent orientation ways of suggesting change that do not necessarily commit them publicly to a particular policy (e.g., by proposing the need for change in other nations than their own).

Looking at the individual characteristics, we note support for the hypotheses for nationalism, need for power, and need for affiliation under various of the interest and training conditions. For nationalism and need for power, the correlations are significant and in the predicted direction for heads of government with low interest and for heads of government with little training. On the contrary, for need for affiliation, the correlations are significant and in the predicted direction for heads of government with high interest and for heads of government with much training. Conceptual complexity was related in the opposite direction from that predicted for each group of heads of government.

High conceptual complexity was related to little professed need for change.

Independence/Interdependence of Action

Independence/interdependence of action is concerned with the amount of autonomy that a nation maintains in its foreign policy actions. At issue are whether foreign policy actions are taken alone or in concert with other nations, and whether such actions are initiated by a nation or in response to a prior stimulus directed at the nation. Actions taken alone and initiated by the nation are considered to denote independence of action, while actions taken in concert with other nations and in response to a prior direct stimulus denote interdependence of action. . . .

In some sense, this foreign policy behavior gets at the essence of the conceptual difference between the independent and participatory orientations toward foreign affairs. Heads of government with the independent orientation are likely to want to act alone and to initiate behavior on their own terms. They will seek to maintain autonomy, that is, to control their own national behavior. Such leaders believe that they can have some effect on events. Moreover, they distrust the leaders of other nations. These two traits coupled with a desire to maintain their own and their nation's position and power base suggest an emphasis on independence of action. Heads of government with a participatory orientation, on the other hand, are probably willing to relinquish some autonomy or control over their own behavior. An individual (or nation) can benefit from working with rather than against others. Building on their low level of distrust in others, heads of government with a participatory orientation perceive little harm in acting in consort with others if by doing so they can achieve an objective. Moreover, such leaders are likely to be sensitive to stimulation from the environment, picking up on behaviors directed toward them. . . .

The relationships for the participatory orientation may be low, because the emphasis for such heads of government is less on elicited behavior than on acting with other nations. In other words, heads of government with a participatory orientation may be interested in initiating behavior but prefer to include other nations in their activity. . . . The percentage of such actions during a head of government's tenure in office was the dependent variable. Examining these relationships, we note that one for the participatory orientation is significant and two approach significance. These correlations occur for the sample of heads of government as a whole, for the heads of government with low interest, and for the heads of government with little training. Moreover, all five of the individual personal characteristics involved in the participatory composite have correlations with initiative-multilateral actions that are significant or that approach significance.

Commitment

A commitment is a behavior which limits a government's future capacity to act either because it uses up physical resources, involves pledges of resources in the future, or involves a statement of intent to use resources for a specific purpose. In other words, commitments reduce the pool of available resources for dealing with other problems or generate expectations that limit future behavior. . . .

By limiting future behavior, commitments reduce the independence and maneuverability of a government's policy makers. They are no longer completely in charge of their nation's behavior. As such, commitments are seen as inappropriate foreign policy behavior by heads of government with an independent orientation. Reducing control over one's resources and putting constraints on one's ability to act, particularly if it involves trusting leaders in other nations—this is anathema to independent heads of government. They are interested in increasing their power and maintaining their nations' separateness, not limiting their power and reducing their nation's separateness. On the other hand, the heads of government with a participatory orientation are willing to commit their nations' resources, expecting to gain resources from others that are beneficial to their nations in return. They have no predisposition to distrust the leaders of other nations, figuring cooperation may increase their gain in the long run. Moreover, heads of government with a participatory orientation are less concerned about maintaining their nations' separateness; they are willing to become somewhat dependent on other nations, if such dependencies are built on supportive relationships. . . .

One of the individual personal characteristics, distrust of others, is significantly related to commitment for the same three groups of heads of government as the independent orientation. As expected, the more distrusting these heads of government were of others, the fewer commitments their nations made.

Need for affiliation changes the direction of the relationship with commitment depending on which group of heads of government is analyzed. Need for affiliation is positively related—the predicted direction—when the head of government's interest is low and when training is limited, negatively related when the head of government's interest is high and when there is much training. Interest and training may provide the head of government whose need for affiliation is high with less extreme strategies than commitment for maintaining positive relations with other nations.

Affect

Affect denotes the feelings ranging from friendliness to hostility which policymakers of one nation express toward the policies, actions, or government of another nation. . . .

Direction and intensity of affect are expected to relate to scores on the independent and participatory orientations in the following manner. Because heads of government with an independent orientation to foreign affairs are interested in emphasizing the differences between their nation and other nations and because they generally distrust the leaders of other nations, they are likely to express negative affect toward other nations, being fairly intense in the expression of such affect. By using such techniques, heads of government with an independent orientation accentuate their separateness and the fact that they maintain control over their own behavior. They move on their own terms; they are their own bosses. Heads of government with a participatory orientation, on the contrary, have as a basic premise of their world-view a desire to maintain friendly

relations with others. Moreover, they do not distrust others nor are they overly concerned with the differences between their nation and other nations. Such heads of government are likely to emphasize the positive in their relations with other nations and to not "rock the boat" by being too intense in the expression of their affect. They perceive that consistent, positive reinforcement to others enables them to participate freely in the international environment. A "low, positive profile" keeps channels and opinions open.

. . . The results suggest support for the hypotheses for both orientations. For all groups of heads of government, the correlations are in the predicted direction. Moreover, sixteen of the twenty correlations for the orientations are significant or approach significance. With regard to the individual characteristics, all but belief in one's own ability to control events have correlations in the predicted direction that are significant or approach significance with these two affect variables. The largest number of significant or near significant correlations occur for nationalism and distrust of others.

Feedback from the Environment

How do other nations respond to the foreign policy behavior of a specific nation, i.e., what is the nature of their feedback? Is it favorable or unfavorable, accepting or rejecting? . . .

Our hypotheses for feedback follow from the previous hypotheses on affect. Heads of government with an independent orientation to foreign affairs are prone to actions that are negative in tone and fairly intense. Such behavior is likely to elicit mirror image behavior from other nations if they bother to respond at all. Because more independent heads of government do not develop relations with other nations and seek to maintain an independent status in the international arena, it may be easy to reject their behavior. There are fewer strings attached and probably fewer repercussions to such a rejection than would be the case with a more involved nation. Turning this rationale around, we expect more positive feedback for heads of government with a participatory orientation. Such heads of government tend to be positive toward other nations, eliciting positive behavior in return. Moreover, heads of government with a participatory orientation actively involve their nations in the international system so that a rejection of their nation's behavior may have repercussions not desired by the responding nation. If any feedback is to be given, positive feedback is probably safest.

. . . For all the groups of heads of government except those with high interest in foreign affairs, the correlations were in the predicted direction for the independent and participatory orientations. Of those eight relations in the predicted direction, one was significant and four approached significance. The significant correlation occurred for heads of government with low interest in foreign affairs.

Only need for affiliation in the individual characteristics does not have a correlation with feedback that is significant or approaches significance. For nationalism, need for power, and distrust of others, the correlations are reversed in sign for heads of government with low and high interest and for heads of government with little and much training. The correlations are all negative, as hypothesized, for heads of government with low interest and for heads of government with little training, but they are positive for heads of government with high interest and for heads of government with much training. Interest and training may increase the foreign policy stature of heads of government with these characteristics and/or make them more adept in foreign policy-making so that positive rather than negative feedback is directed toward their nations.

CONCLUSIONS

The research reported in this article has examined how six personal characteristics of heads of government interact to form two orientations to foreign affairs. Based on a set of premises about the ways heads of government with these two orientations will urge their governments to act, we have related the two orientations to six foreign policy behaviors. . . .

The results suggest the need to reconceptualize the impact of interest in foreign affairs on the relationship between personal characteristics and foreign policy behavior. Much like the lack of training in foreign affairs, low interest appears to provide heads of government with little to tap but their predispositions when they must make a foreign policy decision. With high interest in foreign affairs, the heads of government have probably read about, discussed, and formulated positions on foreign policy issues before taking office, and, after taking office, have kept themselves informed on problems in the foreign policy arena. They have developed some basis on which to make a decision other than their predispositions. Interest, like training, appears to increase the range of activities which heads of government can consider in dealing with foreign affairs. Instead of relying on strategies and styles dictated by their personal orientations, interested heads of government have a choice of several ways of acting and some knowledge of the probable outcomes when these alternative strategies and styles are used. Interested heads of government have a broader repertoire of possible behaviors.

Before leaving this discussion of interest and training, we should note that we learned as much about the particular foreign policy variables examined in this research by focusing on the sample of heads of government as a whole as from looking at the effects of interest and training in foreign affairs. The numbers of correlations with $p < .10$ are virtually the same for the whole sample as for those heads of government with little interest or with little training. In other words, the relationships between these personal characteristics and foreign policy behaviors tend to show up without taking such mediating variables as training or interest in foreign affairs into account. However, a closer examination of the correlations indicates that they are stronger—the personal characteristics account for a larger percentage of the variance in the foreign policy behaviors—for heads of government with little interest or with little training in foreign affairs than for the whole sample of heads of government. . . . Specifying the conditions under which personal characteristics can affect foreign policy behavior appears to enhance the explanatory power of the personal characteristics.

We have examined in this study the direct effects of leaders' personal char-

acteristics on their governments' foreign policy behavior and several conditions that appear to enhance this direct effect. Many other conditioning variables can be posited (see Hermann, 1976, 1978; Hermann and Hermann, 1979). Some other possible enhancing conditions involve being a predominant as opposed to nonpredominant leader (i.e., having a disproportionately large amount of power in the government), being part of a cohesive as opposed to a fragmented regime, facing an ambiguous as opposed to a structured situation, and having to deal with a small as opposed to a large bureaucracy. An important objective of the CREON Project, of which this study is a part, is the building of integrative links among these types of variables in explaining governments' foreign policy behavior. We are interested in developing models showing how national attributes, regime factors, decision structures and processes, situational variables, and external relationships interrelate in affecting foreign policy activities (see Salmore et al., 1978). The present study suggests that the personal characteristics and orientations to foreign affairs of political leaders are worth including in this integrative effort. It is, however, only a first step in the process of trying to explain why governments do certain things in the foreign policy arena.

NOTES

1. The conceptual scheme sketched here appears in a more detailed form in Hermann (1978).
2. The reader will note that although we are examining six personal characteristics, each of the orientations is composed of five characteristics. The orientations differ

in motivating forces. Need for power is included in the independent orientation but not in the participatory orientation; need for affiliation is included in the participatory orientation but not in the independent orientation. It was unclear conceptually that need for affiliation was relevant to an independent orientation or that need for power was relevant to a participatory orientation; thus, both motives were not included in each orientation.

REFERENCES

Atkinson, J. W. (1958) *Motives in Fantasy, Action, and Society.* New York: Litton.

Axelrod, R. (1976) *Structure of Decision: The Cognitive Maps of Political Elites.* Princeton, NJ: Princeton Univ. Press.

Barber, J. D. (1972) *The Presidential Character.* Englewood Cliffs, NJ: Prentice-Hall.

——— (1965) *The Lawmakers.* New Haven, CT: Yale Univ. Press.

Callahan, P., L. P. Brady, and M. G. Hermann (forthcoming) *Events, Behaviors, and Policies: Measuring the Foreign Activities of National Governments.* Columbus: Ohio State Univ. Press.

Christie, R. and F. L. Geis (1970) *Studies in Machiavellianism.* New York: Academic.

Crow, W. J. and R. C. Noel (1977) "An experiment in simulated historical decision making," pp. 385–405 in M. G. Hermann (ed.) *A Psychological Examination of Political Leaders.* New York: Free Press.

De Rivera, J. H. (1968) *The Psychological Dimension of Foreign Policy.* Columbus, OH: Merrill.

Driver, M. J. (1977) "Individual differences as determinants of aggression in the Internation Simulation," pp. 337–353 in M. G. Hermann (ed.) *A Psychological Examination of Political Leaders.* New York: Free Press.

Eckhardt, W. and R. K. White (1967) "A test of the mirror-image hypothesis: Kennedy and Khrushchev." *J. of Conflict Resolution* 11: 325–332.

Falkowski, L. (1978) *Presidents, Secretaries of State, and Crises in U.S. Foreign Relations: A Model and Predictive Analysis.* Boulder, CO: Westview.

Frank, J. D. (1968) *Sanity and Survival.* New York: Random House.

George, A. L. (1969) "The 'operational code': a neglected approach to the study of political leaders and decision-making." Int. Studies Q. 13: 190–222.

Guterman, S. S. (1970) *The Machiavellians.* Lincoln: Univ. of Nebraska Press.

Hermann, C. F., M. A. East, M. G. Hermann, B. G. Salmore, and S. A. Salmore (1973) "CREON: A foreign events data set." *Sage Professional Papers in International Studies* Vol. 2, No. 02-024. Beverly Hills, CA: Sage.

Hermann, M. G. (1979) "Who becomes a political leader? Some societal and regime influences on selection of a head of state," in L. Falkowski (ed.) *Psychological Models in International Politics.* Boulder, CO: Westview.

——— (1978) "Effects of personal characteristics of leaders on foreign policy," pp. 49–68 in M. A. East, S. A. Salmore, and C. F. Hermann (eds.) *Why Nations Act.* Beverly Hills, CA: Sage.

——— (1977) "Some personal characteristics related to foreign aid voting of congressmen," pp. 313–334 in M. G. Hermann (ed.) *A Psychological Examination of Political Leaders.* New York: Free Press.

——— (1976) "Circumstances under which leader personality will affect foreign policy: some propositions," pp. 326–333 in J. N. Rosenau (ed.) *In Search of Global Patterns.* New York: Free Press.

――― (1974) "Leader personality and foreign policy behavior," pp. 201-234 in J. N. Rosenau (ed.) *Comparing Foreign Policies: Theories, Findings, and Methods.* New York: Sage-Halsted.

――― and C. F. Hermann (1979) "The interaction of situations, political regimes, decision configurations, and leader personalities in interpreting foreign policy: leader effects when controlling for selected variables." Presented at the Moscow International Political Science Association Congress, August 12-18.

Hofstadter, R. (1965) *The Paranoid Style in American Politics and Other Essays.* New York: Knopf.

Holsti, O. R. (1977) "The 'operational code' as an approach to the analysis of belief systems." Report to the National Science Foundation.

――― (1967) "Cognitive dynamics and images of the enemy." *J. of Int. Affairs* 21: 16-39.

Jervis, R. (1976) Perception and Misperception in International Politics. Princeton, NJ: Princeton Univ. Press.

Johnson, I. (1977) "The operational code of Senator Frank Church," pp. 82-119 in M. G. Hermann (ed.) *A Psychological Examination of Political Leaders.* New York: Free Press.

Levine, R. A. (1966) *Dreams and Deeds: Achievement Motivation in Nigeria.* Chicago: Univ. of Chicago Press.

Osgood, C. E., and L. Anderson (1957) "Certain relations among experienced contingencies, associative structure, and contingencies in encoded messages." *Amer. J. of Psychology* 70: 411-420.

Rutherford, B. M. (1966) "Psychopathology, decision-making, and political involvement." *J. of Conflict Resolution* 10: 387-407.

Salmore, S. A., M. G. Hermann, C. F. Hermann, and B. G. Salmore (1978) "Conclusion: toward integrating the perspectives," pp. 191-210 in M. A. East, S. A. Salmore, and C. F. Hermann (eds.) *Why Nations Act.* Beverly Hills, CA: Sage Publications.

Shneidman, E. S. (1963) "The logic of politics," pp. 177-199 in L. Arons and M. A. May (eds.) *Television and Human Behavior.* Englewood Cliffs, NJ: Prentice-Hall.

Thordarson, B. (1972) *Trudeau and Foreign Policy: A Study in Decision-Making.* Toronto: Oxford Univ. Press.

Tucker, R. C. (1965) "The dictator and totalitarianism." *World Politics* 17: 55-83.

Verba, S. (1969) "Assumptions of rationality and non-rationality in models of the international system," pp. 217-231 in J. N. Rosenau (ed.) *International Politics and Foreign Policy.* New York: Free Press.

Winter, D. G. (1973) *The Power Motive.* New York: Free Press.

――― and A. J. Stewart (1977) "Content analysis as a technique for assessing political leaders," pp. 28-61 in M. G. Hermann (ed.) *A Psychological Examination of Political Leaders.* New York: Free Press.

QUESTIONS

1. According to Hermann, what impact does training (or the lack of training) have on the foreign policy behavior of a leader?

2. What evidence does Hermann provide to support her contention that the personal characteristics of leaders affect their governments' foreign policy behavior?

38.   Perception and Misperception in International Politics

Robert Jervis

In this introductory chapter to his book, *Perception and Misperception in International Politics* (1976), Robert Jervis provides an examination of each of the generally accepted levels of analysis for decision-making—the international system, the state system, the bureaucracy, and the individual. He argues that scholars have ignored the influence that perception and image have on each of these levels, especially that of the individual leader. In addition, Jervis critiques each of the levels of analysis and concludes that the perceptions of the individual leader needs to be examined further.

Robert Jervis is the Adlai E. Stevenson professor of International Relations and a member of the Institute of War and Peace Studies at Columbia University. His other works include *The Illogic of American Nuclear Strategy* (1984), as well as numerous contributions to various political science journals.

DO PERCEPTIONS MATTER?

Before discussing the causes and consequences of the ways in which decision-makers draw inferences from the world, we must ask a preliminary question: do the decision-makers' perceptions matter? This is an empirical question. Logic permits us to distinguish between the "psychological milieu" (the world as the actor sees it) and the "operational milieu" (the world in which the policy will be carried out) and to argue that policies and decisions must be mediated by statesmen's goals, calculations, and perceptions.[1] But it does not follow from this that we must deal with these intervening variables in order to understand and predict behavior. This is not an uncommon claim:

> One may describe particular events, conditions, and interactions between states without necessarily probing the nature and outcome of the processes through which state action evolves.

However, and the qualification is crucial, if one wishes to probe the "why" questions underlying the events, conditions, and interaction patterns which rest upon state action, then decision-making analysis is certainly necessary. We would go so far as to say *that the "why" questions cannot be answered without analysis of decision-making.*[2]

But theory and explanation need not fill in all the links between cause and effect. Indeed, this is impossible. One can always ask for the links between the links. High density theories have no privileged status; they are not automatically illuminating or fruitful.[3] It is true that re-creating a decision-maker's goals, calculations, and perceptions is a satisfying method of explaining his behavior because the scholar, sharing as he does the decision-maker's characteristics of being a thinking, goal-seeking person, can easily say: "If that is the way the statesman saw the situation, it is no wonder that he acted as he did." But the comfort we feel with this form of explanation should not blind us to the fact that, unless there are significant variations in the ways people see the world that affect how they act, we need not explore decision-making in order to explain foreign policy. Most case studies assume that the details presented significantly affected the outcomes. This may not be true, however. "Pleikus are streetcars," McGeorge Bundy said in explaining that the Viet Cong attack on the American installation in February 1965 had affected only the timing of the American bombing of North Vietnam.[4] If you are waiting for one, it will come along. The specifics of the triggering event cannot explain the outcome because so many probable events could have substituted for it. To understand the American policy of bombing the North we should not examine the attack on Pleiku. Had it not occurred, something else would have happened that would have permitted the same response. Logic alone cannot tell us that a similar claim about the decision-making process is invalid: the way people perceive others and make decisions only marginally influences outcomes. So we must seek empirical evidence on the question: do the important explanatory variables in international relations involve decision-making? In terms of perceptions this can be separated into two subsidiary questions: "are important differences in policy preferences traceable to differences in decision-makers' perceptions of their environments?" and "are there important differences between reality and shared or common perceptions?"[5] Detailed affirmative answers to these questions will emerge in this book, but a brief general discussion is in order here.

These questions raise the familiar level of analysis problem. Although it has been much debated, agreement is lacking not only on the substantive dispute but even on the number of levels. Arnold Wolfers proposes two, Kenneth Waltz three, and James Rosenau five.[6] To fill in the sequence, we will discuss four. One is the level of decision-making, the second is the level of the bureaucracy, the third is that of the nature of the state and the workings of domestic politics, and the fourth focuses on the international environment.[7] Which level one focuses on is not arbitrary and is not a matter of taste—it is the product of beliefs (or often hunches) about the nature of the variables that influence the phenomena that concern one. To restate the first question in terms of the level of analysis problem, we need not adopt a decision-making approach if all states behave the same way in the same objective situation, if all states of the same kind (i.e. with the same internal characteristics and politics) behave the same way in the same objective situation, or if state behavior is determined by bureaucratic routines and interests.

Although the empirical questions are central here, we should also note that the level of analysis problem has important moral implications. When all people would respond the same way to a given situation, it is hard to praise or blame the decision-maker. Thus, those accused of war crimes will argue that their behavior did not differ from others who found themselves in the same circumstances. And the prosecution will charge, as it did against Tojo and his colleagues, that, "These defendants were not automatons; they were not replaceable cogs in a machine. . . . It was theirs to choose whether their nation would lead an honored life . . . or . . . would become a symbol of evil throughout the world. They made their choice. For this choice they must bear the guilt." Similarly, if all nations follow similar courses of action, one cannot argue that some deserve to be branded as immorally aggressive. Thus in 1918 Bethmann-Hollweg rebutted those who blamed Germany for the war by pointing to the "general disposition towards war in the world . . . how else explain the senseless and impassioned zeal which allowed countries like Italy, Rumania and even America, not originally involved in the war, no rest until they too had immersed themselves in the bloodbath?"[8]

The three non-decision-making levels assert the importance of various aspects of the objective situation or the actor's role.[9] They say that if we know enough about the setting—international, national, or bureaucratic—we can explain and predict the actor's behavior. An interesting sidelight is that if other actors believed that the setting is crucial they would not need to scrutinize the details of the state's recent behavior or try to understand the goals and beliefs held by the state's decision-makers.[10] It would be fruitless and pointless to ask what the state's intentions are if its behavior is determined by the situation in which it finds itself. Instead, observers would try to predict how the context will change because this will tell them what the state's response will be. Decision-makers could then freely employ their powers of vicarious identification and simply ask themselves how they would act if they were in the other's shoes. They would not have to worry about the possibility that the other might have values and beliefs that differed from theirs. It is interesting, although not decisive, to note that

decision-makers rarely feel confident about using this method. They usually believe both that others may not behave as they would and that the decision-makers within the other state differ among themselves. So they generally seek a great deal of information about the views of each significant person in the other country.

Of course it is unlikely that there is a single answer to the question of which level is most important. Rather than one level containing the variables that are most significant for all problems, the importance of each level may vary from one issue area to another.[11] Furthermore, which level of analysis is the most important may be determined by how rich and detailed an answer we are seeking. The environment may influence the general outline of the state's policy but not its specific responses. Thus it can be argued that, while decision-making analysis is needed to explain why World War I broke out in August 1914, the external situation would have led the states to fight sooner or later. Or the importance of variables at each level may vary with the stages of a decision. For example, domestic politics may dictate that a given event be made the occasion for a change in policy; bargaining within the bureaucracy may explain what options are presented to the national leaders; the decision-maker's predisposition could account for the choice that was made; and the interests and routines of the bureaucracies could explain the way the decision was implemented. And the same variable may have different effects at different stages of the decision-making process—for example, conflicts among subordinates may increase the variety of information and the number of opportunities for decision that the top decision-maker gets, but may simultaneously decrease his ability to see that his decisions are faithfully implemented.

The importance of variables at one level can also vary with the state of variables at other levels. Rosenau suggests that the international environment is more important in determining the policy of small states than it is of large ones, and Stanley Hoffmann argues that nuclear weapons and bipolarity have reversed this relationship.[12] More generally, the importance of the other levels decreases if the variables in one level are in extreme states.[13] Thus, maneuvering within the bureaucracy may be more important when the top decision-makers are inexperienced or preoccupied with other matters.[14] And Wolfers argues that states tend to behave the same way when they are faced with extreme danger or extreme opportunity, but that when environmental constraints are less severe there will be differences in behavior that must be explained at the decision-making level. More complex interactions among the levels are also possible. For example, the effect of internal instability on expansionism could vary with the opportunities for success in war. Unstable states may be more prone to aggression than stable ones when the chances of victory are high but might be more cautious than others when their leaders perceive a significant probability of defeat or even of temporary setback. Or the stability of the regime might influence its propensity for aggression, but the nature of the regime (e.g. whether it is democratic or dictatorial) might be more important in explaining how it makes peace.

To deal with all these questions would require another book. Here all I will try to do is to outline the kinds of evidence necessary to establish the validity of simple propositions about the importance of the various levels. In doing so, I will sketch the most extreme arguments for the importance of each level. It is obvious that the questions and arguments could be rephrased in more subtle terms but since I am concerned with the kinds of evidence that the propositions call for the gain in analytical clarity is worth the sacrifice involved in ignoring more complete explanations that combine a multitude of variables at many levels.

The International Environment

To argue that the international environment determines a state's behavior is to assert that all states react similarly to the same objective external situation. Changes in a state's domestic regime, its bureaucratic structure, and the personalities and opinions of its leaders do not lead to changes of policies. Changes in the external situation, however, do alter behavior, even when variables on the other levels remain constant. To test these claims, we would need good measures of all the variables, especially the nature of the objective situation and the state's policies.[15] Even if we had such indicators, we would have to cope with the paucity of the most desired kinds of comparisons. This is easily understood by glancing at the similar issue in the study of individual behavior—the debate over the relative importance of situation and role versus idiosyncratic variables in determining individual behavior.[16] Because so many people of widely differing backgrounds, personalities, and opinions fill the same role and because the same person fills many different roles, we can try to determine the relative impact of situational and idiosyncratic variables by examining how a person's behavior varies as his role changes and how people of widely differing characteristics perform in similar situations.

It is much harder to make the analogous comparisons in international relations. In only a few international systems do we find many cases in which states play, either simultaneously or consecutively, several roles and in which each role is filled by states that are otherwise quite different. This would occur in a long-lasting system where there were frequent changes in the relations among the actors. Thus each state might at one time be a neutral, a "holder of the balance," a state with aggressive designs, a defender faced by a state whose intentions are difficult to determine, and so on. To a limited degree this test is possible in a balance-of-power system. But it is not available for most other systems, for example the one prevailing since World War II. Most nations have not changed roles, and indeed cannot do so because of such permanent factors as size and geography. The United States can never play the role of a second-ranking state caught between two blocs of greater powers. France can never be the leader of one of two dominant blocs. And while the United States and France may have played roles similar to these in the past, the extensive differences in the situation mean that any differences in response that might be found would not show that roles are unimportant.

COMPULSION IN EXTREME CIRCUMSTANCES?

It is worthwhile to look at cases of the kind that are supposed to show most strongly the influence of external conditions. If there are differences of behavior here, the argument for not ignoring the other levels of analysis will apply a fortiori to a wider domain of cases. Arnold Wolfers argues that, the greater the external compulsion, the greater the homogeneity of behavior and therefore the less the need to study decision-making. In a well-known passage he says: "Imagine a number of individuals, varying widely in their predispositions, who find themselves inside a house on fire. It would be perfectly realistic to expect that these individuals, with rare exceptions, would feel compelled to run toward the exits. . . . Surely, therefore, for an explanation of the rush for the exits, there is no need to analyze the individual decisions that produced it."[17]

But the case is not as clear as this analogy suggests. If a situation were so compelling that all people would act alike, decision-makers would not hesitate nor feel torn among several alternative policies, nor would there be significant debates within the decision-making elite. In fact, key decisions that are easily reached, such as those involving the Truman Doctrine and Marshall Plan, stand out because they are so rare. For despite the implication of Wolfers' proposition that we know when we are faced by extreme danger, just as we can tell when the house is on fire, in fact this question is often bitterly contested. (To say that once decision-makers perceive the fire they will head for the exits leads us back to decision-making analysis.) For Churchill, the house was burning soon after Hitler took power in Germany; for Chamberlain, this was the case only after March 1939; and for others there never was a fire at all. To some decision-makers, the Soviet Union is a threat to which the United States is compelled to respond. To others the threat passed years ago. Again, to a growing number of scholars it never existed. Similarly, American statesmen see a much greater threat from communism in both Europe and Southeast Asia than do the leaders of our allies. Decision-makers may even agree that their state's existence is threatened but disagree about the source of the threat. This was true, for example, in the United States around the turn of the nineteenth century, when the Federalists believed France so much a menace that they favored war with her. At the same time, the Republicans believed England an equal menace. (It should be noted that this disagreement was rooted as much in differences in values and interests as in divergent empirical analyses of the situation.)

In extreme cases we can specify with some certainty an indicator of the "fire" that all decision-makers will recognize—for example a large armed attack—and we can be relatively certain that the state will react. But even then the objective situation will not determine all aspects of the state's response. There are apt to be several exits from the burning house. Will the state limit the extent of its involvement? What will its war aims be? While the United States may have had no choice but to declare war on Japan after Pearl Harbor, the major decisions that followed were less compelled and require further explanation. For example: the United States decided not to concentrate its energies on the country that had attacked it but to fight Germany first; the war was to be fought with few considerations for the shape of the postwar world; and no compromise with the enemies would be accepted (had the Japanese realized this would be the case, they almost certainly would not have attacked).

Even if all states and all statesmen responded similarly to similar high threats,

we have to explain how the threat arose—i.e. why the adversary was so aggressive. In some cases we may be able to do this by reference to the other's objective situation, for example by focusing on the anarchic nature of the international system and the resulting security dilemma that we will discuss in detail in Chapter 3. But when this analysis is insufficient, the state (and later scholars) must examine variables at other levels of analysis to establish some of the most important facts about the objective situation that the state faces.

Finally, one cannot prove that the external environment determines the response by simply showing that the decision-makers believed this to be the case. It is not enough to say with Kecskemeti that "In tense war situations, the decision-maker is likely to feel that he is acting from necessity rather than from deliberate choice." Nor is it sufficient to cite Holsti's finding that the decision-makers on both sides in July 1914 felt that they had no choice but to make the decisions they did, or to show that when "Mr. Acheson was advised not to favor the production of the first thermonuclear bomb, he is reported to have declared that its production was a matter of necessity and not of choice: in other words, that he was experiencing 'compulsion.' "[18] The subjective feeling of determinacy is interesting and may lead decision-makers unnecessarily to restrict their search for alternatives, but it does not show that other decision-makers in the same situation would have felt the same compulsion and acted in the same way. Indeed the theory of cognitive dissonance (Chapter 11) and other theories of irrational cognitive consistency (Chapter 4) lead us to expect that decision-makers may avoid psychological conflict by thinking that they had no choice but to act as they did. This also means that, when scholars claim that a situation permitted no policy other than the one that was adopted, it may be that at least part of the reason why the circumstances appear overwhelming in retrospect is that they were claimed to be so by the decision-makers.

These arguments are, of course, far from conclusive. The necessary comparisons have merely been mentioned, not made. But, as we have seen, there are many points at which people can disagree about what the objective situation is or what policies will best cope with it, and there is little evidence for the existence of the homogeneity of behavior that would allow us to ignore everything except the international setting.

Domestic Determinants

Even if all states do not behave similarly in similar situations, the details of decision-making and images may not be significant. Instead, the state may be the appropriate level of analysis—i.e. variations in decision-makers' policies may be accounted for by variations in social and economic structure and domestic politics of the states they are serving. Wilsonian and Marxist theories are examples of this position. Other theories at this level of analysis argue for the importance of a state's geographical position, its traditions, its national style, or the consequences, often unintended, of domestic conflicts. Extreme formulations hold that the state's internal system determines its foreign policy, while weaker versions claim that foreign policies are a product of both domestic politics and international circumstances.

The forms of the assertions correspond to those discussed in the previous section. States with the same critical internal attributes behave the same way in similar situations—and often behave the same way in the face of significant variations in the environment—and this behavior is different from that displayed by other states with different attributes even when the setting is the same. The latter claim denies the overriding importance of the international environment. Thus while Cold War revisionists stress the importance of America's domestic political and economic needs, others reply that American actions were heavily influenced by external constraints and that her behavior was not peculiarly American or peculiarly capitalist but rather was typical of any great power in such a situation.[19] Because we are concerned with examining the importance of decision-making, we will not treat this part of the argument that deals with conflicts between claims for two other levels of analysis.

If states of the same type behave in the same way, then changes in a state's leadership will not produce significant changes in foreign policy, and we need not examine the images, values, and calculations of individual decision-makers. Unfortunately, claims about continuity in a state's foreign policy are notoriously difficult to judge. We might try to see whether we could deduce changes in the identities of the state's decision-makers from the course of its foreign policy. Could we tell when Democrats replaced Republicans or Conservatives replaced Labour governments? Scholars used to agree that Stalin's death led to major foreign policy changes, but now even this is in doubt.[20] Before taking office, decision-makers often claim they will introduce new policies. But these promises are often neglected. Eisenhower's foreign policy more closely resembled that of his predecessor than it did his campaign rhetoric. Gladstone pledged himself to avoid immoral and wasteful imperialism, and, although he successfully extricated Britain from some entanglements, he was eventually drawn into commitments similar to those made by Disraeli. And while in 1937 Clement Atlee said that "the foreign policy of a Government is the reflection of its internal policy," when his party took power the foreign secretary declared that "Revolutions do not change geography, and revolutions do not change geographical needs."[21]

Many arguments about the wisdom of policies can be understood in terms of claims about the autonomy of the decision-making level. Those who praise Bismarck's diplomacy claim that, had he continued in office, he would have been able to maintain German security by avoiding the errors of severing Germany's ties to Russia, being forced to rely on Austria, and recklessly antagonizing several powerful countries. The rejoinder is that the dynamics of German domestic society and of the international system would have destroyed Bismarck's handiwork no matter who was in power. The glittering skill of Bismarck's diplomacy could not alter the underlying forces at work. Debates about the origins of the Cold War must deal with the similar question of whether Roosevelt's death changed American policy. Most traditional accounts argue that F.D.R. was coming to an anti-Soviet position and would have acted much as Truman did. This view is shared by those revisionists who look to the American political and economic sys-

tem for the roots of foreign policy but is disputed by those who see the Cold War as avoidable. Similarly, those who defend President Kennedy but opposed the war in Vietnam argue that he would not have acted as Johnson did. Those who either favored the war or opposed not only it but also most recent American foreign policies argue that the policies of these— and other—presidents were consistent. While those who supported the war see the determinants as international and those who criticize the general lines of America's postwar policy see the causes as domestic, both argue that few significant differences can be traced to the identity of the president.

These questions are so difficult to resolve partly because the situation facing the new government always differs from that which confronted the old. Kennedy was never forced to choose between defeat in Vietnam and fighting a major war. F.D.R. did not live to see Russia consolidate her hold over East Europe. The questions must then be hypothetical, and the comparisons that underlie our judgments are often strained. This problem can be avoided by using alternative comparisons—by examining the views of members of the elite to see whether they favor the policy that was adopted.[22] Of course disagreement with a policy does not prove that a person would have acted on his views were he in office. His opposition might be rooted in his role in the government, lack of information, freedom from the pressures that accompany holding power, or the belief that opposition is politically expedient. But when these explanations are not satisfactory, internal elite disagreement reveals the limits of the impact of both domestic politics and the international situation.

The Bureaucracy

Even if state behavior cannot be explained by the state's internal politics and external environment, we still may not need to examine the perceptions and calculations of the top decision-makers. The workings of the bureaucracy may determine policy. It is not enough for proponents of this position to show that the state's course of action appears inconsistent and lacks value integration. Such inadequacies can be the product of individual decision-making. As we will show later, normal human behavior often does not fit even a loose definition of rationality. Individuals as well as organizations fail to coordinate their actions and to develop carefully designed strategies. The fact that people must reach decisions in the face of the burdens of multiple goals and highly ambiguous information means that policies are often contradictory, incoherent, and badly suited to the information at hand. Unless we understand this, puzzling state behavior will automatically be seen as the product of either internal bargaining or the autonomous operation of different parts of the government. Thus if we did not know better it would be tempting to argue that the contradictory and erratic behavior displayed by Richard Nixon in Watergate and related matters shows that "Nixon" is not a single individual at all, but rather a title for the set of behaviors that are produced by the interaction of conflicting entities, each pursuing its own narrow interests in ignorance of or indifference to any wider goal of the "general Nixon interest." Similarly, if we were to insist that theories of individual behavior apply only when the actor is following a coherent path guided by his self-interest, we would have to say that Spiro

Agnew was an uncoordinated bureaucracy rather than a person because he simultaneously accepted kickbacks and sought the presidency.

Because incoherent policy is insufficient evidence for the importance of bureaucracies, the "pure" theories of this type must make two basic assertions. First, bureaucrats' policy preferences are determined by their positions in the government: "Where you stand is determined by where you sit." The external environment and the nature of the state and domestic politics have only limited and indirect impact on these preferences. Of course if the concept of bureaucratic interest is to be more useful than the concept of national interest, we must be able to specify in advance what the bureaucratic position will be.[23] Even if we cannot do this, it would still be significant if everyone in each unit of the government had the same position on a given issue. If, on the other hand, there is a good deal of disagreement within the organization about the goals to be sought or the means that are appropriate, then we would have to apply decision-making analysis to the bureaucratic level, and so this approach would lose much of its distinctiveness. More importantly, if people in different units share the same policy preferences or if preferences are distributed at random throughout the government, then the first assertion would be undermined.

The second basic claim of theories on this level of analysis is that the state's policies are formed by bureaucratic bargains and routines. Bureaucratic actions either determine the statesman's decision or else implement it in a way that renders the decision largely irrelevant to what is actually done. This point is vital because, even if bureaucrats' policy preferences were linked to their positions within the

government, this would be relatively unimportant unless these preferences explain policy outcomes.[24] But we should
note at the start that even if this were true
we would have to explore the sources of
power of parts of the bureaucracy. If we
find, for example, that the military often
prevails in conflicts with the organization
in charge of arms control, this may be because over a period of years the state's
leaders have supported the former more
than the latter. Sometimes we can go
back some years to find a decisive action
that set the guidelines for both the policy
and the distribution of power within the
bureaucracy. In less dramatic cases the
relative strengths of interests represent
the standing decision of the decision-
makers—and often of wider publics—
and their choices among competing policies and values. To the extent that this
distribution of power is both important
and accounted for by factors outside the
bureaucracy, an explanation of specific
outcomes in terms of bureaucratic maneuvering will be superficial at best.

Are policy preferences determined
by one's role within the government?
With the important exception of questions of military hardware and doctrine,
the evidence is limited and ambiguous. It
is not hard to find examples of units taking consistent and unified stands and political appointees adopting their units'
views and thus expressing different opinions depending upon their positions in
the government. "General Marshall,
while Chief of Staff, opposed the State
Department's idea of using aid to promote reforms in the Chinese government. Then, when he became Secretary
of State, he defended this very idea
against challenges voiced by the new
chiefs of Staff." In "1910, Winston
Churchill, as Home Secretary, led the at-

tack upon the demand of McKenna, First
Lord of the Admiralty, for more ships; by
1913 they had exchanged offices and
each, with equal conviction, maintained
the opposite view." When Samuel Hoare
was secretary of state for air, he strongly
fought against naval control of the Fleet
Air Arm; when he later served as first lord
of the Admiralty he took the opposite position. When Théophile Delcassé was the
minister of colonies in France before the
turn of the century, he supported an expedition to the Nile that would give
France a lever to use against Britain. As
foreign secretary, he sought to recall the
adventure.[25]

But not all policy disagreements are
traceable to roles. Organizational perspectives and loyalties are less important
when issues are unusual rather than
routine, necessitate relatively quick
decisions, and involve important and
generally shared values. Beliefs about the
most important issues of foreign policy—
those involving war and peace—are usually unrelated to roles. When we look at
the major decisions of American foreign
policy—those that set the terms for future debates and established the general
framework within which policy was then
conducted—it does not seem to be true,
at least for the top decision-makers, that
"where you sit determines where you
stand."

In several important cases what is
most striking is the degree of unanimity.
In the spring of 1947 there was general
agreement within the government that
massive aid for Europe was needed.
Three years later most officials felt that
foreign policy considerations argued for
large-scale rearmament, although there
was a disagreement—which was not
tightly connected with bureaucratic interests—over whether domestic political

and economic constraints made such a policy feasible. Once the Korean War removed this opposition, government officials were again in general agreement. In other important cases there are basic disputes, but the key to them is not divergent bureaucratic interests. Doves and hawks on Vietnam were to be found in all parts of the American government. Views on whether to take a hard line toward Japan before World War II, and specifically on the crucial issue of embargoing oil and other vital raw materials, were only loosely related to organizational affiliations. The advice that Truman received at the start of the Berlin blockade and the Korean War and most of the differences that emerged in the discussions during the Cuban missile crisis were not predictable by the participants' roles.

In the missile crisis none of the leading officials espoused views that were linked to his position within the government. The Republican secretary of the treasury was concerned about the effects of a "soft" response on the fortunes of the Democratic party in the coming elections; the secretary of defense at first argued that the missiles did not present a major military threat; the secretary of state did not take a strong position and did not pay special attention to the political consequences of various moves; and the attorney general opposed an air strike. (It should also be noted that his view carried great weight not because of his governmental position or independent political resources, but because he was thought to speak for the president.)

The other claim—that policies can be explained by bureaucratic maneuvering—could be supported in either of two ways. First, it could be shown that different parts of the government carry out, or fail to carry out, policies in ways that are consistent with their preferences and routines rather than with the decisions of the national leaders. But the other possible linkage in the second point—the argument that authoritative decisions can be explained by the interaction of bureaucratic stands—raises difficulties that go deeper than the temporary absence of evidence. To verify this claim we must be able to specify the expected relationship between the variety of bureaucratic positions on the one hand and policy outcomes on the other. It is not enough to show that the outcome can be seen as a compromise among views that have been advocated by various parts of the government. Almost any decision could fit this description. The theory must provide generalizations that tell us more exactly what the outcome will be. If the goals of different parts of the bureaucracy are complementary, then presumably each agency will give up its position on the part of the program it cares least about in order to gain a larger voice on those issues that are more important to it. Presumably the success of an organization in conflicts with others is related to its strength (determined independently of outcomes), although as we noted this raises further questions. Still another likely pattern is that the symbols will be given to one side in a bureaucratic conflict and the substance to the other. But much more detail is needed. Furthermore, these generalizations must not involve the values and beliefs that vary with the identity of the top decision-makers, and they must be able to explain how policies change. The latter task poses great problems since bureaucratic structures and interests often remain constant over periods in which policies shift.

Although the paucity of research on this level makes conclusions especially tentative, it is hard to see how any of the major decisions of American foreign policy in recent years could meet this test. The Marshall Plan, the establishment of NATO, the crucial decisions in Korea, the rearmament that followed, the decision to integrate West Germany into West Europe, the New Look in defense, American policy in the Suez crisis, Kennedy's attempt to increase conventional forces in Europe, the major decisions to fight and later withdraw from Vietnam, and crucial choices in the Cuban missile crisis cannot be explained as the outcome of intrabureaucratic conflict. That these decisions combined major elements of positions held within the bureaucracy is hardly surprising because different parts of the bureaucracy serve and represent divergent values that the president seeks to further. Thus what seems to be a clash of bureaucratic interests and stands can often be more fruitfully viewed as a clash among values that are widely held in both the society and the decision-makers' own minds. What embarrasses the theories under consideration here is that, while the decisions listed above did embody some of the preferences that had been articulated by parts of the bureaucracy, they did not combine them in a way that can be predicted by rules of bureaucratic politics. Or, to put the argument more exactly, until we have a theory that specifies how policy is formed out of conflicting bureaucratic perspectives and preferences, we cannot tell whether any given outcome can be explained by this level of analysis. As things stand now, there is no way to explore the extent to which bureaucratic factors cause the outcome because we have no grounds for claiming that a different constellation of bureaucratic interests and forces would have produced a different result or that the outcome would have been different were there no bureaucracies at all.

PERCEPTIONS, REALITY, AND A TWO-STEP MODEL

Our discussion thus far leads to the conclusion that it is often impossible to explain crucial decisions and policies without reference to the decision-makers' beliefs about the world and their images of others. That is to say, these cognitions are part of the proximate cause of the relevant behavior and other levels of analysis cannot immediately tell us what they will be. And even if we found that people in the same situation— be it international, domestic, or bureaucratic—behave in the same way, it is useful to examine decision-making if there are constant differences between the decision-makers' perceptions and reality. In this case all people might react in the same way to the same situation, but this behavior would puzzle an observer because it was self-defeating, based on incorrect beliefs about the world, or generally lacking in a high degree of rationality.[26] Many of the propositions advanced in this book fit in this category: they are generalizations about how decision-makers perceive others' behavior and form judgments about their intentions. These patterns are explained by the general ways in which people draw inferences from ambiguous evidence and, in turn, help explain many seemingly incomprehensible policies. They show how, why, and when highly intelligent and conscientious statesmen misperceive their environments in specified ways and reach inappropriate decisions.

Other propositions in this book deal with cases in which an analysis of decision-making is necessary because people in the same situations behave differently. This is often the case because people differ in their perceptions of the world in general and of other actors in particular. Sometimes it will be useful to ask who, if anyone, was right; but often it will be more fruitful to ask why people differed and how they came to see the world as they did.

The exploration of the images actors hold and the development of the two kinds of propositions discussed above should be seen in the context of a mediated or two-step model.[27] Rather than trying to explain foreign policies as the direct consequence of variables at the three levels of analysis previously discussed, we will examine the actor's perceptions as one of the immediate causes of his behavior. Thus Britain and France felt that their security was endangered by Germany before both world wars. They may have been mistaken in the first case and correct in the second, but both cases can be grouped together in discussing the immediate causes of their responses.

Our understanding of the actor's images and beliefs affects the further question that we ask about that event and the behavior that we expect of the actor in other cases. For example, when it was believed that most American decision-makers had thought that escalation would bring a quick victory in Vietnam, the interesting questions concerned the reasons for this error and the ways by which successive small steps increased the stakes of the conflict. If the decision-makers believed that victory was cheap, it is not surprising that they acted as they did. But by revealing that the decision-makers had a relatively accurate view of the chances of success, the Pentagon Papers and related commentaries have shown that the crucial question is why saving Vietnam was considered important enough to justify the high expected price. This then leads us to look at this and other American actions in terms of beliefs about "domino effects" rather than directing our attention to commitments that develop inadvertently and "quagmires" that trap unwary statesmen. Similarly, the question about Russian behavior raised by the Cuban missile crisis probably is not "What Soviet calculus and risk-taking propensity could explain this bold and dangerous step?" but rather "How could they have so badly misestimated the probable American response?"[28] And previous Soviet behavior can be re-examined to see if it could be explained by similar misperceptions. . . . actors as well as scholars must engage in these kinds of analyses.

Of course perceptions, and more specifically perceptions of other actors, are not the only decision-making variables that are important. That two actors have the same perceptions does not guarantee that they will adopt the same response. But their responses will often be the same, and, when they are not, it is usually relatively easy to find the causes of the differences. Although people with different images of an adversary may agree on the appropriate response, just as people may favor the same policy for different reasons, this agreement is apt to be short-lived. . . . The roots of many important disputes about policies lie in differing perceptions. And in the frequent cases when the actors do not realize this, they will misunderstand their disagreement and engage in a debate that is unenlightening.

Images, however, are not first causes, and so we will try to find the causes both of common misperceptions and of differences in perceptions. Thus the second step in the model involves relating the images held, if not to reality, then at least to the information available to the actor. How, for example, do statesmen come to develop their images of other actors? What evidence do they pay most attention to? What makes them perceive threat? Under what conditions do they think that the other, although hostile, has only limited objectives? What differentiates legitimate inducements from bribes? What kinds of behavior are most apt to change an established image?

This is not to claim that we will be able to explain nearly all state behavior. As we will discuss in the context of learning from history, propositions about both the causes and the effects of images can only be probabilistic. There are too many variables at work to claim more. In the cases in which we are interested, decision-makers are faced with a large number of competing values, highly complex situations, and very ambiguous information. The possibilities and reasons for misperceptions and disagreements are legion. For these reasons, generalizations in this area are difficult to develop, exceptions are common, and in many instances the outcomes will be influenced by factors that, from the standpoint of most theories, must be considered accidental. Important perceptual predispositions can be discovered, but often they will not be controlling.

NOTES

1. See especially the following works by Harold and Margaret Sprout: *Man-Milieu Relationship Hypotheses in the Context of International Politics* (Princeton, N.J.: Center of International Studies, 1956); *The Ecological Perspective on Human Affairs* (Princeton, N.J.: Princeton University Press, 1965); and *An Ecological Paradigm for the Study of International Politics* (Princeton, N.J.: Center of International Studies, Princeton University, Research Monograph No. 30, March 1968).

2. "Decision-Making as an Approach to the Study of International Politics," in Richard Snyder, H. W. Bruck, and Burton Sapin, eds., *Foreign Policy Decision-Making* (New York: Free Press, 1962), p. 33. For a similar argument see Fred Greenstein, "The Impact of Personality on Politics: An Attempt to Clear Away Underbrush," *American Political Science Review* 61 (September 1967), 631–33. This is related to the debate about the significance of developmental sequences. For differing views on this question see Herbert Hyman, *Survey Design and Analysis* (Glencoe, Ill.: Free Press, 1955), pp. 254–63, and Travis Hirschi and Hanan Selvin, *Delinquency Research* (New York: Free Press, 1967), pp. 82–85. (The latter book [republished in paperback as *Principles of Survey Analysis*] has much broader relevance than its title indicates and is extremely valuable not only for its explanation of the use of survey research data but for its treatment of general questions of theory, causation, and evidence.)

   This issue is also related to the broader debate between what Maurice Natanson has called the "Two distinctively opposed philosophic attitudes . . . underlying the social sciences: . . . [the] 'objective' and 'subjective' *Weltanschauungen.*" ("Foreword" in Natanson, ed., *Philosophy of the Social Sciences* [New York: Random House, 1963], p. viii.) This reader is a good introduction to the arguments.

3. Hirschi and Selvin, *Delinquency Research,* p. 38. As Abraham Kaplan puts it, "I would not wish to say that something has been explained only when we have traced the microconnections with their antecedents, or even only when we can

believe that such conditions exist." ("Noncausal Explanation," in Daniel Lerner, ed., *Cause and Effect* [New York: Free Press, 1965], p. 146.)

4. Quoted in Townsend Hoopes, *The Limits of Intervention* (New York: McKay, 1969), p. 30.

5. The question of the existence and nature of reality need not be treated here in its profound sense. For our purposes the consensus of later observers usually provides an adequate operational definition of reality.

6. Arnold Wolfers, "The Actors in International Politics," in *Discord and Collaboration* (Baltimore, Md.: Johns Hopkins Press, 1962), pp. 3-24; Kenneth Waltz, *Man, the State, and War* (New York: Columbia University Press, 1959); James Rosenau, "Pre-Theories and Theories of Foreign Policy," in R. Barry Farrell, ed., *Approaches to Comparative and International Politics.* (Evanston, Ill.: Northwestern University Press, 1966), pp. 29-92.

7. We refer to the international environment rather than the international system because we are not dealing with systems theories. Our concern is with explaining specific foreign policies rather than finding general patterns of interaction.

8. Quoted in Robert Butow, *Tojo and the Coming of the War.* (Princeton, N.J.: Princeton University Press, 1961), p. 506; quoted in Egmont Zechlin, "Cabinet versus Economic Warfare in Germany," in H. W. Koch, ed., *The Origins of the First World War* (London: Macmillan & Co., 1972), p. 165.

9. See K. J. Holsti, "National Role Conceptions in the Study of Foreign Policy," *International Studies Quarterly* 14 (September 1970), 233-309.

10. It is interesting to note that in interpersonal perception people tend to overestimate the degree to which the other's behavior is determined by his personality and underestimate the impact of the external situation. See, for example, Gustav Ichheiser, *Appearances and Realities* (San Francisco: Jossey-Bass, 1970), pp. 49-59. But when the person explains his own behavior, he will attribute his actions to the requirements of the situation, not to his own predispositions. See Edward Jones and Richard Nisbett, *The Actor and the Observer: Divergent Perceptions of the Causes of Behavior* (New York: General Learning Press, 1971).

11. Two recent articles explore the utility of the concept of issue areas in foreign-policy research, but they are not concerned with the level of analysis problem. See Thomas Brewer, "Issue and Context Variations in Foreign Policy," *Journal of Conflict Resolution* 17 (March 1973), 89-114, and William Zimmerman, "Issue Area and Foreign-Policy Process," *American Political Science Review* 67 (December 1973), 1204-12.

12. James Rosenau, "Pre-Theories and Theories of Foreign Policy," pp. 47-48; Stanley Hoffmann, "Restraints and Choices in American Foreign Policy," *Daedalus* (Fall 1962), 692-94.

13. Most of the propositions in Greenstein, "The Impact of Personality on Politics," about the conditions under which personality is most important can be subsumed under this heading.

14. Thus the famous remark by a cabinet officer that you only have to obey the president when he repeats an order for the third time.

15. An excellent discussion of the evidence on this point derived from quantitative studies is Dina Zinnes, "Some Evidence Relevant to the Man-Milieu Hypothesis," in James Rosenau, Vincent Davis, and Maurice East, eds., *The Analysis of International Politics* (New York: Free Press, 1972), pp. 209-51. But these studies have limited utility for the questions being asked here because they do not provide adequate measures of the similarity of the objective situation and the similarity of the state's responses. This is also true for

the growing body of literature that examines these questions using event-scaling techniques. For a study that copes with these problems relatively well and finds that differences in perceptions among decision-makers decrease as tension increases, see Ole Holsti, "Individual Differences in 'Definition of the situation,'" *Journal of Conflict Resolution* 14 (September 1970), 303-10.

16. For a general discussion, see Herbert Blumer, "Society as Symbolic Interaction," in Arnold Rose, ed., *Human Behavior and Social Processes* (Boston: Houghton Mifflin, 1962), pp. 180-91. For an inventory of findings see Kenneth Terhune, "Personality in Cooperation and Conflict," in Paul Swingle, ed., *The Structure of Conflict* (New York: Academic Press, 1970), pp. 193-234. This subject has received much attention from psychologists in the past few years. For a review of the literature and an excellent argument, see Daryl Bem and Andrea Allen, "On Predicting Some of the People Some of the Time," *Psychological Review* 81 (1974), 506-20.

17. Wolfers, *Discord and Collaboration,* p. 13.

18. Paul Kecskemeti, *Strategic Surrender* (New York: Atheneum, 1964), pp. 19-20; Ole Holsti, "The 1914 Case," *The American Political Science Review* 59 (June 1965), 365-78; Wolfers, *Discord and Collaboration,* p. 14.

19. See, for example, Charles Maier, "Revisionism and the Interpretation of Cold War Origins," *Perspectives in American History* 4 (1970), 313-47; Robert Tucker, *The Radical Left and American Foreign Policy* (Baltimore, Md.: Johns Hopkins Press, 1971); James Richardson, "Cold-War Revisionism: A Critique," *World Politics* 24 (July 1972), 579-612; and Ole Holsti, "The Study of International Politics Makes Strange Bedfellows: Theories of the Radical Right and the Radical Left," *American Political Science Review* 68 (March 1974), 217-42. Comparisons with the reactions of European statesmen would also shed light on the question of whether there was anything peculiarly American in the United States' perceptions.

20. Marshall Shulman, *Stalin's Foreign Policy Reappraised* (Cambridge, Mass.: Harvard University Press, 1963).

21. Michael Gordon, *Conflict and Consensus in Labour's Foreign Policy, 1914-1965* (Stanford: Stanford University Press, 1969), p. 6; M. A. Fitzsimons, *The Foreign Policy of the British Labour Government, 1945-1951* (Notre Dame, Ind.: University of Notre Dame Press, 1953), p. 26.

22. In this group we include potential leaders who could come to power without drastic changes in the state's internal political system. Dissent from those outside this group does not undermine the arguments for the importance of the nature of the state, and, indeed, if such people have been rejected as possible powerholders because of their foreign policy views, this would demonstrate the importance of this level of analysis rather than showing the autonomy of the decision-making level.

23. Most light is shed on this subject by the writings of Philip Selznick. See his *TVA and the Grassroots* (Berkeley and Los Angeles: University of California Press, 1947) and *Leadership in Administration* (Evanston, Ill.: Row, Peterson, 1957). Also see Morton Halperin, "Why Bureaucrats Play Games," *Foreign Policy,* No. 2 (Spring 1971), 74-88, and *Bureaucratic Politics and Foreign Policy* (Washington: Brookings Institution, 1974), pp. 26-62.

24. During the Second World War the British set up an intelligence section to try to recreate the German perspective. They did well at predicting the positions taken by various parts of the German bureaucracy but could never adequately predict when Hitler would side with a particular faction or impose his own solution.

(Donald McLachlan, *Room 39* [New York: Atheneum, 1968], pp 252–58.)

25. Ernest May, "The Development of Political-Military Consultation in the United States," in Aaron Wildavsky, ed., *The Presidency* (Boston: Little, Brown, 1969), p. 668; Patrick Gordon Walker, *The Cabinet* (New York: Basic Books, 1970), p. 67; W. J. Reader, *Architect of Airpower: The Life of the First Viscount Weir* (London: Collins, 1968), p. 270; Roger Brown, *Fashoda Reconsidered* (Baltimore, Md.: Johns Hopkins Press, 1970), pp. 24–32, 85.

26. The knowledge gained by studying how people view the world and process incoming information can lead to the discovery of patterns in state behavior that would not be apparent to an observer who had ignored decision-making. We may be able to say, for example, that two kinds of situations, although not seeming alike to later scholars, will appear to be similar to contemporary decision-makers and will be seen to call for similar responses. Thus, once we have examined a number of cases, detected common deviations, and isolated their causes, we could apply this knowledge to theories that do not call for intensive analysis of decision-making.

27. See Charles Osgood, "Behavior Theory and the Social Sciences," in Roland Young, ed., *Approaches to the Study of Politics* (Evanston, Ill.: Northwestern University Press, 1958), pp. 217–44. For a recent discussion and application, see Richard Jessor and Shirley Jessor, "The Perceived Environment in Behavioral Science," *American Behavioral Scientist* 16 (July/August 1973), 801–27. In an interesting critique, Robert Gorman asks "Must we look into the perception of the decision-maker at the time the decision was being made by centering our political analysis on the decision-maker himself? Or, should we concentrate on the social organization of which the decision-maker is a part and the social environment in which both the organization and the individual function? If we accept the first choice, then social factors assume a secondary, instrumental purpose. If we choose the second framework, the perceptions of the decision-maker would seem to be *logically* dependent on external rules, and investigation into the nature of individual perception would be absurd. If we combine the two, as the decision-making theorists seem to have done, we are left with a theory in which each premise is negated by the existence of the other, and the general theory itself is left to flounder in a formalistic but meaningless syncretism." ("On the Inadequacies of Non-Philosophical Political Science: A Critical Analysis of Decision-Making Theory," *International Studies Quarterly* 14 [December 1970], 408.) The use of a two-step model avoids this contradiction.

28. Daniel Ellsberg, "The Quagmire Myth and the Stalemate Machine," in *Papers on the War* (New York: Simon and Schuster, 1972), pp. 42–135; Leslie Gelb, "Vietnam: The System Worked," *Foreign Policy* No. 3 (Summer 1971), 140–67; Klaus Knorr, "Failures in National Intelligence Estimates: The Case of the Cuban Missiles," *World Politics* 16 (April 1967), 455–67. Theodore Draper fails to see the significance of these kinds of questions in explaining the American intervention in the Dominican Republic. ("The Dominican Intervention Reconsidered," *Political Science Quarterly* 86 [March 1971], 26–28.) To take an example from another field, the fact that young people in less politicized homes share fewer of their parents' political views than do those in more highly politicized families is not to be explained by the former group having less desire to adopt their parents' beliefs, but by their lack of knowledge about what their parents believe. (Richard Niemi, *How Family Members Perceive Each Other* [New Haven: Yale University Press, 1974], pp. 200–201.)

QUESTIONS

1. What are the inherent problems of the levels of analysis in explaining the influence of perception?

2. What are the two propositions that Jervis identifies regarding his perceptions model?

---

39.   The Beliefs of Leaders: Perceptual and Ideological Sources of Foreign Policy After the Cold War

Mark P. Lagon

In this article, Mark P. Lagon argues that elites inside and outside of the government are a major determinant of United States foreign policy. Using their beliefs about world politics, they help define the so-called national interest. The end of the Cold War has caused an even greater change in the consensus among elites about United States foreign policy than the Vietnam War did in the early 1970s. Lagon contends that a complex realignment is taking place, overshadowing the traditional spectrum of "left" versus "right." He identifies six ideological categories of political leaders, all with varying beliefs about the political, military, and economic role of the United States in the world today.

Mark P. Lagon is research associate at the American Enterprise Institute and adjunct professor of government at Georgetown University. He is also the author of *The Reagan Doctrine: Sources of American Conduct in the Cold War* (1994).

Contemporary forms of the realist theory explain the everyday workings of world politics in terms of the international system. The actions of states are constrained by the "structure" of the global distribution of power, and motivated by an objective "national interest." More and more, political scientists are recognizing the role of elites and their ideas in determining the behavior of states in world politics.[1] Elites are the decision-makers in a government, plus those experts and opinion shapers outside of government—in universities, interest groups, think tanks, the press, and other elite circles—who focus day to day on what the foreign policy of their nation should be. Based on their ideas—their worldviews, their principled beliefs about right and wrong, and their causal beliefs about what actions lead to what outcomes—they define the national interest.[2] Perhaps elites are the arbiters of that mysterious national interest realists always speak of.

Scholars who looked at elite beliefs during the Cold War as a source of American foreign policy observed a consensus among political leaders in favor of the Containment policy. Then the Vietnam War exploded that consensus. Arguably, however, the end of the Cold War has caused an even more substantial change in the landscape of elite beliefs about U.S. foreign policy. This essay will set out to describe what that new landscape of elite beliefs is. Instead of a chaotic dealignment of elite beliefs, it appears a complex realignment is taking place, which above all is removing the difference between "left" and "right."[3]

CATEGORIES OF ELITE BELIEFS DURING THE COLD WAR

Before discussing post-Cold War elite beliefs, it will be useful to examine categorization schemes proposed by scholars to describe the foreign policy beliefs of American elites during the East-West conflict. These categorization schemes serve as a point of reference for understanding continuities with and changes from the Cold War era which elite beliefs exhibit today. The ideological groupings identified by international-relations scholars for the early Cold War era, the transition period of the Vietnam War, and Reagan's return to confrontation with the Soviet Union all hark back to studies of the United States' exceptionalist political culture in the pre-1945 period.[4] The tension between self-interested pragmatism and an altruistic idealism has been highlighted by a number of students of pre-World War II American foreign policy, most notably Robert Osgood.[5] A secondary tension been isolationism and crusading moralism in the American culture has created a paradox in American foreign policy. If a moral mission is not aptly de-

fined by the rhetoric of political leaders, then the basic default preference of the public is insularity.

The first set of categories of elite beliefs scholars identified during the Cold War period related to the creation of the containment policy. The conclusion of a battle between competing elites resulted in the announcement of the Truman Doctrine, the Marshall Plan, the Four Point program, and the North Atlantic Treaty all within a few months in the late 1940's. Daniel Yergin described the consensus which had emerged by that time: "The development of bipartisanship—general agreement and cooperation between Congress and the executive, and between the two parties—meant that foreign policy no longer was a divisive domestic-policy issue."[6] The influence of a consensus among elites who sought to implement the formula first enunciated by George Kennan in *Foreign Affairs* has been the subject of several historical and biographical studies.[7] More rigorous treatments of leaders' beliefs include Deborah Larson's *Origins of Containment* and Gaddis Smith's writings attributing the Truman policy to a fear of appeasing totalitarians, based on the Munich analogy.[8]

Daniel Yergin describes the "Yalta" and "Riga" axioms as alternative interpretations of the Soviet Union. Those in the Yalta school believed that the Soviet Union and the United States could have intersecting interests as great powers—as they had in their World War II alliance. Yergin takes the "Yalta axioms" label from the cooperative spirit of the Yalta conference of 1945. Proponents of the Riga view believed that the Soviet Union was naturally going to be a menacing rival to the United States, given its Russian imperialist traditions and its Communist revolutionary aims. The "Riga axioms" label comes from the diplomatic outpost in Latvia where many foreign service officers studied Soviet behavior in the pre-1941 period. The Riga position won out in elite circles, and led in Yergin's estimation to the construction of the "national security state."[9] Robert Osgood describes a similar pair of categories, which he objectively calls "Analysis A" and "Analysis B," corresponding to the Riga and Yalta views respectively.[10]

While the Riga position represented a bipartisan consensus among elites—as its success in creating the containment policies of the late 1940s attests—the Yalta view remained. A majoritarian view among elites that Soviet power must be contained was opposed by a minoritarian view that the United States was unnecessarily fixated upon the Soviet threat until the Vietnam War.

After Vietnam, thinking about America's role in the world changed. The failure of the United States to achieve victory or even to define what its aims were in the war caused a realignment of views amongst elites. The most tangible manifestation of this realignment in intellectual circles was the increasing discussion of an interdependent world in which force was no longer as useful an instrument of foreign policy, and in which the "high politics" of security no longer overshadowed the "low politics" of economic affairs.[11]

Ole Holsti and James Rosenau identify three diverging views in elite circles resulting from contrasting answers to the question of why the U.S. intervention in Vietnam was a failure.[12] "Cold War internationalists" remained committed to containment given their conviction that the East-West conflict was the key prob-

lem in world politics, even after Vietnam. "Post–Cold War internationalists" sought to shift the foci of American engagement in the world, namely to the North-South conflict and to economic affairs generally. The third group, "neoisolationists," reacted to the Vietnam experience by rejecting internationalism altogether; the chief threats to and problems of the United States were at home.[13]

The Reagan era represented a return to an aggressive anti-Soviet policy.[14] The work of two political scientists is representative of the scholarly classifications of elite views in the 1980s. Alexander Dallin and Gail Lapidus pinpointed three views of the Soviet Union among American political leaders. "Essentialists" like Richard Perle and Richard Pipes considered the Soviet Union to be destabilizing and tyrannical in its essence, and considered it as an intractable foe. Dallin and Lapidus explain:

> The essentialist approach focuses not on what the Soviet Union does, but rather what it is. This highly deterministic approach defines the Soviet system as inherently evil, sees little prospect for change, and denies the benefits of piecemeal accommodation.[15]

"Mechanists"—such as Henry Kissinger, Zbigniew Brzezinski, and George Shultz—saw the rivalry between the United States as the function of incompatible interests of great powers in the international system. Dallin and Lapidus note:

> The mechanist approach is concerned with Soviet behavior, not essences. It views the threat as primarily geopolitical and takes the traditional view that power can and must be checked with equal or superior power: The answer to Soviet ambitions is containment.[16]

"Interactionists" saw the Cold War as a big misunderstanding to be solved by increased interaction between Americans and Soviets; getting to know one another better could eliminate perceived differences. Sovietologists Marshall Shulman, Jerry Hough, and Stephen Cohen embody "interactionism." Dallin and Lapidus observe:

> [T]he interactionists see the sources of the Soviet-American conflict in both structural—superpower—elements and in mutual misperceptions. They are more likely to emphasize elements of diversity, if not pluralism, in Soviet elite politics and to anticipate the possibility of significant evolution in the Soviet system.[17]

The Carter Administration was characterized by a coalition of mechanists and interactionists in constant conflict. Subsequently, the Reagan Administration was characterized by a bitter battle between essentialists and mechanists, evolving from the dominance of the former to the dominance of the latter.[18]

COMPLEX REALIGNMENT AFTER THE COLD WAR

It appears a new array of elite beliefs is taking shape now that the Cold War is over. First, elites are divided into three views on what the United States' role in the world should be with regard to "high politics." *High politics* is the term traditional realists used to describe the issues of peace and war, the politico-military aspects of international relations. In this area, elites are now divided among those who seek to continue the global engagement which characterized U.S. foreign policy in the Cold War: those who seek to scale back American commitments to become selectively engaged based on case-by-case judgments of immediate American interests, and those who seek a more insular American posture, withdrawn from political and military conflict.

With the rise of an increasing interdependent world economy in an information age, economic foreign policy in the post–Cold War era is as important as this political and military dimension of American foreign policy. What realists called "low politics" in the past are no longer a secondary concern. On economic matters, American elites are divided into two basic groupings: those who favor a pure free market orientation based on minimal government intervention in the private sector, and those who favor a more nationalist orientation, willing to use the state to serve American interests in the form of regulation, protectionism, and industrial policy. The basic difference between the two views is that the first is based on a "positive sum" image of mutual benefit gained by the U.S. and other nations in the economic interaction, and the latter is premised upon a "zero sum game," where the successes of other economic powers come at the expense of the United States and vice versa.

If one accounts for both the three positions on high politics and the two positions on so-called low politics together, one sees that six categories of elites are emerging today in the discussion of the U.S. role in the world. Combining a preference for global engagement in political and security affairs with a free market orientation, one can an identify an ideological grouping that could be called "market internationalists." Examples of these include Republican Senator Richard Lugar, Democratic Senator Bill Bradley, think tank scholar Joshua Muravchik, and Harvard political scientist Joseph Nye (a Carter and Clinton appointee).

Linking a selective engagement posture in high politics with a laissez-faire economic worldview, one pinpoints a rather common elite grouping: "market pragmatists." Examples of these are George Bush and most of his foreign policy advisers, as well as publisher of the journal, *The National Interest,* Irving Kristol.

Those who believe in both strategic withdrawal from high politics and in economic liberalism are appropriately dubbed "libertarians." They represent a coherent—if not necessarily appealing—philosophical approach. They believe that both in political-military affairs *and* in economic affairs, the government that governs least governs best. In the Cold War, liberals and Democrats for the most part favored limited government in high politics, so as to scale back the expensive "national security state," but sought extensive government intervention in economic matters. Alternatively, conservatives favored building up a substantial government apparatus to fight the Cold War, but wanted to limit the government's role in the economy. Libertarians are consistent in their preference for very limited government in both spheres. The most notable examples are the thoughtful affiliates of the libertarian CATO Institute, Ted Galen Carpenter, Doug Bandow, and Christopher Layne.

Another coherent philosophical position is produced by the combination of global engagement in political-military affairs with a nationalist economic orientation. Because these thinkers favor an extensive state role in geopolitical and economic affairs, one might call them "interventionists." Richard Gephardt, Majority Leader in the House of Representatives, and Lane Kirkland, head of the AFL-CIO—the chief advocates of the interests of labor in and out of government—are perhaps the best examples of this interventionist worldview among elites.

Those supporting prudential selective engagement in high politics and a retaliatory nationalist approach to maximizing American economic interests are "mercantilists." *Mercantilism* was the term for the policy pursued by European states in the 17th and 18th centuries. The power of states was judged by the amount of specie, or precious metal, collected by the state. The zero-sum assumptions behind this view, and the emphasis on the power of the state in economic affairs as well as geopolitical matters make the term *a propos* for this contemporary perspective. Ross Perot arguably represents this form of nationalism. The ever-blunt Senator Ernest Hollings does too. In the extragovernmental world of scholars and publicists, Paul Kennedy, Michael Lind, and Alan Tonelson are three of the most thoughtful exponents of this perspective.

If a preference for isolationism in political and military affairs and one for statism in economic affairs are linked, the product is a sixth and final elite grouping. That grouping deserves the label "autarkists." *Autarky* connotes self-reliance, which is precisely what this brand of opinion shapers seek in both geopolitical and economic spheres of policy. Examples are strange bedfellows indeed. In the 1992 presidential primaries, the pugilistic candidates Pat Buchanan, a Republican, and Tom Harkin, a Democrat, both enunciated autarkist themes.

What makes the debate over the U.S. role in the world complex is not just that there are six apparent worldviews, which do not form a unilinear spectrum from the far left to the far right. What further complicates the debate is the pattern of cross-cutting cleavages which appear according to what foreign issue is being debated. For instance, if one were to ask elites whether the promotion of democracy should be the primary goal of American foreign policy, what National Security Adviser Anthony Lake called a doctrine of "enlargement" in a 1993 speech,[19] the six groupings would likely line up as follows: market internationalists and interventionists as advocates of global engagement would back this core policy, and the other four groupings would not.

If one were to ask whether the United States should leave a substantial number of troops in Western Europe under NATO auspices—say at least 100,000—the dividing line would be different. Then the proponents of global and selective engagement in high politics (market internationalists, market pragmatists, interventionists, and mercantilists) would probably back that troop presence; isolationists (libertarians and autarkists) would not.

Finally, if one were to examine where these six groupings lined up on the North American Free Trade Agreement, the cleavage would form between advocates of free market liberalism and advocates of retaliatory nationalism. Market internationalists, market pragmatists, and libertarians likely approved of Congress passing NAFTA; interventionists, mercantilists, and autarkists no doubt opposed NAFTA's passage.

The result of these cross-cutting cleavages is the appearance of utter chaos in the discussion of American foreign policy after the Cold War. But views of elites, as the true arbiters of the national interest, are actually more in conflict than they are confused. The complex realignment of elite beliefs after the Cold War—more complex than the mere tripartite realignment after Vietnam posited by Holsti and Rosenau—shapes the debate after the Cold War. But it is important to bear in mind that elite ideologies may be undergoing a realignment, not a dealignment. The hope for the coalescence of a new elite consensus is not as bleak as one might initially suspect. A broad alliance of two, three, or four groupings may emerge. If an issue is so galvanizing—such as fascism arising in Russia—or a rising ideological movement perspective is so abhorrent—such as one promoting isolationism or protectionism—that alliance may be forged sooner rather than later.

AN AGENDA FOR FUTURE RESEARCH

The array of six elite perspectives set out above has not been verified by comprehensive empirical study of elite attitudes. Until it is, it remains only a hypothetical construct to be validated or invalidated. Future research should undertake the rigorous examination of elite attitudes through surveys and even the in-depth interviews some social scientists consider old-fashioned and cumbersome. This empirical research would see if the deductively-derived classification scheme outlined here indeed exists, and whether the six categories are both mutually exclusive and exhaustive in describing elite worldviews.

Moreover, future research might address the various types of elites to see whether opinion shapers in particular professions belong wholly or largely in one category or another. For instance, are people in the media typically "mercantilists," or government officials "market internationalists"? The Times Mirror Center for the Study of the People and the Press has initiated research helpful in this regard. In a study entitled "America's Place in the World,"[20] the Times Mirror Center has polled no less than nine groups of "influentials." These elites include members of the news media, leaders in business and finance, artists and writers (the "cultural elite"), foreign affairs specialists, experts on national security, officials in state and local government, scholars in universities and think tanks, clergy, as well as scientists and engineers. Further study of such types of elites could yield a better sense of how their respective views correlate (if at all) with the ideological groupings identified here.

The *Times Mirror* study suggests one last avenue for fruitful scholarship. "America's Place in the World" compares the views of the public with those of various types of influentials. Future research should seek to identify which of the six ideological perspectives cited above are prevalent in mass attitudes and which are prevalent in elite attitudes. The consonance or disjunction between mass and elite attitudes would be interesting to investigate in and of itself. Still more significant would be the question of whether mass opinion or elite opinion is a more salient predictor of which course the United States will pursue in its foreign policy. If the U.S. pursues a foreign policy representative of a dominant perspective among elites and not among the general public, it has enormous implications for understanding just how democratic the foreign policy making in the American democracy is.[21] Defined in terms of the relative weight of elite and mass opinion, it would be particularly valuable to learn whether American foreign policy is becoming more or less democratic now that the Cold War is over.

NOTES

1. See Judith Goldstein, *Ideas, Interests, and American Trade Policy* (Ithaca, NY: Cornell University Press, 1993); Judith Goldstein and Robert O. Keohane (eds.), *Ideas and Foreign Policy: Beliefs, Institutions, and Political Change* (Ithaca, NY: Cornell University Press, 1993); Peter Haas, "Introduction: Epistemic Communities and International Policy Coordination," *International Organization*, vol. 46, no. 1 (Winter 1992): 1-35; and Mark P. Lagon, *The Reagan Doctrine: Sources of American Conduct in the Cold War's Last Chapter* (Westport, CT: Praeger Publishers, 1994).

2. See Judith Goldstein and Robert O. Keohane, "Ideas and Foreign Policy: An Analytical Framework," in Goldstein and Keohane (eds.), *Ideas and Foreign Policy*, pp. 8-11.

3. On the irrelevance of left and right in the discussion of post-Cold War American foreign Policy, see Alan Tonelson, "Beyond Left and Right" *The National Interest* 34 (Winter 1993/94): 3-18.

4. See Michael H. Hunt, *Ideology and U.S. Foreign Policy* (New Haven: Yale University Press, 1987).

5. See Robert Endicott Osgood, *Ideals and Self-Interest in America's Foreign Relations* (Chicago: University of Chicago Press, 1953.)

6. Daniel H. Yergin, *The Shattered Peace: The Origins of the Cold War and the National Security State* (New York: Penguin Books, 1977), p. 47.

7. The best autobiographical account of this effort is found in Dean Acheson, *Present at the Creation: My Years at the State Department* (New York: W. W. Norton, 1969). A particularly useful recent history of the small group of establishment foreign policy advisers to Truman is Walter Isaacson and Evan Thomas, *The Wise Men: Six Friends and the World They Made* (New York: Simon and Schuster, 1986).

8. Deborah Welch Larson, *Origins of Containment: A Psychological Explanation* (Princeton: Princeton University Press, 1987); and Gaddis Smith, "The Ghost of Hitler: Lessons of the Past," in *The Origins of the Cold War,* ed. Thomas G. Paterson, 2nd ed. (Lexington, MA: D. C. Heath, 1974).

9. See Yergin, pp. 193–220.

10. See Robert E. Osgood, et al., *Containment, Soviet Behavior, and Grand Behavior, and Grand Strategy* (Berkeley: Institute of International Studies, 1981).

11. See Robert Keohane and Joseph Nye, *Power and Interdependence,* 2nd ed. (Glenview, IL: Scott, Foresman, 1989); Edward Morse, *Modernization and the Transformation of International Relations* (New York: Free Press, 1976); and Richard Rosecrance (ed.), *America as an Ordinary Country: U.S. Foreign Policy and the Future* (Ithaca: Cornell University Press, 1976).

12. See Holsti and Rosenau, "Vietnam, Consensus, and the Beliefs Systems of American Leaders," p. 13.

13. Holsti and Rosenau, *American Leadership in World Affairs.*

14. See Raymond Garthoff, *Detente and Confrontation: American-Soviet Relations from Nixon to Reagan* (Washington: Brookings Institution, 1985).

15. Alexander Dallin and Gail W. Lapidus, "Reagan and the Russians: American Policy Toward the Soviet Union," in *Eagle Resurgent? The Reagan Era in American Foreign Policy,* ed. Kenneth A. Oye, Robert J. Lieber, and Donald Rothchild (Boston: Little, Brown, 1987), p. 200.

16. *Ibid.*

17. *Ibid.*

18. *Ibid.,* p. 202. See also Stephen M. Walt, "The Case for Finite Containment: Analyzing U.S. Grand Strategy," *International Security,* vol. 14, no. 1 (Summer 1989). For an excellent table comparing the various propositions of the worldviews he identifies, see Walt, p. 14.

19. Anthony Lake, "From Containment to Enlargement," address at the Johns Hopkins School of Advanced International Studies, Washington, D.C. (21 September 1993).

20. "America's Place in the World: An Investigation of the Attitudes of American Opinion Leaders and the American Public about International Affairs," Times Mirror Center for the People and the Press (November 1993).

21. On this point, see Jeane J. Kirkpatrick, "A Normal Country in an Normal Time," *The National Interest* 21 (Fall 1990): 41–42.

QUESTIONS

1. Why are the ideological beliefs of "elites" important in understanding the conduct of American foreign policy?

2. Identify and define the six "new" ideological categories of political leaders discussed in the article.

Chapter 9

FEMINIST THEORY

INTRODUCTION

Our discussion in both this chapter on feminist theory and the one that follows on peace studies focuses on two relative newcomers to the international relations theory stage. Certainly, there is important scholarship being done on the feminist perspective in a number of fields—literature, history, and sociology, to name just a few. These efforts have also extended into political science and provide some welcome and unique insights and perspectives to the study of world affairs.

The analysis and articles presented here examine international relations and established theories of international relations from a feminist viewpoint. That is, they introduce the element of gender into our understanding of foreign policy and the behavior of states. Gender, with respect to political science, does not narrowly adhere to the traditional biological delineation between men and women. Rather, the term **gender** encompasses the social and cultural distinctions, as well as the differences in traditional roles between the two sexes, not simply clinical or biological classifications.

When we associate a particular **role** with an individual or group, we generally mean the function or behavior patterns normally connected with a particular position. **Gender roles,** therefore, are the jobs, tasks, and activities that are traditionally associated with either men or women as a group. It may seem a bit of a stretch to categorize a theory dealing with a group that makes up half of the world's population in the individual level of analysis. The reason feminist theory of international relations is placed in this level is because it addresses world politics and the behavior of states from a perspective that originates from the unique role and characteristics most commonly associated with women.

WHAT IS FEMINIST THEORY?

To begin our discussion of feminist theory, we will resort to the technique of first ruling out what it is *not.* While acknowledging that the distribution of power is a key component in the behavior of and relations between states as the system currently stands, feminist theorists question the validity of this set-up. They do not believe that the accumulation of power, balance of power politics, and domination implicit in such an arrangement represent viable standards for the conduct of international affairs. Feminist theory also argues that the current system fails to promote the interests and roles of women in the world community. By ignoring women's contributions and issues, the history and present system of, as well as the approach to, international politics is considered one-sided, masculinist, and not fully representative.

What feminist theory *is* might be viewed as a multifaceted effort to change the course and conduct of international relations in a way that includes and incorporates the unique character and contributions of women. Since feminist theory is a relatively new approach in the study of international relations, it might be helpful to distinguish a few of the different branches within the theory and how they apply the role of gender to their interpretations. One aspect of feminist theory focuses both on the unique perspective and contributions that women bring to human relations and an analysis of human relations. In this way, feminist theorists highlight the distinctions between men and women in terms of role, interests, capabilities, etc., arguing that women do not need to compete with or surpass men on every issue. Rather, it is the differences in women's expertise and perspective on various issues that bring vitality, expand possibilities, and offer a new breadth of understanding to accepted norms and established theories of international affairs. For example, women's traditional skills and experience as primary caregiver and nurturer in the family setting and in society would presumably give a woman a greater range of abilities in the public spheres of conflict resolution, negotiation, and diplomacy. Overall, her greater capacity to bond, form lasting relationships, and empathize with others provides a woman with a natural advantage over men in these situations.

Not all proponents of feminist theory would necessarily agree with this approach. A second branch of feminist theorists de-emphasizes these differences and, instead, focuses on promoting greater participation of women within the existing framework of international relations and international relations theory. They tend to view the problem as one of exclusion, rather than emphasis. That is, expanding the proportion of women in positions of power throughout the world community would fundamentally change the character of global affairs without having to develop specific areas of women's special interest. In essence, given an equal opportunity, women can compete with men at what has traditionally been a man's game, succeed, and, in so doing, change the entire nature of the game itself.

One final aspect of feminist theory suggests that the problems of traditional approaches to international relations theory do not lie with whether they emphasize the perspectives and experiences of women or include women in sufficient numbers. Rather, they are found in the gender-related—often oppressive—themes and subtexts that litter a field dominated by men since its inception and still dominated by men today. A **subtext** is a hidden, underlying meaning or interpretation that can presumably be discerned by close examination of the words and phrases chosen by the author. Thus, both overtly and unconsciously, the structure of analysis, worldview, and terminology that are widely used and accepted in the study and practice of international affairs are dominated by a male perspective. Feminist theorists often use the term **androcentric** (male-centered) to describe the idea that traditional theories of international relations (particularly realism) ignore alternative viewpoints and, instead, rely on essentially masculine interpretations of world affairs. The male approach—filled with images of power, strength, domination, and war—is quite distinct from the female approach—characterized by images of peace, equity, social justice, and environmental balance. By recognizing these inherent and pervasive inequalities and exposing the hidden masculinist agenda in the world political system, these feminist theorists hope to create a broader overall setting for enlightened discourse. And, since women have classically been outsiders in this global power game, this new approach would likely benefit peripheral nations (Third World, less-industrialized societies) that have also commonly found themselves on the fringes of political influence.

Obviously, feminist theory encompasses several viewpoints in a progressive dialogue on international relations theory. There is, however, agreement within the ranks of the debate on some key issues. First, the frameworks for both the practice of and theorizing about international affairs have been constructed to fit male conceptions of the world, life, and human interaction. In addition to setting up these frameworks, men have played and continue to play the primary role within them. Feminist theorists generally agree that the inclusion of women, in any of the forms mentioned above, would have a significant, positive impact on the policymaking process and the policies themselves. Such changes would stem from the perspective and experience of women in society and would benefit the world community by promoting greater equality throughout the system, as well as policies emphasizing nonviolent solutions and alternatives.

WRITINGS IN FEMINIST THEORY

The articles selected for this chapter represent a sampling of the work being done on feminist theories of international relations. Sandra Whitworth, in "Gender in the Inter-Paradigm Debate," examines three existing paradigms of international relations to determine whether and how well these theories can accept the introduction of gender into their analysis. The author uses three criteria to evaluate each paradigm. First, does the theory allow for a discussion of "the social construction of ideas or meanings"? In other words, Whitworth examines whether the theories look at explanations or interpretations for various terms, groupings, and norms within society, including gender. Second, does the theory permit a discussion of differing interpretations of history? This question takes into account that past events can be viewed differently by different people, depending on their perceptions and experiences. Finally, proceeding from the assumption that inequalities in the power relationships within the political process can be overlooked or hidden, Whitworth asks whether the theories allow for speculation about international relations that might uncover these inequities.

J. Ann Tickner's "Hans Morgenthau's Principles of Political Realism" makes some broader assumptions about the nature of international relations theory as a discipline. Tickner examines the core assumptions of Morgenthau's realism from a feminist viewpoint in order to demonstrate how traditional theories of international relations reflect a masculine bias and exclude the role or perspectives of women. In addition, Tickner tries to expose *why* men continue to dominate this field and the reasons that women are, consequently, under-represented. As she admits, the article does not offer self-help strategies for how women can break into the foreign policy establishment but, instead, exposes existing inequalities and examines why international politics is still perceived as a "man's world."

V. Spike Peterson and Anne Sisson Runyan argue that it is not just international politics that is viewed through this gender lens, but specific constructs throughout our society that perpetuate this cycle of inequality. A **gender lens** can be described as a prism, either masculine or feminine, that colors how individuals view life and the world around them. This excerpt from their book *Global Gender* suggests that generally men benefit from the masculinism endemic to the system, which, at the same time, relegates women's "energies, lives, intellects, demands, and needs" to secondary status. Hence, according to Peterson and Runyan, this gender division tends to create and perpetuate a world shaped by forces hostile to women.

A CRITIQUE OF FEMINIST THEORY

One of the greatest strengths and contributions of feminist theory is that it serves to highlight issues such as these. It stands to reason that if the course and conduct of international relations has been dominated by men, and theories on this subject have been designed predominantly by men, that our overall perceptions have been gender influenced. Just as two people witnessing the same event might describe it differently due to their unique backgrounds and preconceptions, it is likely that the predominance of men in international affairs has had an affect on the foreign policy behavior of states and theories about world politics.

Feminist theory has also made important headway both in uncovering the masculinist approach to international relations theory and in promoting the interests, goals, and equality of women in the field. Essentially, feminist theorists have moved beyond isolating the gender inequities in our traditional ways of looking at things and have established various methods for redressing these inequities, as well. These methods seek to incorporate a greater number of issues important and relevant to women's lives or to expand the percentage of women in the foreign policy establishment. As the disparities in power and influence between men and women equalize, the nature and conduct of international politics will change.

A major critique of the feminist paradigm, however, is its failure to provide a comprehensive theoretical construct for analyzing international relations. Traditional theorists might suggest it is not sufficiently rigorous, lacking an organized, cohesive framework. As a prescriptive theory, feminism falls into the trap of focusing too much of its efforts on how the situation in world politics, and the study of world politics, might be changed. What feminist theory does *not* supply are the explanatory and theoretical tools to conduct a thorough analysis.

We might also question some of the standards that are established in the context of feminist theory. Are feminists guilty of relying on their own stereotypes of gender characteristics? By using selective characterizations—women are more cooperative and peaceful, while men are more violent and aggressive—feminist theorists risk reinforcing the same gender stereotyping they are trying to overcome.

Despite our initial point, crediting feminist theory with uncovering gender bias in a male dominated field, there are skeptics who question the utility of this view. Critics contend international relations theory should explain and predict behavior based on how the world actually operates. Since men hold the vast majority of leadership positions, scholars must study their behavior. Critics also point out that gender may not provide a sufficient explanation for past and contemporary international politics. Larger forces (human nature, disparities in wealth and power, anarchic world system, to name just a few) shape the behavior of various actors on the world stage, irrespective of gender. As evidence, critics point to the fact that when women have assumed leadership positions and confronted the same global problems that men have confronted, women have acted in a similar fashion.

Feminist theorists respond to these arguments in a number of ways. First, feminists contend that illustrating that women and men behave differently is not engaging

---

KEY CONCEPTS

Androcentric   (male-centered) describes the idea that traditional theories of international relations (particularly realism) ignore alternative viewpoints and, instead, rely on essentially masculine interpretations of world affairs.

Gender   encompasses the social and cultural distinctions, as well as the differences in traditional roles, between the two sexes, not simply clinical or biological classifications.

Gender lens   can be described as a prism, either masculine or feminine, that colors how individuals view life and the world around them.

Gender roles   are the jobs, tasks, and activities that are traditionally associated to either men or women as a group.

Role   is the function or behavior patterns normally connected with a particular position.

Subtext   is a hidden, underlying meaning or interpretation that can presumably be discerned by close examination of the words and phrases chosen by the author.

---

in stereotypes. It simply challenges scholars to appreciate the extent to which traditional theories of international relations rely solely on male conceptions of reality and ignore the perspectives and concerns of women. Second, they argue that feminist theories of international relations should not be judged by conventional, male-dominated rules of objectivity and analysis. Feminism is an innovative approach that seeks to inject a "feminine" perspective into the study of international relations. With this new perspective come new ways of analyzing global politics that cannot, and should not, be judged merely on how well the theories hold up to conventional social science methodologies and practices.

Whether we agree or disagree with these critics, feminist theory is now an important perspective in the field of international relations. In our study of how individuals behave in a global setting, differences between the sexes cannot be ignored. As men and women address gender issues in practice within society at large, it must certainly be time to address them in theory.

40.   Gender in the Inter-Paradigm Debate

Sandra Whitworth

In this article, Sandra Whitworth examines the possibilities for putting together a feminist theory of international relations from the realist, pluralist, and critical paradigms. Whitworth argues that realism offers more opportunities for theorizing about gender than pluralism. Furthermore, the author suggests that while the critical theory of international relations does provide some stimulus for theorizing about gender, the limited literature and analyses on the role of gender in international relations theory presents a fundamental challenge to feminists in the field. This selection is from the journal *Millenium* (1989).

Sandra Whitworth is a lecturer in Political Science at York University in Ontario, Canada.

Two important but, sadly, parallel debates have appeared recently in the pages of *Millennium*. The special issue devoted to "Women and International Relations" was a first of its kind and contained path-breaking work.[1] Similarly, a series of articles examining critical international relations theory has done much to generate interest and exchange over the state of the field in international relations.[2] That these debates have taken place largely in isolation of one another, however, is not merely regrettable but alarming.[3] For feminists concerned with developing an international relations theory which is sensitive to gender, the continued silence of critical international relations in relation to gender presents a fundamental challenge, perhaps even more so than from within the mainstream of international relations. Realism, for example, has been accused of a variety of "absences," not least of which is its inability to theorise its own central unit of analysis, the state.[4] Within this context, an inability or unwillingness to theorise about gender does not seem so unusual. However, critical international relations purports to contemplate the social and political complex as a whole and to understand the process of change within both the whole and its parts.[5] In this context, the failure to acknowledge, let alone analyse, the character and bases of female subordination within both the study and practice of international relations is untenable.[6]

Simply to note the absence of gender within international relations theory, critical or otherwise, does not take us very far. The rest of this paper will be devoted to an examination of whether one *could* theorise about gender from international relations theory; that is, to extrapolate from what *is* written within international relations theory to what is not, thus creating the possibility, at least, of a gendered account of international relations.[7] What I propose to do here is to provide a reconstruction of the inter-paradigm debate from a feminist perspective. In this way, I will be paralleling the format which Mark Hoffman[8] used to locate critical theory within international relations theory; however, I will alter that format somewhat by including critical international relations theory as one of the paradigms.[9] I should note also that my intention here is not to carry out what Stanley Hoffman warns against, a "wrecking operation,"[10] but rather to explore possibilities for a gendered account of international relations from within each of the paradigms.

GENDER

Gender refers not to women or to men *per se,* but to the ideological and material relation between them, which historically has been an unequal relationship. Additionally, gender is not given biologically, as a result of the sexual characteristics of either women or men, but is constructed socially. As Catherine MacKinnon writes:

> . . . gender is an outcome of a social process of sub-ordination that is only ascriptively tied to body and doesn't lose its particularity of meaning when it shifts embodied form. Femininity is a lowering that is imposed; it can be done to anybody and still be what feminine means. It is just women to whom it is considered natural.[11]

Thus, the pertinent feature of the notion of gender is that it is a socially constructed inequality between women and men.

It is important to emphasise here that the choice of the word gender is not a theory-neutral one; that is, there is a reason why this article refers to "gender" rather than to "women." Indeed, the approach to feminist theory which is suggested here explicitly rejects the notion that the pursuit of feminist international relations scholarship is or should be to bring women into the discipline of international relations. As Sarah Brown notes, the assumption that women need to be brought into international relations is a largely liberal-feminist concern which assumes that women were not there in the first place.[12]

The silence of international relations scholars about women is significant, and has been taken to mean in the past either that international relations is gender neutral or that women are not part of the subject matter of international relations at all.[13] It is argued here, by contrast, that the theory and practice of international relations have always been gendered, and that international economic and political institutions contain, affect and are affected by understandings of gender.[14] To suggest that they are not, by implying some sort of gender neutrality, only serves to sustain the power relations embedded in this sort of silencing within international relations. The absence of women in international relations is hegemonic, in a Gramscian sense, insofar as that absence is considered natural.[15] This project, then, is not one which deplores the apparent absence of women in international relations but is one which asks, as Sarah Brown does, why a theory and history which sustains this appearance is accepted.[16]

GENDER AND THE INTER-PARADIGM DEBATE

Given what has been suggested thus far about gender, several criteria for the project of uncovering a space for a feminist international relations theory from within traditional international relations theory should be apparent.[17] For one, such a theory should allow us to talk about the social construction of ideas or meanings. As gender is itself a "constructed" concept (there is nothing essentialist about the term), there must be room within international relations theory to talk about that fact. Second, such a theory should allow us to talk about historical variability, for gender is not constructed at one point in time once and for all, but is a concept that has changed, depending upon both changing material conditions and the various struggles in which actors engage. Third, such a theory should allow us to talk about power, for implicit in the notion of gender is an understanding of power and an inequality of power. Such a discussion of power should not focus simply on overt expressions of force, however, but on the ways in which power relations between women and men, and gender (as a concept) itself, are made invisible.[18] There are three criteria, then, by which to evaluate international relations theory: whether it permits us to discuss the social construction of meaning, whether it permits us to discuss historical variability, and whether it permits us to theorise about power in ways that uncover the very masking of those power relations.

Realism and Gender

Realism constitutes the central tradition of international relations theory, but there is little in realism that seems conducive to theorising about gender. And indeed, it is unlikely that most realists *would* theorise about gender. Morgenthau defines international politics

as the struggle for power, which he defines as the ability of the state representatives of one nation to control the minds and actions of another nation's representatives.[19] He argues further that international relations that are not concerned with the pursuit of power are simply not about international politics.[20] Examples of international relations that are *not* international politics by this definition would include the activities of international organisations, the exchange of goods and services among nations, or the co-operation among nations in providing relief from natural disasters.[21] More recently, Kal Holsti has argued against the increasing fragmentation and overspecialisation which he claims currently characterises the field of international relations. He describes some such work as bordering on trivia (*e.g.* the co-ordination of labour policies among Scandinavian states), and calls for a return to the fundamental purpose of the discipline: the investigation into the causes of war, and the condition for peace, order and security.[22] From this perspective, any analysis of gender would not and should not be included within the discipline of international relations.

Realists themselves may not be inclined to theorise about gender, and would argue from their ontological assumptions against such a project. However, I would argue that there are a number of spaces within realist theory which would at least not foreclose such a possibility. Two brief examples will illustrate this point, one the classical realist work of Morgenthau and second, the neo-realist contributions of regime theory. I would argue that while neither classical realism nor regime theory open up a sufficient space for a feminist theory of international relations and, in fact, their ontological commitments necessarily preclude such an outcome, both *do* suggest a necessary epistemological space within which such a project could begin.

My choice of Morgenthau may be surprising to some, but I would follow the earlier work of Richard Ashley here and argue that in its commitment to practice (the practice of diplomats), the classical realism of Morgenthau rejects the "antihistorical enclosure" of much neorealist thought that came after it.[23] By this understanding of realism, it is not the case that notions such as national interest, power, the states system, and so on, are not clearly defined by realists, as some neorealists charge. Rather, realists such as Morgenthau recognise that such concepts are given meaning only within an historical context through the practices and struggles of individuals, *i.e.,* diplomats.[24] There is nothing essentialist about the national interest, by this account. Rather, it is given meaning in different historical periods, within different material and ideological constraints, through the often 'strategic artistry' of the practitioners of international diplomacy.[25]

Such an interpretation of classical realism acknowledges that meaning is contingent and socially constructed and, further, acknowledges historical variability. While of course no explicit reference to gender is, or would be, made here, such an account creates a space for the analysis of gender and international relations discussed above: that gender is socially and historically constructed and is manifest within the operation of numerous international activities. How those meanings are constructed depends upon the activities and struggles of individuals and collectivities acting within particular historical conjunctures and constrained by particular material conditions.

While classical realism opens up an epistemological space for feminist international relations, its ontological commitments to states and states*men* ultimately preclude any incorporation of gender into its analysis. Further, its conception of power is one that recognises only the overt ability to control action, through force or coercion, and not one in which the management of power relations tends to recede into the background of consciousness.[26] Neo-realist regime theory is similar in this regard. Regimes are defined as "principles, norms, rules and decision-making procedures around which actor expectations converge."[27] As Ruggie and Kratchowil note, "The emphasis on convergent expectations as the constitutive basis of regimes gives regimes an inescapably intersubjective quality."[28] Like classical realism, regime theory suggests an epistemology (but does not carry through with it, as Ruggie and Kratchwil argue) which is more interpretive, one in which meaning is not given, but is constituted through the shared meanings of international actors. But again, as with classical realism, regime theory's ontological commitment to states as the most important actors ultimately precludes analysis of gender.

Pluralism and Gender

The pluralist paradigm, in contrast to realism, would appear at first glance to be conducive to theorising about gender. In its many guises, from the early work of Keohane and Nye, to the World Order Models Project, to the World Society perspective of Burton, it has sought to enlarge the purview of international relations theory away from the strictly state-centric concerns of realism.

One of the most dramatic departures from realism within the pluralist paradigm may be that of the world society perspective.[29] It was launched in the late 1960s by John Burton when he argued that global politics resembled more a "cobweb" in which a large proportion of international relations and transactions take place between non-governmental actors, than the "billiard-ball" model of the realists.[30] In this, problems of international politics such as war, terrorism, arms races, ideological conflict and famine are conceptualised along with other apparently unrelated problems such as alcohol and drug abuse, crime and racial conflict as having common origins. Conflictual relationships of all varieties have as their origin, according to Burton, the denial of human needs. He thus argues that such conflicts are not over some material good or symbol which cannot be shared, but over commonly held goals or universal needs. The goal of conflict resolution is to uncover these underlying conflicts, which are expressed in terms of conflicts over scarce resources.

In expanding the purview of international relations theory to include various non-state and sub-state actors, Burton seems to open up a larger ontological space than realism might for considerations of gender and international relations. I would argue, by contrast, that while there is certainly room here to incorporate an analysis of *women* and international relations, Burton's account forecloses any possibility of discussing *gender* and international relations be-

cause it is ahistorical and denies the material bases of conflict, inequality and power. Women as a category may figure in conflicts over security and recognition, just as an ethnic group might in Burton's problem-solving approach. In this way Burton's project, if it were applied to women, would be very much that of liberal feminists: to bring women into international relations. But this understanding of conflict and human needs suffers from the limitations inherent in liberal feminism: it fails to analyse the structural features of women's oppression.[31] Burton's approach ignores structural sources of inequality and conflict and, as Brian Fay writes, "makes it sound as if all conflict . . . is generated by mistaken ideas about social reality rather than by the tensions and incompatibilities inherent in this reality itself."[32]

Thus, it is argued here, counterintuitively perhaps, that there are more spaces within realism to discuss gender, at least insofar as some of its epistemological suggestions do not foreclose this possibility, than there are within pluralism.

Critical Theory and Gender

I have left critical theory until this point not only because it is the most recent approach to the study of international relations, but because it holds out the greatest promise for incorporating gendered analyses into international relations. As Mark Hoffman describes critical international relations theory, it stands apart from the prevailing order and asks how that order came about. It entails a theory of history and questions the origins and legitimacy of social and political institutions; it contemplates the social and political complex as a whole.[33] Clearly, such a view replicates almost precisely the gender and international relations project outlined, which attempts to theorise about historical variability, power and the social construction of meaning. Moreover, it is only through a 'critical' interpretation of realism, outlined above, that the spaces for a feminist international relations theory within realism were uncovered.[34]

But because critical international relations is, in some ways, one of the most recent entries into the field, its prescriptions for a critical theory of international relations are not yet fully developed. For example, it is only recently that scholars working within the World Order Models Project have begun to discuss *how* the transformations they envisage, the alternative world orders, may come into being. They have only recently, that is, begun to theorise agents of change and thus incorporated notions of historical variability.[35]

So, while critical international relations theory seems to open up a space for theorising about gender, it is as yet quite undeveloped, and as such, the prospects for gender and international relations from within this approach are still undetermined. In addition, it should be noted that a space created within critical theory would not launch gender analyses into the mainstream of international relations: critical theory is as much on the peripheries of international relations as is feminist analysis.

Finally, and most importantly, while critical theory may be the most hospitable to theorising about gender, the fact that no critical international relations theorists have yet discussed gender in any sustained fashion is the most damning criticism that can be made of it. As Nancy Fraser notes, Marx's definition of critical theory as "the self-clarification of the struggles and wishes of the age" positively demands an account of gender.[36] If one of the most important struggles of our age has been that of women, and I would argue that it has been, then critical international relations is simply not deserving of the name until it develops an analysis of gender.

The relationship between critical international relations and feminist international relations should be a reciprocal one. While critical international relations theory is as yet underdeveloped, there is much within feminist theory from which it can draw. The feminist insight that "women are made not born," as Jane Jenson writes, "compels us to think not only about the social construction of gender relations but also about the ways in which *all* social relations are constructed."[37] Examinations of the social construction of meaning pointed to by feminist analysis can be applied to a variety of traditional international relations concerns such as international organisations, militarism, the state system and so on.[38] Thus, the "next stage" of international relations theory will not be one which is merely "critical," but one which is *both* critical *and* feminist.

NOTES

1. *Millennium: Journal of International Studies* (Vol. 17, No. 3, Winter 1988).
2. Mark Hoffman, "Critical Theory and the Inter-Paradigm Debate," *Millennium* (Vol. 16, No. 2, Summer 1987), pp. 231–49; see also N. R. Rengger, "Going Critical? A Response to Hoffman," *Millennium* (vol. 17, No. 1, 1988), pp.

81–90; M. Hoffman, "Conversations on Critical International Relations Theory," in *ibid.;* Y. Lapid, "*Quo Vadis* International relations? Further Reflections on the 'Next Stage' of International Theory," *Millennium* (Vol. 18, No. 1, Spring 1989); Y. Lapid, "The Third Debate: On the Prospects of International Theory in a Post-Positivist Era," *International Studies Quarterly* (forthcoming).

3. The extent to which any discussion *has* taken place between feminist and critical IR theorists has been largely feminist IR scholars noting that examinations of gender inequality is a "requirement for a critical theory of international relations." See Sarah Brown, "Feminism, International Theory and International Relations of Gender Inequality," *Millennium* (Vol. 17, No. 3, Winter 1989), p. 472.

4. See Richard K. Ashley, "The Poverty of Neorealism," in R. O. Keohane (ed.), *Neorealism and its Critics* (New York: Columbia University Press, 1986); and Fred Halliday, "State and Society in International Relations: A Second Agenda," *Millennium* (Vol. 16, No. 2, Summer 1987).

5. Hoffman, *op. cit.,* p. 238.

6. For a parallel discussion, see Nancy Fraser, "What's Critical about Critical Theory? The Case of Habermas and Gender," in S. Benhabib and D. Cornell, (eds.), *Feminism and Critique* (Minneapolis, MN: University of Minnesota Press, 1987), pp. 31–55.

7. *Ibid.,* p. 32.

8. Hoffman, *op. cit.*

9. Michael Banks suggests that there are currently three paradigms within IR: realism, pluralism and structuralism. Michael Banks, "The Inter-Paradigm Debate," in M. Light and A.J.R. Groom (eds.), *International Relations: A Handbook of Current Theory* (London: Frances Pinter, 1985), pp. 7–26. The last of these, structuralism, is a rather confused collection of theories in which, for example, he in-

cludes both Richard Ashley and Robert Cox, two writers who explicitly reject purely structural accounts of IR and which has not engaged in "debates" with realism in the same way as the pluralist paradigm during the 1970s and 1980s. Because of this, I have replaced structuralism with critical IR theory and include a variety of approaches which, in Robert Cox's words, "do not take institutions and social power relations for granted but calls them into question by concerning itself with their origins and whether they might be in the process of changing." Writers such as Wallerstein, and more recently Ashley, Hoffman, Rengger and Cox would be included in this approach.

10. *C.f.,* R. O. Keohane, "Theory of World Politics: Structural Realism, and Beyond," in R. O. Keohane, *op. cit.,* p. 160.

11. Catherine A. MacKinnon, *Feminism Unmodified: Discourses on Life and Law* (Cambridge, MA: Harvard University Press, 1987), p. 234; *c.f.,* Brown, *op. cit.,* p. 469.

12. Brown, *op. cit.,* p. 464.

13. Paraphrased from Alison M. Jaggar, *Feminist Politics and Human Nature* (Brighton: Harvester, 1983), p. 21.

14. Paraphrased from Joan Wallach Scott, "The Modern Period," *Past and Present,* (No. 101, November, 1983).

15. *C.f.,* R. W. Cox, "Production and Hegemony: An Approach Towards a Problematic," paper prepared for the IPSA Congress, Moscow, 12–18 August 1979, p. 1.

16. Brown, *op. cit.,* p. 464.

17. Much of the conceptual work for this section has been inspired by numerous recent writings by Jane Jenson. See, for example, "Gender and Reproduction: Or, Babies and the State," *Studies in Political Economy* (No. 20, 1986), pp. 9–46; "Changing Discourse, Changing Agendas: Political Rights and Reproductive Policies in France," in M. Katzenstein and

C. Mueller (eds.), *The Women's Movement of Western Europe and the USA: Consciousness, Political Opportunity and Public Policy* (Philadelphia, PA: Temple University Press, 1987); and "The Talents of Women, The Skills of Men: Flexible Specialization and Women," in S. Wood (ed.), *The Transformation of Work* (London: Unwin Hyman, 1989).

18. K. J. Holsti, *The Dividing Discipline: Hegemony and Diversity in International Theory* (Boston, MA: Allen and Unwin, 1985), p. 8.

19. H. J. Morgenthau, *Politics Among Nations,* Fifth Edition (New York: Alfred A. Knopf, 1978), pp. 9, 30.

20. *Ibid.,* pp. 12, 29–30.

21. *Ibid.,* pp. 29–30.

22. Holsti, *op. cit.,* pp. 139–40.

23. Ashley, *op. cit.,* p. 270.

24. *Ibid.,* pp. 270–71; see also Keohane, *op. cit.,* p. 168.

25. Ashley, *op. cit.,* pp. 270–71.

26. R. W. Cox, "Social Forces, States and World Orders: Beyond International Relations Theory," *Millennium* (Vol. 10, No. 2, Summer 1981), p. 137.

27. Stephen Krasner, "Structural Causes and Regime Consequences: Regimes as Intervening Variables," in Stephen Krasner (ed.), *International Regimes* (Ithaca, NY: Cornell University Press, 1983).

28. Friedrich Kratchowil and J. G. Ruggie, "International Organisation: A State of the Art on an Art of the State," *International Organisation* (Vol. 40, No. 4, 1986), p. 764.

29. Ernie Keenes, Gregg Legare and Jean-Francois Rioux, "The Reconstruction of New-Realism from Counter-Hegemonic Discourse," *Carleton University Occasional Papers* (No. 14, Spring 1987), p. 15.

30. John W. Burton, "World Society and Human Needs," in M. Light and A. J. R. Groom, *op. cit.,* p. 47; C. R. Mitchell, "World Society as Cobweb: States, Actors and Systemic Processes," in Michael Banks, *Conflict in World Society,* pp. 59–61.

31. See Jaggar, *op. cit.,* p. 199 and chapter 7 for a review of liberal feminism and its critics.

32. Brian Fay, *Social Theory and Political Practice* (London: George Allen and Unwin, 1975), pp. 90–91.

33. Hoffman, *op. cit.,* pp. 237–8 and passim.

34. And, of course, this interpretation of realism is a contentious one, even among critical IR theorists. See especially the exchange between Richard Ashley, Ramashray Roy and R. B. J. Walker in *Alternatives* (No. 13, 1988), pp. 77–102.

35. See, for example, R. B. J. Walker and Saul H. Mendlovitz, "Peace, Politics and Contemporary Social Movements," and Richard A. Falk, "The State System and Contemporary Social Movement," in S. H. Mendlovitz and R. B. J. Walker (eds.), *Towards a Just World Peace* (Toronto: Butterworths, 1987).

36. Fraser, *op. cit.,* p. 31.

37. Jane Jenson, "Different but not Exceptional: the Feminism of Permeable Fordism," *Studies in Political Economy* (forthcoming).

38. Sandra Whitworth, "What Next? Gender and IR?," mimeo.

Questions

1. Identify the reasons why a gender bias exists within each of the international relations paradigms.

2. In your view, is the question of gender relevant to the systemic and domestic levels of analysis?

41. Hans Morgenthau's Principles of Political Realism: A Feminist Reformulation

J. Ann Tickner

In this article, J. Ann Tickner argues that the existence and composition of gender bias in international relations is revealed, to a certain extent, by how the subject is taught. Tickner evaluates Hans Morgenthau's realism and provides a feminist perspective on the theory. This essay contends that the perception of "reality" has excluded gender questions. Tickner introduces a feminist perspective into Morgenthau's six principles of realist theory. This selection is from the journal *Millennium* (1988).

J. Ann Tickner is assistant professor of Political Science at the College of the Holy Cross.

It is not in giving life but in risking life that man is raised above the animal: that is why superiority has been accorded in humanity not to the sex that brings forth but to that which kills.

—SIMONE DE BEAUVOIR[1]

International politics is a man's world, a world of power and conflict in which warfare is a privileged activity. Traditionally, diplomacy, military service, and the science of international politics have been largely male domains. In the past, women have rarely been included in the ranks of professional diplomats or the military: of the relatively few women who specialise in the academic discipline of international relations, few are security specialists. Women political scientists who do international relations tend to focus on areas such as international political economy, North-South relations and matters of distributive justice.

Today, in the United States, where women are entering the military and the foreign service in greater numbers than ever before, rarely are they to be found in positions of military leadership or at the top of the foreign policy establishment.[2] One notable exception, Jeane Kirkpatrick, who was US ambassador to the United Nations in the early 1980s, has described herself as 'a mouse in a man's world'. For in spite of her authoritative and forceful public style and strong conservative credentials, Kirkpatrick maintains that she failed to win the respect or attention of her male colleagues on matters of foreign policy.[3]

Kirkpatrick's story could serve to illustrate the discrimination which women often encounter when they rise to high political office. However, the doubts as to whether a woman would be strong enough to press the nuclear button (an issue raised when a tearful Patricia Schroeder was pictured sobbing on her husband's shoulder as she bowed out of the 1988 US presidential race) suggest that there may be an even more fundamental barrier to women's entry into the highest ranks of the military or of foreign policy-making. Nuclear strategy, with its vocabulary of power, threat, force, and deterrence, has a distinctly masculine ring:[4] moreover, women are stereotypically judged to be lacking in qualities which these terms evoke. It has also been suggested that, although more women are entering the world of public policy, they are more comfortable dealing with domestic issues such as social welfare that are more compatible with their nurturing skills. Yet the large number of women in the ranks of the peace movement suggests that women are not uninterested in issues of war and peace, although their frequent dissent from national security policy has often branded them as naive, uninformed or even unpatriotic.

In this article I propose to explore the question why international politics is perceived as a man's world and why women remain so under-represented in the higher echelons of the foreign policy establishment, the military and the academic discipline of international relations. Since I believe that there is something about this field which renders it particularly inhospitable and unattractive to women, I intend to focus on the nature of the discipline itself rather than on possible strategies to remove barriers to women's access to high policy positions. As I have already suggested, the issues that get prioritised in foreign policy are issues with which men have had a special affinity. Moreover, if it is primarily men who are describing these issues and constructing theories to explain the workings of the international system, might we not expect to find a masculine perspective in the academic discipline also? If this were so, then it could be argued that the exclusion of women has operated not only at the level of discrimination but also through a process of self-selection which begins with the way in which we are taught about international relations.

In order to investigate this claim that the discipline of international relations—traditionally defined by realism—is based on a masculine world view, I propose to examine Hans Morgenthau's six principles of political realism. I shall use some ideas from feminist theory to show that the way in which Morgenthau describes and explains international politics, and the prescriptions that ensue, are embedded in a masculine perspective. Then I shall suggest some ways in which feminist theory might help us begin to conceptualise a world view from a feminine perspective and to formulate a feminist epistemology of international relations. Drawing on these observations, I shall conclude with a reformulation of Morgenthau's six principles. Male critics of contemporary realism have already raised many of the same questions about realism that I shall address. However, in undertaking this exercise, I hope to link the growing critical perspective on international relations theory and feminist writers interested in global issues. Adding a feminist perspective to its discourse could also help to make the field of international relations more accessible to women scholars and practitioners.

HANS MORGENTHAU'S PRINCIPLES OF POLITICAL REALISM: A MASCULINE PERSPECTIVE?

I have chosen to focus on Hans Morgenthau's six principles of political realism because they represent one of the most important statements of contemporary realism from which several generations of scholars and practitioners of international relations have been nourished. Although Morgenthau has frequently been criticised for his lack of scientific rigour and ambiguous use of language, these six principles have significantly framed the way in which the majority of international relations scholars and practitioners in the West have thought about international politics since 1945.[5]

Morgenthau's principles of political realism can be summarised as follows:

1. Politics, like society in general, is governed by objective laws that have their roots in human nature which is unchanging: therefore it is possible to develop a rational theory that reflects these objective laws.

2. The main signpost of political realism is the concept of interest defined in terms of power which infuses rational order into the subject matter of politics, and thus makes the theoretical understanding of politics possible. Political realism stresses the rational, objective and unemotional

3. Realism assumes that interest defined as power is an objective category which is universally valid but not with a meaning that is fixed once and for all. Power is the control of man over man.

4. Political realism is aware of the moral significance of political action. It is also aware of the tension between the moral command and the requirements of successful political action.

5. Political realism refuses to identify the moral aspirations of a particular nation with the moral laws that govern the universe. It is the concept of interest defined in terms of power that saves us from moral excess and political folly.

6. The political realist maintains the autonomy of the political sphere. He asks "How does this policy affect the power of the nation?" Political realism is based on a pluralistic conception of human nature. A man who was nothing but "political man" would be a beast, for he would be completely lacking in moral restraints. But, in order to develop an autonomous theory of political behavior, "political man" must be abstracted from other aspects of human nature.[6]

I am not going to argue that Morgenthau is incorrect in his portrayal of the international system. I do believe, however, that it is a partial description of international politics because it is based on assumptions about human nature that are partial and that privilege masculinity. First, it is necessary to define masculinity and femininity. According to almost all feminist theorists, masculinity and femininity refer to a set of socially constructed categories that vary in time and place rather than to biological determinants. In the West conceptual dichotomies such as objectivity *vs.* subjectivity, reason *vs.* emotion, mind *vs.* body, culture *vs.* nature, self *vs.* other or autonomy *vs.* relatedness, knowing *vs.* being and public *vs.* private have typically been used to describe male/female differences by feminists and non-feminists alike.[7] In the United States, psychological tests conducted across different socio-economic groups confirm that individuals perceive these dichotomies as masculine and feminine and also that the characteristics associated with masculinity are more highly valued by both men and women alike.[8] It is important to stress, however, that these characteristics are stereotypical; they do not necessarily describe individual men or women who can exhibit characteristics and modes of thought associated with the opposite sex.

Using a vocabulary which contains many of the words associated with masculinity as I have defined it, Morgenthau asserts that it is possible to develop a rational (and unemotional) theory of international politics based on objective laws that have their roots in human nature. Since Morgenthau wrote the first edition of *Politics Among Nations* in 1948, this search for an objective science of international politics, based on the model of the natural sciences, has been an important part of the realist and neo-realist agenda. In her feminist critique of the natural sciences, Evelyn Fox Keller points out that most scientific communities share the 'assumption that the universe they study is directly accessible, represented by concepts shaped not by language but only by the demands of logic and experiment'.[9] The laws of nature, according to this view of science, are "beyond the relativity of language." Like most feminists, Keller rejects this view of science which, she asserts, imposes a coercive, hierarchical and conformist pattern on scientific inquiry. Feminists in general are sceptical about the possibility of finding a universal and objective foundation for knowledge that Morgenthau claims is possible. Most share the belief that knowledge is socially constructed: since it is language that transmits knowledge, the use of language and its claims of objectivity must continually be questioned.

Keller argues that objectivity, as it is usually defined in our culture, is associated with masculinity. She identifies it as "a network of interactions between gender development, a belief system that equates objectivity with masculinity, and a set of cultural values that simultaneously (and cojointly) elevates what is defined as scientific and what is defined as masculine."[10] Keller links the separation of self from other, an important stage of masculine gender development, with this notion of objectivity. Translated into scientific inquiry this becomes the striving for the separation of subject and object, an important goal of modern science and one, which Keller asserts, is based on the need for control; hence objectivity becomes associated with power and domination.

The need for control has been an important motivating force for modern realism. To begin his search for an objective, rational theory of international politics, which could impose order on a chaotic and conflictual world, Morgenthau constructs an abstraction which he calls political man, a beast completely lacking in moral restraints. Morgenthau is deeply aware that real man, like real states, is both moral and bestial but, because states do not live up to the universal moral laws that govern the universe, those who behave morally in international politics are doomed to failure because of the immoral actions of others. To solve this tension, Morgenthau postulates a realm of international politics in which the amoral behavior of political man is not only permissible but prudent. It is a Hobbesian world, separate and distinct from the world of domestic order, in which states may act like beasts, for survival depends on a maximisation of power and a willingness to fight.

Having long argued that the personal is political, most feminist theory would reject the validity of constructing an autonomous political sphere around which boundaries of permissible modes of conduct have been drawn. As Keller maintains, "the demarcation between public and private not only defines and defends the boundaries of the political but also helps form its content and style.''[11] Morgenthau's political man is a social construct which is based on a partial representation of human nature. One might well ask where the women were in Hobbes' state of nature; presumably they must have been involved in reproduction and childrearing, rather than warfare, if life was to go on for more than one generation.[12] Morgenthau's emphasis on the conflictual aspects of the international system contributes to a tendency, shared by other realists, to deemphasise elements of cooperation and regeneration which are also aspects of international relations.[13]

Morgenthau's construction of an amoral realm of international power politics is an attempt to resolve what he sees as a fundamental tension between the moral laws that govern the universe and the requirements of successful political action in a world where states use morality as a cloak to justify the pursuit of their own national interests. Morgenthau's universalistic morality postulates the highest form of morality as an abstract ideal, similar to the Golden Rule, to which states seldom adhere: the morality of states is an instrumental morality which is guided by self-interest. Morgenthau's hierarchical ordering of morality contains parallels with the work of psychologist Lawrence Kohlberg. Based on a study of the moral development of eighty-four American boys, Kohlberg concludes that the highest stage of human moral development (which he calls stage six) is the ability to recognise abstract universal principles of justice; lower on the scale (stage two) is an instrumental morality concerned with serving one's own interests while recognising that others have interests too. Between

these two is an interpersonal morality which is contextual and characterised by sensitivity to the needs of others (stage three).[14]

In her critique of Kohlberg's stages of moral development, Carol Gilligan argues that they are based on a masculine conception of morality. On Kohlberg's scale, women rarely rise above the third or contextual stage but Gilligan claims that this is not a sign of inferiority, but of difference. Since women are socialised into a mode of thinking which is contextual and narrative, rather than formal and abstract, they tend to see issues in contextual rather than in abstract terms.[15] In international relations, the tendency to think about morality either in terms of abstract, universal and unattainable standards or as purely instrumental, as Morgenthau does, detracts from our ability to tolerate cultural differences and to seek potential for building community in spite of these differences.

Using examples from the feminist literature, I have suggested that Morgenthau's attempt to construct an objective, universal theory of international politics is rooted in assumptions about human nature and morality that, in modern Western culture, are associated with masculinity. Further evidence that Morgenthau's principles are not the basis for a universalistic and objective theory is contained in his frequent references to the failure of what he calls the ''legalistic-moralistic'' or idealist approach to world politics which he claims was largely responsible for both the World Wars. Having laid the blame for the Second World War on the misguided morality of appeasement, Morgenthau's *realpolitik* prescriptions for successful political action appear as prescriptions for avoiding the mistakes of the 1930s rather than as prescriptions with timeless applicability.

If Morgenthau's world view is embedded in the traumas of the Second World War, are his prescriptions still valid as we move further away from this event? I share with other critics of realism the view that, in a rapidly changing world, we must begin to search for modes of behaviour different from those prescribed by Morgenthau. Given that any war between the major powers is likely to be nuclear, increasing security by increasing power could be suicidal.[16] Moreover, the nation-state, the primary constitutive element of the international system for Morgenthau and other realists, is no longer able to deal with an increasingly pluralistic array of problems ranging from economic interdependence to environmental degradation. Could feminist theory make a contribution to international relations theory by constructing an alternative, feminist perspective on international politics that might help us search for more appropriate solutions?

A FEMINIST PERSPECTIVE ON INTERNATIONAL RELATIONS

If the way in which we describe reality has an effect on the ways we perceive and act upon our environment, new perspectives might lead us to consider alternative courses of action. With this in mind, I shall first examine two important concepts in international relations, power and security, from a feminist perspective and then discuss some feminist approaches to conflict resolution.

Morgenthau's definition of power, the control of man over man, is typical of the way power is usually defined in international relations. Nancy Hartsock argues that this type of power as domination has always been associated with masculinity since the exercise of power has generally been a masculine activity; rarely have women exercised legitimised power in the public domain. When women write about power they stress energy, capacity and potential says Hartsock, and she notes that women theorists, even when they have little else in common, offer similar definitions of power which differ substantially from the understanding of power as domination.[17]

Hannah Arendt, frequently cited by feminists writing about power, defines power as the human ability to act in concert, or action which is taken in connection with others who share similar concerns.[18] This definition of power is similar to that of psychologist, David McClelland's portrayal of female power which he describes as shared rather than assertive.[19] Jane Jaquette argues that, since women have had less access to the instruments of coercion, women have been more apt to rely on power as persuasion; she compares women's domestic activities to coalition-building.[20]

All of these writers are portraying power as a relationship of mutual enablement. Tying her definition of female power to international relations, Jaquette sees similarities between female strategies of persuasion and strategies of small states operating from a position of weakness in the international system. There are also examples of states' behaviour which contain elements of the female strategy of coalition-building. One such example is the Southern African Development Co-ordination Conference (SADCC) which is designed to build regional infrastructures based on mutual co-operation and collective self-reliance in order to decrease dependence on the South African economy. Another is the

European Community, which has had considerable success in building mutual co-operation in an area of the world whose history would not predict such a course of events.[21] It is rare, however, that co-operative outcomes in international relations are described in these terms, though Karl Deutsch's notion of pluralistic security communities might be one such example where power is associated with building community.[22] I am not denying that power as domination is a pervasive reality in international relations, but sometimes there are also elements of co-operation in inter-state relations which tend to be obscured when power is seen solely as domination. Thinking about power in this multidimensional sense may help us to think constructively about the potential for co-operation as well as conflict, an aspect of international relations generally downplayed by realism.

Redefining national security is another way in which feminist theory could contribute to new thinking about international relations.[23] Traditionally in the West, the concept of national security has been tied to military strength and its role in the physical protection of the nation-state from external threats. Morgenthau's notion of defending the national interest in terms of power is consistent with this definition. But this traditional definition of national security is partial at best in today's world.[24] When advanced states are highly interdependent, and rely on weapons whose effects would be equally devastating to winners and losers alike, defending national security by relying on war as the last resort no longer appears very useful. Moreover, if one thinks of security in North-South rather than East-West terms, for a large portion of the world's population, security has as much to do with the satisfaction of basic material needs as with military threats. According to Johan Galtung's notion of structural violence, the lowering of life expectancy by virtue of where one happens to be born is a form of violence whose effects can be as devastating as war.[25] Basic needs satisfaction has a great deal to do with women, but only recently have women's roles as providers of basic needs, and in development more generally, become visible as important components in devising development strategies.[26] Traditionally the development literature has focused on aspects of the development process which are in the public sphere, are technologically complex and are usually undertaken by men. Thinking about the role of women in development and the way in which we can define development and basic needs satisfaction to be inclusive of women's roles and needs are topics which deserve higher priority on the international agenda. Typically, however, this is an area about which traditional international relations theory, with its prioritising of order over justice, has had very little to say.

A further threat to national security, more broadly defined, which also has not been on the agenda of traditional international relations, concerns the environment. Carolyn Merchant argues that a mechanistic view of nature, contained in modern science, has helped to guide an industrial and technological development which has resulted in the environmental damage that is now becoming a matter of global concern. In the introduction to her book, *The Death of Nature,* Merchant suggests that, "Women and nature have an age-old association—an affiliation that has persisted throughout culture, language, and history."[27] Hence she maintains that the ecology movement, which is growing up in response to these environmental threats, and the women's movement are deeply interconnected. Both stress living in equilibrium with nature rather than dominating it; both see nature as a living non-hierarchical entity in which each part is mutually dependent on the whole. Ecologists, as well as many feminists, are now suggesting that only with such a fundamental change in the way we view the world could we devise solutions that would allow the human species to survive the damage which we are inflicting on the environment.

Thinking about military, economic and environmental security in interdependent terms suggests the need for new methods of conflict resolution which seek to achieve mutually beneficial, rather than zero-sum, outcomes. One such method comes from Sara Ruddick's work on "maternal thinking."[28] Ruddick describes "maternal thinking" as focused on the preservation of life and the growth of children; to foster a domestic environment conducive to these goals, tranquillity must be preserved by avoiding conflict where possible, engaging in it non-violently and restoring community when it is over. In such an environment the ends for which disputes are fought are subordinated to the means by which they are resolved. This method of conflict resolution involves making contextual judgements rather than appealing to absolute standards and thus has much in common with Gilligan's definition of female morality.

While non-violent resolution of conflict in the domestic sphere is a widely accepted norm, passive resistance in the public realm is regarded as deviant. But, as Ruddick argues, the peaceful resolution of conflict by mothers does not usu-ally extend to the children of one's enemies, an important reason why women have been ready to support men's wars.[29] The question for Ruddick then becomes how to get "maternal thinking," a mode of thinking which she believes can be found in men as well as women, out into the public realm. Ruddick believes that finding a common humanity among one's opponents has become a condition of survival in the nuclear age when the notion of winners and losers has become questionable.[30] Portraying the adversary as less than human has all too often been a technique of the nation-state to command loyalty and increase its legitimacy in the eyes of its citizens but such behaviour in the nuclear age may eventually be self-defeating.

We might also look to Gilligan's work for a feminist perspective on conflict resolution. Reporting on a study of playground behaviour of American boys and girls, Gilligan argues that girls are less able to tolerate high levels of conflict, more likely than boys to play games which involve taking turns and in which the success of one does not depend on the failure of another.[31] While Gilligan's study does not take into account attitudes toward other groups (racial, ethnic, economic, or national), it does suggest the validity of investigating whether girls are socialised to use different modes of problem-solving when dealing with conflict, and whether such behaviour might be useful to us in thinking about international conflict resolution.

TOWARD A FEMINIST EPISTEMOLOGY OF INTERNATIONAL RELATIONS

I am deeply aware that there is no one feminist approach but many which come out of various disciplines and intellectual traditions. Yet there are common themes in these different feminist literatures that I have reviewed, which could help us to begin to formulate a feminist epistemology of international relations. Morgenthau encourages us to try to stand back from the world and to think about theory-building in terms of constructing a rational outline or map that has universal applications. In contrast, the feminist literature reviewed here emphasises connection and contingency. Keller argues for a form of knowledge, which she calls "dynamic objectivity," "that grants to the world around us its independent integrity, but does so in a way that remains cognizant of, indeed relies on, our connectivity with that world,"[32] Keller illustrates this mode of thinking in her study of Barbara McClintock, whose work on genetic transposition won her a Nobel prize after many years of marginalisation by the scientific community.[33] McClintock, Keller argues, was a scientist with a respect for complexity, diversity and individual difference whose methodology allowed her data to speak rather than imposing explanations on it.

Keller's portrayal of McClintock's science contains parallels with what Sandra Harding calls an African world view.[34] Harding tells us that the Western liberal notion of rational economic man, an individualist and a welfare maximiser, similar to rational political man upon which realism has based its theoretical investigations, does not make any sense in the African world view where the individual is seen as part of the social order acting within that order rather than upon it. Harding believes that this view of human behaviour has much in common with a feminist perspective. If we combine this view of human behaviour with Merchant's holistic perspective, which stresses the interconnectedness of all things including nature, it may help us to begin to think from a more global perspective which appreciates cultural diversity but at the same time recognises a growing interdependence which makes anachronistic the exclusionary thinking fostered by the nation-state system.

Keller's "dynamic objectivity," Harding's African world view and Merchant's ecological thinking all point us in the direction of an appreciation of the "other" as a subject whose views are as legitimate as our own, a way of thinking that has been sadly lacking in the history of international relations. Just as Keller cautions us against the construction of a feminist science, which could perpetuate these same exclusionary attitudes, Harding warns us against schema which contrast people by race, gender or class and which originate within projects of social domination. Feminist thinkers generally dislike dichotomisation and the distancing of subject from object that goes with abstract thinking, both of which, they believe, encourage a we/they attitude so characteristic of international relations. Instead this literature points us toward constructing epistemologies which value ambiguity and difference, qualities that could stand us in good stead as we begin to build a human or ungendered theory of international relations containing elements of both masculine and feminine modes of thought.

MORGENTHAU'S PRINCIPLES OF POLITICAL REALISM: A FEMINIST REFORMULATION

In the first part of this article I used feminist theory to develop a critique of

Morgenthau's principles of political realism in order to demonstrate how the theory and practice of international relations may exhibit a masculine bias. I then suggested some contributions which feminist theory might make to reconceptualising some important concepts in international relations and to thinking about a feminist epistemology. Drawing on these observations, I will now conclude with a feminist reformulation of Morgenthau's six principles of political realism, outlined earlier in this paper, which might help us to begin to think differently about international relations. I shall not use the term realism since feminists believe that there are multiple realities: a truly realistic picture of international politics must recognise elements of co-operation as well as conflict, morality as well as *realpolitik,* and the strivings for justice as well as order.[35] This reformulation may help us begin to think in these multidimensional terms:

1. A feminist perspective believes that objectivity, as it is culturally defined, is associated with masculinity. Therefore, supposedly "objective" laws of human nature are based on a partial masculine view of human nature. Human nature is both masculine and feminine: it contains elements of social reproduction and development as well as political domination. Dynamic objectivity offers us a more connected view of objectivity with less potential for domination.

2. A feminist perspective believes that the national interest is multidimensional and contextually contingent. Therefore it cannot be defined solely in terms of power. In the contemporary world the national interest demands co-operative rather than zero-sum solutions to a set of interdependent global problems which include nuclear war, economic well-being and environmental degradation.

3. Power cannot be infused with meaning that is universally valid. Power as domination and control privileges masculinity and ignores the possibility of collective empowerment, another aspect of power often associated with feminity.

4. A feminist perspective rejects the possibility of separating moral command from political action. All political action has moral significance. The realist agenda for maximising order through power and control prioritises the moral command of order over those of justice and the satisfaction of basic needs necessary to ensure social reproduction.

5. While recognising that the moral aspirations of particular nations cannot be equated with universal moral principles, a feminist perspective seeks to find common moral elements in human aspirations which could become the basis for de-escalating international conflict and building international community.

6. A feminist perspective denies the validity of the autonomy of the political. Since autonomy is associated with masculinity in Western culture, disciplinary efforts to construct a world view which does not rest on a pluralistic conception of human nature, are partial and masculine. Building boundaries around a narrowly defined political realm defines political in a way that excludes the concerns and contributions of women.

In constructing this feminist alternative, I am not denying the validity of

Morgenthau's work. Adding a feminist perspective to the epistemology of international relations, however, is a stage through which we must pass if we are to begin to think about constructing an ungendered or human science of international politics which is sensitive to, but goes beyond, both masculine and feminine perspectives. Such inclusionary thinking, which, as Simone de Beauvoir tells us, values the bringing forth of life as much as the risking of life, is becoming imperative in a world where the technology of war and a fragile natural environment are threatening human existence. This ungendered or human discourse becomes possible only when women are adequately represented in the discipline and when there is equal respect for the contributions of both women and men alike.

NOTES

An earlier version of this paper was presented at the symposium on Women and International Relations at the London School of Economics in June 1988. I am grateful to Hayward Alker, Jr. and Susan Okin for their careful reading of the manuscript and helpful suggestions.

1. Quoted in Sandra Harding, *The Science Question in Feminism* (Ithaca, NY: Cornell University Press, 1986), p. 148.
2. In 1987 only 4.8 per cent of the top career Foreign Service employees were women. Statement of Patricia Schroeder before the Committee on Foreign Affairs, US House of Representatives, *Women's Perspectives on US Foreign Policy: A Compilation of Views,* (Washington, DC: US Government Printing Office, 1988), p. 4. For an analysis of women's roles in the American military, see Cynthia Enloe, *Does Khaki Become You? The Militaris-*

ation of Women's Lives. (London: Pluto Press, 1983).
3. Edward P. Crapol (ed.), *Women and American Foreign Policy* (Westport, CT: Greenwood Press, 1987), p. 167.
4. For an analysis of the role of masculine language in shaping strategic thinking see Carol Cohn, "Sex and Death in the Rational World of Defense Intellectuals," *Signs: Journal of Women in Culture and Society* (Vol. 12, No. 4, Summer 1987), pp. 687–718.
5. The claim for the dominance of the realist paradigm is supported by John A. Vasquez, "Colouring it Morgenthau: New Evidence for an Old Thesis on Quantitative International Studies," *British Journal of International Studies* (Vol. 5. No. 3, Oct. 1979), pp. 210–28. For a critique of Morgenthau's ambiguous use of language, see Inis L. Claude Jr., *Power and International Relations* (New York: Random House, 1962), especially pp. 25–37.
6. These are drawn from the six principles of political realism in Hans Morgenthau, *Politics Among Nations: The Struggle for Power and Peace,* 5th Revised Ed. (New York: Alfred Knopf, 1973), pp. 4–15. I am aware that these principles embody only a partial statement of Morgenthau's very rich study of international politics, a study which deserves a much more detailed analysis than I can give it here.
7. This list is a composite of the male/female dichotomies which appear in Evelyn Fox Keller, *Reflections on Gender and Science* (New Haven, CT: Yale University Press, 1985) and Sandra Harding, *op. cit.*
8. Inge K. Broverman, Susan R. Vogel, Donald M. Broverman, Frank E. Clarkson and Paul S. Rosenkranz, "Sex-Role Stereotypes: A Current Appraisal," *Journal of Social Issues* (Vol. 28, No. 2, 1972), pp. 59–78. Replication of this research in the 1980s confirms that these perceptions still hold.
9. Keller, *op. cit.,* p. 130.

10. *ibid.,* p. 89.

11. *ibid.,* p. 9.

12. Sara Ann Ketchum, "Female Culture, Womanculture and Conceptual Change: Toward a Philosophy of Women's Studies," *Social Theory and Practice* (Vol. 6. No. 2, Summer 1980), pp. 151–62.

13. Others have questioned whether Hobbes' state of nature provides an accurate description of the international system. See, for example, Charles Beitz, *Political Theory and International Relations* (Princeton, NJ: Princeton University Press, 1979), pp. 35–50, and Stanley Hoffmann, *Duties Beyond Borders* (Syracuse, NY: Syracuse University Press, 1981), ch. 1.

14. Kohlberg's stages of moral development are described and discussed in Robert Kegan, *The Evolving Self: Problem and Process in Human Development* (Cambridge, MA: Harvard University Press, 1982), ch. 2.

15. Gilligan's critique of Kohlberg appears in Carol Gilligan, *In a Different Voice: Psychological Theory and Women's Development* (Cambridge, MA: Harvard University Press, 1982), ch. 1.

16. There is evidence that, toward the end of his life, Morgenthau himself was aware that his own prescriptions were becoming anachronistic. In a seminar presentation in 1978, he suggested that power politics as the guiding principle for the conduct of international relations had become fatally defective. For a description of this seminar presentation, see Francis Anthony Boyle, *World Politics and International Law* (Durham, NC: Duke University Press, 1985), pp. 70–4.

17. Nancy C. M. Hartsock, *Money, Sex and Power: Toward a Feminist 'Historical' Materialism* (Boston, MA: Northeastern University Press, 1983), p. 210.

18. Hannah Arendt, *On Violence* (New York: Harcourt, Brace and World, 1969), p. 44. Arendt's definition of power, as it relates to international relations, is discussed more extensively in Jean Bethke Elshtain,

"Reflections on War and Political Discourse: Realism, Just War, and Feminism in a Nuclear Age," *Political Theory* (Vol. 13, No. 1, Feb. 1985), pp. 39–57.

19. David McClelland, "Power and the Feminine Role" in David McClelland, *Power, The Inner Experience* (New York: Wiley, 1975), ch. 3.

20. Jane S. Jaquette, "Power as Ideology: A Feminist Analysis" in Judith H. Stiehm, *Women's Views of the Political World of Men* (Dobbs Ferry, NY: Transnational Publishers, 1984), ch. 2.

21. These examples are cited in Christine Sylvester, "The Emperor's Theories and Transformations: Looking at the Field Through Feminist Lenses" in Dennis Pirages and Christine Sylvester (eds.), *Transformations in the Global Political Economy* (New York: Macmillan, forthcoming).

22. Karl W. Deutsch, *Political Community and the North Atlantic Area* (Princeton, NJ: Princeton University Press, 1957).

23. "New thinking" is a term that is also being used in the Soviet Union to describe foreign policy reformulations under Gorbachev. There are indications that the Soviets are beginning to conceptualise security in the multidimensional terms described here. See Margot Light, *The Soviet Theory of International Relations* (New York: St. Martin's Press, 1988), ch. 10.

24. This is the argument made in Edward Azar and Chung-in Moon, "Third World National Security: Toward a New Conceptual Framework," *International Interactions* (Vol. 11, No. 2, 1984), pp. 103–35.

25. Johan Galtung, "Violence, Peace, and Peace Research" in Johan Galtung, *Essays in Peace Research,* Vol. 1 (Copenhagen: Christian Ejlers, 1975), ch. 1.4.

26. See, for example, Gita Sen and Caren Grown, *Development, Crises and Alternative Visions: Third World Women's Perspectives* (New York: Monthly Review

Press, 1987). This is an example of a growing literature on women and development which deserves more attention from the international relations community.

27. Carolyn Merchant, *The Death of Nature: Women, Ecology and the Scientific Revolution* (New York: Harper and Row, 1982), p. xv.

28. Sara Ruddick, "Maternal Thinking" and Sara Ruddick, "Preservative Love and Military Destruction: Some Reflections on Mothering and Peace" in Joyce Treblicot, *Mothering: Essays in Feminist Theory* (Totowa, NJ: Rowman and Allanheld, 1984), ch. 13-4.

29. For a more extensive analysis of this issue, see Jean Bethke Elshtain, *Women and War* (New York: Basic Books, 1987).

30. This type of conflict resolution bears similarities to the problem solving approach of Edward Azar, John Burton and Herbert Kelman. See, for example, Edward E. Azar and John W. Burton, *International Conflict Resolution: Theory and Practice* (Brighton: Wheatsheaf Books, 1986) and Herbert C. Kelman, "Interactive Problem Solving: A Social-Psychological Approach to Conflict Resolution" in W. Klassen (ed.), *Dialogue Toward Inter-Faith Understanding,* (Tantur/Jerusalem: Ecumenical Institute for Theoretical Research, 1986), pp. 293-314.

31. Gilligan, *op. cit.,* pp. 9-10.

32. Keller, *op. cit.,* p. 117.

33. Evelyn Fox Keller, *A Feeling for the Organism: The Life and Work of Barbara McClintock,* (New York: Freeman, 1983).

34. Harding *op. cit.,* ch. 7.

35. "Utopia and reality are . . . the two facets of political science. Sound political thought and sound political life will be found only where both have their place." E. H. Carr, *The Twenty Years Crisis, 1919-1939* (New York: Harper and Row, 1964), p. 10.

QUESTIONS

1. According to Tickner, what elements of realism are defined in masculine terms? What weaknesses does Tickner identify with this?

2. Describe the elements of the feminist perspective on international relations. How do they differ from the traditional realist view?

42.   The Gender of World Politics

V. Spike Peterson and Ann Sisson Runyan

In this excerpt from their book *Global Gender Issues.*, V. Spike Peterson and Ann Sisson Runyan discuss the "hidden gender at work in conventional" international relations theory. In addition, the authors analyze gender in world politics along three lines: normatively, conceptually, and organizationally.

V. Spike Peterson is assistant professor of Political Science at the University of Arizona. Anne Sisson Runyan is associate professor of Political Science at the University of New York at Potsdam.

POLITICS AND POWER

Masculinism pervades politics. Wendy Brown wrote: "More than any other kind of human activity, *politics* has historically borne an explicitly masculine identity. It has been more exclusively limited to men than any other realm of endeavor and has been more intensely, self-consciously masculine than most other social practices."[1]

In IR, as in political science, power is usually defined as "power-over," specifically, the ability to get someone to do what you want. It is usually measured by control of resources, especially those supporting physical coercion. This definition emphasizes separation and competition: Those who have power use it (or its threat) to keep others from securing enough to threaten them. The emphasis on material resources and coercive ability obscures the fact that power reckoning is embedded in sociocultural dynamics and value systems. Also obscured is the way that power presupposes relationships—among actors, resources, meaning, situation—and its inability to be accurately understood when separated from these relationships.

In IR the concept of "political actor"—the legitimate wielder of society's power—is derived from classical political theory. Common to constructions of "political man"—from Plato and Aristotle to Hobbes, Locke, and Rousseau—is the privileging of man's capacity for reason. This unique ability distinguishes man from other animals and explains his pur-

suit of freedom—from nature as well as from tyranny. Feminists argue that the models of human nature underpinning constructions of "political man" are not in fact gender neutral but are models of "male nature," generated by exclusively male experience. They are not universal claims about humankind but masculinist claims about gendered divisions of labor and identity that effectively and sometimes explicitly exclude women from definitions of "human," "moral agent," "rational actor," and "political man."

Conceptually, "woman" is excluded primarily by denying her the rationality that marks "man" as the highest animal. Concretely, women have historically been excluded from political power by states' limiting citizenship to those who perform military duty and/or are property owners. Under these conditions, most women are structurally excluded from formal politics, even though individual women, in exceptional circumstances, have wielded considerable political power. In this century, women have largely won the battle for the vote, though definitions of citizenship continue to limit women's access to public power, and their political power is circumscribed by a variety of indirect means. . . . Most obvious are the continued effects of the dichotomy of public-private that separates men's productive and "political" activities from women's reproductive and "personal" activities.

These constructions—of power, "political man," citizenship, public-private, and so on—reproduce, often unconsciously, masculinist and androcentric assumptions. Sovereign man and sovereign states are defined not by connection or relationships but by autonomy in decision-making and freedom from the power of others. Security is understood not in terms of celebrating and sustaining life but as the capacity to be indifferent to "others" and, if necessary, to harm them. Hobbes's androcentrism is revealed simply when we ask how helpless infants ever become adults if human nature is universally competitive and hostile. From the perspective of child-rearing practices, it makes more sense to argue that humans are naturally cooperative: Without the cooperation that is required to nurture children, there would be no men or women. And although Aristotle acknowledged that the public sphere depends upon the production of life's necessities in the private sphere, he denied the power relations or politics that this implies.

Gender is most apparent in these constructions when we examine the dichotomies they (re)produce: political-apolitical, reason-emotion, public-private, leaders-followers, active-passive, freedom-necessity. As with other dichotomies, difference and opposition are privileged and context and ambiguity are ignored. The web of meaning and human interaction within which political man acts and politics takes place remains hidden, as if irrelevant. The point is not that power-over, aggressive behavior, and life-threatening conflicts are not "real" but that they are only a part of a more complicated story. Focusing on them misrepresents our reality even as it (to some extent unnecessarily) reproduces power-over, aggressive behavior, and life-threatening conflicts.

SECURITY AND VIOLENCE

Claims about men's superior strength are favored justifications for gender hierarchy. But such claims are misleading. On the one hand, men's strength varies cross-culturally and within cultures, and a considerable number of women are in fact stronger than men. On the other hand, what do we mean by strength? Anyone who has observed women of Africa on lengthy treks carrying heavy loads of firewood and water cannot help seeing how arbitrary our indicators of strength are. Why do we consider men's upper-body muscular strength more significant than women's burden-carrying strength and greater endurance? On what basis do we assume that bigger is better? (Consider the plight of dinosaurs!) Ashley Montagu undertook a comprehensive review of scientific literature and concluded that only androcentric lenses prevent our acknowledging the "natural superiority of women." Specifically, "the female is *constitutionally* stronger than the male": She has greater stamina, lives longer, fights disease better, and endures "all sorts of devitalizing conditions better than men: starvation, exposure, fatigue, shock, illness and the like."[2] Superiority is often defined in terms of the most effective survival traits—but not when women's abilities are assessed.

Historically, the greater muscular strength of (some) males has been a crucial factor when the outcome of conflicts depended on this particular strength. Today's technology dramatically alters the relationship of muscular strength to success in battle or in the workplace. But there continues to be a preoccupation with power and strength defined in masculine terms—upper-body strength as well as access to and use of weapons. And there is no denying that men, worldwide, engage in violent behaviors more frequently and with greater negative effect than do women. Males are encouraged to act aggressively in more situations than females and are systematically placed in situations where proving their manhood requires aggressive behavior. In fact, most models of masculinity include elements of courage and ambition that are difficult to disassociate from physical aggression and even violence. Ancient, classical, and modern depictions of warriors and political actors typically identify risking life—one's own and that of others—as the surest mark of a free man: "A real man lays his life on the line. For what is death risked? For honor, for glory, for a value greater than life, for freedom from enslavement by life, for immortality, or for the 'ultimate value' of the state."[3]

A willingness to engage in violence is built into our constructions of masculinity and is exacerbated by militarization—the extension of military practices into civilian life. And to the extent that we define national security as the defense and protection of sovereignty, militarization becomes hard to avoid. Believing that peace requires preparation for war, we become locked into arms races and other self-perpetuating cycles. These involve sacrificing social welfare objectives in favor of defense spending and training young people—men and women—to risk lives and practice violence in the name of putatively higher objectives.

There are no simple formulas for determining appropriate trade-offs between "butter" and "guns," and we are not suggesting that security concerns are illusory or easily resolved. But in a climate of militarization, we must be careful to assess the ostensible gains from encouraging violence because the actual costs are very great.

Moreover, the construction of security in military terms—understood as direct violence—often masks the systemic insecurity of indirect or structural violence.[4] The latter refers to reduced life expectancy as a consequence of oppressive political and economic structures (e.g., greater infant mortality among poor women who are denied access to healthcare services). Structural violence especially affects the lives of women and other subordinated groups. When we ignore this fact we ignore the security of the majority of the planet's occupants. Finally, because violence is gendered, militarization has a reciprocal relationship to masculinist ideologies: The macho effects of military activities, the objectifying effects of military technologies, and the violent effects of military spending *interact,* escalating not only arms races but also sexual violence.

What the gendered division of violence constructs is a world shaped by hostile forces. In a self-repeating cycle, threats (real or fictive) increase preparations for defense and/or retaliation that are inextricable from conditions of structural violence. An oppositional lens magnifies and legitimates self-other, us-them, friend-enemy, aggressive-passive, soldier-victim, and protector-protected dichotomies. The latter dichotomy is institutionalized in protection rackets: creating a threat and then charging for protection against it. Some theorists argue that nation-states engage in such rackets by creating a system of mutually threatening centralized governments and charging citizens taxes and military service to support effective defense of state boundaries.[5] Feminists have similarly identified marriage as a protection racket. Under conditions of systemic male violence, women are forced to seek protection by entering into disadvantageous marriages to individual men.[6] People often fail to see the repetition of the same pattern in different situations, recognize the self-perpetuating and costly nature of this violence, and seek a way to break these self-destructive cycles.

ECONOMICS AND LABOR

The division of gender and identities is nowhere clearer than in the ways we define "work" and in which kinds of work are most valued, who does what, and how much they are paid. The stereotypes of women and femininity here interact powerfully with the ideology of public-private to generate quite rigid patterns in what men and women do. Just as the public is seen as more important than the private, women's jobs and the status and pay they are accorded tend to be seen as "secondary," as providing the support system for "more important"—the "primary"—work that men, especially elite men, do. Thus we find that women's work is largely of a servicing nature: taking care of the emotional (e.g., counseling, nursing), "entertainment" (e.g., performing arts, sex industries), production (e.g., word processing, assembly-line jobs), and maintenance (e.g., cleaning, clerical, child care, teaching) needs of men as individuals and the masculinist social system generally.

Treated as secondary, these jobs are not assigned high status and are not well paid. And women who earn a paycheck rarely do less unpaid work at home. Instead, women worldwide have a "double workday": earning money for the family while also being held responsible for child care and household maintenance. It seems that women are expected, consistent with the stereotype of femininity, to labor both at home and in the workplace, not for status or income as we expect men to do, but purely for the joy of serving others. Whereas men may be asked to volunteer their time and energy for a special cause or specific occasion, women are expected to volunteer their entire lives in the service of male needs and masculinist social orders. Of course women are not entirely without benefits in these societies. Nor do *all* men benefit equally from the exploitation of women's labor. But as a generalization, all men do benefit in various ways from the systemic masculinism that treats women's energies, lives, intellects, demands, and needs as secondary.

Economic relations are addressed in IR almost exclusively through the lens of neoclassical economics. The ostensible "free market" of capitalist global relations is assumed to be the most efficient and therefore most desirable approach to national and international economic relations. Through this lens, an expanding world economy provides an ever-larger pie and, through a process of "trickle down," ever-bigger pies translate into larger slices, theoretically, even for those with few initial resources. Economic-development policies promote growth as the way to provide more goods and services to the world's rapidly increasing population. And capitalism is identified as the most effective system for securing growth.

In addition, formal modeling of exchange relations and market systems are popular in IR. These models appear to provide analytically powerful tools for understanding human decision-making and its cumulative consequences. On the basis of a rational actor's ("his") utilitarian assessment of market trade-offs, projections of other decision-making activities and their consequences are mapped. Thus game theory models are said to illuminate a wide range of human behaviors, such as responding to deprivation, making threats, risk-taking, and developing nuclear strategies. All such models leave out the complexity of human behaviors in real life because to make models workable, the variables they include must be reduced to a very few. The complex, ambiguous, and nuanced *context* of decision-making must be sacrificed to generate clear patterns that accommodate quantifiable analysis.

Left out are the hard-to-quantify dimensions of social reality, such as culture, emotional investments, and normative commitments. And once preference formation, prior conditions, and the context are considered irrelevant, it becomes hard to say what the relevance of the actual findings is. What does the study of behavior in poorly modeled situations tell us about behavior in the real world, in real-life decision-making? We do not argue that rational-actor modeling is useless. Rather, we ask and attempt to evaluate whether, in a context of scarce research resources, different approaches to IR would not contribute more to our ability to resolve global crises and reduce global inequality.

On the face of it, advocates of traditional approaches tend to reproduce rather than challenge the status quo because the questions they frame result in answers that confirm the assumptions upon which the questions are based. Gender dichotomies are built into the dualities favored by economic analysis: paid-unpaid work, providers-dependents, production-reproduction, and independence in the marketplace versus dependence. Just as women are deemed feminine by their dependence within the family, the Third World is "unmanned" by its position of dependence in the global economy. Finally, "trickle down" theories tend to benefit those who control the most resources by promoting the continued growth that delivers the biggest pieces of pie to those in power. Many argue that not only do the poorest never see the benefits of "trickle down" but even if they get marginally larger pieces, today's ecological crises (which hurt the poorest most) challenge the entire premise of ever-expanding growth.

EQUITY, ECOLOGY, AND RESOURCES

Traditional texts in world politics often contrast "high" and "low" politics. High politics are state-centric security and military affairs; low politics, economic relations. Even more removed from the traditional core of IR concerns are matters of ecology, which are often called "soft politics." Once again, a hierarchy is at work, pitting high over low and hard over soft politics. In recent years, the seriousness of environmental degradation and the dependence of *all* of us on sustainable ecology have prompted much greater attention to environmental issues. When we begin to take the environment seriously, we are forced to examine how resources are distributed and who controls them. It is not simply an increasing population but also the disproportionate and to a large extent irresponsible consumption of resources on the part of industrialized nations that exacerbate resource depletion.

What are the causes of ecological irresponsibility? We observe first that numerous variables interact in sometimes unpredictable ways to shape environmental use. Industrialization promotes resource consumption because it accelerates the consumption of fuels and other raw materials and fosters a growth mentality that condones environmental destruction and the waste of material and human resources. Tragically, the "success" of industrialization and expansion leads to many failures. For example, in the United States the apparent wealth of resources contributes to wasteful attitudes like "bigger is better" and "growth is the answer," which dull environmental sensibilities, discourage recycling, and ignore the need to reduce consumption. We put short-term profit and convenience ahead of long-term security.

Nonindustrialized peoples rarely have the luxury of a throw-away mentality. Without the illusion of constant growth, many live in a symbiotic relationship with their environment. There is neither need nor advantage in wasteful or unnecessary consumption. However, the presence of growing populations in resource-poor environments also creates environmental degradation. People are forced to secure their everyday subsistence by depleting the very resources they depend upon. Water, food, and fuel for domestic use are essential for life, but the acquisition and consumption of these goods in much of the Third World conflict with long-term ecological planning and resources. At the macrosocietal level, development policies—whether securing foreign currency through the sale of timber or building an industrial base with fossil-fuel-driven factories—often have costly ecological consequences. The choices are not easy.

Gender divisions are played out in terms of who has access to what resources, who controls resources and to what ends, who suffers most from environmental degradation, and how gender stereotypes relate to irresponsible resource use. At core, the characteristically Western ideology of limitless growth presupposes a belief in "man's" dominion over nature (promoted, for example, in Christian and capitalist belief systems) and the desirability of "man's" exploiting nature to further his own ends. Conquering nature, digging out her treasure and secrets, proving man's superiority through manipulation of nature—these are familiar and currently deadly refrains. The identification of nature as female is not an accident but a historical development that is visible in justifications by elites for territorial and intellectual expansion. Exploitation is most readily legitimated by "objectifying"—treating something or someone to be exploited as an "object" devoid of intelligence or feelings. Thus, "natural resources" are deemed exploitable by right, no questions asked, "there for the taking." Historically, women, colonies, and the earth's bounty have all been treated as such natural resources. The gendered dichotomies of culture-nature, subject-object, exploiter-exploited, agency-passivity, and leader-follower are reproduced in the process and justification of exploiting human mothers and "mother nature."

Sustainable ecology and the equity it entails is gendered. Worldwide, females are more dramatically affected by environmental degradation than males. As food providers, the work load of women increases when water, food, and fuel resources deteriorate; as caretakers, they have to work harder when family and community members are victims of environmental disasters; as last and least fed, they suffer most from starvation and malnutrition; as poorest, they are least able to quit jobs, acquire adequate health care, purchase safer products, or move away from immediate environmental threats. As we illustrate in this text, women have long been active in ecological movements. But it is no longer "just women" who are systemically threatened by environmental crises.

CONCLUSION

We conclude . . . by looking at gender in world politics along three dimensions: normatively (how we evaluate), conceptually (how we categorize and think), and organizationally (how we act). In contrast to our approach, . . . writers of conventional accounts tend to deny the importance of gender, its relation to social inequalities, and, therefore, the moral costs imposed by gender hierarchy. In regard to the *normative dimension,* blindness to gender inequality is a consequence of reigning ideologies—religious and secular—that naturalize status quo masculinism. A paradox operates here because the exaggeration of gender differences both confirms the existence of gender inequality and depoliticizes that inequality by reducing it to "natural" gender difference.

Some writers "ignore" the politics (and costs) of gender hierarchy by claiming that gender is irrelevant to topics such as presidential politics or national security. Therefore, they "avoid" acknowledging gender inequality and the moral issues it raises. In this case, the moral costs of masculinism remain invisible on the false assumption that unless women are explicitly part of the picture or sexuality is central to the topic, gender is irrelevant. In contrast, stereotypical differences between men and women and the lives they lead are not only acknowledged by some writers—they are celebrated. In those accounts, the moral costs of masculinism remain invisible on the false assumption that gender differences are not *political*—and bear moral costs—but are natural, the inevitable consequence of biological difference. In both cases, denying the pervasive effects of gender has the consequence of obscuring gender inequality and the moral issues it raises.

Not only difference but also the privileging of men and masculinity over women and femininity are "justified" by the assumption that male being and knowing is the norm and is more valuable than female being and knowing. Androcentric moralities thus do not take into account how men's and women's lives differ and that such differences limit the applicability of evaluations based on male experience only. The problem is twofold: Androcentric moralities exclude or silence women's experience and moral orientations and also fail—normatively—to be critical of gender inequality and injustice.[7] In sum, gender remains normatively invisible as long as we do not see how extensively it operates and as long as we take the differences we see for granted, as givens rather than as political problems.

In world politics, the inequalities of power, the effects of direct and indirect violence, the disparities between rich and poor, and the unequally distributed costs of environmental degradation are most often deemed the regrettable but unavoidable price of "progress." Through a gender-sensitive lens we begin to ask how the highly acclaimed benefits of progress are distributed and who pays the greatest costs for them. We also ask what kind of morality operates to keep current inequities and their individual and systemic costs from becoming daily matters of public outrage.

We observe that progress looks most acceptable, even desirable, to those most advantaged by the status quo. If system transformations had only win-lose ramifications, these people would have the most to lose. Those who benefit the most are seldom aware of the extent of their privilege or its relation to the poverty of others (as most residents of the First World remain ignorant of Third World poverty and its relation to First World abundance). Of course, some of those who benefit endorse improvements for "others" who are "less fortunate" (trickle down). The point is that no conspiracy of greed or malintent need be posited. And although we can identify particular groups as generally benefiting more than others from systemic inequities, it is neither adequate nor accurate to hold any particular group solely responsible for structural effects. What we want to emphasize is that, however they originated in historical time, systemic or structural inequities are reproduced through the interaction of multiple variables, including the internalization of oppression by subordinated individuals, the abuse of power by those who wield it, the unaccountability of the marketplace, the institutional structures of racism, classism, ageism, and heterosexism, and it is these we must become aware of and transform.

It is in this sense that masculinism is key to understanding how we normatively accept rather than struggle against systemic inequities. As we argue in this text, masculinism and its twin, androcentrism, are ideologies that pervade our thinking, doing, and evaluating. They are ubiquitous and largely unquestioned. They not only institutionalize the particular hierarchy of masculine over feminine but also perpetuate belief in the inevitability of hierarchies in general. They emphasize abstract reason, objectification, and instrumentalism too often at the expense of attention to context and normative consequences. Their codification of oppositional, nonrelational categories promotes a silence on responsibility: By denying the *relationship of (inter) dependence* between fact and value, subject and object, exploiter and victim, and culture and nature, they obscure who has the greatest power—and therefore responsibility. Finally, these ideologies, to the considerable extent that they inform other normative orientations, blind us to how gender both creates and reproduces a world of multiple inequities that today threatens all of us.

The *conceptual dimension* refers to how patterns of thought make gender invisible. This includes the forms our thought takes (e.g., categories, dichotomies, stereotypes) and more encompassing or more structured systems of thinking (e.g., ideologies, theoretical frameworks, religion, science). Language is extremely important for patterning our thought; a vast literature now documents how gender—and the hierarchy it constructs—is built into the English language. As Laurel Richardson and Verta Taylor noted:

> Embedded in the language are such ideas as "women are adjuncts to men" (e.g., the use of the generic "man" or "he"); women's aspirations are and should be different than men's (e.g., "The secretary . . . *she*," "the pilot . . . *he*"); women remain immature and incompetent throughout adult life (e.g., "The girls—

office staff—have gone to lunch''); women are defined in terms of their sexual desirability (to men) whereas men are defined in terms of their sexual prowess. (Contrast the meanings of the supposedly equivalent words *spinster* and *bachelor, mistress* and *master, courtesan* and *courier,* etc.) As long as we speak the language we have acquired, we are not only speaking but also thinking in sex-stereotyping ways.[8]

English and other languages structure our thinking in dichotomies that emphasize difference, suggest timeless polarities, and thus obscure the interdependence, mutability, and complexity of the social world. The ideology of scientific objectivity structures subject-object and fact-value in dichotomies and thus directs our attention away from the actual and relevant sociopolitical relations of context. Finally, the privileged status of claims to "objectivity"—like claims to "reality"—marginalizes potential critiques.

The systematic effect of thinking in nonrelational categories is to exaggerate difference, separation, and inevitability. Rather than intimate a longer story and larger picture, nonrelational categories render events and beliefs as "givens," appearing inevitable because they are ahistorical and decontextual. If we are looking through the lens of "naturally given," we cannot even ask a variety of questions and cannot take seriously other challenges. Normative questions appear irrelevant or pointless and alternative visions appear necessarily utopian. If we think only in dichotomies—of objective-subjective and realist-idealist, then our attempts to criticize objectivity and realism are rendered immediately suspect—as irrational, illogical, idealistic, unreal. And it

looks as though any critique of objectivity or realism *must* entail its opposite: a complete denial rather than a partial critique.[9]

Gender is at work here because dichotomies, masculinism, and androcentrism are present. In academe as elsewhere, we rely on what men have thought, written, and concluded to establish the "givens" of our discourses. That which pertains to the lives and experience of elite males is taken as the norm and defined as good. Thus, autonomy and freedom, independence from and power over others, separation from and control over nature, military and technological mastery, exploring and taming frontiers—these are given privileged status and held to be good for everybody. However, these values not only fail to benefit everybody; they no longer (if ever) unproblematically benefit elite men. And they have never afforded accurate understandings of the world. These orientations are not all bad, but their pursuit at the expense of other values has always been costly. Without exposing and examining the trade-offs, we continue to live irresponsibly and limit ourselves intellectually.

In terms of the *organizational dimension,* gender is rendered invisible primarily by the androcentric focus on what men do. By taking male experience as the norm and privileging it as the most important to know about, we find ourselves focusing on some activities at the expense of others. This is most obvious in terms of public-private domains and the elevation of men's issues, experiences, and activities over women's. But it is also present in academe, where "hard sciences" (chemistry, biology) and fields noted for logic (physics, philosophy) and instrumentalism (engineering, business administration) are male dominated and accorded the greatest prestige and authority. Outside of the academy, we pay more attention to areas of masculine interest (heart disease, rocketry, corporations) over feminine concerns (breast cancer, contraception, child care). In world politics we focus on national and international leaders, wars and militarization, and the high stakes of global economics.

What these patterns obscure are the relationships between activities, how they are mutually structured, and how alternatives can be pursued. They also obscure the social costs of separating production from reproduction, science from social values, politics from economics, and public from private life. Losing sight of history—forgetting that we *make* our world—locks us into patterns that have never served global justice and may now threaten even the most advantaged. For example, the expansion of global capitalism is associated with the increasing power of transnational corporations and their decision-making elites as well as with a greater reliance on high technologies and the professional class they foster. These developments threaten the majority of the planet's inhabitants in at least two profound ways.

First, the concentration of resources and power in the hands of a few is always suspect; when those few are not accountable to any public constituency, the threat is even greater that they will abuse their power. Second, the consumption of resources in relation to global ecology is dramatically shaped by the operations of giant corporations. The abuse of power through its concentration and the misuse of resources through their control by a small elite in the pursuit of profit combine in today's world. This restricts the opportunities available to the vast majority in every country and throughout the world. In various ways, we *all* participate in reproducing the inequity and imbalance that maintains the status quo. And in quite different but also costly ways, we *all* are impoverished by the status quo and the structural violence it entails.

NOTES

1. Wendy Brown, *Manhood and Politics* (Totowa, N.J.: Rowman and Littlefield, 1988), p. 4.
2. Ashley Montagu, *The Natural Superiority of Women* (New York: Collier Books, 1974), pp. 61–62.
3. W. Brown, *Manhood*, p. 182.
4. See Simon Dalby, "Security, Modernity, Ecology: The Dilemmas of Post Cold War Security Discourse," *Alternatives* 17 (1992): 95–133; V. Spike Peterson, "Security and Sovereign States: What Is at Stake in Taking Feminism Seriously?" in *Gendered States,* ed. V. Spike Peterson (Boulder, Colo.: Lynne Rienner Publishers, 1992), pp. 31–64.
5. For example, see Charles Tilly, "War Making and State Making as Organized Crime," in *Bringing the State Back In,* ed. Peter Evans, Dietrich Rueschemeyer, and Theda Skocpol (New York: Cambridge University Press, 1985).
6. Peterson, "Security and Sovereign States."
7. Historically, moralities generated from women's lives and experiences have been silenced or subordinated. In regard to facing difficult moral choices, Carol Gilligan argued that women are more likely to emphasize responsibility and care, whereas men are more likely to emphasize a weighing of rights. See Gilligan, *In a Different Voice* (Cambridge: Harvard University Press, 1982). Important feminist treatments of justice include Susan Moller Okin,

Justice, Gender, and the Family (New York: Basic Books, 1989); Iris Marion Young, *Justice and the Politics of Difference* (Princeton: Princeton University Press, 1990).

8. Richardson and Taylor, *Feminist Frontiers,* p. 2.

9. For a discussion of the implications for international relations of postpositivist and feminist critiques, see V. Spike Peterson, "Transgressing Boundaries: Theories of Knowledge, Gender, and International Relations," *Millennium* 21 (Summer 1992): 183–206.

QUESTIONS

1. What new insights do the authors contribute to the study of international relations?

2. Do you agree with the authors' contention that the study of international relations is based on "masculinist" notions of power and competition?

Chapter 10

PEACE STUDIES THEORY

COMPONENTS OF PEACE STUDIES THEORY

Focus of Analysis ········▶	• Promoting principles of positive peace
Major Actors ········▶	• Individuals • Individuals working through groups
Approach of Peace Studies ········▶	• Interdisciplinary • Value-oriented
Goals of Peace Studies ········▶	• Social justice, human rights, economic opportunity, and political equality • Building bridges between nations through person-to-person contact
Key Concepts ········▶	• Negative peace; Personal transformation; Positive peace; Value

INTRODUCTION

We complete our look at the individual level of analysis with an examination of peace studies theory. Like feminist theory, it is a relatively new approach to the study of international relations and pushes boldly past many of the guiding principles that commonly characterize the study of foreign policy and the behavior of states. That is, peace studies theorists argue that the study of international affairs should reach beyond the more traditional evaluations and measurements of power, balance of power, and national security. Particularly in our increasingly interconnected world, issues such as poverty, social injustice, and environmental destruction, to name only a few, reach to the heart of our security as human beings. We might say that peace studies suggests there can be no national security in the traditional sense until there is social, economic, and political justice on a global scale.

These elements come together to form a foundation for a theory emphasizing nonviolence, equality, and working—both independently and together—for the collective good. As the name implies, peace studies involves the study of peace and ways to promote peace within the international community. Though proponents aspire to this global cause, we have included peace studies in our look at the individual level of analysis. The reason behind this classification is, as we will discuss in greater detail later, that profound change on an international level begins with personal transformation. **Personal transformation,** in this sense, is a change or shift in an individual's outlook, habits, or worldview in a way that makes that individual more socially conscious of the global affect of his or her actions. The implication is that each of us, working as individuals, can have a positive influence on a much larger, even global, scale—a positive energy "ripple effect," if you will. In this way, peace studies opens up some new possibilities about how we might view the world and our own role within the global community.

PEACE STUDIES: AN INTERDISCIPLINARY APPROACH TO INTERNATIONAL RELATIONS THEORY

Though the study of international relations, with its theories and levels of analysis, generally falls in the realm of political science, peace studies is actually an interdisciplinary field. In incorporates information, analyses, and discourse from not only political science but also the traditional hard sciences (such as physics and mathematics), psychology, anthropology, sociology, and areas of the humanities (such as literature and linguistics). In our first article "The Evolution of Peace Studies," Carolyn M. Stephenson points to this intellectual crossover as one of several key characteristics that distinguish peace studies theory from other paradigms found in the study of international affairs. Using this broad base of information, the theory can examine a full range of human activities and behavior—from peaceful to violent—and can analyze these activities from hard science and social science perspectives.

Another inclusive characteristic of peace studies as a theory and method for studying international relations is its broad historical look at human interaction. The historical reach of peace studies extends farther back than most other fields in examining the patterns and traditions in our relationships with one another. It also projects various scenarios for future world orders. These projected scenarios are based, according to Stephenson, on alternatives to the traditional nation-state structure commonly used as a standard for analysis by other theorists in the international relations field. What is meant by this is that links between individuals or groups might be based not simply on territorial boundaries or geographic proximity (states or blocs of states within a region), but on common interests, ideas, beliefs, or goals (religion, environmental concerns, etc.).

In addition to the inclusive approach of peace studies theory, Stephenson emphasizes that it is also a prescriptive, rather than simply descriptive, paradigm. A prescriptive theory is a set of principles and guidelines that contain overt value judgments about how the world ought to be, rather than how the world actually is. A prescriptive theory actually contains specific recommendations with regard to foreign policy and the conduct of international relations. Peace studies does offer policies, political agendas, and other criteria and conditions designed to promote nonviolence and achieve peace. Thus, just as a physician prescribes medicine to cure an illness, these theorists prescribe a particular course of action to attain a particular end.

Peace studies also evaluates existing policies made and actions taken by governments with an eye to their impact—both direct and indirect—on society. By assessing actions and motives in this way, peace studies is considered a value-based theory. A **value** is an ideal or principle that people generally consider worthwhile and desirable. Peace studies assigns value to the actions, policies, activities, and methods of governments and individuals based on their benefit or harm to society. We might say that rather than the end justifying the means, both the means *and* the end are judged with respect to values and moral appropriateness.

And the ideal end for Stephenson and other proponents of peace studies is not simply peace but positive peace. **Positive peace** is the absence of war in combination with the establishment of broader, worldwide forms of social justice, economic prosperity, and political power-sharing. This notion is contrasted with what some peace studies theorists call "negative peace." **Negative peace** is defined only as the absence of war; a condition in which direct forms of organized violence are absent but the underlying reasons for war, such as social injustice and economic exploitation are left unresolved. Peace studies theorists would point to the end of World War I as an example of negative peace. Although military operations and violence had ended, broader social violence (widespread homelessness and hunger, for example), as well as political and economic retribution on the part of the victors continued, helping to sow the seeds for World War II. True peace, positive peace, could not be achieved under such conditions, according to the principles of peace studies.

It would be important to point out here that advocates of peace studies differentiate between violence and conflict. Even in a situation of positive peace, peace is not necessarily the absence of conflict. Conflict—as opposed to violence—is viewed by peace studies theorists as healthy debate, disagreement, or dialogue and an integral part of life and growth in human existence. The key, according to Stephenson, is to manage and resolve conflict and prevent an escalation to violence, while preserving justice and freedom within society.

Part of prevention, according to peace studies theorists, is to look at the tools of violence. Here, we see the crossover between various fields of study that was discussed earlier. In peace studies, scientists and researchers are asked to look at the consequences (environmental, social, economic) of their work. The invention of the atomic bomb, chemical weaponry, and other such devices cannot be disassociated from their violent purpose. Peace studies encourages scientists, scholars, and social activists from all fields to work together in assessing the potential political, social, and environmental ramifications of these instruments, as well as future technologies and innovations. In short, the variety of work under the rubric of peace studies seeks not only to understand the many causes of war and conflict but seeks to go beyond them in its quest for possibilities of peace building.

As Robin J. Crews points out in her article "A Values-Based Approach to Peace Studies," the search for complete knowledge or "truth" cannot be conducted in separate inquiries among divergent parts of the scientific community. An interconnected inquiry is the only way to reach this goal. Crews emphasizes that epistemological issues—issues dealing with the nature and roots of knowledge—need to be addressed as part of reducing society's violent tendencies. Learning changes our experience as humans in numerous ways, and peace studies, as part of that process, is geared to help channel an individual's search for knowledge, enlightenment, and "truth" in positive directions. She suggests that we need to instill love in our search for truth, make appropriate changes in the curricula of our schools and universities, and take social responsibility for what knowledge brings to, and can do, in our lives. We can begin this process by analyzing current values, norms, standards, and practices within society in order to understand how and what must be done to improve our future.

As we touched on earlier, this kind of global improvement begins with the person's potential for growth and deeper understanding. Our final article, "The Individual and Global Peace-Building: A Transformational Perspective," by Arthur Stein, focuses on the transformational approach to peace studies. The transformational or transformative approach examines the relationship between thought and deed, and seeks to reconcile the two. For example, concern for the preservation of our environment and natural resources must be accompanied by actions that promote this goal. One might begin by recycling on an individual basis, then take action to help develop a comprehensive town or county program. Besides ecological awareness, Stein highlights several key areas as targets for personal transformation, including human rights, civic responsibilities, shared economic well-being, and nonviolent social change. He illustrates the potential of each individual not only to change themselves but, through their example, to make a positive contribution in transforming family, friends, neighborhoods, states, and the international community. Stein emphasizes the importance of the qualities of inclusiveness, civility, and empathy to the development of truly participatory democracies.

Certainly, the transformational perspective of peace studies—or peace building—theory clearly shows the proactive nature of this paradigm. Peace studies theorists are not content simply to describe the behavior of states and its impact on the international system. They begin by ascribing value to this behavior and proceed to make recommendations on how it might be improved. There is, as we have seen, a significant amount of thought, effort, and research behind such an innovative approach to international relations. We must now ask where peace studies theory excels and where it might fall short.

A CRITIQUE OF PEACE STUDIES THEORY

As we have indicated, peace studies theory can hardly be faulted for simply describing the behavior of states in the international system. The prescriptive, interdisciplinary, value-oriented nature of this theory is actually one of its primary strengths. Peace studies outlines specific goals and offers underlying principles and, in some instances, courses of action designed to fulfill them.

The goals are noble and broad-based: social justice, human rights, building positive peace, and changing the fundamental way we view ourselves and the world. Peace studies theorists suggest promoting these goals by creating a more communitarian, global ethic in which the fundamental causes of violence might be overcome by better understanding human nature. Such understanding can be enhanced by person-to-person contact that crosses boundaries and builds bridges of knowledge and communication on an individual level, yet in a global context.

Another goal of peace studies looks for balance within these new relationships. That is, we should strive for global equilibrium between the powerful and the powerless, the wealthy and the poor. Personal and community security, which then translates to global security, can be achieved by providing food and shelter to those in need, justice to those who are persecuted, and a voice to those who have been politically silenced.

It may appear somewhat like bursting the proverbial bubble to point out that a critique of peace studies can legitimately question its idealistic worldview, which some might even call utopian. Peace studies theorists, indeed, have developed such an optimistic outlook that some critics argue it could be potentially dangerous in real-world situations. Though noble in intent, the policies fostered by peace studies could subtly weaken the resolve of people and states to resist or combat a nation bent on extending its power or influence through aggressive actions.

On a theoretical level, peace studies has been similarly criticized for underestimating the inherent conflict between nation-states. Certainly, a realist would describe the international environment as anarchic and characterized by the violence of an ongoing struggle for power between states. Under this scenario, peace studies falls short in explaining present conditions and projecting future behavior. As a theoretical construct, it is considered by critics as disjointed and unable to offer a coherent framework for analyzing international relations.

Peace studies theorists respond to these arguments by stating that the only way to change the international environment is to build bridges (through both person-to-person and government contacts), which, in turn, will reduce the fear and insecurity that lead to war. They recognize that this kind of change comes about incrementally but believe it is a logical, productive course of action. By focusing on disparities of wealth and power, individuals, communities, non-governmental organizations, and governments can formulate effective policies to redress these imbalances and create greater stability within the system. If these global disparities continue in a world of growing environmental, economic, and political instability, even powerful nations will no longer be safe.

KEY CONCEPTS

Negative Peace is the absence of war. Direct forms of organized violence are absent, but the underlying reasons for war, such as social injustice and economic exploitation, are left unresolved. This term is contrasted with what peace studies theorists refer to as positive peace.

Personal Transformation is a change or shift in an individual's nature, outlook, habits, or worldview in a way that makes that individual more socially conscious of the global effect of his or her actions.

Positive Peace is the absence of war in combination with the establishment of broader, worldwide forms of social justice, economic prosperity, and political power-sharing. This notion is contrasted with what peace studies theorists call negative peace.

Value is an ideal or principle that people generally consider worthwhile and desirable. Peace studies assigns value to the actions, policies, activities, and methods of governments and individuals based on their benefit or harm to society.

The peace studies path to this kind of change is long and gradual. Proponents suggest, though, that the prescriptive nature of the approach and the transformational aspects may offer the only realistic route for long-term, positive change in our world. This transformational process generally proceeds upwards, from individuals to states to the global system, and relies on the idea that people's attitudes and actions can affect international relations. Within its value-based, moral context, peace studies theory emphasizes positive change, social justice, and greater balance between the weak and the powerful.

We might question, however, how successful such a social contract might be. The goals of peace studies contain what were many traditional leftist elements: to more equitably redistribute wealth, to empower the poor and powerless, and to equalize the distribution of power. At a time when we see more and more developing nations turn to capitalism and a free-market system, peace studies theory could face some significant challenges. Then again, peace studies theorists might suggest that we can only change the world by changing ourselves, and that effort begins with one individual at a time.

43.   The Evolution of Peace Studies

Carolyn M. Stephenson

In this excerpt, Carolyn M. Stephenson traces the evolution of peace studies as a systematic interdisciplinary field of study. Stephenson offers five characteristics that distinguish peace studies from other fields, such as security studies, international relations, and conflict resolution. This selection is from *Peace and World Order Studies: A Curriculum Guide* (1989).

Carolyn M. Stephenson is assistant professor of Political Science at the University of Hawaii at Manoa, where she serves as a member of the Executive Committee of the Institute for Peace. She is editor of *Alternative Methods for International Security* (1982).

Peace studies is commonly defined as the systematic interdisciplinary study of the causes of war and the conditions of peace. It arose as an academic field in the aftermath of World War II, for many of the same reasons that the field of international relations had started in the aftermath of World War I. . . .

Despite differences of opinion within the field on important topics such as the nature of "peace," there is general agreement that peace studies is interdisciplinary, international, and policy oriented—that is, intended to have some impact on the real-life political environment of both policymakers and peace movements. While both peace research and peace studies are interdisciplinary, peace *research* is concentrated largely within the social sciences, having begun with a positivistic, behavioral data-based approach to the study of conflict and having later expanded to embrace a wide variety of research methods. Peace *studies* (which is generally defined in the United States to include both research and education), on the other hand, has a broader disciplinary base, drawing on all of the social sciences, as well as history, anthropology, psychology, philosophy, physics,

biology, religion, art, linguistics, and other fields.

Peace studies courses and programs often have titles that suggest the differentiation within the field, and the relationship of the central core of peace studies to other fields. Thus, in addition to just "peace studies," they include "peace and security studies" (or global or world security studies), "peace and justice studies," "peace and world order studies," "peace and global studies," "peace and conflict studies," and "peace and conflict resolution studies." Even though most would agree that the central core of peace studies includes the study of peace as the absence of violence, there is disagreement as to what constitutes "peace" and "violence." While it is not the province of this paper to analyze each of the various approaches to peace studies, a basic recounting of this debate is necessary for understanding the historical evolution of the field. . . .

DEBATES ON "PEACE"

Probably the most significant division in the field of peace studies concerns the definition of peace. The major debate has been whether to define peace simply as the absence of war (often called "negative peace") or whether the concept encompasses both the absence of war and the presence of social and economic justice (often called "positive peace"). Those who argue that peace should be defined narrowly hold that broadening the concept reduces its clarity; those who favor the broader conception argue that the violent life-threatening characteristics of various forms of systemic repression and underdevelopment often approach or exceed that of overt warfare. Just as there is no consensus in political science regarding the concepts of "power" or "politics," the disagreement in peace studies over the central object of our study contributes to the vitality of the inquiry.

To some degree this division in peace studies can be traced geographically: In northern Europe and much of the Third World, the concept of positive peace is more widely accepted; in the United States, a larger number of peace researchers limit their inquiry to negative peace. The two individual researchers most often associated with the poles of this debate are Johan Galtung (1975) of Norway, who is credited with inventing the term "positive peace" in the mid-1960s, and Kenneth Boulding (1977) of the United States, among whose "twelve friendly quarrels" with Galtung include this one.

In practice, however, there is probably more consensus than this conceptual schism would seem to suggest. For example, few scholars would contest the argument that there is a relationship between the absence of war and the presence of other social values such as justice and freedom, even if we cannot articulate

those relationships precisely in a general theory acceptable to the whole of the field. Also, most would not be satisfied with a notion of peace that did not imply some degree of long-term stability. As Karl Deutsch put it, a security-community is one in which there are "dependable expectations of peaceful change" for the foreseeable future (1957, p. 5). Similarly, in advocating the "negative peace" definition, Herbert Kelman includes in that definition "the absence of systematic, large-scale collective violence, accompanied by a sense of security that such violence is improbable" (1981, p. 103). Although he makes the case that peace as "the preservation of human life and the avoidance of violence and destruction are *extremely high values*" in their own right (p. 105), he also sees justice as having a strong bearing on the feasibility, stability, universality, and quality of peace (p. 109).

If one accepts Kelman's definition, as well as his ancillary advice that the study even of negative peace requires also the study of justice, as this author suspects the majority of the field does, then one is left with the notion that peace studies as a field must focus its teaching and research on the various possible relationships between "negative" and "positive" peace, rather than being doctrinaire in definitional matters. In the end, it may be clearer to define peace as the absence of organized violence; but to limit one's study to this formulation alone would not be productive in advancing either the theory or the practice of the field.

A final important point of definition regards the inevitability and the desirability of conflict. By and large, peace researchers reject the commonly shared public definition of peace as the absence or suppression of conflict. Rather, they accept conflict (which, of course, is not the same as violence) as a normal part of human life and international relations. The challenge for peace analysts is to determine how to manage and resolve conflict in ways that reduce the possibility or the level of violence without diminishing other values, such as justice or freedom.

DISTINCTIONS BETWEEN PEACE STUDIES AND ITS SISTER FIELDS

It is important to clarify some of the characteristics that separate peace studies from other closely related fields such as security studies, international relations, and conflict resolution. In fact, some would argue that these areas are totally different from peace studies, while others would argue that one is a branch of the other. These arguments aside, there are at least five features of peace studies that distinguish it from the "sister" fields: (1) Peace studies generally focuses on the security of the whole international or global system, while security studies scholars tend to focus on the security of a single state or alliance. (2) Peace studies covers the full continuum of violent versus peaceful activity (from the individual to the group to the global level), with the primary emphasis at the group and global levels, while international relations focuses on relations between states, and conflict resolution focuses primarily on individual and group conflict, usually in the domestic arena. (3) Peace studies tends to focus on a longer time period than international relations. Whereas the study of international relations generally covers the period since the creation of the nation-state system in 1648, peace studies goes both further back in history and further "forward" through a systematic study of the future. Accordingly, international relations accepts the nation-state and the existing international system as givens whose fundamentals are unalterable, while peace studies examines as well a wide variety of potential alternative world order systems, centralized and decentralized, hierarchical and nonhierarchical. (4) Peace studies incorporates the social sciences, the humanities, and the natural and physical sciences, while international relations tends to be limited to the social sciences, and especially to political science. (5) Peace studies is explicitly policy oriented in the sense that it aspires to describe, explain, and recommend policy relating to the conditions of peace to both governments and social movements, while a substantial number of those in international relations see themselves as limited to description and explanation. (6) Finally, peace studies is value-explicit, while in international relations research, values tend to be more hidden; indeed, some international relations scholars still claiming that research can be "value-free," a conception that most of the sciences have rejected for more than a decade. The most notable consequence of this difference is that the dominant paradigm in international relations tends, at least in practice, to be more accepting of the utility of coercive power and threat systems than is peace studies. The value of conflict, integration, disintegration, equality, justice, freedom, and the relative trade-offs between these factors, as well as the appropriateness of various methods for achieving those valued positively, are widely debated within as well as between both fields. . . .

REFERENCES AND BIBLIOGRAPHY

Alternative Defence Commission (1983). *Defence Without the Bomb.* London: Taylor and Francis.

Boulding, Kenneth (1977). "Twelve Friendly Quarrels with Johan Galtung." *Journal of Peace Research,* Vol. 14, pp. 75–86.

Chatfield, Charles (1979). "International Peace Research: The Field Defined by Dissemination." *Journal of Peace Research,* Vol. 16, No. 2, pp. 161–179.

Dedring, Juergen (1976). *Recent Advances in Peace and Conflict Research.* Beverly Hills, Calif.: Sage.

Deutsch, Karl (1957). *Political Community and the North Atlantic Area.* Princeton, N.J.: Princeton University Press.

Galtung, Johan (1975). *Essays in Peace Research,* Vol. 1. Copenhagen: Christian Ejlers.

Kelman, Herbert C. (1981). "Reflections on the History and Status of Peace Research." *Conflict Management and Peace Science,* Vol. 5, No. 2 (Spring), pp. 95–110.

Korany, Bahgat (1986). "Strategic Studies and the Third World. *International Social Science Journal,* Vol. 35, No. 4, pp. 547–562.

Mack, Andrew (1985). *Peace Research in the 1980s.* Canberra: Australian National University.

Richardson, Lewis F. (1960). *Statistics of Deadly Quarrels.* Pittsburgh, Pa.: Boxwood.

Sharp, Gene (1985). *Making Europe Unconquerable.* Cambridge, Mass.: Ballinger Publishing Co.

Singer, J. David (1981). "Accounting for International War: The State of the Discipline." *Journal of Peace Research,* Vol. 18, No. 1.

Stephenson, Carolyn M., ed. (1982). *Alternative Methods for International Security.* Washington, D.C.: University Press of America.

Varis, Tapio. "Introduction," in Liparit Kiuzadjan, Herberta Hogeweg-de Haart, and Werner Richter, eds. (1986). *Peace Research: A Documentation of Current Research.* Moscow: European Coordination Centre for Research and Documentation in the Social Sciences.

Wiberg, Hakan (1983). "The Peace Research Movement," paper delivered at the Tenth General Conference of IPRA, Gyor, Hungary.

Wright, Quincy (1965). *A Study of War,* 2 vols. Chicago: University of Chicago Press, revised edition (originally published in 1942).

QUESTIONS

1. What are the five features of peace studies that distinguish it from other fields?

2. What does the author say is the difference between "negative peace" and "positive peace"?

---

44.   A Values-Based Approach to Peace Studies

Robin J. Crews

In this excerpt, Robin J. Crews describes the goals of peace studies as including, among other things, the pursuit of knowledge about peace and its development. He reminds the reader that approaches to the study of peace are as varied as approaches to the pursuit of knowledge. Finally, he develops an approach to the study of peace that is informed by sociological analysis, principles of Gandhian nonviolence, and notions of epistemology. This selection is from *Peace and World Order Studies: A Curriculum Guide* (1989).

Robin J. Crews is chair of the Peace Studies Department at Bethel College, and director of the Kansas Institute for Peace and Conflict Resolution. He is also director of the Peace Studies Association.

The goals of peace studies include, among other things, the pursuit of knowledge about peace and its development. Approaches to the study of peace are as varied as approaches to the pursuit of knowledge in general. In this essay, I develop an approach to the study of peace that is informed by sociological analysis, principles of Gandhian nonviolence, and notions of epistemology.

THE ROLE OF PEACE STUDIES IN THE UNIVERSITY

It is sometimes assumed that there is such a thing as purely theoretical learning—learning wherein one investigates reality at the level of theory without affecting reality itself. This assumption (which is closely associated with the Cartesian delineation between mind and matter, and which underlies the belief that learning should not be involved with the application of knowledge, i.e., with social change) contradicts the fact that our familiarity with reality is based upon our perceptions of it. As we comprehend existing symbols or create new theoretical constructs to help explain the world around us, that world changes because our perceptions of it are no longer the same. When a student understands relativity theory in physics, the physical world has changed for that student forever.

Thus all learning contributes in essential ways—some enormous, some minute—to a restructuring of the human experience. Peace studies specifically and intentionally constitutes such learning. It is generally accepted that at the heart of the undergraduate educational process is the goal of learning about the world in which we live. In this way the formal training of the university experience contributes to the universal and ultimate human quest for meaning.

Fundamentally, the role of peace studies in the university is to assist in the human quest for meaning—and to do so in such a way that the world benefits from this search in the process. This quest has many manifestations, including the empirical pursuit of physical "truth" entailing the scientific measurement and interpretation of sensate perceptions; the pursuit of metaphysical "truth" through faith; the search for social linkage by belonging to a community of others; and the elemental process of growth by choosing among alternative futures, both immediate and distant. A key aspect of peace studies is the examination of these images—an enterprise that the field approaches in many diverse ways.

Examining and Challenging Values

Underlying the search for modes of learning that lead to constructive social change and a more peaceful world is a consensus about the inadequacy of present directions—a shared belief that we will not achieve a peaceful world in the future if we continue down the road we are on now. Because the future reality that humanity will create depends upon our *image* of that reality, we must develop new, more humane visions of the future. And because those visions depend upon our culture, a fundamental task for peace studies is the critical examination of our values, beliefs, and assumptions as well as of our hopes and fears, our rituals and our traditions.

The objectives of this examination are liberation from those parochial ideologies and provincial dogmas of the past that prevent us from envisioning and creating a peaceful world, and the development, in their place, of those value constellations that contribute to the full potential of peaceful coexistence in life. The controversial questions about what we leave behind and what we take with us from the past into the future are difficult to formulate and often more difficult to articulate. They are at the heart of peace studies.

Human values—and the methods by which they are shaped—are central to our quest for meaning. We teach them through actions and words, through role modeling, through traditions and rituals. As noted earlier, they underlie our images of meaning, which include, among others, our images of truth, belonging, and choosing.

Images of Truth

In Western scientific culture, we have historically chosen to pursue knowledge about physical reality through the use of scientific methods. This knowledge has often been equated with immutable "Truth." We have also pursued metaphysical dimensions of truth through faith. Both avenues of understanding have contributed much to our larger pursuit of truth. Yet the assumption that these are the only two avenues available to us, and that they are intrinsically antithetical and mutually exclusive of each other, has contributed to a competition for ideological primacy between them—a competition that has persistently hindered the search for truth.

Truth Through Science. The assumptions that objectivity is an achievable goal, that the pursuit of knowledge is a priori beneficial, that value-neutrality is possible, that "Truth" can be discovered through the scientific pursuit of knowledge in the physical world, that scientific inquiry can exist in a vacuum apart from social reality, that increased material well-being is an inevitable result of economic and technological growth, and that it is inherently useful and appropriate to seek technological solutions to social problems—these are all tenets of the social institution of science that contemporary society has come to accept and demand as it waits passively for its scientists to solve the problems that loom ever larger on our ecological and economic horizons.

These assumptions of the Newtonian, mechanistic world view are in part responsible for the unthinkable massacres that transpired on August 6 and 9, 1945. And it is these assumptions that contribute to the current research, development, testing, and deployment of space weapons and chemical munitions that threaten to rival existing technologies of mass destruction. It is these values that allow young scientists at Livermore and Los Alamos, and in weapons development firms in all industrial societies, to rationalize that their work on weapons is a noble and humane endeavor.

To alter fundamentally the course of the arms race requires a willingness to examine the values that underlie our society's pursuit of truth. After centuries of perceiving and defining reality almost exclusively in terms of the sensate world, we are finally coming to understand that science and empiricism are social institutions based upon historically and culturally specific social values.

In the teaching of Mohandas Gandhi, we are told that truth cannot be attained without love—truth, or the overcoming of injustice, is not possible unless we transform our adversaries through loving nonviolence. Indeed, for Gandhi, nonviolence is the pursuit of truth through love. Quite to the contrary, Western scientific culture has sought to separate truth and love through science. Not only does this result in a cultural acceptance and fascination with the implements of mass destruction, but it has also created an intellectual framework that has paralyzed alternative modes of seeking truth and conducting international relations. This framework has denied the legitimacy of viewing peace as the pursuit of truth through love. Many people accept our current prostitution of science as its only identity and as an historical inevitability. However, as science is a social institution—something we create—it is also something we can transform.

The challenge, then, is to critique the ethical and logical dimensions of science, to contribute to the rebirth of sciences that pursue truth through love, rather than through the design of weapons of mass destruction. The task is to reintegrate ethics and other critically essential social values into new ways of teaching science; to alter our own images of truth so as to include other ways of knowing; to assume responsibility for the development of technology in society; and to be more selective and humane in those technologies that we do elect to design and build. In other words, the role of peace studies is to comprehend more fully this empowering knowledge and to assist in the transformation of scientific approaches to truth.

In order to treat the empirical pursuit of truth through science appropriately, peace studies faculty should inject as much natural and physical science as is possible into the curriculum—and not just in "nuclear war" courses. Courses should be designed and team-taught by natural and physical scientists as often as teaching schedules allow. Peace studies faculty outside the "hard" sciences should also seek to be included in the teaching of science courses.

An understanding of scientific methods and competency in analytical problem-solving are essential if peace studies is to maintain intellectual rigor and to progress at a sufficient rate and in the appropriate directions for it to make a difference in the world of tomorrow. Therefore, scientific research methods and theory construction should be taught and used in peace studies courses as well as in physical science courses. Once introduced, logic and analytical approaches to understanding can then be employed in examinations of the assumptions of science; in other words, the methods and rules of science can be used in an examination of science itself.

Although some of this agenda must wait for students at the upper division and graduate levels, introductory courses can and should include units on science that introduce it as a social institution, and that identify it as one of *a number of* legitimate approaches to perceiving and understanding the world (rather than as the only legitimate approach). To succeed in this task, teachers should demystify images of science and technology that reinforce the "leave it to the expert" syndrome regarding policy choices, examine how the compartmentalization of science obscures social and ecological consequences, and explore the nature of "pure" versus "applied" science, including the development of civilian and military technologies.

It is important that science not be perceived as a target at which faculty in the social sciences and humanities can direct unwarranted criticism. We must examine fully the contributions of science to war (especially the history of the Manhattan Project and the resulting arms race up until the present), but such critiques should be balanced with an appreciation of the constructive uses of modern science. Finally, students should gain an understanding of the difficulty in making choices about science and technology, of the problems involved in applying ethical and moral criteria to those choices, and of the absolute necessity of doing so.

Truth Through Faith. Another way that humanity has pursued truth is through faith. In its more organized forms, this search has taken place through the development and maintenance of religious ideologies. Our religious images are based upon values taught to us through the process of inculcation as we are socialized into the world in which we live. Nothing else explains the fact that Jews produce children with an understanding of Jewish ritual and tradition, while Catholics somehow have children that understand Catholic ritual and tradition; nothing else explains the fact that Mennonites perceive an image of god significantly different from that of Muslims.

Despite the fact that few of us are specifically capable of completely and comprehensively describing our images of the divine, these images are somehow communicated to the young and then shared throughout a lifetime with others of their faith. Somehow we know how to create an image of god in our children, yet we cannot put that image into words. Clearly, these images are incredibly powerful.

However, we do use words to convey what we mean when talking about god; and the words we use to generate images of our god are often quite limiting—that is, exclusive of others' images. If this is indeed the case, then our faiths—even though they are fundamentally important and constructive for us—stand between us and a peaceful world. It is a cliche, but also a truism, that more blood has been shed in the name of god than for any other reason. This is so because our images of god are so powerful, so primary in our belief systems. And so long as some peoples' images of god exclude the viability of other people's images of god, then we will continue to live in a world beset by bloody and intractable conflicts between Protestants and Catholics, Jews and Muslims, and Sikhs and Hindus, to mention a few.

Peace will remain a fantasy as well as a slogan for the initiation of combat so long as our images of god do not allow for others to have their images of god, and so long as the agenda is social conformity and missionary conversion rather than tolerance of diverse images. Accordingly, one role of peace studies is to identify and examine beliefs that contribute either to exclusiveness or inclusiveness. This does not mean that we need to abandon our images of god. It only means that we need to transform them into images that benefit from the knowledge that peace is predicated on tolerance, not on its antithesis. We will achieve peace when our religious ideologies and dogmas allow us to value diversity and to accept the sanctity of other people's spiritual paths.

Peace studies curricula can improve their treatment of the pursuit of metaphysical truth by examining the nature of "truth" as such. Here, secularly oriented programs need to balance their agendas by incorporating units on religious contributions to peacemaking. On the other hand, programs predicated on primarily theological world views should seek as ecumenical a perspective on religion as possible. In so doing, such programs must examine the assumptions and values of religious belief systems, describe the many images of god, assess the implications of these values, assumptions, and images for the production and management of conflict in the world, and address the issues of inclusiveness, diversity, and tolerance.

Images of Belonging

There are many different types of human communities, some less voluntary than others. All of them contribute to a sense of belonging in the world; many, however, foster a desire to exclude the rest of the world. In this way, most communities offer the benefits of relationship, as well as the potential for exclusiveness, intergroup competition, ethnocentricity, xenophobia, intolerance, discrimination, and unnecessary conflict. This is true of prisons and the military as well as of gender, family, ethnicity, and the nation-state. Put differently, the obverse of belonging has many faces and regularly contributes to the violent conflict and structural violence we see in the world today. The dynamics and ideologies of "us" versus "them" (as expressed, for in-

stance, in nationalism and excessive patriotism, gender-based chauvinism, religious self-righteousness, and racial prejudice) are antithetical to the development of peace. Thus an important role of peace studies is to explore new ways of creating community that value uniqueness while minimizing exclusiveness and unnecessary competition.

Peace studies has already progressed far in this dimension. Robert Jay Lifton's (1987) seminal research into the concept of a "species self" is a major recent contribution in the field of psychology to the evolution of a global identity. Elise Boulding's new book, *Building a Global Civic Culture* (1988), is a profoundly important treatise on the creative and cooperative work involved in learning about species identity, in discovering our commonalities, and in building a shared global community. Boulding's book is essential reading for everyone in the field, because it comprehensively addresses so many aspects of the role of peace studies. Hence, in this area, we in the field of peace studies are challenged with the exciting task of building upon the work of Lifton, Boulding, and others.

College and university curricula can address problems inherent in the more traditional images of belonging in at least three basic ways: (1) by helping students identify their own images of belonging (an endeavor that includes assessments of the origins of identities, and expectations of and responsibilities to the communities involved); (2) by presenting information about communities of belonging not familiar to most students (e.g., public interest groups, the various agencies of the United Nations, peace organizations and their national and local chapters, cultural exchange programs, and so on); and (3) by jointly (with students) developing or "mapping" new constellations of communities (from local to global) that allow for overlap and mutual identification without exclusiveness or inherent competition for primacy.

Images of Choosing

"Images of choosing" is a metaphor for the ways in which we exist in the present and create our future out of it. Within the systemic limitations of genetics and history, we—as individuals and as a society—*choose* our future. The amount of freedom available for choice varies considerably with individuals and social groups, but even the poorest of the poor make choices.

Images of choosing are important to the field of peace studies because they allow for an examination of the degree of human empowerment that competes with systemic limitations. Apathy, monolithic power models, belief in technological determinism or in salvation through armageddon, and ideologies which proclaim that violence is the outcome of instinctual human characteristics all share a denial or devaluation of the element of human choice and human potential. Peace studies can and should explore the ways in which we create the future, and how we might expand that potential for creation over time. This field of inquiry involves the subject of our choices, as well as our means and structures of choosing, the role of creativity and cooperation in choice, and the consequences of refusing to acknowledge that choices exist.

Specifically, we need to ask questions about how we make these choices now, within our political and economic systems. What is democracy? How closely does our current system approach this ideal? How does this system work? Does it require participation? What form of socioeconomic organization of society is most compatible with democracy? Is the use of military force to coerce others into organizing their societies in certain ways congruous with the basic tenets of democracy? Is the possession of thermonuclear weapons of mass destruction—or the threat to use them to protect that which we choose to define as our national interests—in accordance with the principles and purposes of democracy? We also need to ask similar sorts of questions about other political systems and about the international system as a whole.

At the same time, peace studies should develop methods for *imaging the future*—that is, it should encourage students to visualize multiple world futures that incorporate new and visionary modes of social and political organization. In developing such techniques we can draw on Elise Boulding's "Imaging a World Without Weapons" workshops, which encourage a multiplicity of alternative futures and allow for new visions of practical, peaceful worlds to be created "outside" the realm of today's dominant world views.

There are many ways for images of choosing to be incorporated into peace studies curricula.

■ First, the apathy and alienation that appear as normative aspects of our culture, and that result in large part from the "psychic numbing" produced by our inability to deal with the ever-present risk of nuclear holocaust as well as from the compartmentalization of our complex and technical society, must be named and confronted. Connections to, and responsibility for, our lives and the world of which they are part have to be re-identified and rediscovered as important individual and social values.

- Second, students must be given the opportunity to entertain the notion that social reality is constructed, and that many of the limits to what is possible that were previously assumed to be valid are in fact arbitrary and outmoded; in other words, they are the products of dogma and ideology, rather than of "truth." Here, curricula need to incorporate experiential learning through "imaging the future" exercises.

- Third, the learning process needs to examine the dynamics of action. Clearly, the relationship between means and ends is an essential theme that relates in important ways to our processes of choosing. Simple slogans such as "peace through strength" should be examined logically and their influence on society assessed. At the same time, curricula need to include units on our knowledge of conflict and its resolution, and to provide training in specific skills for conflict resolution, negotiation, and mediation.

- Finally, curricula need to be designed in such a way that students are empowered as they learn about the complex problems we face in the world today, rather than frightened into acquiescence—indeed, into careers with ostrich-like characteristics.

THE PEDAGOGICAL IMPORTANCE OF VALUES

It is neither useful nor appropriate to ask whether values should be taught. In one way or another they are taught or shaped in every social interaction and institution, including those whose goal is formal learning (i.e., schools). The disciplines we emphasize, the curricula we select, the authors we choose for our students to read and analyze—all of these choices impart values. The more appropriate question is to ask *how* we can teach about values in a positive, pluralistic, and empowering way. In this regard, the most important single thing we can do is to train students to ask critical epistemological questions, rather than to accept dominant ideas as "given," as "the truth," or as "the way the world is."

In this context, peace studies is especially challenged to teach about values ethically and honestly. We can do so by incorporating into our curricula the rigorous examination of competing normative positions, with an eye toward understanding how they underlie all policies and world views. When students learn to challenge and examine values successfully, at least three essential pedagogical transformations will have transpired. First, they will have learned to critically examine ideas and values, and to evaluate them on their own merit. Second, they will have come to appreciate the existence of relationships between ideas and values. Finally, and perhaps most important, they will be better prepared to select from among the examined values and ideas for themselves—better prepared to shape a philosophy of life that reflects sound ethical and logical inquiry.

To teach values by examining and challenging them is critical because the values assumed by each new generation are the essential ingredients of our common future. Drawing on metahistory and deconstructionism, we are now learning that much of the power of those who perpetuate the arms race may be hidden in the cognitive and emotive images of discourse. We must be willing to unravel those images if we wish to create new thought-worlds.[1] At the heart of old and new thought-worlds are values.

Of course, peace studies curricula must be designed so that those entering the field do not seek to exploit it as a forum for political, ideological, or religious proselytizing. When abused as such, peace studies invites criticism and loses legitimacy in the eyes of its students. Value formation and selection on the part of students should come from an examination of various ideologies about the pursuit of truth, not from their inculcation *as* truth.

PRACTICING A NEW PROCESS

In addition to analyzing the relationship between cultural content (as it exists today or as we envision it in the future) and truth, peace studies has the potential to offer a profoundly alternative view of the search for truth. Not only does this view require further definition and articulation, but its validity is predicated upon *practice.* To identify cooperation, tolerance, holistic analysis, interdisciplinary examination, and metacultural critique as elements of the search is not sufficient: Those in the field must challenge themselves with the experience of actually *practicing* the processes they seek to institutionalize in the future. What matters here is neither content nor rhetoric about process, but *process itself.* Getting beyond the dogmas of Western scientific culture that have allowed for the illogical

separation of means and ends can be accomplished only by perceiving and practicing the means as ends-in-process.

The success of peace studies is dependent upon the ability of faculty in the field to (1) become cooperative in their shared endeavors; (2) minimize competition among disciplines, ideologies, and affiliations; (3) learn enough of the language, theories, and methods of other disciplines to apply interdisciplinary approaches in their own teaching and research; (4) respect different perspectives and others in the field; and (5) seek multiple alternatives rather than singular prescriptions.

Ultimately, faculty are charged with the task of learning to get beyond ideological labels in order to respect, if not to love, others. For those researching the phenomenon of nonviolence, this means interaction with arms control analysts; for devotees of international relations, it means identification with those focusing on themes of justice, gender, or environmental respect; for theologically inspired faculty, it means active listening to secular colleagues (and vice versa).

The practicing of process also may entail renaming the concepts of "negative" and "positive" peace, so as to avoid denigrating those who focus on the former, while retaining the substantive distinction between peace as the absence of war and militarism (i.e., "negative peace") and peace as the presence of justice (or "positive peace"). Whether individuals in the field choose to focus their inquiry and their curricula on ways to reduce violence in the international system, or on the conditions and characteristics of peace, all perspectives are valid and constructive, and must be pursued through cooperative interaction.

Another challenge to the field of peace studies is to fulfill the potential of its interdisciplinary character. Although some progress has been made here, that quality is still predominantly latent. Most research and teaching in peace studies is conducted within one discipline or another, or it is conducted in a superficially interdisciplinary fashion—that is, the sociologist contributes a sociological perspective in tandem with the psychologist who offers a psychological one, and so on. To the extent that it is humanly and professionally possible, individuals in the field must seek to develop their own interdisciplinary competencies and perspectives while still enhancing their specific areas of expertise and interest.

The practicing of process also suggests that those in the field focus on the development of means suitable to the development of peace. Pedagogically, the emphasis on means implies imparting healthy modes of seeking knowledge, rather than inculcating specific values or ideas as content. Intellectually, it denotes the search for a balanced relationship between traditional academic teaching styles and new experiential modes of learning. Beyond these manifestations of an emphasis on means, the practicing of process ultimately means creating learning structures that contribute to seeking truth through love and exposing those which separate the means from the end.

Seeing the world from as many vantage points as possible is a fundamental task of peacemakers. Therefore, the practicing of process also means developing the ability to engage in what might be called "transperceptual learning"—that is, the learning that comes from perceiving reality from the perspectives of others to the degree possible. Ultimately, the best solutions to our common challenges are the product of joint visualization and cooperative response. This is so because good solutions represent the truth we collectively seek, which in turn is the result of our ability to visualize the perceptions, identify the needs, and respect the rights of others. The sorts of solutions we seek are those that result from cooperative interaction, and that honor the perceptions and needs of others. Transperceptual learning, then, is the dynamic process that comes on the heels of love and precedes the discovery of truth through love.

CONCLUSION

Relationships between means, ends, meaning, truth, and values inform this approach to the construction of peace studies curricula and to the formulation of their role in the Academy. This perspective is only one of many. Peace studies invites the participation of all those whose vision affirms peace as a positive goal and as a concrete process requiring the development of specific social and technical knowledge. The field is open to all who are willing to challenge and transform outdated world views through the creation of new visions of what is necessary, desirable, and possible.

NOTES

1. "Thought-world" was a metaphor used by Pam Solo in a talk given at a conference on "The New Security Debate: Challenges and Strategies for the Peace Movement" sponsored by the Institute for Peace and International Security in Cambridge, Massachusetts in January 1987.

REFERENCES

Boulding, Elise (1988). *Building a Global Civic Culture: Education for an Interdependent World.* New York: Teachers College Press.

Lifton, Robert Jay (1987). *The Future of Immortality: And Other Essays for a Nuclear Age.* New York: Basic Books.

QUESTIONS

1. What does the author mean by the phrase "images of truth"?

2. What are the fundamental values associated with peace studies?

---

45. The Individual and Global Peace Building: A Transformational Perspective

Arthur Stein

In this article, Arthur Stein contends that the potential role of the individual is underestimated in humanity's quest for a more just and peaceful world order. Stein believes that the possibility of significant positive change is based on the premise that people increasingly understand the benefits of living within safe and sustainable environments and over time will commit themselves to working toward these goals. As more people take part in this process, relations among nations will improve.

Professor Stein teaches courses on Peace and World Order Studies in the Political Science Department at the University of Rhode Island. A long-time student of international relations, he has written extensively and worked personally in the field of peace building. His most recent books include *Seeds of the Seventies: Values, Work and Commitment in America (1985),* and *Heart of Compassion* (forthcoming in 1996).

Some contemporary scholars of international relations, following in the footsteps of Hans Morgenthau, doubt whether humankind is innately capable of eliminating war and organized violence. These scholars point to the undeniable fact that conflicts between peoples have been occurring in one place or another from the beginning of recorded history. Sometimes the widespread occurrence of systemic violence is seen as being as natural as an earthquake or hurricane.

By contrast, other theorists contend that organized violence is not inevitable, and that humanity has the capacity to eliminate, or greatly reduce, the incidence of war. I find this contention to be more convincing and believe the cumulative evidence of historical experience shows that humans are capable of a wide range of behaviors and that "human nature" per se can be quite malleable. The very thought of international wars in the nuclear age is appalling to many people. War, then, is not inevitable. Indeed, there are indications of a new global awakening that could bring the peoples of the world together in unprecedented and cooperative ways.

This trend presents a great challenge, for the weapons of destructiveness are too great, and the ecological crises too pressing for global "business" to continue on "as usual." Creative, non-violent ways need to be developed to prevent potentially explosive conflict situations from developing and to defuse those which do exist. Humankind is being challenged to stretch its collective imagination to envision itself as a planetary family living in peace and with social justice. An "end of history" is not at hand, but an end is required to many of the old ways of doing things. In this, the potential transformative role of the individual person is critical.

As we discuss the role of the individual in the process of peacebuilding, a number of questions arise. Each question will be addressed by looking at historical theoretical patterns, as well as contemporary events. First, do humans have the capacity to change?

The Human Nature Debate

There persists the age-old question: Are we perpetually victims of our biology and our history? Socio-biologist E. O. Wilson has observed that, from their origins, homo sapiens genetically have a potential both for peaceful and for aggressive be-

havior. And aggression does not have to manifest in violence. This premise leaves open a number of possibilities, depending on the circumstances in which we find ourselves and those we create. Wilson concludes that violent behavior itself is learned, not inborn.[1]

Beliefs about human nature can become self-fulfilling prophesies. If you believe that human beings are naturally violent or bad, you may be persuaded that it is "realistic" to be that way yourself. In short, humans have both the capacity for good and negative thoughts, words, and actions. Our behavior is rarely all black or white. There are numerous areas of grey in between. As individuals, we only have to look closely at our daily ups and downs to ascertain this.

THE KEY ROLE OF THE INDIVIDUAL IN TRANSFORMATIVE CHANGE[2]

In order to respond to the challenges of our rapidly changing age, we need to develop fresh perspectives. One emerging approach, which can be called transformative or transformational, asserts that more is required than to call for needed reforms or restructuring of political institutions. This approach stresses the need to examine the existential question of what it is to be fully human and the relationship between our psyches and social behaviors. Implicit in this notion is the belief that humans do have the capacity to develop a level of self-understanding that will enable us to deal more effectively with violence and other social disfunctions.

Writing from a transformationist perspective, political scientist Louis Rene Beres, in *People, State and World Order,* emphasizes that it is necessary to balance a person's individual needs and aspirations with the needs of society as a whole. "The core of a good world order inheres originally in each individual person." Beres contends that humans are born into a world of unconsciousness with respect to understanding the evolutionary potential and prospects of the human race. He adds, though, that "we are capable of upward development of consciousness and ascent into reaches where personal growth easily harmonizes with the good of the whole."[3]

In this scenario, the role of the individual person is central. The possibility of meaningful societal change is based on the premise that enough people want to have a good quality of life for themselves and their families and to live in a world that is peaceful and life sustaining. These people would, therefore, commit themselves to working toward these goals. In short, those individuals who discover new feelings of kinship, unity, and creativity within themselves will begin to help shape social orders more hospitable to human imagination, growth, and cooperation.

The individual, then, is the key to peace building and other transformative changes. However, "no man [or woman] is an island." Through cooperative activity utilizing the principle of synergy, creative ideas, feelings, and emotions can then be shared and further developed by the interaction with others.

Looking at the history of social change in the United States as an example, virtually all major social or political changes—whether they be anti-slavery or civil-libertarian, working class rights, feminist, or anti-war—started with an individual or small group of concerned citizens. Sometimes the person with a new

approach might be, in the name of I.F. Stone's newsletter of the 1960s–70s, *A Minority of One.* These concerns expanded outward, invoking more people and gaining momentum until they were gradually accepted (or co-opted) into the mainstream political process or social fabric. These ideas were not always popular, especially in the earlier years of struggle, but if individuals persevere in their perceptions of truth and justice, the ideas will ultimately be heard. It may not happen in the person's lifetime, but seeing oneself in a long tradition of peacemakers often provides the impetus to "carry-it-on."

It is encouraging to hear the views of those who see the positive aspects of human possibility. Affirmative vision sometimes gets reduced to simplistic clichés, however, and there are no ready-made blueprints for a "New Age." As poet-futurist David Spangler aptly put it, "When it comes to the evolution of a new culture there are no experts, but we can figure it out together and build as we go along. [It] is something that must be lived into beingness. It is not a product to be manufactured like a new car."[4]

The real energy crisis is within the human psyche. An abundance of human energy can be generated by working together in common cause, bringing the principle of synergy into play. This principle was employed by Buckminster Fuller in the construction of his geodesic domes. In essence it holds that the sum is greater than the total of its component parts. The concept is also applicable to efforts involving human interaction. If each member of a group puts forth his or her best efforts, the result will be greater than the mere sum of individual inputs. Also, the synergy, "shared energy," that the collective effort has produced will return more than the original investment of time, efforts, or resources to the participating individuals.

Often programs that encourage person-to-person interaction can expand knowledge of other cultures and further the cause of global goodwill. During the Cold War years, reciprocal exchanges of thousands of students, researchers, artists, and factory workers helped to break down the barriers that ideological differences had created. Other forms of citizen diplomacy also take place when people volunteer to serve in another country. Those who have participated in the Peace Corps, World Friends Service Committee, Oxfam, or similar organizations generally feel that they have provided some useful service to the host countries. Almost universally, however, these individuals acknowledge receiving even more from the experience than they have given. Those who serve in poor areas of their own countries report a similar experience.

PEACEBUILDING, NON-VIOLENCE AND PEACE EDUCATION

Peace, both within oneself and within the world, is probably the most common human desire. Peace on earth must begin within the hearts and minds of individuals. This is something that has been understood by enlightened teachers through the ages. In the 6th century B.C., Lao Tse said, "Force is not the Tao or Way for human beings to follow." Jesus of Nazareth, in his message of peace and non-violence spoke: "My peace I give unto you, a peace which passes all understanding."

The yearning for peace can also be found in the languages of many cultures. Both the Hebrew greeting *shalom* and the Arabic *salaam* embrace peace and well-being not only for oneself but for everyone. The Chinese word *ping* implies harmony, the emergence of unity out of diversity. The Russian word for peace, *mir*, also means world—suggesting the notion, perhaps, of a world at peace. Peace obviously is far more than the absence of war. The period between World War I and II, for example, were hardly years of peace, for the seeds of the next international conflict were being sown.

What we will describe as "peace" has certain positive qualities that are built through transformative processes. American peace activist A. J. Muste often said, "There is no way to peace. Peace is the way." For him, "to fight for peace" was an oxymoron. Muste believed that the key to peace within communities, nations, and, ultimately, the world is the development of peace-full individuals.[5] The Vietnamese teacher Thich Nhat Hanh provides an eastern perspective suggesting that it is not enough to talk about peace; we have to learn to be peace. A prerequisite for inner peace is the development of a harmonious balance between one's mind, body, and spirit.[6]

Indian scientist and spiritual teacher, Sant Rajinder Singh, describes the potential multiplier effect that truly peaceful individuals can have: "Transformed individuals can transform families, transformed families can transform communities, transformed communities can transform nations, and transformed nations will transform the world."[7]

The principle of non-violence is the primary component of peace building.

For India's Mohandas Gandhi, ahimsa (non-violence) was not a philosophy of passivity but was an active and principled response based on a profound respect to all life forms. He set forth ahimsa as the central principle to freeing India from colonial rule, and satyagraha (which means "grasping on to truth") as the basis for his non-violent campaigns. The means were (and are) as important as the ends to be accomplished. If the means were distorted, so would be the goal. Success was not measured in terms of just achieving immediate goals, but in terms of how those goals were obtained.[8] Gandhi once told his followers that if India could not rid itself of its debilitating caste system, and if Hindu, Moslem, and Sikh could not reconcile their differences peacefully, then India did not deserve to gain its independence. These words remain relevant today not only for the Indian subcontinent but for the world.

Dr. Martin Luther King brought the philosophy of non-violence to the Afro-American's struggle for civil rights. King emphasized: "Nonviolence is the answer to the crucial political and moral questions of time. . . . Man must evolve for all human conflict a method which rejects revenge, aggression and retaliation. The foundation of such a method is love."

Freedom and racial harmony were also part of the message espoused by the first two Africans to receive the Nobel Peace Prize, Chief Luthuli and Bishop Desmond Tutu.[9] Both men are South Africans who opposed apartheid and sought a free and racially harmonious society. The words of Bishop Tutu reinforce those uttered by Dr. King almost three decades ago, "We know that darkness can overcome evil, that light overcomes darkness, and love can overcome hatred."

Peace building and world order studies are the focus of many new courses and programs at the university level. Sometimes Peace and Global Security are linked together in the titles, because until people and nations experience a sense of security from the fear of aggressive behavior by others, there will not be any real possibility for a peaceful new world order. Professor David Barash explores some facets of this new discipline in his book *Introduction to Peace Studies.* While acknowledging there are no simple solutions to the problems of war and violence, he suggests that humankind has the potential to move toward a more cooperative, just, and sustainable world.

There is reason for hope, not just as an article of faith but based on the premise that once human beings can understand the larger situation and recognize their own best interests, they can behave rationally, creatively, and with compassion. Positive steps can be taken that will diminish humanity's reliance on organized violence to settle conflicts.[10]

Johan Galtung, one of the pioneers of Peace Studies, established the world's first Peace Research Institute in 1959 in Oslo, Norway. He is an advocate of "positive peace building" in which the basic systemic causes of war and violence are eliminated. In a condition of "positive peace," the exploitation of one person or society by another would be minimized or eliminated. There would be no overt violence nor, in a more subtle form, structural violence.[11]

Admittedly, these are difficult goals, not easily achieved. It is the ideals, however, that these scholars believe are worth pursuing, studying, and codifying. The pursuit of peace and justice in society cannot be considered utopian idealism. From a theoritical standpoint, it is up to mankind to build personal, national, and systemic frameworks for peace.

On a practical level, there are three basic approaches to teaching peace studies: reformist, reconstructionist, and transformational. Betty Riordan of Columbia University considers the transformational approach the most comprehensive. She writes:

> It espouses as its overarching goal nothing short of profound social change. This approach puts equal emphasis on behavioral and structural change but it views as the most essential development a transformation of consciousness, asserting that the fundamental causes of war, violence and oppression lie in the way we think. Only through fundamental changes in values and modes of thinking, this approach posits, can we achieve a comprehensive global peace that rejects all forms of violence and coercive authority in favor of a social order held together by communal values and consensual politics.[12]

Because we often fail to grasp the full complexity of the problems that produce war and violence, we tend to focus on the symptoms, rather than the root causes. With the goal of creating new understanding, the transformational approach emphasizes "transdisciplinary, synthesizing, extending scholarly methods and where necessary inventing new ones. The method integrates fields such as macro-history, feminist scholarship, human ecology, process theology and action research in developing its content," and encourages integrative and holistic learning by the students.

The transformational approach is basically a normative one and deals with the often neglected areas of personal and societal values. Professional associations of scholars, such as the International Politi-

cal Psychology Society, are just now beginning to advance studies in this field. There are four general areas of focus: human rights, ecological wholeness, economic well-being, and non-violent social change.

In 1947, the United Nations adopted its Universal Declaration of Human Rights, championed in the United States by Eleanor Roosevelt. The Declaration spells out specific inalienable human rights. Individuals have the right to be involved in making the basic decisions that affect their lives, and the right to security for themselves and their families. There is also the inherent right to freedom of conscience, self-expression and assembly, and freedom from want and fear.

In 1988, a Declaration of Human Responsibilities was drawn up by an international conference meeting at the University for Peace. The Declaration spells out the linkages between human rights and responsibilities. The document calls for strong commitments by individuals as well as governmental authorities because the signators recognize that meaningful change begins within individuals and communities. The more advantaged have a responsibility to share their resources with others to advance these goals.[13]

The Declaration of Human Responsibilities issued a strong challenge. But to what extent are we willing in fact to take responsibility to secure the rights of others? What will be our ability to respond, individually and collectively to the urgent challenges of our era. But who will take the responsibilities to fulfill these rights? What will be our ability to respect, individually and collectively, to the urgent challenges of our era?

Peace implies a state of personal tranquility and satisfaction, but it is very hard to be calm when denied basic such needs as food, clothing, shelter, education, and medical care. To put it bluntly, a hungry person is more often than not an angry person. New models for "third-world" development are needed, involving widespread participation by the people who are themselves most directly affected—involving grass-roots decentralized programs.

In 1993, John K. Galbraith warned, "If we don't address the needs of the have-nots, the have-nots will address the haves—there's no question about it." Globally, we have to provide a more level playing field. The problems of poverty and economic scarcity are not insoluble. Solutions do exist, invoking various redistribution strategies, development programs, family planning, etc. As we have seen, theses solutions can begin with the concern and commitment of a single individual. New programs and fields of study in peacebuilding can make that beginning possible.

EXEMPLARY PEOPLE AND VOICES OF HOPE

The development of a new awareness by humankind involves the participation of individuals throughout the world. Indeed, a positive view of human potential is necessary if widespread change is to be achieved.

This perspective energizes a practical visionary like Robert Muller, who served as United Nations Undersecretary General, coordinating the thirty-two U.N. specialized agencies for three decades. Born in Alsace-Lorraine, long a focal point for German-French armed conflicts, Muller became a strong advocate of European unity. Among his colleagues at the United Nations, he was known as the

"philosopher of hope." In *New Genesis: Shaping a Global Spirituality,* Muller foresaw the dawning of a global age and the development of a sense of community among all people.[14] Despite the international conflicts currently facing the United Nations, Muller sees nations slowly overcoming their divisiveness, as well as a re-formed U.N. helping humanity to realize the goal of peace. As incipient signs of an emerging worldwide consciousness, he points to global conferences on disarmament, ecology, the aged, the malnourished, AIDS, and "the year of the child." Muller had a major role in preparing the groundwork for many of these conferences. Now in his seventies, Muller is the pro bono Chancellor of the University for Peace in Costa Rica, and is committed to the notion that "everything depends upon personal commitment."

Muller is supportive of groups and programs that seek to realize the inherent potential of the United Nations, such as the series of annual international Conferences for a More Democratic U.N. (CAMDUN). These conferences have been co-sponsored by over two hundred Non-Governmental Organizations (NGOs) and have produced scores of ideas for U.N. reform. Their recommendations include the development of new conflict resolution mechanisms, especially preventative diplomacy to reduce international tensions before violence occurs.

The year 1995 will mark the fiftieth year of the United Nations. CAMDUN will put forth a detailed proposal for the creation of a new bicameral legislature for the U.N. consisting of the present general assembly (representing national governments) and a newly-created peoples assembly. The peoples assembly would have elected delegates from all the world's regions directly representing the diversity of peoples and cultures and their non-governmental organizations.[15]

There are many people internationally whose work is not widely known, but who offer practical and hopeful approaches to resolving problems of resource depletion, environmental degradation, and societal injustice. In 1980, Jakob von Uexkull, a Swedish-German writer and philatelic expert, set up The Right Livelihood Awards to honor those working on practical and exemplary solutions to the real problems facing humankind, locally and globally. The foundation recognizes activists, researchers, scientists, and social movements for their work. In its first decade, forty-four people and organizations (out of over 250 nominees from fifty countries) received these awards, presented annually in the Swedish Parliament in Stockholm on the day before the Nobel Prize presentations.[16]

In 1979, Mildred and Glen Leet, who had worked for many years as international civil servants, decided to do something worthwhile with part of their retirement pension. They started the Trickle Up Program as an "independent non-profit organization dedicated to creating new opportunities for employment and economic and social well-being among the low income populations of the world." In the early 1980s, Trickle Up opposed the tide of "trickle down" development projects and "trickle down" economics. The "experts" scoffed at the concept that poor people in Africa, Asia, and Latin America could create small business enterprises and solve their own problems. Trickle Up provides small loans of $50 or $100 as start-up funds for self-sufficiency projects to families or small groups. For example, five women

from Guatemala, who had lost their husbands during the civil violence, started up a local business raising baby chicks. A family in Nepal, which had long aspired to own a small bakery, received start-up funds to bake and market their own special rotis (breads). The recipients of the loans are linked up with volunteer field coordinators who understand the local infrastructures and who can help with the initial paper work.

Accounts are kept on the operation, using on a computer in New York. As of the end of 1992, 29,000 businesses and close to 200,000 small entrepreneurs in ninety-eight countries had taken advantage of the Trickle Up Program, and repayment of the initial loans was at over ninety percent.

Today, even the larger development agencies such as the World Bank (whose failure rate in its large development projects has been acknowledged at over eighty percent) have accepted people-oriented trickle-up development as an effective and efficient way to create purposeful change—and are seeking the organization's advice. The concept of involving people in creating their own solutions is becoming more universally accepted. World political, social, and economic thinking is gradually shifting, and the trickle-up process is used by many as an example that proves the practicality of empowering people at the grass roots level.

In Africa, Asia, and Latin America, Trickle Up is promoting cooking and water purification with solar energy. Workshops in over a dozen countries have provided an opportunity for the indigenous poor to learn how to produce, use, and market Solar Box cookers in a cost effective way. Women are usually the actual users of the technology.

In a project with women in rural Nigeria, local coordinator Christopher Ugwu wrote, "With our women's groups we are emphasizing local action for maintaining bio-diversity. . . . No environmental crusade has even the slightest chance of succeeding without women being pivotal in the execution."

Even in circumstances of natural or man-made disasters, Trickle Up works effectively with indigenous organizations. In the Philippines, victims of volcanic eruptions have been helped to rebuild their lives and restart their own businesses. Indigenous-run organizations in war-torn Sudan and Haiti are helping people to create their own income and jobs amid political upheaval.[17] With their small but effective program, John and Mildred Leet illustrate how individuals can make a difference in the movement toward global transformation.

ENVIRONMENTAL AWARENESS

Scholars and activists in many parts of the world are advocating the idea of sustainable development.[18] This notion is similar to the Native American ideal that each individual and society should assess the impact of its actions not only on one's own generation but for seven generations to come.

Conservation and environmental protection are growing trends in global politics. Many organizations—Greenpeace, the Friends of the Earth, the Sierra Club, The Nature Conservancy, and green political parties—have sprung up in many countries.[19] Since there is so much to be done, international agreements on the ozone layer and on the protection of biodiversity have been steps in the right direction. There are signs of hope as governments and citizenry alike attempt to find appropriate responses to uniquely global problems.[20] At the UNCED Conference held in Rio de Janeiro in 1992, economists, environmentalists, and the world's national leaders got together in large numbers for the first time to try to find a common language and to work together cooperatively for the rehabilitation of Mother Earth and her inhabitants.

Increased amounts of information on the condition of the world's environment, natural resources, and peoples is increasingly accessible through the publications of the Worldwatch Institute and other sources.[21] Each of us can continue to educate ourselves on how to be better stewards of our planet, learning new information, and sharing it with others.

The word "ecology" derives from the Greek word *oikos,* meaning *house.*[22] Broadly defined, it refers to the relationship between living things and their environment. As a newly emerging global society we have to get our common home in order, and to do so we have to get our priorities straight.

The search for ecological "wholeness" leads to a recognition that there is an underlying unity between all life forms. Scientists such as the late David Bohm of Oxford, England, developed holographic models to help visualize the notion of an "implicate order" linking and embracing all of reality. He hypothesized that ultimately each person is connected to the totality of the life force in the universe, and believed that people will soon come to better comprehend this linkage.[23] Our new ecological and environmental understanding is teaching us that everyone and everything on the planet is linked together in an interconnected web of life. Part of the new transformative movement toward peace on the planet is this focus on environmental education, especially for the young people.

Courage is a word derived from the French *coeur,* meaning *heart.* We are indebted to courageous people throughout the world, such as Russian physicist Andrei Sakharov and the American chemist, Linus Pauling, who in 1963 convinced their nations' leaders of the necessity for a ban on nuclear testing in the atmosphere. Further activism on nuclear education over the years was carried out by such groups as the International Physicians for Social Responsibility, the Union of Concerned Scientists, and by individuals like Australia's Dr. Helen Caldicott. Internationally, we acknowledge the exemplary courage of people like Cesar Chavez of the United Farm Workers, the Mothers of the Missing (in Argentina and Chile), and the young people who confronted the tanks in Peking's Tienamman Square. It takes a certain fortitude to "buck the system" and make it work, as PIRG organizer and educator Ralph Nader can testify. Another person who exemplifies working with great effectiveness within the system is civil rights trial lawyer Morris Dees, co-founder of the Southern Poverty Law Center. Dees has used the legal system to successfully bring lawsuits against the Ku Klux Klan, and has made the Teaching Tolerance program available to tens of thousands of schoolchildren.

Education, in its many forms, is the most essential ingredient in the long-term quest for a peaceful world. Peace education, mediation training, and conflict resolution are necessary at all levels. The following are a number of organizations designed to further this endeavor: The Fellowship of Reconciliation, based in Nyack, New York, has pioneered conflict resolution workshops for public schools, peace activists, and the general public. On the college campus, sociologists Elise and Kenneth Boulding and activist-writer Joanna Macy are among those who have linked academic and community peace-building concerns. Professors Richard Falk and Saul Mendlovich focus on the role of international law and institutions in the ongoing search for a just, new world order. Peace conversion work was pioneered by economist Seymour Melman. The Carter Center of Emory University provides mediation assistance in global and civil conflicts.[24] And centers like the United States Institute of Peace, based in Washington, D.C., provide a needed link between academic research, the government, and the public.

The Harvard University group headed by Dr. Roger Fisher, through its books, *Getting to Yes* and *Getting Together,* has made conflict resolution techniques, in politics, business, and daily living, accessible to millions. Fisher and his colleagues have also applied their "win-win" approach by themselves serving as mediators in various international crisis situations.[25]

Another kind of conflict is addressed by psycho-linguist Deborah Tannen in her insightful study, *You Just Don't Understand,* in which she addresses the different communication styles of men and women. In some respects, males and females have grown up in separate subcultures. In today's world, the traditional "battle of the sexes" has intensified, and better levels of communication and understanding between the genders are necessary if our species is to have domestic tranquility, let alone, global community.[26]

ROLE OF RELIGION

One area that the discipline of international relations does not sufficiently address is the complex role of religion in the contemporary world. Organized religions, throughout history, have alternately been "part of the problem and part of the solution."

The Parliament of the World's Religions, held in Chicago in August, 1993, was probably the largest and most inclusive gathering of world religious and spiritual leaders, lay people, and scholars in history. Christians, Zoroastrians, Buddhists, Native Americans and other indigenous peoples, Jains, Taoists, Hindus, and practically every other tradition met for eight days and shared ideas and fellowship. They sought to identify the shared values that are at the core of all religions and to respect the diversity of human spiritual experience.

It was encouraging at the Parliament to witness Moslems and Jews getting to know each other's traditions better and listening to the other's concerns. Such interfaith dialogues will help to build the welcome breakthrough between Israel and the PLO into a just and lasting peace.

Things have come a long way since the original Parliament in 1893 in which American Indians, for example, were not even recognized as having a legitimate spiritual tradition. Still, the organized religions that have given so much to what is valued in human culture are still the source of much intolerance and discord. In many of 50 major conflicts around the globe, from Northern Ireland to the former Yugoslavia to the Indian subcontinent, ethnic and religious differences often fuel the fires of misunderstanding and hatred.

Two important aspects of the Parliament of Religions received little media coverage. The first was the active participation of the secularly-oriented Council for the 21st Century, which focused on the linkages between religion in its broader sense and the economic, social, and ecological issues confronting humanity. In a document prepared by the Council, "Global 2000 Revisited: The Critical Issues for the 21st Century," Dr. Gerald Barney challenged the religious leaders to respond creatively to the crises and new opportunities facing the planet.

Thirteen years earlier, Barney directed the Global 2000 Report upon the request of then President Jimmy Carter. At that time, he did not see the role of the religious community as important in peacebuilding. But in 1993, Barney was convinced that without active participation and cooperation of religious and spiritual groups, it would be impossible for political leaders to muster the vision and leadership to move forward successfully into the next century.

Another significant aspect of the conference was the adoption of a "Declaration of a Global Ethic" by the great majority of the religious leaders there. The document, prepared by German reformist theologian Dr. Hans Kung, provides a declaration of responsibility for the leaders to work for interfaith understanding, for just and peaceful resolution of conflicts throughout the world, and for the healing of Mother Earth.

The Global Ethic provides a touchstone of accountability, declaring that "Any form of aggression or hatred in the name of God or religion is soundly condemned." The denunciation of genocide and ethnic cleansing, for example, is directly applicable to the Bosnian tragedy. As the Da'lai Lama of Tibet put it, the declaration can provide a focal point where world religious and spiritual communities and concerned individuals everywhere can find a united voice to help prevent future Bosnias.

On the last evening of the Parliament, an African-American woman of the Ba'hai faith read the Preamble to the Global Ethic to the assemblage: "We make a commitment to respect life and dignity, individuality and diversity, so that every person is treated humanely, without exception. . . . We consider humankind our family. We commit ourselves to a culture of non-violence, mutual respect, justice and peace." Each person on earth, whether of a religious inclination or not, is invited to join in the commitment to nurturing these basic ethical values."

The Council of the Parliament plans to cooperate with other groups in fostering activities at the global, regional, and local levels. In the Chicago area, the Parliament's positive example has spurred representatives of 130 religious and other organizations to establish an organization to facilitate interfaith dialogue and community action programs. This is the kind of response that the Parliament would like to stimulate world-wide, putting the ideals expressed in the new Global Ethic into practice.

Some of the themes concerning peace making discussed at the World Parliament were further developed at the World Fellowship of Religions Conference held in Delhi, India, in February, 1994. One practical result, put in the form of a formal request to the Secretary-General of the United Nations calls, for the creation of a U.N. Center for Nonviolent Conflict Prevention and Resolution, with a full-time staff of trained personnel.

The proposal for the new U.N. center points out that "the Cold War was characterized by a cycle of fear where armaments bred insecurity and insecurity bred more armaments. We believe it is time to create a new cycle of life where trust, confidence, and non-violent preventative diplomacy" can become the new norm. The permanent center at the U.N. (and regional centers elsewhere) would utilize all available means of mediation, negotiation, conciliation, and conflict resolution techniques known to humankind. Since this center could not be most effectively created by the U.N. alone, non-governmental organizations, academic institutions, parliamentarians, business and professional communities, and media and the public at large all need to be involved. "The faith-based communities also need to be included, since so much conflict has roots in ethnic and religious misunderstanding." Offering to be of service themselves, the signatories of the proposal point out that some within the religious communities already have had experience with mediation techniques that can be utilized in conflict resolution and preventative diplomacy. The request closed: "This is the time and the opportunity to bring into action the deepest intentions for peace which are at the heart of humankind."

AMERICA'S ROLE

Virtually all the world's racial, religious, ethnic, and cultural traditions are found in the United States. In this sense, the United States is a microcosm of the world's peoples, and is an ongoing experimental workshop in the evolution of democratic theory and practice.

America today is at a crossroads. Without discernment, the American dream at times can easily fade into a nightmare, leading on the personal level to a desire for excessive wealth and power, and on the societal level to a nation with little purpose or direction.

At its best, though, the American dream could be more accurately described as a vision. Unlike an ordinary dream, a vision connotes a deeper level of truth. This vision is of a society that allows each person—regardless of race, religion, creed or class—the opportunity to fulfill his or her unique aspirations. It is of a land where people care for and help one another, where children can grow up safely and realize their full potential as human beings. This view of America is one in which each person has the inalienable right to live without fear or want. To paraphrase Mahatma Gandhi, the world has enough to meet each person's need, but not enough to meet anyone's greed. The same principle applies to the United States.[27]

The U.S. plays a pre-eminent political, economic, and military role in the world. As a nation that proclaims high principles, the United States is often judged critically when it fails to live up to its own ideals or others' expectations. We are challenged to develop more fully the humility and compassion that are evidences of a mature people.

There are a number of qualities that might promote and enhance positive social change.

1) Develop a life pattern based more on voluntary simplicity so that America uses its resources more wisely and is less of a drain on the rest of the world. This would improve the quality of our individual lives, create fewer antagonisms, and lessen the divisions between haves and have-nots at home and abroad.

2) Learn to work together in human-scaled groups to hone the skills of participatory democracy. Get involved in organizations that emphasize ethical standards, cooperation and inclusiveness, those which will help lay the groundwork for a more egalitarian, non-sexist and non-racist society.

3) Recognize the importance of life-affirming practices to help save and restore the environment, from urban centers to the wilderness.

4) Be willing to help others and promote human dignity.

5) Be open, appreciative of life, and remember to maintain a sense of humor. Become centered, more fully integrated human beings with a greater sense of purpose.

6) Recognize that education is a life-long process. Listen with empathy, learn about other cultural traditions, and realize that there is something to be learned from everyone and from every situation in which we find ourselves.

7) When discouraged, remember the words of anthropologist Margaret Mead: "Never doubt that a small group of thoughtful committed citizens can change the world. Indeed it is the only thing that ever has."

Those who will lay the groundwork for positive change at home and abroad include educators who encourage in their students the spark of honest inquiry, students who are responsive and exercise their own creative capacities; public servants who practice the art of politics with integrity; those in the healing arts who take a holistic and people-oriented approach toward their profession; and creative writers and musicians who help sensitize us to the human condition and awaken our shared humanity. Each person's input is significant in that oft-elusive pursuit of finding our common ground.

WHERE DO WE GO FROM HERE?

In 1776 Thomas Paine wrote that "we have the power to begin the world again." But what we are talking about today, more than 200 years after the American Revolution, is something far more complex than gaining political independence. It is a struggle that cannot be won with bullets and barricades, neither in America nor elsewhere in the world. It involves a different kind of revolution— the working through of a process, and not just a final climactic political act. Revolution in the full sense, literally a complete turning around, appears necessary if we are not only to survive but to become more humane in the process.

What is most needed is an opening of the heart, a deepening of insights, and a willingness to listen with empathy to others. Such a "turning" by a substantial portion of the population would be truly revolutionary.

Sant Darshan Singh of India insightfully writes that the greatest revolutionary change can only be brought about by a change of attitude within the human heart: "We are witnessing the dawn of a spiritual revolution. By definition, such a revolution, unlike political, social or economic ones, cannot be enforced from without. It is an inner revolution which centers on a change of consciousness. We cannot convert others, we can only convert ourselves."[28]

Thoughtful people from many backgrounds and disciplines have suggested ways to attain a more peaceful world. Unfortunately, articulation of our goals and even of the methods to attain them are not enough to bring about substantive change. What is required additionally is a re-visioning of our values and developing a clearer understanding that we are all linked together as members of the human family. In short, what we need additionally, individually and collectively, is a change of perspective.

Just as the breakthroughs in the discoveries of quantum physics brought about a paradigm shift in understanding the physical world so a paradigm shift may well be necessary in the social sciences for us to better understand the human psyche and social evolution in our complex times. A greatly accelerated understanding of our physical universe also necessitates a parallel growth in the metaphysical (philosophical) realm. Just as scientific inquiry has led to exciting discoveries both in subatomic matter and in outer space, humanity is now recognizing the need to probe more deeply into the far reaches of the frontiers of inner space.[29]

Global change will begin with personal transformation that will help us to become more integrated human beings. But the transformation of individuals is itself predicated on a fundamental shift in that which we value in our lives. What we seek in our search for personal happiness needs to be expanded to include the well-fare of all.

This transformation of the human spirit has been experienced and spoken of in the esoteric teachings of virtually all the world's religious and spiritual traditions. The process by which a person "taps within," recognizes and develops spiritually oriented values, and then puts these values into action within families, communities, nations, and, transnationally, can contribute to the development of an enriched political democracy in which the human spirit will prevail.[30]

The great majority of countries today say they wish to implement political democracy. But without a reawakening of the human spirit that we can experience for ourselves, acknowledging that our lives and fate are inextricably linked together, there can be no true political democracy. Nor will there be the impetus and motivation to create truly participatory systems that respect cultural differences and promote societal equity.

As we approach the year 2000 A.D. questions are often raised about the future of humankind. In what basic direction is our world heading? What might our lives be like in the years to come? Can we continue to keep "muddling along," pursuing business as usual?

Among the responses to these fundamental questions two increasingly polarized points of view have emerged. In broad terms, one viewpoint holds that great ecological disasters and social chaos lie ahead; the other contends that transformative responses are emerging to meet the challenges of our era and that somehow humankind can learn to resolve its differences and live sensibly.

Both positions can muster "evidence" to support their views. Those with a more optimistic vision adhere to the belief that the forces of life will yet prevail, that over the next several decades, humanity will become increasingly aware of, and will act on the necessity to lay the groundwork for, a peaceful planetary order. This perspective is less visible to the general public and receives less media attention. It draws ultimately on the innate human capacity to care for and cooperate with one another and is evidenced by the goodwill that many people extend daily.

Should we become discouraged at times, our spirits are renewed when we witness an unexpected handshake between Yasser Arafat and Yitzak Rabin on the front lawn of the White House, bringing new hope to the Middle East, or the Mandela-deKlerk accords ending the scourge of apartheid in South Africa. And there are the countless daily acts of random kindness by people everywhere who choose to lend a helping hand, or share the warmth of a smile with friend or stranger.

A growing number of people in all parts of the world are developing a "one-humanity" consciousness and sharing what they have learned with others. The practice of "thinking globally, acting locally," is beginning to take root. This involves working within one's own community and simultaneously being aware of the planetary implications of one's actions.

Sanity and human dignity can yet prevail.

NOTES

1. Edward O. Wilson, *On Human Nature* (Harvard University Press: Cambridge, 1978). Also see a succinct discussion on "Violence and Human Nature" in Howard Zinn, *Declarations of Independence: Cross-Examining American Ideology.* (Harper-Collins: San Francisco, 1990) 32–47.

2. One definition given to the word "transform" in *Webster's Dictionary of the English Language* (1987) is "to change the character or nature of radically."

   Transformational change in our time needs to be radical in the etymological sense of getting to the roots (or the heart) of a situation, but not in the way that the word is often used to describe political radicalism.

3. Louis Beres, *People, States and World Order* (S. E. Peacock: Itasca, IL, 1981) 139–140. Also see Richard Falk, *Explorations*

on the Edge of Time: The Prospects for the World Order, Philadelphia PA.: Temple University Press, 1992.

4. David Spangler, "On the New Humanity," a transcribed talk at the Omega Institute's 1979 summer conference held at Bennington College, Vermont.

    See in David Barash, *Introduction to Peace Studies* (Wadsworth: Belmont, CA, 1991), the sections on Eastern and Judeo-Christian Concepts, 6-7, and Ethical and Religious Perspectives, 439-457.

5. See the chapter on A. J. Muste in Charles DeBenedetti (Ed.), *Peace Heroes In Twentieth Century America* (Indiana University Press: Bloomington, 1986) 149-167.

6. Thich Nhat Hanh is a Buddhist teacher who advocated a "middle-way" approach to resolving the Vietnam Conflict. Harrassed by both sides, he escaped to France where he founded the Plum Village community. He has led the resettlement movement for refugee Vietnamese boat people in the United States and France, and has brought together groups of former American servicemen and Vietnamese citizens in order to bring about healing and reconciliation. Among his most recent books is *Peace Is Every Step: The Path of Mindfulness in Everyday Life* (Bantam Books: New York City, 1991).

7. Quoted from Rajinder Singh's "Peace Begins Within You: A Message to the 1993 Parliament of the World's Religions" held in Chicago in August-September.

8. M. K. Gandhi, *Non-Violent Resistance* (Schocken Books: New York, 1951). For a book of interviews with a dozen remarkable people, Western and Eastern, whose life philosophies and work have been influenced by Gandhi, see Catherine Ingram, *In The Footsteps of Gandhi: Conversations With Spiritual Social Activists* (Parallax Press: New York, 1990).

9. An insightful portrait of the life and work of Desmond Tutu is included in Leonard S. Kenworthy, *Twelve Trailblazers of World Community,* Kenneth Square, PA.: The Friendly Press, 1988. pp. 210-231.

10. David Barash, op. cit. 5.

11. See e.g., Johan Galtung, *The True Worlds: A Transnational Perspective. Free Press: New York,* 1980).

12. Betty Riordan, "Pedagological Approaches to Peace Studies," in Daniel Thomas and Michael Klare (Eds), *Peace and World Order Studies (5th edition)* (Westview Press: Boulder, CO, 1989).

13. Arthur Stein and Eileen Borris, "Towards a More Peaceful Planet," *Peacehaven Winter,* 1990, 18-21. See Also Abelardo Brenes-Castro (ed.) *Seeking the True Meaning of Peace,* San Jose, Costa Rica: University for Peace Press, 1991.

14. Robert Muller, *New Genesis: Shaping A Global Spirituality* (Doubleday: New York, 1982). His most recent book is *The Birth of a Global Civilization,* (World Happiness and Cooperation: Anacorter, WA, 1991).

15. The CCCUN Newsletter, published by the Communications Coordinating Committee of the United Nations provides a comprehensive source of information about CAMDUN and other areas of work being done by the several hundred NGOs functioning to assist the work of the United Nations. Also see the *United Nations Observer.*

16. Paul Ekins, *A New World Order: Grassroots Movements for Global Change,* (Routledge: London, 1992). Right Livelihood Awards were given, for example, for converting the Kenyan ecological debate into mass action for reforestation (1984), for organizing to protect rights of the Indians in the Amazon Basin (1986), and for reversing economic decline in rural areas of Finland (1992).

17. See *Trickle Up Program: The Second Decade* (Trickle Up Program Inc.: New York, September 1, 1993).

18. See Jeremy Seabrook, *Pioneers of Change* (New Society: Philadelphia, 1993).

19. John Rensenbrink, *The Greens and the Politics of Transformation* (R. & E. Miles:

San Pedro, CA, 1992). Magazines containing articles with transformative perspectives include: *The Futurist, Peacework, Transpersonal Perspective, Re-Vision, Utne Reader, Common Cause,* and *Fellowship in Prayer.*

20. As a follow-up three years after the publication of *Our Common Future,* the report of the World Commission on Environment headed by Norway's Gro Harlem Brundtland, the Center for Our Common Future published Linda Starke, *Signs of Hope: Working Towards Our Common Future* (Oxford University Press: New York, 1990).

21. Beginning in 1984, under the leadership of Lester Brown, the Worldwatch Institute has published annually the *State of the World.* The 1993 edition was published in twenty-seven languages worldwide. For the first time, teachers and students, government officials and environmentalists, and others from many parts of the globe at the same time can be reading and discussing the same planetary issues, and can have access to comprehensible statistics from a variety of sources. Worldwatch also facilitated the ten-part television series "Race to Save the Planet."

22. To enhance our understanding, such books are available as Thomas Berry, *Dream of the Earth* (Sierra Club Books: San Francisco, 1990) and David Ehrenfeld, *Beginning Again: People and Nature in the New Millennenium* (Oxford University Press: New York, 1993).

23. David Bohm, *Wholeness and the Implicate Order* (Kegan Paul: Boston, 1980).

24. Former President Jimmy Carter remains active in his role of senior statesman. His civic concerns and energies are seen is his hands-on work with Habitat for Humanity and in such books as *Talking Peace: A Vision for the Next Generation* (Dutton's Childrens Books: New York, 1993).

25. Roger Fisher and Scott Brown, *Getting Together: Building a Relationship That Gets To Yes* (Houghton Mifflin Co.: Boston, 1988).

26. Deborah Tannen, *You Just Don't Understand* (William Morrow: New York, 1990).

27. See Arthur Stein, *Seeds of the Seventies: Values, Work and Commitment in Post-Vietnam America* (University of New England Press: Hanover, NH, 1985).

28. Darshan Singh, *Spiritual Awakening* (S. K. Publications: Bowling Green, VA, 1982) p. 7.

29. For a dialogue exploring the frontiers of science, society, and spirituality, see Fritjof Capra and David Stendl-Rast, *Belonging to the Universe* (Harper: San Francisco, 1991).

30. Arthur Stein and Daniel Campbell, "Personal Transformation, Spiritual Democracy and Global Change," in *General Systems Approaches to Alternative Economics and Values.* Proceedings of the 36th Annual Conference of the International Society for the Systems Sciences (1992), vol. 2, 818–828.

QUESTIONS

1. According to the author, what role can the individual play in the peace-building process?

2. Compare and contrast Stein's conception of human nature with that of Sigmond Freud and Thomas Hobbes.

CREDITS

Allison, Graham T., "Bureaucratic Politics," adapted from *The American Political Science Review*, Volume 63, Number 3, September 1969. Reprinted by permission of American Political Science Association and the author.

Ajami, Fouad, "The Summoning," from *Foreign Affairs*, September/October 1993. Reprinted by permission of *Foreign Affairs*, September/October 1993. Copyright 1993 by the Council on Foreign Relations, Inc.

Aristotle, excerpt from *The Politics*, edited by Stephen Everson. Copyright © 1988 by Cambridge University Press. Reprinted by permission of Cambridge University Press and the editor.

Bull, Hedley, excerpt from *The Anarchical Society*, by Hedley Bull. Copyright © 1977 by Columbia University Press, New York. Reprinted with permission of the publisher.

Carr, Edward Hallet, excerpt from *The Twenty Years' Crisis*, by Edward Hallet Carr. Reprinted by permission of The Macmillan Press Limited.

Crews, Robin J., "A Values-Based Approach to Peace Studies," from *Peace and World Order Studies: A Curriculum Guide*, 5e, edited by Daniel C. Thomas and Michael T. Klare. Copyright © 1989 by Robin J. Crews. Used with permission of the author.

Dos Santos, Theotonio. "The Structure of Depression," from *American Economic Review*, Volume LX, Number 2, May 1970. Reprinted by American Economic Association.

Fukuyama, Francis, "The End of History?" from *The National Interest*, Summer 1989. Reprinted by permission of International Creative Management, Inc. Copyright © 1989 by Francis Fukuyama.

Gilpin, Robert, "The Nature of Political Economy," pp. 20–43, 264–266 from *U.S. Power and the Multinational Corporation* by Robert Gilpin. Copyright © 1975 by Basic Books, Inc. Reprinted by permission of HarperCollins Publishers, Inc.

Halliday, Fred, "A Singular Collapse: The Soviet Union, Market Pressure and Inter-State Competition," from *Contention*, Volume 1, Number 2, Fall 1991. Reprinted by permission.

Henkin, Louis, "Influence, Marginality, and Centrality in the International Legal System," reprinted from *Jerusalem Journal of International Relations*, Vol. II, No. 3, 1989, by permission of the Johns Hopkins University Press. Copyright © 1989 by The Hebrew University of Jerusalem.

Hermann, Margaret, adapted from "Explaining Foreign Policy Behavior Using the Personal Characteristics of Political Leaders," from *International Studies Quarterly*, Volume 24, Number 1, March 1980. Reprinted by permission.

Hobbes, Thomas, excerpt from *Leviathan*, edited by Richard Tuck. Copyright © 1991 by Cambridge University Press. Reprinted by permission of Cambridge University Press and the author.

Huntington, Samuel, adapted from "The Clash of Civilizations," from *Foreign Affairs*, Volume 72, Number 3, Summer 1993. Reprinted by permission of *Foreign Affairs*, Summer 1993. Copyright 1993 by the Council on Foreign Relations, Inc. "No Exit: The Errors of Endism," reprinted with permission of *The National Interest*. Copyright © 1989, No. 17, *The National Interest*, Washington, DC.

Jervis, Robert, excerpt from *Perception and Misperception in International Politics*. Copyright © 1976 by Princeton University Press. Reprinted by permission of Princeton University Press.

Keohane, Robert O., excerpts from *After Hegemony*. Copyright © 1984 by Princeton University Press. Reprinted by permission of Princeton University Press.

Kennan, George, "The Sources of Soviet Conduct," from *Foreign Affairs*, Spring 1987 (reprint), July 1947 (original). Reprinted by permission of *Foreign Affairs*, Spring 1987 (reprint), July 1947 (original). Copyright 1987 (reprint), July 1947 (original) by the Council on Foreign Relations, Inc.

Lagon, Mark P., "The Beliefs of Leaders: Perceptual and Ideological Sources of Foreign Policy After

Whitworth, Sandra, "Gender in the Inter-Paradigm Debate," from *Millennium: Journal of International Studies*, Volume 18, No. 2, Summer 1989. Reprinted by permission of Millennium Publishing Group.

Wilson, Woodrow, "The Fourteen Points," reprinted from *Speeches of the American Presi-*

dents, edited by Steven Ansouin and Janet Podell. New York: H. W. Wilson, 1988.

Zakaria, Fareed, "Is Realism Finished," reprinted with the permission of *The National Interest*. Copyright © Winter 1992/93, No. 30, *The National Interest*. Washington, DC.